THE SOCIAL DYNAMICS OF
FAMILY
VIOLENCE

The Social Dynamics of Family Violence explores family violence throughout the life course, from child abuse and neglect to intimate partner violence and elder abuse. Paying special attention to the social character and institutional causes of family violence, Hattery and Smith ask students to consider how social inequality, especially gender inequality, contributes to tensions and explosive tendencies in family settings. Students learn about individual preventative measures and are also invited to question the justice of our current social structure, with implications for social policy and reorganization. Hattery and Smith also examine violence against women globally and relate this to violence in the United States. Unique coverage of same-gender and multicultural couples, as well as of theory and methods, make this text an essential element of any course considering the sociology of family violence.

Angela J. Hattery is Professor of Sociology and serves as the Director of the Women and Gender Studies Program at George Mason University. Her research focuses on social stratification, gender, family, and race. She is the author of numerous articles, book chapters, and books, including her latest titles, *Gender, Power and Violence* (2019), *Policing Black Bodies* (2017), *African American Families: Myths and Realities* (2012/2016), *Prisoner Reentry and Social Capital* (2010), *Interracial Intimacies* (2009), *Interracial Relationships* (2009), *Intimate Partner Violence* (2008), and *Women, Work, and Family* (2001).

Earl Smith is Professor of Sociology and Anthropology at George Mason University and Emeritus Professor of Sociology and the Rubin Distinguished

Professor of American Ethnic Studies at Wake Forest University. Dr. Smith was the Chairperson of the Department of Sociology, Wake Forest University, from 1997 to 2005. He is the author of numerous distinguished works, including *Gender, Power and Violence* (2019), *Policing Black Bodies* (2018), *Prisoner Reentry and Social Capital* (2010), *Sport and Social Theory* (2010), *Race, Sport and the American Dream* (2014/2009/2007), *Interracial Intimacies* (2009), *Interracial Relationships* (2009), and *African American Families* (2007).

Third Edition

THE SOCIAL DYNAMICS OF
FAMILY
VIOLENCE

ANGELA J. HATTERY AND EARL SMITH

Routledge
Taylor & Francis Group

NEW YORK AND LONDON

Third edition published 2020
by Routledge
52 Vanderbilt Avenue, New York, NY 10017

and by Routledge
2 Park Square, Milton Park, Abingdon, Oxon, OX14 4RN

Routledge is an imprint of the Taylor & Francis Group, an informa business

First edition published by Westview Press in 2012
Second edition published by Westview Press in 2016

Library of Congress Cataloging-in-Publication Data
A catalog record has been requested for this book

ISBN: 978-1-138-32604-0 (hbk)
ISBN: 978-1-138-32605-7 (pbk)
ISBN: 978-0-429-45008-2 (ebk)

Typeset in Garamond
by Swales & Willis Ltd, Exeter, Devon, UK

To Travis, Emma, and Porter: Gandhi said, "Be the change you want to see in the world." I've been dedicating my work to you since you were in elementary school. You are adults now, pursuing your dreams and passions, and I'm genuinely awed by you and your dedication to being the change you want to see in the world.

—Love, Mom

To Earl: As always, in everything we do, our partnership focuses me on the things that matter, motivates me when the days are long and the work is difficult, and sustains me through it all.

—Angela

To Angela: Perfect. This work, in the third edition, underscores all that we have done together examining what sociologists continue to describe as "life chances." As the society we live in becomes better, hopefully there will not be the need for a book of this type again.

—Earl

To Travis, Emma, and Porter: Gandhi said, "Be the change you want to see in the world." I've been dedicating my work to you since you were in elementary school. You are adults now, pursuing your dreams and passions, and I'm genuinely awed by you and your dedication to being the change you want to see in the world.

—Love, Mom

To Earl: As always, in everything we do, our partnership focuses me on the things that matter, motivates me when the days are long and the work is difficult, and sustains me through it all.

—Angela

To Angela: Perfect. This work, in the third edition, underscores all that we have done together examining what sociologists continue to describe as "life chances." As the society we live in becomes better, hopefully there will not be the need for a book of this type again.

—Earl

CONTENTS

EXPANDED TABLE OF CONTENTS

EXPANDED TABLE OF CONTENTS

CHAPTER 3
Theories for Studying Family Violence   49

CHAPTER 10
Cultural Factors and Intimate Partner Violence   273

CHAPTER 11
Religion and Family Violence   317

ACKNOWLEDGMENTS

Many of our students contributed to the third edition of *The Social Dynamics of Family Violence*. Thank you to Lna Eljaafari, Arizthia Espino, Delaney Kirk, and Aurora Murrills who read the entire manuscript and provided well-researched updates to every single statistic as well as updated tables and figures as necessary. We could not have done this without your dedication and hard work. Thank you to the George Mason students enrolled in Gender, Power and Violence in the spring 2019 semester. Each of you contributed thoughtful ideas to the book manuscript itself, as well as creating all of the ancillary materials that are available to instructors. If you find the PowerPoint presentations and test banks useful, you can thank these students: Luke Hellyer, Liz Hinkel, Katie Hinkell, Aurora Murrills, Nakhla Noakes, Rhyanna Oneal, Chris Slotten, Cece Steinbach, and Luke Waltermire. L'Erin Garner-Holden, Lna Eljaafari, and Delaney Kirk served as reviewers of the student work and their contributions made the materials that much stronger. A special thank you to Luke Waltermire for suggesting we add financial abuse to our discussion of intimate partner violence. Being able to use our book in our courses and receive feedback from our students is the perfect feedback loop. We hope your students enjoy the book as much as ours do!

PREFACE TO THE THIRD EDITION

It is with great pleasure that we were offered the opportunity to revise *The Social Dynamics of Family Violence* and produce a third edition. Many things have changed in the landscape of families and violence since our original book was published in 2012, and again in 2016, and thus the opportunity to revisit our arguments and refine our analysis could not be timelier. Specifically:

- The United States Supreme Court ruled that bans on gay marriage are unconstitutional, and in the summer of 2015, marriage equality became the law of the land.
- #MeToo. The hashtag #MeToo erupted on the scene in the fall of 2017 when women in Hollywood began to come out publicly and speak about the alleged sexual harassment they had experienced at the hands of men like Harvey Weinstein. Tarana Burke, a black woman, actually began the movement a decade earlier, and it spread slowly until the onset of the social media #MeToo movement, which then spread quickly. During 2017 and 2018 many high-profile men, including Bill Cosby, were held responsible. The summer of 2018 also brought the case of child sexual abuse to the forefront when Larry Nassar was convicted and sent to prison for the rest of his life for the sexual abuse of more than 300 women. This is the backdrop for the third edition of *The Social Dynamics of Family Violence*.
- The Violence Against Women Act (VAWA), which was originally passed in 1996, was reauthorized in 2013 under a great deal of contention. Revisions to the Act included provisions for intimate partner violence in the LGBTQ community, for cases involving immigrant women, and for cases on Native American reservations. Sadly, VAWA remains threatened under the Trump administration.
- Donald Trump was elected President of the United States, and under his administration he appointed Betsy DeVos as Secretary of Education. Secretary DeVos has expressed concern that campus sexual misconduct processes are not attentive enough to the *accused*, and as a result, the new policies coming to colleges and universities are turning the clock back on the gains made under the Dear Colleague Letter of the Obama administration.

We address each of these events as they impact the issues we include in the book.

One of the best things that can happen to authors is when our colleagues think enough of our book to use it in their own courses. One of our colleagues, Professor Veronica Tichenor, has been using our book for years. In a conversation with Professor Tichenor about the book and the opportunity to prepare a third edition, she urged us, and we agreed, to add a new chapter on sibling abuse. Sibling abuse is the most common and yet least reported form of family abuse. It is significantly more common than bullying or other forms of peer violence that receive significantly more attention; even First Lady Melania Trump is in on that act. And it can have long-term and devastating consequences for victims and perpetrators, both of whom remain at higher risk of committing acts of violence in their adult relationships, as partners and parents. Professor Tichenor agreed to do the research and write this new chapter, and the book is unbelievably more comprehensive and powerful thanks to her.

While considering these developments, as well as teaching and writing about gender-based violence and child sexual abuse, we identified four institutions that we had previously treated only minimally (or not at all) in the first edition: the military, the Catholic Church, fraternities, and sports. First, we expanded our discussion of child sexual abuse in the Catholic Church to include the recent developments in civil lawsuits.

We are grateful to the anonymous reviewers, many of whom have used the book in their classes, for their honest and helpful critiques and recommendations. Based on their recommendations, we have enhanced our discussion of violence in the LGBTQ community as well as expanded our discussion of responses to violence by the criminal justice system, law enforcement, and social services.

Finally, we have identified and highlighted more best practices, including the Emerge! Center Against Domestic Abuse in Tucson, Arizona, so that the reader will have more illustrations of initiatives that are successful as examples that they can bring to their own communities and workplaces.

As in any third edition, we have of course updated illustrations and data to the most current available.

It has been a joy to return to this manuscript and rework it so that, we hope, it is even more impactful than the original text, of which we remain so very proud. We invite the reader into a revised, updated, and expanded journey exploring the dark side of family life.

Angela Hattery and Earl Smith
Fairfax, Virginia
March 2019

SETTING THE STAGE

She died in September by the ugliest means, weighing an unthinkable 18 pounds, half what a 4-year-old ought to. She withered in poverty in a home in Brooklyn where the authorities said she had been drugged and often bound to a toddler bed by her mother, having realized a bare thimble's worth of living . . . Marchella weighed 1 pound 4 ounces when she was born, prematurely, on April 3, 2006. A relative recalls thinking she was about the size of a one-liter Pepsi bottle. A twin sister, born first, died. Her name was Miracle.

—**N. R. Kleinfield and Mosi Secret**, "A Bleak Life, Cut Short at 4,
Harrowing from the Start," *New York Times*, May 8, 2011

This chapter will set the stage for an in-depth, theoretically framed discussion of various types of family violence, including elder abuse, intimate partner violence, and child abuse. In addition to defining key terms, we will also discuss the concept of family violence itself, which is, perhaps surprisingly, contested; compare and contrast scholarly approaches to thinking about family violence; and offer a reconceptualized model for considering family violence.

OBJECTIVES

- Provide the latest empirical data on a variety of types of family violence
- Define critical concepts and recognize key issues relevant to the study of family violence
- Identify and introduce the theoretical paradigms that have been employed to analyze and understand family violence: (1) the family violence approach, (2) the feminist approach, and (3) the race, class, and gender (RCG) approach
- Illuminate the ways in which social structures and institutions, such as the economy, cultural norms, religious ideologies, and the military, shape violence in families
- Illuminate the ways in which social statuses—race, social class, gender, age, and sexuality—shape patterns of violence in families
- Provide an honest discussion of the issues that families living with violence face

---

KEY TERMS

family	economy
violence	cultural norms
family violence	religion
family violence theory	the military
feminist theory	social status variation
race, class, and gender theory	

INTRODUCTION

From their earliest formation families have been complex and dynamic units that have evolved in order to meet the changing needs of both individuals and societies. Although families are inherently private, they are also public. In the United States alone the government has, on many occasions, involved itself in family life, most frequently by passing laws or deciding court cases that determine the structure of the family and establish the rules about families and marriage. For example, one of the major issues of the early twenty-first century entails various branches of state and federal governments—legislatures, voting referenda, and courts—engaged in shaping the legal structure of families through the debate on gay marriage; in the summer of 2015 the United States Supreme Court ruled in a 5–4 decision that the prohibition against gay and lesbian marriage was unconstitutional, and marriage equality became the law of the land.

Although discussions of gay marriage range from the uninterested to the frantic, just like the discussions of interracial marriage in the 1960s (Smith and Hattery 2009), most Americans focus on their personal beliefs about sexuality rather than the legal aspects of defining family. For example, when we ask students in our classes to conjure up an image of a wedding and share it with the class, most describe a religious ceremony in a church, temple, or mosque. They describe clothes: tuxedos for men and white wedding dresses for women. And, unlike the tuxedo, the white dress has values and norms attached: it denotes that the woman is a virgin. They describe music, dancing, and food rituals. Despite some variation by race, religion, social class, or region of the country, there is a high level of agreement among the students about the necessary elements of a wedding. What students rarely, if ever, describe is the signing of the marriage license. Yet it is the marriage license that is the most critical part of the wedding, far more important than the selection of the wedding dress, despite what Randy, the fashion consultant on TLC's *Say Yes to the Dress*, might say, because it is the legal contract that binds two people and their future children together and defines them as a legitimate family.

This legal contract impacts everything from taxes to health insurance to inheritance (Jackman 2011). Furthermore, the legal definition of *family* is an important aspect of the ways in which violence that occurs in families is treated by the criminal justice and legal systems.[1] For example, there are likely to be differences in the way judges issue protective orders to cohabiting couples as opposed to married couples, or gay or lesbian couples as opposed to heterosexual couples. However, the sting of a slap, the gasp for air when one is punched, and the frantic desire to be safe from violence do not differ across the individuals in these different types of couples. Whether the *law* recognizes the relationship may shape the way individuals are treated, but it does not shape the feelings of hurt and disillusionment that individuals in these families experience. As important as legal definitions are to shaping the response to violence by the criminal justice and legal systems, for individuals living in families, the definitions of *family* otherwise have little impact on the actual experience of violence. Therefore, other than when necessary, our discussions of **family violence** will not be limited by legal definitions. Rather, we will operate under the assumption that families can be, and often are, defined by their members in much broader ways.

Our primary objective in writing this book is to examine the state of violence in families in the United States at the beginning of the twenty-first century. In this book, we examine through a sociological lens the most important issues that researchers, policymakers, social service providers, and families themselves face. These issues, which are central to the academic discussions of family, include child abuse, both physical and sexual; elder abuse; intimate partner violence (IPV); and violence in subgroups, such as among gay and lesbian families and families in the military. We also include a discussion on the role that social institutions and structures—such as the **economy, religion, the military**, and college campuses (fraternities and sports groups in particular)—play in structuring family violence. Last, we explore variations across family groups, including differences across race and ethnicity, social class, and sexuality. We do all of this using a straightforward approach to these issues, many of which have reached the level of crises of epic proportions in families yet remain largely ignored. We begin, as any discussion of a complex phenomenon should, with some basic definitions. This allows us all to "be on the same page" as we begin our discussions.

DEFINITIONS

Family

Family scholars have developed several different definitions of the term **family**. We discuss five:

1. Family is a set of people with whom you live and with whom you share biological and/or legal ties (Burton and Jayakody 2001).

   This definition focuses on what many of us refer to as the nuclear family. This definition restricts family primarily to parents (who are married) and their biological and/or adopted children. This is the definition of family that is used by the census, and it is the most common definition of family in use by both scholars and the average American.

2. Family is a set of people you may or may not live with but with whom you share biological and/or legal ties (Cherlin 1999).

   This definition of family is often referred to as the "extended family." As such, it is used to acknowledge that both in the past and continuing today, many households include extended family members such as grandparents. It also recognizes the continued importance of family once children have permanently moved out of the house.

3. Family is a set of people you live with but with whom you may or may not share biological or legal ties (Landale and Fennelly 1992).

   This is a much more contemporary definition of family that is designed to acknowledge several changes in family life, specifically the rise of cohabiting couples, who in the twenty-first century are increasingly likely to be raising children together. Specifically with regards to the African American family, this definition recognizes both higher rates of cohabitation and the practice of sharing child-rearing with nonrelatives in response to a variety of forces, such as incarceration. This definition was developed, in part, to recognize same-gender couples as "families" long before the law did. And, though we will devote an entire chapter to LGBTQ families, it is important to note here that the law has been applied in various and often confusing ways to LGBTQ families. Although some stability has been brought to the discussion of same-gender families by the US Supreme Court decision in 2015, which ruled that prohibitions against gay and lesbian marriages are unconstitutional and marriage equality—the legal marriage between two members of the same gender—is the law of the land, there continue to be many areas of the law, especially as it relates to trans-identified people, that do not guarantee civil rights, including the right to marry, to all, and thus this definition of the family remains necessary.

4. Family is a set of people with whom you share social, physical, or financial support or a combination thereof (Sarkisian and Gerstel 2008).

   This definition is very inclusive and was developed, as noted above, primarily to acknowledge the existence of gay and lesbian households, which at the time were not legally recognized (which was, of course, reversed by the

2015 US Supreme Court decision). Furthermore, this definition is designed to emphasize a key feature of families: the fact that members are interdependent. Families generally provide support of various sorts for their members. The flow and direction of this support may change over time—for example, from parent to child during the period of child-rearing and from child to parent during later years. For the purposes of our discussion in this book, *family* can also characterize one's involvement in a variety of social institutions, including the military, fraternities—where members refer to themselves as *brothers*—elite sports teams, and the Catholic priesthood, whose members work, play, and live together.

5. Family is a set of people whom you love (Neff and Karney 2005).

The most inclusive of all definitions, this one recognizes that, increasingly, people create their own "families" that may or may not be based on formal ties (biological or legal), and that these important people may or may not live together. The classic example used to illustrate this concept is the popular television program *Friends*. *Friends* depicts a group of young men and women who provide support for each other and love each other but do not necessarily share any biological or legal ties (of course, there are two exceptions to this rule: Ross and Monica are siblings and Chandler and Monica eventually marry). Some of the "friends" lived together, but others did not. Yet they provided for each other most of the very things that have historically been provided by people with formal family ties. Family scholars often refer to this form of family as *fictive kin*, and this is especially common when referring to African American family relationships. Some may find the term *fictive kin* offensive because it assumes that some relationships (those based on biology or law) are real and that others (those *not* based on biology or law) are "fictive"—that is, not real. Thus, we refrain from this kind of distinction and suggest that the initial development of the term carried no such qualifier.

The final two definitions are critical to the focus and discussion of this book because they both highlight what is perhaps the most devastating aspect of family violence: that whatever form it takes, family violence shatters notions of love, respect, interdependence, and mutual support. Whether the violence involves a man beating to death the woman he claims to love, an adult daughter emotionally and financially blackmailing her elderly parents, or an uncle engaging in incest with a young niece or nephew, family violence *always hijacks safety and security*, the very notions on which family is built. Thus, regardless of who is the victim and who is the perpetrator in any specific example, this shattering of the safety and interdependency is universal.

Violence

Often when we think of violence, we think only of physical abuse: hitting, kicking, slapping, beating, and so forth. Yet central to any discussion of *family violence* are acceptance and recognition of the fact that much of the abuse that occurs in families is emotional and psychological as well as physical. Emotional and psychological abuse often takes the form of name-calling and verbal degradation. For example, battered women we interviewed as part of a larger project (Hattery 2008; Hattery and Smith 2012) reported that their husbands and boyfriends frequently referred to them as "bitch" or "slut" and that they constantly, even incessantly, accused them of sleeping around or nagged them about not keeping up with the housework. Similar types of verbal abuse take place when children are involved as well. The toll that this type of abuse takes can be, and often is, significant.

For as little attention as physical, psychological, and emotional abuse receives among scholars and in popular discourse, perhaps the darkest secret of family violence is sexual abuse. More than a quarter of young girls report that they have been sexually abused by someone they are related to—most often their mother's boyfriend or another male relative—and one in seven boys reports the same (Steese et al. 2006; Tjaden and Thoennes 2000). In fact, as part of another project (Hattery and Smith 2010), we interviewed two sex offenders who were returning home after periods of incarceration, and in the course of the interviews both revealed that they were themselves victims of child sexual abuse. The impact of sexual abuse, especially when the victims are children, is severe, long-lasting, and often nothing short of devastating (Hattery 2009; Kaiser Family Foundation 2003; Tresniowski 2011).

Violence in families can also take the form of financial abuse. This is most common in battering relationships and in cases of elder abuse. In these situations the abuser typically denies the victim access to financial resources, which, among other things, prevents them from leaving the abusive situation. In the case of elder abuse, adult children often trick vulnerable parents—who are often suffering from some form of dementia—into changing their will or giving them power of attorney that allows them to drain their parents' financial assets from bank accounts, investments, and so on. This is nothing short of embezzlement, only the victim is one's parent, not one's boss (Fox et al. 2002).

It is also important to recognize, based on the definitions of *family* we offered previously, that family violence is not limited to individuals whose relationships meet the legal definitions of family—for example, the most common perpetrator of child sexual abuse is the new boyfriend of the victim's mother. Nor is family violence limited to people who live together. In fact, the most common time for intimate partner violence homicide to occur is after a battered woman has already physically separated from her abusive partner. And intimate partner violence is equally present in cohabiting relationships and legal marriages. Thus, unless there is some reason to do so, we will not utilize a single definition of *family* but rather will report on the violence that takes place between people who love each other—or claim to—and who consider themselves to be part of an intimate relationship or family.

THEORETICAL APPROACHES

Our second objective in this book is to provide a theoretical framework for understanding family violence. Chapters 3 and 4 will be devoted to a lengthy and in-depth discussion of the theoretical and methodological approaches to the study of violence in families. That said, we would like to take the opportunity here to briefly introduce some of the theoretical frameworks that are employed to study violence in families. There are essentially three main approaches: (1) **family violence theory**, (2) **feminist theory**, and (3) **race, class, and gender theory**.

Family Violence Theory

Family violence theory was developed largely by Murray Straus and Richard Gelles (1995). Straus and Gelles were among the theory's early pioneers, and their work has shaped the field of family violence for the past thirty-plus years. As family sociologists, they conceptualized families as a set of interconnected relationships, and they looked for commonalities among the various types of family violence, from incest to elder abuse. In short, they recognized that families are constructed around relationships that involve, among other things, obligations and responsibilities but also status and power. For example, their perspective identifies a key pattern in family violence: the tendency for it to be perpetrated by people with power against those without power; that is, stronger, older people abuse weaker, younger people. Of course, this trend reverses when parents are elderly and vulnerable to their adult children. People with more resources (parents, adult children, husbands) are more likely to be abusive toward those without resources (children, elderly adults, wives) than the reverse. Last, they suggest that people engage in abusive behavior because they can and because it works. When a parent spanks a child there are generally no consequences ("they can"), and it generally changes a child's behavior in the desired direction ("it works"). Building on these basic tenets, family violence theory is the most widely accepted theoretical framework among scholars of the family who study violence.

Feminist Theory

Feminist theory approaches the analysis of any social phenomenon by assuming first and foremost that gender stratification, which is rooted in patriarchy, is universal and that it produces a system of inequality that creates opportunities and offers rewards that privilege men and disadvantage women. Thus, the approach of feminist theory to the study of family violence is focused on the ways in which family violence is a *gendered phenomenon*. In other words, more often than not, the victims of family violence are women and the perpetrators are men. Feminist theorists expand the work of family violence theorists by suggesting that who "can hit" is not random; that is, the ability to access the power necessary to engage in physical, emotional, psychological, and sexual abuse is structured by the system of gender stratification. Thus, although there are exceptions to the rule, as we will explore in Chapter 3, even when women make more money than men or have access to other types of power, they are rarely the perpetrators of violence in families, even when boys or men are the victims. Family violence, feminist theorists argue, should be understood as an extension of other types of gender-based violence, such as rape and sexual harassment, rather than being understood inside the various configurations of the institution of the family. We use the term *gender-based violence* to call attention to the gendered nature of intimate partner violence. This term extends beyond the term previously employed, *violence against women*, because it focuses our attention on both the gender of the victim and the gender of the perpetrator.

Race, Class, and Gender Theory

Race, class, and gender theory is an extension of feminist theory in two key ways: it was developed by a subset of feminist scholars—African American feminists such as Bonnie Thornton Dill and Patricia Hill Collins—and it builds on the idea of structured inequality and power. Distinct from feminist theory, race, class, and gender theory is built on the assumption that there are *multiple systems* of oppression that independently and collaboratively create complex systems of stratification that produce interlocking systems of inequality.

Sometimes it is useful to consider an illustration that is disconnected from the topic we are considering. This strategy prevents us from conflating the theory with what we know about the issue. Let's consider an example from the area of health care. A core tenet of race, class, and gender theory is the assumption that every system of domination has a counter system of privilege. In other words, oppression is a system of both costs and benefits; when one person receives a "benefit" (such as a lower probability of experiencing intimate partner violence or a higher probability of getting an education), someone else experiences a "cost" (such as a higher probability of experiencing intimate partner violence or a lower probability of graduating from college). In other words, the benefit does not accrue from an infinite pool of resources; it is extracted at a cost to someone else. For example, we know that African American men die prematurely, seven or eight years earlier than their white counterparts (Hattery and Smith 2007). Generally, discussions of this gap in life expectancy focus on the reasons African American men die early—for example, because they are more likely to hold jobs that involve physical labor, they are more likely to live in poverty, they are more likely to lack access to health care, and they are more likely to experience racial discrimination and the stresses associated with being an African American man. Yet a race, class, and gender framework forces us to also ask the opposing question: why is it that white men live so much longer?

When we pose the question this way, we realize that the gap is also created by the fact that white men tend to have more access to white-collar employment and the best-quality health care, and their affluence affords them the ability to pay for the "dirty" work in their lives to be taken care of by others, mostly African American men and women. Thus, the intersection of race and social class creates *simultaneously* a disadvantage for African American men *and* an advantage for white men. Furthermore, when we dig deeper into this question of life expectancy, we see that there are significant gender differences as well. Specifically, not only do women live longer than men, but the racial gap is also significantly smaller for women than for men. In short, our understanding of racial disparities in life expectancy is improved when we layer these explanations together, focusing not only on gender or race but also on the ways in which they interact to produce outcomes that vary by both statuses.[2] In terms of family violence, the race, class, and gender paradigm allows us to better understand the fact that African American children are at a higher risk for experiencing child abuse, both because they are more likely to live in families that are at higher risk for child abuse, including single-parent families and poor families, and because they are nearly twice as likely as white children to be placed in foster care (ChildWelfare.gov 2016), where they face a substantially higher risk for child abuse.

SOCIAL STRUCTURES

One of the most important aspects of this book is the time we dedicate to understanding the social and institutional forces that shape family violence. As sociologists, our focus is less on the individual themself—we leave those discussions to our colleagues in psychology—and more on the role that social structures such as the economy and religion play in shaping both the risk for family violence as well as the ways in which it is perpetrated and experienced.

The Economy

It will come as no surprise that money is a major poin[t] of contention in any household. Couples fight about money—how to spend it, [who should] bring it into the household, and so forth. Parents a[nd children fight about] money—how much allowance should be paid for ho[usehold chores]

Breadwinner / Homemaker

money = power control

macro / micro

will have access to a car when turning sixteen and what kind of car that should be, how much money the family is willing to invest in paying college tuition, and so forth. Adult siblings fight with each other and with their aging parents over "the inheritance." Money is a site of contest no matter which relationships we are discussing and how they are configured. And it will probably come as no surprise that, as one might predict, some types of family violence—specifically, violence between intimate partners—increased substantially during the recession of 2007–2009. There is some evidence that intimate partner violence rates have stabilized since the end of the recession. In the environment of the postindustrial service economy, however, that characterizes the post-2000 United States, an economy with slow growth, stagnant wages, and wealth transfers from the middle classes to the very wealthy, many families remain under significant financial pressure and intimate partner violence continues. This point brings us to the role of the larger economy.

In addition to examining the ways in which money becomes a source of stress and conflict in families, in Chapter 9 we explore the ways in which the role and structure of the *economy* itself shape patterns of family violence. In addition to examining the ways in which individual couples fight about money, we will look carefully at the ways in which wages, discrimination, the definition of the term *worker*, and other economic factors shape the patterns of family violence that we see. For example, we will argue that one of the reasons women make up the vast majority (85 percent) of the victims of intimate partner violence is because they are economically vulnerable and dependent upon their partners. As a result of the static and persistent wage gap, women continue to earn only 80 percent of what men earn, and women of color earn far less (Hegewisch 2018). Thus, because money is often linked to power, intimate partner violence takes the shape of men placing expectations on women in exchange for providing for their financial needs. When women fail to meet these expectations—which might be as insignificant as not having dinner on the table at the "proper" time—violence may erupt. When women attempt to leave these types of abusive relationships, the critical factor that prevents them from doing so is often their lack of access to money and their inability to earn a living wage with which to support themselves and their children. In Chapter 9 we explore these issues as well as the recent data on the role the recession of 2007–2009 played in shaping intimate partner violence.

Cultural Norms

Just as women's economic vulnerability s ~~edacation,~~ potential victims of intimate partner violence, beliefs about appropria ~~patriarchal structure~~ ntial batterers and women as potential victims. S ~~gender~~ apter 10, **cultural norms**—for instance, the rig ~~relationships~~ primary

media,
military
education,
patriarchal structure
gender
relationships
sports,
law enforcement
class

breadwinners in their families—create ground that is fertile for intimate partner violence. As we will demonstrate using both the work of other scholars and our own interviews, when men feel their masculinity is threatened they often respond with violence. One of the primary "triggers" to this violence is a threat to their identity as the family breadwinner. This response can be triggered interpersonally— for example, when a wife complains to her husband that he does not make enough money for them to pay their bills or when she "nags" him about being laid off. This response can also be triggered by the structure of the economy itself, whereby men of color, in particular, face hiring and wage discrimination and men in certain sectors—such as manufacturing—face high levels of layoffs in times, such as the years of the Great Recession (2007–2009), when the overall economy is in recession, making it difficult for these men and their families to achieve and maintain financial success. This inability to achieve success as a breadwinner may result in intimate partner violence that unfolds over many years—even decades in some families.

Additionally, an economic trend that began in the 1980s is the rise of women in the paid labor market. Kimmel (2005) and others have argued that this shift in the workplace and at home has resulted in a form of alienation from the masculine identity. The Pew Research Center reported that in 2013, 40 percent of married mothers were breadwinners—they earned more than their husbands (Wang, Parker, and Taylor 2013). We will examine the ways in which these kinds of changes—and their impact on masculine identities—as well as the recession in general have shaped the levels of intimate partner violence we see at the end of the second decade of the twenty-first century.

Religion

A primary source of cultural information regarding appropriate roles in families comes to us from *religion*. In Chapter 11 we exam~~ine specifically the role that~~ religion has played in shaping expectations for famil~~y roles and in creating a ter~~rain that is ripe for family violence. In addition to the ~~...~~ religions have for women's submission, they also have ~~...the behavior~~ of children and parents, particularly fathers. In all of ~~...religions across the~~ globe, and indeed in the United States, religious doctr~~ines...~~ decrees—as well as the beliefs of religious leaders rein~~force...~~ to be the heads of households and both women and ~~children...~~ submissive to them. This ideology contributes to the ~~...~~ linity and femininity, which, as we noted above, lay ~~...~~ partner violence as well as child abuse. For example, when discussing the role that parents, particularly fathers, play in disciplining their children, Proverbs 13:24 is

[handwritten margin notes:] Values, traditions, Catholicism: children & women are property. Mainstream religion is powerful

often cited: "Whoever spares the rod hates his son, but he who loves him is diligent to discipline him." This teaching, especially when coupled with the adage "Spare the rod, spoil the child," is part of the landscape in which corporal punishment occurs. In fact, some cases of child abuse can be best analyzed as parents, usually fathers, taking this belief to the extreme.

Additionally, most, if not all, major religions are built around the belief that religious leaders are distinct from and superior to "regular" believers. This belief lays the groundwork for the abuse of women and children inside the institution of religion—for example, the Catholic Church sex scandal that has plagued the United States beginning in 2001. Although the sex scandal will not be the sole focus of our subsequent discussion, we will explore the ways in which institutionalized sexism and violence can contribute to the perpetration and perpetuation of family violence. For example, in a survey of battered women, more than 70 percent said that when they consulted religious counselors about the abuse they were experiencing at home, they were told to go home and be better wives. Thus, we devote Chapter 11 to the role that religion plays in family violence.

Institutionalized Violence

In Chapter 12, we expand our discussion of institutionalized violence beyond the military to include violence on college campuses, which is located primarily in two institutions: fraternities and sports teams. These institutions share certain features that facilitate gender-based violence: they are highly sex-segregated, they have a "fraternal" quality that privileges loyalty to the organization over the individual's identity, and they have internal systems of justice that by and large protect perpetrators and fail to hold them accountable, so that they are free to continue engaging in sexual and intimate partner violence. Though at the outset these institutions may not appear to be explicitly familial, in fact the relationships inside each institution often mimic families—people live together, work together, eat together, and study together, and thus when one member engages in violence against another, it can be experienced by the victim in similar ways to family violence. We provide a detailed discussion of the structural features of each institution in Chapter 12.

SOCIAL STATUS VARIATION

Our discussion of **social status variation** in family violence is different from the way in which it is typically approached. Unlike the majority of texts, which include separate chapters on family violence in different racial or ethnic groups, for example, we will weave into each chapter discussions of the ways in which two key statuses—race or ethnicity and social class—shape family violence. For example, in Chapter 6 on child abuse, we examine the disproportionate risk of sexual abuse that low-income African American girls face as a result of the prevalence of liquor houses and prostitution—a form of local sex trafficking—in low-income African American neighborhoods. Similarly, in the chapter on cultural norms, though we will not explore it in depth, we note the disproportionate risk that immigrant women face for intimate partner violence related to a series of factors, including their citizenship status, which is often linked to their husbands'; their lack of English-language proficiency; strong cultural norms that demand women's submissiveness and even polygyny; and their relative isolation. We take this approach because we believe that there is nothing distinct about either racial and ethnic or class groups with regards to family violence. In other words, no group is inherently more or less violent than another. However, because various racial or ethnic and class groups have different lived realities, with different access to resources and different experiences with discrimination in the labor market, for example, it is critical to examine the ways in which social status—specifically, race or ethnicity and social class—shapes one's risk for and experiences with family violence. Thus, we will explore variations in the discussions of the structures—the economy, culture, and religion—that shape family violence.

There are two exceptions to this approach: age and sexuality. Although, when appropriate, we weave discussions of age and sexuality into each chapter, we intentionally dedicate separate chapters to age (Chapter 5 focuses on elder abuse and Chapter 6 focuses on child abuse) and sexuality (Chapter 13) because we believe there are some distinct differences in family violence with regards to age and sexuality that merit focused discussions. For example, although the vast majority of victims of intimate partner violence are women, and although the strongest case for understanding why is rooted in discussions of masculine power and privilege, the same patterns do not necessarily apply with regards to either age or sexuality. The majority of victims of elder abuse, for example, are women, which may have more to do with the fact that women outlive men and thus the proportion of the elderly who are women is significantly greater. Another indication of this type of difference is the fact that although men are the perpetrators of the majority, by far, of intimate partner violence, this is not necessarily the case with elder abuse. Women, too, abuse their aging parents, and in fact because women are far more likely to be the caregivers for aging parents with dementia or Alzheimer's, more women than men are perpetrators of elder abuse.

Similarly, although the majority of child physical and especially sexual abuse is perpetrated by men, women also engage in child abuse, especially physical abuse and neglect. With regards to physical abuse, young men are, in some cases, more likely to be the victims than their sisters, though the reverse is true for sexual abuse.

Although the underlying principles of power and privilege that permeate intimate partner violence also permeate elder and child abuse, the gender dynamics are somewhat different. When we consider the cases of elder and child abuse in particular, the key power dynamic at work is far more likely to be age than gender.

Though there are many things about intimate partner violence in same-gender relationships that are identical to the patterns in heterosexual relationships—and we will highlight these parallels as they arise—gender is a critical distinction. Obviously, in lesbian relationships there is no male partner and in gay men's relationships there is no female partner. As with child and elder abuse, the dynamics of power and privilege remain, but they break down on lines other than gender. Sometimes the lines of demarcation are masculinity and femininity—the more "feminine" partner is more often the victim. But this is not always the case. Sometimes abuse in same-gender relationships is structured by each partner's risk for being "outed," their status as a parent, and a variety of other ways in which precarity can be created. Additionally, because there are many ways in which same-gender relationships are unique—for example, though gay marriage is legal, members of the LGBTQ community continue to face discrimination in institutions like employment and housing, and they are often taken less seriously by the police or emergency room staff—we devote Chapter 13 to discussions of the experiences of violence in LGBTQ families.

New to the third edition of *The Social Dynamics of Family Violence* is a discussion of sibling violence, which is the new Chapter 7. Our colleague, Veronica Tichenor, who has been using *The Social Dynamics of Family Violence* in her courses, urged us to include a chapter on sibling abuse. We agreed that this was a much-needed chapter and Professor Tichenor agreed to author that chapter. In this new chapter, Professor Tichenor explores the most common, least reported, and least talked-about form of family violence: sibling abuse. From bullying to physical abuse to psychological abuse and sexual abuse, the data and interviews that Professor Tichenor draws on paint a picture that is both disturbing and will likely be all too familiar to the reader.

A NOTE ABOUT DATA SOURCES

We rely on a variety of data sources in order to tell the story of family violence. Of particular note, however, and part of what makes this book unique, is that we personally conducted interviews with nearly one hundred men and women—African American and white, middle-class and poor—who live with violence, and these data form the basis of our research. Throughout the book we use these interviews (qualitative data) to provide empirical support for our arguments. We include descriptions of particular people we interviewed, and we present their stories as direct, unedited quotes. Qualitative interviews are an important and rich data source: for sociologists, the quotes that are generated by qualitative interviews enhance statistics in much the same way as photographs enhance written descriptions or text. We use the qualitative interviews to paint pictures of violence in family life. And because we believe that understanding a phenomenon like family violence depends upon understanding the science used to generate the theories and analyses, we devote an entire chapter, Chapter 4, to a discussion of the methods that scholars of family violence use and the strengths and weaknesses of the various data collection techniques that build our scientific understanding of this complex social issue.

Although the interviews that we, and others, have conducted help to paint a picture of family violence, in order to truly understand the broader implications of that picture, we also need to examine statistics. Statistics provide the kind of empirical data needed to make broad, sweeping generalizations about a particular phenomenon. So, for example, reading about what it feels like to be hit in the head with a ball-peen hammer provides an illustration of intimate partner violence, but it does not tell the researcher anything about how common this experience is. Thus, in each chapter, for each topic, we provide statistical data so that the reader can understand the prevalence of various types of violence within a population. Although we are careful to provide citations for the statistical evidence we include (both in the text and in tables), we note here that most of the statistical evidence comes from a few sources: the US censuses conducted in 2000 and 2010, the Centers for Disease Control and Prevention (CDC), and the Violence Against Women Act (VAWA), all of which collect data continuously and produce both monthly and annual reports. All of these data sources are the "official" sources and include data from the entire US population (or appropriate subsamples based on the US population). Thus, this book combines the best of both qualitative and quantitative data to help improve our understanding of contemporary family violence.

ORGANIZATION OF THE BOOK

The table of contents makes clear the topics that will be covered in this book. However, we want to expound on them, as several are somewhat different from what is typically found in a text on family violence. We begin the book with an overview of the history of family violence in the United States. Our third chapter provides an in-depth discussion and review of the various theoretical frameworks that have been employed in studies of family violence along with a description of the theory framing our analysis: the race, class, and gender paradigm. This allows the reader to examine for themself the analytical power and shortcomings of the various perspectives. In Chapter 4 we provide an in-depth discussion and review of the methods that are typically used to study family violence. In particular, we identify the problems inherent in studying family violence and how these barriers shape what we know about violence in families.

As noted above, we devote Chapters 5 and 6 to discussions of age-based violence: elder abuse and child abuse, respectively. Chapter 7 is the new chapter on sibling abuse, and Chapter 8 is designed as a transition or bridge chapter, moving us from age-based violence to the most common form of violence: intimate partner violence. Specifically, Chapter 8 will examine perhaps the most tragic outcome of child abuse: an increased risk for experiencing violence—either as a perpetrator or as a victim—in adulthood. We devote the middle chapters (9–12) to a discussion of intimate partner violence. Each chapter will take as its main focus a distinct social structure or institution: the economy, culture, and religion, respectively. Rounding out our discussion of intimate partner violence, Chapter 12 is devoted to a discussion of institutionalized violence in the military and on college campuses. Chapter 13 is devoted, as noted above, to an exploration of violence in same-gender families.

The final section of the book, Chapters 14–16, focuses on prevention and avoidance strategies (Chapter 14), the criminal justice, social service, and legal responses to family violence (Chapter 15), and our conclusions and recommendations for future research and policies (Chapter 16).

SUMMARY OF OUR APPROACH IN THIS BOOK

There are several key features to our book that are unique. First and foremost, not only does it explore the myriad of ways in which violence in families is shaped and perpetuated, it also has a unique focus on structural and institutional factors. As noted earlier, the majority of textbooks on family violence focus on the experiences of individuals. As sociologists, we recognize the need, especially in courses on family violence taught in sociology departments, for a book that is organized around and explores the role that institutions, such as the economy, religion, and the military, and cultural norms play in structuring the prevalence and experiences of family violence. Additionally, this approach allows us to consider the reasons that not all families or individuals are at equal risk for victimization or perpetration, as well as the reasons certain forms of family violence are more common than others. For example, men who grew up witnessing domestic violence are three times more likely to batter their wives and girlfriends than men who did not. Last, this approach takes the focus away from "bad people" and examines the ways in which we are all at risk—though differentially—for family violence; any of us can experience the kinds of stresses associated with caregiving that are the cause of a significant portion of both child and elder abuse. In short, we all have a stake in reducing family violence by disrupting the messages of support created and provided by institutional entities, such as religion, the military, fraternities, and sports groups, and by increasing the support for caregivers and families at risk.

Our book is also unique in its reliance on the race, class, and gender theoretical framework as the lens for analyzing and interpreting the empirical data on family violence. This approach rests on the assumption that systems of oppression (specifically, race, class, and gender) intersect to create a web that shapes access to opportunities and experiences that vary depending on the actor's position in the social hierarchy (their race, class, and gender). Because the theoretical framework that underlies our discussion is based on an intersectional approach, the organization of our book reflects this fact. In other words, in most textbooks each topic—child abuse, sexual abuse, intimate partner violence—is written from the perspective of, and with a focus on, the experiences of white people, the default category of citizens, and separate chapters are devoted to the "unique" experiences of individuals of various other races or ethnicities. In each of these "special" chapters, it is assumed that the experiences of nonwhites are unique and that all family violence experienced by nonwhites is the same. For instance, the assumption is that all family violence that African Americans experience—child abuse, sexual abuse, elder abuse—is the same across type and distinct from every type of abuse that white people experience. Rather than taking this approach, we assume that for the most part, with small variations that we will address, family violence is shaped not so much by race or ethnicity or social class as by the relationship between the perpetrator and the victim. Thus, we organize our book around types of violence—child abuse, elder abuse, intimate partner violence—and discuss racial or ethnic and class variation within each type. This novel approach turns the typical assumptions made by scholars of family violence on their heads.

Last, our approach is unique because we are scholars of family violence who have studied it rigorously by employing both qualitative methods (interviews) and quantitative methods (analysis of large-scale data sets). Our book is not simply a review of other people's research; it utilizes our own research to explore the complexities and tragedies of family violence. Because social science research is rigorous, it takes a long time from start to finish. Thus, the greatest sources of contemporary trends in virtually any social phenomenon are often news accounts, and we employ such sources to illustrate these trends when appropriate. We are also classroom teachers and bring to this textbook combined decades of teaching students about the darker side of family life.

We move now to Chapter 2, in which we provide an overview of the history of family violence—and family more generally—in the United States. Although family violence has always existed, it has been ignored by researchers and the legal system until relatively recently. Our responses to family violence today are largely shaped by this history of sweeping it under the rug, and thus a discussion of this history is critical to understanding the phenomenon of family violence today.

NOTES

1. This will be our major focus in Chapter 15.
2. Deborah King refers to this concept as "double jeopardy" (1988), and Maxine Baca Zinn and Bonnie Thornton Dill refer to it as the "matrix of domination" (2005).

REFERENCES

Burton, Linda, and Rukmalie Jayakody. 2001. "Rethinking Family Structure and Single Parenthood: Implications for Future Studies of African-American Families and Children." In *The Well-Being of Children and Families: Research and Data Needs*, edited by A. Thornton, 125–153. Ann Arbor, MI: University of Michigan Press.

Cherlin, Andrew. 1999. *Public and Private Families*. New York: McGraw-Hill.

ChildWelfare.gov. 2016. "Racial Disproportionality and Disparity in Child Welfare." *Issue Brief*. November 2016. www.childwelfare.gov/pubPDFs/racial_disproportionality.pdf.

Fox, Greer Litton, Michael L. Benson, Alfred A. DeMaris, and Judy Van Wyk. 2002. "Economic Distress and Intimate Violence: Testing Family Stress and Resources Theories." *Journal of Marriage and the Family 64(3)*: 793–807.

Hattery, Angela J. 2008. *Intimate Partner Violence*. Lanham, MD: Rowman and Littlefield.

Hattery, Angela J. 2009. "Sexual Abuse in Childhood and Adolescence and Intimate Partner Violence in Adulthood Among African American and White Women." *Race, Gender, and Class 15(2)*: 79–97.

Hattery, Angela J., and Earl Smith. 2007. *African American Families*. Thousand Oaks, CA: Sage.

Hattery, Angela J., and Earl Smith. 2010. *Prisoner Reentry and Social Capital: The Long Road to Reintegration*. Lanham, MD: Lexington Books.

Hattery, Angela J., and Earl Smith. 2012. *African American Families: Myths and Realities*. Lanham, MD: Rowman and Littlefield.

Hegewisch, Ariane. 2018. "The Gender Wage Gap: 2017; Earnings Differences by Gender, Race, and Ethnicity." Institute for Women's Policy Research. Fact Sheet: Pay Equity & Discrimination. ID: C473. September 13, 2018. https://iwpr.org/publications/gender-wage-gap-2017.

Jackman, Tom. 2011. "Gene Upshaw's Dramatic Death-Bed Scene: The Rest of the Story." *Washington Post*, May 5. www.washingtonpost.com/blogs/the-state-of-nova/

post/gene-upshaws-dramatic-death-bed-scene-the-rest-of-the-story/2011/05/04/AFSF86tF_blog.html.

Kaiser Family Foundation. 2003. "National Survey of Adolescents and Young Adults: Sexual Health Knowledge, Attitudes, and Experiences." http://kff.org/hivaids/report/national-survey-of-adolescents-and-young-adults.

Kimmel, Michael. 2005. *Manhood in America*. New York: Oxford University Press.

King, Deborah. 1988. "Multiple Jeopardy, Multiple Consciousness: The Context of a Black Feminist Ideology." *Signs 14(1)*: 42–72.

Kleinfield, N. R., and Mosi Secret. 2011. "A Bleak Life, Cut Short at 4, Harrowing from the Start." *New York Times*, May 8. www.nytimes.com/2011/05/09/nyregion/short-bleak-life-of-marchella-pierce-emaciated-4-year-old.html.

Landale, Nancy, and Katherine Fennelly. 1992. "Informal Unions Among Mainland Puerto Ricans: Cohabitation or an Alternative to Legal Marriage?" *Journal of Marriage and the Family 54(2)*: 269–280.

Neff, Lisa, and Benjamin R. Karney. 2005. "To Know You Is to Love You: The Implications of Global Adoration and Specific Accuracy for Marital Relationships." *Journal of Personality and Social Psychology 88(3)*: 480–497.

Sarkisian, Natalla, and Naomi Gerstel. 2008. "Till Marriage Do Us Part: Adult Children's Relationships with Their Parents." *Journal of Marriage and Family 70(2)*: 360–376.

Smith, Earl, and Angela Hattery. 2009. *Interracial Intimacies: An Examination of Powerful Men and Their Relationships Across the Color Line*. Durham, NC: Carolina Academic Press.

Steese, Stephanie, Maya Dollette, William Phillips, and Elizabeth Hossfeld. 2006. "Understanding Girls' Circle as an Intervention on Perceived Social Support, Body Image, Self-Efficacy, Locus of Control, and Self-Esteem." *Adolescence 41(161)*: 55–75.

Straus, Murray A., and Richard J. Gelles. 1995. *Physical Violence in American Families*. New Brunswick, NJ: Transaction.

Tjaden, Patricia, and Nancy Thoennes. 2000. *Full Report of the Prevalence, Incidence, and Consequences of Violence Against Women: Findings from the National Violence Against Women Survey*. Washington, DC: US Department of Justice. www.ncjrs.gov/pdffiles1/nij/183781.pdf.

Tresniowski, Alex. 2011. "5 Browns: A Family Shattered." *People*, March 21. www.people.com/people/archive/article/0,,20472972,00.html.

Wang, Wendy, Kim Parker, and Paul Taylor. 2013. "Breadwinner Moms: Mothers Are the Sole or Primary Provider in Four-in-Ten Households with Children; Public Conflicted About the Growing Trend." *Pew Research Center*, May 29. www.pewsocialtrends.org/files/2013/05/Breadwinner_moms_final.pdf.

Zinn, Maxine Baca, and Bonnie Thornton Dill. 2005. "Theorizing Differences From Multicultural Feminism." In *Gender Through the Prism of Difference*, edited by M. B. Zinn, P. Hondagneu-Sotelo, and M. A. Messner, 23–28. Oxford: Oxford University Press.

HISTORICAL PERSPECTIVES ON FAMILY VIOLENCE

2

This chapter will trace the history of family violence and its study in the United States. We will review trends in family violence and changes in the laws that address family violence. In addition to noting the changes in the laws, we will identify the social changes that precipitated the changes in the law.

OBJECTIVES

- To examine the historical definitions of each type of family violence, including child abuse, sexual abuse, elder abuse, and intimate partner violence
- To examine the history of the legal treatment of each type of family violence
- To explore the social and environmental changes that led to revisions in definitions and legal treatments of each type of family violence
- To demonstrate the role that the historical construct and legal treatment of family violence plays in the contemporary definitions and legal responses

KEY TERMS

special populations	age of consent
Child Protective Services (CPS)	incest
child welfare services/laws	patrilineal
Personal Responsibility Work Opportunity Act (PRWOA)	cross-cousin marriage
	parallel cousins
Temporary Aid for Needy Families (TANF)	statutory rape
	Megan's Law
cap babies	Amber Alert
battered child syndrome	rule of thumb
medical neglect	mandatory arrest
anti-immunization movement	order of protection
child sexual abuse (CSA)	Violence Against Women Act

INTRODUCTION

For many social phenomena, the ways in which the phenomenon is constructed and interpreted at a specific moment in time are shaped by the history of that phenomenon. So, for example, the belief that people of African descent were less than fully human shaped both beliefs and laws about interracial marriage well into the early twentieth century. By the late 1960s, after decades of the civil rights movement and historic legal decisions such as the landmark US Supreme Court decision *Brown v. Board of Education*, which opened the door to integration in schools and other public settings, beliefs about interracial marriage had moderated to the point that laws prohibiting them were declared unconstitutional in the 1967 US Supreme Court ruling *Loving v. Virginia* (Smith and Hattery 2009). Such is also the case with the evolution of beliefs about discipline versus abuse, children and wives as possessions as opposed to independent beings, and the role of corporal punishment in the socialization of both.

Understanding the evolution of both beliefs and the legal treatment of phenomena helps us to understand the current climate with regard to all forms of family violence. In this chapter we will explore the evolution of these beliefs and practices for each of the types of family violence. We will conclude this chapter by examining the degree to which there are parallel and overlapping evolutions, the ways in which evolution in thinking around one type of family violence influenced beliefs about other forms, and the ways in which various types of family violence are unique in their history and evolution. We will also examine the ways in which recognizing **special populations**—minorities, "at-risk" youth, the differently abled, children of parents who are incarcerated, and so forth—shapes the development and implementation of unique policies, moving us beyond a one-size-fits-all approach to dealing with family violence. We begin with a discussion of child abuse.

CHILD ABUSE

Most people are familiar with the notion that beliefs about child abuse have developed and evolved and that the legal response to it changed significantly across the last half of the twentieth century. It wasn't that long ago that corporal punishment could be (and was) used in schools, when spanking was not a topic of conversation among parents of young children, and when grandmothers used phrases like "Spare the rod, spoil the child." And when we look back even further we see that there is a long and complex history surrounding child discipline and child abuse. Of course, you will also recall from our discussions in Chapter 1 that child abuse can be sexual as well as physical. Because these types of abuse have very different histories and trajectories, we will discuss them separately. We begin with a review of the history of what is routinely referred to simply as "child abuse"—the physical abuse of children.

Child Physical Abuse

Child abuse has existed for all of recorded history, and in fact only recently, at the beginning of the twentieth century, did commonly held beliefs about it begin to change. Child abuse can take many forms, including the physical beating of a child, infanticide and child murder, neglect, abandonment, and selling a child into slavery. As we shall see throughout this chapter, the customs, norms, and laws in the United States have their roots in the British system—which drew significantly on Roman and Greek law—and thus an examination of the state of children in Britain and across "civilized" Europe prior to the birth of the United States is helpful.

A look at the assumptions and laws in the early Greek and Roman societies is revealing. "In Roman society the father had complete control over the family, even to the extent that he could kill his children for disobedience" ("Child Abuse—A History" 2005).

Simultaneously, early religious beliefs were being institutionalized, and many of the tenets extolled by these religious teachings contributed to the further codification of the rights of fathers and children. For example, in Catholicism, which was formally institutionalized as part of the Roman Empire, fathers were charged with the proper socialization of their children. Because children were seen as being unable to engage in rational thought and abstract reasoning (the same notions were applied to women as well), it was believed that physical punishment was often necessary and appropriate as a strategy for the proper training of children. There are many examples from the Middle Ages (eleventh through fourteenth centuries) of parenting manuals that advocated beating children as an important part of their socialization ("Child Abuse—A History" 2005).

The notion that children were the property of their parents pervaded beliefs, norms, and practices across Europe throughout the Middle Ages, Renaissance, and early modern period and traveled with the colonists who arrived in the United States in the seventeenth century. While families remained patriarchal, both mothers and fathers were expected to socialize their children through discipline. Some colonial legislatures even passed "stubborn children laws," giving parents the legal right to kill unruly children. According to journalist Roger Rosenblatt (1995), Massachusetts enacted a law in 1646 that allowed the death penalty for a rebellious child, though the law was never applied.

Abandonment was a common strategy for dealing with unwanted or unruly children, and it was practiced extensively in Europe through the apprenticeship system.

Obviously, the child then gained a skill, but the winner in this system was typically the child's master, who was able to extract free labor for a number of years from a child who had no other recourse or way to escape. Similar to the situation in sweatshops in the late eighteenth and nineteenth centuries, the treatment children received as apprentices could often be characterized as abusive.[1]

During the Industrial Revolution, the factory replaced the apprenticeship as a site for abandoning unwanted or unruly children. According to historical records, it was not unusual for children as young as five to be literally turned over to factories that were free to exploit their labor. Children were forced to work sixteen hours a day, and not uncommonly they were shackled to the machines. These children were housed in public poorhouses and almshouses alongside indigent adults ("Child Abuse—A History" 2005). One can only imagine that the living conditions alone constituted abuse by modern standards.

Child neglect, a common experience in the modern era, was not even a concept in the United States until midway through the twentieth century. As the United States transitioned out of an agricultural economy where food was perhaps plentiful but other necessities were often lacking—including shoes, access to an education, and so forth—into an industrial economy where food became far more scarce and living conditions were deplorable in the rapidly growing urban centers created by industrialization, the conditions most people lived under would today be considered substandard. Imagine for a moment a charge of neglect during the Great Depression. The inability to adequately feed and clothe a child during a decade when many adults relied on soup and bread lines for their only meal of the day would have been disregarded in light of the overall standards most adults lived under. (See Gordon 1988 for a lengthy discussion of the status of children during the Great Depression.) Thus, it was not until the plentiful period after World War II that child neglect—other than the most severe—was a matter of public concern.

Today, despite a dramatic revision to our beliefs, norms, and practices, child abuse, abandonment, and neglect are not only common but also frequently reach devastating conclusions because of our reluctance to intrude on the private sphere of the family.

Legal Response

The primary agency charged with the protection of children is the Department of Health and Human Services (DHHS). Additionally, most jurisdictions have an office of **Child Protective Services (CPS)** that has the legal authority to remove children from their homes and put them into foster care.

As noted above, it was not until midway through the twentieth century that child abuse, abandonment, and neglect became something of public concern.

Given both the dire circumstances of the Depression as well as the dawn of the New Deal programs begun under President Franklin D. Roosevelt, it is not surprising that the first child welfare laws were enacted in the mid-1930s.

The federal government first provided **child welfare services/laws** with the passage of the Social Security Act of 1935 (49 Stat. 620). Under Title IV-B (Child Welfare Services Program) of the act, the federal Children's Bureau received funding to grant to states for "the protection and care of homeless, dependent, and neglected children and children in danger of becoming delinquent." Prior to 1961, Title IV-B was the only source of federal funding for child welfare services. It is important to note that the expansion of child welfare legislation, though partly a response to changing attitudes about children, was more about changing attitudes about the poor; Roosevelt's New Deal programs included the development of Social Security—designed to alleviate poverty among the elderly—and other social programs.

The laws to protect children and provide for their welfare were greatly expanded in the 1960s when President John F. Kennedy began enlarging safety-net programs and peaked during the Johnson administration. The 1962 Public Welfare Amendments (Public Law 87–543) required each state to make child welfare services available to all children. It further required states to provide coordination between child welfare services (under Title IV-B) and social services (under Title IV-A), which served families on welfare. The law also revised the definition of "child welfare services" to include the prevention and remedy of child abuse. Finally, in 1980 Congress created the separate foster care program under Title IV-E. Title IV-A became Title XX ("Block Grants to States for Social Services and Elder Justice") in 1981, which gave states more options regarding the types of social services they could fund. Today child abuse prevention and treatment services remain an eligible category of service.

The period immediately following World War II saw some of the biggest changes in family life in United States' history, including a reversal in the trend toward later marriages and childbearing as well as a reversal in the trend toward lower fertility rates. Women began marrying earlier, having children earlier, and having more children than their mothers did; as a result, the children born between 1945 and 1965 are referred to as "baby boomers." This period also saw a reversal in the trend for women to be employed outside the home. During World War II, with so many men off in the various war theaters, women went to work in factories building the "war machine." After the war, when veterans returned, they went back to their jobs in the factories and women went back home. In addition, the GI Bill greatly expanded home ownership for veterans. Thus, the era of the stay-at-home mom—the *Leave It to Beaver* era—was ushered in. These changes in the family led to a greater appreciation for the welfare of children.

As previously noted, the most significant force that influenced the expansion of child welfare legislation was an overall focus on the poor. Beginning in the late 1950s, through Democratic leaders, including John F. Kennedy and Lyndon B. Johnson, and public figures like Martin Luther King Jr., as well as the social upheaval created by the civil rights movement, the plight of the poor in the Deep South, Appalachia, and urban centers was exposed nationally. In response, the government substantially expanded all social welfare, including programs that were designed to provide for the welfare of children.

The vast majority of social welfare programs—with the exception of the largest one, Social Security—are actually administered at the state and local levels, even though the rules governing them and the money funding them are provided by the federal government. Therefore, we focus our discussion here on state-level programs.

There are two distinct types of programs that are designed to address issues of children: "welfare" and protective services. Before receiving welfare, individuals, including children, must be approved by the local welfare agency in the community in which they live. In other words, children themselves are required to endure a process of qualification before their custodial parent(s) or guardian(s) is awarded access to programs on the part of these children. For example, when a low-income woman goes to the welfare office to apply for welfare, her award will be based on the number of people in her household who qualify. Though one might assume that that all of her minor children (those under age eighteen) are automatically covered, in fact one of the more troubling aspects of the welfare reform laws of 1996, which "reformed" welfare into the **Personal Responsibility Work Opportunity Act (PRWOA)**, established guidelines that prohibit babies born after a mother has begun receiving **Temporary Aid for Needy Families (TANF)** from being eligible for TANF. Referred to as "**cap babies**" (Hays 2003), these children *do not qualify* for welfare and thus *are not covered by the child welfare laws designed specifically to protect them, in this case from the severest poverty.* The authors of this legislation developed the notion of cap babies in order to discourage women already receiving welfare from having more children. The logic behind the development of this policy can be attributed to the stereotype of the "welfare queen" made popular in the 1980s by President Ronald Reagan. (For a comprehensive discussion of these reforms, as well as evidence that contradicts the rationale for them, we highly recommend Dorothy E. Roberts's book *Killing the Black Body*.)

The second goal of child welfare laws is to protect children from neglect and abuse. Under the Title IV-B Child Welfare Services (Subpart 1) and Promoting Safe and Stable Families (Subpart 2) programs, families in crisis receive preventive intervention so that children will not have to be removed from their homes. If this cannot be achieved, children are placed in foster care temporarily until they can be reunited with their families. If reunification is not possible, the parents' rights are terminated and the children are made available for adoption. Practically speaking, this is the law that allows social services to investigate accounts of child neglect and abuse and, if necessary, to remove children temporarily from their homes and even revoke parental custody.

For a variety of reasons, including a long history of not only tolerating but also advocating for the use of physical force on children—defined conveniently as "punishment"—and the long-held belief that family life is private, one of the barriers to protecting children from neglect and abuse is the simple fact that it is almost always hidden. One important change that has impacted this barrier—though it is difficult to quantify how much—was the development of the notion of "mandatory report-ers." The impetus for the development and implementation of a mandatory reporting law came, interestingly, from a pediatric radiologist. In 1961 Dr. C. Henry Kempe coined the term **battered child syndrome** at the annual meeting of the American Academy of Pediatrics, and a year later his findings were published (Kempe 1962). Kempe's research focused on the specific collection and pattern of injuries among children who were being physically abused or neglected or both. Relatively rapidly, by 1967, there was widespread acceptance among health-care and welfare workers such that Kempe's findings were expanded to include not just physical abuse and neglect but also sexual and emotional abuse, maltreatment, malnourishment, **medi-cal neglect,** and failure to thrive. This expanded definition was critical in shaping current beliefs about child abuse and the treatment of it. Additionally, Dr. Kempe felt strongly that physicians should be required by law to report abuse when they observed it. By 1967 forty-four states had implemented mandatory reporting laws for a series of occupations, including health-care providers, teachers, coaches, and others who frequently interact with, observe, and supervise children. The majority of cases that are referred to Child Protective Services come through the channels cre-ated by the mandatory reporting laws.

Definitions of child abuse have continued to expand, and beginning in the mid-1980s and continuing today, modifications have been made to the child welfare statutes, largely in response to social pressures and research that demonstrated gaps. After ignoring child abuse for centuries, there was a push following the initial legis-lation designed to protect children, and by 1980 there was concern among both the public and social workers that the foster care system was overwhelmed with chil-dren. As a result, with the goal of promoting family reunification, Congress passed the Adoption Assistance and Child Welfare Act of 1980 (Public Law 96–272). Less than two decades later, based on research and the reports of social work-ers, it became apparent that reuniting abused children with their families did not always work in the best interests of the children. Congress revisited the "reasonable efforts" for family reunification originally mandated by the Adoption Assistance and Child Welfare Act. Under the 1997 Adoption and Safe Families Act (Public Law 105–89), "reasonable efforts" was clarified to mean that the safety of the child comes first. States were directed to indicate circumstances under which an abused child *should not* be returned to the parents or caretakers.

Special Populations

In order to address the needs of children in special populations, a series of laws were passed. In 1994 Congress passed the Multiethnic Placement Act (Public Law 103–382), which directs states to actively recruit adoptive and foster families, especially for minority children waiting a long time for placement in a home. The Promoting Safe and Stable Families Amendments of 2001 (Public Law 107–133) was enacted partly to address the rising number of children with incarcerated parents. Currently, 2.7 million children have a parent in prison, including one million who are the children of incarcerated mothers (Hattery and Smith 2018). The majority of children whose fathers are incarcerated live with, and are cared for, by their mothers. However, when mothers are incarcerated, the percentage of children who live with their fathers is significantly lower, 37 percent. About half are cared for by their grandmothers or another woman relative, but nearly 11 percent are placed in foster care (Hairston 2009). Thus, there is a great need for services for children whose mothers are incarcerated.

In order to respond to the challenges faced by the nearly three million children with incarcerated parents, in 2013, Sesame Street introduced a new character, Alex, whose father is incarcerated. You can watch the episode where Alex reveals his father's incarcerated status on YouTube: www.youtube.com/watch?time_continue=119&v=yk3SxyPW6lA.

The Child Abuse Prevention and Treatment Act (Public Law 93–247), which was enacted in 1974 and amended and reauthorized most recently in 2010 with the CAPTA Reauthorization Act (Public Law 111–230), directed more comprehensive training of Child Protective Services personnel, including a mandate that they inform alleged abusers, during the first contact, of the nature of complaints against them. The law called for child welfare agencies to coordinate services with other agencies, including public health, mental health, and agencies serving those with developmental disabilities. In some states, this coordination has been utilized in order to address another special population: children who witness the abuse between their parents. In Minnesota, for example, when an officer arrives on an intimate partner violence call, if there are children "within sight or sound" of the intimate partner violence, the officer is required to refer the children to CPS. This launches a series of services, including counseling and the development of safety plans, especially if the parents decide to continue living together. This progressive law recognizes that children who witness abuse are themselves victims. This notion will be a central part of our discussion in Chapter 7. The law also directed the collection of data for the fourth, and most recent, *National Incidence Study of Child Abuse and Neglect*, the first of which was initiated in 1988 with the Child Abuse Prevention, Adoption, and Family Services Act (Public Law 100–294), which mandated, among other things, the establishment of a system to collect national data on child maltreatment.

MEDICAL NEGLECT AND THE ANTI-IMMUNIZATION MOVEMENT

Medical neglect, which is a very new phenomenon, refers to the fact that because parents have the legal right to make all medical decisions for a child, children may be denied medical care that they need if receiving such care violates an ideological or religious belief held by the parents.

For example, one case of medical neglect arose around a young cancer patient named Daniel Hauser, of New Ulm, Minnesota. Daniel, who was thirteen years old at the time of the controversy, suffered from Hodgkin's lymphoma. His mother believed that natural, homeopathic remedies were appropriate for Daniel and that the chemotherapy he had been prescribed—which was administered previously—was killing him. Despite the fact that chemotherapy was the only way to treat Daniel's tumors, his mother refused to allow him to be treated. In spring 2009, a medical exam revealed that his tumors had grown since the first round of chemo, and the court ordered him to undergo chemotherapy. With no more legal remedies for resistance, his mother, Colleen, fled with her son. In May 2009, mother and son returned to Minnesota and a judge took control of Daniel's "medical custody", ordering him to return to his treatment protocol. In November 2009 he received his last treatment and his medical report suggested he was in remission. This controversial case raises the question of who has the right to determine a child's medical needs. In this instance, the court argued that because the probability of remission was high if Daniel received chemotherapy—around 90 percent—and that death was nearly certain if he did not, the court had the right to protect the medical needs of the child, and this right superseded his parents' rights to restrict his access to medical care. It is also noted that Daniel himself did not want the chemotherapy treatments. Thus, this case also raises the question of the age of consent for medical treatment. Novelist Jodi Picoult explores this controversy in her 2005 book

My Sister's Keeper, in which a younger sister seeks medical emancipation in order to prevent further medical procedures used to prolong her older sister's life.

One of the most recent controversies surrounding medical neglect is the **anti-immunization movement**. The goals of public health infectious disease programs are achieved largely through widespread immunization; ideally, nearly the entire population would be immunized. This strategy is central to the eradication of disease because the scientific data demonstrate that over a period of time, if the vast majority of a population is immunized against a particular disease, not only will cases of that disease diminish, but the disease itself may be eradicated entirely from the human population. The case of smallpox is often cited as one of the biggest success stories for immunization.

Beginning in the mid-1990s, many parents began to question the role of immunizations in their children's health and some refused to immunize their children. Separate from the case in which parents without health care or easy access to clinics simply cannot get their children to the well-baby checkups where immunizations are provided, the anti-immunization movement is based on the belief in the individual right of a parent to decide whether to have a child immunized. Though parents in this movement clearly understand the overall benefits to the population when children are immunized, they believe that some children may be harmed by immunizations, and that their children should not be forced to be immunized because it could pose a risk to their health. Central to this movement is the belief that at least some proportion of autism cases are caused by vaccinations given to children, *though there is no scientific evidence to support this belief.* In fact, the research of the physician who proposed this relationship, Dr. Andrew Wakefield, was discredited when one of the most prestigious medical journals, *The Lancet*, which ironically published his original paper, retracted it after numerous follow-up studies found no evidence of a link between autism and vaccinations (Ziv 2015). Public health officials are rightly concerned that, as a result of the decrease in vaccinations, we will see the resurgence of devastating childhood diseases that we now consider to be "extinct" in the developed world, including whooping cough, measles, mumps, and diphtheria. And, in fact, because the anti-immunization movement is fairly localized, in white, upper-middle-class, "progressive" enclaves, there has been a spike in diseases like measles and whooping cough in these communities where a majority of parents refuse immunization. Troubling to public health officials is the fact that children living in these communities who cannot be vaccinated for medical reasons, for example if they have leukemia and the vaccine itself would kill them, now face exposure to deadly diseases because their neighbors, whose children are healthy and able to be vaccinated, refuse to do so. At the time of this writing, refusing to have one's child immunized does not constitute medical neglect. It will be interesting to watch the development of this movement in light of a lack of medical research that establishes a link between immunizations and autism coupled with the potential threat to public health that failing to immunize creates.

CHILD SEXUAL ABUSE

As is the case with the physical abuse of children, the history of **child sexual abuse (CSA)** is complicated by the fact that definitions and norms have changed significantly over time. Specifically, definitions of both family and the appropriate age for marriage—which generally signals the age one is considered old enough to freely consent to have sex—have changed over time and continue to vary dramatically from place to place. That said, some aspects of this phenomenon are so nearly universal that we can examine them in order to establish some common understanding of the history of CSA. Last, it is important to recognize that even more so than physical abuse, sexuality has always been considered something that is private and belongs inside the family. Only when sexual expression was perceived as threatening did it ever receive public attention. For example, when the open expression of homosexuality raised concerns in a local community or in the wider public, then public attention—including the enforcement of archaic sodomy laws that remained on the books in most states, until they were ruled unconstitutional by the Supreme Court in 2003—focused on what is otherwise a private matter. Rarely has CSA been considered a public matter—the only exceptions being when sex offenders kidnap, sexually abuse, and murder a child, and cases involving the widespread abuse of many children by a single public figure (for example, a teacher, coach, or Catholic priest)—and thus there is very little in the historical record of individual cases of CSA. Sex between family members, even if they are of the **age of consent**, is considered abuse. Thus, one of the complexities of defining CSA involves defining who is in the family.

DEFINITIONS OF FAMILY

The majority of CSA occurs inside of the family, and there is every reason to believe that this has always been the case. **Incest**, or sexual contact between relatives, depends upon how family is defined. For example, in the majority of states in the US, marriage and sex are illegal between any relatives closer than second cousins (Figure 2.1). As a result, sex with a child by a parent, grandparent, uncle, aunt, sibling, or first cousin is defined as incest. However, in a handful of states, marriage—and therefore sexual behavior—is allowed between first cousins. Thus, sex between married first cousins in Florida would be legal, whereas the same sex between the same first cousins in Minnesota would be illegal. The fact that in some states marriage between first cousins is allowed only when one of the potential spouses is infertile is indicative of the concerns surrounding sexual behavior in families and its potential outcome: children.[2]

In order to better understand the ways in which definitions of family are malleable, and thus why definitions of incest are variable, it is instructive to look at other cultures. For example, highly **patrilineal** and rural communities, such as the Cree—an American Indian Nation that thrived in what is now Canada and Minnesota, whose members now live on reservations in Montana—practiced **cross-cousin marriage** (Flannery 1938). Cross-cousin marriage, particularly the form in which a son marries his mother's brother's daughter, developed as a strategy for concentrating wealth and power based on a patrilineal structure of inheritance—all wealth is passed down through the men—as well as for alleviating concerns about paternity. The latter was accomplished by ensuring that all sexual access would take place among brothers, and thus even if an individual man was not the father of the children his wife bore, his brother would be, and thus his investment in the children was still an investment in passing on his family's genes.

Cross-cousin marriage is coupled with beliefs about incest and is built on pre-established notions of family. In a highly patrilineal culture, one's family is

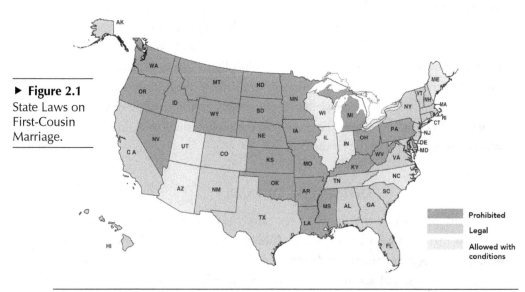

▶ **Figure 2.1**
State Laws on First-Cousin Marriage.

In twenty-four states (dark gray), first-cousin marriages are illegal. In nineteen states (medium gray), first cousins are permitted to wed. Seven states (light gray) allow first-cousin marriage but with conditions. Maine, for instance, requires genetic counseling; some states permit it only if one partner is sterile. North Carolina prohibits marriage only for double first cousins.

Source: CousinCouples.com, www.cousincouples.com/?page=states.

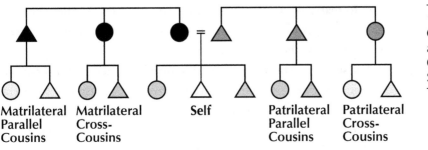

◀ **Figure 2.2**
Cross-Cousin
and Parallel-
Cousin
Structure.

Triangle = Male   Circle = Female

traced through one's father, not one's mother. Thus, one's father's family is one's family—for example, one's father's brother is one's uncle—but one's mother's family is not one's family. Thus, marriage and sex with one's father's family is incest, but marriage and sex with one's mother's relatives is not defined as incest and is actually preferred to marriage with other, nonrelated members of the community, as illustrated in Figure 2.2.

To further complicate matters, in some cultures, both sides of the family are considered relatives, but there is a distinction made between cross-cousins and **parallel cousins**, in which case "cross" refers to opposite-gender siblings in the parent generation and "parallel" refers to same-gender siblings in the parent generation. My cross-cousins are my father's sister's children and my mother's brothers' children. My parallel cousins are my father's brother's children and my mother's sister's children. Parallel cousins are considered "relatives" and cross-cousins are not.

To illustrate, a boy's (Self is male) "relatives" are his father's brother's children and his mother's sister's children. His ideal marriage partners are his female cross-cousins, his father's sister's daughter and his mother's brother's daughter.[3] Rather than focusing on the intricacies of the patterns, the most important point here is that parallel and cross-cousins share the same amount of genetic material, yet sex with a parallel cousin would violate the incest taboo, whereas cross-cousins are defined as ideal marriage—and by default sexual—partners. Thus, the definition of incest is not always determined by shared genetics but may be determined by other social forces as well.

CHANGING DEFINITIONS OF THE AGE OF CONSENT

Currently in the United States the age of consent for marriage is eighteen, with two exceptions: Nebraska's age of consent is nineteen, and Mississippi's age of consent is twenty-one. With parental consent, teenagers in most states can marry at age sixteen, with some states allowing children as young as fourteen (Texas) and twelve

(Massachusetts) to marry with parental consent. The majority of states allow for teenagers between the ages of fourteen and sixteen to marry when the girl is pregnant, in some cases even without parental consent.

The rules that surround **statutory rape** are somewhat different. For example, the age of consent to sex in most states is sixteen. However, in response to several tragic cases, including that of Genarlow Wilson in Georgia, who was convicted of statutory rape and spent two years in prison after he had consensual oral sex with a fifteen-year-old when he was seventeen, many states have modified their laws to require that there must be an *age difference* of more than two years between the parties when either party is under the age of consent in order for statutory rape laws to be applicable.[4]

One aspect that makes defining CSA complex is that the age of consent has changed dramatically over time and especially across space, and just as is the case with cross-cousin marriage, a situation that would be categorized as CSA in the United States at the beginning of the twenty-first century might not be in another culture. For example, Kristoff and WuDunn (2009) chronicle the pattern of child marriage, especially for girls, that continues to persist across rural regions of the Middle East, the Far East, Southeast Asia, and Africa. UNICEF reports on its website that more than sixty-four million women between the ages of twenty and twenty-four were married as children—under the age of eighteen years old. In Southeast Asian countries and the majority of African countries, more than 45 percent of women were child brides, and in countries in central Asia and the Middle East, rates hover just below 17 percent (UNICEF 2017). Though these marriages are technically illegal—most countries worldwide raised the formal age of consent to eighteen after pressure from the United Nations—because cultural beliefs and practices, not legal practices, dominate the lives of rural citizens, there has been very little change in the rate of child marriage in the developing world. We argue that all of these women are victims of CSA, regardless of the cultural traditions under which they live, yet, as one can see, defining CSA is problematic when ages of consent, cultural practices, and variations in definitions of family vary across time and place.

Child Sexual Abuse Laws in the United States

Though incest and CSA have always existed in the United States, and there has likely been little change in the rates across time, the primary motive for changing the laws around CSA was the dramatic increase in *stranger abductions* that typically involved sexual abuse and often murder.

Beginning in the early 1980s, the nation's attention was piqued and focused on several tragic child abduction cases, including that of Adam Walsh in 1981 and

Jacob Wetterling in 1989. Adam's decapitated head was found a month or so after his abduction, and Jacob's remains were found in September 2014. These cases, though a tiny minority of all CSA, were so horrific and the parents, especially John Walsh, so vocal that national attention began to be focused on CSA—at least that which is perpetrated by strangers.

In December 1995, with growing acknowledgment of and concern about sex crimes against minors, Congress passed the Sex Crimes Against Children Prevention Act (Public Law 104–71). The act increased penalties for those who sexually exploit children by engaging in illegal conduct or via the Internet, as well as for those who transport children with the intent to engage them in criminal sexual activity.

BOX 2.1	"MY BABY IS MISSING"

My Baby Is Missing
By Mark Gado (2014)
TruTV Crime Library

Adam Walsh was a happy six-year-old boy living in Florida with his parents, John and Reve Walsh. On July 27, 1981, Adam and his mother went to a mall in Hollywood, Florida, on a shopping expedition. They went into a Sears store, where Adam took an interest in a video game display. Mrs. Walsh continued shopping while Adam played the game. With the exception of several minutes, Adam was within his mother's eyesight nearly the entire time. When the mother returned for Adam, he was not where she had left him. Adam's severed head was found two weeks later. He had been sexually abused and tortured by a convicted sex offender.

In 1996 the US Congress passed **Megan's Law** as an amendment to the 1994 Jacob Wetterling Crimes Against Children and Sexually Violent Offender Registration Act (Public Law 103–322). It required every state to develop some procedure for notifying a community when a sex offender is released into their area. Different states have different procedures for making the required disclosures. Megan's Law was inspired by the case of seven-year-old Megan Kanka, a New Jersey girl who was abducted from her bedroom, raped, and killed by a known child molester who had moved across the street from her family. The Kanka family fought to have local communities warned about sex offenders in their area. The New Jersey legislature passed Megan's Law in 1994. Since the passage of the federal law in May 1996, all states have passed some form of Megan's Law.

Two years later, Congress enacted the Protection of Children from Sexual Predators Act of 1998 (Public Law 105–314), which, among other things, established the Morgan P. Hardiman Child Abduction and Serial Murder Investigative Resources Center (CASMIRC). The purpose of CASMIRC, as stated in the text of the act, is

> to provide investigative support through the coordination and provision of Federal law enforcement resources, training, and application of other multidisciplinary expertise, to assist Federal, State, and local authorities in matters involving child abductions, mysterious disappearance of children, child homicide, and serial murder across the country.

Congress passed the Prosecutorial Remedies and Other Tools to End the Exploitation of Children Today (PROTECT) Act (Public Law 108–21) on April 30, 2003. Among other things, the act established a national **Amber Alert** program for recovering abducted children and mandated that there will be no statute of limitations for sex crimes and the abduction of children. (Under previous laws, the statute of limitations expired when the child turned twenty-five.) The law also provided for severe penalties for sex tourism and the denial of pretrial release for suspects in federal child rape or kidnap cases. As is the case with so many CSA laws, the Amber Alert program is named after a victim, Amber Hagerman of Texas, who was abducted and murdered in 1996. She was nine years old. A witness notified police, giving a description of the vehicle and the direction it had gone, but police had no way of alerting the public.

The fact that the majority of CSA laws are named for victims is not serendipitous. As with the first case—Adam Walsh's murder—the legal response to CSA is driven almost entirely by high-profile, horrific, individual cases. This reactive rather than proactive approach is largely the reason there has been significantly less progress with regards to the laws involving incest—which is by far the most common form of CSA. Incest, as with other forms of family abuse, remains largely hidden behind the privacy of the family, and though we have better estimates of its prevalence—which we will discuss in Chapter 6—there has been little change in the legal approach; the majority of convicted child molesters serve less than three years in prison, and most return to their abusive behavior within a year of their release. In order to truly understand the impact of CSA on its victims, we need to focus our attention on cases of incest rather than the high-profile cases that, though horrific, are extremely rare.

ELDER ABUSE

The term *elder abuse*, which did not enter the national vocabulary until the 1970s, commonly refers to the physical abuse of an adult by their younger relatives, usually adult children, though it may also include other forms of abusive behavior, especially financial abuse, and fits under the larger rubric of "adult abuse" (Bonnie and Wallace 2003). Awareness about elder abuse is relatively recent in comparison to some other forms of abuse; for instance, the reader will recall that attempts to address child abuse and neglect began in the 1930s. There are a variety of reasons for the timing. First, perhaps obvious but not often considered, the elderly population in the United States did not make up a substantial part of the overall population until around 1970, when those over age sixty-five made up 10 percent of the population of the United States. In 2016, the most recent year for which data are available, that age group had risen to approximately 15 percent. As a result, it is not surprising that the early 1970s marks the beginning of a national focus on elder abuse.

One distinct element of elder abuse, as it is treated by the legal system, is that some victims are not elderly but adults, over the age of eighteen, who are vulnerable in some way as the result of a disability. This includes adults with mental and physical impairments or chronic diseases or injuries that require more or less constant care and supervision. Prior to the early 1980s this population was unlikely to survive into adulthood, and those individuals who did were institutionalized. Certainly, there is no question that abuse of these individuals existed, but it was hidden far from view as long as they remained locked in state hospitals and private facilities. Once this population began to be deinstitutionalized and cared for at home, the abuse that they experienced entered the mainstream consciousness as well.

This deinstitutionalization led to an increased awareness not only of elder abuse but also of additional factors that contributed to it, namely the fact that care was increasingly provided by relatives rather than paid staff. This shift changed elder abuse in two ways: it moved it under the rubric of "family violence," which meant that it came to the attention of scholars of family violence, and it spawned a new set of theories for explaining it (Bonnie and Wallace 2003). We will return to a discussion of the theoretical explanations in the next chapter. Like all other forms of abuse, it also generated legislation designed to protect this vulnerable and growing population.

Legal Response to Elder Abuse

About twenty years before the term *elder abuse* became mainstream, Congress became aware of an increasing number of aging adults who could not take care of their daily needs. In response, in the 1950s, as part of the Social Security Act, Congress provided funds to states on a three-to-one matching basis to set up protective service units for the elderly. Interestingly, in several matched sample studies, which compared adults receiving services via protective units with those who did not, those receiving services had both higher mortality rates and higher rates of institutionalization in nursing homes (Bonnie and Wallace 2003). *Despite increasing evidence that protective service units were in fact detrimental to the health and well-being of aging Americans*, in 1974 the US Congress amended the Social Security Act to provide funding to set up protective units in each of the fifty states and extended the services to all individuals over the age of eighteen (Bonnie and Wallace 2003).

Attention on elder abuse waned until the end of the 1970s, when Claude Pepper, a representative from Florida—one of the "grayest" of all states—held hearings in which the term *granny battering* was introduced. Across the decade of the 1980s, the focus on elder abuse grew beyond the need for protection from neglect and physical abuse to an understanding of the needs elderly Americans had for expanded access to medical, legal, and financial services, as well as other social and protective services. The transformation from an *abuse concept* to an *aging concept* paved the way for the 1990 expansion of the 1965 Older Americans Act (Public Law 89–73),[5] which, among other things, established a national center for the study of aging and elder abuse (Bonnie and Wallace 2003). In the early 1990s, the then secretary of health and human services, Louis Sullivan, held a national conference on family violence, and he chose to include elder abuse as a topic under this rubric. This act cemented the notion that elder abuse is one type of family abuse and thus generated and encouraged research by both gerontologists and family violence scholars (Bonnie and Wallace 2003).

INTIMATE PARTNER VIOLENCE

Like all forms of family abuse, intimate partner violence can be characterized as being hidden from view and subject to changing definitions and cultural norms. In nearly every culture and across all historical periods, women have been relegated to an inferior status legally as well as socially (Epstein 2007).[6] Scholars who have studied the history of intimate partner violence note that there is significant evidence to conclude that as a result of women's inferior status—as established by both religious doctrine and legal statutes—the physical abuse of women was not only legal but endorsed, especially when it was used as a form of discipline (Graetz 1998; Kelly 1994). Specifically, for most of recorded history, across most cultures, the belief was that women's constitutions—their inferior intellect, lack of rationality, and tendency to become overemotional—resulted in their needing guidance first from their fathers and, once married, from their husbands. Thus, the belief was that when a woman behaved inappropriately it was not only legal but, indeed, necessary for her husband to discipline her, and often this discipline took the form of physical abuse. Individual men found support for this behavior from their leaders—both civic and religious. Around AD 300, the Roman emperor Constantine burned his wife alive because he no longer had a use for her (Lemon 1996).

For many in the Western world, the inferiority of women was based on and reinforced by biblical texts, especially Ephesians 5:22–33, which dictates that wives are to be submissive to their husbands:

> 22 Wives, submit yourselves to your own husbands as you do to the Lord. 23 For the husband is the head of the wife as Christ is the head of the church, his body, of which he is the Savior. 24 Now as the church submits to Christ, so also wives should submit to their husbands in everything. 25 Husbands, love your wives, just as Christ loved the church and gave himself up for her 26 to make her holy, cleansing her by the washing with water through the word, 27 and to present her to himself as a radiant church, without stain or wrinkle or any other blemish, but holy and blameless. 28 In this same way, husbands ought to love their wives as their own bodies. He who loves his wife loves himself. 29 After all, no one ever hated their own body, but they feed and care for their body, just as Christ does the church—30 for we are members of his body. 31 "For this reason a man will leave his father and mother and be united to his wife, and the two will become one flesh." 32 This is a profound mystery—but I am talking about Christ and the church. 33 However, each one of you also must love his wife as he loves himself, and the wife must respect her husband.

As stated in verses twenty-five through thirty-three, husbands are required to love their wives, but there is no indication that this requires them to refrain from physically abusing them. In fact, as the reader shall see in later chapters, many of the men we interviewed who battered their partners fiercely claimed to love them and justified their physical abuse based on this love. One woman's partner proclaimed that he would not beat her if he did not love her so much. Therefore, we argue that it is reasonable to conclude that individual men, religious leaders, and political leaders throughout the Western world, and through most of recorded history, would have come to the conclusion that the Bible required men to love their wives, but it also required them to demand women's submission, for which discipline could be utilized to enforce submission when women "forgot their place."

Much like child abuse, intimate partner violence has a long legal history, the vast majority of which protects men's legal right to beat their wives. The commonly held principle with regards to intimate partner violence was that it was legal—and tolerable—for a man to beat his wife as long as the rod he used to do so was smaller than the diameter of his thumb (Kelly 1994). This law was referred to as the **rule of thumb**, though obviously the phrase has a different meaning when used today. In 1824 the Mississippi Supreme Court in *Bradley v. State* allowed a husband to administer only "moderate chastisement" in cases of emergency (Lemon 1996; Martin 1976).

> In 1867 a North Carolina court acquitted a man who had given his wife three licks with a switch about the size of one of his fingers, but "smaller than his thumb." The reviewing appellate court upheld the acquittal on the ground that a court should "not interfere with family government in trifling cases."
>
> (Martin 1976: 31)

Though several states had begun to rescind a man's legal right to beat his wife, again in North Carolina in 1874, the "finger-switch" rule was disavowed when the Supreme Court of North Carolina ruled that "the husband has no right to chastise his wife under any circumstances." However, the court went on to say, "*If no permanent injury has been inflicted, nor malice, cruelty nor dangerous violence shown by the husband, it is better to draw the curtain, shut out the public gaze and leave the parties to forget and forgive*" (Martin 1976: 32; emphasis added). Thus, the message is loud and clear: domestic violence will be tolerated—even as it is becoming illegal—and the best approach to dealing with domestic violence is to consider it a private matter.

This notion that intimate partner violence is a private matter, as with child abuse and elder abuse, has shaped much of the manner in which the phenomenon continues to unfold in the contemporary United States. Though intimate partner violence is now illegal in all states and the marital rape exemption has been removed from all state statutes, it remains very common for intimate partner violence to either go undetected entirely or be ignored because people continue to perceive it as a private matter. Interviews with battered women reveal that it is commonplace for them to experience a severe beating in an apartment with thin walls, in an apartment complex hallway, in public—often outside of a bar or restaurant—or to be stalked at work or church, and no one intervenes or calls the police. The fact that our public response to intimate partner violence remains passive is highly indicative of our history of treating it as a private matter between a husband and wife.

A Brief History of the Intimate Partner Violence Movement

The earliest research on intimate partner violence dates back to the 1970s. In fact, it was not until 1970 that the index for the *Journal of Marriage and the Family*, the premier journal for sociologists who study the family, included the term *violence*. The second wave of feminism, with all of its consciousness-raising and support groups and public marches and rhetoric, brought battering to the mainstream discourse. Women like Susan Brownmiller and Lenore Walker helped to bring battering to the attention of lawmakers, law enforcement agencies, and research scholars.

During the late 1970s and early 1980s, shelters for battered women began to spring up all over the country, though they are still outnumbered three to one by shelters for abandoned animals (Browne 1989; Koss et al. 1994). More recently, advocates and researchers have put together protocols for dealing with intimate partner violence that have been codified in the form of legal codes such as **mandatory arrest** laws. Despite all of this, we still know very little about the inner workings of intimate partner violence, and we are still relatively unsuccessful in reducing its prevalence.

Intimate partner violence remains a misdemeanor in most states, punishable by probation rather than jail time. In fact, in many communities batterers can opt for a diversionary treatment program (as NFL player Ray Rice did, as did many of those interviewed for this book) and forgo jail time altogether. In these diversionary treatment programs batterers learn the rhetoric but they seldom cease battering. Most of the men whose stories are told in this book admitted openly and freely that they were still abusing their partners, and some admitted, or their partners confessed, that battering episodes had occurred within just a day or two of the interview.

Today, the movement around intimate partner violence has moved toward increasing inclusivity in all forms. Intimate partner violence advocates now focus not just on the physical and sexual abuse that victims experience but also the emotional and psychological trauma. Intimate partner violence advocates increasingly recognize the need for prevention and intervention programs that target young people, as dating violence rates are high (between 6.5 and 10.2 percent) among teens ages thirteen to eighteen (Centers for Disease Control 2018). Additionally, there is a growing awareness of the need for prevention and intervention strategies that are sensitive to racial or ethnic, religious, and other cultural differences. In fact, in a community in which we lived during the 2000s, Winston-Salem, North Carolina, there has been a decade-long attempt to address intimate partner violence through partnerships between advocates and religious leaders. Last, the intimate partner violence movement has expanded to incorporate issues of sexuality, not only violence in gay and lesbian relationships but also violence against transgender individuals.

Legal Response to Intimate Partner Violence

As noted earlier, by the mid-1880s some states, Alabama being the first, began to modify their laws by rescinding men's legal rights to beat their wives. However, the enforcement of these laws was highly contested, and in 1886 the North Carolina

Supreme Court ruled again that "a criminal indictment cannot be brought against a husband unless the battery is so great as to result in permanent injury, endanger life and limb, or be malicious beyond all reasonable bounds" (Martin 1976: 44).

A significant shift in the enforcement and handling of intimate partner violence began in 1911 with the establishment of the first family court, in Buffalo, New York. This movement is significant in that it shifted intimate partner violence from criminal court to family court. The belief was that family courts would be better suited to handling domestic disputes. Perhaps that is true. But, by moving intimate partner violence out of criminal court, the ability to impose sanctions and require accountability, which criminal courts have, was diminished. For example, in most states this means that a man convicted of battering will not face the harsher penalties associated with an assault conviction in criminal court. We will return to this point later.

By the 1960s, the dominant belief was that arresting batterers was an inadequate solution to the complexities of intimate partner violence, and thus police officers were trained in crisis intervention techniques. The most common tactic was to calm the abuser down by walking him around the block. Research on intimate partner violence demonstrated that this approach tended to intensify rather than reduce the violence. Men who were not arrested believed that they would not be held accountable, and they believed this translated into free rein to batter their wives and girlfriends (Browne 1989). Many battered women who have been interviewed for documentaries, including the powerful *Defending Our Lives*, report this experience as common.

By the late 1980s, based on the recommendations of advocates, a return to arresting abusers was implemented on a trial basis in a small number of jurisdictions. In Minnesota, for example, a mandatory arrest law was established that required officers who were called to intimate partner violence incidents to arrest the perpetrator. This approach was deemed successful and by the mid-1990s most states had laws that required that perpetrators be arrested and detained for seventy-two hours. The laws vary from state to state and various attempts to modify them have taken place, beginning in the early 2000s. For example, in North Carolina the domestic violence statute is termed *assault on a female*, which indicates that the crime is limited to cases with women victims. This creates serious problems for straight and gay men who are victims. In states like Minnesota, where intimate partner violence laws are gender-neutral, social workers who saw the traumatic outcomes for children who witness violence advocated for requiring children of all genders in these cases to be referred to social services.

As noted earlier, one of the most important decisions to impact intimate partner violence policy was moving these cases out of criminal court and into family court, where cases involving family matters, including divorce and adoption, take place. Family court operates much more like civil court in the sense that the most common decisions focus on legal relationships that have contract implications, such as child custody or adoption. Rarely are punishments per se associated with family court. Again, the specific laws vary from state to state and we are, of course, most familiar with those in states where we have lived and been actively engaged in antiviolence movements. To use North Carolina as an example, when a man is convicted of "assault on a female"—the charges are dropped more than 50 percent of the time—he is typically offered the opportunity to participate in a batterer intervention program in lieu of jail time or probation. On the one hand, this might seem like a progressive option, especially in light of the fact that by avoiding jail the man can continue to work—if he is employed—and contribute to the financial well-being of his family. However, in practical terms, because family court judges have no ability to require accountability, the court has no power to enforce his attendance at an intervention program and, as a result, the majority of the men we studied rarely attended the program. Of those who did, few completed more than 25 percent of the program's sessions. Whether this influences recidivism rates is still unclear, but what is clear is that in criminal court, assault is treated very differently from the way the same type of physical abuse is treated in family court when it occurs between intimate partners. The lack of accountability in batterer intervention programs is in stark contrast to cases in which individuals are sentenced to drug or alcohol rehabilitation as part of the terms required to getting a driver's license reinstated after a DUI. In other words, our courts require accountability in cases of drug or alcohol abuse but not in cases of intimate partner abuse.

Another aspect of the criminal justice response to intimate partner violence is the availability and implementation of an **order of protection**, which prevents someone who poses a threat from having any contact with the person who files for the order; contact can be defined as physical or via e-mail, phone, text, and so forth. Like so many other aspects of intimate partner violence, orders of protection are granted and enforced by civil, family courts. Thus, though they may initially make a battered woman feel more secure, in practice, because they are civil and not criminal orders, they are nothing more than pieces of paper with very little power to protect.

More recently, states have developed and implemented a series of stalking laws. In part, these laws developed out of recognition that batterers often terrorize their intimate partners by stalking them—popping up unexpectedly, following them in their cars, calling their phones at all hours of the day and night—a point that we will return to later. However, the need for stalking laws increased substantially as the technology of the late twentieth and early twenty-first centuries has exploded:

in an age of cellphone tracking devices, the ability to hack into computers and mobile devices, e-mail harassment, and various forms of harassment associated with social networking—such as posting threats or derogatory comments or pictures on Facebook or Instagram—the ability a batterer has to harass his victim has increased exponentially. In addition, stalking laws have been a major boost to the prevention and intervention strategies associated with teen violence. Because young men in high school and college often engage in harassing strategies long before they are married to or cohabiting with their partners—indeed, in the case of high school students, both parties usually still live with their parents—stalking laws have provided an avenue for early intervention for teens.

One of the most significant developments in the overall approach to intimate partner violence comes from the passage of the **Violence Against Women Act** (VAWA) in 1994.

VAWA was drafted by then senator Joseph Biden's office with support from a number of advocacy organizations, including the National Organization for Women. VAWA was passed as Title IV, section 40001–40703 of the Violent Crime Control and Law Enforcement Act of 1994, which was signed into law as Public Law 103–322 by President Bill Clinton on September 13, 1994. It provided $1.6 billion to enhance the investigation and prosecution of violent crime perpetrated against women, increased pretrial detention of the accused, imposed automatic and mandatory restitution on those convicted, and allowed civil redress in cases that prosecutors chose to leave unprosecuted. VAWA was reauthorized by Congress in 2000 and again in December 2005, and in both cases it was signed by President George W. Bush. VAWA was again reauthorized, though after contentious debate, in 2013, and ultimately signed by President Barack Obama (Sacco 2015). Under the administration of President Trump, VAWA is once again being threatened and, at the time of this writing, it is not clear if it will be reauthorized.

One of the most important outcomes of VAWA was the establishment of an office within the Department of Justice that deals exclusively with violence against women. Statutorily established following the reauthorization of VAWA in 2000, the Office on Violence Against Women has the authority to administer the grants authorized under VAWA—which is how many of the shelters and prevention and intervention programs across the nation are funded, including on college campuses—as well as to develop federal policy around issues relating to intimate partner violence, dating violence, sexual assault, and stalking. Of course, one of the negative, and perhaps unintended, consequences of gender-based laws like this is that they often leave out men who are victims—both gay and straight. For example, because many shelters receive the majority of their funding from VAWA, they are restricted from providing shelter to men, including teenage boys who arrive with their mothers attempting to escape abusive households (Sacco 2015; www. faithtrustintitute.org).

CONCLUSIONS

In this chapter we have reviewed the overall history of various types of family violence in the United States. As we have noted, some of the common principles of family violence—regardless of the form it takes—are that it has been accepted historically and cross-culturally, it has often been endorsed by religious teachings, and the first key to beginning to address it has been to redefine both people and actions. All of these issues are important. For example, like virtually any practice, attitudes and norms of behavior typically change at a snail's pace compared to changes in the law. Think for a moment about the famous desegregation case *Brown v. Board of Education*, decided by the US Supreme Court in 1954. Despite its power, changes to segregated patterns were heavily resisted by those in power (whites), and it took decades to achieve any meaningful change. And some fifty-five years after *Brown*, attitude polls continue to reveal that a strong minority of whites continue to believe that African Americans are less capable, less intelligent, and lazier than whites, attitudes that persist despite electing the first African American president of the United States, twice (Hattery and Smith 2012).

So it is with family violence. Recall the many changes in the law and in court cases just in the state of North Carolina during the late nineteenth century. A man's right to beat his wife was rescinded, but that did not necessarily mean that battering was illegal. Once battering was declared illegal, that did not necessarily translate into charging individual men with intimate partner violence. Indeed, as late as 1874 the North Carolina Supreme Court ruled that even if intimate partner violence was illegal, unless the man killed his wife or abused her so badly that it became a public matter, it should remain "behind the curtain" and be treated as any other family problem; that is, it should be ignored. Our current mechanisms for dealing with intimate partner violence have been largely shaped by the very long history of failing to define it as a problem and tolerating or ignoring it. The same is true for child abuse and elder abuse. Additionally, the fact that Americans continue to attend religious services in which passages from holy books—the Bible, the Talmud, the Qur'an—that endorse women's submissiveness are read and "preached" has a profound impact on our attitudes regarding intimate partner violence and our approach to dealing with it when it occurs. As we will discuss at length in Chapter 10, 70 percent of women who sought counseling from a religious leader—a pastor, rabbi, or imam—reported that they were first told to go home and try to behave "better" so that their husbands would not be tempted to beat them (Nason-Clark 2009).

Religious institutions are not the only institutions that facilitate abuse or combat it; where appropriate, individual chapters interrogate the roles of various institutions in perpetuating family violence, and intimate partner violence in particular. And, as noted in the Preface, an entire chapter on institutionalized violence (Chapter 12) is devoted to this type of discussion.

Understanding something about the history of family violence is the first step in understanding the phenomenon. In the next chapter, we will examine the theories that are used to explain family violence.

NOTES

1. We argue that any situation that one cannot enter or exit freely is, by definition, abusive. Thus, even in apprenticeship arrangements where the masters were reasonable, the very situation itself constituted abuse.

2. For an interesting discussion of this, see Kershaw 2009.

3. The opposite pattern would apply when Self is a girl.

4. For more on Genarlow Wilson's story, see Dewan 2006.

5. This amendment was sponsored by Claude Pepper.

6. For an excellent examination of domestic violence, including bride burning and dowry murders, see Kristoff and WuDunn 2009.

REFERENCES

Bonnie, R. J., and R. B. Wallace, eds. 2003. *Elder Mistreatment: Abuse, Neglect, and Exploitation in an Aging America.* Washington, DC: National Academies Press.

Browne, A. 1989. *When Battered Women Kill.* New York: Free Press.

Centers for Disease Control (CDC). 2018. *Youth Risk Behavior Survey: Data Summary and Trends Report 2016–2017.* www.cdc.gov/healthyyouth/data/yrbs/pdf/trendsreport.pdf.

"Child Abuse—A History." 2005. *Information Plus Reference Series*, 1st ed. Farmington Hills, MI: Gale/Cengage Learning.

Dewan, S. 2006. "Georgia Man Fights Conviction as Molester." *New York Times*, December 19. www.nytimes.com/2006/12/19/us/19georgia.html.

Epstein, C. 2007. "Great Divides: The Cultural, Cognitive, and Social Bases of the Global Subordination of Women." *American Sociological Review* 72(*1*): 1–22.

Flannery, R. 1938. "Cross-Cousin Marriage Among the Cree and Montagnais of James Bay." *Primitive Man* 11(*1–2*): 29–33.

Gado, Mark. 2014. "My Baby Is Missing!". *Child Abduction, Analysis of This Crime and Major Cases, Crime Library on truTV.com.* www.trutv.com/library/crime/criminal_mind/psychology/child_abduction/4.html.

Gordon, L. 1988. *Heroes of Their Own Lives: The Politics and History of Family Violence.* New York: Penguin.

Graetz, N. 1998. *Silence Is Deadly: Judaism Confronts Wifebeating.* Northvale, NJ: Jason Aronson.

Hairston, Creasie. 2009. *Kinship Care When Parents Are Incarcerated: What We Know, What We Can Do*. Baltimore, MD: Annie E. Casey Foundation.

Hattery, A. J., and E. Smith. 2012. *African American Families: Myths and Realities*. Lanham, MD: Rowman and Littlefield.

Hattery, A. J., and E. Smith. 2018. *Policing Black Bodies: How Black Lives Are Surveilled and How to Work for Change*. Lanham, MD: Rowman and Littlefield.

Hays, S. 2003. *Flat Broke on Welfare*. New York: Oxford University Press.

Kelly, H. 1994. "Rule of Thumb and the Folklaw of the Husband's Stick." *Journal of Legal Education 44(3)*: 341–365.

Kempe, C. H. 1962. "The Battered-Child Syndrome." *Journal of the American Medical Association 181(1)*: 17–24.

Kershaw, S. 2009. "Shaking Off the Shame." *New York Times*, November 25. www.nytimes.com/2009/11/26/garden/26cousins.html.

Koss, M. P., L. A. Goodman, A. Browne, L. F. Fitzgerald, G. P. Keita, and N. F. Russo. 1994. *No Safe Haven: Male Violence Against Women at Home, at Work, and in the Community*. Washington, DC: American Psychological Association.

Kristoff, N., and S. WuDunn. 2009. *Half the Sky: Turning Oppression into Opportunity for Women Worldwide*. New York: Alfred A. Knopf.

Lemon, N. 1996. *Domestic Violence Law: A Comprehensive Overview of Cases and Sources*. San Francisco, CA: Austin and Winfield.

Martin, D. 1976. *Battered Wives*. New York: Pocket Books.

Nason-Clark, N. 2009. "Christianity and the Experience of Domestic Violence: What Does Faith Have to Do with It?" *Social Work and Christianity 36(4)*: 379–393.

Protection of Children from Sexual Predators Act of 1998. Pub. L. 105–314, 11 Stat. 2974 §703(b).

Rosenblatt, R. 1995. "The Society That Pretends to Love Children." *New York Times Magazine*, October 8. www.nytimes.com/1995/10/08/magazine/the-society-that-pretends-to-love-children.html.

Sacco, L. N. 2015. The Violence Against Women Act: Overview, Legislation, and Federal Funding. *Congressional Research Service*, May 26. www.fas.org/sgp/crs/misc/R42499.pdf.

Smith, E., and A. Hattery. 2009. *Interracial Intimacies: An Examination of Powerful Men and Their Relationships Across the Color Line*. Durham, NC: Carolina Academic Press.

UNICEF. 2017. www.unicef.org/rosa/what-we-do/child-protection/child-marriage.

Ziv, Stav. 2015. "Andrew Wakefield, Father of the Anti-Vaccine Movement, Responds to the Current Measles Outbreak for the First Time." *Newsweek*, February 10. www.newsweek.com/2015/02/20/andrew-wakefield-father-anti-vaccine-movement-sticks-his-story-305836.html.

3

THEORIES FOR STUDYING FAMILY VIOLENCE

This chapter introduces the three different theoretical frameworks for studying family violence. Each will be reviewed and critiqued on both its strengths and its weaknesses. Additionally, the chapter covers the key figures associated with each theory and provides examples of their contributions to the field.

OBJECTIVES

- To introduce the primary theories that are used to study family violence
- To provide an assessment of each theoretical framework, highlighting both its pros and its cons
- To identify the scholars who have developed each theory

KEY TERMS

grand theories
conflict theory
structural-functionalism
symbolic interaction theory (SI)
"doing gender"
theories of the middle range
feminist theory
race, class, and gender theory (RCG)
criminology theories
strain theory
conformists
rebels
retreatists
ritualists

innovators
social control
theory social bonds
differential association theory
family violence theory
Conflict Tactics Scale (CTS)
mutual combat
intimate terrorism
situational couple violence
psychological theories
situational theory
exchange theory
social learning theory

INTRODUCTION

Theory has the reputation of being boring, dense, and static, and as a result, courses on theory and philosophy are often undersubscribed. Though we would agree that the paradigms developed by early social theorists are often difficult to read—most were written in French or German and the translations are often dense—in fact, theory is neither static nor irrelevant. Theories are developed to provide a general framework for understanding social phenomena and making predictions. In this chapter, we provide an overview of the founders of social theory and then systematically review all of the theoretical frameworks that have been developed and/or applied to understanding the family and family violence in particular.

THEORETICAL APPROACHES TO FAMILY VIOLENCE

The unique focus on structure and institutions that sociologists take is often less familiar to non-sociologists. In our own classrooms, we find that this framework is very difficult for students to feel completely comfortable with, which stands to reason since the "fathers" of sociology—whose work contributed significantly to our focus on structures and institutions—failed to include the family in their work, as their attention was elsewhere.

Lester Frank Ward, for example, whom many consider the "father of American sociology" (Calhoun 2007; Ward 1963), spent his time examining issues related to evolutionary processes and eugenics, like other early sociologists in the United States and elsewhere. Early on, sociologists were concerned about issues such as charities and correction, labor problems, statistics, social reform, social control, personality and social adjustment, and urban and rural sociology.

Urban sociology was popular in places like the University of Chicago, but so was the study of immigration, settlement patterns, and ethnicity. We cannot forget, though, that early sociologists were very interested in putting forth the perspective that sociology was a "real" science and spent enormous time on the burning issues of their time (Weber 1949).

The family only became a central issue in American sociology around the time of the Great Depression. Beginning on Black Tuesday, October 29, 1929, the Great Depression catapulted Americans into a life of despair. The struggles for food, work, living space, and a more normal life did not end until around the time of America's entry into World War II in 1941.

All of this is important in terms of family violence. To understand what was happening in the American home, it stands to reason that someone had to be studying it. Family sociologists were at this time those people engaged in chronicling the life chances of American families.

One of the first things that students want to know is why they should care about theory and why they should have to learn it. Most of our own students remark that theory is boring, that it was written by a bunch of dead white men—that, in short, it has no relevance. In fact, the development and understanding of theories are important not only for the scholars who do the research on family violence and the practitioners who work with families who are experiencing it, but also for students of family violence because it provides a sort of road map that helps us to see the patterns in family violence, rather than seeing it as a set of disconnected and isolated events.

But first, a few caveats. Social theory has been built upon the same principles as theories of the natural world—the theory of relativity, Boyle's law, Newton's laws—which are more like guidelines than exact rules. Everyone who has taken a physics or chemistry class in a lab knows that the theories that guide these disciplines provide precise and repeatable "laws" that describe how the physical world works. So, for example, one learns early on that when heat is applied to water, it turns to steam, and that the point at which this transformation begins to occur is when the water reaches a temperature of approximately 212 degrees Fahrenheit. Similarly, when water is subjected to cold temperatures, it turns to ice, at approximately 32 degrees Fahrenheit. Yet every meteorologist knows that predicting when a February storm will yield snow, when it will yield ice, and when it will yield rain is difficult at best. And though we often "blame the weatherman," the truth is that predicting the weather—which relies on a variety of complex factors, including air temperature, wind, ground temperature, cloud cover, and so on—is a lot like developing theories of family violence: it is mushy.

Social and psychological theories are often critiqued for being imprecise and for not being able to explain every variation of a phenomenon, yet just like the weather, individual people are infinitely complex and unique, and when they are in groups—as they are in a family—the complexity of possible outcomes grows exponentially. Thus, predicting any one person's behavior, let alone their behavior when they are acting inside a group or relationship, is difficult at best and impossible at worst. Social and psychological theories, then, are not designed to predict with certainty the behavior of an individual person; rather, they provide a road map that identifies patterns and the strength that these patterns have in explaining most of human behavior. Social and behavioral scientists make clear that these theories cannot explain or predict every single person's behavior, but they are useful in painting a broad picture of the overall shape of particular social phenomena.

Sociological theories come in three types: grand theories, theories of the middle range, and theories that attempt to explain a single phenomenon, such as prisoner reentry (for instance, see Hattery and Smith 2010).

GRAND THEORIES

Grand theories, most notably conflict theory, structural-functionalist theory, and symbolic interactionist theory, were developed in order to explain all of the vastness of human behavior. Each is built on the assumption that all types of human behavior—both at the micro or individual level and at the macro or institutional level—are organized around several key principles.

Conflict Theory

Developed by Karl Marx (Marx, Engels, and Struik 1971), **conflict theory** argues that all of the social world can be understood as a battle over resources. This battle is structured around the antagonistic *class* relationship between those who have access to "the means of production" (the bourgeoisie, or capitalists, who own land and factories) and those who do not (the proletariat, or workers). Marx argued that this fundamental and antagonistic relationship based on class could explain all of human behavior. Marx's conceptualization developed primarily as an economic theory and has been used to explain labor market behavior, wages, the development of unions, and so on. That said, Marx and his colleagues and, more recently, neo-Marxist theorists have modified and developed the basic tenets of conflict theory to explain a wide range of phenomena, from the exploitation of student athletes and the big business of sports (Smith 2014) to the covert and overt goals of the criminal justice system (Wacquant 2001; Wright 1997), to the development of social capital networks (Lin 2000), and to family violence.

Conflict Theory and Family Violence

Friedrich Engels, Karl Marx's coauthor of the *Communist Manifesto*, modified their theory of capitalism and exploitation and applied it to the family. Engels (1884) argues that the family, as an institution, can be understood and analyzed like the economy. Writing during the height of the Industrial Revolution, when men increasingly worked in the public sphere and the majority of women stayed at home, taking care of the family and doing other home-based work, such as piecework for factories, sewing, taking care of small gardens, and so forth, Engels argues that the husband can be compared to the bourgeoisie and the wife to the proletariat. According to Engels, because the husband worked for wages, like the bourgeoisie, he had access to capital, whereas the wife, because her work did not generate wages, was like the proletariat. Under this conceptualization, women could have their labor exploited because they did not have ownership rights or rights to money, but rather had to rely on their husbands who provided for them in exchange for their domestic labor and sexual availability.

Engels extends this argument by suggesting that wives serve in a critically important capacity in a capitalist economy: they are responsible for the reproduction of labor. Engels conceptualized this in two ways, as the daily reproduction of labor and as the generational reproduction of labor. Engels's argument is that women's reproductive capacity and their role as mothers were central to the literal reproduction of the labor force; they gave birth to children who grew up to be the next generation of workers. Additionally, Engels argues that in their capacity as caregivers and caretakers of the home, women's daily cooking, cleaning, and doing laundry allow the worker—her husband—to come home to an environment in which, relieved of these responsibilities, he can convalesce and be ready to return to his labor the next day. Though Engels was writing during the peak of the Industrial Revolution, when many men worked in factories and coal mines and their labor was often dirty and physically demanding, his logic can be applied to today's families as well. In many working-class families, men work more than one job, and though women are often employed as well, they still do the majority of the housework (Bianchi, Robinson, and Milkie 2007), and their relegation to the duties associated with household labor relieves their husbands or partners of this work and thus facilitates their ability to work more than one job. In many professional households, men work in jobs that require them to travel or to work extraordinary hours—sixty to eighty hours per week for many lawyers, physicians, financial consultants, and accountants—and once again it is the household labor done by their wives, who are somewhat less likely to be employed, that allows these men to rejuvenate at home and return to work rested.

Conflict theory focuses on the fact that institutions—economies, families—that are built on inherently unequal relationships are thus designed for exploitation, and abuse may be an intended or unintended consequence (Merton 1968). In terms of the economy, for example, the antagonistic relationship between capitalists—or owners of the means of production—and workers centers primarily on wages and working conditions. Owners can increase their profits substantially by paying lower wages. This has always been a core tenet of capitalism, and we see it in the United States as more and more companies outsource manufacturing to developing countries, where labor is cheap (Friedman 2006). Owners also seek to limit the benefits they pay for as well as refuse to spend money updating the workplace environment—for example, many institutions, including colleges, delayed removing asbestos in ceiling and floor tiles until lawsuits for asbestos exposure escalated. In contrast, the workers' self-interests are in earning a fair wage, receiving benefits such as health insurance and retirement contributions, and working in an environment that is comfortable, safe, and free from exposure to toxins like asbestos. Because the self-interests of the owners are in direct opposition to the self-interests of the workers, their relationship is inherently antagonistic. Furthermore, when there is a surplus labor force, as exists in the United States in the mid-2010s, coupled with stagnant wages (Lazear 2015), the owner has the power to enforce their self-interests and lower wages, reduce benefits, and refuse to improve the working environment. Workers are forced to either accept this exploitation of their labor or find themselves unemployed.

Engels argues, as we do elsewhere (Hattery 2008), that one can conceptualize the family in a similar manner. Conflict theorists would argue that because men tend to make higher wages and have access to other types of power in families, it is not surprising that men are more likely to be the perpetrators of intimate partner violence and women the victims. Comparatively, because similar power dynamics—though even more pronounced—exist between parents and children, including adult children and elderly parents, the direction of violence tends to be from those with more access to resources toward those who have less access to resources and are thus vulnerable to exploitation and abuse.

The strength of this approach is that it explains the majority of violence in families. The weakness of this approach is that it has difficulty explaining certain patterns of violence, such as violence perpetrated by women against their partners or violence by adult children who stand to gain a great deal through inheritance or who are benefiting financially from contributions by their aging parents. This approach also fails to explain much about sibling abuse and is more difficult to apply to gay and lesbian couples where the power dynamic may not be as obvious, if it exists at all, based on conventional identities.

Structural-Functionalist Theory

Structural-functionalism was perhaps the most popular theoretical approach utilized in sociology across the twentieth century. Many well-known and frequently studied sociologists interpreted the world through the structural-functionalist lens, including Émile Durkheim, Talcott Parsons, and Robert K. Merton. Like conflict theory, structural-functionalist theory attempts to explain the entire range of human behavior and has been utilized across the discipline, by criminologists and family sociologists alike.

In brief, structural-functionalist theory was developed in the mid-nineteenth century in response to the claim that sociology was not a "real" science. Early theorists like Durkheim went to great lengths to convince the scientific community of the power of sociology, and apparently he and other early social theorists believed that linking sociology to the natural sciences would yield the most compelling argument for the acceptance of sociology as a bona fide science. Thus, the language and assumptions of structural-functionalist theory look very similar to those that are utilized in the natural sciences. Structural-functionalist theory is built on the core assumption that society is like an organism that has many different parts that all work together to keep the society working in harmony. So, for example, the human body has many different organ systems and individual organs; the organs all have distinct functions that, when coordinated with other organs, keep the body in equilibrium. Structural-functionalists argue that, likewise, institutions and individuals all serve different functions in society, but it is the coordination of these functions that keeps society running smoothly. For example, just as the human body would not work if an individual had two livers and only one kidney, or if organs duplicated functions, in society we designate roles to different institutions because this is more efficient than replication or overlap. We have one system of government, one system of education, one system of health care, and so forth. Schools provide education but do not provide health care, for example. And if they did, or when they do, this is less efficient.

The second core assumption of structural-functionalist theory is that change occurs only in cases of dysfunction. For example, the human body evolved in response to changing environmental pressures, and this response is what kept the human race thriving across many millennia. When things are working properly, according to structural-functionalists, there is no incentive to change, for change might make the system less efficient. In other words, "if it ain't broke, don't fix it."

The election of 2008 produced much change in the federal government. Presidential candidate Barack Obama ran on the slogan "Change we can believe in," and dissatisfaction with the Bush administration not only helped Obama attain the presidency but also led to the complete turnover of both houses of Congress. The midterm elections in 2010 and 2014 saw a reversal of the trends of 2008, due to frustration that though the recession of 2007–2009 had officially ended, the economy had not improved and the United States was still fighting two wars, and analysts suggested that more upheaval was to be expected. And they were right. Since the 2016 election, the political world has been in utter turmoil as it reacts to and attempts to deal with the presidency of Donald J. Trump. Attempting to understand how a businessman and celebrity with no political experience could be so successful, most analysis settles on the dissatisfaction that many Americans are experiencing; unemployment may be down but underemployment is common, wages have stagnated for most Americans, and the United States is still engaged in military action in the Middle East, with there appearing to be no end in sight as Syria sheds millions of refugees and ISIS continues to terrorize Western Europe. The midterm elections of 2018 brought change yet again; most analysts agree the dramatic shift in electoral politics was a direct response to Donald Trump. Specifically, women and minorities gained increased representation at both state and federal levels. At the federal level there were several firsts; the first Native American women, Muslim women, and Hispanic women (representing Texas) were all elected to Congress. In the Senate, the first women representing both Tennessee and Arizona were elected. At the state level, Colorado elected the first openly gay governor and South Dakota elected their first woman governor.

But government is not the only institution that has experienced pressure to change. In 2015, the US Supreme Court heard a case over which there had been much public pressure and also much controversy: *Obergefell v. Hodges*, a case about marriage equality. The plaintiffs argued that the ban on gay marriage was out of date and denied gay Americans the "equal protection of the laws" guaranteed by the Constitution. In contrast, opponents of marriage equality argued that marriage was defined by the Constitution as being limited to one man and one woman and that therefore marriage equality would violate the Constitution. In June 2015, the court ruled that prohibiting same-gender couples from marrying was unconstitutional, and marriage equality became the law of the land. Thus, the Supreme Court changed the institution of civil marriage. Though not all Americans agreed with this ruling, just as many did not agree with the landmark *Brown v. Board of Education* decision in 1954, the plaintiffs argued persuasively that there was a cost to not modifying the institution of marriage, namely that it would deny some Americans their constitutionally guaranteed civil rights.

As with Jim Crow segregation (see Hattery and Smith 2012), there were economic costs associated with the ban on gay marriage as well. In the Jim Crow era, not only did white business owners fail to make a profit off of the black customers they refused to serve, but municipalities often had to build two of everything—schools, hospitals, swimming pools, even movie theaters—in order to guarantee the races remained segregated. In the case of marriage equality, many businesses argued that the ban on gay marriage was economically costly: in states without marriage equality, businesses had difficulty recruiting gay and lesbian employees. Change is not proactive but reactive, and it's often spurred by the growing acknowledgment that discrimination violates Americans' sense of equality as articulated in the Constitution, as well as a realization that discrimination is economically costly. In other words, change doesn't occur on its own; it is propelled by a threat to the efficiency and ideological tenets of the state.

Structural-Functionalist Theory and the Family

One of the first sociologists to attempt to analyze the institution of the family through the structural-functionalist lens was Talcott Parsons. Parsons began writing about the family in the early 1950s, and much like Engels did a century earlier, he attempted to transform a "grand theory" and make it applicable to a single institution.

As a structural-functionalist, Parsons began with the assumption that if a family form existed and continued to exist over time, then it must be functional. His logic, built on the assumptions of structural-functionalist theory, is that if the form were dysfunctional, the family would have changed and evolved to a more functional form. Thus, any long-standing form was, by definition, functional. Parsons and Bales (1955) argues, for example, that the gendered division of household labor—namely, the fact that regardless of women's hours of paid employment, they do, on average, two-thirds of the household labor (Bianchi, Robinson, and Milkie 2007)—can be traced back to prehistoric times. Specifically, he argues that during the days of the "hunter and gatherer" economies, men needed to be able to range widely to hunt big game, while women—who were often pregnant or nursing small children—were confined to the "home." Over time, these patterns of social behavior evolved into our genetic structure such that in the modern era, men are wired genetically to be able to be away from their families for long stretches of time, whereas women are not. In contrast, women, having spent all of those centuries doing the work of the home and family, have evolved skills that make them better at this type of work. For example, he argues, women can distinguish among a baby's cries more easily than men (Parsons and Bales 1955). The notion of sociobiological evolution is at the core of the application of structural-functionalist theory to the institution of the family.

Though there are few, if any, examples of the strict application of structural-functionalist theory to the study of family violence, we can extend Parson's general thesis and see its influence on family violence theory, mostly through the conduit of gender role theory. Parsons endorsed a division of household labor in the family because it is functional, and he believed that the most efficient division is strictly by gender. Though he never approaches the topic of violence, we can see, at least with regards to intimate partner violence, that a strict and rigid construction of gender roles leaves open the possibility that frustrations may lead to violence. For example, if wives' duties are to please their husbands by maintaining calm and decorated homes, providing tasty and nutritious meals, taking care of children, and being sexually available, then husbands may view any failure at these tasks as an occasion requiring discipline (recall our discussion in Chapter 2). We will return to a lengthier discussion of the role that gender roles and cultural constructions of gender play in intimate partner violence in Chapter 10.

With regard to other forms of family violence, we can speculate that structural-functionalist theorists would attribute child abuse and elder abuse to the frustrations that caretakers sometimes feel when they are faced with the difficult and seemingly never-ending task of caretaking. The strength of this approach is that its tenets, were they to be applied, are consistent with the patterns present in the majority of violence in families. The weakness of this approach is that it could be understood as accepting violence as an unintended but unavoidable outcome of the ways in which families are structured. This approach would then let perpetrators "off the hook" and leave victims wondering when and how change will occur, much as modern disgruntled wives doing all of the household labor report feeling frustrated (Hattery 2001).

Symbolic Interaction Theory

The fathers of **symbolic interaction theory (SI)** are widely considered to be two social psychologists, George Herbert Mead and Charles Horton Cooley. In contrast to both conflict theory and structural-functionalist theory, SI is a micro-level theory that focuses on the interactions that people have and the ways in which these interactions create reality. Herbert Blumer (1969), a second-generation SI theorist, laid out the following three principles as central to SI theory:

1. Human beings act toward things based on the meanings they ascribe to those things.
2. The meaning of things derives from, or arises out of, the social interaction that one has with others and the society.
3. These meanings are handled in, and modified through, an interpretative process used by the person in dealing with the things he or she encounters.

In sum, SI theorists argue that the interactions that humans have with each other create meaning and that without interaction and interpretation, nothing—including relationships or institutions—has any meaning. In contrast to conflict theorists, for example, SI theorists would argue that "work" exists only insofar as we ascribe meaning to it through relationships and interpretation. For example, let us consider the case of cooking as analyzed through SI theory. When I cook at home for myself and my family, a task in which I have a great deal of autonomy—I get to decide what to cook, when to cook, what methods to use, and so forth—and for which I am not paid, this labor is not defined as "work." In contrast, if I go to a local restaurant, put on a white coat and a specific type of white hat, and respond to the directions of the executive chef with regards to what is to be cooked, how, and when, after doing this for forty hours, I am given a paycheck. It is then that my cooking is transformed into "work" (Wilson 1996).

Symbolic Interaction Theory and the Family

Family scholars working from an SI framework developed "role theory" as a way of understanding the forms that families take and the ways in which they operate on a daily basis. For example, when two children are fighting over a toy and a parent interrupts and instructs the children to share the toy, this interaction is reinforcing the roles of both parent and child. Similarly, when a wife greets her husband at the end of the day with the remote control (the modern-day version of the newspaper) and a cocktail and asks about his day at work, the couple is engaging in their roles as husband and wife.

This may sound a lot like structural-functionalist or even conflict theory, but SI is unique in that it does not adhere to the rigid constructions of these roles. Rather, SI focuses on *the ways* in which the roles are played and reinforced through interaction. For example, the script above could easily be switched, as it may be in modern-day households, with the husband greeting his husband at the door with the remote control and his favorite cocktail and inquiring about his day at work. The interaction would be analyzed similarly: the two adults are playing out the roles of spouses. What SI theorists would focus on is the degree to which men and women or gay and lesbian couples "do spouse" differently (Erickson 2003).

Furthermore, in examining the issue of elder abuse, SI would focus on the ways in which the interaction between child and parent changes over time, from the scenario described above to one in which an adult child talks abusively to his or her aging parent. SI theorists would analyze this interaction as an example of how adult children and aging parents "do child–parent interaction" later in life as compared to during childhood.

Specifically with regard to family violence, West and Zimmerman's (1987) work on **doing gender** is useful to consider. They argue that when men and women interact in ways that reinforce or challenge gender role stereotypes, they are in fact "doing gender." Thus, intimate partner violence can be understood as an extreme form of "doing gender" (a point to which we will return in Chapter 10). When a man responds violently to his partner, this can be understood as an assertion of his masculinity, or an occasion of "doing gender." Similarly, when a battered woman tries to avoid a future incidence of violence by "behaving properly"—being home on time, having dinner on the table on time—she is also "doing gender." Similarly, one could argue that when a parent disciplines a child, which is part of their role as a parent, they are "doing parent," and when abuse occurs, it is a matter, like intimate partner violence, of "doing parent" to an unnecessary extreme (Hattery 2008).

The strength of this approach is that it largely makes intuitive sense. Following a lengthy history in our culture of allowing men to physically discipline their wives and parents to physically discipline their children, understanding abuse as an extreme form of behavior that is otherwise central to one's role as a husband or parent makes sense. This approach does not explain well violence that does not follow this pattern (for example, wives who abuse husbands). The primary weakness of this theory is that it attributes phenomena such as child abuse to individual choices and actions and minimizes the role that institutional structures play in shaping the patterns of violence that we see—for example, the role that patriarchy plays in structuring intimate partner violence as a *gendered* phenomenon.

THEORIES OF THE MIDDLE RANGE

Theories of the middle range are those designed to analyze and predict phenomena in one area or one institution rather than the entirety of human existence. In addition, according to Merton (1968), who coined the term, theories of the middle range, unlike grand theories, require more than abstract arguments but must be supported by empirical evidence. For example, feminist theory—which feminists would argue is a grand theory but general sociologists consider a theory of the middle range—seeks to explain a wide range of *gendered* phenomena using verifiable empirical evidence. For example, feminist researchers have examined sex segregation in the workplace, the division of household labor, differential treatment in the criminal justice system (feminist criminology), different health behavior as well as differential access to health care, the wage gap, gender stratification in the military and in churches, and of course violence against women—or what is commonly referred to as *gender-based violence*.

Each theory of the middle range is built on a set of assumptions. As with the grand theories, we will lay out the assumptions of each theory, summarize the overall position taken by the theory, and provide examples of the ways in which it is used to explain family violence.

Feminist Theory

Feminist theory is built on the assumption that patriarchy—a gender-based hierarchy on which rewards, privileges, and power are distributed—undergirds every human society (Epstein 2007). In her presidential address to the American Sociological Association, Cynthia Fuchs Epstein offers a straightforward summary of feminist theory and its universal applicability:

> The divide of biological sex constitutes a marker around which all major institutions of society are organized. All societal institutions assign roles based on the biological

sex of their members. The divisions of labor in the family, local and global labor forces, political entities, most religious systems, and nation-states are all organized according to the sexual divide.

(2007: 4)

Thus, feminist theorists assume that a system of stratification based on gender structures all institutions and thus all human behavior.

Feminist Theory and Family Violence

Because a tremendous amount of family violence is gendered, feminist theory, alongside race, class, and gender theory, is one of the few theories of the middle range that has been utilized to explain family violence. (Note that none of the grand theories explicitly addresses family violence, though, as we discussed previously, several contribute to specific theories that have attempted to address family violence.) Indeed, one of the earliest areas examined by feminist scholars was gender-based violence, specifically rape (Brownmiller 1975; Griffin 1979), sexual harassment (MacKinnon 1991), and intimate partner violence (Walker 1984). These early feminists, as well as contemporary feminist scholars, including ourselves (Hattery 2008; Hattery and Smith 2007, 2019; Smith 2008), argue that the system of patriarchy that bestows power and privilege on men and oppresses women creates a situation in which men beat their wives *because they can.* Additionally, because institutions are also structured around gender inequality, men beat their wives because there are few consequences of doing so, especially legally. Readers will recall the lengthy discussion of the history of intimate partner violence in Chapter 2 and the fact that for centuries, intimate partner violence was legal as long as the perpetrator was a man. Additionally, even once there were laws that made battering illegal, the criminal justice system, including state supreme courts, worked out a sort of "don't ask, don't tell" policy. As long as the woman was not severely injured or killed, then battering was considered a private matter between a man and his wife and was not a matter for the courts. These types of laws, along with the statistics on intimate partner violence, which reveal that the majority of victims of lethal and near-lethal violence are women— indeed, *half* of all homicides of women are the result of intimate partner violence (Petrosky et al. 2017)—are at the core of the feminist argument that battering is a gendered phenomenon. Additionally, the strength of feminist theory is that it focuses on the structural rather than individual nature of gender-based violence. In other words, the focus is less on individual men and more on the role that patriarchy plays in structuring both individual power within households—based on widely held cultural norms about gender relations—and institutional power, such as in the criminal justice system, which contributes to or reinforces and supports intimate partner violence. Feminist theorists argue that men hit because they can and because they can get away with it. Therefore, one of their solutions to the endemic problem of intimate partner violence is the dismantling of patriarchy, or at the very least a change in the way that intimate partner violence is handled by the criminal justice system. If men were held accountable for intimate partner violence—if there were a cost to engaging in it—then we would likely see a decline in its prevalence.

The weaknesses of feminist theory are several. First, it does not adequately explain the "exceptions to the rule"—the cases in which women beat their partners. Similarly, it does not address violence in LGBTQ communities adequately. Third, feminist theory has much less to contribute to our understanding of child abuse and elder abuse, though it is very powerful in explaining child *sexual* abuse. And last, feminist scholars have a tendency to treat gender-based violence as "violence against women," which keeps the focus on the victims rather than on the perpetrators (see especially Hattery 2008 and Hattery and Smith 2019). This final point is controversial. Messner (2016) argues that feminist scholars and activists should further interrogate and deconstruct the language used to examine gender-based violence:

> Here, "violence against women" is recast as "gender-based violence," opening space for thinking about the connections between violence against women with violence against gay, lesbian, queer and transgender people, sexual assaults of boys and men, as well as gender-based bullying in schools . . .. While anti-violence professionals view this expansion of the anti-violence field as important, many of them are concerned that the language and pedagogy of this new paradigm risks eclipsing a feminist language of collective social transformation, and *de-centering women*, who are still the major victims of gender-based violence, and are still also the major source of activist response to it.
>
> (Messner 2016: 61, emphasis ours)

This final point illustrates the ways in which feminist theorists and activists continue the long tradition of grappling with language, power, and, most of all, gender.

Race, Class, and Gender Theory

Developed by black and multiracial feminists, including Maxine Baca Zinn, Bonnie Thornton Dill, Dorothy Roberts, Kimberlé Crenshaw, Patricia Williams, Audre Lorde, bell hooks, Patricia Hill Collins, and others, **race, class, and gender**

theory (RCG) was a response to the alienation that many women of color felt in the feminist movement. Building on the principles of both feminist theory and conflict theory, in essence RCG is built on the assumption that there are multiple systems of oppression—patriarchy, capitalism, racial domination, heteronormativity—that work independently and in tandem to structure both institutional and individual inequality.

RCG assumes that every system of domination has a counter system of privilege. In other words, oppression is a system of both disadvantages and advantages. For example, we know that African American men die prematurely—seven or eight years earlier than their white counterparts (Hattery and Smith 2007). (You may recall this example from our discussion of RCG in the first chapter.) When it comes to life expectancy, the intersection of race and social class creates *simultaneously* a disadvantage for African American men and an advantage for white men. Furthermore, when we dig deeper into this question of life expectancy, we see that there are significant gender differences as well. Specifically, not only do women live longer than men but the racial gap is significantly smaller for women than for men. In short, our understanding of racial disparities in life expectancy is improved when we layer these explanations together, focusing not only on gender or race but also on the ways in which they interact to produce outcomes that vary by both statuses.[1]

At the structural level, the race, class, and gender framework illuminates the ways in which different systems of domination are mutually reinforcing: patriarchy is woven with racism (or racial supremacy), both of which are woven with capitalism. It is critical to point out that the race, class, and gender paradigm requires more than simply including individuals of different racial or ethnic groups, social classes, and genders in research studies. The race, class, and gender paradigm requires that researchers design their studies and analyze empirical evidence with attention to the inequality regimes that are based in the systems of patriarchy, capitalism, and racial domination (Acker 2006).

Race, Class, and Gender Theory and Family Violence

Compared to feminist theory, RCG not only provides a more complex way of understanding gender-based violence but also has the strength of being able to explain other forms of family violence as well. For example, the ways in which white affluent men feel threats to their masculinity, or beat their wives, or are dealt with at the police station are very different from the experiences of African American men, who may, for example, experience different threats to their masculinity and are certainly exposed to a criminal justice system that can only be characterized as racially unjust (Hattery and Smith 2007, 2012; Smith 2008).

RCG would analyze both child and elder abuse as forms of violence perpetrated by an individual with privilege against an individual who is oppressed. For example, age is a major system of stratification in the United States, as it is in most cultures, with those at both ends experiencing the most oppression and the least power. Though we are a culture of youth, we do not really extend privileges to young people until they are adults. Additionally, recalling both our discussion of the history of child abuse in Chapter 2 and the evidence provided by Kristoff and WuDunn (2009), we see that both infanticide (killing a baby before its first birthday) and leaving the elderly to die—in places like sub-Saharan Africa—or engaging in euthanasia suggest that in most cultures, power and privilege belong to those in early and middle adulthood. Thus, RCG theorists would suggest that both child abuse and elder abuse can be explained through this paradigm. RCG theory is also able to explain IPV in same-gender couples by focusing on other status systems, including perceived identity—for instance, butch versus femme and "out" versus "closeted." In the case of the latter, an out partner has more power than one who remains closeted, and the out partner may use the threat to out the closeted partner as part of a system of intimate terrorism.

CRIMINOLOGY THEORIES

Criminology theories are designed specifically to explain all sorts of deviant behavior, including behaviors that are illegal and those that are unusual but not illegal—for example, cheating on a test. We find this interesting because until relatively recently, most family violence was not dealt with as a crime. Therefore, the attempt to retroactively apply theories that were developed when family violence was not on the radar screen of criminologists seems absurd. That said, working under the assumption that family violence is a crime and will be dealt with as a crime—a tentative assumption at best—we review some of the key criminology theories and suggest ways in which they can be utilized to explain family violence.

Strain Theory

Robert K. Merton, who was trained as a structural-functionalist theorist by Parsons, developed a theory of social structure and anomie that he then applied to criminal behavior. Merton's basic argument in "Social Structure and Anomie" (1938), which was developed to respond to the critique that structural-functionalist theory did not explain institutional change, explores the way in which changes in social structure—namely, norms—can lead to the alienation of the individual, which can in turn produce a response that, when experienced on a macro level, may lead to structural change. So, for example, Merton argues that as social norms began to change with regard to achieving success, such as the increased focus on and need for education, those who did not have the tools necessary to achieve educational success would feel alienated from the process. In an attempt to deal with this alienation, individuals would develop alternative strategies—other than educational attainment—in order to obtain success. Alternative strategies might include pouring their resources into educating their children (conforming) or seeking avenues for success in the illegitimate economy—for example, through the Mafia or gangs—where education is unnecessary (innovation). This process, an unintended consequence of social change, would then produce additional change in the social system (Merton 1938; Zuckerman 1998).

It is relatively easy to see how Merton transformed his general theory into one that could be used to explain crime. He termed this application **strain theory** (see Figure 3.1). Merton (1968) argues that when an individual or a set of individuals experience anomie, or strain, their responses to this anomie can be analyzed through the lens of deviance; responses are either consistent with traditionally held norms or deviant in relation to these norms. We illustrate with an example of strategies a variety of individuals may employ in attempting to achieve the American dream.

Conformists accept the norms of success as well as the pathways toward getting there. Conformists will stay in school, seek more education and training, and work hard in order to achieve the American dream.

Rebels and **retreatists** reject both the norms of success and the normative pathways. Rebels will establish a different set of norms of success—for example, they might reject the notion of acquiring and building wealth and instead seek the freedom associated with not being beholden to material wealth and tied down by concrete things like a mortgage and car payment. They will also seek alternative ways of getting what they desire, such as engaging in the illegitimate economy or participating in marginal economies. The beatniks and hippies of the 1960s are a good example of rebels. In contrast, retreatists more or less "check out" altogether. These individuals tend to be highly alienated and live on the margins. Ted Kaczynski, the "Unibomber," would be an example of a retreatist.

Ritualists are individuals who have rejected the norms of success—usually because they have become uninterested like the rebels or view them as unattainable—yet they continue, usually out of habit, to participate in the pathways to success. An example of a ritualist is someone who continues to go to school despite the fact that they have given up on the idea of graduating, or the employee who continues

▶ **Figure 3.1**
Merton's
Strain Theory.

Category	Acceptance of Norms	Acceptance of Pathways
Conformist	ACCEPT	ACCEPT
Rebel	REJECT	REJECT
Retreatist	REJECT	REJECT
Ritualist	REJECT	ACCEPT
Innovator	ACCEPT	REJECT

to work in the factory even though he or she realizes that doing so will never lead to the acquisition of the tenets of the American dream. Ritualists are often very disenchanted people.

Innovators are individuals who continue to accept the norms of success but reject the accepted pathways for achieving it. Examples of innovators are students who cheat rather than study for a test and adults who make their money through the illegitimate economy—by selling drugs, engaging in prostitution, working with the Mafia or gangs—rather than work in a legitimate job in order to achieve success and acquire the accoutrements of the American dream.

Merton's typology has been used to explain criminal behavior. When individuals experience strain, in this case the kind of strain that leaves them feeling alienated from the standard routes to success, they may begin to engage in "deviant" behavior in order to either achieve success or to reject it altogether.

Merton's typology has not been applied to discussions of the family, or family violence in particular, except by one of the authors. Smith (2008: 173–174) argues that one way of understanding and explaining the intimate partner violence perpetrated by African American men is to employ Merton's strain theory. In particular, Smith argues:

> My analysis demonstrates that though the "causes" and the "triggers" for violence may not vary across race, the structural inequalities that African American men face—specifically discrimination in the labor market and incarceration—lead to higher levels of alienation, stronger threats to one's masculine identity, and consequently the utilization of more severe violence to alleviate the high levels of strain. In addition, African American men are disproportionately likely to have experienced violence in the families in which they grew up. This exposure to violence puts them at increased risk for battering in adulthood. Merton's framework provides a unique and useful way of thinking about the racial variation evident in the statistics on IPV.

In addition, we would suggest that just as Smith utilizes Merton's framework to deconstruct racial variations in intimate partner violence, other forms of family violence might be analyzed utilizing this framework as well. So, for example, we know that the rate of child abuse is higher in single-parent families. We might conclude that single parents experience strain in child-rearing both because they are the only parent engaged in the day-to-day work of child-rearing and because the pressures on them to earn a living and provide for the child, simultaneously and on their own, are greater. The strain produced by these two conditions may result in well-meaning parents engaging in physical discipline that "gets out of control," rather than the more emotionally costly and time-consuming strategies, including "time out," reasoning with children, and so forth.

The strength of Merton's theory is that it takes into consideration the role that institutional pressure and structures play in criminal behavior. Merton's theory is unique among criminology theories in this regard, as the majority focus solely on the individual. And, as Smith has argued, it does have some applicability to some forms of family violence.

The weakness of Merton's theory is that it was not designed to address this kind of "deviant" behavior and thus has not been widely utilized by family scholars, in general, and family violence scholars, in particular. Additionally, though Merton's theory focuses on structure in shaping human behavior, it does not focus on the role of gender, age, or any form of inequality in structuring family violence. Finally, an application of Merton's theory implies that family violence is "deviant," when in fact it may simply be an exaggeration of traditional gender norms and parenting strategies.

Social Control Theory

Social control theory, developed by Travis Hirschi, derives its assumptions largely from both structural-functionalist theory and social psychological theories of socialization. Hirschi (1969) argues that socialization, and specifically the development of social bonds, leads to the type of social control that is necessary to prevent one from engaging in criminal behavior. A core assumption of Hirschi's theory is that individuals are born without any ability to engage in social control. Additionally, the implied assumption is that engaging in deviant or criminal behavior is more desirable than not, and thus internal mechanisms of social control must be developed. The development of these internal mechanisms occurs through what Hirschi refers to as **social bonds**. The more a child is concerned about the assessment of parents, teachers, and other important adults, and the closer the child feels to each of the individuals—in other words, the stronger the social bonds—the less likely he or she is to engage in deviant or criminal behavior. Thus, a parent may refrain from hitting a child, a husband may refrain from beating his wife, or a stepparent may refrain from sexually abusing a stepchild because of the embarrassment and shame that would result if another adult found out. For example, a man might refrain from beating his wife because he is worried that his mother and father would think less of him. Or, in a more generalized way, in adulthood he might fear the embarrassment that would ensue if a police officer arrested him and his mug shot were taken at the local police department. Though not widely used to examine family violence—primarily, as we noted, because family violence has not been considered an area of interest for criminologists—this approach does offer some insight into behavior at the individual level.

The strength of this approach is that it is intuitive: it makes sense. Second, the solutions that arise from it also make sense: if we can work with parents and spouses to help them develop deep social bonds, we can reduce family violence.

The weakness of this approach, as with many criminology theories, including Merton's, is that it assumes that family violence is the same as other acts of deviance or criminal behavior. We will argue in later chapters that family violence is not like other criminal activity or deviant behavior; rather, building on the historical development of family violence, we will argue that it arises out of constructions of power and privilege, norms of behavior and accountability, and ideological distinctions between discipline and abuse. Additionally, social control theory is an individual-level theory and does not consider the role of structures and institutions in shaping any deviant behavior—family violence in particular. Last, applying social control theory to family violence relies on the assumption that engaging in family violence would bring shame upon the perpetrator. When considered alongside the history of various forms of family violence, this seems likely to be a stretch. When we discuss the role of child abuse in the development of batterers, we will see that this assumption is likely false; indeed, for many individuals living with family violence—intimate partner violence and child abuse—family violence is so pervasive that it does not produce shame in the perpetrator.

Differential Association Theory

Developed by Edwin Sutherland out of the symbolic interaction perspective, **differential association theory** is built on the assumption that deviance is behavior that it is learned through exposure to others who are engaging in it. Sutherland (1924) argues that behaviors take on different meanings based on the groups with which they are associated. Thus, for example, shaking down a "mark" might be considered deviant and criminal under normal circumstances, but inside of a gang or a group of individuals who are engaged in crime, it might be understood as a means of getting the money that is needed for another activity. Similarly, murder, especially among gang members, may be understood as an action necessary to prove allegiance or to avenge the murder of one's own by a rival gang; thus, it is justified and not necessarily defined as a criminal act.

Key to differential association theory is the notion that deviant and criminal behavior is learned through exposure to it. Thus, the likelihood of an individual engaging in deviant or criminal behavior is directly linked to the probability that an individual is exposed repeatedly to it and develops intimate types of relationships with individuals and groups that are engaged in it. This theory is widely used to explain the way in which young children living in low-income communities, for example, get involved in deviance and crime vis-à-vis their exposure to gangs who meet many of the social and economic needs faced by those living in neighborhoods with concentrated poverty.

We are unaware of any attempts to apply differential association theory directly to the study of family violence, but the process it proposes for learning behaviors does make sense with regard to family violence. For example, when we discuss the role that boys' exposure to intimate partner violence plays in the likelihood that they will grow up to perpetrate intimate partner violence, the tenets of differential association theory apply. Young men who witness domestic violence are three times more likely than their counterparts to grow up to abuse partners. Differential association theory would suggest that this is because when a young boy witnesses his father or stepfather beating his mother, he is both learning the "tools of the trade" and also learning that this behavior produces an outcome that his father or stepfather seems to desire. Just like the young boy hanging out on the corner with gangbangers or the suburban youngster hanging out in the basement with older siblings who are smoking pot, the lessons and skills for deviant behavior are transmitted through exposure. This is the main contribution this approach can make to the study of family violence.

As with all of the other criminology theories, differential association theory is an individual-level theory that does not take into account the structural forces that shape family violence. Additionally, differential association theory does not adequately explain the person who is exposed to deviance but chooses not to engage in it—as is the case for 50 percent of the boys who observe intimate partner violence in the families in which they grew up but do not go on to perpetrate it. Nor does it explain the individual who engages in deviant or criminal behavior yet has not been exposed—or who has been exposed only minimally—to this activity.

THEORIES SPECIFIC TO THE STUDY OF FAMILY VIOLENCE

Last, we turn to a discussion of the theories that are specific to family violence. We will begin with family violence theory as it was designed to understand, explain, and predict all forms of family violence. Second, we will discuss theoretical approaches that were developed specifically to address one form of family violence and are unlikely to be transformed to discussions of other forms.

Family Violence Theory

The "fathers" of **family violence theory** are Richard Gelles and Murray Straus (1988). In addition to developing a general theory of family violence that is based on conflict theory, they also developed an instrument—which we will discuss in Chapter 4—to measure family violence. This instrument is called the **Conflict Tactics Scale (CTS)**. In a discussion of the CTS, Straus summarizes the theory of family violence:

> CTS is based on conflict theory. This theory assumes that conflict is inherent in all human groups, including the family. It is inherent because group members, while sharing many interests, also have different interests. These range from specifics, such as what color to paint the bedroom, to the desire of those in power to stay in power and of those at the bottom to gain more control of their lives. Conflict is also a key part of the feminist theory of family violence . . . The version of conflict theory on which the CTS is based assumes that *any* inequality in the family, including dominance by a *female* partner, increases the probability of violence because the dominant partner may use violence to maintain his or her position, or the subordinate partner may use violence to try to achieve a more equitable relationship. Thus, a key feature of the CTS is that it measures violence by both partners in a relationship.
>
> (1999: 195)

In short, family violence theory assumes that violence arises out of conflict and that the person perpetrating the violence does so because they have the power to do so and because it works: it tends to end the conflict, at least temporarily. Additionally, Straus and Gelles and other family violence theorists argue that violence is a response, albeit an undesirable one, to disagreement or conflict. Family violence theorists note that violence erupts in families when individuals lack the skills to make other, more appropriate responses. Additionally, they argue that violence may be employed because, as noted above, it is an "easy" response, especially for individuals who are otherwise overburdened or stressed—single parents, families living in poverty, or young couples who have not developed the communication skills and patience necessary to address conflict. In short, individuals in families who have power engage in violence because they can and because it works (Gelles and Straus 1988). Gelles and Straus (1988) also note in their theoretical discussion of the CTS that violence may be attempted by a subordinate partner, who is usually a woman, in order to level the playing field and gain status in the relationship.

Family violence theory has many strengths and shares some overlap with the other major theory used to examine family violence: feminist theory. Both family violence theorists and feminist theorists agree that violence in families is shaped by inequality and power and that those who engage in it do so because they can; they are not challenged by other family members, and they are not held accountable by the criminal justice system. A second strength of family violence theory is that it is gender-neutral—in other words, it takes into account the possibility that men can be, and are, victims of family violence and women can be, and are, perpetrators of family violence.

There are two major critiques of family violence theory and the CTS in particular. We will discuss the critique of the CTS in the next chapter, which is devoted to methodological approaches to studying family violence. The second critique, made by feminists, of family violence theorists is that they ignore the role of patriarchy in shaping power and inequality in families. As we will document in Chapter 9, though many women in today's households earn more money than their partners, this rarely translates into power in the relationship. And specifically with regard to intimate partner violence, women who out-earn their partners are not only no more likely to be violent toward them but are *actually at increased risk* for being the target of IPV because their economic power upsets the traditional gender roles of the family. This upsetting can be interpreted as a threat to masculinity by men who may respond and reassert their masculinity through violence (Hattery 2008; Smith 2008). Additionally, our research (Hattery 2008; Smith 2008) confirms what feminist scholars have noted for decades: that only *rarely* do women—who are subordinate in relationships by virtue of their second-class status in our patriarchal system—use violence against their partners, and when they do, it is almost always in response to violence they are experiencing (that is, they are fighting back) rather than violence that they instigate in order to "level the playing field," as Straus and Gelles suggest.

Intimate Terrorism Versus Situational Couple Violence

Among scholars of intimate partner violence there is a critical debate centering on **mutual combat**, a term coined by Gelles and Straus (1988) that refers to families in which both partners engage in violence against each other. Based on their findings in studies that utilized the CTS, which revealed that in some families both partners engage in violence against each other, Straus and Gelles developed the concept of "mutual combat."

Michael P. Johnson and his colleagues have extended this debate and attempted to distinguish between two different forms of intimate partner violence: intimate terrorism and situational couple violence. These corresponding forms of violence against women differentiate themselves in terms of the *lethalness* of the violence—the likelihood that it will produce severe injury or death—and the *level of control* in the relationship.

Intimate terrorism: Johnson and his colleagues (Johnson and Ferraro 2000; Leone et al. 2004) describe **intimate terrorism** as "a partner's attempt to exert control over his partner using a broad range of power and control tactics, which include physical violence" (Leone et al. 2004: 473).

Situational couple violence: In contrast, **situational couple violence** "does not exist within a general pattern of controlling behavior. This form of violence is not motivated by a desire to control and exert power over a partner or in a relationship, but rather occurs when specific conflict situations escalate to violence" (Leone et al. 2004: 473).

The strength of Johnson's framework is that unlike other theories, including feminist theory, it allows for the fact that not all violence is the same. And certainly in our interviews, we met people whose relationships were highly conflictual—they fought, sometimes physically—but their fights could be understood in the context of conflict, and there were no other types of abuse present (sexual abuse, emotional abuse, or psychological abuse). Additionally, the violence was rarely severe, and it was generally perpetrated more or less equally. The weaknesses of Johnson's approach, similar to those associated with the family violence framework, are that, first, this distinction often blurs or hides the ways in which intimate partner violence is about gender and power and that when we look at lethality and injury and remove conflict as a required context, women are far more likely to be the victims and men the perpetrators, and, second, in many violent relationships, both types of violence—intimate terrorism and situational couple violence—exist. Last, we note that this approach is limited to explaining only intimate partner violence and not other forms of family violence. This is not a weakness but a distinction.

Psychological Theories

We conclude our discussion of theories of intimate partner violence with a brief overview of psychological theories. Because we are sociologists and this book is rooted in the sociological tradition, we do not feel it is necessary to provide an in-depth discussion of these theories, but students, scholars, and activists should be familiar with them.

Psychological theories of intimate partner violence were developed primarily through either experimentation by psychologists or research conducted by therapists whose work is limited to that context. Psychologists have long been interested in understanding why human beings engage in violence. This interest reached a peak in the 1960s, following the fallout from World War II and the knowledge of the incredible atrocities perpetrated by the Nazis.

One of the landmark studies on the psychology of violence was performed in 1961 by Stanley Milgram (1974). Milgram recruited white middle-aged men to participate in a "learning" study. His subjects arrived at his lab and were told that they were part of a study that focused on techniques for improving learning; they would play the role of "teacher." The "student," played (unbeknownst to the participants) by a confederate of Milgram's, was seated in an adjacent room. The teacher could hear but not see the student. As the experiment began, Milgram introduced the teacher and student and showed the teacher that he was hooking the student up to a series of electrodes that would, he told the teacher, deliver electric shocks every time the student failed a task. He then closed the door and moved the teacher to his station, which included a "shocking" device labeled from 5 volts to XXX. The experiment involved the teacher reading word pairs to the student. The teacher then requested that the student repeat the word pairs back to him. The student intentionally missed some of the word pairs, and when he did, Milgram instructed the teacher to administer a shock (which was of course not real). Each subsequent miss required a more severe shock. Unbelievably, Milgram reported that 50 percent of the subjects went all the way up to the end of the scale and delivered the XXX shock. In the film that documents the experiments, we see the incredible anxiety on the faces of the subjects, their verbal resistance to Milgram, their ultimate complicity, and finally their intense relief when they realize that the student is fine and everything was just an act of theater.

The conclusion Milgram reached is that under certain constrained circumstances, anyone can be propelled to perpetrate violence. Thus, extensions of Milgram's work would theorize that individuals who engage in any kind of family violence are not necessarily mentally ill but rather are victims of contexts and pressures that lead them to engage in violence. The work of Philip Zimbardo, who performed the Stanford Prison Experiment in 1971 and revisited it in his most recent book (2008), confirms these basic findings. We should note that there are no more recent studies that confirm or extend the Milgram and Zimbardo studies because institutional review boards determined that these studies violated the rights of human subjects and banned any further study that involved this level of deception.

Much of the psychological literature derived from counseling settings that is focused on batterers clearly identifies two predictors of family violence: mental health—such as the presence of anger and control problems or intermittent explosive disorder—and substance abuse. David Adams, a specialist in batterer intervention in the Boston program Emerge, argues that although battering is not typically a result of mental *illness*, it is a result of a mental health *issue* and must be treated rather than punished. Though we will not discuss interventions here, as these will be reserved for Chapter 15, these intervention models provide insight into the psychology of an individual who engages in intimate partner violence. Often batterers have anger management issues, or they are unable to take the role of the other (Scully 1990). For example, they may not be able to put themselves in the shoes of their victims and thus fail to understand fully the impact of their abusive behavior. Additionally, their abusive behavior may be influenced by, though not necessarily caused by, the use or abuse of alcohol and drugs. As the Emerge website notes:

> While alcohol and other drugs can certainly escalate abuse, neither cause a batterer to abuse his partner. Substances will lower inhibitions, and many abusers believe they have less responsibility while using substances. Under the influence, abusers may have fewer barriers on how abusive they will be, so the abuse tends to be more violent.
>
> (2016)

Thus, in summary, psychological theories of violence in general, such as Milgram's, and family violence in particular offer two critical concepts: first, that violence is not limited to individuals who have mental defects or mental illness (in fact, anyone under the right circumstances will engage in violence), and, second, violent behavior can result from mental health issues, including anger management problems and substance abuse, and it should thus be treated rather than criminalized. It is important to point out that both of these imply, and psychologists generally agree, that violence is *learned behavior*; it is rarely the result of capacities with which people are born and therefore destined.

THEORIES OF ELDER ABUSE AND CHILD ABUSE

The research on child and elder abuse often overlap, as do the theories developed to explain them. This is not surprising because the primary focus of scholars of child abuse and elder abuse is on individual explanations, and most of the abuse is categorized as situational or acute rather than chronic. Because the scholars of these two specific types of family abuse have relied so heavily on each other's work, it makes sense for us to treat them together for the purposes of examining specific theories focused on child and elder abuse.

A variety of theories have been developed specifically to explain elder abuse (Bonnie and Wallace 2003). One of the most popular is **situational theory**. Situational theory is based on the assumption that the abuse itself is situational or acute, rather than chronic, and arises primarily from the overburdening of a caregiver. Scholars of child abuse have adopted this perspective as well (Gelles and Straus 1988). Situational theory is appealing because it is based on intuitive assumptions, namely that the majority of abuse occurs when caregivers are tired, stressed, overcommitted, and generally overburdened. And any of us who have been parents—as both the authors are—know how this feels and can relate to the parent who "loses it" as a result of being stressed and overburdened. This theory is also appealing because the research on both parenting and taking care of the elderly is full of empirical support for the notion that caregivers in either situation are often overburdened as they attempt to balance caregiving with other responsibilities, like paid work and managing their other relationships, for example, with spouses. In fact, beginning in the mid-1990s, family scholars developed the term *sandwich generation* to refer to adults in their forties and fifties (most often women) who were parenting and caring for aging parents at the same time. Situational theory is particularly useful in thinking about situations such as this where there are simply too many demands on an individual and their frustrations are occasionally expressed through abusive or neglectful behavior, or both.

Several additional theories have been used to explain elder abuse and have been adapted to research on child abuse as well. **Exchange theory** focuses on the role that patterns of dependency that exist in families play in abuse. These patterns are developed in family life and often continue across the life course. If these patterns have been unhealthy or harmful, as roles in the family switch from parents caring for children to adult children caring for aging parents, these patterns of abuse may continue in a new form.

Social learning theory is another major theory that has been used to explain both child and elder abuse. Social learning theory is based on the principle that children are socialized to behave in particular ways by socializing agents—parents, teachers, coaches, Scout leaders—and that once these behaviors are learned, they are part of an individual's "tool kit" and guide an individual's behavior. With regards to child abuse and elder abuse, the argument is essentially that when children grow up learning that conflict is resolved through hitting or that physical punishment is appropriate, then they are more likely to use these techniques when they are caregivers themselves—either for children or for their aging parents. Like situational theory, social learning theory is popular because it is intuitive and useful in explaining the high rates of intergenerational patterns of abuse.

The weaknesses of these specific theories are several. First, like Johnson's typology for understanding intimate partner violence, these specific theories are limited to specific forms of family violence—elder abuse and child abuse—and do not offer a framework for understanding, analyzing, and explaining family violence as a unique phenomenon. Second, like many of the other theories we have outlined in this chapter, these theoretical perspectives—situational theory, social learning theory, and exchange theory—are all individual-level theories and do not account for structural factors that shape elder and child abuse. So, for example, the focus on overburdened caregivers considers individuals' experiences with stress and treats this as a problem of individuals who are overburdened, without attention to the role that status location plays in *structuring who* is overburdened (Hattery 2001). For example, single mothers, low-income families, and women in the sandwich generation are more likely to perpetrate situational abuse caused by being overburdened than women who do not fall into these categories. Additionally, situational theory is of little use in explaining chronic abuse and abuse that is transmitted intergenerationally. Social learning theory suffers from additional weaknesses as well, including the tendency to paint abusers as "bad people" rather than understanding the structural and individual forces that shape their behavior. For example, as horrific as the abuse wrought by a sex offender can be, in our interviews with sex offenders we heard about their own experiences with horrific sexual abuse by their mothers' boyfriends and pimps (Hattery and Smith 2010). This knowledge does not lessen the impact of their abusive behavior, but it provides clues to how it came about and how it might have been prevented with appropriate interventions.

Even though most scholars adhere to one specific theoretical paradigm and devote decades of research to testing it and demonstrating its utility, many also acknowledge that the most effective way in which to understand family violence is to analyze it through a lens provided by taking a comprehensive approach that draws on the strengths of multiple theoretical approaches.

CONCLUSIONS

If you come away with nothing else, we hope you finish this chapter with a few key thoughts. First, the theories used to understand family violence are relatively underdeveloped for several key reasons. As noted in the previous chapter, defining violence in families as something worthy of attention is a relatively recent development.

As we alluded to here, and as we will discuss in the next chapter, measuring family violence is contentious! Because the sociological model of theory and methodologies relies on the interplay between theory and methodologies, a lack of well-established theories to guide research will result in an ad hoc approach that fails to generate the kinds of data necessary to confirm, reject, and advance the existing theoretical frameworks. Instead, these ad hoc approaches to research will result in a tendency to build ad hoc theories.

Second, though there are some scholars who align themselves exclusively with one theoretical paradigm or use only one method (for instance, Straus and Gelles and the CTS), many scholars, ourselves included, have found that the most powerful and comprehensive explanations of family violence arise when they are not afraid to call on many different theoretical traditions and methodological approaches. In our own work, for example, we have found that there are useful aspects to conflict theory (especially that written by Friedrich Engels), feminist theory, and the race, class, and gender paradigm. The reader will see firsthand how we combine these approaches in subsequent chapters. We turn now to a discussion of the methods used to investigate family violence.

RESOURCES

Emerge: www.emergedv.com.
Milgram experiments: www.dailymotion.com/video/x24guhr_the-milgram-experiment_shortfilms.

NOTE

1. Deborah King refers to this as "double jeopardy" (1988), and Maxine Baca Zinn and Bonnie Thornton Dill refer to it as the "matrix of domination" (2005).

REFERENCES

Acker, Joan. 2006. *Class Questions, Feminist Answers*. New York: Routledge.

Bianchi, Suzanne, John P. Robinson, and Melissa A. Milkie. 2007. *Changing Rhythms of American Family Life*. New York: Russell Sage Foundation.

Blumer, Herbert. 1969. *Symbolic Interactionism: Perspective and Method*. Berkeley and Los Angeles, CA: University of California Press.

Bonnie, Richard J., and Robert B. Wallace. 2003. *Elder Mistreatment: Abuse, Neglect, and Exploitation in an Aging America*. Washington, DC: National Academies Press.

Brownmiller, Susan. 1975. *Against Our Will: Men, Women, and Rape*. New York: Simon and Schuster.

Calhoun, Craig J. 2007. *Sociology in America: A History*. Chicago, IL: University of Chicago Press.

Emerge. 2016. "Domestic Violence FAQ." www.emergedv.com/index.php/f-a-q/domestic-violence-faq.

Engels, Friedrich. 1884. *The Origin of the Family, Private Property, and the State.* Introduction by Eleanor Leacock. New York: International Publishers.

Epstein, Cynthia. 2007. "Great Divides: The Cultural, Cognitive, and Social Bases of the Global Subordination of Women." *American Sociological Review 72(1)*: 1–22.

Erickson, Rebecca. 2003. "The Familial Institution." In *Handbook of Symbolic Interactionism*, edited by L. Reynolds and N. Herman-Kinney, 511–538. Lanham, MD: Rowman and Littlefield.

Friedman, Thomas. 2006. *The World Is Flat: A Brief History of the 21st Century.* New York: Farrar, Straus, and Giroux.

Gelles, Richard J., and Murray A. Straus. 1988. *Intimate Violence.* New York: Simon and Schuster.

Griffin, Susan. 1979. *Rape: The Politics of Consciousness.* New York: Harper & Row.

Hattery, Angela. 2001. *Women, Work, and Family: Balancing and Weaving.* Thousand Oaks, CA: Sage.

Hattery, Angela. 2008. *Intimate Partner Violence.* Lanham, MD: Rowman and Littlefield.

Hattery, Angela J., and Earl Smith. 2007. *African American Families.* Thousand Oaks, CA: Sage.

Hattery, Angela J., and Earl Smith. 2010. *Prisoner Reentry and Social Capital: The Long Road to Reintegration.* Lanham, MD: Lexington Books.

Hattery, Angela J., and Earl Smith. 2012. *African American Families: Myths and Realities.* Lanham, MD: Rowman and Littlefield.

Hattery, Angela J., and Earl Smith. 2019. *Gender, Power and Violence: Responding to Sexual and Intimate Partner Violence in Society Today.* Lanham, MD: Rowman and Littlefield.

Hirschi, Travis. 1969. *Causes of Delinquency.* Berkeley and Los Angeles, CA: University of California Press.

Johnson, Michael P., and Kathleen J. Ferraro. 2000. "Research on Domestic Violence in the 1990s: Making Distinctions." *Journal of Marriage and the Family 62(4)*: 948–963.

King, Deborah. 1988. "Multiple Jeopardy, Multiple Consciousness: The Context of a Black Feminist Ideology." *Signs 14(1)*: 42–72.

Kristoff, Nicholas, and Sheryl WuDunn. 2009. *Half the Sky: Turning Oppression into Opportunity for Women Worldwide.* New York: Alfred A. Knopf.

Lazear, Edward. 2015. "Ed Lazear: This Is the Real Unemployment Rate." *Washington Post,* November 6. www.washingtonpost.com/news/wonk/wp/2015/11/06/ed-lazear-this-is-the-real-unemployment-rate.

Leone, Janel M., Michael P. Johnson, Catherine L. Cohan, and Susan E. Lloyd. 2004. "Consequences of Male Partner Violence for Low-Income Minority Women." *Journal of Marriage and Family 66(2)*: 472–490.

Lin, N. 2000. "Inequality in Social Capital." *Contemporary Sociology 29(6)*: 785–795.

MacKinnon, Catharine. 1991. *Toward a Feminist Theory of the State.* Cambridge, MA: Harvard University Press.

Marx, Karl, Friedrich Engels, and Dirk Jan Struik. 1971. *Birth of the Communist Manifesto, with Full Text of the Manifesto, All Prefaces by Marx and Engels, Early Drafts by Engels, and Other Supplementary Material.* New York: International Publishers.

Merton, Robert K. 1938. "Social Structure and Anomie." *American Sociological Review* 3(5): 672–682.

Merton, Robert K. 1968. *Social Theory and Social Structure.* New York: Free Press.

Messner, Michael. 2016. "Bad Men, Good Men, Bystanders: Who Is the Rapist?" *Gender and Society 30(1)*: 57–66. doi: 10.1177/0891243215608781.

Milgram, Stanley. 1974. *Obedience to Authority: An Experimental View.* New York: Harper.

Parsons, Talcott, and Robert Bales. 1955. *Family, Socialization, and the Interaction Process.* Glencoe, IL: Free Press.

Petrosky, E., J. M. Blair, C. J. Betz, K. A. Fowler, S. P. Jack, and B. H. Lyons. 2017. "Racial and Ethnic Differences in Homicides of Adult Women and the Role of Intimate Partner Violence—United States, 2003–2014." *MMWR Morbidity and Mortality Weekly Report 66*: 741–746. doi: http://dx.doi.org/10.15585/mmwr.mm6628a1.

Scully, Diana. 1990. *Understanding Sexual Violence: A Study of Convicted Rapists.* Boston, MA: Unwin Hyman.

Smith, Earl. 2008. "African American Men and Intimate Partner Violence." *Journal of African American Studies 12*: 156–179.

Smith, Earl. 2014. *Race, Sport, and the American Dream.* Durham, NC: Carolina Academic Press.

Straus, Murray A. 1999. "The Controversy over Domestic Violence by Women: A Methodological, Theoretical, and Sociology of Science Analysis." In *Violence in Intimate Relationships*, edited by X. B. Arriaga and S. Oskamp, 17–44. London: Sage.

Sutherland, Edwin. 1924. *Criminology.* Philadelphia, PA: Lippincott.

Wacquant, Loïc. 2001. "Deadly Symbiosis: When Ghetto and Prison Meet and Mesh." *Punishment and Society 3(1)*: 95–134.

Walker, Lenore E. 1984. *The Battered Woman Syndrome.* New York: Springer.

Ward, Lester Frank. 1963. *Lester Frank Ward: Selections From His Work.* New York: Crowell.

Weber, Max. 1949. *The Methodology of the Social Sciences.* Edited by Edward A. Shils and Henry A. Finch. Glencoe, IL: Free Press.

West, Candace, and Don H. Zimmerman. 1987. "Doing Gender." *Gender and Society 1(2)*: 125–151.

Wilson, Williams J. 1996. *When Work Disappears: The World of the New Urban Poor.* New York: Alfred A. Knopf.

Wright, Erik O. 1997. *Class Counts: Comparative Studies in Class Analysis.* New York: Cambridge University Press.

Zimbardo, Phillip. 2008. *The Lucifer Effect: Understanding How Good People Turn Evil.* New York: Random House.

Zinn, Maxine Baca, and Bonnie Thornton Dill. 2005. "Theorizing Differences from Multicultural Feminism." In *Gender Through the Prism of Difference*, edited by M. B. Zinn, P. Hondagneu-Sotelo, and M. A. Messner, 23–28. Oxford: Oxford University Press.

Zuckerman, Harriet. 1998. "Accumulation of Advantage and Disadvantage: The Theory and Its Intellectual Biography." In *Robert K. Merton and Contemporary Sociology*, edited by Carlo Mongardini and Simonetta Tabboni, 136–162. New Brunswick, NJ: Transaction Books.

4

METHODS FOR STUDYING FAMILY VIOLENCE

This chapter will be devoted to a discussion of the methodological approaches to studying family violence. In addition to outlining each approach, we will critique each and identify its strengths and weaknesses. We will also provide examples of the outcomes of each type of research and resources—including data sets—that you can use to learn more and even conduct your own analysis.

OBJECTIVES

- To give an overview of the methodological approaches that have been used to study family violence
- To assess the strengths and weaknesses of each approach
- To provide access to sources of data so that readers can explore family violence on their own

KEY TERMS

objectivity
generalizability
repeatability
replicability
experiment
random assignment
manipulation of the independent
    variable
control of third variables
correlational
sampling
qualitative research
face-to-face interviews
ethnography

observational methods
epistemology
quantitative methods
survey research
National Violence Against Women
    (NVAW) Survey
random digit dialing (RDD)
Bureau of Justice Statistics (BJS)
National Crime Victimization Survey
    (NCVS)
Uniform Crime Reports (UCR)
ecological fallacy
Conflict Tactics Scale (CTS)

INTRODUCTION

One of the most important aspects of social science research is the methodological approaches that we use to gather empirical data. Whereas theory provides the framework for analyzing and interpreting what we see in the social world, methodologies ensure that when we collect empirical data in order to test hypotheses and determine the utility of theoretical frameworks, these data are collected systematically, rigorously, and in ways that are repeatable.

OBJECTIVITY, GENERALIZABILITY, AND REPEATABILITY

Objectivity: The absolute core tenet of the scientific method is objectivity. This means nothing short of removing the researcher from the process—much easier said than done in social science research! If you have taken even the most rudimentary natural science class at the high school level you will be familiar with this core tenet. Objectivity relies on removing the researcher from the process by assigning the measurement or observation to instruments that can be calibrated. For example, disciplines such as chemistry rely heavily on perfectly calibrated titration equipment, and physics relies on perfectly calibrated scales. Measurement tools such as litmus paper, for example, are responsible for determining if a chemical reaction produces a base or an acid; this type of analysis is not left up to a human being, who might otherwise eyeball the results and inaccurately assess the reaction. Fundamentally, objectivity is considered important because it prevents the scientist from generating data and results that intentionally confirm their hypothesis rather than allowing the outcomes of the research to occur "naturally" and without the intent of the scientist being injected.

Generalizability: Another core tenet of the natural science method is the ability to generalize the findings from one sample to another. Simply put, this means that every time heat is applied to water, it should boil at precisely 212 degrees Fahrenheit. This process should work with any sample of water, in any location, and always at the same temperature, not at 211 degrees or 213 degrees, but at precisely 212 degrees. The assumption is that when a finding is generalizable, then it is "real."

Repeatability: Repeatability, or **replicability**, is the notion that a finding can be repeated by any scientist under any condition. Similar to the notion of generalizability, which focuses on the replicability across different samples and conditions, repeatability focuses on the replicability across scientists. This is perhaps the primary test that confirms that a finding is "real"; if a scientist had inserted his or her own biases into the research—the opposite of objectivity—then another scientist, without the same biases, would not be able to replicate the findings.

A BRIEF HISTORY OF SOCIOLOGICAL METHODS

Sociology is one of the youngest sciences—perhaps senior only to computer science—and thus draws heavily on the methodologies utilized by natural and other social and behavioral sciences in developing its own set of methods for research. Specifically, sociological methods have attempted to recreate the key tenets of natural science methods—objectivity, generalizability, and repeatability—in the social world.

MENDEL: AN ILLUSTRATION OF SCIENTIFIC ETHICS

Gregor Mendel is probably best known for discovering the laws of inheritance as they relate to dominant and recessive genes. Mendel bred and cross-bred green (dominant) and yellow (recessive) pea plants and discovered that when cross-bred, the dominant gene is always expressed. Recessive traits are expressed only when both parents carry a recessive gene. When both parents express the recessive trait (for the pea plants, the color yellow), both parents carry only the recessive gene, so 100 percent of the offspring will express the recessive trait. When one parent carries two dominant genes (for the pea plants, genes for the color green), then 100 percent of the offspring will express the dominant trait, even if the second parent carries a recessive gene (Figures 4.1 and 4.2).

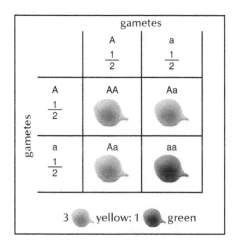

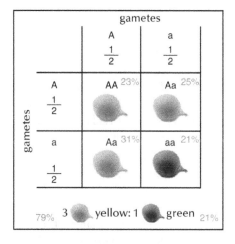

▲ Figure 4.1
Mendel's Pea Plant Experiments.

▲ Figure 4.2
Mendel Revised.

However, when both parents express the dominant trait but carry a recessive gene, 25 percent of the offspring will express the recessive trait.

Though many people have heard of Mendel and the pea plants, fewer people are familiar with the evidence that Mendel fudged his data. British statistician and biologist R. A. Fisher analyzed Mendel's data and concluded two important things: first, Mendel's law is right, and, second, Mendel was afraid that people would not believe his experiments unless the findings were "clean," 75 to 25, and thus he fudged his data in order to make his findings more compelling. This is precisely the reason natural science and social science, its younger sibling, are based on the principle of objectivity.

There are several important issues that distinguish the natural sciences from the social and behavioral sciences that impact methodological approaches. First, because the majority of social science research is conducted on living people, there are many restrictions on the types of research we can conduct relative to the natural sciences. For example, the hallmark of natural science research—the **experiment**—is often difficult to perform on the research questions many social scientists are the most interested in exploring.

EXPERIMENTAL CONDITIONS

An experiment requires three conditions:

1. **Random assignment:** This refers to the process by which subjects are assigned to their conditions randomly rather than based on some quality or characteristic that they have. For example, in an experiment that involves more than one gender, the experimenter might flip a coin to determine which treatment condition each subject receives. Because a coin flip is a random event, the researcher can be sure that the subject was assigned to the treatment group or the control group based on the coin flip, not their gender. In order to be certain that it is the independent variable and not something else that is causing a change in the dependent variable, two additional requirements must be met.
2. **Manipulation of the independent variable:** In order to isolate the cause of a change, the researcher must control the variation in the independent variable and not allow it to vary on its own. Recall our discussion of boiling water. In order to be sure that it was heat that was causing water to boil, early scientists had to apply heat incrementally to the pot of water—and measure the temperature—in order to determine that heat, and not something else, like time, was the cause of boiling water.
3. **Control of third variables:** This allows the researcher to isolate the independent variable they are manipulating in order to be certain that it is the single cause of the change in the dependent variable. Again, returning to our discussion of water boiling, early scientists applied only heat and did not allow any other factor—such as light or wind—to vary, in order to isolate heat as the single factor that causes water to boil.

For example, in order to truly test the "intergenerational transmission of violence" thesis, social scientists would have to identify hundreds of children at birth, randomly assign them to a condition—either exposure to violence in childhood or no exposure to violence in childhood—and then track their experiences with violence in adulthood. It should be obvious why this research could never be conducted but, for the record, so we can be perfectly clear about the pitfalls to social science research, let's review the concerns.

First, we as a society believe it is unethical to remove children from their parents at birth and assign them to live in different families. What parent would agree to this?! Second, it is unethical to *knowingly* expose children to violence. Third, it is unethical to know that adults are perpetrating violence against children or among themselves and not intervene. Thus, the experiment would be impossible to conduct. Yet from a methodological perspective, it is the *only* way to determine if exposure to violence in childhood *causes* children to grow up to perpetrate violence in adulthood. As a result, social science research that investigates this topic is limited to drawing **correlational** conclusions—indications or evidence that events coexist—based on surveys and interview research.

A second and important way in which sociological research is distinct from virtually all other sciences is that we believe that the individuals that we study are infinitely unique. Whereas a chemist can assume that any sample of hydrochloric acid that they utilize in the lab is chemically consistent with all other samples of hydrochloric acid, sociologists know that no two human beings—not even twins—are interchangeable. And although much psychological research on the brain assumes that, with the possible exception of gender or race, all brains work in the same way, sociologists believe that every aspect of our lives, from biology to gender to race to sexual orientation to religion to social class to geography, shapes us and our experiences. Thus, **sampling** is a critically important matter in sociology. Because we assume that none of our subjects are interchangeable, we seek to design sampling techniques that capture as much of the range of human experience as is relevant to our research questions. This is difficult, time-consuming, and very expensive, and these constraints further shape much of the way our research is conducted. This is what makes sociological research unique from all other disciplines.

The majority of sociological research falls into two categories: interviews and surveys. Though sociologists also conduct experiments, analyze historical records, and engage in other methodological techniques like ethnography, because the vast majority of research on family violence has relied on the two most common methods, we will focus on both and provide information on data sets where you can conduct your own secondary analysis.

Qualitative research includes any of a number of techniques that involve researching phenomena in a natural setting or through interactions with individuals experiencing the phenomenon being researched. Qualitative methods generate descriptive data, rather than numbers, which are analyzed by identifying themes or "qualities" rather than by utilizing typical statistical methods.

INTERVIEWS AND QUALITATIVE RESEARCH

Researchers may conduct in-depth **face-to-face interviews** with victims and perpetrators of intimate partner violence, as we did (Hattery 2008; Hattery and Smith 2007, 2019). The interview method is a complement to survey methods—which we will discuss below—in terms of understanding the quality of family violence.

For example, reading the results of research conducted on intimate partner violence by utilizing survey methods can help people to develop an understanding of the frequency of violence in American society—or any other society—because the reports are based on the percentage of people who answer a question such as: "In the last year, did your partner slap or hit you?" In contrast, reports derived from qualitative interviews that provide the details of a violent episode (see Browne 1989 and Hattery 2008 for examples) offer an opportunity to understand the severity of the violence that is typical in violent families as well as to develop sympathy for the victims, whom they have grown to "know" through reading the intimate details of their lives. How do interviews produce this kind of data? Often, a seasoned interviewer can build rapport with a subject rather quickly and, once trust is established, subjects will often disclose extremely painful and intimate details of their lives that help the researcher to develop an accurate picture of the phenomenon. We illustrate with a brief example from our own research. A young African American man we interviewed told us about the violence he grew up with and recounted the day his mother shot his father:

She would go downtown and take out warrants on him and restraining orders, and he'll go back, and one night she took and killed him. You know, they got into a fight, and one night she took and got it. They got into a fight, and she grabbed a pistol and shot him in the head, and he got killed the day before I had to go to court and go to training school, and uh, I went to training school at the age of fourteen years old. I didn't know where my mother was at, she was going with guys that would sell her drugs, you know, she was doping, you know.

(**Eddie**, fortysomething African American man, North Carolina)

This type of thick description (Geertz 1974) paints a picture of the violence and allows the reader to experience the violence—by reading—as it was recounted by the victim. Additionally, the reader can interpret and analyze the data presented in the subject's own words on their own. Last, this type of description is likely to be remembered far longer than a statistic, and this is often useful from the perspective of educating the public about a particular issue, such as child abuse or intimate partner violence.

As implied above, another strength of interview data is that the questions posed by researchers are typically open-ended and allow the subject to interpret the question through their own lexicon, and respond based on that interpretation and in their own words. The challenge for the interviewer is often to guide the subjects, especially if they seem to misunderstand the intent of a question, as well as to generate "data" in the form of quotes that are clear and distinct enough to be published. For example, in our interviews with men and women who had recently been released from prison (Hattery and Smith 2010), the individuals we were interviewing were not terribly articulate, and many of their responses not only used slang but were also peppered with references to aspects of life in prison or drug use that would be meaningless to readers not familiar with these terms. Thus, whereas the statistician is charged with analyzing complex survey data, the researcher who utilizes interview data must often provide a translation of the interview for the reader while managing to retain the intent and voice of the subject. Or, as in the case of a battered woman we interviewed who had been a child prostitute and was severely ashamed of it, the researcher must rely on nonverbal clues to be able to accurately interpret and translate the subject's experiences for the reader.

EVIE

The following is a quote from Evie, an African American woman we interviewed in North Carolina. She was in her fifties and was living in the battered women's shelter as she attempted to leave her abusive partner.

You can't imagine what it's like to have to sit on the laps of men when you are a ten-year-old. I hadn't even learned to ride a bike yet.

Reading the quote apart from the rest of the interview, one might not be struck by it and could conclude that it simply suggested that Evie was talking about an unfortunate childhood, one that was void of the simplest childhood pleasures: a bike.

Reading the entire interview, the researcher would have a context for the quote that might change the analysis. We provide some of the context here in order to demonstrate the ways in which contextualizing a single quote can significantly alter the interpretation.

Evie grew up in a liquor house, or drink house. Liquor houses are a sort of unregulated social club; usually, they are created in a townhouse-style apartment in a public housing project. In a typical liquor house, a man allows a woman (and often her children) to live rent-free upstairs in exchange for her (and her children) running the liquor house on the main level of the home. This arrangement also usually involves sex with the woman whenever he desires it.

continues

EVIE *continued*

When we asked Evie about the men who frequented the drink house where she grew up, she told us that the primary customers were white executives from R. J. Reynolds Tobacco Company (our research was conducted in Winston-Salem, North Carolina). One cannot underestimate the degree to which Winston-Salem is a "company town" even today. (Note that two brands of Reynolds's cigarettes, Winston and Salem, bear the names of the town.) These men would come during their lunch hour and at happy-hour time (usually four o'clock) to consume alcohol, smoke, and have sex before returning to their quiet, white middle-class neighborhoods.

Now that the analyst has a greater context for the original quote, he or she would come to the conclusion that Evie was most likely involved in some level of illegitimate activity. She confirms this with the following quote:

> *Some of the Reynolds men got paid on Wednesday. They'll come in, maybe, and buy . . . give me a five, and maybe they done bought four drinks and I would have the change. Sometimes they would sell fish in there. And a lot of times, some of the guys would get the cigarettes and change cigarettes for drinks.*

Evie continues to describe her role in the liquor house:

> *And it was just like, I wonder that the people that lived out by a car [meaning out in the suburbs]. There was nice section. But they would come in our neighborhood, and drink, and buy women and stuff like that.*

When combined with the initial quote, and with our observation of her nonverbal body language—Evie lowered her face, her eyes became dark and teared up, and she turned toward the woman researcher and decidedly away from the man who was also interviewing—we, as the researchers, came to the conclusion that Evie was in fact prostituted to the men in the liquor house, the customers. At ten years old, Evie was a victim of childhood prostitution.

In addition to interviewing, other qualitative techniques include ethnography and observational methods. **Ethnography** is a methodological approach that requires embedding oneself deeply into the community that one is studying and typically involves both observations and interviews. Ethnographies often take years to complete and the data they yield provide an in-depth and very detailed description and analysis of the people and community that are being investigated. **Observational methods** require the researcher to embed themself in a naturalistic setting and observe behavior. Compared to a full-blown ethnography, observational methods may be more limited in terms of both time and scope. Examples related to family violence would include volunteering at a shelter for battered women and their children and observing the experiences of the women and their children as they attempt to escape the violence or sitting in an emergency room at a local hospital to observe the kinds of injuries that victims of domestic violence or child abuse seek treatment for. Researchers might also observe in family court in order to better understand orders of protection and child custody, or they might ride along with police officers responding to intimate partner or family violence calls. The former examples, such as volunteering over a long period of time in a shelter, are more typical of an ethnographic approach and would likely result in opportunities for the researcher to conduct interviews as well as make long-term observations. The latter examples are typical of standard observational research, such as observing in an emergency room or courtroom or participating in ride-alongs with police officers, and would likely not include interviews, primarily because the lack of opportunity to have anything more than a short interaction with the subjects—if they were allowed to interact at all—would preclude the opportunity to develop rapport and conduct a formal interview. Additionally, these environments are not conducive to interviews because the researcher is relying on other parties whose professional concerns do not include research—emergency room nurses, whose job is to provide medical care; judges, whose job is to approve legal instruments; or police officers, whose job is to protect the public—and who may not be able or willing to allow the researcher the time to conduct an interview or who may be concerned that conducting an interview would disrupt the primary goal of the interaction. In all of these instances, these professionals' jobs require that they move on to the next case once they have met their professional goals—stabilized a patient, made an arrest, and the like. The only exception to the lack of opportunity for interviews is the possibility, if it is the focus of the research, to interview the professionals about their attitudes, observations, and so forth.

Strengths

In all of these cases that utilize ethnographic or observational methodologies, as with interview methods, the data that are collected and analyzed are rich and thick and provide a tremendous level of detail regarding the phenomenon. And though all data are sifted through the lens of the researcher, as demonstrated by the box on p. 88, one of the great strengths of qualitative methods is that the data generated are produced by the subjects themselves; their experiences are not forced into a set of checkboxes that may or may not capture those experiences accurately. For example, as we shall see below when we discuss the Conflict Tactics Scale in detail, one of the main criticisms, waged especially by feminist scholars, is that the questions used to solicit experiences with intimate partner violence include contextualizing language—for example, "During the past year, how many fights with your partner resulted in (you/him/her) hitting, shoving, or throwing things at (you/him/her)?"

Scholars, and feminist scholars in particular, who utilize qualitative methods to study family violence note that often the violence seems to lack a context at all, especially for victims, who often report that there was no fight that led up to the violence and they struggled to figure out what they had "done wrong" to provoke it. Thus, questions that include a context may result in underreporting of violence, especially for victims who live in extremely violent households like those described by Browne (1989), where violence is an almost daily event. Thus, the strengths of qualitative research—interviews, ethnography, and observational methods—are that these methods provide opportunities for researchers to hear about the violence in the subject's own voice and interpreted through their own framework. It also produces the kind of data that are very compelling to consumers of the research—students, policymakers, funders.

Weaknesses

The primary weaknesses of qualitative methods are directly tied to the development of sociological methods: replicability and generalizability. Interviews, for example, are designed on the premise that questions need not be standardized and that interviewers can rephrase questions, adjust the order in which questions are asked, ask follow-up questions as well as those that seek clarification, and redirect the interviewee. As a result, though most interview schedules—the term we use to describe the flow of questions that will be asked during an interview—are standardized enough to cover the same material with each subject, because of the flexibility of the process of the interview, each interview will also produce data that are not standardized across each interview. Thus, not only are the interviews conducted by one interview team not necessarily standardized across the sample, but the likelihood that they can be reproduced—the key to replication—across samples with different interviewers is limited.

Additionally, a strong literature generated primarily by both feminist and minority scholars illustrates the role that the race and gender of the interviewer and interviewee play in the data that are generated in an interview (Hawkesworth 2006; Zuberi and Bonilla-Silva 2008). Specifically, Zuberi and Bonilla-Silva focus on the role that power plays in designing studies, choosing research questions, selecting samples, and interpreting data. They note that race and gender shape every aspect of research. And of importance to our discussion here is the fact that when the phenomenon itself is strongly shaped by power—in this case gender and age—the biases of the researcher can be even more damaging to the integrity of the study. The criticism that feminist scholars have made about the use of survey questions that situate experiences with violence in a context of "conflict" is an example of this overall concern; the researcher is imposing their judgment on the experience of the respondent. Another example of a concern is related to the way in which rapport is established in an interview. If the subject feels that the researcher uses their power in ways that are coercive and thus blur the lines of consent, then the integrity of the interview itself, and the data, are compromised. Thus, especially in research with disadvantaged or marginalized populations—women, minorities, and members of the LGBTQ community—researchers who have power need to be aware of this dynamic. One solution is to design diverse teams of researchers. This both addresses concerns about power and has the potential to ease the establishment of rapport.

THE IMPORTANCE OF DIVERSITY IN RESEARCH TEAMS

Our own experience illustrates the ways in which research teams that are diverse can produce better data than teams that are not. As an African American man and a white woman, we often found that rapport developed with subjects based either on race or on gender. And in some cases, rapport would "switch" and "move" during the course of a single interview. For example, we were conducting an interview with an African American woman who was living in the shelter for battered women as a result of the violence in her home. When she talked about the violence she experienced at the hands of the man who claimed to love her and when she described the sexual abuse her stepfather perpetrated against her, she looked almost exclusively at Hattery, and it was as if Smith was not in the room. Later in the interview, when she described her neighborhood and seeing the occasional white person, she looked directly at Smith and said, "The only time white people come through the projects is when they are lost or looking to buy drugs." This example, though perhaps extreme, illustrates the concerns raised by Zuberi and Bonilla-Silva, and others, and makes a strong case for the importance of diverse research teams, especially when the issues being researched are themselves racialized and gendered.

Hawkesworth (2006) raises the more theoretical question of the distinction between methodology and epistemology. As noted above, research methods are a tool for ensuring that data are gathered or generated, analyzed, and reported in a manner that is as objective as possible and reduces the influence of the researcher's own implicit biases. In contrast, **epistemology** refers to "ways of knowing." As Hawkesworth argues, the way we know things is significantly shaped by our social location—our place in the world. For example, Hattery argues in her work on rape (Hattery and Kane 1995) that women in general have a more complex understanding of sexual abuse because it has always been part of their landscape. Parents warn young girls about the evils that lurk in dark alleys and, more recently, about the risks of date-rape drugs. By their teen years, most young women know of at least one friend who has experienced sexual abuse or rape, for the truth is that by that time perhaps one in five girls (20 percent) have had at least one experience with sexual violence. In contrast, parents, teachers, and other adults, such as coaches, rarely talk with young boys about sexual abuse or rape. The perception is that they are not at risk. And although this perception is wrong—as many as one in seven boys will be sexually abused before reaching adulthood—the truth is that their risk is significantly less than girls', which is at least part of the justification for the silence. Additionally, boys are less likely to know if their friends—both boys and girls—have been sexually abused or raped, in part because the perpetrators are almost always men, and as a result the victims often respond by limiting their relationships with boys and men; they rarely disclose such a painful experience to someone who looks like the person who hurt and violated them. Thus, the landscape for girls and women is one where rape and sexual abuse are a constant, whereas the landscape for men is one where rape and sexual abuse are rarely visible despite their existence at epidemic proportions.

This example illustrates the fact that regardless of their individual experiences, women and men have different "ways of knowing" about sexual abuse and rape. This knowledge is likely to influence every aspect of the research process, including the choice of research questions, the selection of subjects, the methods chosen, and the analysis. For example, especially with regard to research about gender issues, feminist scholars are somewhat more likely to employ qualitative methods such as interviewing and ethnography. This may be partly because they are comfortable with and experienced in listening to women talk about their experiences and partly because, with their more complex understanding of these phenomena, they deliberately choose to employ methods that will reveal rather than minimize its complexities. Despite the fact that one might draw the conclusion that this means that one must be an "insider" (Merton 1972) in order to study a phenomenon that is racialized or gendered—such as intimate partner violence—in fact, scholars such as Hawkesworth and Merton, as well as ourselves, use this fact to advocate for diverse research teams; we believe strongly that the best body of research is generated when a phenomenon is studied by people with various epistemological standpoints. And, we note, generally when issues that are gendered or racialized are studied, it is rarely the case that white men are excluded from studying these phenomena; rather, women and minorities are accused of being too close to the subject to be able to be objective. We argue that as long as objective methods are employed that reduce the subjectivity of the scientist, we do not need to worry about the "outsider" or "insider" status of the researcher.

The second key weakness of qualitative methods is generalizability. As we noted previously, because sociologists operate under the assumption that all individuals are unique and that their experiences are strongly shaped by their social location and geographic location, we must accept the fact that a study performed on a small sample, typically in one geographic location, may not accurately represent the myriad ways in which the phenomenon actually occurs. For example, our interviews with twenty-five men and women who were returning home from prison to a midsize city in the Southeast in 2008 may not represent the experiences of men and women returning from prison to rural South Dakota in 2020. And because qualitative research is very expensive and time-consuming to conduct, the samples are almost always small and almost always limited by geography. Imagine flying around the United States to interview a single person in each of the more than three thousand counties, for example. It would take a long time and be very expensive. In order to counteract this limitation, qualitative researchers often interpret their own data and draw conclusions in the context of other qualitative research conducted by other researchers, with different populations, in different geographic locations, and over time, as well as compare the rates they discover to those generated by studies that utilize national probability samples.

SURVEY RESEARCH AND QUANTITATIVE METHODS

> **Quantitative methods** include techniques or strategies for collecting numeric data—and usually vast quantities of it—that are analyzed using statistical techniques.

The majority of sociological research that is performed—and this also holds for family violence research specifically—is **survey research**. Survey research can be, and is, performed in many different ways, including in the study of family violence, and in this section we will provide a brief overview of survey methods as well as examine several ways in which it has been utilized to generate data regarding family violence.

Most of you have probably taken a survey. The use of surveys begins early in our lives—often in school—and most of us probably do not even realize the extent to which we have participated in survey research. For example, every ten years we participate in the biggest survey ever undertaken: the decennial US census (Figure 4.3). The census is a set of survey questions designed to count the population and gather data on relationships, families, the economy, work, and housing, which can then be used to create a portrait of the US population. For example, the census allows us to estimate the racial composition of the US population and to track trends in marriage rates and fertility, as well as study phenomena such as home ownership.

On the other end of the scale, many or perhaps most of us have completed surveys about who we are likely to vote for in the next election, for example, or how likely we are to buy a new car or some other product in the next six months. These types of surveys—often only a single question—are the hallmark of political science and market research. And college students are certainly accustomed to surveys, as all incoming students are typically surveyed about their social behavior—including their use of alcohol and drugs—and they are often surveyed about potential changes being proposed on campus, including dining plans and housing.

Survey research involves two key elements: designing the survey itself so that the questions asked generate data that researchers can use to address larger research

▶ **Figure 4.3**
The 2010
Census Form.

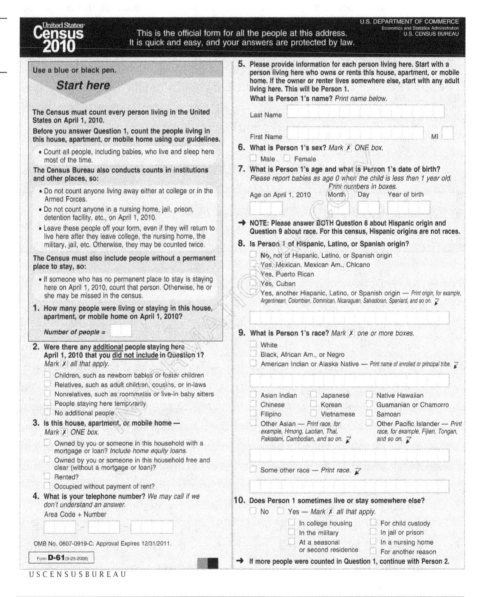

Source: www.census.gov/schools/pdf/2010form_info.pdf.

questions, and constructing the sample. When constructed properly, samples of as few as one thousand can predict within two or three percentage points the outcome of national elections. However, in order to produce this level of reliability and generalizability, the measurement and sampling must be extremely well designed, and when they are not, which is often the case, data that are significantly flawed are nonetheless entered into the public discourse and taken as fact. We will illustrate this point later when we critique specific surveys that are used to generate data on family violence.

SURVEYS AND FAMILY VIOLENCE

There are two types of surveys that are used to generate data about various forms of family violence: self-report research and crime reports. Because they have different purposes, they generate different types of data. We begin with an overview of each and then provide information so that interested students and researchers can access these data themselves.

Scholars who are interested in using survey methods to study family violence typically intend to take advantage of the strengths of survey design: replicability and generalizability. Thus, they design surveys with closed-ended questions that require respondents to choose from a fixed number of predetermined responses. By developing measures and pretesting them in different populations, researchers can be sure that the questions they ask will be interpreted nearly the same way by each respondent, and thus if used repeatedly and in different populations, these items should measure the same thing. We illustrate with an example from the **National Violence Against Women (NVAW) Survey** (Tjaden and Thoennes 2000).

In the last twelve months has your partner ever hit you with an object?

Yes   No

One can see that this question seems very straightforward and should elicit the same response from *any person* who has been hit with an object. Thus, the survey meets the standard of replicability that is so heavily valued in the natural sciences.

In order to generate responses that are generalizable, a sample must be constructed that is representative of the entire population of the United States. The NVAW Survey utilized one of the most common and powerful sampling designs in order to gather data from a nationally representative sample of men and women. This method is referred to as **random digit dialing**, or **RDD**. Random digit dialing combines the survey with computer technology that aids in both the sampling and the administration of the survey. The survey is loaded into a computer system, and a trained phone interviewer administers the survey to respondents over the telephone. When the interviewer is ready to conduct an interview, he or she instructs the computer to generate a telephone number, which is then dialed by the computer. This phone number is generated by randomly selecting ten digits. The number of ten-digit combinations that can be generated is enormous! And because the phone numbers are generated randomly, any one of us has the same probability for having our phone number called as the next person. This is the biggest strength of this design because it ensures that no group of people can be intentionally or unintentionally left out of the study. Additionally, because phone numbers are assigned in a manner that is also random—aside from the fact that area codes and some prefixes indicate a certain geographic region—and all numbers are equally likely to be generated by the computer, we can be sure that everyone has the *same probability* of being included in the study. An additional strength, which is especially important in the twenty-first century, is the fact that because the phone numbers are generated through a random digit process rather than by using phone books or other phone listings, the sample will include unlisted phone numbers as well as cell phone numbers, thus ensuring that young people, for example, who may have cell phones and not landlines, are as likely to be surveyed as older folks, who may have landlines and not cell phones. The one group that is excluded by this design is people who do not have phones. Thus, there is a social class bias to this design, though in terms of surveying the very poor, sociologists have yet to design something better.

There are a couple of drawbacks to this design that are of varying consequence. First, because the numbers are generated randomly, some percentage of these will not actually be phone numbers, or they may be phone numbers to large institutions or offices—for example, the general phone number for the University of Wisconsin Hospital and Clinics. Obviously, the interviewer would realize that the operator answering the phone is not an eligible subject, based on this sampling design, and would apologize for taking up their time and hang up. This is a not a major concern, but it does mean that time will be spent that fails to generate a usable survey response. Though this is not always the case, the NVAW Survey has a Spanish-language option, but it does not offer the administration of the survey in any other languages. Thus, non-English- or non-Spanish-speaking individuals, though they will be included in the initial sample, are not able to participate in the study. As the population of the United States continues to become increasingly diverse, scientists who develop surveys would be best served by developing Spanish versions of any survey—as Hispanics, according to the 2010 census, now make up nearly 20 percent of the US population—as well as survey options in other languages. For example, in our community of Fairfax County, Virginia, officers respond to intimate partner violence calls in 131 languages. When a survey is available only in English, its generalizability is significantly limited to the English-speaking US population.

Last, and of more serious concern to this study—and indeed any study of intimate partner violence—is the possibility that a battered woman is selected as a respondent, but when the interviewer calls she is unable to participate or participate honestly because she is being carefully watched or monitored by her abusive partner. Thus, there is some possibility that underreporting of violence may occur, and it is *most likely* to occur in the *most violent and abusive homes*, which typically also include extreme levels of controlling behavior. This is problematic because it may lead to an underestimation of the most severe violence that is occurring in families in our communities.

The second category of surveys that generate data on family violence is conducted by government and law enforcement agencies. In some instances, these surveys are designed specifically to gather information on family violence, and in others they are part of the larger reporting system in which law enforcement agencies are required to participate. For example, the **Bureau of Justice Statistics (BJS)**, the government clearinghouse for all data related to crime, the criminal justice system, law enforcement, and corrections, conducts the **National Crime Victimization Survey (NCVS)** every six months. The major source of information on all types of criminal victimization, the survey involves contacting one hundred thousand persons aged twelve or over, either in person or by telephone, and asking them about their experiences as victims of crime. Demographic data on the victim and the offender (if known) are collected, as well as information about the relationship between the victim and the offender, the crime itself, and whether the victim reported the crime to law enforcement. Though it focuses on all types of crime, including being the victim of a robbery or stranger assault, it does contain data on various types of family violence, including intimate partner violence, sexual abuse, and child abuse.

This type of crime survey suffers from the same weaknesses that other surveys do, namely the exclusion of small pockets in the population who may not have access to a telephone or speak a language in which the survey is being conducted. Additionally, the primary flaw of this type of survey in estimating levels of family violence is that it requires the respondent to conceptualize or frame her or his experience as a crime. In many cases of family violence, the victims do not frame their experiences as crimes. This can occur for a variety of reasons, including the fact that they simply may not believe the behavior they are experiencing constitutes a crime. For example, a victim of child abuse may believe that their parents have a right to engage in physical forms of discipline and that their experience does not constitute a crime. Second, it is not uncommon for victims of family abuse, both child abuse and intimate partner violence, to have reported the experience, sometimes even to a law enforcement agent, only to have the complaint dismissed. Thus, they may assume, usually wrongly, that their experiences do not qualify as crimes when in fact they do. Taken together, these design issues will result in underreporting of family violence. Often the underreporting leads to severe underestimations that, when used by funding agencies to allocate resources to organizations serving victims of family violence, result in their being severely underfunded and deprived of much-needed resources.

The third type of "survey" involves the reporting that all law enforcement agencies are required by law to perform. The **Uniform Crime Reports (UCR)** require that all law enforcement agencies, including municipal police departments and county sheriff offices, send a report each month directly to the FBI. Though these reports include "crime counts"—how many crimes of various types were reported in the previous month—they also include data on crimes cleared and persons arrested (age, race, gender), characteristics of homicides and assaults, and homicides of police officers. As an aside, as a result of political pressure, these reports also contain data on each and every stop an officer makes. These data are used to track racial differences in stops and arrests, or what we commonly refer to as *racial profiling* (Hattery and Smith 2007, 2018).

Strengths

As already mentioned, one of the primary strengths of survey data is the fact that standard questions offer the possibility for replication. For example, the Conflict Tactics Scale (which we will discuss at length later) has been administered to tens of thousands of individuals over a period of thirty or so years. This allows researchers to develop reliable gauges of trends. For example, has the physical abuse of children increased or decreased over time? Have boys become more vulnerable to child sexual abuse since the 1970s? And, if so, does this represent an actual change in the phenomenon or a change in the willingness of boys to report sexual abuse? This is a very important characteristic of survey research that contributes significantly to our understanding of trends in various types of family violence.

Of equal or perhaps even greater importance is the fact that survey research allows scholars and policymakers to estimate the prevalence of various types of family violence both overall and in distinct populations. Having some ability to estimate how often violence is occurring and who the victims and perpetrators are is essential for many reasons. First, it is important to understand the level of violence that is occurring in our families and homes. Second, in order to adequately staff a variety of agencies, from shelters for battered women to emergency rooms to intimate partner violence units in police departments, we need an estimate of the rate of violence in our local communities. Third, nonprofit agencies that serve victims and provide intervention services for offenders rely on these numbers not only for staffing purposes but also for seeking the funding necessary to provide these services. In order to justify proposals that seek hundreds of thousands, if not millions, of dollars in both federal and private funding, agencies need to provide an estimate of the need that exists for their services. Last, these types of data are the best way of estimating difference among populations, especially race, gender, age, sexual orientation, religious, and geographic groups. For example, the most recent data on intimate partner violence indicate that for the first time ever, the rate of intimate partner violence is significantly higher among African American women than among white women (Violence Policy Center 2008), an issue we will explore at greater length in subsequent chapters.

Weaknesses

Of course, the weaknesses of survey research are the flip side of the strengths of interview data, namely that numbers tell a different kind of "story" than the stories told by individual men, women, and children. When we read a statistic that 70 percent of women worldwide (World Health Organization 2013) will experience an episode of intimate partner violence in her lifetime, we may be shocked. But that shock is soon forgotten if we cannot connect that statistic to the actual experiences of battered women. Thus, one of the weaknesses of survey data is that surveys are designed to elicit standard responses to short questions or statements and very rarely include the kinds of questions that will elicit detailed responses. In fact, one critique of many surveys designed to estimate family violence is that they do not include measures of frequency. So, as noted above, we may gather data on how many people have been hit with an object by their partner in the past twelve months, but we cannot distinguish between those who were hit only once and those who were hit many times in a single episode, let alone in many different episodes. And though violence is violence, it is clear that it can be qualitatively different, and we should be designing survey questions and response options that better capture these qualitative differences. Another way to think about this is the adage that "a picture is worth a thousand words." Qualitative data, though built on words, generate a picture in ways that quantitative data rarely can.

As noted above, one of the main potential weaknesses of all types of survey research is the very real possibility of inaccuracies in reporting. And though some types of surveys or survey populations may be predisposed to suffer from overreporting, in all cases of research on family violence, the real concern is in underreporting. There is less to be concerned about when the underreporting is not specifically linked to the phenomenon of family violence, but there is reason to be concerned when it is. So, as noted previously, if the context of the survey itself (as is the case with the NCVS) or the questions (as with the Conflict Tactics Scale) shape the types of incidents that victims and perpetrators report and if this results in underreporting, then the data that are generated will be *less accurate* than we anticipate, and in ways that we cannot adjust for. Additionally, as noted with regards to the NVAW Survey, if the design relies on calling household phone numbers, we can assume that the greatest risk for underreporting will be *directly related to the experiences of violence*; namely, the surveillance that many severely battered women experience will prohibit them from participating in the survey. When conclusions about the prevalence of violence and the levels of it are based on these reports, then we will be underestimating the problem and underfunding our responses to it.

Last, we simply want to point out a rarely discussed, but extremely common, error that people make when interpreting and applying survey data. The term **ecological fallacy** describes this error, which involves the attempt to predict individual experiences or outcomes from aggregate-level data. So, for example, just because we know that 70 percent of women will experience an episode of intimate partner violence in her lifetime, and that this rate increases for women who are poor, are nonwhite, marry young, have more than the average number of children, and live with a partner who abuses alcohol or drugs, or who live in countries outside of the United States, we cannot predict the likelihood that an individual with these traits will be abused. So, if you are reading this book and you have these traits, all we know is that people like you have a higher risk for being a victim, but we cannot predict the likelihood that *you as an individual person* will be victimized. Similarly, if you are reading this book and you have none of these traits, all we know is that your risk for experiencing intimate partner violence is low, but we cannot ensure that you aren't already, or won't become, a victim. Thus, we need to be very cautious when we attempt to generalize these types of findings to individuals in their own lives.

CONFLICT TACTICS SCALE

The **Conflict Tactics Scale (CTS)** is the most widely utilized and most controversial of the large-scale surveys that have been used to measure family violence. Created by Murray Straus and Richard Gelles in the early 1970s, this was the first attempt to develop a tool that could be used to measure the prevalence of family violence nationally. Straus and Gelles, who are trained as psychologists, have primarily conducted their research on samples of college students. However, according to Straus (1999), the CTS has been administered in more than one hundred empirical studies. We were unable to find any instances in which the survey was administered to a nationally representative sample. Rather, the CTS seems to be utilized most often by psychologists using college samples and therapists who administer it in a therapy setting. Thus, one shortcoming of the actual implementation of the CTS is that any findings generated through its use may not represent the experiences of the majority of adults living in the United States. As we know, college students represent a very small subset of Americans—a subset that is both "whiter" and wealthier than the overall population. Additionally, though dating violence is on the rise (an issue we will be exploring in subsequent chapters), the majority of intimate partner violence is perpetrated and experienced in adulthood, and thus a college student sample will certainly underestimate its prevalence.

As Strauss himself points out in response to criticisms of the CTS, it was not designed to measure power or intent but is strictly limited to measuring behavior. On the one hand, this is quite important because it means that the findings are based on things that happened rather than on one person's assessment of why the behavior happened or what caused it. Below are some of the items that are found in the CTS.

When you had an argument with your partner in the past year, how many times have you threatened to hit or throw something at him or her?

Never   Once   Twice   3–5 times   6–10 times   11–20 times   More than 20 times

How many times has he or she threatened to hit or throw something at you?

Never   Once   Twice   3–5 times   6–10 times   11–20 times   More than 20 times

As noted, there are many critiques of the CTS. Feminists and others critique the CTS for *not* measuring perceived intent. They argue that although all hits may be the same in terms of the potential harm done, a hit in the context of an argument might indicate something different about the couple's relationship than a hit that comes out of nowhere. The former would likely be an indicator of what Johnson and colleagues refer to as *situational couple violence*, and the latter might indicate a case of *intimate terrorism* (Leone et al. 2004). Similarly, the CTS includes measures of injury, but it does not measure the extent of an injury. Thus, incidents that require a bandage will be categorized in the same way as those that involve broken bones, emergency room visits, and even surgery. The same is true of frequency. The CTS does not measure multiple incidents of the same behavior; it measures only if the behavior occurred at all. And last, as noted above, contextualizing the violence for the respondent by using the term *conflict* or the phrase *when you had an argument* is far more likely to capture situational couple violence—which by definition is violence that occurs during an argument or is the result of conflict—rather than the more serious violence that is associated with intimate terrorism, which often seems to the victim to "come out of the blue."

Thus, studies that rely on the CTS alone, by failing to distinguish between certain types of violence, frequency, level of injury, and so on, may tend to over-estimate situational couple violence and underestimate intimate terrorism. This is problematic because intimate terrorism is far more likely to result in an escala-tion of violence that may result in serious injury, the very real need for a victim to escape, and even homicide.

You will recall from the discussion of theory in Chapter 3 that feminist theorists make specific critiques of family violence research and the CTS in particular. Here we summarize the feminist critique of the CTS.

The CTS is a set of questions designed to measure conflict and violence in families (Straus 1999). Yet feminists argue that at least some incidents of inti-mate partner violence do not occur around a conflict. In interviews with battered women we (Hattery 2008; Hattery and Smith 2007) and our colleagues (Browne and Finkelhor 1986; Browne 1989; Koss et al. 1994) document many incidents of violence—some of it very severe—that seemed, according to the victims, to arise out of nowhere. In these cases women report that their partners simply came home and started beating on them, for example, and that there was no context of conflict or argument in which to locate the violence. Thus, feminist theorists argue that the CTS underreports the intimate partner violence women experience because it focuses the questions only around occasions of conflict.

Additionally, feminist theorists argue that much of the violence that is perpe-trated by women and reported in the CTS is violence that must be characterized as self-defense. For example, we interviewed a woman who was court-ordered to an intervention program for batterers. Her husband had her arrested after she bit his arm severely and the judge ordered her to attend the intervention program. In our interview she revealed, and we confirmed this with the staff of the program, that she bit her husband's arm *while he was banging her head against the dashboard of the car while he was driving!* The CTS would have captured her behavior as an inci-dent of female-perpetrated violence—because it also met the criterion of occurring within the context of an argument—but it would not have captured the fact that this behavior was self-defensive, not an attack. Thus, feminists argue that complete gender neutrality and the limiting of experiences with violence to those that occur in the context of conflict—as opposed to including violence that just seems to come out of nowhere—both arise from the tendency by family violence scholars to ignore the system of gendered inequality (patriarchy) that undergirds most pat-terns of violence in the United States, and indeed globally (see Acker 2006; Epstein 2007). Additionally, as noted, family violence scholars who employ tools like the

CTS fail to distinguish acts of self-defense from attacks—thus overestimating both women's perpetration of violence and situational couple violence—and in doing so they conclude, as Johnson and his colleagues do (Leone et al. 2004), that situational couple violence is the more prevalent type of intimate partner violence and that the more severe form, intimate terrorism, is rare. This contradicts the findings of other quantitative research as well as qualitative, interview-based research. This is an important weakness in family violence theory that unfortunately infiltrates both the academic literature on family violence and the media—which loves these types of reports—and these then shape, inaccurately, the perceptions of the general public, including many of those in professions that deal with intimate partner violence, including police officers, judges, and divorce attorneys (Martin 2005).

CONCLUSIONS

We have always believed in the triangulation of methods: we look to both survey data and interview data in order to better portray the face of family violence. Because different methods have different purposes as well as different strengths and weaknesses, rather than preferring one over the other, we believe the most effective approach is to take the best of each and combine these "bests" in order to create a more complex picture of family violence. This process can be performed by individual scholars—and in subsequent chapters you will gain insight into how we accomplish this—as well as by scholars working together in the field. For example, edited books and journals that take family violence, child abuse, or intimate partner violence as their focus would be best served by selecting chapters and research essays in such a way as to represent the range of methodological and theoretical approaches. By incorporating the best and most advanced statistical measures of family violence alongside the more compelling stories generated by interviews and observation, the scholar, the practitioner, and the student can develop the most comprehensive understanding of family violence.

Last, because of the various ways in which quantitative data on family violence are collected and because of the relative accessibility of much of the quantitative data, we strongly advocate this approach for the student or scholar who wishes to see for themself: we find that, although it may be tedious, the best way to accurately estimate the prevalence of family violence that is *reported* is to build cross-checking tables from all of the sources of data available—the BJS, NCVS, and UCR. Estimates can then be derived from data from survey sources such as the NVAW Survey and the CTS. We note that some websites developed by policy and advocacy groups have done this as well, and some data may be available in a form that is "ready to use." The Resources section contains a review of data sources that can be accessed by individual researchers and students. These are excellent sources of data for research papers. They can provide the most recent data for funding reports, and because several surveys allow the researcher to conduct their own analysis, they can be an excellent source for an honor's or master's thesis, or even a doctoral dissertation.

Studying family violence is a challenging but very rewarding experience, and we look forward to taking you through the phenomenon in the next several chapters.

RESOURCES

Inter-University Consortium for Political and Social Research (ICPSR): www.icpsr. umich.edu.

The CTS is available at the following website: www.icpsr.umich.edu/icpsrweb/ PHDCN/descriptions/cts-partner-spouse-PAS-w1-w2-w3.jsp.

The Bureau of Justice Statistics: http://bjs.ojp.usdoj.gov.

The UCR data are available at the FBI website: www.fbi.gov/ucr/ucr.htm.

Intimate Partner Violence

National Coalition Against Domestic Violence: www.ncadv.org.

United States Department of Justice Office on Violence Against Women: www.justice. gov/ovw.

Many states also have websites for data related to intimate partner violence inside the state.

Child Abuse

National Children's Advocacy Center: www.nationalcac.org.

Prevent Child Abuse America: www.preventchildabuse.org.

National Children's Alliance: www.nationalchildrensalliance.org.

Elder Abuse

Center of Excellence on Elder Abuse and Neglect: www.centeronelderabuse.org.

National Committee for the Prevention of Elder Abuse: www.preventelderabuse.org.

REFERENCES

Acker, Joan. 2006. *Class Questions, Feminist Answers*. New York: Routledge.

Browne, Angela. 1989. *When Battered Women Kill*. New York: Free Press.

Browne, Angela, and David Finkelhor. 1986. "Impact of Child Sexual Abuse." *Review of the Research Psychological Bulletin 99(1)*: 66–77.

Epstein, Cynthia. 2007. "Great Divides: The Cultural, Cognitive, and Social Bases of the Global Subordination of Women." *American Sociological Review 72(1)*: 1–22.

Geertz, Clifford. 1974. *Myth, Symbol, and Culture*. New York: W. W. Norton.

Hattery, Angela J. 2008. *Intimate Partner Violence*. Lanham, MD: Rowman and Littlefield.

Hattery, Angela J., and Emily W. Kane. 1995. "Men's and Women's Perceptions of Non-Consensual Sexual Intercourse." *Sex Roles 33(11)*: 785–802.

Hattery, Angela J., and Earl Smith. 2007. *African American Families*. Thousand Oaks, CA: Sage.

Hattery, Angela J., and Earl Smith. 2010. *Prisoner Reentry and Social Capital: The Long Road to Reintegration*. Lanham, MD: Lexington Books.

Hattery, Angela J., and Earl Smith. 2018. *Policing Black Bodies: How Black Lives are Surveilled and How to Work for Change*. Lanham, MD: Rowman and Littlefield.

Hattery, Angela J., and Earl Smith. 2019. *Gender, Power and Violence: Responding to Sexual and Intimate Partner Violence in Society Today*. Lanham, MD: Rowman and Littlefield.

Hawkesworth, Mary E. 2006. *Feminist Inquiry: From Political Conviction to Methodological Innovation*. New Brunswick, NJ: Rutgers University Press.

Koss, M. P., L. A. Goodman, A. Browne, L. F. Fitzgerald, G. P. Keita, and N. F. Russo. 1994. *No Safe Haven: Male Violence Against Women at Home, at Work, and in the Community*. Washington, DC: American Psychological Association.

Leone, Janel M., Michael P. Johnson, Catherine L. Cohan, and Susan E. Lloyd. 2004. "Consequences of Male Partner Violence for Low-Income Minority Women." *Journal of Marriage and Family 66(2)*: 472–490.

Martin, Patricia Yancey. 2005. *Rape Work: Victims, Gender, and Emotions in Organization and Community Context*. New York: Routledge.

Merton, Robert K. 1972. "Insiders and Outsiders: A Chapter in the Sociology of Knowledge." *American Journal of Sociology 78(1)*: 9–47.

Straus, Murray A. 1999. "The Controversy Over Domestic Violence by Women: A Methodological, Theoretical, and Sociology of Science Analysis." In *Violence in Intimate Relationships*, edited by X. B. Arriaga and S. Oskamp, 17–44. London: Sage.

Tjaden, Patricia, and Nancy Thoennes. 2000. *Full Report of the Prevalence, Incidence, and Consequences of Violence Against Women: Findings from the National Violence Against Women Survey*. Washington, DC: US Department of Justice. www.ncjrs. gov/pdffiles1/nij/183781.pdf.

Violence Policy Center. 2008. *When Men Murder Women: An Analysis of 2006 Homicide Data*. Washington, DC: Violence Policy Center. www.vpc.org/studies/ wmmw2008.pdf.

World Health Organization, Department of Reproductive Health and Research, London School of Hygiene and Tropical Medicine, South African Medical Research Council. 2013. *Global and Regional Estimates of Violence Against Women: Prevalence and Health Effects of Intimate Partner Violence and Non-Partner Sexual Violence*. www.who.int/reproductivehealth/publications/violence/9789241564625/en.

Zuberi, Tukufu, and Eduardo Bonilla-Silva. 2008. *White Logic, White Methods: Racism and Methodology*. Lanham, MD: Rowman and Littlefield.

5

ABUSE ACROSS THE LIFE COURSE

Elder Abuse

Financial scams targeting seniors have become so prevalent that they're now considered "the crime of the 21st century." Why? Because seniors are thought to have a significant amount of money sitting in their accounts. Financial scams also often go unreported or can be difficult to prosecute, so they're considered a "low-risk" crime. However, they're devastating to many older adults and can leave them in a very vulnerable position with little time to recoup their losses. It's not just wealthy seniors who are targeted. Low-income older adults are also at risk of financial abuse. And it's not always strangers who perpetrate these crimes. Over 90% of all reported elder abuse is committed by an older person's own family members, most often their adult children, followed by grandchildren, nieces and nephews, and others.

—**National Council on Aging**, "Top 10 Financial Scams Targeting Seniors"

This chapter will focus on the abuse of the elderly, primarily by their children but also by nonrelative caregivers, in both the home setting and institutional settings. We will review the research on elder abuse and the laws that deal with elder abuse and provide a conceptual framework for understanding the significance of elder abuse. As will be the case in all chapters, we will not limit our discussion to physical abuse but will include lengthy discussions of psychological abuse—especially of individuals suffering from dementia or Alzheimer's—and, as noted in the epigraph that opens this chapter, financial abuse.

OBJECTIVES

- To identify the changing demographics of the US population, specifically with regards to age
- To describe the trends in life expectancy and health in later life
- To explore trends in caregiving patterns for the aging
- To identify common patterns of abuse of the elderly by their children
- To explore patterns of abuse of the elderly by nonrelative caregivers in both home and institutional settings
- To illuminate patterns and trends in various types of elder abuse, including physical, psychological, and financial
- To examine the ways in which elder abuse is being dealt with by law enforcement and legal and social welfare institutions
- To offer some ideas for the prevention of and early intervention in elder abuse

KEY TERMS

age pyramid	ageism
life expectancy	sexual abuse
sandwich generation	psychological model
financial abuse	social learning theory
neglect	symbolic interaction theory
active neglect	social exchange theory
passive neglect	situational theory
self-neglect	ecological theory
physical abuse	feminist theory
psychological abuse	

INTRODUCTION

As we noted in our discussion of the history of various types of abuse (Chapter 2), elder abuse is relatively recent, both as a phenomenon and as a social problem. As is the case with all forms of family violence, elder abuse has long been invisible, hidden from view by the fact that it most often occurs in the privacy of one's home—either the caregiver's or the victim's. And though we now have a much greater awareness of elder abuse, our ability to estimate its prevalence is limited by the fact that the majority of elderly victims continue to be cared for and abused in the privacy of the home. That said, it is critical to develop an understanding of both the prevalence of elder abuse and the changing demographics that impact the rate of elder abuse. We begin by discussing the changing demographics.

CHANGING DEMOGRAPHICS

One important dimension of elder abuse, its history, and its current prevalence, is the changing age structure of the United States, especially across the twentieth century and into the second decade of the twenty-first century. At the beginning of the twentieth century, children under the age of eighteen made up the largest portion of the US population. The second-largest group were people who in 1900 would have been defined as "middle-aged," and by far the smallest proportion of the US population was aging or elderly. In contrast, as birth rates have steadily declined and life expectancy has steadily increased, the US population of the first decades of the twenty-first century is more evenly spread across age categories, with just as many young people (under age eighteen) as those over age fifty-five. In the twenty-first century, for the first time in history, a significant portion of the US population can be defined as "elderly."

An **age pyramid** is an excellent visual to illustrate the changes in the composition of a population. The age pyramids shown in Figures 5.1 and 5.2, one from 1900 and the other from 2000, clearly illustrate the shifts and trends in the US population by age. In the 1900 figure, the pyramid is truly a pyramid, with the base, composed of the youngest members of our population, being the largest, and the top, composed of the elderly, being the smallest. In the 2000 figure, the age pyramid is not really a pyramid at all but more like a rectangle; this shape indicates that currently the US population has *nearly* equal proportions of citizens in every age category except at birth and after about age fifty-five, the two age groups with somewhat smaller shares of the US population. Thinking toward the future, as birth rates continue to decline and life expectancy continues to increase, demographers predict that by the mid-twenty-first century or sooner, the US population will be best illustrated by an inverted pyramid. Already the age pyramid for the European Union has begun to shift from a rectangle shape very vaguely toward the shape of an inverted pyramid, and we anticipate a similar shift in the US population as well.

What does all of this mean with regards to elder abuse? First, it helps to explain a part of the *history* of elder abuse. As noted in Chapter 2, in addition to the fact that elder abuse had not been defined and that it was largely hidden from public view and considered a private family matter, it is also true that a very small percentage of the population lived long enough to become elderly. And if we assume that only a small fraction of elders will be abused, the prevalence of elder abuse was likely very low for the first half of the twentieth century simply because to live long enough to be considered elderly was indeed a rare event.

Today, as the population of elders continues to grow, the prevalence of abuse will undoubtedly increase. Quite simply, there are more potential victims. Additionally, there are a number of changes that produce key stressors that increase

▶ **Figure 5.1**
Distribution of
US Population
by Age and
Gender (1900).

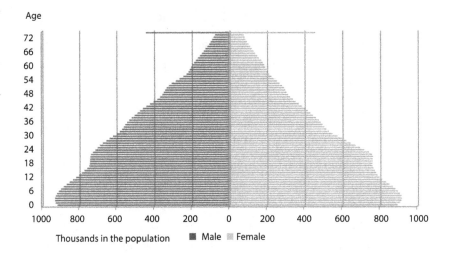

Source: US Census Bureau. "Resident Population—Estimates by Age, Sex, and Race: July 1, 1900." www.census.gov/popest/data/national/asrh/pre-1980/tables/PE-11-1900.pdf.

▶ **Figure 5.2**
Age Pyramid,
2000.

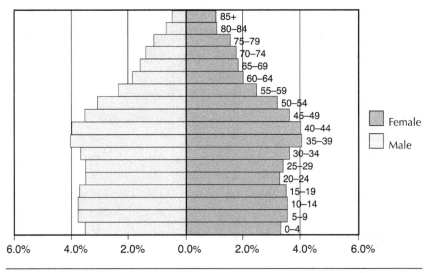

Source: www.censuscope.org/us/chart_age.html.

the likelihood of elder abuse, and we will discuss these below. That said, one of the important lessons we can, and should, draw from the changes in the age pyramids is that as the pyramid transitions from the rectangular shape we see today to eventually—as birth rates continue to decline and life expectancy continues to expand—something resembling an inverted pyramid, the number of people needing elder care will increase while the number of people available to provide care and pay for it will dramatically decrease. This fact alone suggests that the age structure of a society itself shapes the likelihood of elder abuse and its prevalence and patterns. Even with the acknowledgment of elder abuse, education about it, and the existence of prevention programs, the likelihood that it will continue to increase is high given the limited human resources—family members and potential care providers—that are available for each aging person in the population.

CHANGING LIFE EXPECTANCY

Among the best indicators of the changes in the health and well-being of Americans across the twentieth century is the rapid increase in **life expectancy**—or the number of years the average person can expect to live—which rose from 47.3 years in 1900 to 78.8 years in 2013 (National Center for Health Statistics 2015). As noted above, though many factors have contributed to the changes in the age pyramid in the United States, the greatest contributing factor is no doubt the incredible rise in life expectancy in a relatively short period of time: thirty years in a century. As life expectancy has increased, so has the potential for elder abuse.

Race and Gender Variation in Life Expectancy

It is important to note that both race and gender significantly shape life expectancy. For example, in 1900 the life expectancy for white men was 46.6, and for white women it was 48.7. In comparison, African American men's life expectancy was only 32.5 years, and African American women could expect to live only one year longer: 33.5 years. Interestingly, across the twentieth century the racial gap of more than ten years narrowed slightly for men and significantly for women, while the gender gap for both racial groups increased. In 2013 (the latest year for which data are available), life expectancy for white men was 78.7 years, and for white women it was 81.4 years. In contrast, African American men's life expectancy increased to 72.3 years (more than double the figure in 1900), and African American women's rose to 78.4—nearly equivalent to the figure for white men (National Center for Health Statistics 2015).

The overall increase in life expectancy has been driven primarily by a few key factors: public health policies, an increase in the standard of living, and changes in medicine. Consider the factors that continue to depress life expectancy in developing nations—access to clean water and sewage removal, a lack of the widespread use of vaccinations, and access to a nutrient-rich diet—and it is easy to understand the types of changes that took place in twentieth-century America.

The increase in the gender gap in life expectancy is a bit harder to explain, but most scholars who study life expectancy point out a few key factors: stress and violence. Men of all racial and ethnic groups live lives that are more marked by stress than their women counterparts. This includes stress at work—both psychological and physical—and a lack of intimate relationships that are believed to reduce stress. For example, men are more likely to work in fields that generate stress, such as medicine and finance, as well as those that are difficult or physically demanding, including construction, heavy manufacturing, mining, over-the-road trucking, and road work; quite simply, they are more likely to be injured or even die on the job than women. Second, men are less likely than women to be married—a factor that has been shown to enhance overall health and extend life expectancy—and they are less likely to report that they have close personal friendships that involve regular contact (Reis and Franks 1994), a factor that is likely to shape health and life expectancy in many different ways. Also, it is believed that intimate relationships and friendships improve mental health in ways that affect both physical health and life expectancy. One measurement of the impact of psychologically related stress is that suicide is the eighth leading cause of death for white men (National Center for Health Statistics 2015).

All of the data on violence indicate that although women are far more likely to be victims of lethal and near-lethal intimate partner violence, men are *far more likely* to be victims of violence, especially homicide. And this is exacerbated by race. In fact, homicide is the fifth most common cause of death for African American men (National Center for Health Statistics 2015). Thus, as the health of men and women of all racial and ethnic groups has improved across the twentieth century, thanks to advances in public health and sanitation, work-related stress and violence have differentially gendered life expectancy. Differences in life expectancy related to race and gender shape patterns of elder abuse, specifically who is at greatest risk of becoming a victim.

RACE AND GENDER AS PREDICTORS OF ELDER ABUSE

According to the Centers for Disease Control and Prevention (CDC), with the exception of abandonment—which refers to the situation in which a caregiver simply stops providing any care and even stops having any contact with the elderly person, as compared to neglect, in which case the caregiver continues to provide care but that care is inadequate—older women are far more likely to be victims of all forms of elder abuse than older men. In fact, most research, including that reported by the Centers for Disease Control (National Center for Injury Prevention and Control 2016) as well as scholarly publications (Mouton et al.

2004), indicates that elderly women experience levels of physical abuse that are similar to younger women, and the prevalence of verbal abuse is actually higher among elderly women (44 percent) than among younger women (7.5 percent) (Mouton et al. 2004).

Scholars suggest that gender shapes the experiences of elder abuse in patterns similar to those of other forms of family violence. Indeed, in some cases the abuse is a continuation of intimate partner violence that began when the women and their husbands or partners were much younger.

With regard to race, there are significant differences. Mouton and colleagues (2004) followed ninety-one thousand postmenopausal women for three years and found that African American women were 2.84 times more likely to report that they had experienced an act of physical violence than their white counterparts. In contrast, white women were more likely than all other women to report verbal abuse. This study, which looked at functionally independent older women, reflects findings that are more consistent with the literature on intimate partner violence rather than elder abuse. Women's greater life expectancy, regardless of race, and their vulnerability to other forms of violence, namely sexual abuse and intimate partner violence, result in the fact that among the elderly, women are far more likely to be the victims of all forms of elder abuse, except neglect, which is experienced more frequently by men (Figure 5.3).

INDIRECT AND DIRECT CAUSES OF ELDER ABUSE

Because the vast majority of elder abuse is born out of a set of factors, including access to the elderly person, the elderly person's level of physical and cognitive

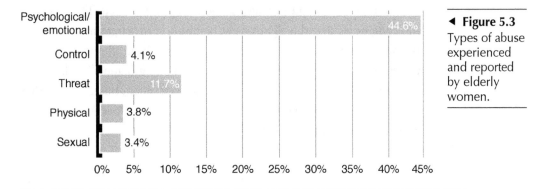

◀ **Figure 5.3**
Types of abuse experienced and reported by elderly women.

Of 842 women aged sixty or over seen in primary-care settings in three states, nearly half had experienced psychological or emotional maltreatment. Women who had encountered one type of mistreatment were often found to have encountered other types as well.

Source: Data from Fisher and Regan 2006.

functioning, the elderly person's level of vulnerability, and so forth, race and gender are indirect rather than direct factors in shaping patterns of elder abuse. For example, because elderly women are perceived as being less capable and knowledgeable about finances, and because white women have the longest life expectancy as well as higher levels of wealth (Hattery and Smith 2012; Shapiro 2003), we can anticipate that white women will constitute the largest segment of the population of victims of financial abuse. It is not so much their gender or their whiteness explicitly that leaves them vulnerable to financial abuse but rather the ways in which their race and gender shape their life expectancy, wealth, and stereotypes—especially of not being fiscally capable—that render them vulnerable to financial abuse.

Finally, it is important to note that unlike the other forms of family violence that we are exploring in this book, elder abuse is unique in that it is often perpetrated by nonrelatives. Though family caregivers perpetuate abuse, so do nonfamilial caregivers and strangers. For example, in response to longer life expectancy and the accompanying array of physical and cognitive diseases that often plague those of us who live to advanced old age, during the latter half of the twentieth century the United States experienced a dramatic rise in the number of nursing home facilities, long-term care facilities, Alzheimer's care facilities, and so forth—a trend that is likely to increase well into the twenty-first century. "Warehousing" the elderly, especially those who are dependent and suffering from physical and cognitive decline, opens up the opportunity for paid caregivers and institutional staff to engage in all of the various types of abuse that the elderly experience. In addition, especially with regard to financial abuse, the elderly are often targets for scams—for example, one in which the victim pays for home improvements in advance with cash and the work is never completed. The elderly are also more vulnerable to pressure from salespeople who earn their money by commission and may sell vulnerable elderly people financial services they do not need. The National Council on Aging notes that the eighth most common scam targeting the elderly is selling them reverse home mortgages, ads for which we have all seen repeatedly on daytime television ("Top 10 Financial Scams Targeting Seniors" n.d.). That said, family members are most often the perpetrators of elder abuse, committing 90 percent of the abuse according to the National Center on Elder Abuse ("Elder Abuse: The Size of the Problem" n.d.).

SANDWICH GENERATION

While often elder abuse is really an *extension* of intimate partner violence that has occurred in a victim's life, possibly across decades, some scholars of elder abuse point to one significant change in family structure that makes the elderly more vulnerable to neglect and abuse. The emergence of the **sandwich generation** of the late twentieth century was a structural change in the institution of the family that created the types of stresses that some scholars argue may be linked to elder abuse. Specifically, the term *sandwich generation* refers to the concept that many middle-aged women are caring simultaneously for young children and aging parents. Carol Abaya, a syndicated news columnist, coined the term in 1992 when she started a syndicated news column, "The Sandwich Generation."

According to research conducted by the Pew Research Center, as many as one in eight Americans have an older relative living with them, and as many as 10 million are part of the sandwich generation, providing daily care, financial assistance, and often supervision for both their own children and their aging parents and, in some cases, grandparents (Parker and Patten 2013).

The sandwich generation is the result of a number of changes in family structure that have occurred almost simultaneously. Though the focus in this chapter has been on the significant increase in life expectancy that has dramatically extended the lives of older adults, at least three other structural changes have occurred as well: delayed childbearing, the prolonging of the onset of adulthood, and the reduction of funded retirement plans.

Beginning in the late 1960s, more and more young adults deferred adulthood by attending college; today many young adults are further delaying adulthood by pursuing training, professional school, or graduate school, all of which can extend until their late twenties or early thirties. Coupled with a tightening job market and the skyrocketing costs of higher education, which often lead to students exiting institutions of higher education with student loans in the six digits, many parents find that they are still providing significant financial support to their children until they reach their early thirties. Increasingly commonly, they are also providing housing—either by paying rent or by allowing their grown children to live with them—a phenomenon referred to as *boomerang children*. Many adults may have expected to care for aging parents, but few thought they would also have children at home simultaneously!

One significant consequence of both increased longevity and the deferral of adulthood in the late twentieth century—often in response to involvement in higher education—was a significant delay in childbearing. Whereas at the turn of the twentieth century most American women had their first child in their late teens, today, on average, women have their first child at twenty-six and men at twenty-seven. Thus, most adults who became parents after 1990, in their mid- to late twenties, will be in their forties before their children graduate from high school, and they may be in their early fifties when these children graduate from college. Thus, as adult children defer adulthood until their late twenties and early thirties, their parents find that they are providing significant support for their children until they themselves are in their early sixties and just on the cusp of retirement!

The structures of the workplace have also changed in the last quarter-century in ways that have significantly shaped retirement. Employees and workers of the mid-twentieth century benefited from both union pressures and government policies that created rather generous retirement benefits. Specifically, most employees of companies and the government could expect a pension that they were eligible to collect beginning in their late fifties, or at the latest by age sixty. Pensions of this era, which are today collected by a significant number of adults over the age of sixty, provide relatively generous monthly stipends and comprehensive health benefits. Additionally, the prevailing belief was that workers should be able to enjoy the fruits of retirement, and thus benefits commonly "kicked in" by age sixty at the oldest. Today, there are very few businesses that offer the traditional pension. Pensions have been replaced by retirement plans—which vary but fall under the umbrella term *401k*—that generally allow employees to contribute a predetermined percentage of their income, prior to being taxed, into investment accounts that can then be accessed when one retires. Additionally, most employers have some sort of "matching" plan whereby the company also contributes a percentage of the employee's salary—often between 5 percent and 10 percent, depending on the number of years of employment—into the employee's account.

The shift away from pension-style retirement to investment retirement is considered by some to be positive for employees. First and foremost, it allows individuals to take control of their own retirement funds and, if all goes well, offers them the opportunity to produce greater gains in their investment accounts than might be possible when pension funds are invested without employee input. The reader may recall that this was an argument made by then president George W. Bush when he proposed a similar change to Social Security. Additionally, CEOs prefer investment retirement accounts because they are far less expensive for companies. Investment retirement accounts give control to the employee, but they also rely on the employee to make the bulk of the contributions and determine individually when to retire and how to withdraw the funds. In contrast, the typical pension of the mid- to late twentieth century guaranteed specific payouts at retirement as well as cost-of-living increases over time. Furthermore, the bulk of the money in pension funds was contributed by the employer and current employees. These pension funds operated much more like Social Security, where employees pay ahead but are ensured a certain monthly payout at retirement. These funds often allowed individuals to retire at age fifty-five and often required retirement by age sixty. In contrast, investment retirement accounts depend entirely on the contributions by the employee; their performance and payout structure are the responsibility of the employee; and they often have no upper age limit for retirement. The individual who has not contributed, has contributed only the minimum to their retirement account, or who has managed the investments poorly, or who planned to retire just when a recession hit and their investment accounts suffered significant losses as the stock market crashes—during the Great Recession of 2007–2009, retirement accounts lost billions of dollars—may find that they are unable to retire because there are not enough funds in the account. Additionally, whereas pensions paid out until death, investment accounts pay until they are empty. Thus, individuals may be hesitant to retire until they are sure the funds they have amassed are adequate and the time they have left to live is minimal. These structural changes in retirement policies mean that the majority of caregivers in the sandwich generation are also full-time workers. The pressures and costs of elder care may prolong their careers and delay retirement, and simultaneously, this continuation of employment often leads to an additional stress on the day-to-day activities of the caregiver, who has one more role and one more set of expectations and requirements to balance.

CAROL ABAYA

In the late 1980s Carol Abaya, a syndicated news columnist, found herself in what was then considered a unique situation. After her mother suffered a severe and debilitating injury, Carol felt she had no choice but to "take the reins" of her mother's life, including taking over her finances, supervising her health care, and moving her into Carol's own home. Meanwhile, Carol was also raising a teenager. She soon began to recognize the stresses associated with not only elder care but also providing care and, in this case, breadwinning for a multigenerational family. And although there are many advantages to having family members of multiple generations in the household, the stresses associated with this arrangement are significant as well, primarily because children (including adolescents and teenagers) require supervision, attention to daily needs, financial support, and often "chauffeuring," all of which significantly constrain the daily lives of the caregiver. People of the sandwich generation wonder when, if ever, they will be able to reclaim their lives and focus on themselves—something many Americans assume will happen when they have an "empty nest" and in the period prior to, as well as during, retirement. Though Carol never became neglectful or abusive toward either her son or her mother, one can imagine how the stresses on people—mostly women—living in the sandwich generation create a situation ripe for neglect and even abuse.

PREVALENCE OF ELDER ABUSE

Research on the prevalence of elder abuse is scarce, in part because the issue has only recently been defined, but primarily because it is difficult to conduct research on a problem that is hidden and in a population that is often experiencing declining cognitive abilities, which render them unavailable for surveys and interviews. However, the National Center on Elder Abuse estimated that in 2004, between one and two million people over the age of sixty-five were victims of abuse (Elder Mistreatment: Abuse, Neglect and Exploitation in an Aging America 2003). Research published by the prestigious medical journal *The Lancet* reports that from 2 percent to 10 percent of the elderly have experienced some form of elder abuse (Lachs and Pillemer 2004), and the National Center on Elder Abuse confirms the finding that 10 percent of the elderly experience some form of elder abuse ("Elder Abuse: The Size of the Problem" n.d.).

Furthermore, based on qualitative research on injuries that require medical treatment, and on calls for assistance, particularly regarding financial abuse, scholars estimate that for every act of abuse that is reported, there are at least five acts that go unreported. Thus, there is a "widely held consensus" that elder abuse is severely underreported and that as many as 2.5 million people over the age of sixty are the victims of abuse each year (Bonnie and Wallace 2003). Last, an additional problem we face in attempting to estimate the prevalence of elder abuse is the fact that there are many different types of elder abuse, and the risks associated with each are not only different but also shaped by factors such as gender, race, and socioeconomic class as well as living arrangements—whether one is living alone, with one's children, or in an assisted-living facility—health, and cognitive functioning. We turn now to a discussion of the various types of elder abuse that occur in the United States.

TYPES OF ELDER ABUSE

Scholars of elder abuse and advocates for the elderly identify at least five categories of elder abuse: financial abuse, neglect, physical abuse, psychological abuse, and sexual abuse. Although there are many cases in which an elderly person is the victim of more than one type of abuse, it is also common for abuse to be segmented, or not overlapping, and thus the victim may experience abuse of only one type or the abuse may occur discretely, with different types not overlapping and occurring at very different times in the elder's later years. We begin with a discussion of financial abuse.

Financial Abuse

Elder **financial abuse** involves a variety of behaviors—the majority of which are criminal and can be prosecuted—that involve improperly taking money or other financial assets from the elderly. Sometimes the abuse is forceful, sometimes it involves deceit, and frequently it is predicated on the older person's diminished cognitive capacity. Of all reported elder abuse, 12.3 percent is financial abuse, which is a rate higher than self-reports of physical, sexual, or emotional abuse or neglect (Acierno et al. 2010). Elder financial abuse spans a broad spectrum of conduct, including:

- taking money or property
- forging an older person's signature
- getting an older person to sign a deed, will, or power of attorney through deception, coercion, or undue influence
- using the older person's property or possessions without permission
- promising lifelong care in exchange for money or property and not following through on the promise
- the use of deception to gain victims' confidence ("cons")
- fraudulent or deceptive acts ("scams"), through the use of deception, trickery, false pretense, or dishonest acts or statements for financial gain
- telemarketing scams, a specific and widespread fraud in which perpetrators call victims and use deception, scare tactics, or exaggerated claims to get them to send money or disclose credit card information, allowing the scammer to make charges against victims' credit cards without authorization.

Who Are the Perpetrators?

One of the unique aspects of financial abuse, as opposed to the other types of abuse, is that the abuse, though most often perpetrated by family members—according to a study reported by Nursing Home Abuse Center n.d.), 90 percent of elder financial abuse that involved Adult Protective Services *involved family members*—is also perpetrated by nonfamilial caregivers. Furthermore, unlike any other form of family abuse, the elderly face a high risk of being victimized by scams and swindles that are perpetrated by nonfamily members. As we shall see in the next chapter, children are also at risk for child abuse by nonfamily members, but it is much less common than in cases of elder abuse. Research indicates that although financial abuse may be perpetrated by both family members and nonfamily members—both acquaintances and strangers—family members and nonfamily members may have very different motives for perpetrating the abuse (Acierno et al. 2010). Some of the motives that family members have for perpetrating financial abuse against the elderly include:

- They have substance abuse, gambling, or financial problems and believe that they can solve these problems by taking money from an elderly relative. They may even convince themselves that they will make restitution once they get out of their own financial trouble.

- Because they will eventually inherit from their elderly relative, they may feel justified in taking what they believe is "almost" or "rightfully" theirs already.

- As those responsible for the care of an elderly relative, they may fear that their older family member will get sick and use up their savings, depriving the abuser of an inheritance or even costing them money if they anticipate that they will have to pay some, or all, of the financial costs of caring for the elderly relative who has exhausted his or her funds.

- They may have had a negative relationship with the older person and feel a sense of entitlement but worry that because the relationship is negative, they have been or will be denied "their fair share" when the elderly person dies.

- They may have negative feelings toward siblings or other family members, whom they want to prevent from acquiring or inheriting the older person's assets.

It is important to point out that the types of abuse discussed above may not begin maliciously. For example, an adult son or daughter may begin by paying an elderly parent's bills out of his or her checking account, and only when a stressful event arises does he or she begin stealing from the parent.

In contrast, predatory individuals seek out vulnerable seniors with the intent of exploiting them. They generally come in two categories: those who seek relationships or find means to exploit an existing relationship, with motives similar to those outlined above, and those who have no particular relationship with the person they exploit and simply identify the most vulnerable senior, whom they then victimize. In the first case, they may:

- Profess to love the older person in what are commonly known as "sweetheart scams" and then often seek a marriage without a prenuptial agreement, so that they can access financial assets while the elderly person is still alive, as well as at the time of their death.

- Seek employment as personal care attendants, counselors, and so forth to gain access to financial assets or even be written into a will; in some extreme and sophisticated cases, individuals who become trusted attendants turn the elderly person against his or her own family members and assist him or her in writing these relatives out of the will.

The second type of perpetrator is rarely motivated by a personal relationship with an elderly person and rarely seeks a relationship in order to accomplish the financial abuse. Rather, these are scams that target a large number of people with the hopes of snaring a few. Common techniques include:

- Identifying vulnerable persons by driving through neighborhoods (to find persons who are alone and isolated) or contacting recently widowed persons they find through newspaper obituaries.
- Moving from community to community to avoid being apprehended (transient criminals).
- As unscrupulous professionals or businesspersons, or posing as such, overcharging for services or products, using deceptive or unfair business practices, or using their positions of trust or respect to gain compliance.

One of the most common scams of this type is to pose as a repair person at an elderly person's home. The scammer convinces the elderly person that they are desperately in need of home repairs; among the most common is the claim that the senior needs a new roof. They demand payment, often five to ten thousand dollars, in advance. They may show up once or twice, but typically they do not complete any of the work, and they vanish with the money. During the spring and fall it is not uncommon to see billboards on local roads or public service announcements on television warning the elderly of this type of scam. The following is an example of such a scam, which was reported in the *Houston Chronicle* as both news and a warning to local seniors.

BOX 5.1	SCAM WARNING

In January 2011, an article in the *Houston Chronicle* (Zheng 2011) warned of a local financial scam targeting seniors. Con artists in Fort Bend County, Texas, in the Houston-Galveston area, were going door-to-door visiting seniors and claiming to need access to their Social Security numbers, computers, credit card information, and so on, in order to assist them in updating their data or to help with their finances. After this was discovered, caregivers helped those affected close down credit card accounts and protect other personal information.

SENIOR CITIZENS AND NATURAL DISASTER SCAMMERS

American seniors have lost upwards of $5 billion dollars to criminals who scam them on everything from home repair scams, investment scams, travel scams and other cons that target older people. Elder abuse scams are illustrated starkly and disturbingly in cases of natural disasters like hurricanes. Hurricane Florence caused severe damage in the Carolinas between August 31, 2018 and September 19, 2018. Before Hurricane Florence had even vacated

continues

SENIORS CITIZENS AND NATURAL DISASTER SCAMMERS *continued*

the coastal areas, scammers and con artists descended, targeting anyone in need but especially senior citizens. One of the most persistent and concerning scams involved scammers calling up senior citizens on the telephone impersonating US government officials and extending offers of home repairs that were never intended to be completed, to finance deals too good to be true, to funeral scams. These offers price gouged and forcibly attempted to capitalize on the agony and despair impacting senior victims of natural disasters like hurricanes.

Source: Jamie Gold. 2018. "Top Hurricane Home Repair Scams—And How Florence Homeowners Can Avoid Them." *Forbes*. http://bit.ly/2CO1zvP.

Who Is at Risk?

According to the National Committee for the Prevention of Elder Abuse, there are certain conditions or factors that increase an older person's risk of being victimized (Acierno et al. 2010). These include:

- isolation
- loneliness
- recent losses
- physical or mental disabilities
- lack of familiarity with financial matters
- having family members who are unemployed or have substance abuse problems.

What role do these factors play in increasing the probability of being victimized? The first three factors (isolation, loneliness, and recent losses) are common to many types of abuse—both of the elderly and of other populations—because they indicate an overall vulnerability. Individuals who are lonely or isolated may be far hungrier for interaction with others and thus somewhat less discriminating in terms of whom they interact with or the types of information they share. These feelings of loneliness are common among adolescent girls who were sexually abused in childhood and often contributes to their choosing romantic partners who are abusive toward them. We will return to a lengthy discussion of this in both Chapters 8 and 15.

The three other factors (physical or mental disabilities, lack of familiarity with financial matters, and having family members with financial or substance abuse issues) make elderly individuals particularly vulnerable to financial abuse primarily because they can be easily targeted and victimized by family, nonfamilial caregivers, and strangers. For example, their lack of familiarity with financial matters may mean that they do not know what kinds of transactions in their bank accounts are normal and which are questionable, or they may be vulnerable to scams like the one highlighted above because they do not have a good understanding of computers. Thus, those who have elderly family members with these risk factors and practitioners who work with the elderly should be particularly vigilant about watching for early warning signs—new "friends" and so forth—as these may be indicators that an elderly person is about to be scammed or has already been groomed for abuse.

Why Are the Elderly Attractive Targets?

There are many reasons, in addition to the above risk factors, that the elderly are attractive targets for potential financial crime. According to the Center for American Progress (Cawthorne 2008) and the National Council on Aging, the poverty rate among the elderly is 9.4 percent, well below the average poverty rate for all Americans, but without Social Security benefits, 44 percent of the elderly would be living in poverty. This is important for two reasons. First, because the majority of the elderly qualify for and receive Social Security, scams that involve stealing these kinds of benefits, once mastered, can be applied to a large population. Additionally, the very receipt of benefits such as Social Security makes the elderly vulnerable to exploitation because of the uniformity in the way they are handled. For example, Social Security checks arrive in every recipient's mailbox or, if delivered via direct deposit, are deposited the same day each month, which leads to the elderly developing easily discernible patterns in their movements, making them easier targets.

Second, though it has been noted that many of the elderly are poor, this age group nevertheless controls 70 percent of the nation's wealth ("Boomers to Control" 2012). How can these two things be true at once? The elderly tend to have fewer fixed expenses—such as mortgages and college tuition, though health-care costs are an exception—than younger Americans, and thus, if they are healthy or have excellent health insurance, even after they retire they are likely to have more disposable income per month than their younger counterparts. Second, the elderly who have managed to work hard and save have simply, over time, accumulated more wealth than those who are younger and have worked fewer years. For those elderly who have investment incomes, time is their asset, and as they age their investments and wealth grow. For all of these reasons, the elderly have access to more wealth than younger Americans, and thus they can be construed as targets for both scam artists and desperate relatives.

Despite having more wealth, as a group, than younger Americans, many seniors do not recognize the value of their wealth. This can be for reasons related to time, such as the marked appreciation of a home they have owned for forty or fifty years, as well as gender. For example, many elderly women, if they have not managed the family investments, may have no idea how much their investments or even bank accounts are worth. This fact alone puts elderly women at greater risk for financial abuse for several distinct reasons. First, although there is strong evidence that this is changing, historically gender roles were divvied up in such a way that men controlled the household finances: men were believed to be better at math, the man was often the only member of the household earning a wage, and men remain more likely to own businesses than women, even in the twenty-first century, and the financial skills they develop and use at work can be translated to the home. Thus, it is not unusual for older women to have very little financial experience. Second, because women outlive men in every racial and ethnic group, older women may find that their first experience dealing with financial matters is when they are widowed. Both their inexperience and the loss of their spouse—which, as noted above, is a major risk factor for being a victim—put them at greater risk. In addition, women are more likely to live well into their eighties, when other diseases, especially cognitive decline, become more common. This both increases their risk for financial abuse in and of itself and also means that they are more likely to need assistance at home or move into an assisted-care facility—a fact that also increases their risk for financial abuse. Last, as the scam explained previously illustrates, women are at greater risk for scams that involve not only finances but also home maintenance because, once again, due to historical patterns of the division of household labor, they have less experience in dealing with these matters.

These risk factors for financial abuse are increasing as financial transactions and markets have become digitized. Whereas the typical working American in their thirties or forties may appreciate the fact that bank accounts, mortgage assets, and investment accounts may be monitored 24/7 through online accounts and even through apps on smartphones, many of the elderly, who are often afraid of technology and may have limited, if any, access to or experience with computers, the Internet, and especially smartphone technology, may actually have less access to the value of their wealth and investments than they did ten years ago, when they received quarterly paper records in the mail. Again, the scam already described in the box illustrates this point.

Elderly men and women who have disabilities and are dependent on others for help, including daily care, are seen as ideal targets. The "helper"—whether a relative or nonrelative—may gain easy access to financial records and, after having developed a rapport with the elderly person, may be able to exert undue influence over them. Imagine, for example, that a middle-aged grandchild or a nonrelative caregiver offers to show the elderly person how to set up online banking to view their assets and accounts and make transactions. This offer may be quite helpful in that it will save the elder having to physically go to the bank, which may be a challenge if they have difficulty walking or cannot drive. It is quite plausible that during the process the elderly person—who may not realize their own vulnerability—may share passwords, Social Security numbers, and other private information that the "helper" can then use to access the accounts directly and steal money.

Last, and perhaps most insidious, is the fact that many people who engage in financial abuse of the elderly may believe that, because their victims are physically frail and dependent and old, they may not live long enough to make a complaint or testify in a hearing should the abuse be discovered. This kind of "cost–benefit analysis" adds to the vulnerability of the elderly and their value as targets for abuse.

What Are the Indicators?

The National Committee for the Prevention of Elder Abuse has put together a list of indicators or signs that abuse has occurred based on the research of Reeves and Wysong (2010). This list was compiled by examining hundreds of cases of financial abuse of the elderly. They note that some of the indicators listed below can be explained by other causes or factors, and thus no single indicator should be taken as conclusive proof. Rather, one should look for patterns or clusters of indicators, which could suggest a problem. That said, even one indicator should be explored to be sure that it is not the first sign of the beginning of an abusive process. Finally, many of these early warning signs are significant enough that even if they are not caused by abuse, they should be investigated so that problems that may stem from another cause—perhaps the elderly person is not receiving enough benefits to pay his or her bills, or perhaps their health benefits are not covering their medical costs—can be addressed. The following is a comprehensive list of indicators that should be explored:

- unpaid bills, eviction notices, or notices to discontinue utilities
- withdrawals from bank accounts or transfers between accounts that the older person cannot explain
- a change in where bank statements and canceled checks are sent (they no longer come to the elder's home), or the discontinuation of all paper statements in favor of electronic statements
- new "best friends"
- legal documents, such as powers of attorney, that the older person did not understand at the time they signed them
- unusual activity in the older person's bank accounts, such as large unexplained withdrawals, frequent transfers between accounts, or ATM withdrawals
- home services whose costs are not commensurate with the size of the elder's estate—for example, hundreds of dollars spent on lawn mowing or house-cleaning for a relatively small yard or house

- a caregiver's excessive interest in the amount of money being spent on the older person
- missing belongings or property
- suspicious signatures on checks or other documents
- absence of documentation about financial arrangements
- implausible explanations about the elderly person's finances from the elder or the caregiver
- the elder's lack of awareness or understanding about financial arrangements that have been made for him or her.

Neglect and Self-Neglect

Neglect is the failure of caregivers to fulfill their responsibilities to provide needed care. There are many different types of abuse that are considered under the general rubric of neglect and self-neglect. We begin with a few distinctions.

Active **neglect** refers to behavior that is willful—that is, the caregiver intentionally withholds care or necessities. The neglect may be motivated by financial gain (for instance, the caregiver stands to inherit) or reflect interpersonal conflicts.

Passive **neglect** refers to situations in which the caregiver is unable to fulfill their caregiving responsibilities as a result of illness, disability, stress, ignorance, lack of maturity, or lack of resources.

Self-neglect refers to situations in which there is no perpetrator, and neglect is the result of the older person's refusing care despite their need for it. Self-neglect is not technically a form of family violence, but we include the definition here because it might occur alongside caregiver neglect—either passive or active—and an individual who suspects neglect is taking place may want to explore the possibility of self-neglect occurring as well.

Who Are the Perpetrators?

Unlike financial abuse, where the perpetrators may be strangers who are engaged in a scam to swindle money from the elderly, in cases of neglect, the perpetrators are always people who have agreed to—in the case of family members—or been hired to provide care for the elderly person. Thus, in general the perpetrators may be paid attendants, family members, or employees of long-term care facilities, hospital facilities, or nursing homes. Unlike parental responsibilities to care for children under the age of eighteen, there are no laws that require a child to care for aging parents, nor is there any law that requires a spouse or any other relative to provide this care. Thus, when relatives do serve as caregivers, this is a voluntary activity—though we can imagine cases in which there is coercion or pressure involved on the part of the elder needing care (financial or inheritance promises) or on the part of other family members, who might in fact offer some compensation to the relative who agrees to serve as the caregiver.

Often, but not always, the perpetrators are individuals—family members or paid professionals—who lack adequate skills, training, time, or energy. Sometimes the perpetrators are caregivers who are mentally ill or who have alcohol, substance abuse, or other mental health problems. In some cases the perpetrators are spouses who are providing care and who suffer from their own dementia or other cognitive or physical impairments that compromise their ability to give appropriate care.

Who Is at Risk?

Quite obviously, the number-one factor that contributes to the vulnerability of an elderly person for this type of abuse is their mental or physical capacity and subsequent need for care. Individuals who are self-sufficient and intellectually sharp and have limited or no physical incapacities are not at risk for this type of abuse.

Though anyone who depends on others for some or all of their care is at risk, there are certain conditions that elevate the likelihood of this type of abuse. Individuals with high care needs are more likely to experience neglect than those with low care needs. For example, elderly persons who need assistance with tasks like grocery shopping, cooking, and cleaning are at a lower risk for neglect than those who require assistance with all of the aforementioned tasks as well as more personal "daily care" tasks, such as bathing. Those who have particularly challenging needs such as incontinence—and thus must wear "depends"—or those with complex medical needs, such as the regular delivery of medications, especially suppositories, are more likely to have their needs neglected. And, sadly, those with significant cognitive impairments, especially diseases such as Alzheimer's and advanced-stage Parkinson's, are the most vulnerable to neglect. Elderly patients with Alzheimer's and Parkinson's are particularly vulnerable both because their needs are great and often difficult to meet—they can be belligerent—and because their cognitive impairments may make them less able to detect the neglect when it is occurring in ways that a cognitively intact elderly person with physical impairments would be able to detect.

What Are the Indicators?

Indicators of neglect include the condition of the older person's home (environmental indicators), physical signs of poor care, and behavioral characteristics of the caregiver and the older person. Some of the indicators listed below may not signal neglect but rather reflect a lack of resources or mental health problems. However, the presence of any factor should encourage a conversation or mild investigation to be sure there are not deeper underlying problems, and of course when a pattern or cluster of indicators co-occurs, this should raise greater concern that there might be a problem that requires immediate investigation and action. The following are checklists of things to look for as evidence that neglect may be a concern.

INDICATIONS OF NEGLECT

Indicators Observed in the Home

- absence of necessities, including food (an empty refrigerator), water, and heat in the winter or air-conditioning in the summer (as dictated by the environment)
- inadequate living environment, evidenced by lack of utilities, sufficient space, and ventilation
- animal or insect infestations
- signs of medication mismanagement, including empty or unmarked bottles and outdated prescriptions
- unsafe housing as a result of disrepair, faulty wiring, inadequate sanitation, substandard cleanliness, or architectural barriers.

Indicators Related to the Person's Physical Condition

- poor personal hygiene, including soiled clothing, dirty nails and skin, matted or lice-infested hair, odors, and the presence of feces or urine
- lack of clothing, or improper clothing for the weather
- decubiti (bedsores)
- rashes
- dehydration, evidenced by low urinary output, dry and fragile skin, dry and sore mouth, apathy, lack of energy, and mental confusion
- untreated medical or mental conditions, including infections, soiled bandages, and unattended fractures, or the presence of conditions that should be controlled by medication, such as diabetes
- absence of needed dentures, eyeglasses, hearing aids, walkers, wheelchairs, braces, or commodes
- exacerbation of chronic diseases despite a care plan
- worsening dementia.

Behavioral Indicators

The caregiver or abuser:

- expresses anger, frustration, or exhaustion
- isolates the senior from the outside world, friends, or relatives
- obviously lacks caregiving skills

continues

INDICATIONS OF NEGLECT *continued*

- is unreasonably critical and dissatisfied with social workers and health-care providers and changes providers frequently
- refuses to apply for economic aid or services for the senior and resists outside help.

The victim:

- exhibits signs of emotional distress, such as crying
- exhibits symptoms of depression or despair, including being disengaged or despondent, having a flat affect, or talking about suicide
- has nightmares or difficulty sleeping
- has had a sudden loss of appetite that is unrelated to a medical condition
- is confused and disoriented (this may be the result of malnutrition or being improperly medicated)
- is emotionally numb, withdrawn, or detached
- exhibits regressive behavior (which may include a sudden inability or lack of interest in performing daily care tasks that were previously manageable)
- exhibits self-destructive behavior
- exhibits fear of the caregiver
- expresses unrealistic evaluations of their care (e.g., claiming that their care is adequate when it is not or insisting that the situation will improve).

All of these indicators can be present in cases of neglect by a caregiver as well as self-neglect. Relatives, care providers, and advocates for the elderly should be aware of these indicators and investigate any situation in which an indicator is present. Because there can be many causes of neglect, including poverty, solutions will be highly situationally dependent, and it may take multiple attempts to address a case, especially if the neglect is severe.

Physical Abuse

Because much of this book is about physical abuse, it is not necessary to review the definition of **physical abuse**, which can be found in Chapters 1 and 2. Physical abuse of the elderly can occur at the hands of family members or paid caregivers. Most common, as noted earlier in the chapter, is physical abuse that is a continuation of intimate partner violence that has been a part of the victim's life previously and typically began long before they were considered "elderly." Though the source of physical abuse will dictate interventions and solutions, the indicators of physical abuse are not likely to vary by the relationship between the victim and the perpetrator—spouse, adult child, paid caregiver—but rather will be shaped by the individual qualities of both the victim and the perpetrator and may be present in other relationships that involve the same perpetrator. For example, a husband who beats his wife with objects may also beat his children in similar patterns, or a paid caregiver whose abusive behavior involves tying an elderly victim to their bed may exhibit the same behavior with other elderly people for whom they are providing care.

What Are the Indicators?

As with other types of elder abuse, there are multiple types of indicators that physical abuse is taking place. Physical indicators may include injuries or bruises, while behavioral indicators are the ways victims and abusers act or interact with each other. Like the indicators of other types of abuse, many of the indicators listed below can be explained by other causes (for example, a bruise may be the result of an accidental fall), and no single indicator can be taken as conclusive proof. Rather, one should look for patterns or clusters of indicators that suggest a problem. That said, no indicator should be ignored because it likely indicates something. If a bruise is not the result of physical abuse but instead of a fall, then one would need to explore both the health of the elderly person (is their sense of balance declining?) and the overall environment—for example, if they live in a home with stairs, accommodations may need to be made.

INDICATIONS OF PHYSICAL ABUSE

Physical Indicators

- sprains, dislocations, fractures, or broken bones
- burns from cigarettes, appliances, or hot water
- abrasions on arms, legs, or torso that resemble rope or strap marks
- internal injuries, evidenced by pain, difficulty with normal functioning of organs, and bleeding from body orifices
- bruises—the following types of bruises are rarely accidental:
  - bilateral bruising to the arms (may indicate that the person has been shaken, grabbed, or restrained)
  - bilateral bruising of the inner thighs (may indicate sexual abuse)
  - "wrap-around" bruises that encircle an older person's arms, legs, or torso (may indicate that the person has been physically restrained)
  - multicolored bruises (indicating that multiple bruises were sustained in the same location over a period of time)
- injuries healing through "secondary intention" (indicating that they did not receive appropriate care)
- signs of traumatic hair and tooth loss.

continues

INDICATIONS OF PHYSICAL ABUSE *continued*

Behavioral Indicators

- when inquiries about injuries are made, they are unexplained or explanations are implausible (they do not fit with the injuries observed)
- caregivers provide inconsistent explanations of how injuries were sustained
- there is a history of similar injuries or numerous or suspicious hospitalizations
- victims are brought to different medical facilities for treatment (to prevent medical practitioners from observing a pattern of abuse)
- there is a delay between when the injury occurs and when medical care is sought.

In summary, physical abuse of the elderly may have "elderly onset"—it begins after someone grows old and requires care and supervision—or it may be a continuation of intimate partner violence that began decades earlier, such as when the victim was newly married. In the case of violence that is a continuation of abuse, the indicators may be less visible because the perpetrator has had years to practice hiding the evidence of the abuse. In either case, our elderly deserve to live lives free of all types of abuse, whether it has only recently begun or has been a part of an elderly person's life for decades.

Psychological Abuse

Psychological abuse is the willful infliction of mental or emotional anguish by threat, humiliation, or other verbal or nonverbal conduct. Cultural values and expectations play a significant role in how psychological abuse manifests and how it affects its victims. For example, in cultures where the elderly are revered for their cultural capital and historical knowledge, and their sheer survival—this is very typical in developing cultures across Asia and Africa—psychological abuse of the elderly is uncommon. Among nomadic peoples who range across sub-Saharan Africa, day-to-day living is very difficult. The infant mortality rate is high, and life expectancy is short. Thus, when people live to be "old"—perhaps forty-five— they are considered to be special; they have clearly been blessed with a long life, and because the history of the people and the family is entirely oral, they possess important information. For example, among the !Kung, a nomadic group who live in Botswana, just north of South Africa, an elder not only carries the family and group history but also, based on their longevity, possesses information about weather and seasonal patterns that are critical to surviving the next weather crisis; they may remember the last severe drought and strategies for finding water when the rivers are dry. Thus, to abuse an elder in the !Kung society would be to seriously disrespect and disadvantage the rest of the group.

In contrast, in Western postindustrial cultures like the United States, where aging is considered to be negative and the elderly are devalued, psychological abuse of the elderly is more common. Think, for example, of the images of the elderly that we see on television and in the movies. How are they depicted? In our economy, people who are past middle age are considered incompetent and behind the times and have a difficult time gaining employment if they find themselves in need of a job. For example, women who are divorced or widowed in middle age and middle-aged men and women who have been laid off often face serious age discrimination when they seek a new job. In the 2009 film *Up in the Air*, the director included several real people—not actors—who had been recently laid off. The majority of those featured are middle-aged. One woman, in her forties or fifties, notes, "There will be people more qualified than me now," in recognition of the fact that young people just coming out of college will have the up-to-date skills that employers are looking for, whereas she views herself as more or less "past due."

Who Are the Perpetrators?

Perpetrators may be family members, caregivers, or even acquaintances—basically, anyone with whom the elderly person has any regular or ongoing contact.

Who Is at Risk?

Persons who are isolated and lack social or emotional support are particularly vulnerable. Additionally, because psychological abuse is built on cultural ideologies of age and because these ideologies are gendered, racialized, and shaped by factors such as disability, women, racial and ethnic minorities, and elderly individuals with physical disabilities are at greater risk of suffering psychological abuse because they fit the stereotypes invoked by **ageism**—a set of beliefs that construct the elderly as less competent, dumb, behind the times, forgetful, lacking in physical abilities, and even asexual.

What Are the Indicators?

As with other types of abuse, there can be both physical and behavioral indicators. Physical indicators may include somatic changes or decline, while behavioral indicators are the ways victims and abusers act or interact. As always, some of the indicators listed below can be explained by other causes, and no single indicator can be taken as conclusive proof; patterns or clusters of behaviors are more likely to be present when psychological abuse is taking place. And as always, because any indicator, regardless of its origin, may be a symptom of a problem, the presence of any indicator warrants an examination so that its cause can be determined and solutions identified.

INDICATIONS OF PSYCHOLOGICAL ABUSE

Physical Indicators

- significant weight loss or gain that is not attributed to other causes
- stress-related conditions, including elevated blood pressure, irritable bowel syndrome, unexplained and frequent headaches, or the onset of any other somatoform disorder.

Behavioral Indicators

The caregiver or abuser:

- isolate the senior emotionally by not speaking to, touching, or comforting them.

Behavioral Indicators

The victim:

- difficulty sleeping
- depression and confusion
- cowering in the presence of abuser
- emotionally upset, agitated, withdrawn, and unresponsive
- unusual behavior usually attributed to dementia (e.g., sucking, biting, rocking).

Like other forms of family abuse, psychological abuse is often "undervalued." People often assume that if there are no bruises or cuts or broken bones, the abuse is not as harmful. Yet the impact of psychological abuse is often as significant, if not more significant, than physical abuse. It can cause physical outcomes and stress-related diseases as well as psychological trauma that can cause severe damage to the elderly victim. In surveys, elderly women reported that not only was psychological abuse the most common form of abuse they experienced, but when several types of abuse were present, they ranked it as the most devastating (Mouton et al. 2004).

Sexual Abuse

Sexual abuse is any form of nonconsensual sexual contact, including rape, molestation, or any unwanted or coerced touching. Sexual abuse also includes *any* sexual conduct with a person who lacks the *mental capacity* to exercise consent or the physical capacity to exercise refusal; for example, an elderly person who has suffered a stroke may be unable to speak despite having the cognitive capacity to understand the situation.

Who Are the Perpetrators?

Perpetrators of sexual abuse include attendants, employees of care facilities, family members (including spouses), and others who have the opportunity to have unsupervised contact with an elderly victim. Facility residents sometimes assault fellow residents.

Who Is at Risk?

The majority of identified victims are women, but older men have been sexually abused in both domestic and institutional settings. Others at risk include:

- those with physical or cognitive disabilities
- those who lack social support and are isolated
- those who the abuser believes will not be able to reveal that the abuse is taking place because they either lack the physical capacity to do so (perhaps they have had a stroke and cannot speak), are afraid to report the abuse, or lack the cognitive capacity to understand what is happening to them or report it.

This last risk factor is important because it is similar to that which puts children at risk for sexual abuse, especially by family members. Family members who sexually abuse children or the elderly often rely on the fact that the victim is too vulnerable and scared to reveal that the abuse is taking place. This vulnerability is a critical quality that the abuser uses when they select a victim. Thus, very careful attention must be paid to elderly individuals and children who carry this "risk factor."

What Are the Indicators?

As with the other forms of abuse, there can be both physical and behavioral indicators. Physical indicators may include injuries or bruises, while behavioral indicators are the ways victims and abusers act or interact with each other. Some of the indicators listed below can be explained by other causes (for example, inappropriate or unusual behavior may signal dementia or drug interactions), and no single indicator can be taken as conclusive proof. Rather, one should look for patterns or clusters of indicators that suggest a problem. For example, one of the more recent controversies in retirement communities and assisted-living centers is the rise of sexual activity among senior residents, and with it a rise in the rate of sexually transmitted infections (STIs). That said, in the case of sexual abuse there are very few physical or behavioral indicators that could be attributed to any other cause, and thus any indicator should be investigated immediately. For example, though one might suffer a hip fracture by falling—as opposed to being pushed—a woman is unlikely to develop vaginal tearing from anything other than aggressive sexual contact.

INDICATIONS OF SEXUAL ABUSE

Physical Indicators

- genital or anal pain, irritation, or bleeding
- bruises on external genitalia or inner thighs
- difficulty walking or sitting
- torn, stained, or bloody underclothing
- sexually transmitted infections.

Behavioral Indicators

- inappropriate sexual interactions between victim and suspect
- inappropriate, unusual, or aggressive sexual behavior.

THEORETICAL EXPLANATIONS

Several theoretical models have been developed or adapted in an attempt to explain elder abuse. Here we will briefly review each and provide a discussion of the strengths and weaknesses of each.

Psychological Models

Psychologists and public health researchers have investigated the support for a **psychological model** for explaining elder abuse. This model focuses primarily on individual factors in predicting perpetrators of elder abuse. The most common psychological factors that emerge from these studies are histories of violent behavior, mental illness, and substance abuse (Wang et al. 2009). Pillemer and Finkelhor (2010) found that when surveyed, care providers for the elderly identified their own psychological problems as a greater cause of elder abuse than the qualities of the person being cared for. The data and case studies that we have provided in this chapter suggest that psychological models have many strengths in explaining elder abuse. One may recall, for example, that financial abuse often occurs when a care provider who suffers from substance abuse is looking for money to either pay for the abused substance or handle debts that have accrued as a result of the substance abuse. Psychological models fail to explain cases of abuse when the care provider is not suffering from either mental health issues or substance abuse, nor do they explain other patterns of elder abuse, such as the fact that in family settings, it is often perpetrated by women, while it appears to be an "equal opportunity" crime when it occurs either in institutions or as part of a scam.

Social Learning Theory

Social learning theory could be applied to understanding elder abuse, though it is not commonly done. Social learning theory argues that socialization creates patterns of behavior: children watch how their parents and other important adults—teachers, religious leaders, coaches—behave, and they pattern their own behavior on what they observe. According to social learning theorists, an adult caregiver who engages in elder abuse would have likely grown up in a situation where they were exposed to abuse. One of the strengths of this theoretical perspective is that it explains the intergenerational transmission of violence; in particular, boys who grow up in violent homes are far more likely to be abusive as adults, especially with their partners (Ehrensaft et al. 2003). There are several weaknesses of social learning theory as it would be applied to the case of elder abuse. First, the majority of elder abuse is not physical; rather, it is neglect and psychological and financial abuse. It is unlikely that these forms of abuse would be learned unless they are witnessed repeatedly. Second, the evidence for intergenerational transmission of violence focuses on the experience of boys; yet, men and women perpetrate elder abuse at about the same rates (Cooper, Selwood, and Livingston 2008). Last, in general, social learning theory is not widely used by family violence scholars because it fails to address patterns of abuse and fails to hold abusers accountable.

Symbolic Interaction Theory

Though **symbolic interaction theory** is not applied to the study of family violence in general, or elder abuse in particular, one of its components, role theory, is useful in explaining this form of family abuse. Role theory postulates that there are prescribed roles for the elder and the care provider. When individuals behave in ways that are aligned with our expectations for these roles, then interactions go smoothly; when behaviors are contradictory to our expectations, then conflict will arise. In the case of elder care, abuse is more likely to occur when the expectations the caregiver has for the elder's behavior are not met—for example, if the elder is demanding or difficult to deal with. Indeed, in their meta-analysis, Cooper and colleagues (2008) argue that paid care providers are less likely to abuse their charges because they work fewer hours and have more realistic expectations for the experience of providing care.

Social Exchange Theory

Pioneers of family violence research Richard Gelles and Murray Straus developed a specific form of **social exchange theory** in order to explain family violence. One may recall a lengthy discussion of family violence theory in Chapter 3. In sum, social exchange theory purports that abuse and neglect are more likely to occur when the balance of power in the relationship shifts. This theoretical perspective is quite useful in explaining neglect and abuse that is perpetrated by adult children caring for their aging parents: the long-standing flow of resources from parents to children is reversed, and resources must now flow from child to parent. This theoretical perspective, however, is not as useful for explaining abuse and neglect perpetrated by paid care providers and intimate partner violence that has been ongoing and continues into the later years in life.

Situational Theory

One of the theories most commonly used to understand and explain family violence, and elder abuse and child abuse in particular, is situational theory. **Situational theory** suggests that the strains, stresses, and burdens that are typically part of long-term caregiving to needy individuals—the elderly and young children—can lead to abuse. Thus, elderly persons who have many of the risk factors that we presented earlier in this chapter (for example, having dementia and other cognitive diseases, suffering with incontinence, and requiring extensive care for daily needs) are at a higher risk for being abused. Similarly, care providers who are ill-equipped to provide care, who lack the resources necessary to provide appropriate care, and those with other life stressors, including being part of the sandwich generation, are predicted by situational theory to perpetrate abuse at higher rates. Again, as with social exchange theory, the primary weakness of situational theory is its limited ability to explain long-term intimate partner violence that continues into old age.

Ecological Theory

Similar to situational theory, **ecological theory** focuses attention on the other contexts in which the victim and the abuser "reside"—for example, their other relationships, including marriages and friendships, and their involvement in work, church, or any other institution that might provide social support. Again, though seldom used to explain the causes of family violence, ecological theory is useful in that it elucidates the role that social support networks can play in *reducing* the likelihood of abuse or neglect occurring. When paired with situational theory—which best explains the risks for abuse—it is useful for explaining the *protective qualities* that researchers have identified and we have discussed in this chapter, including the reduced likelihood for abuse when victims are ambulatory and cognitively intact. As with the other theories, its major weakness is that it cannot explain long-term intimate partner violence.

Feminist Theory

Feminist theory, which we discussed at length in Chapter 3, is based on the assumption that patriarchy creates a gender-based hierarchy that structures all of social life. Feminist theory is the only theory that adequately explains elder abuse when it is the continuation of intimate partner violence. Given that this remains the most common form of violence experienced by the elderly (Pillemer and Finkelhor 2010), it is critical to include a feminist perspective in analyzing, understanding, and predicting violent elder abuse. Feminist theory is also the most appropriate model for understanding and explaining sexual abuse, which is primarily perpetrated by men regardless of the gender of the victim. That said, the primary weakness of feminist theory is its inability to adequately explain all other forms of abuse and neglect that are experienced by the elderly, including abuse by paid care providers, abuse by children who are caring for aging parents, and abuse that is perpetrated by a spouse—of any gender—who is caring for the other and that does not begin until later in life.

While the field of elder abuse lacks a unifying theoretical framework to guide research, analysis, intervention, and prevention (Bonnie and Wallace 2003), drawing on the strengths of each of the different theoretical frameworks and incorporating the contributions of each can improve our understanding of elder abuse.

CONCLUSIONS

Elder abuse is a relatively new social problem that was first recognized by scholars and practitioners only during the last half of the twentieth century. As noted, this is partly because, like so many forms of family abuse, elder abuse tends to occur behind closed doors in the privacy of an elderly person's home, and partly because of the changing demographics of the United States. The past century has seen a dramatic rise in the life expectancy for all Americans, and thus the percentage of the population that reaches "old age" has also risen dramatically. Quite simply, there is now a larger population of older Americans who can be abused.

Along with the rise in life expectancy comes the likelihood that we will experience both chronic and terminal illnesses that cause us to require significant assistance and may make us dependent upon others not only for our health matters, but for our daily care as well. The stresses associated with caring for an aging, and often ill, parent or grandparent are believed to be part of the cause of certain forms of elder abuse, specifically physical abuse, neglect, and financial abuse. This is exacerbated by the fact that many caregivers are part of the sandwich generation and thus are caring for their own children and families as well.

In addition, because not all adult children are in a position to care for aging parents—whether because they live in different parts of the country, because they cannot afford to retire themselves and devote themselves to the care of their aging parents, or for another reason—and because some of the chronic and terminal diseases that afflict the elderly require some sort of institutional care, the number of elderly living in an institutional setting has risen dramatically over the past half-century, as has, correspondingly, the rate of abuse by nonrelative caregivers.

Elder abuse, like child abuse, is tragic in part because it involves abusing or taking advantage of the most vulnerable persons in our society. Yet there are reasons to be hopeful. First and foremost is the fact that elder abuse is now recognized by researchers and practitioners, and as a result research is being done and policies are being developed to prevent elder abuse and intervene in it when it occurs. For example, we are seeing modifications of Adult Protective Services—the elderly version of Child Protective Services—as a social service option for intervening in elder abuse. Second, as a result of some cases of financial abuse, as well as the growing attention that dementia garners—spurred largely by the cases of former National Football League players, who have some notoriety and celebrity, tragically developing dementia very early in life, in their forties and fifties, as a direct result of concussions and head trauma—more and more people are aware of the challenges of aging and the importance of appropriate care. Third, as baby boomers have experienced the sandwich generation and soon will begin to be considered elderly, this large demographic group that holds more resources than any other in the United States is beginning to bring its own resources and attention to the issues of aging generally, and this impacts the movement around elder abuse as well. Thus, we have every reason to be hopeful that the next decade will result in improvements in the lives of our elderly. We turn now to a discussion of abuse at the other end of the age spectrum: child abuse.

RESOURCES

National Committee for the Prevention of Elder Abuse: www.preventelderabuse.org.
Journal of the American Medical Association Fact Sheet on Elder Abuse: http://jama. ama-assn.org/cgi/reprint/302/5/588.pdf.

REFERENCES

Acierno R., M. A. Hernandez, A. B. Amstadter, H. S. Resnick, K. Steve, W. Muzzy, et al. 2010. "Prevalence and Correlates of Emotional, Physical, Sexual, and Financial Abuse and Potential Neglect in the United States: The National Elder Mistreatment Study." *American Journal of Public Health* 100(2): 292–297.
Bonnie, Richard J., and Robert B. Wallace. 2003. *Elder Mistreatment: Abuse, Neglect, and Exploitation in an Aging America.* Washington, DC: National Academies Press.

"Boomers to Control 70% Of US Disposable Income." 2012. *MarketingCharts*. August 7, 2012. www.marketingcharts.com/uncategorized/baby-boomers-control-70-of-us-disposable-income-22891.

Cawthorne, Alexandra. 2008. Elderly Poverty: The Challenge Before Us. *Center for American Progress*. www.americanprogress.org/wp-content/uploads/issues/2008/07/pdf/elderly_poverty.pdf.

Cooper, Claudia, Amber Selwood, and Gill Livingston. 2008. "The Prevalence of Elder Abuse and Neglect: A Systematic Review." *Age and Ageing 37*: 151–160.

Ehrensaft, Miriam K., Patricia Cohen, Jocelyn Brown, Elizabeth Smailes, Henian Chen, and Jeffrey G. Johnson. 2003. "Intergenerational Transmission of Partner Violence: A 20-Year Prospective Study." *Journal of Consulting and Clinical Psychology 71(4)*: 741–753.

"Elder Abuse: The Size of the Problem." n.d. *National Center on Elder Abuse*, Department of Health and Human Services. www.ncea.aoa.gov/Library/Data/index.aspx#problem.

Elder Mistreatment: Abuse, Neglect and Exploitation in an Aging America. 2003. Washington, DC: National Research Council Panel to Review Risk and Prevalence of Elder Abuse and Neglect.

Fisher, Bonnie S., and Saundra L. Regan. 2006. "The Extent and Frequency of Abuse in the Lives of Older Women and Their Relationship with Health Outcomes." *The Gerontologist 46(2)*: 200–209.

Gold, Jamie. 2018. "Top Hurricane Home Repair Scams—And How Florence Homeowners Can Avoid Them." *Forbes*. http://bit.ly/2CO12vP.

Hattery, Angela J., and Earl Smith. 2012. *African American Families: Myths and Realities*. Lanham, MD: Rowman and Littlefield.

Lachs, Mark S., and Karl Pillemer. 2004. "Elder Abuse." *Lancet 364(9441)*: 1263–1272.

Mouton, Charles P., Rebecca J. Rodabough, Susan L. D. Rovi, Julie L. Hunt, Melissa A. Talamantes, Robert G. Brzyski, and Sandra K. Burge. 2004. "Prevalence and 3-Year Incidence of Abuse Among Postmenopausal Women." *American Journal of Public Health 94(4)*: 605–612.

National Center for Health Statistics. 2015. *Health, United States, 2014: With Special Feature on Adults Aged 55–64*. Hyattsville, MD: Centers for Disease Control and Prevention. www.cdc.gov/nchs/data/hus/hus14.pdf.

National Center for Injury Prevention and Control. 2016. Understanding Elder Abuse. *Centers for Disease Control and Prevention*. www.cdc.gov/violenceprevention/pdf/em-factsheet-a.pdf.

National Committee for the Prevention of Elder Abuse. n.d. www.preventelderabuse.org/elderabuse.

Nursing Home Abuse Center. n.d. www.nursinghomeabusecenter.com/elder-abuse/statistics.

Parker, Kim, and Eileen Patten. 2013. "The Sandwich Generation: Rising Financial Burdens for Middle-Aged Americans." *Pew Research Center*. January 13, 2013. www.pewsocialtrends.org/2013/01/30/the-sandwich-generation.

Pillemer, Karl, and David Finkelhor. 2010. "Causes of Elder Abuse." *American Journal of Orthopsychiatry 59(2)*: 179–187.

Reeves, Shawna, and Julia Wysong. 2010. "Strategies to Address Financial Abuse." *Journal of Elder Abuse and Neglect 22*(*3–4*): 328–334.

Reis, Harry T., and Peter Franks. 1994. "The Role of Intimacy and Social Support in Health Outcomes: Two Processes or One?" *Personal Relationships 1*(*2*): 185–197.

Shapiro, Thomas. 2003. *The Hidden Cost of Being African American: How Wealth Perpetuates Inequality.* New York: Oxford University Press.

"Top 10 Financial Scams Targeting Seniors." n.d. *National Council on Aging.* www. ncoa.org/economic-security/money-management/scams-security/top-10-scams-targeting-seniors.

Wang, J. J., M. F. Lin, H. F. Tseng, and W. Y. Chang. 2009. "Caregiver Factors Contributing to Psychological Elder Abuse Behavior in Long-Term Care Facilities: A Structural Equation Model Approach." *International Psychogeriatrics 21*(*2*): 314–320.

Zheng, Zen T. C. 2011. "Flimflam Financial Planners Are Making Rounds in Fort Bend." *Houston Chronicle*, January 17. www.chron.com/news/houston-texas/arti cle/Flimflam-financial-planners-are-making-rounds-in-1686859.php.

6

ABUSE ACROSS THE LIFE COURSE
Child Abuse

A trial began in Dallas Wednesday for a man accused of locking his girlfriend's children in a hotel bathroom and starving them for up to nine months . . .

The man charged in the case, Alfred Santiago, had lived in the hotel room with the children's mother, Abneris Santiago. The two share a last name, but were not married. A fourth child, a 1-year-old girl who was Alfred Santiago's biological daughter, was found healthy and unharmed . . . A doctor has said the children appeared to have been starved and that their condition was life-threatening. The 11-year-old said she had been sexually assaulted, and the eldest son was covered in bruises from a beating authorities said was delivered by his mother's boyfriend.

—"Trial Begins for Dallas Father Accused of Starving Kids," *Associated Press,* July 21, 2010

This chapter will focus on various aspects of child abuse. We will include discussions of parental abuse of children, sexual abuse, and abuse by non-relatives that impacts family life—for example, abuse by caregivers, clergy, coaches, and other mentors. In addition to reviewing trends and data on various forms of child abuse, we will review the theories that have been developed to explain it. Finally, we will discuss the legal response to child abuse and the controversies that surround the often highly charged claims of child abuse. This chapter will provide a framework for understanding highly publicized instances of child abuse as well.

OBJECTIVES

- To provide an overview of the prevalence of various forms of child abuse as they occur in the contemporary United States
- To explore the different types of child abuse, including physical abuse, sexual abuse, and neglect

- To provide an overview of physical child abuse by nonfamily members, typically in institutional settings, including juvenile prisons
- To examine the disturbing nature of sexual abuse by mentors—coaches, priests, and others—as well as the rise in sexual predatory abuse that is enhanced by the Internet and social networking sites like Facebook
- To describe the legal responses to child abuse of all forms
- To summarize the recent changes in prevention and intervention strategies that move beyond the criminal justice system and include health-care and social services

---

KEY TERMS

emotional abuse	parent or caregiver risk factors
witnessing violence	cycle of abuse
physical abuse	family structure risk factors
neglect	non-coresidential parents
sexual abuse	child risk factors
mandatory reporters	shaken baby syndrome
Child Protective Services (CPS)	ephebophilia
guardian ad litem (GAL)	environmental risk factors
foster care	protective factors

INTRODUCTION

In the last chapter we examined the phenomenon of elder abuse, in which some of the most vulnerable of our citizens are exploited and, worse yet, abused in large part because of their vulnerability, making it, in many ways, that much more tragic. In this chapter we explore the phenomenon of abuse among another vulnerable group of Americans: children.

A BRIEF OVERVIEW

As discussed at length in Chapter 2, historians and other scholars reasonably argue that child abuse and neglect have occurred throughout most of human history. As we moved into the latter half of the twentieth century and the beginning of the twenty-first century in the United States, our understanding of child abuse has shifted significantly in ways that can be described as "prochild." For example, standards regarding corporal punishment have changed not only in the family but also in institutions such as public schools,[1] and a child's right to an education has been recognized and affirmed by Supreme Court decisions. Thus, the later part of the twentieth century and the early part of the twenty-first century is an era that represents many changes in our collective beliefs about child abuse, as well as significant advancements in our laws regarding the rights and protections for children. Yet despite these advances in broadening the definitions of *child abuse* and revising laws to protect children, child abuse rates continue to rise.

PREVALENCE OF CHILD ABUSE

According to the CDC, which gathers statistics on child abuse monthly and annually ("Child Maltreatment Prevention" 2016):

- There were 676,000 victims of child abuse and neglect reported to Child Protective Services (CPS) in 2016.
- The youngest children are the most vulnerable; about 27 percent of reported victims were under the age of three.
- About 1,750 children (or more than four per day) died from abuse and neglect in 2016.
- The total lifetime cost of child maltreatment is $124 billion each year.

As the data in Figure 6.1 demonstrate, the number of children who die each day due to child abuse and neglect has risen steadily over the past decade, which reflects both an increase in the size of the US population (which neared 330 million in 2018) and our failure as a society to keep our children safe.

TYPES OF CHILD ABUSE

As is the case with elder abuse, there are many different forms that child abuse can take, including physical abuse, sexual abuse, emotional abuse, and neglect. In this section we discuss each type of abuse by providing definitions, warning signs, and illustrations.

Despite the uniqueness of the various forms of child abuse, what they share in common is the emotional impact on the child. As stated on the website of the think tank and resource center HelpGuide.org,

> Children need predictability, structure, clear boundaries, and the knowledge that their parents are looking out for their safety. Abused children cannot predict how their parents will act. Their world is an unpredictable, frightening place with no rules.

▶ **Figure 6.1**
Estimated
Number of
Child Deaths
Per Day Due
to Child
Abuse and
Neglect.

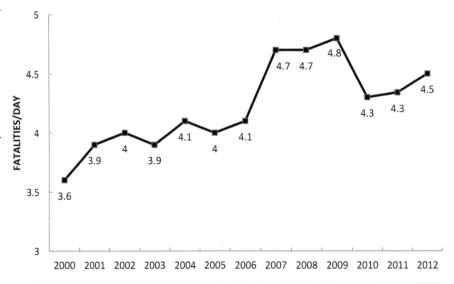

Source: Courtesy of Childhelp (www.childhelp.org). Data from the National Child Abuse and Neglect Data System (NCANDS).

> Whether the abuse is a slap, a harsh comment, stony silence, or not knowing if there will be dinner on the table tonight, the end result is a child that feels unsafe, uncared for, and alone.
>
> (Smith and Segal 2016)

Emotional Abuse

Emotional abuse involves talking to a child in a manner that makes them feel inferior and inadequate. Distinct from discipline, which might involve explaining to a child how their behavior is unacceptable or hurtful, emotional abuse often involves telling children that they are "dumb" or "stupid," or in severe cases blaming them for the parent's problems—for example, by telling a child that the parent would not have lost their job or would not have trouble paying the bills if it were not for the child. Emotional abuse often involves humiliating the child in public—for example, calling a child a "crybaby" or pointing out in public that a child is still wetting the bed or "having accidents." These kinds of comments are humiliating and often leave deep and long-term emotional and psychological scars. Emotional abuse can also involve ignoring a child as part of a punishment, withholding affection, and exposing children to violence in the household, such as the beating of a sibling or the torture of a pet.

Childhelp is a nonprofit foundation that was created to act as a clearinghouse for statistics on child abuse, to develop educational materials and programming designed to prevent child abuse, and to provide intervention programs for victims of child abuse. In addition to being a clearinghouse for statistics and prevention programming, Childhelp is also a reporting agency with direct links to county Child Protective Services in each of the fifty states. The following is a list of warning signs of emotional abuse in children from the Childhelp website ("Emotional Abuse" n.d.):

- appears excessively withdrawn, fearful, or anxious about doing something wrong
- shows extremes in behavior (extremely compliant or extremely demanding; extremely passive or extremely aggressive)
- does not seem to be attached to the parent or caregiver
- acts either inappropriately "adult" (taking care of other children) or inappropriately infantile (rocking, thumb-sucking, throwing toddler-like tantrums).

Witnessing Violence

Relatively recently, scholars of child abuse and practitioners have begun to recognize the effect that **witnessing violence**, especially intimate partner violence, has on young children. In particular, when boys witness intimate partner violence, their risk for growing up to beat their own wives and girlfriends *triples* (Ehrensaft et al. 2003). As a result of this significant outcome—a topic to which we will devote the entire next chapter—scholars and practitioners have begun to formally identify children who witness intimate partner violence as child abuse victims. This label is important for many reasons, first and foremost because labeling the witnesses of intimate partner violence *as victims* entitles them to the types of social services that are otherwise restricted to victims of crime. For example, children who witness intimate partner violence and live in counties where this is labeled as child abuse are entitled to counseling, intervention programs, and the development of family safety plans. Additionally, this identification as victims of child abuse renders them eligible for court interventions. For example, the repeated witnessing of intimate partner violence by a child may result in a hearing to determine whether the child should stay in the home or be removed, either temporarily or permanently. Though jurisdictions vary greatly in terms of their support for defining the witnessing of intimate partner violence as child abuse, one good example comes from the state of Minnesota, where any child determined by the police to have been "in sight or sound" of intimate partner violence is considered a victim of child abuse and is referred to all of the relevant responders, including Child Protective Services.

A child who is witnessing intimate partner violence in the home may exhibit many of the same symptoms as children who are experiencing emotional abuse, including low self-esteem, being withdrawn, and so forth. Unfortunately, the most significant indicator may not be visible for years, and that is the likelihood, especially for boys, of becoming perpetrators of intimate partner violence themselves. As we will discuss at length in the next chapter, attention to child witnesses of intimate partner violence is critical to interrupt the cycle of violence.

Physical Abuse

As the name implies, **physical abuse** entails causing physical injury to a child. Note that the intent of the harmful action does not determine whether it is abusive, only the outcome. For instance, there's often no explicit intent to harm when an adult shakes a baby—the intent may simply be to get the baby to stop crying—but the action can, nonetheless, cause severe injury and, in the case of shaken baby syndrome, even death, and it is considered abuse. Understanding what led to a behavior like shaking a baby may help social workers and agents of the court determine appropriate intervention strategies for the adult who is engaging in child abuse.

As is the case with elder abuse, certainly injuries can and are sustained by children every day in the normal context of their lives; children fall down the stairs, they fall off bikes, and so forth, which can result in the same kinds of injuries that are typical of child abuse, including bruises, lacerations, broken bones, and burns. Thus, any discrete incident is not necessarily an indicator of child abuse. That said, physicians, teachers, coaches, and other adults who interact with children should investigate any injury, and they should pay particular attention to a pattern of injuries that seems to defy explanation. For example, sustaining multiple broken bones during a school year might indicate that abuse is taking place. Similarly, with radiological technologies, physicians can identify patterns of abuse based on recently healed or unhealed injuries that were never treated but appear on an X-ray.

The following is a list of warning signs of physical abuse in children from the Childhelp website ("Physical Abuse" n.d.):

- having frequent injuries or unexplained bruises, welts, or cuts
- being watchful and "on alert," as if waiting for something bad to happen
- having injuries with a distinctive pattern such as marks from a hand or belt
- shying away from touch, flinching at sudden movements, or seeming afraid to go home
- wearing clothing to cover up injuries, such as long-sleeved shirts on hot days.

Neglect

As noted in Figure 6.2, child neglect is the most common type of child abuse; of all abuse cases reported, nearly 80 percent involved neglect. Similar to neglect as a form of elder abuse, **neglect** that constitutes child abuse appears as a pattern of failing to provide for a child's basic needs, whether it be adequate food, clothing, hygiene, or supervision. Child neglect is not always easy to spot. For example, unless a child becomes seriously ill from malnourishment, it may be difficult to spot a child who is not getting an adequate diet. Perhaps the most difficult form of neglect to identify is a lack of supervision. It is not uncommon for low-income single mothers to leave their children unattended at night while they sleep so that the mothers can work a better-paying third-shift job. These instances are difficult to spot unless tragedy strikes. For example, every year children die in home fires that began while their mothers were at work and the children were left unattended. Quite often these mothers were not being intentionally neglectful but were doing their best to provide a steady income for the family in a market where child-care costs often consume an *entire* minimum-wage paycheck.

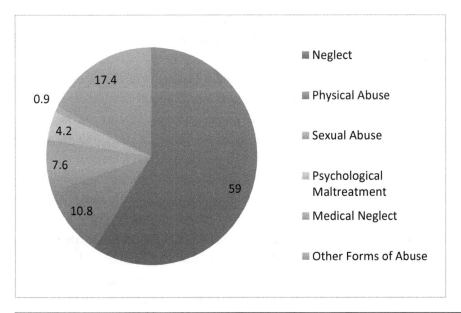

◀ **Figure 6.2**
Types of Child Abuse in 2018.

Percentages are calculated against the number of unique victims (679,000), and a child may see multiple types of abuse or multiple instances of the same type of abuse.

Source: Courtesy of Childhelp.

Similarly, there are many children in extremely low-income families who meet the technical definition of neglect in that they lack adequate food and housing, yet the only real "crime" is that their caregivers—often single mothers or grandmothers—are very poor and do not receive adequate support from the government to provide for the children in their care (Edin and Lein 1997). This situation does not negate the impact of the neglect on the child but rather indicates the need to understand the source of the neglect in order to design appropriate interventions. Poor mothers may not need classes in parenting or the proper care of their children, but what they do often need is income support, housing support, and child-care support so that they can work to earn a living and be sure their children are adequately taken care of while they do so. Thinking about child abuse in this way is part of what distinguishes a sociological approach from some other approaches. Though we acknowledge, and will discuss later in the chapter, individual explanations for child neglect—being a young parent, not having an adequate understanding of what children need, or simply being a neglectful person—as sociologists we believe it is important to keep our focus on structural explanations as well, as these are often ignored by the general public. For example, when newscasters tell a tragic story or politicians discuss the state of the American family, it's rare to hear any mention of the role that poverty plays in a parent's ability to provide adequately for their children. It is far easier to blame bad parenting than to point out that economic inequalities are very real in the United States, and these inequalities produce child victims of neglect.

It is also important to note some of the individual causes of child abuse. In many cases, child neglect occurs when a parent becomes physically or mentally unable to care for a child, such as with a serious injury or untreated depression or anxiety. Other times, alcohol or drug abuse may seriously impair judgment and the ability to keep a child safe. In interviews we conducted with people who had recently been released from prison, we heard countless stories of neglect that were related to untreated drug addiction. Because many drugs suppress an addict's appetite for food, children of drug addicts often live every day with empty refrigerators and cupboards (Hattery and Smith 2010). Depression and other mental illnesses may have this effect as well. Thus, the neglect experienced by children of drug addicts or untreated mentally ill parents may run the gamut from lack of food to soiled clothing, from infrequent bathing to a lack of supervision. In extreme cases, we heard about children growing up without functioning indoor plumbing and being forced to dumpster-dive for food. Again, as with poverty, understanding the source of the neglect does not negate its impact on the child victims. However, failing to understand the source of the neglect limits our ability to propose appropriate interventions.

One final complicating factor in child neglect cases is that older children might not show outward signs of neglect, especially if they have been experiencing it for a long period of time. They may have become used to presenting a competent face to the outside world and figured out how to get access to the things they need, like food and clothing, in order to do so. In many cases, older children adopt the role of the parent—especially in cases of untreated addiction or mental illness—and do their best to prevent or interrupt the neglect of their younger siblings. Though having to take on the role of a parent is a form of abuse or neglect that is difficult to substantiate, according to Childhelp, it may be an indicator of emotional abuse. Either way, one can imagine that having to take on the role of a parent for younger siblings can take a terrible toll on older children.

The following is a list of warning signs of child neglect from the Childhelp website ("Child Neglect" n.d.):

- ill-fitting, filthy clothes, or clothes that are inappropriate for the weather
- consistently bad hygiene (visibly soiled, matted and unwashed hair, noticeable body odor)
- untreated illnesses and physical injuries
- being frequently unsupervised or left alone or allowed to play in unsafe situations and environments
- being frequently late to or absent from school.

In sum, neglected children are not getting their physical and emotional needs met, and as a result they suffer consequences that range from mild to very serious and can be physical, emotional, psychological, or behavioral.

Physical consequences of neglect may be immediate—such as a "failure to thrive" in infants—but they can also be long-term, such as poor brain development, delayed speech, and inhibited growth that result from long-term malnourishment. Emotional and psychological consequences include depression, anxiety, and an inability to bond with a parent and can include an obsession with food, which can lead to behavioral consequences, including hoarding or stealing. Other behavioral consequences include a higher rate of teen pregnancy and a higher rate of contracting a sexually transmitted infection while a teen—both of which may be a result of seeking affection through sex, sexual abuse, and even selling sex in order to get access to money to buy food and clothes. Child victims of neglect, and all forms of abuse, also have higher rates of drug and alcohol abuse, and they are more likely to be involved in the juvenile justice system.

Sexual Abuse

R. KELLY

R. Kelly is a child predator.

R. Kelly is also a talented R&B singer, whose music many of us at some time have had on our iPods. But no matter how much we like his music, the evidence continues to mount that he is a child abuser, much of which became public after the airing of "Surviving R. Kelly" in January 2019 on the Lifetime Network.

People began to talk in 1994 when R. Kelly married an underage teenager by the name of Aaliyah, who was fifteen years old at the time. Both she and Kelly lied about her age to get married.

Sadly, as the documentary also revealed, R. Kelly was, himself, a victim of child sexual abuse at the hands of his uncle. This is not an excuse for his behavior, but it is an explanation. Without an appropriate intervention, R. Kelly grew up to perpetuate the cycle of violence.

Since the 1990s Kelly has been successful in alluding the law. He has been charged several times with having inappropriate relationships with underage girls. Early in the 2000 era the *Chicago Sun Times* broke a story about R. Kelly's behavior but again nothing really happened. He has never been convicted, nor has he served prison time for any sexual crime, including child sexual abuse, rape, or statutory rape.

What is interesting is that Kelly has been protected for a long time by many of the young black girls themselves, their parents and, oddly enough, by the black church. The church went way beyond boundaries to make excuses for Kelly over the years. Why?

After the airing of "Surviving R. Kelly," which in explicit detail illustrates the singer's sexual abuse of black girls, many of whom are featured on camera telling their stories, the gospel music industry has been quiet. Not a word. Some pastors have been quoted as saying they "the Lord works in mysterious ways" and that they are praying for Kelly. Nothing about the many victims!

"Surviving R. Kelly" that aired on the Lifetime Network has subsequently renewed interest in Kelly's purported pedophilia. What the documentary really showed was not only the sexual abuse R. Kelly inflicted on young girls but also heavy, heavy psychological violence as well.

Enter Gloria Allred, the pit-bull lawyer for women's rights. She says she represents several of the women, some of whom are under age. Her strategy is to get facts, data, and then file lawsuits against Kelly and others.

At the end of the day, Robert Sylvester Kelly has been exposed. Exposed in ways that have never before happened across two and a half decades. Police and prosecutors in Chicago and Atlanta have searched Kelly's homes and have asked for documents. At the time of this writing, R. Kelly has been indicted and charged with child sexual abuse. What will happen we do not know, but if similar cases like that of Harvey Weinstein and Bill Cosby are any examples, perhaps justice will finally be served. We know we are no longer willing to include R. Kelly's songs on our iPods.

Unlike adults, children are legally unable to consent to sexual contact, and therefore *any sexual act—consensual or not—with a child under the age of sixteen (or eighteen, in some states) is considered sexual abuse.* **Sexual abuse** may involve sexual intercourse, but it is more likely to be sexual touching or molestation. In addition, it is important to recognize that sexual abuse does not always involve body contact. Exposing a child to sexual situations or sexual material also constitutes sexual abuse, whether touching is involved or not. In one case in which one of the authors was involved as an advocate, the victim was a young teenage girl whose father was taking sexually explicit pictures of her and selling them as part of a child pornography ring. He was prosecuted for both child pornography—which involves possessing nude or sexually explicit images of a child under the age of consent—and sexual abuse, based on the fact that the simple act of taking the pictures constituted a sex crime.

The sexual abuse of children is most likely to take place between the child and an adult the child knows. Often, but not always, this adult is a family member, the most likely perpetrator being the child's stepfather or mother's boyfriend. However, as we have become increasingly aware because of stories in the news media, children are also at a reasonable risk for sexual abuse from adults who work with children, including Catholic priests, coaches, Scout leaders, and other adult mentors. Every year stories are reported in the media about the sexual abuse of young athletes by their coaches. In spring 2018 a scandal similar to the Catholic Church sex scandal (which we will discuss at length in Chapter 10) broke in the USA Gymnastics team in which the team physician, Larry Nassar, was accused and convicted of having sexually molested more than two hundred and fifty young women. During summer 2018 he was sentenced to three consecutive life sentences. Dr. Nassar will die in prison.

RATES OF CHILD SEXUAL ABUSE (CSA)

One in five girls and one in twenty boys is a victim of child sexual abuse (Finkelhor et al. 2005). According to the Centers for Disease Control, 12.3 percent of girls and 27.8 percent of boys who reported being sexually abused were raped *when they were ten years old or younger.*

Source: Finkelhor et al. 2005; "Child Maltreatment Prevention" 2016.

BOX 6.1   LARRY NASSAR

We've chosen the case of Larry Nassar as our illustration of sexual abuse by mentors because of the sheer size of the "footprint" of his abuse, because of the widespread media attention it received, which gives us adequate resources to build our case, and finally because it illustrates all of what goes wrong when leaders value institutions more than the victims.

continues

BOX 6.1   LARRY NASSAR *continued*

On August 4, 2016 the world was alerted to the sexual violence perpetrated at the hands of the Michigan State University osteopathic physician Dr. Larry Nassar. Nassar served nineteen years as a physician with the Michigan State athletic programs and also was a physician with USA Gymnastics for over twenty years, serving as the national team doctor. Larry Nassar began molesting young girls the moment he arrived at MSU and as soon as he was hired with the USA Gymnastics national team. Some of the women who charged him with sexual assault were not even born when he started his serial abuse attacks. Rachael Denhollander is one of the first gymnasts who contacted the *IndyStar* about Nassar and the sexual abuse she endured by him. She wrote: "I recently read the article titled 'Out of Balance' published by the IndyStar. My experience may not be relevant to your investigation, but I am emailing to report an incident . . .."

During his tenure serving as team physician for USA Gymnastics and Michigan State he abused more than three hundred victims, mostly young women gymnasts, but also student athletes competing at Michigan State in sports as varied as gymnastics and softball. Among his accusers is 2012 gold medalist Mikayla Maroney, who says that Nassar molested her more than one hundred times. Reports indicate that leadership of USA Gymnastics and Michigan State athletics were aware of accusations against Larry Nassar as far back as 1997 and protected him, going so far as covering for his absence from major gymnastics events in 2016 while he was being investigated. All the while, Nassar continued his reign of terror on the bodies of *children* who wanted nothing more than to have a chance to compete at the highest level of sports. In the end, the President of MSU was fired; USA Gymnastics went bankrupt, Michigan State University, a public institution, agreed to pay $500 million dollars in fines and settlements, and Nassar was sentenced, in July 2017, to sixty years in federal prison with a lifetime of supervised release and forty to one hundred and seventy-five years in state prison. This is, in fact, a life sentence. The set of stories of the three hundred and thirty-two victims who have accused Larry Nassar of sexual abuse was rated as the Associated Press Sports Story of the Year.

Source: Hattery and Smith 2019; Kwiatkowski, Alesia, and Evans 2016.

The least-common type of sexual abuse, but the one that receives the most attention, is the abuse that typically accompanies abductions and murders of young boys and girls. We will provide illustrations of these types of sexual abuse cases later in the chapter, as they are critical to the development of the legal response to child abuse and child sexual abuse in particular, for example Megan's Law (see Box 6.2).

Finally, we note that, contrary to what many people believe, it is not just girls who are at risk. Boys and girls both suffer from sexual abuse. The shame of sexual abuse makes it very difficult for children to come forward. They may worry that others will not believe them or will be angry with them or that it will split their family apart. Because of these difficulties, false accusations of sexual abuse are not common, so if a child makes an accusation or confides in someone, it should be taken very seriously. In fact, because boys may feel higher levels of shame, because of our culturally dominant beliefs about male sexuality—boys and men are supposed to have a higher sex drive, they are supposed to want more sex partners, adolescent boys are supposed to desire initiation into sex with an older and more experienced woman like a teacher or babysitter, and so on—the sexual abuse of boys is likely to be even more underreported than that of girls. To illustrate, think about the media coverage that boys who are victims of sexual abuse often receive, as was the case of child molester and teacher Mary Kay Letourneau (see Box 6.3).

BOX 6.2	MEGAN'S LAW

Megan's Law is named for Megan Kanka, who was kidnapped from her bedroom, raped, and murdered by convicted sex offender Jesse Timmendequas, who lived across the street from Megan. Megan's Law requires that all convicted sex offenders register with local law enforcement so that their current residence and contact information can be updated in the Department of Justice's National Sex Offender Public Website. Megan's Law is controversial for several reasons, including the fact that there is no evidence that it actually keeps communities safer and the fact that it is not always adjusted for individual factors. As we demonstrated in the second chapter, stranger abduction is the least-common type of sexual abuse, and yet this is the type of crime that drives laws like this. In fact, the most likely perpetrator of child sexual abuse *lives* in the home of the victim or is a close family friend or mentor. Megan's Law is unlikely to prevent these kinds of pedophiles from subsequent abuse. A more effective approach would be holding abusers accountable by giving them appropriate prison sentences.

Source: "Megan's Law Website" 2008.

BOX 6.3	MARY KAY LETOURNEAU

Mary Kay Letourneau was an elementary school teacher who twice (in second grade and sixth grade) had Vili Fualaau as a student in her class and who began a sexual relationship

continues

| BOX 6.3 | MARY KAY LETOURNEAU *continued* |

with him in 1996, when she was thirty-four and he was twelve. She became pregnant by him shortly before she was arrested on child sexual abuse charges in 1997. She was found guilty and sentenced to prison. After serving her sentence, only three months, she was released, and within two weeks she was caught having sex with Fualaau in her car. Since a no-contact order was part of her probation agreement, she was arrested and returned to prison, pregnant with their second child. Fualaau, a *teenager*, raised their children with his mother while she was incarcerated. After serving another six years in prison, Letourneau was released. At that point Fualaau was over eighteen and the no-contact order was lifted, and Letourneau and Fualaau wed in 2005. The event was covered by many news sources, including *Entertainment Tonight*.

Source: "Mary Kay Letourneau Marries Former Victim" 2009.

Teachers, that group of professionals whom Americans trust with their children upwards of seven to eight hours a day for nine to ten months out of the year, have several loopholes they can crawl through to get back to teaching once they have sexually abused schoolchildren.

The national case that first brought to light abusive teachers was that of Seattle middle-school teacher Mary Kay Letourneau, who is featured in Box 6.3. What is interesting about the Letourneau case is that, unlike other teachers from across the United States who were found guilty of having sexually abused schoolchildren and who then received some type of suspended sentence, she did not go back to the classroom.

A *USA Today* investigative news report found that in many cases, teachers who have been convicted of child sex abuse move to another state and continue teaching there (Reilly 2016). A combination of laws, regulations, inconsistencies, and lack of information sharing between states and school districts create cracks in the system, thus allowing child sex abusers to climb back into the classroom.

In the *USA Today* story, it was found that in some cases, a teacher's criminal conviction became known only after the teacher was hired by a district and already back in the classroom. That no records classification system exists in the United States is highly problematic and quite different from, say, Great Britain, where there is a centralized government system for tracking teachers who have been found guilty of child sex abuse.

The following is a list of warning signs of child sexual abuse from the Childhelp website ("Sexual Abuse" n.d.):

- trouble walking or sitting
- displaying knowledge or interest in sexual acts inappropriate to their age, or even seductive behavior
- making strong efforts to avoid a specific person, without an obvious reason
- refusing to change clothes in front of others or participate in physical activities
- an STI or pregnancy, especially under the age of fourteen
- running away from home.

Child Sexual Abuse and the Internet

The Internet has created a whole host of new ways in which sexual predators can engage in child sexual abuse. For example, they often initiate contact with prospective victims using social networking sites like Facebook. Once they establish trust, they arrange to meet their potential victim, often luring them with alcohol or drugs, and then proceed to sexually abuse them. Child trafficking and child pornography, often engaged in by adult relatives of child victims, is also greatly facilitated by the Internet. A parent wishing to sell a child into prostitution can utilize the Internet to find prospective pimps or johns; similarly, a stepfather seeking to circulate images of his stepchild will likely circulate these using the Internet.

BOX 6.4   JARED FOGLE

In summer 2015, longtime Subway spokesperson Jared Fogle, whose notoriety was tied to the fact that he lost more than a hundred pounds by eating nothing but two Subway sandwiches each day, was arrested and pled guilty to charges of child pornography and child prostitution. Fogle sexually victimized fourteen children, sexually abusing two of them and taking, storing, and sharing pornographic images of twelve more. He used the Internet both to distribute child pornography and to arrange for child prostitutes.

Source: Ford 2015.

The stories of child sexual abuse facilitated by the Internet and social media are quite disturbing. Almost daily, a news outlet reports on a sting operation in which undercover police and FBI agents posing as preadolescent girls receive solicitations for sex. In a typical scenario of actual abuse, a sexual predator "friends" a young girl on Facebook. They begin chatting using Facebook, text messages, instant messaging, and e-mail. After "grooming" the victim, the sexual predator arranges for a meeting. When the girl arrives, he often plies her with alcohol or drugs and then proceeds to sexually molest or assault her. Thousands of these cases occur every year, and the sting operations often capture predators who have assaulted dozens of girls by the time they are caught.

The Internet has also allowed for the perpetuation of controversial organizations of men who advocate sex between adult men and preadolescent and adolescent boys. These groups are considered by the majority of the public, as well as all scholars, social workers, and other child safety practitioners, to be engaging in child sexual abuse. The men who belong to these organizations argue that sexuality is not and should not be limited by age; humans are sexual from birth until death, and thus it is unnatural to impose any limitations on children's sexuality. Though scholars of sexuality confirm some sexual function in babies and toddlers—for example, often by the age of two boys will regularly have erections—it is also widely understood that this natural function is not *sexual behavior*. Children lack the cognitive ability to understand sexuality, and thus, as a culture, we in the United States prohibit sexual behavior between adults—who have the cognitive ability to understand sexual behavior—and children.

MANDATORY REPORTERS

One of the aspects of child abuse that makes it distinct from other forms of abuse is the designation of a class of people referred to as *mandatory reporters*. The Child Abuse Prevention and Treatment Act (CAPTA, Public Law 93–247), originally passed in 1974 and renewed most recently in 2010, requires that all fifty states have requirements and processes for the mandatory reporting of the physical or sexual abuse of children or child neglect. **Mandatory reporters** include "health care providers and facilities of all types, mental health care providers of all types, teachers and other school personnel [including coaches], social workers, day care providers and law enforcement personnel. Many states require film developers to report" (Child Abuse Prevention and Treatment Act of 1974). The requirement for film developers to report suspected child abuse arose from the fact that amateur child pornographers were often taking pictures of their own children or of neighborhood children and having these images developed by local companies like Walgreens before circulating the images via mail or on the Internet. Thus, at one time film developers played a critical role in detecting child pornography rings. Today, because most images are taken electronically and uploaded directly to the Internet or printed on home printers, the role of film developers in detecting child pornography has likely decreased.

In the majority of situations, cases reported by mandatory reporters are referred to the state's Child Protective Services.

Child Protective Services is the local agency in each county that is legally charged with investigating allegations of child abuse or neglect.

It is important to note that, while children are not removed from the home in all cases, CPS officials have the legal right to remove children and place them in foster care if the investigation reveals that this is the most appropriate intervention. In addition to any criminal charges that are brought by CPS, child abuse is frequently part of child custody cases—which are family court matters—as well. Because children, especially those who are abused by their parents or parent figures, may be reluctant to speak on their own behalf—for fear of losing their parent(s), being removed from the household, or even just angering a parent who has been abusive to them—many states have established a legal advocate whose sole concern is the best interest of the child.

We encourage anyone who is interested in working for the safety of children to consider being trained to volunteer as a guardian ad litem (GAL); we have taught numerous students who have volunteered as GALs. It is a wonderful experience and can be a great way to determine if one should pursue a career path in a variety of fields that serve child victims, including social work and the law.

A **guardian ad litem (GAL)** is a volunteer who is trained to serve as an advocate for the child. The legal interest of the GAL is only the child, not their parents or anyone else. GALs are typically asked to assist with the investigation of child abuse and child custody cases, and because their sole interest is the best interest of the child, judges often take their recommendations very seriously.

BOX 6.5	GUARDIAN AD LITEM (GAL) PROGRAMS

In 1983, the North Carolina General Assembly established the Office of Guardian ad Litem (GAL) Services as a division of the North Carolina Administrative Office of the Courts. Pursuant to G.S. 7B-601, when a petition alleging abuse or neglect of a juvenile is filed in district court, the judge appoints a volunteer GAL advocate and an attorney advocate to provide team representation to the child, who has full party status in trial and appellate proceedings. All GAL advocates are trained, supervised, and supported by

continues

| BOX 6.5 | **GUARDIAN AD LITEM (GAL) PROGRAMS** *continued* |

program staff in each county of the state. The collaborative model of GAL attorney advocates, volunteers, and staff ensures that all North Carolina children who are alleged by the Department of Social Services to have been abused or neglected receive GAL legal advocacy services.

The role of GAL advocates is to:

- Fulfill state and federal statutory mandates to protect and promote the best interests of juveniles in abuse and neglect court proceedings.
- Help the courts work efficiently toward safety and permanence for children.
- Conduct independent investigations to determine the facts, needs of the child, and the resources appropriate to meet those needs.
- Determine the wishes or expressed preferences of the child and report those to the court.
- Provide a voice for abused and neglected children in every county of the state.

Source: North Carolina Administrative Office of the Courts, October 2010, www.ncgal.org. Reproduced with permission from the North Carolina Court System. www.nccourts.org/Citizens/JData/Documents/Guardian_ad_Litem_Facts.pdf.

Foster care refers to the temporary housing of children under the age of eighteen with an adult care provider.

Foster parents may be relatives, or they may be individuals with whom the child has no relationship. Foster parents receive a small stipend from the government to cover the additional costs of caring for the child. They must also go through a training and certification process to ensure that they are capable of caring for a child. Though it's designed to be temporary—and most children do spend less than two years in foster care—many children live in foster care for the majority of their childhoods; some stay with the same family for so long that they are eventually legally adopted by them. Other children may cycle among different foster care providers (see Figure 6.3), which is very disruptive and less than ideal. Foster care may be invoked when children are removed from their homes, when their custodial parent goes to prison, or in other cases in which their home is determined by a court as less than suitable (see Figure 6.4).

FOSTER CARE IN THE UNITED STATES: THE FACTS

- Annually in the United States there are approximately 2.5 million children who have been removed from their homes or whose parents have relinquished their parental rights and who are receiving services in the foster care system.
- The median age of a child in foster care is nine years old.
- The median length of a child's stay in foster care is nearly two years (23.9 months); 30 percent of children in foster care stay for more than two years.
- Non-white children are over-represented in the foster care system compared to their representation in the US population.

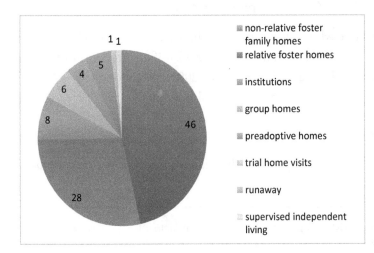

◀ **Figure 6.3**
Types of Foster Care Placement.

■ non-relative foster family homes
■ relative foster homes
■ institutions
▨ group homes
■ preadoptive homes
▨ trial home visits
▨ runaway
▨ supervised independent living

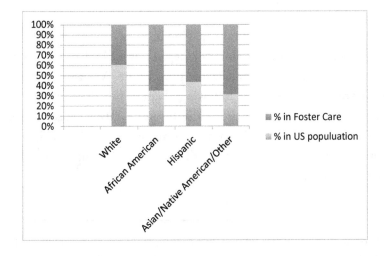

◀ **Figure 6.4**
Race of Foster Care Children.

■ % in Foster Care
▨ % in US populuation

Failure to report suspected child abuse can result in both a criminal charge—typically a misdemeanor—and civil liability. In contrast, those who report have immunity in the case—they cannot be charged with child abuse or neglect—and they are protected from liability if there is no finding of abuse in the case. This is particularly interesting when we consider the sex abuse scandal plaguing the Catholic Church. Legally, priests or bishops who suspected abuse could have reported it without any legal penalty. That they did not in hundreds of cases speaks volumes about the hierarchy of church law over state law. We will feature the case of the Catholic Church in Chapter 10.

RISK FACTORS

Research conducted by the Office of Child Abuse and Neglect, part of the Department of Health and Human Services, identifies four domains of risk factors for child abuse and neglect (Goldman et al. 2003): parent or caregiver factors, family factors, child factors, and environmental factors.

Parent or Caregiver

There is no research to suggest that there is any prototype of an abusive parent.

> **Parent or caregiver risk factors** refers to a set of risk factors for parents or caregivers to become abusive to or neglectful of their children.

One of the primary risk factors for engaging in abusive or neglectful behavior is having been the victim of abuse or neglect as a child or having been exposed to abuse in one's household while growing up. We will explore this link at much greater length in the following chapter, but there are three key factors to address here. First, though the risk for perpetrating abuse or neglect is greater for those who were child victims—as many as one-third of all victims of child abuse grow up to perpetrate it—the majority of child victims do *not* grow up to be abusive parents.

> **Cycle of abuse** refers to the fact that rates of perpetrating child abuse are significantly higher among parents who were abused or who witnessed abuse as children.

The seemingly intergenerational transmission of abuse, or what is often called the "cycle of abuse," has little to do with genetics or biology and much to do with socialization and learned behavior. Parents who grew up without good role models for how to parent lack the information and modeling to be good parents themselves; parents who grew up watching adults "solve" problems through violence, for example, may grow up without the appropriate tools for conflict resolution and may engage in violence to address their own problems. Thus, there is no question that one's childhood impacts the "tool kit" one takes into parenthood. We will explore this in much more depth in the next chapter.

A second risk factor that can affect child neglect is substance abuse and mental illness. Parents or primary caregivers who are substance abusers or addicts are at increased risk for engaging in physical abuse and neglect. One study reports that 40 percent of confirmed child abuse cases involved a parent with substance abuse or addiction problems (Children of Alcoholics Foundation 1996). The same is true for parents with mental illness. In both cases, the parent may have compromised judgment and impaired decision-making skills, which may lead to abuse or neglect.

A third risk factor for engaging in child abuse or neglect is age. Younger parents, especially teenagers, are at a greater risk for engaging in physical child abuse and neglect than older parents. There are a multitude of reasons for this, including the developmental age of most teenagers, their limited ability to handle stress, their lack of realistic expectations for children's behavior—especially infants and toddlers—and their lack of knowledge about appropriate discipline. Additionally, teenage parents are far more likely to hold other risk statuses for abuse; they are more likely to be single parents, less likely to be employed, more likely to be on welfare, and less likely to have graduated from high school all contribute to the relationship between age and risk for perpetrating physical child abuse and neglect (Goldman et al. 2003).

Family Structure

> **Family structure risk factors** refers to the fact that certain family forms or structures create situations in which child abuse is more likely to occur.

Children growing up in single-parent households are at a higher risk for all forms of child abuse and neglect. Indeed, the rate of child abuse for children growing up in single-parent households is double that of children living in two-parent households (Goldman et al. 2003). The sources of increased risk for physical abuse and neglect in single-parent households are similar to those for children of teenage parents—they are more likely to live in poverty, there is stress associated with being the sole care provider, and so forth (Goldman et al. 2003). In addition, children in mother headed single-parent households are at an increased risk for sexual abuse; stepfathers and mothers' boyfriends are the single biggest demographic group perpetrating child sexual abuse. The general understanding is that the incest taboo that prohibits sexual contact between blood relatives, which we discussed at length in Chapter 2, is the strongest factor in reducing or limiting father–daughter incest. In contrast, the connection between stepfathers and stepdaughters appears to be less powerful than social norms against incest, and thus rates of incest are higher in stepfamilies.

Regardless of the marital status of the parents, the presence of a strong relationship between child and father reduces the risks of all forms of child abuse and neglect (Goldman et al. 2003). This finding confirms the argument that it is the stresses of single-parenting that increase a child's risk for being a victim of abuse or neglect, not the individual qualities of the single parent herself. When those stresses are reduced by co-parenting, even by non-coresidential parents, the risk for abuse is diminished.

> **Non-coresidential parents** are parents who do not live together but cooperate or share in child care and child-rearing.

Another pathway by which single-parenting may be linked to greater rates of child abuse and neglect is the instability in the housing of single mothers (Edin and Lein 1997; Seccombe 1998). Children whose mothers have chaotic or constantly shifting housing—often characterized by "doubling up" or living in single-family dwellings with other family members—are at a higher risk for neglect simply because of the instability and the overcrowding of the household (Goldman et al. 2003). In addition, because these arrangements may also involve living temporarily with the mother's or grandmother's boyfriend, the risk for sexual abuse is increased as well.

It is important to point out that children living with single fathers may also face somewhat higher risks for abuse and neglect, but some important differences exist. First, father-headed households are *no more likely* to be poor than two-parent households; thus the risk for abuse and neglect that is associated with poverty is not greater in single-father-headed households than it is in mother-headed households. Second, there are simply too few father-headed households—according to the United States Census, only 4 percent of children live in father-headed households—to conduct reliable research; because the rate of father-headed households is so low, most researchers lump all single-parent families together. Last, it is important to point out that there is no reason to assume that the risk for abuse and neglect that is associated with the stress of being a single parent would be any less in father-headed households than in mother-headed households. Thus, we can expect that the rate of child abuse and neglect would be somewhat higher in father-headed households, but it would not approach the level of mother-headed households because father-headed households are far less likely to be poor. Furthermore, because there is no evidence that stepmothers or fathers' girlfriends are likely to sexually abuse sons (or daughters), the rate of sexual abuse in father-headed households would likely not be higher than in two-parent households.

Based on a national study by the Department of Health and Human Services, Administration for Children and Families (ACF), compared to children in two-parent households, children being raised by single parents had:

- a 77 percent greater risk of being physically abused
- an 87 percent greater risk of being harmed by physical neglect
- a 165 percent greater risk of experiencing notable physical neglect
- a 74 percent greater risk of suffering from emotional neglect
- an 80 percent greater risk of suffering serious injury as a result of abuse
- a 120 percent greater risk of experiencing some type of maltreatment overall.

("Child Maltreatment Prevention" 2016)

Given the fact that at the beginning of the twenty-first century there were increases in both the divorce rate and the rate of nonmarital childbirths, especially to African American mothers (Hattery and Smith 2014), we need to pay special attention to children living in single-parent households to be sure that they are safe and that their parent has adequate resources to provide for the needs of the child.

That said, staying married "for the children" does not ensure their safety. One of the highest risk factors for child abuse is the presence of intimate partner violence. As we will discuss at much greater length in the following chapter, progressive advocates of child safety have begun to argue that exposure to intimate partner violence in and of itself constitutes abuse, and in some states, including Minnesota, where we did research on intimate partner violence, when police officers responding to an intimate partner violence event discover children who are "in sight or sound of" the intimate partner violence, the children are automatically referred to CPS.

Child Factors

> **Child risk factors** are qualities of children that put them at an increased likelihood of being abused.

It is with caution that we write about "child factors," as this can easily be misinterpreted to suggest that certain children are to blame for being abused. Under no circumstances is a child responsible for being abused. Ever. That said, there are "qualities" of children that increase their risk for being victims of abuse: age and disability.

Age

Though the relationship between age and the risk for abuse is not entirely clear-cut, there are several trends that are worthy of exploration. First, the risk for serious physical abuse is highest for children between the ages of one and three; after that, it begins to decline. In contrast, the risk for child neglect increases with the age of the child. These trends are best explained by considering the different needs of children. Infants and young children require the most intense and constant care, and thus the increased risk for physical abuse may be driven by the stresses associated with parenting infants and toddlers. Infants between the ages of three and six months are at increased risk for injury for two reasons. First, because very young children are so small and fragile, it is easier for a parent or caregiver to significantly injure a child by simply shaking them.

SHAKEN BABY SYNDROME

A controversial medical term, **shaken baby syndrome** (see Box 6.6), is used to describe brain trauma in babies that is not accompanied by dramatic exterior symptoms and often leads to death. According to Dr. Thomas Nakagawa, associate professor of neurology at Wake Forest University School of Medicine, what makes the diagnosis of "shaken baby syndrome" problematic is not the injuries but rather linking a particular incident directly to the outcome—it is not always possible to determine that a particular incident of shaking caused the brain injury that resulted. That said, Dr. Nakagawa confirms that there is no controversy surrounding the neurological understanding of the impact of various body movements that result in brain trauma.

BOX 6.6	KEY FACTS ABOUT SHAKEN BABY SYNDROME

Shaken baby syndrome (SBS) results from violent acceleration–deceleration forces that cause brain injury in children.

- SBS is not caused by playful bouncing.
- SBS is not accidental trauma.
- Short falls, from less than four feet, do not result in the type of injury seen in SBS.
- No period of lucidity follows injury caused by violently shaking an infant. Injured infants and children show signs of head trauma almost immediately.
- SBS is not caused by vaccinations.
- Posterior rib fractures are a marker for SBS.
- Diffuse hemorrhagic retinopathy is a sign of abusive head trauma.

Source: Nakagawa and Conway 2004. Reprinted with permission.

The medical data are clear. As shown in Figure 6.5, the acceleration and deceleration that are associated with shaking a baby can result in brain trauma, brain injury, and even death. In exchanges with neurologist Dr. Thomas Nakagawa and his colleague Dr. Joel D. Stizel—a specialist in concussions at Wake Forest University School of Medicine—they confirm that, as has been discussed in the concussion controversy in the NFL, it is difficult to determine which "hits" result in specific brain trauma, but it is well understood that repeated "hits" will eventually result in brain trauma and even injury.

Second, infants at this age are at risk for being shaken because of a phenomenon termed *the period of purple crying*. "The period of purple crying" refers to the fact that at this developmental stage, infants cry more than at any other time in their lives. During this phase, infants not only cry more but often seem inconsolable, there is often no apparent reason for the crying, they may appear to be in pain, and the crying may last for hours and tends to occur at an already stressful time of day: late afternoon and early evening.

Though the risk for being neglected increases with age, infants are far more likely to die from neglect—a phenomenon termed *nonorganic failure to thrive*—than older children. Presumably, this is because older children are more capable of obtaining food from other sources, whereas infants are completely dependent upon their parents or caregivers for their entire nutritional input (Goldman et al. 2003).

▶ **Figure 6.5**
Shaken Baby
Syndrome.

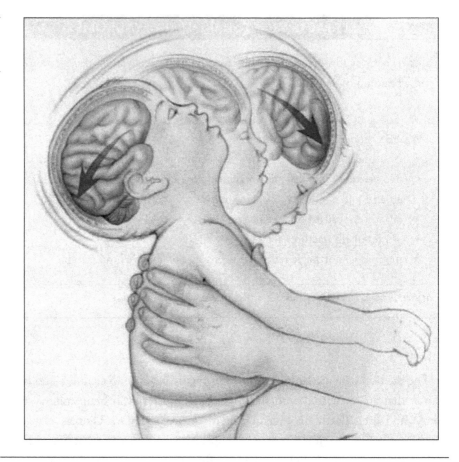

Violent shaking produces acceleration–deceleration forces that cause significant injury to the brain. Rotational forces exerted on the brain result in shear injury.

Source: Image from the article "Shaken Baby Syndrome: Recognizing and Responding to a Lethal Danger," by Thomas Nakagawa, MD, and Edward E. Conway, Jr., MD, MS. Reprinted with permission.

Some research suggests that there is a much less significant relationship between emotional abuse and sexual abuse and age, though preadolescence seems to be the highest-risk age for sexual abuse, especially of girls (Goldman et al. 2003). The lack of a correlation between age and emotional abuse is not surprising; yelling at a child or calling him or her a derogatory name—the hallmarks of emotional abuse—can happen with children of any age. With regard to sexual abuse, the primary factor influencing the high risk that preadolescent girls face for abuse by a male family member—father, uncle, stepfather—is directly related to their sexual development. In order to avoid the complications of pregnancy, much of the child sexual abuse young girls experience— especially by family members and friends—ceases by the time they reach menarche. Of course, there is also a body of scientific research on men who are sexually attracted to adolescent bodies—of all genders. This condition is termed *ephebophilia*.

> **Ephebophilia** is the sexual attraction to adolescent bodies. Though most people diagnosed with ephebophilia are men, they may be attracted to either boys or girls.

Yet it is also important to note that the teenage years hold the greatest risk for both boys and girls for sexual abuse by people outside the household. This is attributable to the fact that it is at this age when parents begin to give their children more freedom from parental supervision; this is also when overnight trips for sports or youth groups begin, and thus the opportunity for abuse opens up in ways that make this age group particularly vulnerable to sexual abuse.

Disabilities

According to Leigh Ann Davis (2009), children with disabilities experience "higher rates of maltreatment than do other children. Children with any type of disability are 3.44 times more likely to be a victim of some type of abuse compared to children without disabilities."

As with age, one of the explanations for this relationship seems to be the additional stress that raising a child with disabilities may place on a parent. Additional sources of stress may come "from the child" in the sense that many physical and cognitive disabilities result in significantly greater caregiving needs, similar to the case with infants and toddlers as well as elders, as we explored in the previous chapter. Additionally, sources of stress may be compounded with certain communication disorders, such as autism, in which the child may have such difficulty communicating that the parent or caregiver feels isolated and unsupported. Another source of stress that is rarely discussed is the economic stress associated with certain physical and cognitive or developmental disabilities. In cases of a child's severe physical disability, parents may face a host of financial burdens, including operations to correct abnormalities, health aids—expensive wheelchairs, for example—and even modifications to the home. Rarely do people realize that the majority of these needs are not covered by any insurance, and thus the financial strain may produce stress that is released in abusive or neglectful ways.

Similarly, having a child with a disability often puts tremendous strain on marital relationships, especially if the disability is the result of genetics, in which case one parent may feel guilt associated with passing on a defective gene and the other may feel anger and resentment. For a variety of reasons—including disagreements over treatment and care—parents of children with disabilities are more likely to divorce, and the strain of being a single parent raising a disabled child may lead to abusive or neglectful behavior (Marshak and Prezant 2007). For a fictionalized account of a family struggling with raising a differently abled child, we recommend

Jodi Picoult's novel *Handle with Care* (2009), which is the fictional account of a family raising a child with osteogenesis imperfecta—a genetic bone disorder.

It is also important to note that children with disabilities are far more likely to be placed for adoption or put into foster care, and any time in foster care increases the likelihood of experiencing abuse or maltreatment. Additionally, the National Council on Disability (2008: 36) reports that once inside the foster care system, children with disabilities are 1.5 to 3.5 times more likely to be abused or neglected than their able-bodied counterparts. Furthermore, they suggest that foster care children with disabilities are one of the most vulnerable populations in the United States, yet their needs are grossly understudied and underfunded.

Last, the National Council on Disability, and scholars including Goldman and colleagues (2003), suggest that an additional problem that disabled children face occurs after the abuse has begun; in cases of development or cognitive delay, children who are being abused may be less able to recognize the abuse as inappropriate, name it, or report it than their similarly aged counterparts. Children with physical disabilities may be less able to protect themselves. For example, in the novel *Handle with Care*, the mother faces inquisitions about child abuse because her daughter, who suffers from "brittle bone" disease, sustains many fractures throughout her childhood. In cases such as this, one can imagine that an abusive parent would be able to easily explain away concerns of abuse by pointing to the characteristics of the child's disease. But in the majority of cases where there is no easily acceptable explanation, it seems probable that interventions come later for abused or neglected children with disabilities, and thus the abuse goes on longer and the possibility for injury and other long-term consequences increases.

Environmental Factors

Goldman and colleagues (2003) identify three **environmental risk factors**—qualities of the physical environment under which children and their families live—that contribute to an increased risk for child abuse and neglect: poverty and unemployment, social isolation and lack of social support, and living in a violent community.

Poverty and Unemployment

We have talked at length about the role that poverty and unemployment play in child abuse and neglect. Statistics compiled by Goldman and colleagues (2003) demonstrate the relationship: "Children from families with annual incomes below $15,000 in 1993 were more than 22 times more likely to be harmed by child abuse and neglect as compared to children from families with annual incomes above $30,000."

Scholars suggest four "theories" for explaining the relationship between poverty and an increased risk for child abuse and neglect (Plotnik 2000).

- As noted above, poverty leads to parental and familial stress, which increases the chances and rates of abuse, and especially neglect.
- Poverty itself compromises a parent's ability to provide adequate care and meet all of the needs of the child.
- There may be a relationship between parental poverty and the likelihood of parental substance abuse.
- Finally, some scholars suggest that the risk for child abuse and neglect is not necessarily higher among low-income families, but rather abuse and neglect are more likely to be detected in low-income families and, ultimately, referred to CPS. This may occur for a variety of reasons, including the stereotypes that professionals such as teachers and health-care providers may hold about the poor as well as a fear of reporting an affluent or well-known family in the community. This explanation has been offered by many feminist scholars of poverty (Chasnoff, Landress, and Barrett 1990; Edin and Lein 1997; Hattery and Smith 2007; Neuspiel 1996).

Social Isolation and Social Support

Goldman and colleagues (2003: 35) review a series of studies that suggest that parents who abuse or neglect their children report experiencing "greater isolation, more loneliness and less social support." Though more research needs to be done to determine whether isolation is a cause or result of abuse, the relationship between social isolation and child abuse is widely accepted by practitioners, and thus programs to alleviate isolation, such as Welcome Baby (which we'll discuss in more detail shortly), were created.

Violent Communities

One of the greatest contributions sociologists make to understanding phenomena such as child abuse is their focus on structural and institutional, rather than individual, factors. Beginning at the very end of the twentieth century, criminologists and sociologists investigating poverty and race or ethnicity began to focus their attention on the role that the environment of a community may play in individual and family life. For example, noted sociologist William Julius Wilson (1996) asked, what role does a high level of unemployment in a neighborhood play in shaping individuals' attitudes toward work? Following this approach, scholars interested in child welfare began to wonder about the role that violence in neighborhoods plays in shaping abuse in individual families.

Protective Factors: Reducing the Risk for Child Abuse and Neglect

Goldman and colleagues (2003) suggest that just as there are factors that increase the likelihood of child abuse, there are protective factors as well.

> **Protective factors** refers to any quality of the child, the parent, the family, or the environment that reduces the likelihood that a parent will be abusive or neglectful and that a child will be victimized.

Obviously, qualities and situations that eliminate certain risk factors will be protective, such as living in a two-parent family, having adequate financial resources, becoming a parent after age twenty-five, having fewer children, and so forth. Of more interest, however, is the ability to reduce the risk for child abuse or neglect by targeting "at-risk families" and changing their risk factors into protective factors. Goldman and colleagues (2003) suggest that social support and a network of resources can serve as a protective factor even for a family that is otherwise at high risk. For example, a parent who was abused as a child will be less likely to become an abusive parent if they have access to appropriate counseling and therapy, parenting classes, and social support. This is the entire premise behind the Welcome Baby program (see Box 6.7), which, though it reaches out to the majority of new parents, targets those with risk factors including poverty; previous abuse; mothers who delivered drug-addicted, underweight, or premature babies; and so forth. This summary comes from the Welcome Baby program in Durham, North Carolina, but many counties around the United States have Welcome Baby programs.

BOX 6.7	WELCOME BABY

The Welcome Baby program of Durham, North Carolina makes contact with new parents when they are at the hospital post-delivery. The program provides nine essential services for at-risk parents:

Parenting education and support: Welcome Baby strives to answer the many child development and infant care questions parents have during their children's first years. We offer weekly classes on a variety of parenting topics. We also distribute developmental guides, offer telephone support to parents of newborns, have a discussion group for parents of newborns, maintain a lending library of books and videos, and our staff is available to discuss your individual parenting concerns.

Car seat safety program: Free classes on the correct use and installation of infant/toddler and booster car seats are offered several times each month. Families who complete the class are eligible to purchase seats on a sliding fee scale.

Cribs for kids: Welcome Baby is the local affiliate of the national Cribs for Kids© program. Through donations, we are able to distribute cribs to families referred through agencies providing in-home services and nurse home visit programs. Families receiving cribs also receive safe sleep educational information. The goal of the program is decreasing SIDS (Sudden Infant Death Syndrome). The program does not accept self-referrals. Prior to making a referral, professionals should contact the Cribs for Kids coordinator.

Developmental guides: Welcome Baby's newsletter, *Welcome Words*, discusses the milestones and challenges of each age. *Welcome Words* covers the changes in children and the concerns of parents at each age. They include specific information about Durham County. The newsletters are available bi-monthly until your child is age 1 and then twice/year until age 5.

Spanish services: All Welcome Baby services are available in Spanish.

The giving closet: Families can visit our free clothing closet four times during the program year (July 1 thru June 30) to select children's clothing, maternity wear and infant equipment when available. Donations of clean infant and toddler clothing are accepted Tuesdays, Wednesdays and Thursdays, between 9 and 4:30 or by appointment. Infant furniture and equipment are especially appreciated. Donations are tax-deductible.

Community resources: Welcome Baby can serve as a link for families to other community resources. This listing describes some of the services available in Durham County. Families can call the Welcome Baby office for additional assistance and professionals can access the confidential referral system.

Volunteer opportunities: Welcome Baby's programs are only possible through the work of many volunteers. Opportunities are flexible, from visiting families at the hospital and offering support to parents of newborns to assisting at the clothing closet and providing childcare during Welcome Baby's parenting classes. Together our volunteers help care for the children of our community.

Lending libraries: Welcome Baby offers a lending library of books and videos on topics pertaining to newborns, their care and development and many other child rearing and parenting topics. The library is located at the Welcome Baby office. The Durham County Library also has information on these topics.

Source: "About Welcome Baby" n.d.

What is missing in this approach is a national-level campaign that focuses on child welfare. For example, given the huge role that poverty plays in both abuse and neglect, if the welfare laws were reworked to focus on the needs of poor children, rather than as a penalty to their parents, who are stereotyped as being lazy and poor decision-makers (Roberts 1997; Seccombe 1998), more resources would be made available to children living in poverty, and this would most likely reduce their risk for abuse and neglect. We will expand this discussion at the end of the chapter and revisit it again in the final chapter of the book, which is devoted to solutions. We turn now to a discussion of the outcomes of child abuse on the victims.

OUTCOMES OF CHILD ABUSE

As we have noted throughout this chapter, one of the saddest outcomes of child abuse is the likelihood that it will be repeated intergenerationally. Because this will be the major focus of the following chapter, here we focus on some of the more immediate outcomes for children who experience abuse and neglect. We focus on three key areas: substance abuse, high-risk sexual behavior, and interactions with the criminal justice system.

Substance Abuse and Mental Health Issues

Mary Pipher, in her book based on working with adolescent girls in therapy, noted a very strong relationship between abuse, especially sexual abuse, and both substance abuse and mental health issues (1994). Quantitative data reviewed and reported by Lalor and McElvaney (2010) noting the relationship between being a victim of child abuse and both substance abuse and mental health issues confirm Pipher's qualitative findings:

- More than 60 percent of people in drug rehabilitation centers report being abused or neglected as a child.
- About 80 percent of twenty-one-year-olds who were abused as children met criteria for at least one psychological disorder; the two most common are anxiety disorder and depression.

In fact, in one of your author's hometowns, the local Boy Scout leader was convicted of sexually abusing the Boy Scouts in his troop. The accusation arose from a Scout who in the seventh grade was being treated for drug addiction. During his therapy he revealed the abuse, and his counselor—a mandatory reporter—brought the tragic accusation to light. This is, unfortunately, an all-too-common scenario.

High-Risk Sexual Behavior

Victims of child abuse, especially sexual abuse, are also at high risk for engaging in risky sexual behavior. We will spend a great deal of time disentangling this very disturbing phenomenon in the next chapter when we examine a specific type of child sexual abuse we term *premature sex engagement* and its relationship to intimate partner violence. But for our purposes here we provide the following statistics (Saewyc, Magee, and Pettingell 2004):

- Abused teens are three times more likely to practice unsafe sex, putting them at greater risk for STIs.
- Abused children are 25 percent more likely to experience teen pregnancy.

Crime

Victims of child abuse are also prone to engage in activities that land them inside the criminal justice system as perpetrators. The statistics provided above contribute to our insight regarding this relationship. As noted, victims of child abuse are far more likely than their peers to use and abuse alcohol and drugs, which is often a pathway into the criminal justice system. For example, among the most common juvenile misdemeanors are citations for underage drinking or possession offenses for either alcohol or marijuana. National statistics on child abuse reveal the following (Saewyc, Magee, and Pettingell 2004):

- Children who have been sexually abused are 2.5 times more likely to abuse alcohol as teenagers and young adults.
- Children who have been sexually abused are 3.8 times more likely to develop drug addictions as teenagers or young adults.

Additionally, as we will discuss at length in the following chapter, girls and women who are victims of child sexual abuse are twice as likely as their peers to become battered women. Experiences with sexual abuse—for both boys and girls—or physical abuse—for girls—often lead victims to seek an escape from the abuse. It is not at all uncommon for the escape to involve behaviors that can also be a pathway to the criminal justice system, including running away or truancy, which can result in juveniles being sentenced to detention centers; passing bad checks or stealing in order to generate the money needed to run away; and prostitution—which is especially common among victims of sexual abuse, both boys and girls—as a strategy to facilitate living on the street once a victim has run away. All of these activities expose the victims to the criminal justice system, and these seem the most likely pathways for victims of child abuse into the criminal justice system (Hattery 2008, 2009; Odem 1995; Pipher 1994). According to Goldman and colleagues (2003):

- While less than 5 percent of all boys were abused as children, 14 percent of all men in US prison were abused as children.
- While less than 20 percent of women experience any type of abuse, 36 percent of all women in prison were abused as children.
- Children who experience child abuse and neglect are 59 percent more likely to be arrested as a juvenile, 28 percent more likely to be arrested as an adult, and 30 percent more likely to commit a violent crime.

Furthermore, the Georgetown Law Center on Poverty and Inequality (Saar et al. 2015) identifies a "sexual abuse to prison pipeline for girls." Though the data varies from state to state, between 80 and 95 percent of girls in juvenile detention were sexually assaulted or raped before they arrived there and more than half had experienced physical abuse or dating violence as well (Saar et al. 2015).

Entering the criminal justice system as a juvenile is problematic for many different reasons, including the stigma and the fact that children who enter the system are three times more likely to be incarcerated as adults than those who were never detained as juveniles. Additionally, juvenile detention centers can also be a site of further abuse: physical, emotional, and sexual (see especially Hattery and Smith 2019). And though we are not advocating for a complete dismantling of the juvenile justice system, as stories of abuse emerge they illuminate not only the horrors of the abuse but also the role the system plays in further abusing children, adding to the already increased risk these children face for being abusive in adulthood. Thus, we are forced to question the system of juvenile detention and recommend that it be overhauled with a rehabilitative goal in mind, rather than a punitive mission that only makes the possibility of transforming youth into productive citizens unlikely at best.

Child abuse can also be systemic in other institutions, including those designed to help children. In June 2011, CNN broke a story about a "therapy" program run at UCLA in the 1960s that encouraged, or even required, parents to engage in physically abusing their children as part of a program designed to cure their homosexuality (Bronstein and

Not long after Donald Trump was elected president, he began implementing one of his signature campaign promises: addressing illegal immigration. Among his controversial policies was a law implemented by then attorney general Jeff Sessions, which changed the rules

continues

continued

around immigrants seeking asylum at the southern US border with Mexico. As a result of these changes, children immigrating with their parents were separated at the border and remanded into immigration detention centers. At the time of this writing, in late 2018, there are more than 14,000 children in detention centers. During summer 2018 as many as 5,000 children, some as young as toddlers, were incarcerated in detention centers without their parents; some parents were detained in adult facilities, some were living with family in other parts of the United States, and others had already been deported to Mexico and other countries in Central and South America with no way to legally enter the United States to reclaim their children. Even those with the most conservative perspectives on illegal immigration agreed that this policy was unacceptable. Others, ourselves included, consider this a form of child abuse . . . perpetrated by the state.

Joseph 2011). In the summer of 2019 news broke that as a result of changes in immigration policy, children were being separated from their parents and detained.

CONCLUSIONS

If you have been lucky enough to have been spared experiencing child abuse or neglect, then you should count your blessings. But whether or not you have, this problem affects you. Child abuse leads to problems that impact all members of society, including increased rates of drug and alcohol abuse and addiction and "deviant" behavior that leads to juvenile detention and incarceration. The annual cost of child abuse and neglect in the United States is estimated by Childhelp to be $124 billion ("Child Abuse Statistics and Facts" n.d.). Thus, it is clear that in order to create a society in which we are all safe and functioning and contributing at our highest levels, it is paramount that we prevent, intervene in, and ultimately reduce the prevalence of all forms of child abuse. Additionally, as noted throughout this chapter, experiencing abuse as a child puts one at significantly higher risk for being in an abusive relationship in adulthood—either as a perpetrator or as a victim, involved in intimate partner violence, child abuse, or elder abuse. Thus, if we are interested in breaking the cycle of violence, then we have an interest in interrupting child abuse when it occurs and seeking better strategies for preventing it.

We conclude this chapter with a discussion of intervention and prevention strategies.

Intervention

Unfortunately, child abuse occurs. Annually, there are more than five million cases of child abuse reported in the United States ("Child Abuse Statistics and Facts" n.d.). Perhaps even more tragic is the fact that many children are "repeat" victims; even after a complaint is filed, it is not uncommon for the abuse to continue. Thus, we must develop more successful intervention strategies. As we have noted throughout this book, and especially in Chapter 2, family violence has long been considered a private problem, and law enforcement and even social service agencies have been reluctant to intervene unless the abuse reaches a certain level. However, this approach leaves millions of children living with neglect and abuse. Tragic as this is on its own, it also puts them at higher risk for substance abuse, risky sexual behavior, and abuse as teenagers and young adults. Thus, we advocate a more proactive approach to intervention. Of course, it is difficult to suggest that in all cases of suspected abuse children should be removed from their homes and put into a foster care system that ultimately puts them at an even greater risk for abuse. In fact, this may always be a last resort. That said, we need to develop intervention strategies that protect children and allow them to stay in their homes, teach parents better parenting skills, and have some measure of accountability. This will not be easy, as these services are expensive to provide and the agencies that currently provide them are understaffed and underfunded, and with the current political climate, there have been cuts to many social service programs, including violence prevention, and it will be difficult to develop and implement these programs in the near future.

Ideally, based on the research of practitioners and scholars who focus on child abuse, we would make the following recommendations:

- Investigate *all* reports of child abuse.
- Create sanctions for mandatory reporters who fail to report suspected abuse.
- Increase training for all mandatory reporters.
- Increase accountability among professional organizations, such as churches and athletic programs, where adults come in regular contact with children and where rates of abuse are unusually high.
- Require parents in any case of suspected abuse to attend mandatory parenting classes and, in cases where the abuse is substantiated, tie the completion of these classes to being released from probation.
- Better supervise the system of foster care, where rates of abuse are higher than in non-foster families.
- Overhaul the system of juvenile detention so that juvenile offenders are rehabilitated and treated, not subjected to further abuse.
- Most importantly, take child abuse seriously, as the damage we are doing to our future generation is nothing less than tragic.

Prevention

As with all forms of family violence, the real difference in child abuse can be made by developing successful prevention programs. If we can prevent abuse and neglect from occurring in the first place, we save not only the tragedy of the abuse but also billions of dollars—in medical costs, court costs, custody costs, and subsequent costly behavior by the child as they enter their teen and young adult years, including substance abuse and deviance. We highlight two areas for prevention: prevention programs and structural changes in the United States.

Prevention Programs

As many people have noted, one has to get a license to drive a car, but one does not need a license to become a parent. We are not advocating that this become the case. We *are* acknowledging that parenting is difficult and that resources should be provided to all new parents. The Welcome Baby program in Durham, North Carolina, one of many iterations in counties around the United States, is an example of a type of program that needs to be available to all new parents nationally. Second, there are risk factors associated with the child, the parents, and the family structure that increase the likelihood of abuse and neglect. Thus, parenting classes and other resources should be readily available and targeted toward these at-risk groups, including teenage parents, single parents, low-income parents, parents on welfare, parents who are struggling with substance abuse, and parents of children with disabilities. Again, these types of programs will cost money, but because models with proven track records, based on best practices, already exist, fully funding these existing programs and expanding them nationally would be steps in the right direction. We will detail more of these programs in Chapter 16.

Structural Changes

As we discussed at length in the section on child neglect, which accounts for more than half of all reported cases of child abuse (see Figure 6.2), there is a strong link between neglect and poverty. Though some parents simply do not know how to care for their children, or choose not to, many other parents know how to care for their children and desperately want to but find themselves in a position where they are unable to meet their child's basic needs. Poverty leaves many families unable to provide for the nutritional needs of their children. According to the US Department of Agriculture, in 2018 nearly thirteen million American children were food insecure; that is, they did not have reliable access to food ("Food Security Status of U.S. Households with Children in 2018" 2017 data). Housing projects create another challenge. Walking through any public housing project in urban or rural America will expose one to a set of circumstances that, by their very definition, can be considered neglect or abuse. Living without adequate heating, cooling, or plumbing, and living with rodent infestations or lead paint are all part of the reality of daily life for low-income people in America; children living in such conditions are suffering from neglect. Additionally, housing projects are notoriously violent places to live, and this exposure to violence constitutes an environmental cause of child abuse. Low wages not only impact parents' ability to provide adequate nutrition, clothing, and shelter for their children but also, when coupled with the high costs of child care, may adversely affect their ability to provide adequate supervision as well. Inadequate supervision can constitute neglect and can lead to abuse, as unsupervised children are more likely to be targets of sexual abuse by babysitters and nonfamily members and more likely to be exposed to drugs.

Thus, we advocate many changes to the United States economy and the system of social welfare that would alleviate multiple problems, including high rates of neglect and abuse among low-income and poor people living in the United States. First and foremost, we advocate that employers be required to pay a living wage. Unlike the poverty line, which is calculated based on formulas established in 1961, a living wage refers to the minimum wage necessary to sustain a reasonable standard of living. Because the cost of living varies from city to city and state to state, the living wage is often calculated locally. While many CEOs make tens or twenties of millions of dollars per year in compensation alone, the people working for them often make just minimum wage, $8.25 an hour (that's the federal minimum wage; individual states may have a higher minimum wage). In fact, the ratio of CEO pay to worker pay has dramatically increased over the last fifty years, from 20 to 1 in 1965 then 361 to 1 in 2017 (Quinnell 2018). If the minimum wage were raised to a living wage, this would provide many parents the resources to provide for the basic needs of their children. Additionally, the current system of social welfare needs to be substantially overhauled so that it is not a punitive system for parents who make bad choices but a safety net for the children of those parents (Roberts 1997). If we were to structure public housing, food stamps, and child-care subsidies with the best interests of children in mind, these programs could significantly change the experiences of many low-income and poor children regardless of the choices their parents made or did not make.

THE FINNISH BABY BOX

Since the middle of the twentieth century, Finland has approached child health by starting at birth and ensuring that each child gets a proper start in life. In Finland, all parents of newborns receive a Baby Box. The Baby Box contains one set of clothing with sizes for the entire first year, including baby's first snowsuit and boots, toys, cloth diapers, and birth control to help the parents better space their children. The box even doubles as baby's

continues

THE FINNISH BABY BOX *continued*

bassinet. Many attribute Finland's low infant mortality rates to this low-cost intervention. What would it be like if we in the United States placed this high value on the life of newborns and set them up with a basic standard of living with the hopes of ensuring better outcomes for them as adults?

Hubert Humphrey once said, "The moral test of government is how it treats those who are in the dawn of life, the children; those who are in the twilight of life, the aged; and those in the shadows of life, the sick, the needy, and the handicapped." Children are, without a doubt, among the most vulnerable of all citizens. And our treatment of them, as a society, by failing to protect them and provide for them when their parents cannot or will not, is a disgrace. If we expect to maintain a position of global leadership in the twenty-first century, we must address issues of child abuse and neglect, take them seriously, and invoke both interventions and preventive measures that reduce the impact of abuse on our most vulnerable yet richest resource: our children.

RESOURCES

Administration for Children and Families, Department of Health and Human Services: www.acf.hhs.gov.
Childhelp: www.childhelp.org.
Maysles, Albert, Deborah Dickson, and Susan Froemke. 2001. *LaLee's Kin: The Legacy of Cotton*. Maysles Films/HBO. (We highly recommend this documentary, which illustrates the ways in which poverty can produce child neglect.)
The Period of Purple Crying, www.purplecrying.info.
Picoult, Jodi. 2009. *Handle with Care*. New York: Washington Square Press.
Welcome Baby program, Durham, North Carolina: www.welcomebaby.org. Many states and locales have Welcome Baby programs. We encourage you to find the local program in your area.

NOTE

1. To read an example see: "The University of Alabama: Where Racial Segregation Remains a Way of Life" 2001.

REFERENCES

"About Welcome Baby." n.d. *Welcome Baby*. www.welcomebaby.org/about_welcome_baby.html.
Bronstein, Scott, and Jessi Joseph. 2011. "Therapy to Change 'Feminine' Boy Created a Troubled Man, Family Says." *CNN.com*, June 10. www.cnn.com/2011/US/06/07/sissy.boy.experiment.

Chasnoff, I. J., H. J. Landress, and M. E. Barrett. 1990. "The Prevalence of Illicit-Drug or Alcohol Use During Pregnancy and Discrepancies in Mandatory Reporting in Pinellas County, Florida." *New England Journal of Medicine* 322(*17*): 1202–1206.

Child Abuse Prevention and Treatment Act of 1974. Pub. *L*. 93–247, 88 Stat. 4, codified as amended at 42 U.S.C. §§5101–5106.

"Child Abuse Statistics and Facts" n.d. *Childhelp*. www.childhelp.org/child-abuse-statistics.

"Child Maltreatment Prevention." 2016. *Centers for Disease Control and Prevention*. www.cdc.gov/violenceprevention/childmaltreatment.

"Child Neglect." n.d. *Childhelp*. www.childhelp.org/child-abuse.

Children of Alcoholics Foundation. 1996. *Collaboration, Coordination, and Cooperation: Helping Children Affected by Parental Addiction and Family Violence*. New York: Children of Alcoholics Foundation.

Davis, Leigh Ann. August 2009. *Abuse of Children with Intellectual Disability*. Washington, DC. The Arc. www.thearc.org/document.doc?id=3666.

Edin, K., and L. Lein. 1997. *Making Ends Meet: How Single Mothers Survive Welfare and Low-Wage Work*. New York: Russell Sage Foundation.

Ehrensaft, Miriam K., Patricia Cohen, Jocelyn Brown, Elizabeth Smailes, Henian Chen, and Jeffrey G. Johnson. 2003. "Intergenerational Transmission of Partner Violence: A 20-Year Prospective Study." *Journal of Consulting and Clinical Psychology* 7(*4*): 741–753.

"Emotional Abuse." n.d. *Childhelp*. www.childhelp.org/child-abuse.

Finkelhor, David, Richard Ormrod, Heather Turner, and Sherry L. Hamby. 2005. "The Victimization of Children and Youth: A Comprehensive, National Survey." *Child Maltreatment* 10(*1*): 5–25.

"Food Security Status of U.S. Households with Children in 2018." 2017. United States Department of Agriculture www.feedingamerica.org/sites/default/files/research/map-the-meal-gap/2016/2016-map-the-meal-gap-child-food-insecurity.pdf

Ford, Dana. 2015. "Jared Fogle Expected to Plead Guilty to Child Porn Charges, Sources Say." *CNN.com*, August 19. www.cnn.com/2015/08/18/us/subway-jared-fogle-charges.

Goldman, J., M. K. Salus, D. Wolcott, and K. Y. Kennedy. 2003. *A Coordinated Response to Child Abuse and Neglect: The Foundation for Practice*. Washington, DC: Office of Child Abuse and Neglect, US Department of Health and Human Services.

Hattery, A. J. 2008. *Intimate Partner Violence*. Lanham, MD: Rowman and Littlefield.

Hattery, A. J. 2009. "Sexual Abuse in Childhood and Adolescence and Intimate Partner Violence in Adulthood Among African American and White Women." *Race, Gender, and Class* 15(*2*): 79–97.

Hattery, Angela J., and Earl Smith. 2007. *African American Families*. Thousand Oaks, CA: Sage.

Hattery, Angela J., and Earl Smith. 2010. *Prisoner Reentry and Social Capital: The Long Road to Reintegration*. Lanham, MD: Lexington Books.

Hattery, Angela J., and Earl Smith. 2014. *African American Families: Myths and Realities.* Lanham, MD: Rowman and Littlefield.

Hattery, Angela J., and Earl Smith. 2019. *Gender, Power, and Violence.* Lanham, MD: Rowman and Littlefield.

Kwiatkowski, Marisa, Mark Alesia, and Tim Evans. 2016. "Out of Balance." *IndyStar* www.usatoday.com/story/news/investigations/2016/08/04/usa-gymnastics-sex-abuse-protected-coaches/85829732.

Lalor, K., and R. McElvaney. 2010. "Child Sexual Abuse, Links to Later Sexual Exploitation/High-Risk Sexual Behavior, and Prevention/Treatment Programs." *Trauma, Violence, and Abuse 11(4)*: 159–177.

Marshak, L. E., and F. P. Prezant. 2007. *Married with Special-Needs Children: A Couple's Guide to Keeping Connected.* Bethesda, MD: Woodbine House.

"Mary Kay Letourneau Marries Former Victim." 2009. *This Day in History, History. com*, May 20. www.history.com/this-day-in-history/mary-kay-letourneau-marries-former-victim.

"Megan's Law Website." 2008. *Pennsylvania State Police.* www.pameganslaw.state.pa.us.

Nakagawa, Thomas, and Edward E. Conway Jr. 2004. "Shaken Baby Syndrome: Recognizing and Responding to a Lethal Danger." *Contemporary Pediatrics 21(3)*: 37–57.

National Council on Disability. 2008. *Youth with Disabilities in the Foster Care System: Barriers to Success and Proposed Policy Solutions.* February 26, 2008, p. 36.

Neuspiel, D. R. 1996. "Racism and Perinatal Addiction, Ethnicity, and Disease." *Ethnicity & Disease 6(1–2)*: 47–55.

North Carolina Administrative Office of the Courts. 2010. www.ncgal.org. Reproduced with permission from the North Carolina Court System. www.nccourts.org/Citizens/JData/Documents/Guardian_ad_Litem_Facts.pdf.

Odem, M. E. 1995. *Delinquent Daughters: Protecting and Policing Adolescent Female Sexuality in the United States, 1885–1920.* Chapel Hill, NC: University of North Carolina Press.

"Physical Abuse." n.d. *Childhelp.* www.childhelp.org/child-abuse.

Pipher, M. B. 1994. *Reviving Ophelia: Saving the Selves of Adolescent Girls.* New York: Putnam Press.

Plotnik, R. 2000. "Economic Security for Families with Children." In *The Child Welfare Challenge: Policy, Practice, and Research*, edited by P. J. Pecora, J. K. Whittaker, A. N. Maluccio, and R. P. Barth, 2: 95–127. New York: Aldine de Gruyter.

Quinnell, Kenneth. 2018. *Executive Paywatch 2018: The Gap Between CEO and Worker Compensation Continues to Grow.* AFL-CIO. https://aflcio.org/2018/5/22/executive-paywatch-2018-gap-between-ceo-and-worker-compensation-continues-grow.

Reilly, Steve. 2016. "Broken Discipline Tracking Systems Let Teachers Flee Troubled Pasts." *USA Today.* http://usat.ly/1R3rsnw.

Roberts, Dorothy. 1997. *Killing the Black Body.* New York: Vintage Books.

Saar, Malika Saada, Rebecca Epstein, Lindsay Rosenthal, and Yasmin Vafa. 2015. *The Sexual Abuse to Prison Pipeline: The Girls' Story.* Washington, DC: Georgetown Law Center on Poverty and Inequality. www.law.georgetown.edu/academics/

centers-institutes/poverty-inequality/upload/2015_COP_sexual-abuse_layout_
web-2.pdf.

Saewyc, Elizabeth M., Lara Leanne Magee, and Sandra E. Pettingell. 2004. "Teenage
Pregnancy and Associated Risk Behaviors Among Sexually Abused Adolescents."
Perspectives on Sexual and Reproductive Health 36(3).

Seccombe, K. 1998. *So You Think I Drive a Cadillac? Welfare Recipients' Perspectives on
the System and Its Reform.* New York: Allyn and Bacon.

"Sexual Abuse." n.d. *Childhelp.* www.childhelp.org/child-abuse.

Smith, Melinda, and Jeanne Segal. 2016. "Child Abuse and Neglect: Recognizing,
Preventing, and Reporting Child Abuse." *HelpGuide.org,* February. www.helpguide.
org/articles/abuse/child-abuse-and-neglect.htm.

"The University of Alabama: Where Racial Segregation Remains a Way of Life." 2001.
Journal of Blacks in Higher Education 32: 22–24.

"Trial Begins for Dallas Father Accused of Starving Kids." 2010. *Associated Press,* July 21.

Wilson, W. J. 1996. *When Work Disappears: The World of the New Urban Poor.* New
York: Alfred A. Knopf.

SIBLING ABUSE

Veronica Tichenor

Recently, I was with a group of friends and we were telling about nicknames we had as children. I said I didn't have any nicknames, but all the while we were laughing and talking, the name I was called by my sister kept going around in my head—*lard ass*. I wouldn't tell them that is how I was known in my house to my sister when I was a child. My parents used to laugh about it. I wasn't laughing; I was crying. My childhood was a nightmare. I don't even want to look at pictures of when I was a child. I threw my school pictures away. The memories hurt so much. At the age of 42 I have finally found the courage to seek counseling. Maybe I can come out of my shell and enjoy the remaining years of my life.

(Adult woman sibling abuse survivor, Wiehe 1997: 1)

This chapter will focus on the abuse of children by their siblings, including physical, emotional, and sexual abuse. We will explore why sibling abuse has received so little attention, and the challenges in defining and studying it. We will examine risk factors in the family and the larger culture, as well as the outcomes associated with this form of abuse. The chapter ends with a discussion of how to intervene effectively in sibling abuse in order to facilitate the recovery of its victims.

OBJECTIVES

- To distinguish between sibling rivalry and sibling abuse
- To describe different types of sibling abuse, including physical abuse, psychological abuse, and sexual abuse
- To understand the cultural and familial risk factors associated with sibling abuse
- To examine the consequences of sibling abuse
- To explore the ways in which parents can effectively intervene in, and respond to, situations of sibling abuse

---

KEY TERMS

sibling rivalry	cultural and familial risk factors for
sibling conflict	sibling abuse
sibling abuse	systems theory
sibling violence	trauma theory
physical abuse	resiliency theory
psychological abuse	feminist theory
sexual abuse	social learning theory
incest	

INTRODUCTION

Sibling abuse is the most common, most damaging, and least reported form of family violence. The harm inflicted can be physical, psychological, and/or sexual. As a culture, we have been very slow to recognize the problem of sibling abuse. This is rather surprising, given that the sibling relationship is likely the longest family relationship one will have. We spend a substantial portion of our lives with siblings, who predate chosen life partners in our biographies and, typically, outlive our parents. The impact of siblings is also felt most keenly in the early stages of our lives, where health and educational experts have long been concerned about the impact of parents and their behavior on our developmental trajectories; the long-term developmental impact of sibling relationships has rarely been considered (Caffaro 2014). We have already seen the long-lasting harm that abuse from parents can cause; the impact of sibling abuse can be just as severe.

One reason abusive behavior between siblings has remained invisible for so long is that it can be mistaken for **sibling rivalry**. Sibling abuse is often normalized or overlooked as "just kids being kids." Of course, conflict between siblings is to be expected. Disagreements, frustrations, even anger are a normal part of human interaction, and siblings (as children) are just learning how to negotiate these relational challenges. Other family dynamics can easily exacerbate those challenges. For example, parents inevitably compare siblings to each other, or children compare themselves. These comparisons can result in bad feelings, jealousy, anger, and retaliation—shifting relational dynamics across the line from rivalry and competition to abuse.

That line between normal sibling behavior and sibling abuse is rarely examined—partly because it can be difficult to determine where that line is. Verbal insults and name-calling, even some pushing and shoving, may be considered "normal" dynamics as children learn to manage their conflicts. Similarly, sexual exploration and "sex

play" may be seen as "developmentally appropriate" in some circumstances. This makes it more difficult for parents and professionals to come to a consensus about where normal sibling behavior ends and abuse begins.

CHALLENGES IN DEFINING SIBLING ABUSE

Studying and documenting sibling abuse presents a number of challenges. First, a range of terms have been used in the research on sibling behavior, including:

- sibling aggression: an umbrella term that may range from conflict to abuse
- **sibling conflict**: often linked to serious cases of parental favoritism
- **sibling violence**: more mutual, with two siblings directing harmful behavior toward each other
- **sibling abuse**: the harm is unidirectional.

(Caspi 2011)

In some cases, these terms are used interchangeably, blurring the lines between harmful and more benign sibling dynamics. Other attempts to define sibling abuse take into account the motivation for the behavior, as well as its severity and duration. In other words, if there is *intent* to harm, there is *actual* harm, and if the behavior is repeated over time, it is defined as abuse (Kiselica and Morrill-Richards 2007). Some definitions include the victim's perception: If the victim *perceives* an intent to harm, and *experiences* harm, it is abuse (Morrill and Bachman 2013).

Because sex play is considered part of normal development in Western societies, it is even more difficult to define sibling sexual abuse. Most definitions highlight behavior that is not motivated by age or developmentally appropriate curiosity, which continues over time. Many definitions of sibling abuse also specify that the age differences between siblings must be substantial (usually five years) to ensure that the behavior is not consensual, but is truly the result of power differences between siblings. However, sexual behavior leading to harm has been documented between siblings much closer in age than five years, and the younger sibling can be the perpetrator—particularly when a younger brother uses his gender advantage over a sister—an argument for removing the large age difference from the definition of sibling sexual abuse (Cyr et al. 2002). The National Task Force on Juvenile Sexual Offending defines sibling **incest** as "sexual acts initiated by one sibling toward another without the other's consent, by use of force or coercion, or where there is a power differential between siblings" (cited in Carlson, Maciol, and Schneider 2006: 20). In many cases, however, the term sibling incest is reserved for sexual intercourse between siblings.

CHALLENGES IN RESEARCHING SIBLING ABUSE

Defining sibling abuse is only one challenge in understanding this form of family violence. Researchers must decide which siblings should be studied: blood/adopted siblings, half-siblings, step-siblings, foster siblings, all of the above? What if the siblings don't live with each other full time, given that many children move between households? And if there are more than two children in the household, will all possible dyads be studied? Typically, researchers focus on full siblings, and on one dyad only—often the first and second born, or first and third—leaving dynamics between other siblings unexplored.

One difficulty in responding to sibling abuse is that most states do not explicitly recognize it as a form of family violence in their criminal codes; there is also no consensus across states on how to define sibling violence, when it *is* addressed. Most state statutes refer to violent behavior between "intimate partners or household members," but then go on to define relationships between various types of adult partners. Many statutes also specify that household members include anyone related by blood, marriage, or adoption, which *could* include siblings, but the law is rarely applied in that way. A few states (e.g., Iowa) specifically *exclude* anyone under the age of eighteen in the statutory language, precluding its application to under-age siblings. When children *are* included in definitions, it is in relation to other adult household members, who are assumed to be the perpetrators. Only a handful of states include specific language regarding siblings:

- Montana lists "brothers" and "sisters" as protected household members in its statute
- South Dakota specifies that "siblings" are protected
- Virginia uses "brothers, sisters, half-brothers, half-sisters" in its language
- West Virginia is the most specific, including "brother or sister . . . half-brother or half-sister . . . stepbrother or stepsister."

With this kind of specificity in the law, it is clear that sibling violence is taken seriously. Without it, victims must rely on the discretion of individual CPS workers and prosecutors (Caffaro, 2014).

Information retrieved from the National Conference of State Legislatures: www.ncsl.org/research/human-services/domestic-violence-domestic-abuse-definitions-and-relationships.aspx.

Much of the research on this topic uses the Conflict Tactic Scale (CTS), modified for siblings. This scale requires individuals to self-identify as being perpetrators of abuse. Since most people don't see themselves as being abusive and, as we've said, sibling abuse is particularly unrecognized as a problem, this methodological practice leads to widespread underreporting of sibling abuse (more below).

Finally, samples in sibling abuse research are heavily skewed toward college undergraduates (especially in psychology courses) and therapeutic samples (including case studies). This means that what we know about sibling abuse largely reflects the experiences of those that are more affluent, and white. These definitional and methodological challenges mean that we are only just beginning to understand the phenomenon of sibling abuse.

PREVALENCE OF SIBLING VIOLENCE

In recent decades, bullying by peers has received a great deal of attention from both scholars and the popular media and has been described as a pressing social problem; however, children are much more likely to be hit by a sibling than a peer, and abuse by siblings persists over a much longer period of time than abuse by someone outside the family (Krienert and Walsh 2011b; Katz and Hamama 2017). Sibling abuse is also more common than violence at the hand of a parent (Kiselica and Morrill-Richards 2007). These two facts alone suggest that sibling abuse is much more prevalent than is commonly believed.

The estimates of the prevalence of sibling abuse range widely, but tend to suggest that experiencing physical and/or psychological abuse at the hands of a sibling may be normative; Caffaro (2014) puts the range at 16–60 percent, Hoffman and Edwards (2004) from 60–80 percent. Ballantine (2012) estimates that the rate of sibling sexual abuse may be five times as common as parent–child incest. Because incidents of family violence in general are underreported, we should view these numbers as *under*estimates of the abuse children endure at the hands of their siblings.

TYPES OF SIBLING ABUSE

Physical Abuse

Physical violence between siblings includes pushing, shoving, pinching, hitting, slapping, biting, pulling hair, punching, kicking, threatening with a weapon, and using a weapon. Many consider lower levels of physical violence (pushing, shoving, pinching) to be normative among siblings. In fact, when children are too young to communicate effectively with words, this behavior is an easy way to show their frustration or displeasure.

DISTINCTIVE FORMS OF SIBLING ABUSE

Vernon Wiehe's (1997) work, in which he surveyed one hundred and fifty adults in the United States, offers rich descriptions of the experience of sibling abuse, and his respondents demonstrate how creatively cruel siblings can be. These survivors report a range of abusive behavior that other family violence victims typically do not:

- *Tickling*: "My brother and sister would hold me down and tickle me until I cried. They considered this play and would usually do it when my parents were gone. They would finally let me go and then laugh because I was a 'crybaby'" (p. 19).
- *Smothering*: "[My brother] put a pillow over my face and smothered me until I almost died. He was twice my size and very big. One time I did pass out and I came to when he gave me mouth-to-mouth resuscitation" (p. 23).
- *Confinement/suffocation*: "My brother forced me to the bottom of my sleeping bag and held the top closed so I couldn't get out or breathe. When I realized I couldn't get out, I became panic-stricken and thought I was going to die. Even as I write this, I am taken back to that moment and feel just the way I felt then. As an adult, I'm claustrophobic and can't have my face covered without panic setting in" (p. 23).
- *Causing blackouts*: "My brother discovered that hitting in the solar plexus caused one to black out. So he would hit me and watch me pass out" (p. 22).
- *Burning in effigy*: "My brothers and a cousin tied me to a stake and were preparing the ground around me to set it on fire. They were stopped and built a dummy of me instead and burnt that" (p. 46).
- *Abandonment*: "They would take my sister and me out into the field to pick berries. When we would hear dogs barking, they would tell us they were wild dogs and then they'd run away and make us find our own way home. We were only 5 or 6, and we didn't know our way home" (p. 51).

The effects of these kinds of traumas last a lifetime.

The available evidence suggests that **physical abuse** begins very early, around age six, and can last for a decade or more (McDonald and Martinez 2016; Meyers 2017). Many victims report that the abuse does not stop until they (or the perpetrating sibling) leave home, creating years of trauma—and even terror in some cases. Witness these examples from Vernon Wiehe's 1997 research, asking adult survivors to write about their experiences of physical abuse at the hands of their siblings:

- A minor argument would erupt into violence when I wouldn't do what my brother wanted me to or I wouldn't agree with his opinion. I was shaken, hit, kicked, and slapped. I was never badly hurt, but the level of my brother's rage was such that I was always afraid of it. I knew what was happening was wrong, but I don't think I thought of it as abuse at the time. I have blocked out my memories of these events for many years and still do not have all of them back (p. 17).

- [My brother] would engage me in wrestling matches daily, typically punching me in the stomach until I could not breathe, torturing my joints, wrists, and knees, spitting on me, putting his knees on my arms, and pinning me down and beating on my chest with his knuckles (p. 16).
- Once my sister was ironing. She was a teenager. I was between 4 and 5. I was curious as to what she was doing. I put my hands flat up on the ironing board and she immediately put the hot iron down on my hand. She laughed and told me to get lost. I still have the burn scar on my left hand (p. 21).
- My oldest brother would put his arms around my chest tight and not let me inhale any air while I had to watch in the mirror as he laughed and explained how I was going to die (p. 22).

In one study, half of the respondents report receiving what they characterized as "severe physical abuse" (Mackey, Fromuth, and Kelly 2010).

Some interesting patterns have been noted in the research in terms of who is victimized more often and under what circumstances. Step-siblings seem to experience lower levels of violence than full siblings, most likely because step-siblings may spend time in separate households, away from each other. There is also evidence that siblings who are more closely spaced together experience greater physical violence. There are some gender variations as well. While girls report more sibling victimization overall, boys report greater injury—especially if the abusive sibling is an older brother (Cicirelli 1995; Hoffman, Kiecolt, and Edwards 2005; Button and Gealt 2010; King et al. 2018). This last dynamic may reflect norms of masculinity that allow, or even encourage, greater physicality and roughhousing between boys, which may increase the risk for abuse and injury.

Psychological Abuse

There is a strong relationship between physical and **psychological abuse**. It is rare to see physical abuse between siblings in the absence of psychological abuse, and physical abuse is often the result of escalating verbal conflict. While the former may seem scarier in the moment, it is the latter that causes the most long-lasting harm, as psychological abuse wears down a sibling's very sense of self. This form of sibling violence is more common than physical abuse, and includes name-calling, taunting, belittling, humiliating, ignoring/rejecting, intimidating, harassing, and terrorizing. According to Mackey, Fromuth, and Kelly (2010), 97 percent of youth experience minor psychological abuse at the hand of a sibling; 80 percent report experiencing severe psychological abuse. The incidence of verbal abuse, in particular, increases with age, as children transition from using physical violence to control siblings and move to the psychological tactics described above. Again, Wiehe's (1997) research provides examples of how siblings wield psychological weapons:

- I was constantly being told I was no good, a pig, a whore, slut, all sexually oriented negatives. I was constantly emotionally being degraded (p. 38).
- My sister would get her friends to sing songs about how ugly I was (p. 41).
- [My siblings] called me names. I was told my parents hated me. If my brothers found out I cared about something—for example, toys—they were taken and destroyed in front of me (p. 52).
- My second oldest brother shot my little dog that I loved dearly. It loved me—only me. I cried by its grave for several days. Twenty years passed before I could care for another dog (p. 54).

This last example represents a level of cruelty that may predict abusive behavior in adult relationships, as we shall see in our discussion of intimate partner violence.

Sexual Abuse

Sexual abuse between siblings has received the most attention by scholars. The most common form of sexual abuse by a sibling is fondling of genitals, breasts, or buttocks; other activities include being forced to fondle others, being forced to expose oneself to others, being forced to witness sex acts or watch pornography, as well as penetration with objects, and vaginal, oral, or anal rape. Because there is such a strong cultural prohibition on nudity and sexual activity for children (especially between family members), there is often a "grooming process" associated with sexual abuse. One sibling will approach another and attempt to desensitize the victim or take advantage of naivete. Young children's normal sexual development is rooted in curiosity and self-exploration; they routinely "play doctor," and delight in using "potty words" and telling dirty jokes. They are curious about their bodies and those of others—particularly the other gender (McVeigh 2003). Siblings can use all of these traits to their advantage when intent on sexual exploitation. They can trick a sibling with "games" that push the norms around bodily integrity and boundaries.

They may bribe a sibling with promises of money or treats in exchange for submitting to their requests, or threaten violence if the victim discloses what the perpetrator has been doing. Sexual abuse is often carefully timed, taking place while parents are away, or at night when everyone in the house is asleep and the perpetrator can sneak into the victim's bed undetected.

Most victims of sibling sexual abuse are under the age of thirteen, and the mean age of victimization is eight (Kreinert and Walsh 2011a). In the great majority of cases, brothers are sexually abusing (typically younger) sisters, though boys also abuse brothers; girls, however, report higher rates of injury from sexual abuse. In addition to gender, other dimensions of social power may also come into play, including age, size, strength, and developmental ability, with older and stronger siblings perpetrating the abuse (Caffaro 2014). It is also common for sibling perpetrators to have their own history of victimization, using their sibling relationships to recreate their own trauma, but this time from a position of power. Step-siblings present another layer of complexity when it comes to sexual abuse. Since they are not biologically related to each other, they do not technically violate the incest taboo (the prohibition on sexual relationships between nuclear family members), but power differentials can still lead to exploitative behaviors and injury.

Wiehe's (1997) respondents again provide examples of the range of sexual abuse children experience at the hands of their siblings:

- I was about 6 years old. My brother persuaded me to lie down on the bathroom floor. There were some neighbor boys in the house. He promised not to let them in. He got me on the floor with my pants down and then opened the door. He laughed about it (p. 66).

- I was 4 years old and my older brother told me that he wanted to show me something that Mom and Dad did. I refused. Then he offered to pay me a quarter and said that I would like it. If I turned him down, it was clear that he would hurt me. So I gave in and he made me perform oral sex with him (p. 64).

- My brother sat on his lower bunk and made me suck his penis. He urinated in my mouth. I was in kindergarten, he must have been in the fourth grade. I remember I became very angry. He laughed. It seems my parents were not at home at this time or in another part of the house (p. 65).

- My brother threatened to kill me if I told our parents about him molesting me. I was 3 or 4 years of age at the time; he was about 18. He showed me the butcher block we kept in the cellar with the ax and blood. He said he'd kill me there if I told (p. 67).

- My earliest memory is of my brother sneaking into my bed while we were on vacation and were sharing one bedroom. This happened while my parents were still out on the town. I pretended I was asleep and it was very difficult to determine what to do about it because of the physical pleasure but inappropriate and selfish behavior on his part (p. 71).
- I would try to put off going to bed. I would try to cover up tight with my blankets. It didn't help. My brother would come into my room and touch me all over. I would pretend I was asleep. After he left, I would cry and cry (p. 76).

In some cases, sexual activity between siblings represents an attempt to meet needs for warmth and attention in a family environment otherwise characterized by emotional abandonment. Parents are not meeting the children's needs and so they turn to each other for physical closeness and comfort. In this situation it is still possible for one sibling to exploit another sexually, but it is also possible that the victim is a somewhat willing participant, viewing the sexual relationship with a sibling as the only available outlet for companionship and caring (Ballantine 2012).

Disclosing sexual abuse presents special difficulties for sibling victims. In many cases, parents do not believe them, or view the behavior as "harmless." They may have their own history of sexual abuse and so view the experience as "normal." Many children never disclose the abuse because they feel partly responsible for what happened. This is particularly true if they experienced any of the activity as pleasurable. It is possible, even under conditions of fear, to experience sexual arousal. If this happens, the victim may believe that s/he secretly wanted or invited it, may feel partially responsible for the abuse, and fear being blamed for it. For these reasons, children sexually abused by siblings are much less likely to disclose this than those abused by adults.

CASE STUDY IN SIBLING ABUSE: IVELISSE'S STORY

Ivelisse attributes much of the violence she experienced in her life to the Hispanic culture in which she was raised. She was born in Puerto Rico. When Ivelisse was about eight years old she moved to the mainland US with her mother, father, and brother (Miguel) who was two and a half years older than she. Gender expectations in the family were very traditional and distinctive. Ivelisse was expected to learn to cook, clean, and perform traditional Latin dances; Miguel was allowed to do whatever he wanted.

continues

CASE STUDY IN SIBLING ABUSE: IVELISSE'S STORY *continued*

The sibling pair had an abusive upbringing. Their parents used to beat them fairly regularly—Ivelisse remembers having to find a way to dress alone in gym class so no one would see her bruises—and when her parents were not home, they were left in the care of a neighbor who would lock Miguel in a closet and wrap a chain around Ivelisse and lock her to a fence all day, out in the blazing sun. When the family moved to the US, the siblings were left alone.

At first, Ivelisse was relieved to be far away from the cruel neighbor. She and Miguel would fight at times, even hitting each other when angry, but they quickly made up and often played together. But once they were left alone, things started to change. Miguel began to sit very close to Ivelisse when they would play, and ask her questions like, "Have you ever kissed someone?" or "Have you ever seen a penis?" She had no idea what he was talking about. Then he began saying things like, "Take off your shirt—it's dirty. Mom's gonna get mad at you." Ivelisse would panic, thinking she would be beaten or locked in a closet, so she would comply. One day Miguel said, "I wanna try something." He called it a "game." He grabbed Ivelisse's face and kissed her on the mouth. She didn't know what was happening, but she knew she didn't like it. Quickly, Miguel moved from using the word "game" to saying, "hey—I need to practice something." Then he began to say, "*we* need to practice."

During this time, Miguel would talk Ivelisse into taking her clothes off, and he would undress as well. He would convince her to shower with him. He would touch her breasts and started "working his way down." Ivelisse didn't quite understand what was happening, but she knew she "didn't like this game." But he was her big brother, and she was scared of her mom and her dad—and, at this point, she was afraid of *Miguel*. Ivelisse was not allowed to lock a door ("You are a child, you don't get privacy," her parents said), so she started to avoid taking showers—she would go as long as two and a half weeks without a shower. Throughout this time, Ivelisse's parents were working hard, trying to support their family; they were not really paying attention to what was happening between the siblings. Miguel eventually attempted to penetrate Ivelisse and she "freaked out." She ran from the room and he did not come after her again.

During the time Miguel was abusing her, Ivelisse began to realize that she was being targeted because she was a girl: "This would not be happening to me if I was a boy." So Ivelisse began to steal Miguel's clothes. Her parents punished her severely for it (physically), but she thought that dressing like a boy would protect her. She also tried to avoid Miguel—by hiding or spending time in the bathroom. At this point, Ivelisse "missed the abusive babysitter." In addition to hiding at home, she joined every club at school she could find so that she could be out of the house as much as possible. Even though she was "terrible at sports," she joined every team—partly to escape her home, and partly to compete with her brother. She channeled her anger with him into determination to best him; she embraced the identity of "tomboy" and attempted to be more masculine than her brother.

continues

CASE STUDY IN SIBLING ABUSE: IVELISSE'S STORY *continued*

Her experience with Miguel made Ivelisse afraid of men in general, so she decided that she needed to gain weight to "protect herself." She binged and developed "body issues." She was active in sports but also eating tremendous amounts of food; she hoped that the extra weight would keep her from attracting men's attention. As she became a young adult she created a completely masculine persona—to the point that she was unable to use a woman's public restroom. She smoked pot "all the time" in an attempt to manage the aftermath of the abuse.

Recovery has been a slow process for Ivelisse. Whenever she was disciplined as a child, Ivelisse was always told that she "deserved what she got." She internalized that message and felt that she deserved what Miguel did to her. Eventually, Ivelisse lost the extra weight and let her hair grow because, above all else, she wanted to feel like a woman and to feel "pretty." She felt that her brother stole her femininity—and her feminine identity—from her, because she had given up being a woman in the hopes that she would never be harmed in that way again.

When, at age twenty, Ivelisse finally found the courage to tell her parents ("your son did this to me . . ."), her mother said, "Well, that's normal. Brothers and sisters do that." They didn't think it was "a big deal," and they continued to minimize and ignore the abuse. This response infuriated Ivelisse, especially since her brother had never apologized or acknowledged the abuse—and still hasn't. The two are still very active in sports, and competitive with each other. Ivelisse had the opportunity to "get Miguel back" one day in the Jiu-Jitsu club they both belong to; the brother and sister were encouraged to wrestle each other. At first Ivelisse was reluctant, but then agreed. She quickly put Miguel in a chokehold and he blacked out; the spectators had to pull her off of him. She had been waiting for that moment:

> He blacked out my entire childhood. He blacked out my womanhood . . . We both went through the abuse. I remember him screaming for getting bad grades, and I would sit and cry in the corner when I would hear him screaming and crying, when my father would be in his room abusing him, and beating him. And there was a few times where I felt sorry for him . . . being locked in a dark closet . . . when my father would beat him and he would scream. I tried to make excuses for him, why he did it . . . but I became the victim. Where we were both the victims before, now you made me the victim . . . "We went through this together, why me? I had your back!" I remember I even got in between him and my father, and taking punches for him. "Why me? . . . You took so much away from me, when I defended you."

At one point, Ivelisse had a "break"; she woke up two days later on a ventilator in hospital due to an overdose, with no memory of how it happened. Ivelisse is in good health now, and married, but she is still working through the anger and the body issues, especially being comfortable in her body. She continues to seek therapeutic help and is just finally starting to feel safe. Reflecting on all that she has endured—the combination of being physically, emotionally, and sexually abused over her childhood, and the impact it has had on her—Ivelisse says, "I would rather be out in the blazing sun, chained to that fence."

RISK FACTORS FOR SIBLING ABUSE

Cultural Risk Factors

Normalization of violence, beliefs about sibling rivalry, and the construction of masculinity are the main **cultural risk factors** associated with sibling abuse. Violent themes in print media, television programming, movies, video games, and Internet content make violence seem pervasive, and often communicate that force is an effective—even permissible—way to get what one wants. The graphic nature and intensity of violent content has accelerated in recent decades, and with the proliferation of computers and mobile devices, children are often viewing this material without adults who could provide critique or moral context that might blunt its impact.

We have seen how the normalization of sibling rivalry can obscure the abuse that occurs in families. If a child discloses abuse, it may be met with disbelief, minimized, or parents may blame *both* children, saying "it takes two to tango" or "you got what you deserve." For these reasons, most perpetrators do not self-identify as being abusive, even when their actions clearly are (Mackey, Fromuth, and Kelly 2010). The normalization of sibling rivalry shapes how parents respond to friction between their children. Many parents, viewing sibling conflict as a normal part of growing up, will leave children to sort out their disagreements among themselves; it is seen as an opportunity for children to learn problem-solving and negotiation skills. Unfortunately, it could also be an opportunity for one sibling to dominate and abuse another outside of an adult's watchful eye.

The cultural construction of masculinity clearly shapes the dynamics of sibling abuse. We have seen a clear gendered dynamic of brothers victimizing sisters (especially sexually), as well as younger brothers (especially physically). Further, if there is a strong pattern of male dominance in the home, the level of sibling violence rises. In such families girls are typically expected to perform household chores, whereas boys are not, and younger sisters are vulnerable to the abuse of older brothers—especially if they refuse to wait on them, or challenge their authority.

Notions of masculinity further shape how this behavior is interpreted. If it comes to light, this abuse is often interpreted as "a stage he's going through" or a "natural" expression of masculinity (i.e., "boys will be boys"). Interestingly, this expectation that boys are the violent ones may also obscure the violence perpetrated by girls. Parents and professionals may not recognize girls as abusers, and may dismiss the damage that they do (Kiselica and Morrill-Richards 2007).

There is very little evidence in the literature about racial/ethnic differences in the rates or dynamics related to sibling abuse. One notable exception is the exploratory work of Rapoza et al. (2010), who find that what constitutes "severe" vs. "mild" violence can vary across cultures. For example, while most racial/ethnic groups view physical aggression as "extreme," and therefore more problematic, Asian Pacific individuals are more likely to view psychological aggression as an extreme form of sibling abuse. White parents report more parenting stress than African American parents, and white children report more abuse (Caffaro 2014). African American parents tend to rely on a wider network of support for caregiving, which may explain this difference.

Familial Risk Factors

Family norms around bathing, sleeping, and nudity have been shown to affect rates of sibling sexual abuse. Family nudity—between children, between parents and children—increases the risk for sibling sexual abuse, as does sharing a bed with the other gender. Co-sleeping, co-bathing, and parent–child nudity may generate confusion around bodily boundaries. These practices also represent grooming opportunities for siblings intent on perpetrating abuse (Johnson, Huang, and Simpson 2009; Griffee et al. 2016).

Family dynamics, especially dysfunction and a parent's own history of abuse, dramatically increase the risk of sibling abuse. There are many ways parents can create an environment that fosters sibling abuse. First, parents themselves may be abusive—to a partner, or to the children—both of which increase the risk of sibling abuse. If a parent is abusing a particular child, it gives siblings a license to join in. In some cases, parents attempt to respond to sibling abuse in ways that make the situation worse; for example, if a parent beats an abusive sibling as punishment for the behavior, the perpetrator may intensify the abuse on the victim in retaliation.

Families may be dysfunctional in absence of any abuse perpetrated by parents. Adults in the home may be overwhelmed by financial or health concerns that prevent them from parenting effectively. In some cases, children may be lacking emotional warmth as well as supervision, which constitutes another risk for sibling abuse—especially sexual abuse. Where there is little emotional support, siblings may develop inappropriate sexual relationships to meet their needs for closeness and caring, as we have already discussed. In some cases, the source of parental dysfunction is their own history of abuse. They may be dealing with the aftermath of their own trauma, which has left them emotionally unavailable to attend to the needs of their children.

Parents may also have unrealistic expectations of what is developmentally appropriate for children. We have already seen that parents may overestimate children's ability to problem-solve effectively (i.e., without violence) on their own. Many also place older siblings in a supervisory role over younger ones. By age twelve, many are seen as capable babysitters. However, not all are emotionally mature enough to handle that responsibility at that age, or they may see it as an opportunity to exercise power over a captive sibling. One final thought: these **familial risk factors** are all exacerbated if a child does not have any support systems *out*side the family to turn to for help.

THEORETICAL EXPLANATIONS

Psychological Theories

These approaches look at individual risk factors for sibling abuse, such as something unusual about a child that siblings can use as an excuse for belittling or harassment. Being overweight or wearing glasses may make one a target, as does having a physical or developmental disability. **Trauma theory** has been used to understand the dynamics between perpetrator and victim. For example, attempting to accommodate or appease an abusive sibling is one hallmark of trauma, as is hypervigilance—being constantly on guard and learning to sense the moods of the abuser as a way to avoid or manage the harm done (Meyers 2016). Trauma theory can also sensitize us to the motivations of the perpetrator. As we've said, in some circumstances the abuser has a history of trauma and is attempting to relive the experience from a position of power, in order to develop a sense of control or mastery over the trauma. Even parents can be traumatized when they eventually learn of the abuse—especially in the case of sibling sexual abuse. **Resiliency theory** highlights the ways that siblings are able to successfully manage, or recover from, the pain that they have endured. Key to resilience is the level of social support available to the child. In many cases, that support comes from a caring adult outside of the family, but it is also possible for another sibling to provide the affection and attention necessary to minimize the damage from sibling abuse and help the victim recover.

Ecological and Systems Theories

These frameworks are social-psychological in nature, and sensitize us to the connectivity between the individual child, the sibling dyad, and the family as a whole. Some ecological approaches would also look at the extended family system and neighborhood or community. The important insight from this perspective is that the child (and the sibling dyad) does not exist in isolation; what goes on around them has an impact on them. **Systems theory** is similar to ecological approaches, though it is primarily used by counselors and family therapists, and typically does not reach beyond the nuclear family. At the heart of this approach is the assumption that all family members play a role in family dynamics, including abuse (Haskins 2003).

This insight can be particularly useful when trying to intervene in sibling abuse, or assist in the recovery from the harm done by it. If others in the family were aware of what was happening, and tacitly endorsed it, or simply allowed it to continue, addressing that dynamic would be key to ending the abuse and improving the long-term health of the family. And since we know that multiple forms of family violence may exist at once, taking a systems approach encourages therapists to look for *other* forms of abuse when the first one comes to light.

Conflict Theories

Conflict theory, broadly, underscores inequalities and abuses of power. We have seen that conflict and competition between siblings, or sibling rivalry, can be a precursor to sibling abuse as struggles for attention and other resources escalate. **Feminist theory** adds to our understanding of sibling abuse by focusing on the effects of patriarchy on social life. The cultural preference for male dominance, and men's disproportionate power, create the strong pattern of brothers abusing sisters—even older sisters. This pattern is particularly pronounced in the presence of other gendered power differentials, such as the expectation that girls should perform household chores while boys should not. Race/class/gender theory has received very little attention in the literature on sibling abuse, and the results that exist are mixed. There is some evidence that low income, low education levels, and race/ethnicity are *not* factors in explaining sibling sexual abuse (Cicirelli 1995; Caffaro 2014). However, other research suggests that cultural practices or economic circumstances that put siblings and cousins in very close proximity, especially sleeping together, may increase the risk of sexual abuse (Bass et al. 2006), and we noted a few racial/ethnic differences in how sibling abuse is defined earlier. Finally, class and race play a role in which cases of sibling abuse receive the attention and help they need. Given the difficulties of accessing mental health care in the United States, this inequality has lifelong implications for a child's ability to recover from the trauma of sibling abuse.

Social Learning Theory

There is a great deal of evidence that a child learns to abuse a sibling by watching a parent being abused by a partner, a sibling being abused by a parent, or through the child's own experience of parental or sibling abuse. A parent who lashes out in anger or frustration and harms another family member teaches a child that behavior is acceptable—and effective. This is true when the parent is abusive, or uses spanking as a form of discipline (Hoffman and Edwards 2004). A child who abuses a sibling may even be rewarded by other family members—this is especially true for boys (Hoffman, Kiecolt, and Edwards 2005). The depictions of violence in our culture more broadly also communicate that the use of force is an acceptable and effective way to get what one wants.

OUTCOMES OF SIBLING ABUSE

Damage to Sense of Self

Sibling relationships have a major impact on psychosocial development. The available evidence strongly suggests that sibling abuse represents an additional source of trauma for children (after controlling for both parental and peer abuse) that has long-lasting effects (King et al. 2018). Some research even suggests that sibling abuse is *more* harmful than parental abuse (Caffaro 2014; Meyers 2017). For many, the greatest damage incurred is to the sense of self. Sibling abuse survivors report low self-esteem or self-worth, in addition to anxiety and depression. Other symptomatology includes eating disorders, substance abuse, and post-traumatic stress disorder (PTSD) (Wiehe 1997), as well as suicidal feelings and a lasting sense of betrayal by parents who did not stop the abuse (Rudd and Herzberger 1999). Sibling abuse is also linked to poorer physical and mental health (Caspi 2011), as well as sexual dysfunction (Wiehe 1997). Individuals who have been especially traumatized may experience gaps in childhood memory that persist into adulthood. Interestingly, *perpetrating* sibling violence, especially emotional and physical, has also been correlated with increased anxiety (Mackey, Fromuth, and Kelly 2010).

One of the most enduring and corrosive effects of sibling abuse is the ongoing self-blame that plagues many survivors. They have been told that they "deserve what they got," and internalized that message. For those who experienced sexual abuse, they may berate themselves for being "stupid" or naïve in "allowing" the abuse to occur and, as mentioned earlier, if they experienced any arousal during the abuse, that only enhances their sense of complicity and deep feelings of shame.

Damage to Relationships

Sibling abuse also damages the victim's ability to form other healthy relationships. Experiencing physical violence increases the risk that one will be physically aggressive toward others. In fact, sibling violence in particular teaches children to escalate with a pattern of attack and counterattack, and they often transfer this knowledge to relationships with peers (Krienert and Walsh 2011b). Survivors also report difficulty in forming successful dating relationships and partnerships. Women, in particular, may hold distorted beliefs about men and how to relate to them

(Carlson 2011), and both men and women report greater use of both emotional and physical violence toward their romantic partners. Interestingly, the kind of abuse endured at the hands of siblings may not predict the type of abuse one uses in the dating context. Simonelli et al. (2002) report that women who were *emotionally* abused were more likely to use *physical* violence against a partner; and for men, *any* type of abuse by a sibling was predictive of dating violence. In short, experiencing a particular type of aggression in childhood does not correlate with using that particular type of aggression in adulthood. Sadly, sibling violence *does* predict later violence toward one's own children (Caffaro 2014).

Sibling abuse also has a lasting impact on relationships in the family. Survivors often resent parents, or other family members, who were in a position to stop the abuse but did not, or who did not show the proper level of outrage once the abuse was disclosed. It is not uncommon for adult survivors to break contact with the offending sibling, or even the entire family, out of anger or in an attempt to heal. In other circumstances, victims may continue to keep the abuse a secret; this is especially true for women who endured sexual abuse at the hands of their brothers. In these cases, the daughters do not think their parents (or the family) are strong enough to handle the disclosure, and so they choose to keep the secret in order to maintain ongoing family relationships (Welfare 2008).

Repeated Victimization

In the absence of full disclosure and proper intervention and recovery, sibling abuse survivors run the risk of repeated victimization. This may occur within the family, where other siblings, or even parents, join in the abuse. It may also happen in peer relationships, or subsequent dating contexts. The damage inflicted on the sense of self can make a survivor a target for others who would seek to be in a relationship where they can exert dominance and use violence with impunity. This makes the intervention and recovery process (which we will discuss below) crucial for the long-term health of sibling abuse survivors.

Criminal Behavior

In addition to aggression in other relationships, experiencing sibling abuse increases the risk of delinquent behavior, including arrests in adolescence (Caspi 2011). Experiencing any kind of sibling abuse increases the risk of sexual offending later in life; sibling incest particularly increases this risk (Hanser and Mire 2008). Taken together, it is clear from the available evidence that the effects of sibling abuse are significant, distinctive, cumulative, and long-lasting.

SIBLING ABUSE INTERVENTION AND PREVENTION

The first step in intervening in sibling abuse is recognizing the magnitude of the problem. We've already seen that parents often do not make a distinction between sibling rivalry and abuse. In many cases this is because they simply have trouble distinguishing between low-risk and problematic behavior. In one study, parents could not reliably discern what is "normal," particularly for children under the age of four, and barely a third could identify the appropriate response to a range of circumstances presented (Marriage et al. 2017). Even when intervention for serious behavior was warranted, parents were much more likely to try to handle the situation themselves, rather than calling in professional help.

Unfortunately, even if parents do turn to professionals, they may not be well educated on sibling abuse either. Most therapists—even those specializing in family dynamics—do not address sibling relationships in their practice (Caffaro and Conn-Caffaro 2005), and very few routinely screen for a history of sibling abuse in their intake assessment. If sibling abuse emerges as part of the therapeutic process, many professionals minimize the impact of it on the presenting problems, focusing instead on parental relationships (Rowntree 2007). Similarly, in a small study assessing school counselors' beliefs about sibling abuse, many reported that this was the first time they had ever thought about the topic (Stutey 2015).

Intervening effectively in sibling abuse requires knowing how to handle the disclosure. Children may not speak about the abuse unless asked directly. And, as we've seen, many victims are met with disbelief when they try to tell others about the abuse; this further traumatizes the individual and increases the long-term harm. Some families are resistant to disclosure because they are worried about the stigma it will bring. They may try to manage the behavior themselves, as noted above.

Disclosure outside the family presents its own challenges. Even if the claim of abuse is deemed credible there may be no mandate to report sibling abuse, in contrast to other forms of family violence (Caspi 2011), or, if it comes to the attention of Child Protective Services (CPS), it may be treated as a case of parental neglect as CPS workers are not always trained to spot sibling abuse (Caffaro 2014).

Once the behavior is disclosed, a thorough assessment should take into consideration the range, severity, duration, and harm caused, in addition to the level of fear the behavior induced in the victim. The ongoing safety of the victim is a concern that raises unique issues in the case of sibling abuse. If the abuser of a child is an adult, it is a much more straightforward proposition to remove the abuser from the home; when it is a sibling, the calculation becomes more complex. Arguably, the perpetrating sibling needs parental time, support, and affection as much as the victim does. Negotiating these relationships, while ensuring the abuse does not continue, can be difficult.

The final intervention stage is successful recovery from the abuse, which typically includes therapeutic intervention. Ideally, the abuse would be disclosed early on and the entire family can benefit from the recovery process. In addition to attending to the needs of the identified victim, the perpetrator would be assessed for a history of victimization, which could be a contributory factor to the abuse. All family members would have the opportunity to process the vicarious trauma endured at the disclosure of the abuse, and to manage any shame or guilt associated with it. Parents, and even other siblings, may grieve over the lost innocence (particularly in the case of sexual abuse) the victim endured, and blame themselves for not having known about the abuse, or coming to the aid of the victim sooner. Successful recovery for the entire family requires parents to support both the victim and the perpetrator, but to also hold the latter accountable for the abusive behavior. Having support outside the family during this process helps build resiliency for all family members and increases the chance of therapeutic success (Welfare 2008). Though families are often resistant to disclosing incidents of abuse, that does not mean they are resistant to change, particularly if family relationships are otherwise close or loving (Bass et al. 2006).

Family response to sibling abuse is not always smooth. If they have few resources of their own, parents may feel their only option to get help is to contact CPS or the police; however, then they lose control of the process and may find these agencies to be intrusive. Or they may find themselves forced into counseling, leaving them feeling that their privacy and autonomy have been breached (Kiselica and Morrill-Richards 2007). And if they do not willingly embrace the therapeutic process, it is unlikely to be successful.

Since sibling abuse is often unacknowledged in families, it is far more likely that therapeutic help will not be sought until adulthood, after the survivor leaves the family of origin. In some cases, this is the first time the survivor labels the behavior as sibling abuse, or discloses it to another person. Even in adulthood, the recovery process remains the same—examining the trauma and its effects, as well as managing relationships with other others, including family members. As noted above, if the abuse is not acknowledged by other family members, the survivor may decide that the best option is to sever ties—either with the perpetrator, or the entire family, in order to facilitate the healing process (Meyers 2016).

Prevention of sibling abuse begins in the home, with the dynamics encouraged by parents. First, they must provide adequate supervision and be realistic in their assessment of when an older child is able to stand in for the parent. Parents must also model healthy communication and help children work through conflicts without resorting to abuse or violence. Children should be given the right to decide who touches their bodies, and discussions of sex and bodily development should be open enough to address questions while maintaining rights to privacy and bodily integrity (Wiehe 1997). Parents should be sensitive to any behavior that suggests fear between siblings, such as crying when the parents are planning to leave the home.

There is much parents can do to encourage healthy relationships between siblings. Positive reinforcement for good behavior, such as when children are playing nicely together, or expressing caring and empathy for each other, is important. Parents can encourage warm relationships between siblings by minimizing comparisons, especially those that would paint one child in a negative light. Parents can also build supportive relationships between siblings by helping them find shared interests and carving out time for siblings to enjoy them together.

Many scholars argue that the best preventive strategy would be a public health approach to sibling abuse, enlisting schools and the community at large in the effort. Schools in particular have an important role to play in addressing sibling abuse, since teachers and school counselors develop long-standing relationships with children; schools also represent the front lines of anti-bullying/anti-violence efforts, and sibling abuse awareness could be part of this (Krienert and Walsh 2011a, 2011b; Caffaro 2014). A public health approach means that in addition to parents, a wide range of professionals, from teachers, therapists, and social workers, to police, court officers, and CPS workers, will need much more comprehensive training on sibling violence. Awareness is the first step in both prevention and intervention.

CONCLUSIONS

While much more research is needed on this topic, the available evidence suggests that sibling abuse is a serious problem that has received insufficient attention. It is more common than both bullying and abuse by a parent, and does more damage. Culturally we view sibling rivalry as a normative experience; sibling abuse appears to be normative as well. Stories shared by survivors demonstrate the trauma and lasting effects from abuse by a sibling. Given just this handful of facts, it is a problem that can no longer be ignored.

Addressing it may well require a public health approach, especially given cultural beliefs about the "naturalness" of sibling rivalry, the common precursor to sibling abuse. Even those who come into contact with children regularly—teachers, school counselors, social workers, and (mental) health professionals—seem uninformed and ill-prepared to manage a disclosure of sibling abuse. Greater awareness of the problem is the first step in crafting an effective response to it—a response that is long overdue.

RESOURCES

American Association for Marriage and Family Therapy: www.aamft.org/Consumer_ Updates/Sibling_Violence.aspx.

REFERENCES

Ballantine, Margaret. 2012. "Sibling Incest Dynamics: Therapeutic Themes and Clinical Challenges." *Clinical Social Work 40*: 56–65.

Bass, Linda, Brent Taylor, Carmen Knudson-Martin, and Douglas Huenergardt. 2006. "Making Sense of Abuse: Case Studies in Sibling Incest." *Contemporary Family Therapy 28*: 87–109.

Button, Deeanna, and Roberta Gealt. 2010. "High Risk Behaviors Among Victims of Sibling Violence." *Journal of Family Violence 25*: 131–140.

Caffaro, John. 2014. *Sibling Abuse Trauma: Assessment of Intervention Strategies for Children, Families, and Adults*, 2nd ed. New York: Routledge.

Caffaro, John, and Allison Conn-Caffaro. 2005. "Threatening Sibling Abuse Families." *Aggression and Violent Behavior 10*: 604–623.

Carlson, Bonnie. 2011. "Sibling Incest: Adjustment in Adult Women Survivors." *Families in Society: The Journal of Contemporary Social Forces 92*: 77–83.

Carlson, Bonnie, Katherine Maciol, and Joanne Schneider. 2006. "Sibling Incest: Reports from Forty-One Survivors." *Journal of Child Sexual Abuse 15*: 19–34.

Caspi, Jonathan. 2011. *Sibling Aggression*. New York: Springer.

Cicirelli, Victor. 1995. *Sibling Relationships Across the Lifespan*. New York: Plenum Press.

Cyr, Mireille, John Wright, Pierre McDuff, and Alain Perron. 2002. "Intrafamilial Sexual Abuse: Brother–Sister Incest Does Not Differ from Father–Daughter and Stepfather–Stepdaughter Incest." *Child Abuse and Neglect 26*: 957–973.

Griffee, Karen, Sam Swindell, Stephen O'Keefe, Sandra Stroebel, Keith Beard, Shih-Y Kuo, and Walter Stroupe. 2016. "Etiological Risk Factors for Sibling Incest: Data from an Anonymous Computer-Assisted Self-Interview." *Sexual Abuse: A Journal of Research and Treatment 28*: 620–659.

Hanser, Robert, and Scott Mire. 2008. "Juvenile Sex Offenders in the United States and Australia: A Comparison." *International Review of Law Computers & Technology 22*: 101–114.

Haskins, Cora. 2003. "Treating Sibling Incest Using a Family Systems Approach." *Journal of Mental Health Counseling 25*: 337–350.

Hoffman, Kristi, and John Edwards. 2004. "An Integrated Theoretical Model of Sibling Violence and Abuse." *Journal of Family Violence 19*: 185–200.

Hoffman, Kristi, K. Jill Kiecolt, and John Edwards. 2005. "Physical Violence between Siblings: A Theoretical and Empirical Analysis." *Journal of Family Issues 26*: 1103–1130.

Johnson, Toni Cavanaugh, Bevan Emma Huang, and Pippa M. Simpson. 2009. "Sibling Family Practices: Guidelines for Health Boundaries." *Journals of Child Sexual Abuse 18*: 339–354.

Katz, Carmit, and Liat Hamama. 2017. "From My Own Brother in My Own Home: Children's Experiences and Perceptions Following Alleged Sibling Incest." *Journal of Interpersonal Violence 32*: 3648–3668.

King, Alan, Sage Ballantyne, Abrianna Ratzak, Shane Knutson, Tiffany Russell, Colton Pogalz, and Cody Breen. 2018. "Sibling Hostility and Externalized Symptoms of Psychological Distress." *Journal of Aggression, Maltreatment, & Trauma 27*: 523–540.

Kiselica, Mark, and Mandy Morrill-Richards. 2007. "Sibling Maltreatment: The Forgotten Abuse." *Journal of Counseling and Development 85*: 146–159.

Krienert, Jessie, and Jeffrey Walsh. 2011a. "Sibling Sexual Abuse: An Empirical Analysis of Offender, Victim, and Event Characteristics in National Incident-Based Reporting System (NIBRS) Data, 2000–2007." *Journal of Child Sexual Abuse 20*: 353–372.

Krienert, Jessie, and Jeffrey Walsh. 2011b. "My Brother's Keeper: A Contemporary Examination of Reported Sibling Violence Using National Level Data, 2000–2005." *Journal of Family Violence 26*: 331–342.

Mackey, Amber, Mary Ellen Fromuth, and David Kelly. 2010. "The Association of Sibling Relationship and Abuse with Later Psychological Adjustment." *Journal of Interpersonal Violence 25*: 955–958.

Marriage, Nathan, Anika Blackley, Karlina Panagiotaros, Soraya Seklaoui, Jed van den Bergh, and Russell Hawkins. 2017. "Assessing Parental Understanding of Sexualized Behavior in Children and Adolescents." *Child Abuse & Neglect 72*: 196–205.

McDonald, Courtney, and Katherine Martinez. 2016. "Parental and Others' Responses to Physical Sibling Violence: A Descriptive Analysis of Victims' Retrospective Accounts." *Journal of Family Violence 31*: 401–410.

McVeigh, Mary Jo. 2003. "'But She Didn't Say No': An Exploration of Sibling Sexual Abuse." *Australian Social Work 56*: 116–126.

Meyers, Amy. 2016. "Trauma and Recovery: Factors Contributing to Resiliency of Survivors of Sibling Abuse." *The Family Journal: Counseling and Therapy for Couples and Families 24*: 147–156.

Meyers, Amy. 2017. "Lifting the Veil: The Lived Experience of Sibling Abuse." *Qualitative Social Work 16*: 333–350.

Morrill, Mandy, and Curt Bachman. 2013. "Confronting the Gender Myth: An Exploration of Variance of Male Versus Female Experience with Sibling Abuse." *Journal of Interpersonal Violence 28*: 1693–1708.

Rapoza, Kimberly, Kelley Cook, Tanvi Zaveri, and Kathleen Malley-Morrison. 2010. "Ethnic Perspectives on Sibling Abuse in the Unites States." *Journal of Family Issues* *31*: 808–829.

Rowntree, Margaret. 2007. "Responses to Sibling Sexual Abuse: Are They as Harmful as the Abuse?" *Australian Social Work 60*: 347–361.

Rudd, Jane, and Sharon Herzberger. 1999. "Brother–Sister Incest—Father–Daughter Incest: A Comparison of Characteristics and Consequences." *Child Abuse and Neglect 23*: 915–928.

Simonelli, Catherine, Thomas Mullis, Ann Elliott, and Thomas Pierce. 2002. "Abuse by Siblings and Subsequent Experiences of Violence Within the Dating Relationship." *Journal of Interpersonal Violence 17*: 103–121.

Stutey, Diane. 2015. "Sibling Abuse: A Study of School Counselors' Shared Attitudes and Beliefs." *The Professional Counselor 5*: 390–406.

Welfare, Anne. 2008. "How Qualitative Research Can Inform Clinical Interventions in Families Recovering from Sibling Sexual Abuse." *The Australian New Zealand Journal of Family Therapy 29*: 139–147.

Wiehe, Vernon. 1997. *Sibling Abuse*. Thousand Oaks, CA: Sage.

8

OUTCOMES OF CHILD ABUSE

Increased Risk for Experiencing Violence in Adulthood

> She would go downtown and take out warrants out on him and restraining orders, and he'll go back, and one night she took and killed him. You know, they got into a fight, and one night she took and got it. They got into a fight, and she grabbed a pistol and shot him in the head.
>
> —**Eddie**, fortysomething African American man, North Carolina

This chapter will focus on the impact that experiences with and exposure to violence in childhood has on experiences with family violence, and intimate partner violence (IPV) in particular, in adulthood. The chapter will be broken into two sections: the impact on girls who experience physical or sexual abuse (or both) in childhood and their probability for experiencing family violence in adulthood, and the impact on boys who witness violence growing up and their likelihood of battering their partners in adulthood. This chapter will include both statistical and ethnographic data that illustrate the significance of these relationships.

OBJECTIVES

- To provide an overview of the three forms that childhood sexual abuse takes: premature sex engagement, incest, and child prostitution
- To provide examples that illustrate the long-term impact of child sexual abuse (CSA) on young women
- To provide examples that illustrate the long-term impact that witnessing IPV has on young boys

- To note the statistical relationship between CSA among girls and the likelihood of being a victim of IPV in adulthood
- To note the statistical relationship between boys witnessing IPV in their home and the likelihood that they will abuse their intimate partners in adulthood

---

KEY TERMS

physical child abuse

intimate partner violence (IPV)

child sexual abuse (CSA)

sexual scripts

premature sex engagement

childhood adultification

situational prostitution

liquor houses

order of protection

intergenerational transmission of

    violence theory

parental violence

INTRODUCTION

This chapter serves as a transition chapter between our discussions of child abuse and IPV; in this chapter, we explore the specific role that experiences with and exposure to violence in childhood play in significantly increasing the risk childhood victims and witnesses face for revictimization and becoming perpetrators of violence in adulthood.

At the beginning of the 2000s, we conducted face-to-face, in-depth interviews with nearly one hundred adult men and women who were living with IPV. Though we had read the literature that demonstrated that girls who grew up experiencing CSA were at risk for revictimization (rape) in adulthood (Lalor and McElvaney 2010 provides an excellent summary of this research), and though we were well aware that boys who witness violence in their households are at significantly higher risk for growing up to abuse their future wives and girlfriends, it was in talking with real men and women who had these experiences in childhood that we learned just how profoundly child abuse shapes victims' and witnesses' lives well into adulthood. The tragedy of their experiences puts a face on the child abuse statistics that we reviewed in the previous chapters. Of equal importance, the voices of real people we interviewed provide the "picture" that qualitative data produce, as we move through our discussion of IPV in the next several chapters.

In this chapter we will explore the experiences of both boys and girls; we begin with a discussion of the ways in which CSA experienced by girls leaves them vulnerable to IPV in adulthood.

OUTCOMES OF CHILD ABUSE FOR WOMEN

In the interviews we conducted with women, we focused on their experiences growing up, dating, and in their adult intimate relationships. Inside of these discussions we were surprised and troubled by the frequency with which stories about experiences with sexual abuse tumbled out of them. The analysis in this chapter highlights the ways in which these experiences with sexual abuse that occurred in childhood and the teen years affect women's ability to cope with violence in their intimate relationships in adulthood. Specifically, abuse in childhood lowers young women's self-esteem and puts them at risk for other behaviors—drug and alcohol abuse and multiple sex partners (Lalor and McElvaney 2010)—that are themselves risk factors for being a victim of IPV (Browne 1989). Childhood sexual abuse in particular seems to erode young women's personal boundaries so that they are less able to protect themselves from exploitation and interpersonal assaults in general, including IPV (Raphael 2004). We begin with a discussion of the statistical data that examine the outcomes of childhood abuse—both physical and sexual—that girls experienced and their probability for revictimization in adulthood and then move to descriptions provided by the women we interviewed. These interviews illuminated the *process* by which child abuse leads to revictimization in adulthood.

Abuse in Childhood and Abuse in Adulthood

In national studies, at least half of all women report at least one incident of *physical abuse* by a parent or caretaker before age eighteen (Tjaden and Thoennes 2000).

Physical child abuse can include beating a child with one's hand or with an instrument; pushing a child; throwing things at a child; burning a child with hot instruments, including cigarette lighters; scalding a child with hot water; tying a child up; or any other sort of action that causes physical injury to a child.

Though not all women who were victims of child abuse grow up to be victims of IPV in adulthood (46.7 percent do, but 53.3 percent do not), they are *twice as likely* to experience IPV as women who were not physically assaulted in childhood (46.7 percent do, compared to 19.8 percent who do not) (Tjaden and Thoennes 2000).

> **Intimate partner violence (IPV)** is abuse that occurs between adults—or teenagers—who are in a relationship with each other; they may be dating, living together, married, or even exes. IPV can include physical, emotional, or sexual abuse. We will have a lengthy discussion of IPV in the next chapter.

In other words, slightly more than half of women who were physically abused in childhood *do not* grow up to be victims of IPV in adulthood (53.3 percent), but the *risk* for IPV is *twice as high—46.7 percent as compared to 19.8 percent*—for girls who are victims of child abuse than for those women who were not abused as children.

The relationship between being sexually abused in childhood and being raped in adulthood follows a similar pattern.

> **Child sexual abuse (CSA)** involves any sort of sexual contact between a child and an adult (or significantly older teenager). Most often CSA involves sexual touching and/or sexual manipulation, but it can also include sexual intercourse—vaginal, oral, and anal. CSA can also involve exposing children to adult sexual images, forcing them to watch pornography, or even witness adult sexual acts.

Women who are raped as minors are *twice as likely* to be raped in adulthood (18.3 percent compared to a rate of 8.7 percent for women who were not raped in childhood). However, as is the case with physical child abuse, most women who are raped in childhood are *not* raped in adulthood—81.2 percent of those raped in childhood are *not* raped as adults (Figure 8.1).

The increased probability of revictimization is confirmed by Lalor and McElvaney's extensive review of empirical studies. They write,

▶ **Figure 8.1** Relationship Between Abuse in Childhood and Being Battered in Adulthood.

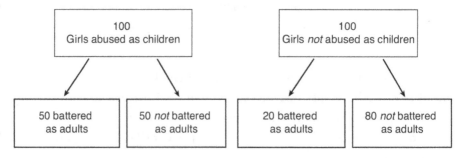

Numerous studies have noted that child sexual abuse victims are vulnerable to later sexual revictimization, as well as the link between child sexual abuse and later engagement in high-risk sexual behaviour. Survivors of child sexual abuse are more likely to have multiple sex partners, become pregnant as teenagers, and experience sexual assault as adults.

(2010: 159)

In short, though most girls who experience sexual abuse or physical violence are not victimized in adulthood, victims of childhood sexual or physical abuse are twice as likely to experience the same type of abuse in adulthood as their counterparts who were not victimized in childhood.

The question becomes how abuse in childhood creates a *pathway* to abuse in adulthood. In her study of stripping and prostitution, Raphael explicates the ways in which sexual abuse and exploitation diminish self-esteem and can create a pathway to IPV. She notes that prostitution and violence destroy one's sense of one's body's boundaries: "If your body does not present limits to other people, you begin to feel that you do not have a right to exist, to take up space" (2004: 164). In other words, once a girl's personal boundaries have been violated by a sexual abuser, it is as if she loses her ability to enforce the boundaries of her body when other people attempt to violate her. Tragically, as Raphael so eloquently articulates, CSA teaches girls and young women that they have *no right* to control their own bodies or limit other people's access to their sexuality.

Beyond Raphael's qualitative research, there is little statistical research on the relationship between sexual abuse in childhood or adolescence and physical abuse in adulthood that allows us to speculate about the probability that girls who are victims of CSA are disproportionately likely to experience IPV in their adult relationships. Based on our interviews with women who reported experiencing sexual abuse as children and who were living with IPV as adults, we identify the *processes* by which early childhood sexual abuse led to revictimization, through two pathways: (1) poor partnering decisions made in an attempt to escape the sexual abuse they were experiencing and (2) their limited agency in ending IPV when it did occur.

INTERVIEWING VICTIMS OF VIOLENCE

People who have never conducted in-depth interviews with victims of violence are often very surprised by the level of intimate details that participants are willing to share with complete strangers. Even for the seasoned researcher, there is often concern that with each

continues

INTERVIEWING VICTIMS OF VIOLENCE *continued*

new project, one will not be able to elicit the information that is most interesting and most pertinent to the project. Across several different projects, we have learned that there are several keys to successful interviewing. First, when one conducts research on a painful topic, it is critically important to establish trust and rapport with the participant. Second, as in therapeutic relationships, sometimes people are more willing to disclose painful and even shameful experiences with a stranger, someone they will never see again, than with their family members or close friends. Thus, it was not unusual for us to learn that our conversation was the first time an individual had talked about their experiences. Third, we have found that victims of gender oppression (rape, IPV) are often ashamed of their experiences, and they have encountered people who are literally shocked by their stories. Therefore, they tend to start out mildly and slowly reveal the real tragedy of their experiences. It is critical that the researcher express sympathy but not shock at these revelations. By accepting the extraordinary experiences of these gracious and generous folks, the researcher develops the trust necessary for the revelation of increasingly intimate and increasingly horrific events.

Though not all girls who are sexually abused in childhood and adolescence grow up to be victims of IPV in adulthood, there does seem to be a significant relationship between being an adult victim of IPV and early experiences with rape and incest (Lawless 2001; Wesely 2006).

Among the women in our study, CSA fell into three distinct categories: premature sex engagement (our term), incest, and childhood prostitution.

We begin with some descriptive data on the forms of childhood and adolescent sexual abuse and then examine the two survival strategies that put victims of CSA at risk of abuse in adulthood: (1) marrying as teenagers to escape incest and prostitution, and (2) choosing intimate partners who could protect them from outside violence but who ended up abusing them.

Child Sexual Abuse: Premature Sex Engagement

One of the first things that struck us in interviewing women who were experiencing IPV was their sexual "initiations"—their first sexual experiences. The *majority* of women we interviewed overall and *all* of the African American women we interviewed experienced sexual initiation at very young ages and with significantly older boys or men, rather than their peers.

There is ample research to suggest that preteens and young teenagers often engage in sexual experimentation with each other. In a common scenario in the United States, preteen and early teenage boys and girls engage in sexual experimentation—kissing, petting, and so forth—in which neither party knows what to expect. In this type of scenario, when neither party has more knowledge or experience, the experimentation is as balanced as possible within the confines of a patriarchal culture in which expectations of boys and girls are different and can shape their behaviors. For example, boys may push for more sexual experiences, and girls may resist based on the sexual scripts that dominate our beliefs about sexuality.

Sexual scripts are the set of cultural norms that govern sexual behavior, including who should or can initiate sex and which role each participant will play in the encounter. The dominant sexual scripts in the United States are gendered: boys and men are supposed to desire sex anytime, anyplace, and any way, whereas girls and women are supposed to have less interest in sex overall, less interest in multiple sex partners, and more conservative beliefs about sex practices (for example, regarding anal sex); to never initiate sex; and to resist men's advances. We note that there are other sexual scripts that are specific to sexual orientation, but for our purposes here, we discuss the heterosexual sexual scripts that dominate teenage sexual experiences in particular.

In contrast, in some cultures—for example, among the Sambia in Papua New Guinea—sexual initiation is believed to be the responsibility of the older members of the community. Older women and especially older men will "initiate" teenagers in order to "teach" them sexual skills. This is believed to be an ideal circumstance because then when they marry, the partners are guaranteed that each will "know what to do" and be a satisfying lover.

What we learned about in our interviews was distinct from this type of culturally institutionalized sexual initiation. For the women we interviewed, the difference in level of experience led to the older participant (always the man) being able to exploit a young woman who did not know what to expect, who did not perhaps understand what was happening, and who could be convinced to engage in activities she might not want to. Think about the ways in which this is illustrated by the urban myths that emerge when we teach courses in human sexuality. When we ask students what myths they have heard about sex, the *women* will admit to having been told by men:

- You cannot get pregnant if you have sex while standing up.
- Douching with Coke will prevent pregnancy.
- "Blue balling" is dangerous for men.

There are other examples as well. The ability to manipulate and exploit in the context of sexual initiation is substantially increased when one partner has significantly more personal experience with sex—and frequently more partners—than the other.

In order to capture the uniqueness of these sexual initiations, we coined the term **premature sex engagement**, which refers to girls' experiencing their first sexual intercourse at a very young age with an older man. The most typical pattern that was presented in our research involved women who recalled that their first sexual experiences occurred when they were thirteen or fourteen years old with men at least ten years older; that is, men in their mid-twenties. In some cases the first sexual experiences of these young teenage girls involved much older men—those in their thirties or forties.[1] Though this fits the definition of statutory rape, these women primarily defined these experiences as consensual. The issue of consent in these cases is a tricky and complex one, as Odem (1995) points out in her historical study of sexuality; the "age of consent" laws effectively remove the possibility that girls under the age of eighteen can legally consent to *any* sexual activity. Recently, some states have modified their statutory rape laws to require age differences of at least two years—for example, sex between a sixteen-year-old and a fifteen-year-old no longer meets the legal requirements of statutory rape, as we noted in Chapter 2.

This issue is further complicated by the blurring of the term *consent*. Diana Scully (1990) points out that convicted rapists' definitions of rape hinge on *their* perceptions of a woman's consent rather than the woman's own perceptions. Research on incest and CSA also notes that in many cases, victims do report "consenting." We argue that the women whom we classify as experiencing premature sex engagement fall into the same category as victims of CSA, and not into the category of those cases now excluded from statutory rape laws. In all cases, the age difference between the girls and the men they had sex with was at least ten years. Furthermore, this age gap results in both a power differential and an experience differential that often left these girls feeling exploited, even when they consented.

Veta, for example, told of her first sexual experience when she was sixteen. Her partner was a forty-two-year-old married man by whom she would eventually become pregnant. In discussing the awkwardness of the age difference, Veta recalled telling her parents she was pregnant and, when they insisted that she bring the father of her child to their home to meet them, she realized she was bringing home to her mother and father a man who was not only married to someone else but also *older than her parents*! Veta's partner was her school bus driver.

Of the twenty African American women we interviewed, nearly all, eighteen (90 percent), experienced premature sex engagement (several via incest or childhood prostitution). Though it's incredibly common among white women as well, somewhat fewer (87 percent) experienced premature sex engagement.

Furthermore, of the white women we interviewed, only one experienced incest and none experienced prostitution.

Not only was early teenage sexual activity common among the women we interviewed, it almost always involved older, and presumably more experienced, first sex partners. For African American women, these sexual experiences at fourteen or fifteen almost invariably led to pregnancy and a birth before the mother turned sixteen. Half of the white women who experienced premature sex engagement also became teen mothers, and they too struggled to complete high school and find jobs that paid enough that they could take care of themselves and their children. With rare exceptions, girls who had their first child by age sixteen dropped out of high school and failed to earn a general equivalency diploma (GED). Race differences exacerbate this problem. Because African Americans have higher levels of *unintended unemployment* (Hattery and Smith 2014; Padavic and Reskin 2002) and because African Americans and women require more education to make the same wages as white men (Padavic and Reskin 2002), the long-term consequences of these experiences significantly shape the life chances of African American girls and their children (Hattery and Smith 2014; Maynard 1997). The failure to complete high school left these women even more vulnerable to IPV—as we will explore extensively in the next chapter—because they have little earning power in a changing economy where low-skilled employment continues to disappear (Browne 1989; Brush 2001).

Clearly, race shaped both the likelihood of experiencing premature sex engagement as well as its consequences. The fact that *nearly all* of the African American women we interviewed experienced premature sex engagement suggests that as scholars and practitioners (teachers, social workers, and health-care providers), we need to adjust our understanding of the "typical" experiences of African American teenage girls to include this type of experience. Second, because we know that premature sex engagement has many consequences for young women, *especially African Americans*, these race differences demand our attention.

Unbeknownst to us at the time when we were conducting these interviews with women who were experiencing IPV and learning about their experiences with premature sex engagement, simultaneously, our colleague Dr. Linda Burton was seeing something similar in her own research. Burton coined the term *childhood adultification* to describe the outcomes of premature sex engagement. We note here that it is not the sexual behavior *itself* that is the issue but the power dynamics associated with the sexual behavior. The consequences associated with premature sex engagement are significantly more serious and concerning and have a longer-term, more negative impact than early sexual intercourse that is consensual and with a same-aged partner.

Childhood adultification involves contextual, social, and developmental processes in which youth are prematurely, and often inappropriately, exposed to adult knowledge and assume extensive adult roles and responsibilities within their family networks. In particular, respondents expressed negative images of African American girls who were described as sexual beings, immanent mothers, girlfriends, and sexual partners (Burton 2007: 329, 338).

Consequences that are also associated with early sexual intercourse that is consensual and with a same-aged partner include (Alan Guttmacher Institute 2004):

- higher rates of unintended pregnancy
- higher rates of STIs
- more sexual partners.

Consequences associated with the exploitation inherent in situations that are characterized as premature sex engagement include (Sweet and Tewksbury 2000; Wesely 2006):

- higher risk for drug and alcohol abuse
- eating disorders
- self-mutilation.

Consequences associated with teen childbearing include (Hattery and Smith 2014; Maynard 1997):

- failing to complete one's education
- long-term dependency on welfare
- overall higher fertility rates or having more children over the course of their lifetime.

Incest and Child Molestation at Home

Twelve to forty percent of adult women report that they experienced incest or molestation as children (American College of Obstetricians and Gynecologists 2017). Several women whom we interviewed, both white and African American, admitted to being sexually abused by fathers, stepfathers, and mothers' boyfriends. Among the thirty-five women we interviewed, five (15 percent) reported at least one experience with incest. Consistent with national-level data

(Tjaden and Thoennes 2000), there were very few race differences with regard to the women's experiences with incest. Regardless of women's willingness to disclose the details, scholars and practitioners need to assume a high probability for CSA when working with young women, especially young women who are in trouble or "at risk" (Gaarder and Belknap 2002; Sweet and Tewksbury 2000; Wesely 2006). We remind the reader of the sexual abuse to prison pipeline we discussed previously (Saar et al. 2015).

Preadolescent Prostitution: The Liquor or Drink House

Among the women we interviewed, none of the white women but 15 percent (three of twenty) of the African American women had experiences as child prostitutes. One case involved "situational prostitution"; the other two cases involved *continuous* child prostitution in drink houses run by their fathers or stepfathers. **Situational prostitution** refers to the circumstance when a woman (or man) engages in prostitution only when it seems the most efficient way in which to meet an immediate need. The most common example of this involves *occasionally* trading sex for drugs.

We must begin the discussion of liquor houses with a caveat. We do not want to imply here that childhood prostitution is a normative experience for young African American women. We do suspect, however, that Winston-Salem, North Carolina, is similar in many regards to other southern communities in which there is a single major employer; in Winston-Salem this employer is R. J. Reynolds Tobacco. (Yes, the cigarette brands Winston and Salem are both named for the town in which they are produced.) As in many southern communities, until very recently work was segregated here (Collins 1994; Hattery and Smith 2014; Shapiro 2003), and R. J. Reynolds was no exception. Though a few African Americans were hired to sweep floors and to do the most menial labor associated with cigarette production, for the most part they were excluded from working at the town's primary company. As is typical in many southern towns, African Americans were, however, called on to "service" the white community as housekeepers, nannies,[2] gardeners, and liquor suppliers (Hattery and Smith 2010; Korstad 2003; Tursi 1994). This was an especially important function during Prohibition, and the habit of going into the housing projects to imbibe that developed then continues today, though today drugs are more likely to be the product being sought for purchase. When conditions like these exist, the environment is primed for many exploitative and oppressive behaviors, among them prostitution. Therefore, we believe there is much to learn from the case of Winston-Salem, North Carolina.

LIQUOR HOUSES

Liquor houses are a sort of unregulated social club. Usually, they are apartments in the public housing projects. In a typical liquor house, a man allows a woman (and often her children) to live rent-free upstairs in exchange for her (and her children) running the liquor house on the main level of the home. So that the man can drink and gamble and enjoy the liquor house he literally lives in, the woman acts as the bartender and the short-order cook (many liquor houses serve simple food such as fried fish or chicken) and generally handles all of the sales—of cigarettes, food, and of course liquor. Additionally, this arrangement usually involves an exchange for sex with the woman whenever he desires it.

Typically, liquor houses are open nearly twenty-four hours a day. The women we interviewed told us that they were horrible places to grow up because customers, mostly men, come in at all times of the day and night to get a drink and a plate of food, play cards, and buy cigars or cigarettes. A typical liquor house not only stocks liquor, wine, and beer but also often serves cold sandwiches during the afternoon and fish, pork chops, and French fries in the evening. One woman we interviewed, Evie, talked almost with pride about how she could make the sandwiches and even pour a shot of whiskey by the time she was ten. But her face turned dark and tears filled her eyes as she talked about the men she encountered there and what they made her do—employing the euphemism that she had to "sit on their laps."

When we inquired about the men who frequented the drink houses, Evie—a fiftysomething African American woman we interviewed in a battered women's shelter in North Carolina—told us that of course there were the locals, men who lived in the projects, but that the primary customers were white male executives from R. J. Reynolds Tobacco Company who lived in the more affluent parts of town. These men would come during their lunch hour and at happy-hour time (usually after four in the afternoon) to consume alcohol and cigarettes and have sex before returning to their quiet, white middle-class neighborhoods.

> Some of the Reynolds men got paid on Wednesday. They'll come in, maybe, and buy . . . give me a five, and maybe they done bought four drinks and I would have the change. Sometimes they would sell fish in there. And a lot of times, some of the guys would get the cigarettes and change cigarettes for drinks. And it was just like, I wonder that the people that lived out by a car [in the suburbs]. There was nice section. But they would come in our neighborhood, and drink, and buy women and stuff like that.

Both of the women we interviewed who worked in (and in fact grew up in) liquor houses, Evie and Shakira, were initially lured into this work—and ultimately into a life of forced childhood prostitution—by their fathers or stepfathers, who told them they could earn a little money making sandwiches and pouring drinks. Evie recalls that by age twelve she was frying fish and managing the food side of the operation. In addition, she admitted that her

continues

LIQUOR HOUSES *continued*

father required her to work regularly as a child prostitute; in her words, she was required to "perform favors" for the men in the liquor house.

You can't imagine what it's like to have to sit on the laps of men when you are a ten-year-old. I hadn't even learned to ride a bike yet.

Thus, as important as it is to be aware of the international world of child sex trafficking, we need to recognize that it is happening in our own communities as well and has devastating consequences on the victims, who often go on to be victims in adulthood too.

What is perhaps most striking about these stories of preadolescent prostitution in liquor houses is the way that they are shaped by both race and social class. Not only were the women African American and poor, but the liquor house itself was, in part, a product of race and class inequalities that existed in the community. In a segregated community like Winston-Salem, there were few legitimate ways for African Americans to earn a living, and those that did exist were primarily restricted to educated, middle-class, and professional African Americans and to women who were employed as domestics (Collins 1994). Poor whites were able to find work in the R. J. Reynolds cigarette factories, but African Americans were excluded from this employment option. Thus, African Americans living in the housing projects created a service economy that filled a niche, one that would never have been allowed to operate in most white neighborhoods regardless of their social class composition (Korstad 2003; Tursi 1994). Thus, race, class, and gender were powerful forces in shaping both the individual experiences these women had with childhood prostitution as well as the phenomenon itself. In order to grasp the power of the institutions of race, class, and gender in shaping this phenomenon, imagine a similar situation in which professional black men go to a house in a middle-class suburb and sexually abuse ten-year-old white girls. It would never happen. The burgeoning international child sex trade is similar. The vast majority of children sold into prostitution not only are poor themselves but also come from some of the poorest countries in the world. We will explore this in a bit more depth in Chapter 10.

In response to the CSA they experienced, the women we interviewed employed two related survival strategies: marrying to escape the abuse and choosing dangerous partners. Both strategies put these women at risk for IPV. We turn now to a discussion of the survival strategies and incredible violence that these women endured at the hands of their abusive partners, opening with the revealing story of Debbie.

Sexual Abuse and a Drive to Escape

By age seventeen, seeking answers and help, Debbie became a disciple of James and Tammy Faye Bakker's Praise the Lord (PTL) ministry. Homeless for a time, she slept in a trailer on the grounds of the PTL club in Charlotte. There she met a young man. After a few weeks they had sex, and, feeling guilty about it, they married. Debbie describes her decision to marry John.

It was three days after we met that we kissed. And we never really discussed that kiss or nothing. We just liked each other right away. So he took me to a jewelry store and bought me an engagement ring and a wedding band. Then he had this necklace around his neck that said "I love you" that somebody gave to him. So he took it off and put it around my neck. Then I put the engagement ring on, and he asked me to go with him. And I said, "Sure." I wanted to be free from my family. I thought, If I get married, my name changes and I'm free from my family.

(**Debbie**, thirtysomething African American woman, North Carolina)

For many women like Debbie, getting pregnant or married is perhaps the only route for escape (Lawless 2001). *All* of the women we interviewed who acknowledged that they had been sexually abused or prostituted in childhood entered their first intimate, romantic sexual *relationships* before they were eighteen. Frequently, these relationships involved living together (married or not) within weeks or months of meeting each other. In their eyes, moving in with another man seemed the most obvious escape route, one that almost always led to physical, emotional, and sometimes sexual abuse at the hands of their lovers (Brandt 2006; Griffing et al. 2005; Lawless 2001). In their attempts to escape the sexual abuse they were experiencing at home, these girls often left with the first man who would take them away (usually by marrying them), and within months it was clear to them that they had traded one sort of violence and abuse for another. Debbie paints a graphic picture:

I wanted to please him [sexually, and] because my mom never talked to me or nothing, I had to figure out what I'm supposed to do. I knew you screwed, but I wanted more than that. So I looked at the videos. And when I did something on him that I learned from the video, he was like, "Oh, where did you learn to do that? You had to do it before somewhere else." But then he got sexually abusive. He wanted to, like, use objects on me and all kinds of stuff. When he did that, that's when I started hating him. And I wouldn't let him do it, and he would get mad. And then he would tear my pictures up of my family and burned them. He tore up some of my clothes he bought me. One time he got so mad, we was going down the road, and he ran his car into an overpass bridge. We were both in it, and he was going eighty miles per hour. He totaled the car, but we both walked out of it. [AH: Was he trying to kill you?] Yeah. He wanted to kill both of us.

(**Debbie,** thirtysomething African American woman, North Carolina)

Many, many women we interviewed reported having sex when they did not want to, though they seldom called it rape. And many reported that sex seemed to be a tool of the violence or an attempt to "make up" after a violent episode. They described not only the hurt of being raped by your intimate partner, the person who claims to love you, but also the consequences, such as unintended pregnancy or possible exposure to STIs, including HIV. Cheri describes her experience:

So, you know, the park. We smoke a little blunt. And then we have sex in the car, which was ironic, 'cause we'd never done this before. Okay, my pants still on my ankles, and then he just starts beating me on my face. Yeah. I mean, his was too [pants were down]. That's how, soon as he done it, it happened. He didn't even get up off of me. He just started beating me, talking about, that's what I was doing, that's what I gave to somebody else, and just rambling on and on and on. And I crawled out of the car and crawled under my car. Then my stubborn butt wouldn't leave 'til he gave me my two hundred dollars back. Then, he was like, he was like, well, go clean your face up. I had about six bones broken over here. And to this day, I can't see out this eye. I have a dislocated retina. And, so, I went a whole day without going to the emergency room 'cause I was scared. So, when I finally went to the emergency room, 'cause the eye wouldn't open up is what made me go, and I was in so much pain, I found out I was pregnant. So, I told . . . so I told the abortion clinic, if y'all don't get this baby out of me, I am. So they got me a volunteer to help pay for it, but by the time they came through, I was five months pregnant. So then that almost killed me.

(**Cheri,** thirtysomething African American woman, North Carolina)

We argue that seeking out sexual partners as a means of escape is similar to stripping and prostitution in that they all involve trading sexual access for economic support, or, as the stories of the women here illustrate, agreeing to marry (and have sex) in exchange for a place to live and an escape from the childhood abuser. The strategies employed by Debbie, like those of so many other women we interviewed, illustrate a well-established finding by scholars who study CSA: that CSA is a major pathway to careers in stripping and prostitution (Monto and Hotaling 2001; Sweet and Tewksbury 2000; Wesely 2006) and juvenile delinquency (Gaarder and Belknap 2002; Goodkind, Ng, and Sarri 2006; Saar et al. 2015). In short, these are the pathways that populate the sexual abuse to prison pipeline.

In contrast, the women we interviewed who had been victims of IPV but who had *not* experienced CSA left intimate partner relationships the *first time* they were hit. As a result, they were seldom forced into the cycle of trading sexual access for the economic support of a man who would help them flee but who would also abuse them. Additionally, our interviews confirm the research of other scholars who have studied women who experienced CSA and IPV as opposed to those who only experienced IPV. An important pattern is revealed:

> Childhood abuse, and particularly childhood sexual abuse, is associated with a pattern in which women are less likely to be in a stable marriage or a long-term cohabiting relationship but are instead more likely to experience multiple short-term unions. Adult abuse, and particularly adult physical abuse, on the other hand, is associated with a reduction in the probability of being in either form of union.
>
> (Cherlin et al. 2004: 784)

Child Sexual Abuse and Economic Dependency in Adulthood

With regard to social class, the strategy of trading sexual access for economic support, though used by many women, for centuries and in all cultures, is by and large a strategy that affluent women do *not* need to rely on. The middle-class women we interviewed *did not* establish a pattern of trading sexual access for economic support to flee abusive relationships. Instead, they were able to rely on their own economic assets to leave relationships when they became abusive. It is, of course, important to realize that women's access to their own resources—either resources they earned or joint checking accounts, credit cards, and so forth—is a relatively recent phenomenon. We turn next to an examination of a severe case of relying on fleeing as a strategy to escape violence, as told to us by Andi.

Andi is an African American woman we interviewed in Minnesota. Andi's is yet another case of premature sex engagement. At age thirteen Andi had her first sexual relationship, with a twenty-three-year-old man. She ultimately bore two children by this man, though they never married. Because he was also a drug dealer and violent with her and the children, she decided that she needed to escape.

I knew this guy who drove a truck, and he had to go back to Chicago—I was living in Mississippi—so he took us to Chicago. I stayed in a hotel for about a week and then went to a shelter. I met this guy one day when I was outside of the shelter. And I do not know what was going through my mind, but I liked him; he was like, "Why don't you come to Minnesota with me?" So I came to Minnesota. I'd been in Chicago for a week and a half. [AH: And how quickly did you move to Minnesota?] The next day after I met him. It was like no, I didn't, it was like one of those stupid, you're-risking-your-life moves, but I was like, "Hey, what do I have to lose right now? I have absolutely nothing." Everything seemed pretty good for a minute. He got a job . . . but then one night he flipped out because he found out I had smoked a blunt and that I had been around some guys . . . We got into this fight and everything . . . he had just grabbed me, and like, slammed me into the wall . . . He ended up hitting my face against the wall.

(**Andi,** twentysomething African American woman, Minnesota)

Andi's story, though perhaps extreme in that it involves moving several hundred miles, is typical of the stories we heard from the women we interviewed. What Andi's story illustrates is the cycle that many of the women we interviewed fell into, specifically their drive to replace the financial security they forfeited when they left abusive circumstances. These women often reported that they felt that their options were limited to either living alone and being poor or taking a chance to improve their economic conditions by moving in with a man, sometimes a total stranger.

Though this may seem obvious, for many of the women we interviewed, leaving a violent or sexually abusive relationship, often involving fathers, stepfathers, or older men, had plunged them into such severe poverty that they were homeless. In addition, moving out often meant that they lost their jobs because they either failed to come to work during the transition or could not continue to go to work *and* care for their children. For example, it is common in low-income families for parents to "split shifts" so that one parent watches the children while the other works, thus eliminating or significantly reducing childcare costs (Hattery 2001a, 2001b). In such instances, leaving the abusive relationship often meant leaving behind the only childcare that was available and affordable. Therefore, the pressures these women felt to find a new relationship were significant and pressing. Most of the women we interviewed reported that after leaving an abusive relationship, they often established a new relationship within weeks, often with someone they barely knew or with someone they knew had a reputation for violence and, more often than not, this new relationship, pursued as an escape, turned violent as well. Other scholars have found similar patterns in studies of homeless women who reported high rates of violence in their relationships (Brush 2011).

It is evident that the women entered into adult relationships for multiple reasons (often related to childhood issues): to escape the home environment, to prove to themselves and others that they could "do it right," to achieve what they discerned as safety, security, comfort, or love (Wesely and Wright 2005: 1089). In short, as Wesely and Wright (2005) note, women who have experienced abuse typically find that their options shrink. And this situation is further compounded by race and social class. Women with fewer of their own economic resources are more likely to jump directly into new relationships in order to avoid what they see as a real chance they would otherwise be homeless. Furthermore, because of the strong correlation between race and social class (Hattery and Smith 2014; Shapiro 2003), this pattern is more pronounced among African American women than their white counterparts. Explicating the links among CSA, IPV, race, and economic instability contributes to our understanding of the complexities of seemingly unrelated phenomena, including the homelessness faced by women and, often, their children. Additionally, our research sheds light on the process by which child abuse, and CSA in particular, has long-term consequences for its victims, including homelessness—as a result of leaving the home of the perpetrator—and, ultimately, for girls who are victims, the revictimization they experience at the hands of the men who help them to escape and then, once they are free, abuse them. Understanding these links is central to reforming our responses to child abuse and responding to adult victims whose fundamental risk for IPV is the abuse they experienced as children.

Trading Sexual Access for Protection

Women who have been raped or sexually assaulted often view men as dangerous (Brownmiller 1975; Griffin 1979; Koss 1985; Koss et al. 1994). If they are sexually assaulted by someone they know, they often report feeling as if they can no longer trust anyone. Women who are raped by a stranger may develop a generalized distrust of the world, including an increased fear of being a victim of natural disasters, accidents, and so forth, as is typical of most people suffering from posttraumatic stress disorder (Griffin 1979; Koss 1985; Koss et al. 1994). Living with such generalized distrust, some women may put up with sexual and physical abuse by their intimate partners in exchange for the protection these men provide from the outside world (MacKinnon 1991; Rich 1980).

Ironically, wanting a protector is, by definition, wanting someone capable of violence. To defend a woman from another man's physical violence, he must himself be capable of inflicting physical harm, or of creating the threat of physical harm. Clearly, not all protectors *use* physical violence, either against women or against men, but the paradox lingers—and it played itself out especially clearly in Candy's relationship.

Candy was molested at age fifteen by her mother's boyfriend. Like many of the other women whose stories are told here, she sought adult intimate partners who would protect her even while abusing her. Candy lives with Mark, a physically dominant man who is horribly abusive. Candy's **order of protection**—a civil order granted by a judge that prohibits any physical contact and often phone, text, and e-mail contact—also prohibits them from living together. However, when we interviewed Candy, she told us they were living with each other off and on and were continuing to have a sexual relationship, another violation of both the order of protection and the terms of Mark's batterer intervention treatment program. This is so common that many social service agencies are beginning to recommend family counseling and safety plans rather than rely on orders of protection, which are often ignored by the couple as well as law enforcement. We will discuss orders of protection at length in Chapter 15.

Among many of the incidents that have taken place over a number of years, Mark choked Candy until she was unconscious, beat her against the stick shift of their car until her pelvis broke—causing her to miscarry their child a few days later—slapped her, pulled her hair, jumped on her and broke several ribs (almost causing an additional miscarriage and landing Candy in the hospital for two days), and bit her in the face at least ten times. At five feet nine and 120 pounds, Candy is extremely thin. At 300 pounds, even Mark's slaps are extremely dangerous. Candy also indicated that Mark had raped her "once or twice." When we met Candy, this level of violence had been going on for four or five years. However, Candy rationalized that although Mark might beat her, abuse her emotionally, and rape her, *he did not allow anyone else to treat her this way.*

Candy stays with Mark because he provides protection from the violence she fears she might otherwise experience at the hands of a stranger. The abuse she experiences with Mark is predictable, making it preferable to the unpredictable nature of sexual harassment and sexual and physical assault that women face in the workplace and outside world (Kearl 2010; MacKinnon 1991; Rich 1980).

When things were good, they were so good. Like I said, I was always secure with him. He might try to hit me and he might try to kill me, but nobody else was going to do it. Nobody else was going to talk bad to me or hurt me or talk bad about me. That just wasn't going to happen. I was secure in that sense with him. He was going to protect me from everybody else.

(**Candy,** twentysomething white woman, North Carolina)

Candy's quote not only illustrates an extreme example of the types of violence these women live with but also demonstrates her cognizance of her situation. Many people believe that battered women have no agency or do not know how to make good choices. Candy's statement is clear: she understands very clearly the trade-off that she is making. And, though extreme, Candy's case illustrates the trade-off that many battered women make: choosing life-threatening violence that is predictable over the kind of random violence they perceive awaits them in the streets. In Candy's case, this choice also puts her at risk of becoming one of the thirteen hundred women who are murdered by their partners and ex-partners each year. And it illustrates, profoundly, the terrible mistake that is made when we teach our young women (in health classes, for example) and our daughters at home that they should fear strange men—and adjust their behavior accordingly (for example, by not walking alone after dark, not jogging on secluded paths, and not accepting drinks from men they do not know). Although this is all good advice, it renders invisible the reality that *their greatest risk for violence is in their own homes.* Last, it seems very clear that Candy's general distrust and fear of the violence that awaits her are a direct result of the molestation she experienced at age fifteen, by a man she had never met, a man her mother had brought home from the racetrack earlier that evening.

A Life of Illegal and Illegitimate Behavior

Sexual assault and sexual abuse are significant events in any woman's (or man's) life. As noted by many scholars, including Pipher (1994), Wolf (1992), and Lalor and McElvaney (2010), many girls and women who are raped or sexually abused rely on dangerous coping strategies: they medicate the pain with alcohol or drugs or attempt to become "sexually invisible" by developing anorexia or bulimia or overeating; some will go so far as to end the pain by committing suicide.

Although rape and sexual abuse are so common in the lives of girls and women—one-quarter will experience sexual abuse by the time they are twenty-five years old—and under these circumstances it is impossible to prevent all rape and sexual abuse, those who deal with its victims note the importance of support and a healthy environment in which to heal. The women that we interviewed had neither a healthy environment nor the financial resources to get the support they needed. For Evie in particular, the effects of being forced to work as a child prostitute in her father's liquor house, living in a violent household, and living in poverty, *all of which amount to child abuse and neglect,* had lifelong effects.

Evie was exposed to many different avenues for making money in the illegitimate economy while she was working at the liquor house. As one can imagine, based on the trauma she experienced as a child prostitute, she escaped prostitution as soon as she could, and as an adult she never returned to this way of life as a long-term solution to earning money, though, like many other victims of CSA, she did sometimes trade sex for the financial support of a partner—a place to live, some food on the table, or some drugs—what we term *situational prostitution.* However, for the majority of Evie's life, she supported herself in all sorts of ways. Her father was a numbers writer[3] and she learned the numbers trade in the liquor house. As a teenager, she began running numbers for her father. She also learned to deal drugs and steal clothes and accessories from stores at the mall and sell them in "after"-market outlets, usually through "fences" who sold stolen property out of the trunks of their cars in the housing projects or in the parking lots of shopping centers in low-income neighborhoods. She worked for a while in a laundry but she was always engaged in running numbers and dealing drugs, even when she was employed, and often she used her job as a distribution point, weaving legitimate work with illegitimate work.

As we talked more and more about her adult life, Evie talked about the only legitimate job she had ever had. For the four years prior to our interview, she had worked as a cook at the county hospital, a job she got when she was forty-six years old. Evie had not had a "real" job, full-time in the legitimate labor market, until she was forty-six years old! This was not because she had been out of the labor market raising children and taking care of a home, or because she was on welfare, but because she had always been able to support herself by working in the illegitimate economy. When we met Evie in the shelter, she had just lost her job at the hospital due to a single absence that resulted from a violent beating at the hands of her partner, a phenomenon we will explore in great depth in the next chapter.

Having grown up with physical, sexual, and emotional abuse, living her entire life in the illegitimate world of liquor houses and drug dealing left Evie with very little hope for her future. Typical of many victims of child abuse, Evie had never experienced any measure of stability, and this adversely affected her decision making. As Evie was describing her foray into legitimate employment, it was, perhaps, the only moment in the interview in which she smiled. She loved to cook and was happy that she could earn a living doing something she loved. The other staff in the kitchen where she worked were impressed by her skills, and when we asked what her signature dish was, she beamed and replied, "My turkey and stuffing! Everything made from scratch."

Yet we were shocked when in the midst of this conversation Evie stopped, opened up her pocketbook, and pulled out a receipt. She had been living at a local flop hotel for the past *four years* and had paid them almost forty thousand dollars in rent! When we remarked that for that sum, with her good job at the hospital, she could have bought a small house or at least paid on a mortgage, her face sank. Yes, she knew that. When we asked her why she had not invested in something more permanent, even an apartment, which would have cost less per month and thus allowed her to save some money, she replied that it was her fear of instability. She *assumed* that she would lose her job. And of course, in the end, Evie's predictions for her life came true. Just prior to our meeting with her, she had lost not only her job but her housing as well. In essence, she had lost nearly everything except a few possessions. To put it simply, sexual abuse in childhood, when coupled with poverty and an unhealthy home life, has long-term, far-reaching, and in fact lifelong effects that extend into nearly all aspects of "typical" adult life, including shaping the aspirations—or lack thereof—of girls who are victims of CSA.

Race and Class Variation

National-level data indicate that African American women are more likely to experience rape and sexual abuse. Among the women we interviewed, though many of the white women had experienced molestation or incest, virtually *all* of the African American women we interviewed had experienced CSA in the form of incest, childhood prostitution, or premature sex engagement. Analysis of National Violence Against Women Act data (see Chapter 4 and its Resources section for a description of this data set) also indicates that African American women are more likely to experience severe IPV than are their white counterparts (Hattery 2008). Though there are many reasons for this, we would argue that *one key issue is the increased exposure of African American women to CSA, which ultimately increases their risk for IPV in adulthood.*

Furthermore, though rates of IPV are relatively stable across time and across racial and ethnic boundaries, our analysis of the NVAW data (Hattery 2008) demonstrates that race and ethnicity shape the *forms* of violence that women experience. Overall, African American women are disproportionately likely to experience lethal and near-lethal violence. For example, they are more likely to have a weapon (knife or gun) used against them, and they are more likely to be "beat up" (Hattery 2008). Our interviews confirmed this quantitative finding as well. White women were less likely to report injuries that required a visit to the emergency room or other forms of medical attention than were their African American counterparts. African American women reported incidents such as being hit in the head with a ball-peen hammer, being hit in the mouth so hard that one woman's teeth punctured both her top and bottom lips, being threatened with a shotgun, and being beaten beyond recognition—by an abusive partner who was also a boxer and had recently killed another boxer in the ring.

Similarly, research on the effects of child physical and sexual abuse demonstrates that African American children who are abused or neglected are more likely

to be involved in criminal activity as juveniles and adults than white children who experienced abuse or neglect in childhood (Widom and Maxfield 2001). For girls, arrests were most often reported for alcohol and drug violations (Saar et al. 2015; Widom and Maxfield 2001), which is consistent with the research on "self-medicating" by girls who are victims of CSA (Browne and Finkelhor 1986; Hanson 1990; Kendall-Tackett, Williams, and Finkelhor 1993; Pipher 1994; Rind, Tromovitch, and Bauserman 1998; Sturza and Campbell 2005), and which also feeds the growing sexual abuse to prison pipeline. Understanding clearly the likelihood of revictimization for girls who are victims of child abuse, and CSA in particular, and based on the realities that minority and low-income girls are more likely to experience CSA as well as be at greater risk for IPV (regardless of their experiences with CSA), *additional attention and resources must be dedicated to our most marginalized and vulnerable citizens.* We turn now to a discussion of the impact of childhood violence on men.

THE IMPACT OF VIOLENCE IN CHILDHOOD ON MEN

Growing up in a violent household, especially one that involves IPV, is a significant predictor of violence in adulthood. Family scholars like Straus and Gelles talk about this as the **intergenerational transmission of violence theory**: the theory that a propensity toward committing violence is transmitted from parent to child, from father to son.

In their study of men, Ehrensaft and Cohen (2003) report that experiencing child abuse *doubles* one's risk for beating one's intimate partner in adulthood. *But witnessing violence in childhood triples one's risk for growing up to become an abusive partner.* Ehrensaft and Cohen also report that child abuse and witnessing parental violence put individuals (both men and women) at risk for drug abuse, mental illness, and a variety of problematic behaviors. Few researchers dispute the fact that child abuse or growing up witnessing intimate partner parental violence is detrimental to the healthy development of children. (We use the term **parental violence** here to refer to violence perpetrated between intimate partners who are raising children. We fully recognize that in many cases, the batterer or the victim may not be a parent to the child. The adults may be stepparents, foster parents, even grandparents who are raising the child. The use of the term *parental* is merely a tool to reduce the cumbersome nature of the discussion and to reinforce the reality that the people engaging in violence are also charged with providing a safe and stable home for the child.)

Discussions of the intergenerational transmission of violence theory are fraught with controversy. Critics of the theory point to the fact that the *majority* of boys who grow up in violent homes do not grow up to abuse either their own children or their partners (Kaufman and Zigler 1987). Others are critical of the term because it implies a genetic transmission. We will discuss this critique in Chapter 16 and argue that the intergenerational transmission of violence can be understood by examining the ways that men, especially violent men, *teach* their sons to be men, rather than by interpreting the cycle of violence as genetic transmission.

To ignore the fact that boys who grow up experiencing violence or witnessing it often grow into men who perpetrate it would be to ignore one of the processes by which violence becomes part of intimate relationships. It would also be dismissive to ignore the powerful impact of child abuse on the men we interviewed. As we noted in the previous chapter, witnessing parental violence is a form of child abuse that has long-lasting and devastating consequences on boys who are victims. Many of the men that we interviewed grew up in households that were violent. Men like Darren grew up in households in which their fathers physically abused their mothers:

I saw the violence growing up. I can remember him standing over my mother with an iron in his hand and me drawing a .22 rifle on him to make him back up. Stuff like that. I can remember him choking my mother when I was seven, eight, nine years old. And all my friends are going to the kitchen window. There he is; he's got her over the sink. It was violent. Nobody was ever hospitalized or anything like that, but it was usually associated with his drinking.

(**Darren,** fortysomething white man, North Carolina)

In addition to the physical violence that occurred between Darren's parents, he described his father as emotionally absent; in fact, he indicated that his father was incapable of expressing emotion. After his parents divorced, he saw his father only five or six times in the next twenty years, until his father's death. On one of the rare occasions that Darren did see his father, they were having an argument about his father's absence and lack of guidance, and Darren's father became physically violent with him.

He got up and he backed me up against a wall, and he was just quivering from head to toe . . . He said, son, I love you, but I'll kill you . . . He was just unable to handle the emotional side about losing his family.

(**Darren,** fortysomething white man, North Carolina)

Other men grew up in homes in which their fathers were physically abusive to them:

Yeah, yeah, but I don't want him [my son], you know what I mean, to grow up and go through what we been through, you know what I'm sayin'. I believe in discipline, I give out spankin's, but I just don't want him to go through what me, my brother, and my sister went through with this dude [his stepfather], you know what I'm sayin', 'cause I still got scars from when he beat us. He beat me with an extension cord, hit me in the face, yeah, he left a scar down my face, you know what I'm sayin', so I had to stay out of school for a while on that, you know. He used to taunt my brother all the time. You're a punk, you're a pussy, you're a pussy, you know what I'm sayin', you ain't never gonna be nothing, you're stupid, dumb, you see what I'm sayin'. So me and him, he had grabbed me by my neck and broke my glasses because this one particular day he kept calling my brother a punk, you're a punk, you're a pussy, you're a punk, so he had went outside and got into some altercation with some dude [laughing], he came home, the dude kicked his ass [laughing], so when he came home I was like I guess you the punk and the pussy now, you know, so I guess that comment made him mad, and he grabbed me by my neck, so me and him start fightin', you know, but just by me making that comment I didn't care about gettin' beat up or gettin' a whippin', I just feel good that he got hit [laughing]. You know what I mean, that was a great feeling, you know what I mean.

(**Manny**, thirtysomething African American man, North Carolina)

Finally, though much less common, several of the men we interviewed grew up in households in which one parent killed the other, as Eddie's mother did.

THE IMPACT OF PROSTITUTION ON SONS

Earlier in the chapter we discussed at length the impact of prostitution on girls and young women. Many of the men we interviewed also grew up with prostitution. In these cases it was their mothers who worked as prostitutes, frequently in tandem with a drug addiction. Again, the impact on these young men was severe. Boys growing up in these households were often introduced to the drug culture and began using drugs themselves at an early age. We would also argue that these boys and young men were learning important lessons about women from the johns they serviced: that women's primary function is to satisfy men's sexual needs, that women's own interests and desires are unimportant, and that women are not to be respected or trusted. Unfortunately, they carried these views into their own adult relationships, as noted by Eddie, whose mother killed his father:

At the course of time I even would see my mother stick needles in her arms, shooting heroin, you know, and it just became a life for me that I had developed some bad habits from the people that I was hanging around and from I seen in my past, all that I knew what I knew. And during the course of years, during the course of these years, in school, I would go to school, you know, lay my head on the desk, wouldn't focus on the work, or cuss the teacher out, skip school, goin' to school, having marijuana, school just wasn't important to me. It had no benefits to me whatsoever, because I had already had made up my mind that I was going to be a drug dealer because, you know, that's all I had seen, that's all I had developed. I thought that getting high and drinking was the way to go because that's all I developed throughout my years of coming to be a early teenager and, uh, because all the abusive and damage I seen from my parents, all the damage of the people that I seen and hung around them. It became a habit to me, and by the time I was sixteen years old I was selling drugs and, uh, toting guns, and snorting cocaine, smoking crack at the age of sixteen years old, um, stealing cars, you know, the situation had gotten worse. I was snorting heroin, you know. The situation had just gotten bad at the age of sixteen, and therefore due to the fact that I had been in so much trouble, the judge sentenced me to go to Morganton High Rise for young men, a young prison camp in Morganton, North Carolina, and I was there and I went there, I caught ten years when I was sixteen years old. The judge gave me ten years.

(**Eddie**, fortysomething African American man, North Carolina)

Race and Class Variation

Much research documents the fact that rates of physical abuse of boys cross all race and class lines (Tjaden and Thoennes 2000). Thus, the role that race and class play in the intergenerational transmission of violence is in some ways minimal. However, the interviews that we conducted with abusive men of different racial or ethnic and class backgrounds illuminate the ways in which race and class *do shape* the relationship between child abuse or witnessing of abuse and perpetrating violence in adulthood. The situation for men is similar to that for women: because minorities and the poor are significantly less likely to report abuse or have it interrupted when it occurs, the cycle of interpersonal violence is significantly more likely to continue.

African American men also face distinct differences that shape their likelihood for seeing interpersonal violence propagated from one generation to the next. Most of these forces, such as unemployment, will be discussed in the next chapter. However, it is important to point out here that there are other individual risk factors, such as drug abuse, prostitution, and homicide, that young African American men are disproportionately likely to be exposed to that shape their decisions and behaviors in adulthood (Wilson 2009). African American men (and women, as noted above) are far more likely than their white counterparts to grow up in families that subsist in the illegitimate economy, a risk factor for exposure to drug abuse and prostitution. Homicide rates are substantially higher in the African American community as well. According to the Centers for Disease Control, homicide constitutes the fifth leading cause of death for African American men (National Center for Health Statistics 2015). In fact, in 2010, the *New York Times* reported the fact that the homicide rate in New York City has actually produced *a one-year drop in average life expectancy for African American men living in New York*, so common is the homicide of young black men (Rabin 2010). In Eddie's case, one can see evidence of the impact that witnessing an IPV homicide had on his own violence in adulthood. This increased exposure to severe violence certainly impacts the likelihood that African American men will grow up to abuse their intimate partners.

CONCLUSIONS

Clearly, the relationships among CSA, IPV, race and ethnicity, and social class are complex. We have argued here that African American women's disproportionate exposure to CSA puts them at increased risk for IPV in adulthood. As noted by sociologist Deborah King (1988), the impact of race, class, gender, and other social statuses is not "additive" but rather intersectional or "multiplicative." In order to truly understand the differences in the experiences of IPV for African American and white women, we need to understand the complexities of being a white woman or being an African American woman and how this status intersects with other systems, such as access to shelters, health care, stable employment, and the criminal justice system, that shape both the risk for IPV as well as the services available for women who find themselves faced with IPV. The same is true of social class. The fact that social class and race are so conflated exacerbates the situation for African American women. In terms of CSA and IPV, the issues we have been exploring in this chapter, we need to pay attention to the fact that African American women who are sexually abused as girls will, on average, have less access to treatment (mental health services, counseling) that, if successful in producing healing, may reduce their risk for IPV in adulthood.

Most boys who grow up in violent homes do not grow up to become abusive themselves. But the impact of the abuse they witness or experience is severe nonetheless. For so many of the men we interviewed, white or African American, the homes they grew up in were extremely violent. In some cases, they experienced violence themselves, but far more commonly they watched their fathers (or stepfathers) beat their mothers. This confirms the finding that Straus and Gelles and others have reported that boys who grow up watching their fathers (or stepfathers) beat their mothers *are at the greatest risk for growing up to beat their own partners* (Ehrensaft and Cohen 2003). Because understanding the concept of the intergenerational transmission of violence theory is critical to the solutions we propose for reducing *all* forms of family violence, we will return to this discussion of intergenerational transmission in Chapter 16.

Furthermore, it is clear that we cannot understand African American women's experiences with IPV until we understand their relation to African American men (Hattery and Smith 2014). Because of a long history of segregation and antimiscegenation laws, coupled with the continued abhorrence by many whites of black–white marriage—a 2011 survey conducted by Public Policy Polling of GOP voters in Mississippi, both white and African American, reported that 46 percent believe interracial marriage should be *illegal* ("MS GOP: Bryant for Gov., Barbour or Huckabee for Pres" 2011)—most African American women who are in relationships are in relationships with African American men, and interracial marriage rates for African American women are less than 2 percent. Thus, an additional "risk" that African American women face is linked to their partnerships with African American men, who, like them, are situated in a particular space in the opportunity structure that heightens the probability that they will engage in violence against their partners (Hattery and Smith 2014; Smith 2008). We will explore this issue at greater length in Chapters 9 and 10.

Finally, we note that one question that is always asked with regard to these women's stories is why these women sought out relationships with men as a route to escape sexual abuse. Part of the answer is quite simple; in most cases, these women were poor and unable to make a living on their own. In short, they were economically vulnerable. Of all the themes that run through the scholarly literature consulted to develop an effective model for understanding, preventing, and interrupting IPV, economic vulnerability was the most frequently cited by scholars and by our interviewees.

Furthermore, the majority of African American women and some (about 25 percent) of the white women we interviewed were pregnant as teenagers; most dropped out of school. Thus, they were extremely limited in their ability to provide for themselves economically and so they sought out relationships with men who they thought could put a roof over their heads, some food in their children's bellies, and provide some level of support for them. This is one of the most powerful ways in which class inequality shapes exposure to IPV. Why? Because women who are marginalized and denied access to the opportunity structure are vulnerable to and at an increased risk of violence both in the streets and at home.

Last, of course, we ask the question in reverse: what girl or young woman would not want to escape incest or childhood prostitution? Given their resources, most relied on very dangerous ways in which to effect the escape. Their response teaches us more about the tragedy of CSA than about their decision-making processes. Their experiences with incest and childhood prostitution left them feeling so desperate that they would have done literally anything to escape.

Though we will make many policy recommendations in the final chapter, we note here that it is clear that because of the strong relationship between CSA and child abuse (for women) and witnessing intimate partner parental violence and IPV in adulthood (for men), interventions with the child victims of abuse, including those who witness it, are critical and are likely to produce a sharp reduction in the incidence of IPV in adulthood. In the next chapter, we will examine the structural causes of IPV, such as unemployment and incarceration.

NOTES

1. As stated, in some cases the age differences were smaller, only ten years. Yet we argue that for a teenager, this age difference still represents a huge gap in knowledge about sex and power in the "relationship."

2. For a carefully researched, award-winning novel on this subject, we recommend Kathryn Stockett's book *The Help*.

3. Individuals will place "numbers" with a bookie on the days of horse races. Depending on the outcome, they can win considerable amounts of money for a small investment, sometimes as little as a quarter. When they "hit," the bookie collects a percentage of the take. See St. Clair Drake and Horace Clayton, *Black Metropolis: A Study of Negro Life in a Northern City* (1945), for a further explanation and discussion of what they refer to as the "policy station" (380–381).

REFERENCES

Alan Guttmacher Institute. 2004. *U.S. Teenage Pregnancy Statistics: Overall Trends, Trends by Race and Ethnicity, and State-by-State Information*. New York: Alan Guttmacher Institute.

American College of Obstetricians and Gynecologists. 2017. *Adult Manifestations of Childhood Sexual Abuse*. Committee on Health Care for Underserved Women. www.acog.org/-/media/Committee-Opinions/Committee-on-Health-Care-for-Underserved-Women/co498.pdf?dmc=1&ts=20181229T0104183777.

Brandt, J. E. 2006. "Why She Left: The Psychological, Relational, and Contextual Variables That Contribute to a Woman's Decision to Leave an Abusive Relationship." PhD dissertation, Department of Psychology, City University of New York.

Browne, A. 1989. *When Battered Women Kill*. New York: Free Press.

Browne, A., and D. Finkelhor. 1986. "Impact of Child Sexual Abuse: A Review of the Research." *Psychological Bulletin 99(1)*: 66–77.

Brownmiller, S. 1975. *Against Our Will: Men, Women, and Rape*. New York: Simon and Schuster.

Brush, Lisa D. 2001. "Poverty, Battering, Race, and Welfare Reform: Black-White Differences in Women's Welfare-to-Work Transitions." *Journal of Poverty 5(1)*: 67–89.

Brush, Lisa D. 2011. *Poverty, Battered Women, and Work in U.S. Public Policy*. London: Oxford University Press.

Burton, L. 2007. "Childhood Adultification in Economically Disadvantaged Families: A Conceptual Model." *Family Relations 56(4)*: 329–345.

Cherlin, A. J., L. M. Burton, T. R. Hurt, and D. M. Purvin. 2004. "The Influence of Physical and Sexual Abuse on Marriage and Cohabitation." *American Sociological Review 69(6)*: 768–789.

Collins, P. H. 1994. "Shifting the Center: Race, Class, and Feminist Theorizing About Motherhood." In *Mothering: Ideology, Experience, and Agency*, edited by E. Glenn, G. Chang, and L. Forcey, 45–66. New York: Routledge.

Drake, S. C., and H. Clayton. 1945. *Black Metropolis: A Study of Negro Life in a Northern City*. Chicago, IL: University of Chicago Press.

Ehrensaft, M., and P. Cohen. 2003. "Intergenerational Transmission of Partner Violence: A 20-Year Prospective Study." *Journal of Consulting and Clinical Psychology 71(4)*: 741–753.

Gaarder, E., and J. Belknap. 2002. "Tenuous Borders: Girls Transferred to Adult Court." *Criminology 40(3)*: 481–517.

Goodkind, S., I. Ng, and R. C. Sarri. 2006. "The Impact of Sexual Abuse in the Lives of Young Women Involved or at Risk of Involvement with the Juvenile Justice System." *Violence Against Women 12(5)*: 456–477.

Griffin, S. 1979. *Rape: The Politics of Consciousness*. New York: Harper & Row.

Griffing, S., D. F. Ragin, S. M. Morrison, R. E. Sage, L. Madry, and B. J. Primm. 2005. "Reasons for Returning to Abusive Relationships: Effects of Prior Victimization." *Journal of Family Violence 20(5)*: 341–348.

Hanson, R. K. 1990. "The Psychological Impact of Sexual Assault on Women and Children: A Review." *Sexual Abuse 3(2)*: 187–232.

Hattery, A. J. 2001a. "Tag-Team Parenting: Costs and Benefits of Utilizing Nonoverlapping Shift Work Patterns in Families with Young Children." *Families in Society 82(4)*: 419–427.

Hattery, A. J. 2001b. *Women, Work, and Family: Balancing and Weaving*. Thousand Oaks, CA: Sage.

Hattery, A. J. 2008. *Intimate Partner Violence*. Lanham, MD: Rowman and Littlefield.

Hattery, Angela J., and Earl Smith. 2010. "Cultural Contradictions in the South." *Mississippi Quarterly 63(1)*: 145–166.

Hattery, Angela J., and Earl Smith. 2014. *African American Families: Myths and Realities*. Lanham, MD: Rowman and Littlefield.

Kaufman, J., and E. Zigler. 1987. "Do Abused Children Become Abusive Parents?" *Journal of Orthopsychiatry 57*(*2*): 186–192.

Kearl, Holly. 2010. *Stop Street Harassment: Making Public Places Safe and Welcoming for Women.* New York: Praeger.

Kendall-Tackett, K., L. Williams, and D. Finkelhor. 1993. "Impact of Sexual Abuse on Children: A Review and Synthesis of Recent Empirical Studies." *Psychological Bulletin 113*(*1*): 164–180.

King, D. 1988. "Multiple Jeopardy, Multiple Consciousness: The Context of a Black Feminist Ideology." *Signs 14*(*1*): 42–72.

Korstad, R. 2003. *Civil Rights Unionism: Tobacco Workers and the Struggle for Democracy in the Mid-Twentieth-Century South.* Chapel Hill, NC: University of North Carolina Press.

Koss, M. P. 1985. "The Hidden Rape Victim: Personality, Attitudinal, and Situational Characteristics." *Psychology of Women Quarterly 9*(*2*): 193–212.

Koss, M. P., L. A. Goodman, A. Browne, L. F. Fitzgerald, G. P. Keita, and N. F. Russo. 1994. *No Safe Haven: Male Violence Against Women at Home, at Work, and in the Community.* Washington, DC: American Psychological Association.

Lalor, K., and R. McElvaney. 2010. "Child Sexual Abuse, Links to Later Sexual Exploitation/High-Risk Sexual Behavior, and Prevention/Treatment Programs." *Trauma, Violence, and Abuse 11*(*4*): 159–177.

Lawless, E. J. 2001. *Women Escaping Violence: Empowerment Through Narrative.* Columbia, MO: University of Missouri Press.

MacKinnon, C. 1991. *Toward a Feminist Theory of the State.* Cambridge, MA: Harvard University Press.

Maynard, R. A. 1997. *Kids Having Kids: Economic Costs and Social Consequences of Teen Pregnancy.* Washington, DC: Urban Institute Press.

Monto, M. A., and N. Hotaling. 2001. "Predictors of Rape Myth Acceptance Among Male Clients of Female Street Prostitutes." *Violence Against Women 7*(*3*): 275–293.

"MS GOP: Bryant for Gov., Barbour or Huckabee for Pres." 2011. *Public Policy Polling,* April 7. www.publicpolicypolling.com/pdf/PPP_Release_MS_0407915.pdf.

National Center for Health Statistics. 2015. *Health, United States, 2014: With Special Feature on Adults Aged 55–64.* Hyattsville, MD: Centers for Disease Control and Prevention. www.cdc.gov/nchs/data/hus/hus14.pdf.

Odem, M. E. 1995. *Delinquent Daughters: Protecting and Policing Adolescent Female Sexuality in the United States, 1885–1920.* Chapel Hill, NC: University of North Carolina Press.

Padavic, I., and B. Reskin. 2002. *Women and Men at Work.* 2nd ed. Thousand Oaks, CA: Pine Forge Press.

Pipher, M. B. 1994. *Reviving Ophelia: Saving the Selves of Adolescent Girls.* New York: Putnam Press.

Rabin, R. C. 2010. "Longevity: For New York Men, a Life Expectancy Gap." *New York Times,* August 30.

Raphael, J. 2004. *Listening to Olivia: Violence, Poverty, and Prostitution.* Boston, MA: Northeastern University Press.

Rich, A. C. 1980. "Compulsory Heterosexuality and Lesbian Existence." *Signs 5(4)*: 631–660.

Rind, B., P. Tromovitch, and R. Bauserman. 1998. "A Meta-Analytic Examination of Assumed Properties of Child Sexual Abuse Using College Samples." *Psychological Bulletin 124(1)*: 22–53.

Saar, Malika Saada, Rebecca Epstein, Lindsay Rosenthal, and Yasmin Vafa. 2015. *The Sexual Abuse to Prison Pipeline: The Girls' Story*. Washington, DC: Georgetown Law Center on Poverty and Inequality.

Scully, D. 1990. *Understanding Sexual Violence: A Study of Convicted Rapists*. Boston, MA: Unwin Hyman.

Shapiro, T. 2003. *The Hidden Cost of Being African American: How Wealth Perpetuates Inequality*. New York: Oxford University Press.

Smith, E. 2008. "African American Men and Intimate Partner Violence." *Journal of African American Studies 12(2)*: 156–179.

Stockett, K. 2009. *The Help*. New York: Amy Einhorn Books.

Sturza, M. L., and R. Campbell. 2005. "An Exploratory Study of Rape Survivors' Prescription Drug Use as a Means of Coping with Sexual Assault." *Psychology of Women Quarterly 29(4)*: 353–363.

Sweet, N., and R. Tewksbury. 2000. "What's a Nice Girl Like You Doing in a Place Like This? Pathways to a Career in Stripping." *Sociological Spectrum 20(3)*: 325–343.

Tjaden, Patricia, and Nancy Thoennes. 2000. *Full Report of the Prevalence, Incidence, and Consequences of Violence Against Women: Findings from the National Violence Against Women Survey*. Washington, DC: US Department of Justice. www.ncjrs. gov/pdffiles1/nij/183781.pdf.

Tursi, F. 1994. *Winston-Salem: A History*. Winston-Salem, NC: John F. Blair.

Wesely, J. K. 2006. "Considering the Context of Women's Violence: Gender, Lived Experiences, and Cumulative Victimization." *Feminist Criminology 1(4)*: 303–328.

Wesely, J. K., and J. D. Wright. 2005. "The Pertinence of Partners Examining Intersections Between Women's Homelessness and Their Adult Relationships." *American Behavioral Scientist 48(8)*: 1082–1101.

Widom, C. S., and M. G. Maxfield. 2001. An Update on the "*Cycle of Violence*." Washington, DC: National Institute of Justice. www.ncjrs.gov/pdffiles1/nij/184894.pdf.

Wilson, W. J. 2009. *More Than Just Race*. New York: W. W. Norton.

Wolf, N. 1992. *The Beauty Myth: How Images of Beauty Are Used Against Women*. New York: Anchor Books.

THE ECONOMY AND INTIMATE PARTNER VIOLENCE

9

Violence by men against members of their own family is one of the most common yet perplexing forms of criminal behavior. One interpretation is that intrafamily violence is instrumental behavior that is used by domineering men to control their partners and children . . . There are 2.5 to 4.5 million physical assaults inflicted on adult women by their intimate partner per year.

Half of female homicide victims in the United States [are] killed by their husband or partner.

—**David Card and George B. Dahl**, "Family Violence and Football:
The Effect of Unexpected Emotional Cues on Violent Behavior"

This is the first of two chapters that are devoted *entirely* to discussions of intimate partner violence (IPV) in heterosexual couples. In contrast to the discussions of child abuse and elder abuse, which were organized around the types of abuse experienced, these two chapters are organized around the two dominant structural forces that shape IPV: the economy and cultural norms. Because this is the first chapter devoted to examining IPV, we begin by providing an overview of IPV, the forms it takes, and its prevalence in the United States population. We then move our discussion to the role that structures play in shaping IPV. Perhaps the most powerful structure shaping IPV is the economy, and of particular concern to researchers and service providers in the second decade of the twenty-first century is the way in which the Great Recession of 2007–2009 impacted IPV. We will also explore the role that an individual's social class plays in shaping their experiences with IPV and how it impacts women's responses to IPV when they find themselves victims of it. Last, we will provide some suggestions for ways in which transformations in the economy would lead to reductions in IPV.

OBJECTIVES

- To provide an overview of IPV and the forms it takes
- To provide some basic statistics on IPV
- To examine the predictors of IPV: individual factors, couple factors, and structural factors
- To explore the ways in which the economy contributes to and shapes IPV
- To identify the role that economic systems play in creating inequality and shaping gender relations
- To examine the ways in which the economic system of a particular culture contributes (or not) to the rates of IPV
- To explore differences in rates of IPV across class groups in the United States, and specifically the role that social class plays in shaping one's risk for IPV

KEY TERMS

intimate partner violence
physical abuse
intimate terrorism
situational couple violence
emotional or psychological abuse
financial abuse
stalking
sexual abuse
intimate partner violence homicide
economic systems

social structure
ecological fallacy
micro level
macro level
social class
status inconsistency
compulsory partnering
labor market
occupational sex segregation
wage discrimination

INTRODUCTION

The first of two chapters devoted to IPV, this chapter will begin by describing IPV as it occurs in the United States and providing statistics on its prevalence. Second, we will examine the factors that shape one's risk for IPV. After we have briefly discussed individual and couple factors, the remainder of the chapter will be devoted to a key structural factor that shapes IPV: the economy. As noted above, we will discuss the role of the economy at the individual level (one's social class) and at the societal level (the overall role of economic systems) in shaping IPV.

This chapter, along with the previous and several of the subsequent chapters, is unique to this text because it includes data that we gathered. As we briefly discussed in Chapter 1, between 2001 and 2004 we conducted interviews with nearly one hundred men and women who live with IPV. We interviewed whites, African Americans, and some Hispanics. About half of the individuals we interviewed were in relationships with each other; this allowed us a unique opportunity to see both sides of the story, so to speak. As we noted in our discussion of methods in Chapter 4, qualitative interviews allow for the exploration of a phenomenon at significantly greater depth. Our interviews allow us to explore the processes by which risk factors for engaging in IPV, for example, lead to actual abusive behavior in one's relationship. Our interviews also provide a much more complex and in-depth view of the ways in which IPV takes place in the contemporary United States. That said, because our work is qualitative, we also examine the work of researchers who conducted broad, national studies in order to provide an expansive, overall view of the prevalence of IPV. One way to think about this is that our interviews provide the contours and shape of the two-dimensional map created by the research conducted on national samples. In several of the subsequent chapters, we will draw on the words of the people we interviewed in order to illustrate key concepts. This allows one to see the world of IPV through the people who are living it. We begin our discussion with an overview—some definitions and some statistics.

DEFINITIONS AND STATISTICS

Intimate Partner Violence

Intimate partner violence refers to physical, emotional, psychological, and/or sexual abuse that takes place between intimate partners. These partners may be married or in a long-term committed relationship, or they may be dating. They may be living together or not living together. They may be separated or even divorced. They may be heterosexual or part of the LGBTQ community. IPV occurs between two people who claim, or claimed, to love each other.

Physical Abuse

Physical abuse refers to violence that is physical. It can range from a slap or a push to kicking, biting, punching, or hitting with an object. Victims of physical abuse often sustain cuts, bruises, and lacerations; they frequently sustain broken bones; and in extreme cases they experience violence that requires hospitalization. When we first began interviewing victims of IPV, we were stunned at the level of physical violence that was going on in our own community. We met a woman who had been hit in the head multiple times with a ball-peen hammer, resulting in wounds that required dozens of stitches; we met a woman who had been slammed so hard into the stick shift of her car that she broke her pelvis; we met a woman who was hit so hard in the mouth that her teeth punched through both her top and her lower lips. We met a woman who was bitten regularly in her face, apparently as a way of "marking" her. At the extreme, physical violence can result in permanent injury and even death. According to the Bureau of Justice Statistics, which counts only those crimes reported to the police, in 2013 more than three-quarters of a million (805,700) acts of IPV were reported (Catalano 2013). Statistics that are based on national samples of women report that about one in four women (31.5 percent) and one in seven men (27.5 percent) have experienced severe physical violence by an intimate partner (for example, they were hit with a fist or something hard, beaten, or slammed against something) at some point in their lifetime (Centers for Disease Control 2017a). Perhaps most disturbing is the fact that reports of severe IPV have increased since 2002 such that in 2013, approximately one-third of all IPV reported was categorized by the CDC as "severe" (Catalano 2013). One will recall from our discussion of methods in Chapter 4 that one of the problems associated with all forms of family violence is the likelihood that they will be underreported; thus, most scholars agree that estimates generated through national probability samples are more accurate than official crime statistics.

As we discussed in Chapter 3, some scholars of family violence believe it is important to distinguish between two types of IPV—intimate terrorism and situational couple violence. We provide a brief overview of our longer discussion in Chapter 3 here.

Intimate Terrorism

Leone and her colleagues describe **intimate terrorism** as "a partner's attempt to exert control over his partner using a broad range of power and control tactics, which include physical violence" (2004: 473).

Situational Couple Violence

In contrast, **situational couple violence**

> does not exist within a general pattern of controlling behavior. This form of violence
> is not motivated by a desire to control and over power a partner or a relationship,
> but rather occurs when specific conflict situations escalate to violence.
>
> (Leone et al. 2004: 473)

Emotional or Psychological Abuse

Emotional or psychological abuse refers to the type of abuse that is designed to belittle and humiliate the victim. It is the most common form of abuse; it coexists with all other forms of abuse. Many victims report that it is as painful as physical violence (Browne 1989; Hattery 2008). Quite often, emotional or psychological abuse is verbal and ranges from name-calling to verbal assault—berating someone for a mistake or for doing something the "wrong way." Emotional or psychological abuse often involves public humiliation—for example, women often reported that their husbands or boyfriends called them names in front of their friends. A common scenario involved the husband inviting friends over to watch a sports event and berating his wife for not providing proper food or enough beer. Public humiliation frequently involves calling one's wife names or referring to her as "dumb" or saying "she doesn't know anything" in a public setting, such as when shopping or doing business at a bank. Emotional or psychological abuse can also involve terrorizing one's partner by tapping her phone, hacking into her email, following her to work or on errands, and so forth. We explore these types of behaviors at length in Chapter 14.

Financial Abuse

Financial abuse refers to many different ways in which abusers restrict access to financial resources. In addition to restricting their intimate partners from working outside the home, an issue we will devote a great deal of time to in this chapter, abusers may also restrict their partners by giving them an "allowance" and not letting them have access to all of the household funds. They may also prohibit their partners from holding individual bank accounts or credit cards to which the abuser does not have access. All of these strategies severely limit routes to escaping the violence.

Stalking

Stalking is a particular kind of psychological abuse that we discuss separately because it has become the focus of recent IPV and dating violence legislation. Stalking can involve some of the behaviors previously mentioned, including tapping phone lines, hacking into email accounts, and following the victim as they travel to work or school, on errands, and so forth. Stalking can also involve harassment, including calling or texting incessantly and banging on the door for hours, demanding to be let into the victim's home. According to the CDC, 10 percent of women and 2 percent of men have been stalked at least once in their lifetime (Centers for Disease Control 2017a). Stalking is particularly common among violent couples who have separated or divorced, and it is also a common part of dating violence, especially among adolescents and college students. One of the authors had a student who shared that her boyfriend demanded that she be on Skype with him at all hours of the day and night—except for when she was in class—and if he could not see her through the webcam he installed on her computer, he would call her cell phone and her roommate's cell phone for hours, until she responded to him. She asked the author if this was unusual; yes, the author responded. It is stalking, it will likely get worse, and she should end this relationship. Stalking came to the attention of IPV advocates in the 1980s, and in 1990 the first anti-stalking legislation was enacted. Because it is so common in certain types of intimate relationships, especially among dating couples and couples who have separated, and because it is relatively easy to document in the age of cell phone technology and computers, it is one of the forms of violence that is more likely to be prosecuted.

Sexual Abuse

Sexual abuse refers to any forced, coerced, or undesired sexual behavior. Though most commonly thought of as rape (we will discuss marital rape at length in the next chapter), sexual abuse typically involves forcing someone to engage in sex acts that they do not desire. So, for example, a woman who might be more than willing to have sexual intercourse with her husband may find that when he is drunk and unable to sustain an erection, he will penetrate her with an object; women have reported being penetrated with curling irons, beer bottles, and many other objects that result in internal injuries. According to the Centers for Disease Control, nearly half, 45.4 percent, of women who reported being raped were raped by their intimate partner and 57.9 percent of women who reported to law enforcement an incident of IPV reported that they were sexually abused (Centers for Disease Control 2017a).

As we will discuss at length in the next chapter, sexual abuse is very common, but for a variety of reasons, including beliefs about sexuality and the lack of physical evidence, it is rarely prosecuted.

Intimate Partner Violence Homicide

Intimate partner violence homicide simply refers to the most severe outcome of physical violence: homicide. IPV homicide can be intentional or result from a severe beating that may take place in minutes or hours and leaves the victim dead. More than thirteen hundred women are murdered per year by their current or former intimate partners, and IPV homicide accounts for *half* of all homicides of women (Centers for Disease Control 2017a). In other words, one in two women who are murdered are murdered by their intimate or ex-intimate partners. This is nothing short of stunning. Not all women face the same risk for IPV homicide, in fact, women of color and African American and Native American women are far more likely to be murdered than white or Asian women.

The report (CDC) also found that black and indigenous women are slain, in general, at significantly higher rates than women of other races. Black women are killed at a rate of 4.4 per 100,000 people, and indigenous women at a rate of 4.3 per 100,000; every other race has a homicide rate of between 1 and 2 per 100,000.

(Centers for Disease Control 2017b)

It is also important to note that in cases of IPV homicide, when the perpetrator is a man, he often kills children, and it is not uncommon for him to attempt or commit suicide. Each year between two and three hundred men are murdered by their spouses or ex-spouses (Catalano 2013). As the research of Angela Browne (1989) reveals, along with the documentary film work on the Framingham Eight, *Defending Our Lives*, and the documentary *Sin by Silence* illustrate, the majority of men who are victims of domestic violence homicide are killed by wives and partners whom they have been abusing.

BOX 9.1   INTIMATE PARTNER VIOLENCE HOMICIDE

Officers were called to the home to conduct a welfare check. When they realized Conley had an outstanding warrant . . . they tried to enter but were met with gunshots. The . . . stand-off resulted in Conley's arrest and the discovery of the eight bodies.

—Elisha Fieldstadt, "Texas Man David Conley
Accused of Killing 2 Adults, 6 Children in Dispute
with Ex," *NBC News*, August 10, 2015

The case of David Conley, Valerie Jackson, her ex-husband, and the six children, one of which was Conley's, illustrates so many of the triggers for IPV and IPV homicide in particular. According to the news account excerpted above, Jackson and Conley had recently broken up and Jackson's ex-husband had moved back in with her. This sent Conley into a jealous rage and is likely the primary trigger for the mass shooting he committed. Additionally, according to reports, Child Protective Services had recently been called to the house to investigate allegations of child abuse, another risk factor for IPV homicide.

IPV homicide is under discussed and under researched in the United States. It takes place on a regular basis and results in approximately 1,500 murders each year. Most victims are women. These homicides happen so often that they rarely make the news, and only when the crime is horrific—as in the Conley case, which left eight dead—will there be a media blitz, but notably, the *New York Times* did *not* pick up this story.

Source: Fieldstadt 2015.

The mass shootings, domestic violence link: this includes school shootings.

On November 19, 2018, 32-year-old Juan Lopez shot and killed his girlfriend, 38-year-old Tamara O'Neal, an emergency room physician at Mercy Hospital in Chicago. He also killed a pharmaceutical resident and a police officer. Lopez was killed by the police.

This incident, like so many other mass shootings, was the tragic conclusion of an argument between Lopez and O'Neal. Yet another example of intimate partner violence homicide.

Of the 156 mass shootings that took place between 2009 and 2016 approximately 54% were related to domestic violence, including the tragedy that unfolded just before Christmas in 2012 when Adam Lanza, a 20-year-old white man, massacred 20 children as well as 6 adults at the Sandy Hook Elementary School in Connecticut. Lanza had been having domestic disputes with his mother Nancy Lanza. He killed her before he went to Sandy Hook to kill all of the young children. Other mass and school shootings that were perpetrated by men, almost all white, that are also linked to intimate partner or family violence include the DC Sniper (Lee Boyd Malvo), the mass shooting in Las Vegas in October 2017 in which shooter Stephen Paddock murdered 59, and the "first" mass shooting, the Texas Tower shooting in August 1966, in which Charles Whitman climbed to the top of the tower on the University of Texas campus and began shooting. Ultimately 11 were murdered and 31 were injured. Whitman's rampage began when he murdered his mother.

Source: Smucker, Sierra. 2017. "Strengthening laws which take guns out of the hands of domestic abusers will help prevent future mass shootings." USApp—American Politics and Policy Blog (November 13). http://bit.ly/2QfxZTn.

The connection between these shootings and IPV is crystal clear. As a society we need to take these relationships seriously. Intervening in IPV may be our best prevention strategy for eliminating mass shootings—even more promising than gun reform.

We turn now to a discussion of the research that has revealed risk factors for experiencing IPV.

RISK FACTORS FOR EXPERIENCING IPV

As with other forms of family violence, there are factors that increase the probability that IPV will occur. There are three types of risk factors: those associated with the individual (either the perpetrator or the victim), those associated with the couple, and structural factors. We begin by examining individual risk factors.

Individual Risk Factors for IPV

There are several factors that increase one's likelihood of perpetrating IPV:

- being a man
- witnessing IPV in the household in which one grew up

- substance abuse or addiction
- poverty
- unemployment
- a history of incarceration
- a history of anger management problems, including fighting and assaults.

Though all of these factors increase one's probability for violence, the two most important predictors are gender, specifically being a man, and witnessing domestic violence in childhood. In the vast majority of cases of IPV, the perpetrator is a man. But of course not all men engage in IPV, and, as we discussed at length in Chapter 8, a man's risk for perpetrating IPV is significantly increased by exposure to IPV in childhood; boys who witness IPV are three times more likely to perpetrate IPV in adulthood than boys who do not. It is important to point out that none of these risk factors guarantees that someone will become abusive; in fact, most people with the greatest risk factors do not become abusive. That said, when we consider prevention strategies, intervention strategies, and dating practices, it is important to understand the differential risk individuals may have for violence.

There are also several factors that increase the probability that one will become a victim of IPV. These include:

- being a woman
- being a victim of child abuse, child sexual abuse in particular
- poverty
- being a woman of color
- unemployment
- becoming pregnant as a teenager
- early sexual initiation
- substance abuse or addiction.

It is important to point out that by far the single greatest risk factor for becoming a victim of IPV is being a woman. Women are the victims in approximately 80 percent of all IPV cases, and additionally, compared to men who are victims, they are more likely to sustain injuries that require medical attention and they are *significantly* more likely to be killed by current or former intimate partners (Center for Disease Control and Prevention 2017a). Furthermore, as we noted, our own interviews confirmed that in the majority of cases in which men report being victims of physical violence at the hands of their wives and girlfriends, the violence engaged in by the women was perpetrated in self-defense; they were fighting back. As we explored at length in the previous chapter, women who are the victims of child abuse are at significantly greater risk for becoming victims of IPV in adulthood. Last, we note that women of color, and African American women and Native American women in particular, experience significantly higher rates of IPV than their white counterparts (Tjaden and Thoennes 2000). As was the case with risk factors for perpetrating IPV, it is important to note that even the presence of several risk factors does not mean that an individual will eventually be abused. It is important to understand these risk factors, however, as we create intervention and prevention programs. In particular, as we noted in the previous chapter, victims of child sexual abuse need significant attention in order to prevent a lifetime of abuse.

Couple Risk Factors for IPV

In addition to factors that place individuals at greater risk for IPV, there are a series of factors that, when present in a couple, increase the likelihood that violence will become part of the relationship:

- marrying before the age of twenty-five
- having a child before the age of twenty-five
- having more than the average number of children, and especially having children close together
- poverty
- unemployment
- substance abuse or addiction.

Like the risk factors for child and elder abuse, many of the "couple" risk factors are related to stress; when a couple has several factors that increase the likelihood that they will have conflict—they are young parents, they have many children, they are facing financial problems—the very presence of the conflict increases the risk of IPV. As always, it is important to point out that this does not mean that all poor people or all teen parents or all large families will experience IPV. Rather, it is important to recognize that these couples face a greater likelihood of violence, and we need to design prevention programs that target at-risk couples.

Structural Risk Factors for IPV

In addition to risk factors associated with either individuals or couples, there are also structural factors that increase the likelihood of IPV occurring in a population. As Sanday (1981) noted in her examination of gender-based violence (sexual and IPV) cross-culturally, in cultures that are characterized by high levels of hierarchy and stratification—where people are ranked by their status, especially gender, age, and social class—that prohibit women's leadership, and that have a double sexual standard for men and women (especially cultures where polygyny, taking several wives, is accepted), all forms of gender-based violence are higher. In cultures that are relatively egalitarian—be they postindustrial cultures like Sweden or Norway or subsistence cultures like the !Kung of Botswana—rates of gender-based violence are significantly lower.

The United States is a culture based on significant stratification—dividing people by race, gender, religion, social class, age, sexuality, and so forth—and a high degree of hierarchy among these competing groups, and thus people living in the United States are at higher risk of living with IPV than individuals in many other cultures. However, women in the United States are at significantly lower risk for experiencing violence than women in parts of Africa and the Middle East (World Health Organization 2015).

Within the United States, since that is the main focus of this discussion, one of the primary structural factors that impact the risk for or rate of IPV is the economy. **Economic systems** that engender equality tend to exist in cultures that are otherwise egalitarian (for instance, Sweden), and economic systems that perpetuate inequality tend to exist in cultures that are otherwise stratified (for instance, the United States). In addition to the overall impact of the economic system operating in a culture, which is relatively fixed across time, the state of the economy itself, whatever its form, also influences the rate of IPV present in a culture. In particular, not only are rates of IPV expected to be higher in a capitalist economy than a socialist one, but rates of IPV are also expected to be higher during periods of economic downturn and recession than during periods of relative prosperity. Because the nature of economic systems and the state of the actual economy both influence rates of IPV in a given culture, we devote the remainder of this chapter to a discussion of the relationship between the economy and IPV.

STRUCTURAL AND INDIVIDUAL FACTORS

One of the distinguishing features of sociology as a discipline is the focus on the structural and institutional aspects of society as opposed to the individual within society.

"**Social structure** refers to the way social positions, social roles, and networks of social relationships are arranged in our institutions, such as the economy, polity, education, and organization of the family. A social structure could be a labor market that offers financial incentives and threatens financial punishments to compel individuals to work; or it could be a 'role' associated with a particular social position in an organization such as a church, family, or university (e.g., pastor, head of a household, or professor) that carries certain power, privilege, and influence external to the individuals who occupy that role" (Wilson 2009: 4).

Source: From *More Than Just Race: Being Black and Poor in the Inner City*, by William Julius Wilson. Copyright © 2009 by William Julius Wilson. Used by permission of W. W. Norton & Company, Inc.

Though, as noted above, there are individual factors and couple factors that shape one's risk for IPV, these lists of factors are simply useful in identifying patterns in IPV; it does not occur randomly. However, unlike in other disciplines, such as psychology, sociologists adhere to a core principle that patterns cannot be used to assess an actual person's risk for experiencing an event; this principle is called the *ecological fallacy*.

Ecological fallacy refers to the fact that aggregate-level data cannot be used to predict individual-level risk for an event or experience. For example, as noted in Chapter 8, boys who witness violence in the households in which they grew up are three times more likely to abuse their partners in adulthood than boys who did not (Ehrensaft and Cohen 2003). That said, if we had one hundred young men enrolled in a course on marriage, and half of them had witnessed violence in the homes in which they grew up, we could not predict with any degree of certainty *which*, if any, of these men would grow up to become abusive, only that the fifty who had witnessed abuse are three times more likely to abuse their own partners compared to the rate among the fifty who had not. Incidentally, some of the fifty boys who had *not* witnessed abuse growing up would also grow up to be abusive partners.

Our argument, then, pertaining to the behavior of abusive men is based on the distinction between what any one individual might do or say and how their actions are shaped by their circumstances. It is, of course, the classic problem that sociologists pose when trying to make sense of unclear or irrational human actions—the tension between individual agency and structural constraints (Connidis and McMullin 2002; Lin 2000).

THE ECONOMY AND IPV

The economy and IPV are interconnected in many different ways, at both the macro and the micro levels.

Sociologists distinguish between individual or **micro-level** experiences and structural/institutional or **macro-level** experiences. Being poor is a micro-level factor related to IPV. Living during or in the aftermath of the recession of 2007–2009 is a macro-level factor related to IPV.

THE MICRO LEVEL: SOCIAL CLASS AND MONEY

At the micro, or individual, level, finances and money are strongly linked to IPV. A common belief about couples is that they fight about two things: money and children. There is no doubt that money is an important part of family life. Generally, couples argue about how to obtain money, how to spend money, how to manage money, who should be earning the money, and by what means it should be earned. As we will discuss at length in Chapter 10, dominant beliefs about masculinity prescribe that "real" men must be successful breadwinners, and as reported by other scholars as well as *all* the men we interviewed, money is something couples that experience IPV argue about often and specifically. For white men, their partners' critique of them as breadwinners was a significant trigger for IPV (Dunleavey 2009; Hattery 2008).

Control of the family's economic resources is important for many different reasons. But in families that involve abuse and violence, the degree to which women have access to these resources is critical to their ability to exit or escape these relationships (Hattery 2008). In addition, access to financial resources is directly linked to the mode of leaving; poor women are forced to seek assistance at shelters, whereas more affluent women may take a hotel room or even rent a separate apartment. However, access to financial resources is by no means a guarantee of exit, as many affluent women do not leave their abusive partners for the same reasons middle-class or poor women do not—they love their partners and because they believe they will change.

Affluence is a complex part of the IPV puzzle because women in affluent households often have the resources to leave but, frequently, they also have a great deal to lose. There are many examples of this in the worlds of sport, business, entertainment, and politics (Hattery 2008: 20). These stories are difficult to unearth. Like Farrah Fawcett, the actress and sex symbol, women in the upper classes have been the victims of IPV, but their stories are rarely heard outside a tight-knit community of close friends and therapists. Why? They, like all women who are the victims of violence, are mostly afraid and ashamed to go public with their pain (Weitzman 2001). For example, Susan Weitzman's unique study of upper-class women who are victims of IPV is possible only because of a particular niche that she occupies—that of therapist. As part of her practice, upper-class women who are "having trouble" in their marriages come to her for therapy and during the course of this therapy, stories of violence tumble out.

One famous example is that of NFL player, Ray Rice. On February 15, 2014, Ray Rice, who was at the time, a star playing for the Baltimore Ravens, punched his then fiancée, Janay Palmer, unconscious in an elevator in Atlantic City, New Jersey. Though the incident was reported to the police immediately and to the NFL within days, the incident was not taken seriously by the NFL until later that fall when the closed-circuit video of the violent incident emerged. Though Palmer reported the incident to both the police and the NFL, and she was interviewed by both the police and NFL officials, Palmer's support for her fiancée never wavered. In fact, within twenty-four hours of his indictment for assault, they wed. At the time of this writing, in the winter of 2018, Janay Palmer Rice continues to appear in public, including on television talk shows defending her husband and begging for others to forgive him (and give him a job!) just as she has.

Why would Janay Palmer Rice defend her husband's extremely violent attack? Why would she be his most ardent supporter and forgiver? We would argue that it's because, on balance, Janay, like many wives of powerful, influential, affluent men, had a lot to lose—mainly money and thus her standard of living. Though she most likely had the assets to exit, she chose not to. It may be that this was the only incident of violence, and this is what Janay has said publicly, and thus perhaps Janay's decision to remain with Ray was also predicated on the cessation of the violence. It is also possible that the experience of being arrested, having his violent rage played out over and over again on YouTube, and ultimately losing his job was potent enough that Ray did in fact stop engaging in IPV. We certainly heard many stories like this from many middle- and upper-middle-class men we interviewed; a foray into the criminal justice system "scared them straight," so to speak. Of course, it's also possible that the violence continued and that her own foray into the criminal justice system scared Janay enough that she never reported it again; this is also consistent with what we heard from women we interviewed. We will never know what happened in the Rices' marriage. What we do know is that money doesn't protect people from experiencing IPV. It is important to point out that there are always push-and-pull factors that make the decision(s) to stay or leave complex.

Though social class may have only a limited effect on *whether* women who are abused leave, it most certainly affects the *ways* in which they do. Affluent women rarely wind up in shelters, for example, because they have access to resources that will facilitate temporary housing arrangements; that is, they can stay in a hotel, rent an apartment, or even live with family or friends, who are also more likely to have the resources necessary to accommodate a long-term guest. In contrast, most of the poor women we interviewed were from poor families who were not in a financial position to help them. If they were to move in with family, as some of them did, this often resulted in two or three whole families living in a two- or three-bedroom apartment.

Though class privilege can provide alternatives to staying in an abusive relationship or fleeing to a shelter, affluence does not protect women from experiencing IPV. When we analyzed data from the National Violence Against Women Survey (Tjaden and Thoennes 2000) specifically to examine the relationship between types of violence experienced and social class, we found that rates of violence remained high among middle-class, upper-middle-class, and affluent women. The data in Table 9.1 are limited to middle- and upper-income households; those who are affluent. In the analysis, the rates of violence reported by middle-class and upper-class women were compared to the rates reported by working-class and poor women. In the Violence Against Women Act (VAWA) data, upper-class women were those designated as living in households earning at least eighty thousand dollars per year, or approximately 1.5 times the median household income at the time. On only a few types of violence (as denoted by the asterisks) were rates of violence *less common* among affluent than working-class and poor women. Thus, it is safe to say that affluence is *not* a buffer from IPV.

Table 9.1 Intimate Partner Violence and Social Class: Percentage of Affluent Women Reporting Physical Violence, 1994–1996

Types of Violence	HOUSEHOLD INCOME	
	Upper Middle ($50–80K)	Upper (<$80K)
Partner throws something at woman that could hurt her[1]	9.4%	7.2%
Partner pulls woman's hair*	9.1%	8.3%
Partner slaps woman	20.2%	18.8%
Partner kicks or bites woman	6.0%	4.3%
Partner chokes or drowns woman*	5.4%	4.9%
Partner hits woman with an object	6.8%	5.4%
Partner beats woman up*	8.7%	8.6%
Partner threatens woman with a gun*	5.1%	2.9%
Partner threatens woman with a knife	3.4%	4.3%
Partner uses a gun on woman	2.0%	1.8%
Partner uses a knife on woman	1.7%	2.4%

Significance based on Chi-Square analysis with p-values <.10

Analyses were performed using the data collected as part of the Violence and Threats of Violence Against Women survey, a national probability sample of men and women. Descriptions and data can be found at: www.icpsr.umich.edu/icpsrweb/ICPSR.

SOCIAL CLASS

When the average person thinks of the term **social class**, they are generally thinking about how much money somebody makes. But sociologists generally define social class as a combination of three variables:

1. income
2. education
3. occupation

In general, though not always, individuals who are members of the upper class make a lot of money (income); they have attained a high level of education, perhaps a professional degree (such as a medical or law degree); and they have prestigious occupations, such as being a doctor, lawyer, college professor, or investment banker. In contrast, people who are of a lower class typically earn low wages, have less education—perhaps they graduated from high school or perhaps not—and they have less-prestigious occupations, such as being a construction worker or secretary, or even working in service jobs, such as in fast food or retail at the local mall.

Sociologists also recognize something we refer to as **status inconsistency**, which refers to the fact that sometimes one or more of the variables that make up social class are inconsistent with the others. For example, teachers have a high level of education and work in a relatively prestigious occupation, but they make relatively low salaries; the average high school teacher, even with a master's degree, will likely make just over fifty thousand dollars per year. Even college professors with a PhD typically earn less than one hundred thousand dollars per year. In contrast, professional athletes, who often have only a high school degree, can earn tens of millions of dollars per year.

Fact: the median household income for the United States is approximately fifty thousand dollars annually. This means that half of all American households earn *less than* fifty thousand dollars per year, and half earn more. Thus, the typical high school teacher is earning only what the average American household earns, despite his or her educational achievements and commitment to the important task of teaching.

We turn now to an exploration of the complex relationship between IPV and economics. This can be best described as a "chicken and the egg" relationship. In some cases, the abusive partner prevents his wife or girlfriend from working or gaining access to economic resources as a way of keeping her in the relationship, and in other cases the violence results in lost wages and even the loss of a job—women are fired for missing work due to injury or because their abusive partners show up at work and harass them. In violent couples, preventing women from working is a tool of control; they are rendered completely economically dependent upon their partners and have few, if any, options for leaving. Stalking women at work is another form of control utilized by abusers; an intended consequence of stalking is controlling the woman's behavior, and an unintended consequence of stalking at work is that it can lead to the victim being fired, thus rendering her economically dependent upon her partner. Additionally, both control strategies increase the difficulty women face as they attempt to leave abusive relationships; they lack not only the financial resources but also the ability to make the types of friendships and connections that can provide the kind of help needed to facilitate leaving an abusive relationship. In the following section, we explore the strategies utilized by abusers and the outcomes of these behaviors.

"You Can't Work": A Tool of Control

Because IPV has its roots in anger and control, as noted in our discussion of intimate terrorism, many abusers seek to control every movement of their partners. Often this includes a prohibition on labor-force participation (Atkinson, Greenstein, and Lang 2005; Hattery 2008). Among the women we interviewed, this was slightly more common in white households, but it was prevalent in African American households as well.

In some violent families, women's employment is threatening to her abusive partner for several practical reasons: it provides income that would allow her to successfully leave by breaking the economic dependency the abuser can extort from his partner; it is often the source of friends in whom the victim can potentially confide about the violence; and it often provides interactions with men of whom the abuser is extremely jealous (this will be explored in more depth in Chapter 14). Thus, many women who are victims of IPV find that they are prohibited from working outside the home (Browne 1989). The story of Josie, a woman we interviewed, illustrates this concept.

Josie's Story

Josie had worked as a nurse her entire adult life. She liked the independence that being employed offered, and she enjoyed the friendships she made at work. But John, her boyfriend, was extremely jealous of these friendships, especially the working relationships she had with men. Many times he showed up unexpectedly at the nurses' station at the hospital where Josie worked. One day, after showing up at her station to find that she was out to lunch with a group of her coworkers, including an older man who she acknowledged was no sort of romantic threat ("Not even Viagra would help him!"), John beat her for the first time. Following this, John forced her to quit her job. He justified this request by saying that he had always wanted to take care of Josie and that he did not want her to have to work so hard.

The rage John expressed at Josie's imagined infidelity was completely consistent with other stories we heard. One young woman, Amy, told us that her partner regarded everyone she worked with as an erotic threat:

He told me—he gave me a certain day I had to quit my job because he didn't trust me with anybody I worked with. Any guy whatsoever, if I talked to them, I was screwing them. It didn't matter. He accused me of stuff all the time.

(**Amy,** twentysomething white woman, North Carolina)

John's attempt to prohibit Josie from working, which was typical of many of the men and women we interviewed, was not really about wanting to "take care of her"; in fact, it was one of the many ways in which he was attempting to control Josie's life. After she disclosed the first beating to a friend at work, this friend, whose husband was a police officer, encouraged Josie to search their house.

Josie's search revealed significant evidence that John was in fact monitoring all of her phone calls and comings and goings. Josie later decided to try to return to work, for both the self-fulfillment and the economic reward. She received her second and final beating the night that John found job applications she was sending out in the mailbox. He beat her severely, and she left John that night and never returned. Ironically, though John feared she was attempting to desert him, Josie had actually prepared the job applications with the intention of finding a new place for both herself and John, including a move to a new community. His temporary job was about to end, and she was planning for their future together.

Josie's story illustrates many of the threats abusers feel from their partners' employment, but it also highlights the power that resources, access, and opportunity create for women who are ready to leave. And it was precisely the resources associated with her employment that allowed Josie to leave. Josie had made friends at work on whom she could rely for help. After the second and final beating, Josie's friend took her to the emergency room and helped arrange for her escape, even sneaking into Josie's house to retrieve the cash Josie had in her pocketbook—saved from her latest paycheck—in order to purchase a bus ticket and flee the state.

Because employment represents women's freedom from economic dependency on men and is thus threatening to an abuser, he will frequently restrict her employment opportunities (Browne 1989). Many women we interviewed reported that if they were allowed to work, their partners controlled the logistics of work—he determined where she worked and who she was allowed to befriend at work, and he demanded her paycheck be turned over entirely to him. Stella notes that often the abuse that Will perpetrated on her was triggered when she did not hand over her paycheck to him:

He didn't become abusive to me until I quit [using crack]. And then, I wouldn't give him any more money. And when he was coming down [from a high], he'd get violent and I'd go to work and have choke marks on my throat. He fractured my shoulder blade once 'cause he threw me in the bathroom and I hit the towel bar. Hitting my head against the wall. His favorite one was the choking, though.

(**Stella**, twentysomething African American woman, Minnesota)

In addition to these restrictions, in a beating or repeated beatings, the abuser essentially destroys his victim's freedom by ruining her career and her physical health in one blow. Symbolically, this is consistent with a variety of the accounts we heard from the women we interviewed. Many of them changed jobs, either to accommodate their partner's wishes or to get away from their abuser. Most of the women also reported having to call in sick on the days following a beating. Josie recalled that after the first beating, her jaw was so swollen that she called in sick and missed a couple of days of work. In some cases, the women were just too physically injured to work. More frequently, however, they were too embarrassed to show up at work with bruises and cuts that they had sustained at the hands of men who claimed to love them.

Many women are beaten so frequently that they cannot afford to miss work every time they are beaten. Several with whom we talked shared their secret techniques for covering up the cuts and bruises, techniques that allowed them to go to work following a beating. In fact, on the day we interviewed Candy, she was bruised and battered from a beating a few days before and showed us, almost with pride, how skillfully she had masked the bruises with makeup. Over a long period of time, however, the loss of wages and the potential loss of one's job due to truancy leave many abused women, even those who remain employed, economically dependent on their partners.

"He Showed Up at Work Brandishing a Gun": Fired Because of IPV

Though injuries account for most absences from work, the action of men showing up unexpectedly at work, as Josie's partner, John, did, is also a problem. Browne (1989) argues that this type of intrusion is yet another form of control and emotional abuse in which abusers engage. This type of intrusion allows abusive men to monitor the actions and interactions of their partners, and because it is random and unannounced, it allows them to create a situation in which the women they are abusing are in a constant state of alert or fear, never knowing when or where their abusive partners might show up unexpectedly. The random nature of this activity makes it a successful strategy for abusive men to indirectly control their partners, who must be always on their "best behavior" so as to avoid being "caught" doing something "wrong"—defined as anything the abuser disapproves of—and then being beaten for it later. Josie describes a day when John showed up unexpectedly at her nurses' station during one of her evening shifts:

I asked him what he was thinking. That was my job. I told him that if he went in there and showed his ass, people were going to think that I get off work and this is what I go home to and this is the way she probably really is. And I told him that I'm a professional at my job. I'm still funny and I'm still mouthy, but I'm professional. I do my job and I do it damn well. And I told him he couldn't go up there and show his behind. I told him I wouldn't put up with it. He would say, "I'm sorry, baby, I'm so sorry." Then three weeks later, everything started coming to a head.

(**Josie**, fiftysomething white woman, North Carolina)

Gus, an African American man who was arrested for beating his wife, told of the day he was arrested. Gus believed that his wife was having an affair. They had an argument and she admitted that she was in love with another man. In addition, she told Gus that she wanted a divorce and that she was moving in with her new boyfriend, which she did soon after. Gus could not believe the relationship was over, he could not believe that she had cheated on him, and he continued to believe that he was the best person for her. He wanted her back. Unable to convince her with words, he showed up at her office—she was a receptionist in a local pediatrician's office—with a gun and insisted that she leave with him. She was unwilling, so he kidnapped her at gunpoint and drove her across state lines to her mother's house, hoping that her mother would "talk some sense" into his estranged wife.

Thus, showing up at working unexpectedly, in and of itself, can be understood as emotional abuse. In addition, it is embarrassing when your angry and loud partner shows up at your job demanding to know where you are, as this behavior is disruptive to the workplace. Brush (2011) refers to this as "domestic violence spilling over into work."

Even if the partner is not angry or armed, such erratic behavior is highly unprofessional. Even if you are not in an abusive relationship, try to imagine your own partner showing up unexpectedly at your job, demanding to know what you are doing and who you are talking to. It would be absurd, just as it is for women who are abused by their partners.

This behavior often leaves a woman even more vulnerable to her abuser, for without a job—Gus's wife *was fired* after he showed up at her office and kidnapped her at gunpoint!—and an independent income, she is that much more economically dependent upon an already controlling and abusive man. We turn now to a discussion of macro-level economic factors that shape IPV.

THE MACRO LEVEL: ECONOMIC SYSTEMS AND THE ECONOMY

In this section we will explore the structural aspects of the economy that contribute to IPV. Specifically, we will examine the ways in which capitalism creates a **labor market** based on wage discrimination, which produces economic dependency at the individual level and compulsory partnering at the societal level.

> **Compulsory partnering**, a term we borrow and modify from Rich (1980), refers to the fact that very few women earn enough money to live independently. Women often feel compelled to partner with men, either cohabiting or marrying, in order to ensure that they have the financial resources to pay the rent, put food on the table, and so on, something they are not able to do on their own.

Wage Discrimination and Economic Dependency

One of the central features of the **labor market** in the United States is stratification by race and gender. This stratification arose from a variety of forces and has several important outcomes, which we will briefly review.

From the initial settlement by Europeans of what would become the United States up through the middle of the nineteenth century, the United States was primarily an agricultural economy. There were two key defining features of this agricultural economy: small family farms and the plantation economy of the South. Both played a role in shaping the segregated labor market that emerged during the Industrial Revolution. On the small family farm, women were an important part of agricultural production. That said, they were often relegated to certain tasks, and among the most important was the care of the house—cooking and cleaning—and the children. On the plantation, people of African descent were held as chattel slaves, and it was on their backs that the huge plantations were not only run but also turned huge profits for the planters. With the dawn of the Industrial Revolution in the middle of the nineteenth century, several key transformations occurred that built on existing patterns, shaping the labor market in ways that continue to persist today.

Specifically, as factories were being built and mines were being established—two of the hallmarks of industrialization—the owners of these factories and mines believed that women were entirely unsuitable for this work (they were too frail and too important to the running of the home), and African American men, though strong enough for the work, were considered too dumb and too lazy for the "new" work that was emerging. Additionally, plantations relied too heavily on the work enslaved bodies for the planters to favor leasing out a significant portion of their labor force to factories or mines. Thus, from the very beginning of the Industrial Revolution, work, which had previously not been segregated by gender, became highly segregated by both race and gender; white men were the exclusive beneficiaries of this new and difficult but highly lucrative work. It would not be until World War II that women or minorities would be able to penetrate the workplaces created by industrialization.

In response to the need for men to fight in World War II, both women and African American men were hired to work in factories and other industries as "replacement" workers. After the war, because women and African American men were still viewed as inferior workers—despite the superiority of their products—as well as to protect the white men who remained or had returned from war, white women and African American men were relegated to the lowest-level jobs, and they were paid inferior wages—which was legal—and many were simply "relieved of their duties" (Hattery 2001; Padavic and Reskin 2002). (African American women were by and large denied access to industrial jobs and continued to work primarily as domestics [P. Collins 1994; see Stockett 2009 for a fictional example].) This set the stage for a labor market that continues to be segregated.

> **Occupational sex segregation** refers to the fact that the majority of jobs are dominated by one gender or the other; men and women do different jobs or work in entirely different industries.

Today, in the top ten occupations that employ men—construction, plumbing and other trades, and truck driving—less than 5 percent of workers are women. Similarly, in the top ten occupations that employ women—teaching (from pre-school through middle school), caregiving (daycare providers, home health aides, and the like), lower-level medical professions (dental hygienists, nurses' aides, and so on), and administrative assistant work—more than 98 percent of workers are women. Similarly, many occupations, especially in certain regions of the country, such as the South, are highly racially segregated as well (Padavic and Reskin 2002).

One of the most significant consequences of occupational sex segregation is wage discrimination. In fact, when every other explanation—differences in education, differences in the number of hours worked, differences in taking time out to raise children, and so forth—is controlled for, the strongest predictor of wages is occupational sex segregation (Padavic and Reskin 2002). Essentially, men work in occupations that pay more than women. As noted above, the majority of white men work in industries with relatively high wages, including occupations that are far more likely to be unionized—such as construction or plumbing or electrical work—which means higher wages and better benefits. In contrast, the majority of women work in occupations that are among the lowest paid, including as teachers, daycare providers, home health workers, and administrative assistants. Thus, by virtue of working in different industries, women suffer from severe **wage discrimination**. In 2018 women still earned, on average, only 80 percent of what men who are their counterparts earned. And, unfortunately, when men and women do the same job, men still out-earn women by 20 percent (American Association of University Women 2018) (Figure 9.1). Similar patterns of occupational segregation persist for African Americans as well. For example, African American men continue to face discrimination as they attempt to integrate into professions such as police work, firefighting, and unionized trades (Hattery and Smith 2014).

One of the clearest and most problematic outcomes of wage discrimination is that, because women earn less than men, they are often *economically dependent* upon them (Browne 1989; Engels 1972; Hattery 2001, 2008; Rich 1980). Economic dependency leaves women vulnerable to IPV for two key reasons: they may feel that they have to put up with the abuse in order to continue having access to the resources the batterer provides—recall Janay Palmer, who made the decision to stay despite the abuse in her marriage—and their economic dependency makes it very difficult for them to amass the economic resources that are critical to leaving abusive relationships. This situation increases a woman's dependency on her partner because she may feel she has no other choice but to return home to her abuser because she has no other way to keep a roof over her head and food in the refrigerator.

Anyone who has talked with or interviewed women in a battered women's shelter knows that in many cases, they flee with only the clothes on their backs and any possessions they can fit in a duffel bag. Many women who flee violence find themselves homeless, living in a shelter, faced with the challenge of setting up a new life, finding a job in a new city or state, and saving up the money for a rent

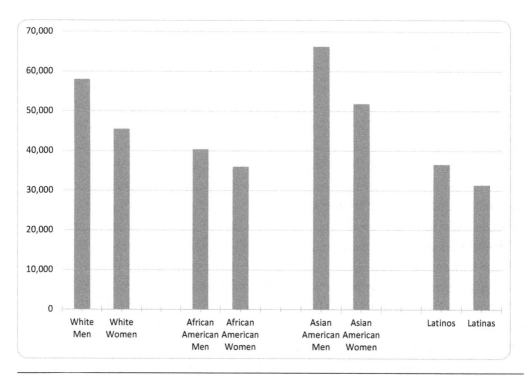

▲ **Figure 9.1**
Women's and Men's Median Weekly Earnings, by Sex and Race/Ethnicity (2018).

Source: US Bureau of Labor Statistics 2018.

deposit—all within sixty to ninety days of arriving at the shelter, depending on the policies of that particular shelter. We turn now to a discussion of the ways in which wage discrimination and the accompanying economic dependency heighten the incentive for women to stay with abusive men or seek out new relationships in order to meet their economic needs.

Wage Discrimination and Compulsory Partnering

One may be surprised to learn that feminists have been debating the costs and benefits of marriage for women for a hundred and fifty years. Among the first marriage "resisters" was Charlotte Perkins Gilman. She argued that marriage required that women give up their identity and their power and become nothing more than cooks and maids and sexual slaves for their husbands.

A hundred years later, Adrienne Rich (1980) argued that beliefs about femininity—that women are "designed" to marry and raise children—and wage discrimination *required* women to seek partnerships with men. Think for a minute about a thirty-five- or forty-year-old single man who, depending on his social status, may be defined as an "eligible bachelor." Yet a woman of similar status is an "old maid." Conventional wisdom holds that a woman is better off with *any* man than *no man at all*. Second, Rich argues, because of the severe wage discrimination women face in the labor market, it is virtually impossible for them to achieve middle-class status, or better, unless they have the benefit of a man's wages (for an update, see Richardson 1996). Thus, marriage—or long-term partnering—is a virtual economic necessity except for the small percentage of women who either inherit wealth or achieve in the well-paying professions.

Often at the end of an interview with a woman who had spent an hour or two or more telling of her experiences with IPV, frequently at the hands of more than one man, we would ask her, "So, what's next? Are you going back to him? Have you had enough of men for a while?" So often the answer she gave was that she was going back, or already had, or had moved on to yet another partner.

Economic dependency can trap women with abusive men, but it can also be a strong pull into relationships. Many of the women we interviewed indicated that the thing that initially attracted them to their boyfriend or husband was his ability to pay the rent or feed her children. Connie recounted meeting a boyfriend, who would later abuse her, this way: She was out in the front yard with several children, some of them hers, many of them the children of friends. It was her birthday. This man drove by and told her she was pretty. He asked if he could get her anything, and she smiled and said lunch for the children. He returned a few minutes later with *two buckets* of Kentucky Fried Chicken, enough to feed all the children. That night they went out on a date, and within weeks they were living together.

When we asked battered women what qualities they hoped or planned to look for in the next man in their lives, the most common response was that he be employed. Clearly, they recognized their own need for the economic support of a partner.

Many of the women we interviewed talked of moving out of the shelter (in North Carolina) and into an apartment with men they had met at the mall only a few days or weeks before. Andi's story, which we presented at length in a previous chapter, is typical and differs from others we heard only in that it involves moving several hundred miles (as opposed to down the street or to the next town).

Andi took a big risk by moving away from her family and friends with a man she barely knew. And, unfortunately for Andi, that risk was realized not long after she moved with "this guy" to Minnesota. Isolated from family and friends, living with his family because they could not afford a place of their own, Andi was in a situation of extreme dependence. She depended on "this guy" for the roof over her head and the food in the refrigerator, and, consistent with Engels's notion of economic exchange (Engels 1972), "this guy" demanded that Andi have sex with him, that she be faithful to him, and that she follow his rules. When she did not, he beat her up, as we recounted in our previous discussion of the relationship between child sexual abuse and IPV.

This form of economic dependency is brutal and sometimes lethal for women, and especially African American women, because generally they have less education and lower wages, and hence are particularly vulnerable to this type of economic dependency. What this type of dependency really means is the selling or trading of one's sexuality in exchange for having one's basic needs met. It is *a trade-off no one should ever have to make.*

RACE AND CLASS ANALYSIS

Women's economic dependence on men, which leads to the demand for compulsory heterosexuality, does vary by one's membership in various social categories. Women with little education, few job skills, and few resources in their extended families, and poor women of all racial and ethnic groups, are more likely to remain with men or move in with them early in the relationship than are middle-class women. Because African American women are more likely to have less education, fewer labor market skills, and fewer resources like bank accounts (or family members with extra resources that could be borrowed) than their white counterparts, they are more vulnerable to IPV than are white women (Hattery 2008; Tjaden and Thoennes 2000).

In contrast, because white women have lower overall rates of being employed—25 percent are stay-at-home mothers—they experience a different vulnerability to IPV. Young white women—who have high rates of employment—may be less likely to seek out a man for economic support initially, but once they are involved in the relationship and have begun childbearing, they are more likely to be out of the labor force as stay-at-home mothers, and thus may be forced to stay with an abusive partner longer. In contrast, African American women, who are more likely to be employed but earning low wages, may seek partners in order to meet their basic financial needs. But because African American women have always had, and continue to have, overall higher rates of employment (P. Collins 1994)—despite the fact that these jobs are most likely to be low wage—by virtue of being employed, African American women have more access to contacts, friends who will intervene or help, and their own wages, all of which are necessary to leave abusive relationships. Thus, African American women may be more likely to *leave* abusive relationships, but they will frequently bounce from one abusive relationship quickly into another—as Andi did—for economic reasons. In other words, just as threats to the breadwinner role exist for all men even while being shaped by race and class, economic vulnerability and compulsory partnering are experienced by all women, though the forms this vulnerability and the responses to this compulsion take are highly shaped by race and social class. We conclude the chapter with a brief discussion of the recent recession.

THE RECESSION OF 2007–2009

Scholarly research often takes many years to move from data collection to publication—where it can be accessed by others. Thus, there is very little research yet available that examines the role of the 2007–2009 recession on changes and trends in IPV. However, a working paper by the scholars at the Bendtheim-Thoman Center for Research on Child Wellbeing reports:

> We find that the Great Recession and other periods of worsening labor market conditions in the 2000s were associated with increases in the prevalence of violent or controlling behavior in marriage, but not cohabitation. Black and Hispanic women and less educated women were more likely to experience intimate partner violence in both low and high unemployment environments. The effect of a worsening economy, however, was stronger for white mothers and for mothers with at least some college education. During the Great Recession, the prevalence of partner violence among white and more educated women rose to the level normally experienced by their more disadvantaged counterparts.
>
> (Schneider, Harknett, and McLanahan 2014)

This research confirms anecdotal data that during the Great Recession, calls to domestic violence hotlines increased, as did the number of women and children seeking help at shelters. Furthermore, their finding elucidates the differential impact of the Great Recession on women of different races and social classes. It is not surprising that they find the biggest impact is felt by white and more educated women, given that the majority of jobs lost were not low wage but rather jobs in the middle sector of the economy, where white women (and men) with some education are more likely to be employed.

CONCLUSIONS

The stories presented in this chapter suggest that at both the micro and the macro levels, the economy is a major structural force that shapes IPV. At the structural level, IPV reinforces men's advantage in the labor market. Abusive men restrict or prohibit women's labor-force participation. Women who are victims of IPV often struggle to advance or even remain employed because in many cases they must miss work due to the physical, psychological, and emotional injuries they experience at the hands of their partners. Another way of seeing this is that IPV reduces the threat of female competitors in the labor force. In this way, all men, even those who are not abusive, benefit from the ways in which IPV eliminates women as competitors in a tight labor market. And there is an overall cost to these days missed at work; it is estimated that IPV costs $8.3 billion annually, which is a significant cost to the US economy ("Intimate Partner Violence: Consequences" 2015).

The effects of IPV on individual women are well documented (Browne 1989; Dobash and Dobash 1979; Hattery 2008; Walker 1979). Although some research has focused on men who perpetrate IPV, most of the attention has been directed toward predicting which men will be abusive and which intervention programs are most successful at treating those who do. There have been even fewer attempts at examining the ways in which IPV operates at both the individual and the structural levels to produce a model for family and the workplace that rewards male privilege (even for men who are not abusive) and limits women's access to the opportunity structure (even for women who are never abused by their partners).

This chapter moves us beyond individual explanations for IPV and analyzes these data with attention to the role that social structures, specifically the economy, play in shaping IPV as it occurs in the United States. As a result, a clearer picture of both the individual and the structural causes and effects of IPV emerges herein. These findings suggest that to reduce or eliminate IPV in the United States will require more than simply teaching individual men not to hit or instructing individual women on how to escape. Rather, the economy of the United States must be transformed such that wage discrimination disappears and women—whether in relationships or single—are no longer economically dependent on men. Reducing economic dependency will reduce women's vulnerability to violence. We acknowledge that this is a hefty recommendation, and we will devote far more time to discussing it in Chapter 16.

In the next chapter we will examine the cultural supports for IPV, namely the ways in which constructions of masculinity and femininity create rigid gender roles that almost inevitably lead to IPV.

RESOURCES

Klaus, Olivia. 2009. *Sin by Silence*. Quiet Little Place Productions. (Filmed behind prison walls, this documentary reveals the lives of extraordinary women who advocate for a future free of domestic violence.)

National Center for Injury Prevention and Control. 2003. *Costs of Intimate Partner Violence Against Women in the United States.* Atlanta, GA: Centers for Disease Control and Prevention. www.cdc.gov/violenceprevention/pdf/IPVBook-a.pdf.

Ruben, Joseph. 1991. *Sleeping with the Enemy.* 20th Century Fox. (Starring Julia Roberts, this film details the experiences of an affluent woman who flees her abusive husband.)

NOTE

1. Indicates physical violence that is significantly *lower* among affluent women than among middle-class and poor women. All other forms of physical violence are *not* significantly different by household income (social class).

REFERENCES

American Association of University Women. 2018. *The Simple Truth About the Gender Pay Gap.* www.aauw.org/research/the-simple-truth-about-the-gender-pay-gap.

Atkinson, Maxine P., Theodore N. Greenstein, and Molly Monahan Lang. 2005. "For Women, Breadwinning Can Be Dangerous: Gendered Resource Theory and Wife Abuse." *Journal of Marriage and Family 67(5)*: 1137–1148.

Browne, Angela. 1989. *When Battered Women Kill.* New York: Free Press.

Brush, Lisa. 2011. *Poverty, Battered Women, and Work in US Public Policy.* New York: Oxford University Press.

Card, David, and George B. Dahl. 2011. "Family Violence and Football: The Effect of Unexpected Emotional Cues on Violent Behavior." *Quarterly Journal of Economics 126(1)*: 103–143.

Catalano, Shannan. 2013. *Intimate Partner Violence: Attributes of Victimization, 1993–2013.* Bureau of Justice Statistics. www.bjs.gov/index.cfm?ty=pbdetail &iid=4801.

Centers for Disease Control (CDC). 2017a. *Fact Sheet.* www.cdc.gov/violenceprevention/pdf/ipv-factsheet.pdf.

Centers for Disease Control (CDC). 2017b. *Racial and Ethnic Differences in Homicides of Adult Women and the Role of Intimate Partner Violence—United States, 2003–2014.* July 21. *66(28)*: 741–746. www.cdc.gov/mmwr/volumes/66/wr/mm6628a1.htm?s_cid=mm6628a1_w.

Collins, Patricia Hill. 1994. "Shifting the Center: Race, Class, and Feminist Theorizing About Motherhood." In *Mothering: Ideology, Experience, and Agency*, edited by E. Glenn, G. Chang, and L. Forcey, 45–66. New York: Routledge.

Connidis, Ingrid, and Julie McMullin. 2002. "Social Ambivalence and Family Ties: A Critical Perspective." *Journal of Marriage and Family 64(3)*: 558–567.

Dobash, R. E., and R. Dobash. 1979. *Violence Against Wives: A Case Against Patriarchy.* New York: Free Press.

Dunleavey, M. P. 2009. "The 12 Biggest Reasons Couples Fight Over Finances." *MSN Money Central*, December 4.

Ehrensaft, Miriam, and Patricia Cohen. 2003. "Intergenerational Transmission of Partner Violence: A 20-Year Prospective Study." *Journal of Consulting and Clinical Psychology 71*(4): 741–753.

Engels, Friedrich. [1884] 1972. *The Origin of the Family, Private Property, and the State*. Introduction by Eleanor Leacock. New York: International Publishers.

Fieldstadt, Elisha. 2015. "Texas Man David Conley Accused of Killing 2 Adults, 6 Children in Dispute with Ex." *NBC News*, August 10. www.nbcnews.com/news/us-news/texas-man-david-conley-accused-killing-2-adults-6-children-n406816.

Hattery, Angela. 2001. *Women, Work, and Family: Balancing and Weaving*. Thousand Oaks, CA: Sage.

Hattery, Angela. 2008. *Intimate Partner Violence*. Lanham, MD: Rowman and Littlefield.

Hattery, Angela J., and Earl Smith. 2014. *African American Families: Myths and Realities*. Lanham, MD: Rowman and Littlefield.

"Intimate Partner Violence: Consequences." 2015. *Injury Prevention and Control: Division of Violence Prevention, Centers for Disease Control*, March 3. www.cdc.gov/violenceprevention/intimatepartnerviolence/consequences.html.

Leone, Janel M., Michael P. Johnson, Catherine L. Cohan, and Susan E. Lloyd. 2004. "Consequences of Male Partner Violence for Low-Income Minority Women." *Journal of Marriage and Family 66*(2): 472–490.

Lin, Nan. 2000. "Inequality in Social Capital." *Contemporary Sociology 29*(6): 785–795.

Padavic, Irene, and Barbara Reskin. 2002. *Women and Men at Work*. Thousand Oaks, CA: Pine Forge Press.

Rich, Adrienne. 1980. "Compulsory Heterosexuality and Lesbian Existence." *Signs 5*(4): 631–660.

Richardson, Diane, ed. 1996. *Theorising Heterosexuality*. Buckingham, UK: Open University Press.

Sanday, P. R. 1981. "The Socio-Cultural Context of Rape: A Cross-Cultural Study." *Journal of Social Issues 37*(4): 5–27.

Schneider, Daniel, Kristen Harknett, and Sara McLanahan. 2014. "Intimate Partner Violence in the Great Recession." Working Paper WP14-04-FF. *Bendtheim-Thoman Center for Research on Child Wellbeing and Fragile Families*. http://crcw.princeton.edu/publications/publications.asp.

Smucker, Sierra. 2017. "Strengthening laws which take guns out of the hands of domestic abusers will help prevent future mass shootings." *USApp—American Politics and Policy Blog* (November 13). http://bit.ly/2QfxZTn.

Stockett, Kathryn. 2009. *The Help*. New York: Amy Einhorn Books.

Tjaden, Patricia, and Nancy Thoennes. 2000. *Full Report of the Prevalence, Incidence, and Consequences of Violence Against Women: Findings from the National Violence Against Women Survey*. Washington, DC: US Department of Justice. www.ncjrs.gov/pdffiles1/nij/183781.pdf.

US Bureau of Labor Statistics. 2018. "Highlights of Women's Earnings in 2014." *BLS Reports*, November. Report 1058. www.bls.gov/opub/reports/cps/highlights-of-womens-earnings-in-2014.pdf.

Walker, Lenore E. 1979. *The Battered Woman*. New York: Harper & Row.

Weitzman, Susan. 2001. *Not to People Like Us: Hidden Abuse in Upscale Marriages*. New York: Basic Books.

Wilson, William J. 2009. *More Than Just Race*. New York: W. W. Norton.

World Health Organization. 2015. "Violence Against Women: Prevalence," *Domestic Violence World Statistics 2015*.

10

CULTURAL FACTORS AND INTIMATE PARTNER VIOLENCE

When I'm old and getting gray, I'll only gang-bang once a day.

—**Fraternity ditty**

This chapter examines the ways in which beliefs about what it means to be a man (masculinity) and what it means to be a woman (femininity) create an environment ripe for intimate partner violence (IPV). In addition, this chapter will explore the ways in which there is racial and ethnic variation in beliefs about masculinity and femininity and how this variation shapes the violence that is perpetrated and experienced. This chapter will conclude with insights into the ways in which prevention and intervention programs need to address cultural differences if partner violence is to be reduced in all communities.

OBJECTIVES

- To explicate the dominant constructions of femininity, which are often invisible because of their widespread acceptance and pervasiveness
- To explicate the dominant constructions of masculinity, which are often invisible because of their widespread acceptance and pervasiveness
- To examine the ways in which cultural constructions of femininity can lead to the acceptance of submissive gender roles for women, which often leaves them vulnerable to IPV
- To examine the ways in which cultural constructions of masculinity can lead to the acceptance of male dominance in relationships, which can lead to tolerance for and even expectations of expressions of men's violence
- To explore the particular case of international abusive marriage migration using the Hmong as an illustration
- To provide a set of recommendations for transforming and expanding cultural expectations for men and women so as to broaden gender roles and reduce IPV

KEY TERMS

culture   sexual prowess
masculinity   sexual double standard
femininity   marital rape exemption
Cool Pose   public–private split
patriarchy   cult of domesticity
gender roles   cult of true womanhood
breadwinning

INTRODUCTION

In the first chapter of our book, we argued that all of the statistics indicate that above and beyond all else, IPV is a gendered crime: women are *by and large* the victims, and men are *by and large* the perpetrators. In this chapter we examine the ways in which American **culture**, and particularly definitions of **masculinity** and **femininity**, contributes to a culture of violence, especially gender-based violence. We begin with some definitions.

Culture: "refers to the sharing of outlooks and modes of behavior among individuals who face similar place-based circumstances . . . or have the same social networks. Therefore, when individuals act according to their culture, they are following inclinations developed from their exposure to the particular traditions, practices, and beliefs among those who live and interact in the same physical and social environment" (Wilson 2009: 4).

Masculinity: What it means to be a man in a given culture; the qualities that we attribute to manliness and the roles we associate with men. Chafetz identified six areas of traditional masculinity: physical, functional, sexual, emotional, intellectual, and interpersonal (1974: 34–35).

Femininity: What it means to be a woman in a given culture; the qualities that we attribute to womanliness and the roles we associate with women. Traditional areas of femininity include verbal, relational, deferential, and submissive roles.

Gender Roles: The concept that certain behavioral patterns are associated exclusively or almost exclusively with a particular gender. For example, men are believed to be workers, the breadwinners; they take out the garbage and wash the cars; at work, they are the boss. Women are believed to be suited to taking care of the home and the family; they are (supposedly) less interested in work and are rarely the boss; they are the emotional center of the family.

Femininity and masculinity and their associated gender roles can be conceptualized as mutually exclusive, binary, and oppositional. In other words, they are two sides of the same coin. Any quality generally attributed to men (masculinity) will have its opposite attributed to women (femininity). For instance, men are aggressive; women are passive. Men are dominant; women are submissive. Men work; women stay at home. Men discipline children; women nurture. Men serve in the military and play sports; women shop and create scrapbooks.

BOX 10.1	GEERTE HOFSTEDE ON MASCULINITY AND FEMININITY

Geerte Hofstede is a European social psychologist who is perhaps best known for developing the cultural dimensions framework for cross-cultural communication. As part of his work, he gathered data from a variety of cultures and developed "dimensions" of masculinity and femininity that were present in the majority of societies and cultures.

The dimensions of masculinity and femininity focus on how, and the extent to which, a society stresses achievement or nurture. Masculinity is seen as the trait that emphasizes ambition, acquisition of wealth, and differentiated gender roles. Femininity is seen as the trait that stresses caring and nurturing behaviors, gender equality, environmental awareness, and more fluid gender roles.

Based on these dimensions, Hofstede developed definitions of masculinity and femininity:

"Masculinity stands for a society in which social gender roles are clearly distinct: men are supposed to be assertive, tough, and focused on material success; women are supposed to be more modest, tender, and concerned with the quality of life."

"Femininity stands for a society in which social gender roles overlap: both men and women are supposed to be modest, tender, and concerned with the quality of life."

Traits of masculinity and femininity:

	High Masculine	*Low Masculine (Feminine)*
Social norms	• Ego-oriented • Money and things are important • Live in order to work	• Relationship-oriented • Quality of life and people are important • Work in order to live
Politics and economics	• Economic growth is high priority • Conflict is solved through force	• Environment protection is high priority • Conflict is solved through negotiation
Religion	• Most important in life • Only men can be priests	• Less important in life • Both men and women can be priests
Work	• Larger gender wage gap • Fewer women in management • Preference for higher pay	• Smaller gender wage gap • More women in management • Preference for fewer working hours
Family and school	• Traditional family structure • Girls cry, boy don't; boys fight, girls don't • Failing is a disaster	• Flexible family structure • Both boys and girls cry; neither fight • Failing a minor accident

Source: Hofstede 2001: 297.

It is important to note that we do not necessarily endorse these constructions of masculinity and femininity; we simply note that they are extremely widely adhered to. It is also important to note that stereotypes do not apply to everyone; rather, they are reflective of both dominant patterns and, more important, beliefs about what men and women *should do*. We know many women who play sports and do not like to shop and many men who enjoy cooking and do not hunt. But we also know that when we measure who is doing what, our behaviors and preferences fall along decidedly gendered lines. In fact, when we do an exercise in our classes asking students to identify traits that are associated with men and women, a list very similar to that in the box above is generated. What is important is not that we endorse these rigid and oppositional constructions of gender roles, but that when we understand not only the social constructions of masculinity and femininity but also the ways in which they are pitted as binary and oppositional, we can begin to see more clearly, as we argue, that IPV is an *almost* inevitable outcome of masculinity and femininity as they are defined in the contemporary United States. We begin with a discussion of masculinity.

BOYS WILL BE BOYS: CONSTRUCTIONS OF MASCULINITY AND INTERPERSONAL VIOLENCE[1]

What do you envision when you think of a man who beats up his woman? Is he a factory worker who comes home, puts on a white "wife beater," drinks a "working-class" beer like Old Milwaukee (as opposed to sipping a Pinot Grigio), and socks his wife in the mouth when the meatloaf she cooked for dinner is not ready on time or, worse yet, is burned? The truth is there is no explicit description of a man who perpetrates IPV. Abusive men are of all races and ethnicities, all ages, all levels of education, and all different occupations, and they live in all different regions of the country. We argue here that if anything distinguishes men who perpetrate IPV from men who do not, it is two things: abusive men are well socialized into hypermasculinity, and their abusive behavior can be best understood as a response to perceived threats to their masculinity (Franchina, Eisler, and Moore 2001). The question for us in this chapter is to what degree do beliefs about what it means to be a man both tolerate (if not require) physical dominance over one's partner and demand a violent reaction when one feels one's masculine identity is threatened?

Masculinity

What does it mean to be a man in our society? Masculinity is a set of characteristics that we often associate with men (Mansley 2007). From an early age, most children raised in the United States ascribe qualities such as strength, power, height, and financial power to boys and men (Connell and Messerschmidt 2005; Connell 1990). What is more, not only do we associate these traits with men, men are *essentialized* by these traits. In other words, men in general are reduced to the qualities and traits that are the core definition of masculinity: physical strength, aggression, economic power, and sexuality. Despite differences by race, ethnicity, sexual orientation, and social class, as well as individual differences—many men are monogamous, many men settle their conflicts through dialogue rather than physical fights—the image by which most men judge themselves and are judged by others can be boiled down to a few qualities or statuses:

> In an important sense there is only one complete unblushing male in America: a young, married, *white*, urban, northern, heterosexual, Protestant, father, of college education, fully employed, of good complexion, weight, and height, and a recent record in sports . . . Any male who fails to qualify in any one of these ways is likely to view himself—during moments at least—as unworthy, incomplete, and inferior.
> (Lemert and Branaman 1997: 78)

In other words, despite individual and population differences, the qualities associated with being a man are relatively universal.

We ask: are these characteristics found among men of other races and ethnicities, or are there alternative constructions of masculinity for men of other racial and ethnic backgrounds? Some say yes.

African American Masculinity: The Cool Pose

The most cited attempt at describing African American masculinity is the work of Majors and Bilson (1992: 44), who make the argument that **Cool Pose** is an attempt to make the African American man more visible. "Cool Pose" is a way to counteract some of the requirements articulated above—white, college-educated—that many African Americans will never achieve and replace them with other qualities that describe a different type of masculinity. They argue:

> Cool Pose is a ritualized form of masculinity that entails behaviors, scripts, physical posturing, impression management, and carefully crafted performances that deliver a single, critical message: pride, strength, and control . . . It eases the worry and pain of blocked opportunities. Being cool is an ego booster for black males comparable to the kind white males more easily find through attending good schools, landing prestigious jobs and bringing home decent wages.
> (1992: 4–5)

Majors and Bilson (1992) argue further that African American men are on a disturbing rollercoaster ride through African American masculine pathology. It is here that one finds not only failure in school but also extreme violence and criminality, hyper drug use and abuse (Majors and Bilson 1992), and an illogical connection to parenting that preferences procreation (making babies) to parenting (raising children) (Sampson 1987). Majors and Bilson conclude that African American men construct their masculinity behind masks, worn to survive not only their second-class status but also their environment. This does not mean, however, that African American men, or any other group, construct their masculine identities only as alternatives, unrelated to normative constructions; rather, they do so *in response to* the dominant constructions of masculinity that are widely available in the culture.

Discourses of Masculinity

Certain well-known men in our culture would be readily identifiable as "men's men" or "manly men." Most of the exemplars, or "ideal types," as sociologist Max Weber would call them, come from the realms of sports, entertainment, politics, and occasionally big business. What do these men have in common? They are successful, affluent, strong, good-looking, and mostly white, and according to popular discourse, they have multiple sex partners. Regular men, masculine men, have access to images of these *quintessential* men by watching mainstream television and movies.

Think for a moment about the images that are transmitted into our homes and that influence our beliefs about masculinity. Arnold Schwarzenegger as "the Terminator," Sylvester Stallone as Rocky Balboa, Denzel Washington as the "entrepreneur" and womanizer in *American Gangster*, and the many actors who have portrayed James Bond, the assassin and womanizer (his image has been part of the discourse on masculinity for four decades). College and professional sports provide yet another genre in which these images are generated, be it LeBron James dunking over his competitors and running down the court pumping his chest, Ndamukong Suh stomping on his opponent after every tackle with the intent of taking him out, or Alex Ovechkin delivering a debilitating check that leaves his opponent unconscious on the ice. All of these images transmit the belief that real men, masculine men, are powerful, strong, dominating, and rich. Consider advertisements, especially those that run during sporting events. The time is filled with ads for trucks "built Ford tough" and "home makeovers" that feature cases of Bud Light. The Marines are looking for "the few, the proud." Either central to the ads or in the background there are always beautiful women who admire the men for their strength, success, and beer-guzzling ability.

These images bombard us from the 24/7 broadcasts on CNN and ESPN as well as in the music videos and shows on networks like MTV, VH-1, and BET, just to name a few. The important point here is that a *specific construction of masculinity* is being transmitted to the young men (and women) who are watching. Not only are boys and men learning how to be "men," but women are learning what they should not only expect but, more importantly, desire in men.

The construction of masculinity that dominates in US culture is not random but is built around the principles of **patriarchy**.

PATRIARCHY

Patriarchy is a social system in which men (and boys) have greater access to opportunities, resources, and power than women (and girls).

Cultural indicators of patriarchy include the following beliefs:

- That men are smarter than women, especially in science and math. Recall former Harvard University president Larry Summers, who argued that the reason men dominated faculty positions in science and math was due to their intellectual superiority (Summers 2005). This assumption and the ensuing stereotype suppress the number of women competing for the top-paying, more prestigious positions in science, engineering, and math.
- That women are more suited to taking care of the home and family, and thus they should focus less on their occupations and professional goals. This assumption reduces the number of women competing for jobs and thus gives men greater access to those jobs.
- That women should defer to their husbands on financial matters. This assumption results in men having more access to resources and more decision-making power when it comes to spending from the family bank account.
- That men are better logical thinkers. This belief results in men having greater access to political and social power as politicians and leaders of all the major industries.

The Roots of Masculinity

Structural-functionalists such as Parsons and Bales (1955) argue that men and women have evolved both biologically and socially toward distinct spheres of specialization. Based on this perspective, men and women are believed to be *biologically* suited for different tasks. As a result, men have come to dominate the *instrumental* sphere, whereas women have been relegated to the *expressive* sphere (Hattery 2001). The instrumental sphere, according to Parsons and Bales (1955), refers to the activities associated with providing for the basic needs of the family. In contrast, the expressive sphere refers to meeting the emotional needs of family members. Parsons and Bales argue that the contemporary division of household labor can be traced back to our earliest roots as humans. For example, they suggest that a man's greater ease at being away from his children for forty-plus hours per week, and even traveling away from home as part of his job, has evolved out of the time in human history when men went on long, extended hunting trips in search of meat. These hunting excursions encouraged a more detached masculine character (Hattery 2001).

With regard to the contemporary American family, the perspective of Parsons and Bales has been used to conceptualize appropriate **gender roles** for men and for women.

For example, we argue that when masculinity (and femininity) is constructed in such a way as to generate these rigid and narrow gender roles, it contributes to a culture of violence against women. Furthermore, when we carry Parsons and Bales's argument that gender roles arise out of biological necessity to its logical conclusion, IPV can be (mis)understood as a "natural" outgrowth of the biology of men and women rather than a "natural" outgrowth of a system of patriarchy. Parsons and Bales's belief that gender roles are based in biology is the underpinning for beliefs among biological as well as social scientists in genetic sex differences. This general belief that men and women are *biologically different* and thus suited to different tasks is both dominant and pervasive today. It is a part of the hegemonic ideology that is derived directly from patriarchy (Epstein 2007).

We illustrate the point with a well-publicized example. In the spring of 2005, then Harvard president Larry Summers, addressing a gathering of science, technology, engineering, and math scientists from the most prestigious institutions—including Harvard, MIT, and Yale—argued that women were underrepresented as tenured and full professors in departments such as math, physics, and engineering because they were *biologically inferior* in math (Bombardieri 2005; Summers 2005).

Biological and genetic explanations for gender differences perpetuate the belief that men beat up women because they are biologically programmed toward violence and that women need to be disciplined for the same reasons, because they are biologically inferior and, like children, need to be trained and "corrected." For example, as we will discuss at length in Chapter 11, much of the support for IPV comes from an interpretation of the Bible that dictates that men are appropriately destined to be the head of the household and women and children are in need of guidance and sometimes punishment. You will also recall from our discussion in Chapter 2 that undergirding the history of America's IPV laws was the belief that men were superior, and thus they were instructed to guide and, if necessary, physically discipline their wives (and children), who were believed to be inferior. This becomes a convenient and popular explanation for IPV that treats it as immutable, inevitable, and individual rather than structural. In other words, as long as IPV is a result of individual men getting "out of control," then one never has to examine the role that male superiority, power, and patriarchy play in IPV. This is akin to focusing on Summers's explanation for the underrepresentation of women in the sciences—women's lack of innate ability at math is an individual problem—rather than on the structural barriers women in the sciences face, including the well-documented inequities in funding, salary, and lab space revealed in studies of gender equity at technology universities. In the 1990s, for example, MIT was forced to conduct a gender-equity study as a result of potential lawsuits by women faculty who were able, in fact, to prove they were victims of gender-based discrimination (Massachusetts Institute of Technology 1999). Though progress has been made, a follow-up study in 2011 revealed that there are still issues to be resolved, especially with regard to recruitment and retention of women faculty (Gillooly 2011).

MASCULINITY AND IPV

When scholars analyze the images that transmit beliefs about masculinity and the rigid construction of gender roles, they note that several traits have come to *signify manhood* in contemporary America, including physical strength and power, aggression, financial success, and sexual prowess (Lemert and Branaman 1997; Kimmel 2005; Messner 2002). With remarkable consistency, the key issues that both violent men and abused women in our study identified as the "triggers" to *violence* are men's successes in **breadwinning** and their performance in the bedroom; what we term *the two Bs.*

Breadwinning

The first *B* is breadwinning. Breadwinning has long been defined by both popular discourse and sociological theory as one of the key roles that men in our society must play. This belief has persisted despite the fact that, beginning in the 1980s, married women's labor force participation and contribution to their overall household incomes have steadily increased (Hattery 2001; Padavic and Reskin 2002).

Kimmel argues that one outcome of the contemporary political, economic, and social climate, replete with declining real wages for men (Padavic and Reskin 2002) and underemployment, which has been rising since the late 1980s when manufacturing jobs began to be shed at rapid rates, is that men's ability to establish a masculine identity vis-à-vis their success in the labor market is tenuous at best and leaves men feeling threatened by the possibility that they are not masculine enough. "At the grandest social level and the most intimate realms of personal life, for individuals and institutions, American men have been haunted by fears that they are not powerful, strong, rich, or successful enough" (Kimmel 2005: 8). One will recall from our lengthy discussion in the previous chapter that all of Kimmel's concerns were likely to be magnified by the 2007–2009 recession. As a result, "American men try to *control themselves*; they project their fears onto *others*; and when feeling too pressured, they attempt to *escape*" (Kimmel 2005: 9; emphasis ours).

Kimmel (2005) calls into question a dilemma for men in the United States. As they are struggling in order to define themselves as "real" men through economic success, they see the rules changing; as women's labor force participation began to rise in the mid-1980s and continues today, men find that they are competing *against* women for jobs they once monopolized. Given Kimmel's argument that in this economic, political, and social landscape masculinity is already at risk, it seems that threats to masculinity—especially those related to the two *B*s (breadwinning and the bedroom), the organizing principles of intimate partner relations—and especially those threats coming directly from men's intimate partners, will be particularly powerful. According to Kimmel's argument, men would be left feeling particularly vulnerable.

The conclusions we drew about the power of masculine identities from our own interviews with abusive men are confirmed by a study published in 2015 that found that, in the context of a hypermasculine culture, men who feel inadequate or that their masculinity is challenged often engage in gender-based violence as a strategy to demonstrate their masculinity:

> Boys who experience stress about being perceived as "sub-masculine" may be more likely to engage in sexual violence as a means of demonstrating their masculinity to self and/or others as well as thwarting potential "threats" to their masculinity by dating partners.
>
> (Reidy et al. 2015: 623)

Why? Because perpetrating violence against women is a straightforward expression that serves two purposes: it confirms the abusive man's sense of his masculinity, and it reinforces the inferiority of women.

Other evidence for this argument that men respond to threats to masculinity by engaging in violence comes from an experiment conducted by Bosson et al. (2009). In their study, men were randomly assigned to one of two conditions.

In both conditions men were asked to braid, and once they completed the braiding, they were offered a choice as to which of two activities they would engage in next. In the control condition, men braided a bundle of rubber bands attached to a basket; in the experimental condition, men braided hair attached to the head of a mannequin. After they completed the braiding task, men were asked to choose the second "task" in which they would engage, either boxing or a brain-teaser puzzle. Men in the control condition were most likely to choose "boxing activity" as their second activity whereas men in the experimental group who had just braided hair, an activity most often characterized as "feminine" or "women's work," overwhelmingly chose "boxing," a decidedly hypermasculine, violent enterprise, as their second activity (Bosson et al. 2009).

We turn now to men's own explanations for their violent episodes. *These are not justifications for IPV and should not be seen as such.* What they do provide is an opportunity to examine IPV through the lens and words used by men who perpetrate it. These are *their explanations for their behavior.* We argue that, although abusive men rarely offer a critical perspective, and neither do they often recognize the position of privilege they occupy in a patriarchy, listening to the voices of men who perpetrate IPV offers insights that are important to incorporate into broader proposals for radical social transformation.

Threats to the Breadwinner Role

Threats to the provider or breadwinner role come in several different forms: men's own failure as providers, not being able to keep up with the demands of their wives or girlfriends, and frustration with wives and girlfriends who wanted to be "kept" when this was simply an unrealistic expectation.

Women as "Nags"

The majority of men we interviewed indicated that their wives and girlfriends failed to recognize *their efforts* as providers. Put in their terms, these men felt "nagged." These men reported that their wives or girlfriends nagged them about not earning enough money, not being able to provide the standard of living they believed they deserved, and not providing them with the means necessary to keep up with their girlfriends and coworkers.

Eddie is an African American man in his late thirties who lives in North Carolina. In addition to owning his own painting company, he is a professional boxer. He has been involved in several *violent relationships* with ex-girlfriends as well as with his wife. When we asked Eddie to talk about conflict in his marriage, he indicated that he and his wife frequently argued about money:

Small stuff, you know. She's always complaining about that I don't treat her like a wife, because I don't buy her what she wants, things like I can't afford. She always throw up in my face like what her friend's husband, what kind of car he bought her and what kind of gifts he bought her. Of course he can buy her a brand-new car when he the assistant chief executive at Wachovia. And uh, she a RN, got a master's degree at Wake Forest, you know, and she complain about, oh and he just bought this $160,000 house and, you know, you married me and you supposed to do this for me and my children, well what you, what you gonna do for yourself? And she always just nick-nagging at me.

(**Eddie,** thirtysomething African American man, North Carolina)

From Eddie's perspective, this nagging is unwarranted—he sees himself as a good provider who is doing the best he can and, meanwhile, his wife is not contributing financially to the household:

My wife hasn't worked, man, right now she don't even work. She, we don't get no kind of assistance, we don't get no kind of assistance, I make the money. She just get a little small child support check from their father, that's it.

Failure as a Provider

Many of the men and women we interviewed identified unemployment or under-employment as significant sources of conflict in their relationships.

Darren is a white man in his mid-forties who resides in North Carolina. When we asked Darren to describe the incident in which he hit his wife and for which he was subsequently arrested, he described an argument about money. He and his wife had a particularly heated debate over a vacation and his perception that his wife had foolishly paid too much for what turned out to be a disastrous airline flight. The argument lasted for a week, during which time Darren attempted to discuss the issue with his wife and she refused to even speak to him. This eventually erupted into a heated debate. While he was yelling at her, his wife ran into the kitchen.

I went into the kitchen. I grabbed my wife around the neck. I laid her on the kitchen floor. She rose up. I slapped her. She rose up again; I slapped her again. And then I made some threats . . . And I told her, listen, let's go sit down in the living room and we're going to talk about this and you're going to listen to me. Okay? I'm taking control of the situation, is how I felt. I'm going to take over. You're going to listen to me, regardless of whether you want to or not. You're not going to turn your back on me, you're not going to give me a sneer, you're not going to make a snide remark, you're going to listen to what I have to say.

(**Darren**, fortysomething white man, North Carolina)

Darren puts his reaction into context (rationalizing their violence is an extremely common reaction and tactic among abusive men):

I was making a lot less money than I was in Washington State. And I was contributing a lot less to the household. I didn't have all the great benefits that I had in Washington. I didn't feel like I was the man of the house, you know. I was kind of hurting here. She had made a couple of cracks, you know, about the way things are different. And about if I was single, I could barely get by [laughing] on what I make, and all this stuff. In the past, she had said these things, and it stuck. We lived in a nice neighborhood—a really nice neighborhood. There was a president of a company next door, a psychiatrist across the street, a business owner down the street. It was a really nice neighborhood. And here I was; I'm a pipefitter, a pipe welder. I came home dirty and I worked with my hands. I started . . . [laughing] the neighbors were really clean when they got home . . . and I started having these, gee . . . self-esteem issues. So, when my wife would reject me and when she would resent me, showed resentment, I'm thinking, well, gee, you know, maybe the money thing is a problem because she inherited a million dollars, more or less. She bought a $625,000 house with it, and furniture and all that stuff. And here I am working at the mill in Concord. And she's making all the major purchases. Things were out of balance financially.

(**Darren**, fortysomething white man, North Carolina)

This imbalance of economic power provided Darren with a justification, in his mind, for beating his wife. He interpreted his wife's economic power as a threat to his self-esteem. In short, Darren beat his wife when he felt his masculine identity vis-à-vis his economic power in the household, a major marker of masculinity, was threatened. We turn now to a discussion of the second measure of masculinity: sexual prowess, otherwise known as the second *B*, the bedroom.

The Bedroom

Sexual prowess encompasses several issues, including men's ability to satisfy their partners and men's ability to be "players" by gaining access to multiple sexual partners, often through sexual conquest. Each year these issues erupt on college campuses when young men—often members of fraternities or football and basketball players—are accused of the sexual conquest of young women on campus. We will highlight several of these cases in Chapter 12.

As old as America, perhaps most of the world, is the **sexual double standard** for men and women. This double standard prescribes that men should or can have more sexual experiences and more sexual partners than women. The evidence for this is overwhelming and far-reaching (see Epstein 2007 for a historical overview). Consider, for example, the fact that polygyny (having more than one wife) was the dominant marriage form throughout history and across the globe (see the Word Cultures Database in Yale University's Human Relations Area Files, www.yale.edu/hraf) and continues to exist in parts of Asia, Africa, and the Middle East (Sanday 1981). Typically, multiple wives are prohibited in these cultures only if a man is unable to provide economically for them. Finally, compare the language we use to describe men who have multiple sex partners to the language we use to describe women who do. We do not have to make a comprehensive list here to demonstrate that virtually all the words for men are positive (*player, stud*) and all the terms for women are negative (*loose, whore, slut*).

Taking together the sexual double standard, the history of polygyny, and the acceptance and praise awarded men who engage in sexual conquest, it is clear that sexual prowess is an important part of masculinity in the contemporary United States—if not in the world more broadly. Given the importance of sexual prowess in constructions of masculinity, the men we interviewed were reluctant to discuss their failures in this area—though they were happy to share with us their successes in the bedroom. However, wives and girlfriends were not so closed-lipped on this issue.

In some cases, wives and girlfriends admitted to us that they were dissatisfied with their sex lives, and they talked about how they expressed this dissatisfaction to their partners. Charlotte is a woman in her early fifties who is married to Perry, also in his fifties. This is Charlotte's second marriage and Perry's first. They married each other when they were well into their forties. Charlotte and Perry are both white and live in North Carolina.

In discussing their relationship, Charlotte talked openly about her dissatisfaction with Perry as a lover. From Charlotte's perspective, their sexual relationship, the second measure of a masculine man, was unsatisfying. Charlotte indicated that she had to beg Perry to have sex with her and that his lack of attention to their sex life contributed to her feeling badly about herself:

A lot of times I would say, "Why? Please. What is your problem?" It would be like two weeks, three weeks. I'm thinking, you know, I'm going to go get sewed up. I told him I was going to go have it sewed up. I did. I would actually tell him that. I said, "I might as well just go to the doctor and have it completely . . ." And he looked at me like, well, can you do that? [laughing]

(**Charlotte,** fiftysomething white woman, North Carolina)

Both Charlotte and Perry admitted that after this accusation, their fight turned violent. Perry not only hit Charlotte but also threw numerous household items at her, including dishes and a lamp. Charlotte sustained facial lacerations and bruising, and Perry was arrested for IPV.

Chris and Wanda also had physical fights that erupted around her dissatisfaction with their sex life:

[Chris] don't appreciate nothing. So now, you know, you're slacking up on everything, even the sex too now. Like sex, like it's a reward or something. NO way. And you know I'm a scuppy. I'm a freak, you know, I like my groove on when I want it. And you're going to tell me no? Oh, hell no. It's time for you to go 'cause I don't need you. 'Cause I got, I can go over here to Lovin' Fun [a lingerie store], I can buy anything, any toy I need and make love to myself 'cause I don't need you. And suck my own titty and everything. I'm just going to be frank. And so, all hell breaking . . . I am so serious! Y'all laugh, but I'm so serious.

(**Wanda,** fiftysomething African American woman, Minnesota)

Because we interviewed both of them, we were able to confirm that they both saw Wanda's accusation that Chris lacked sexual prowess by failing to satisfy her as *triggering* his violent explosion; he had to "put her in her place":

We was in the basement and she wanted more sex or whatever . . . that's when I had to throw the jabs at her and stuff.

(**Chris,** fiftysomething African American man, Minnesota)

Taken together, the sexual double standard and the prevalence of male sexual privilege are evidence of a pervasive sexual ideology that locates sexual prowess at the core of masculinity. Essentializing men as sexual conquistadores results in many problems in relationships, including sexual abuse and marital rape. To recapitulate, it works this way: men grow up learning that conquest is part of the way that men obtain sex. The more women a man can "conquer," the more of a "man" he is. Furthermore, men (and women) are taught that men have a right to seek sex, and they will, and that it is up to women to act as gatekeepers, to decide when to "give it up." This set of antagonistic relationships results in men believing they have a right to sex whenever and with whomever they desire it. When women attempt to act as gatekeepers, saying no, men believe they are being denied what they have a right to have. This is especially the case when the woman saying no is one's wife or long-term partner (Hattery and Kane 1995).

Marital Rape: Sexual abuse of one's spouse or partner is one of the most difficult aspects of IPV for a variety of reasons: it is difficult for the victim, it is difficult to prosecute, and it is the form of IPV that is the least understood by the general public. In her study of women who kill their abusive partners, Angela Browne (1989) found that one of the key factors that differentiated women who left abusive relationships either by divorce or by homicide from those who did not was the presence of marital rape. Browne describes the rape that one of the women she interviewed, Molly, experienced regularly:

> And sometimes he raped her. Molly didn't think you could call it rape, when it was your husband, but he was very rough during lovemaking—pinching and biting and treating her with anger. At these times he was like another person; he didn't seem to know her or realize what he was doing. Molly began to have constant bruises and bitemarks.
>
> (Browne 1989: 39)

In addition, despite changes in the laws around wife abuse across the twentieth century that transformed marital rape into a crime, the marital rape exemption existed in many states well into the 1990s, and remained in some forms in 2015.

The **marital rape exemption** refers to exemptions in state statutes criminalizing IPV that *precluded* marital rape as a form of IPV. Wives, even if they were separated from their husbands, were not legally allowed to bring a charge of rape against them, regardless of the severity of the sexual assault.

Even thirty years after the formal lifting of the marital rape exemption in all fifty states, today it remains extremely difficult for a woman to charge her legal husband or long-time intimate partner with rape, and even more difficult to find a prosecutor who will argue her case. Despite the fact that sexual abuse is common among victims of IPV—one in four women, or 25 percent, report being raped or having sex with their husbands (Russell 1990; Tjaden and Thoennes 2000; Warshaw 1988) or intimate partners (Centers for Disease Control 2017) when they did not want to—that it is violent, that it is a tool of power and control, and that it is devastating to the victim—Americans' attitudes about sex and sexual abuse in relationships are extremely conservative. In a study performed by one of the authors in the mid-1990s, even among college students, only 25 percent of men and 45 percent of women considered a scenario describing marital rape to be "unacceptable," and far fewer indicated that it constituted "rape" or a crime (Hattery and Kane 1995).

Sexual abuse is a common tool for batterers because, as most scholars of rape point out, it is one of the most humiliating experiences for an individual (Brownmiller 1975). Indeed, the *purpose* of sexual assault—whether it be perpetrated by a stranger or by someone the victim knows or is even in a relationship with—is to humiliate the victim and remind her (or him) of the power the perpetrator has over the victim (MacKinnon 1991). This makes it an incredibly powerful tool of IPV as well as a tool of terrorism of marginalized groups—gay men, transgender individuals—and a tool of war (Kristoff and WuDunn 2009; Callimachi 2015). So why is there so much resistance by Americans, as expressed by their attitudes, to defining marital rape as a type of IPV and to supporting its prosecution? We argue, as many others do, that much of this resistance stems from the marital transaction we described in the previous chapter. Marriage has long been based on the understanding that a woman trades access to her sexuality for the economic support and companionship of her husband. Traditionally, and continuing today, this transaction is considered to be permanent—for life—and to hold in any circumstance. This belief was the basis for the marital rape exemption; quite simply, if a woman had agreed to offer free access to her sexuality to her husband without the possibility of refusal, through the civil transaction of a marriage, then he was permitted by tradition and law to have sex with her whenever and however he chose, even if she did not want to and even if they were separated. Under this reasoning, it was quite simply not legally possible to rape one's wife. Though this is no longer the case legally, as we discussed at length in Chapter 2, there is very often a long lag between changes in the law and changes in attitudes and beliefs. We, as a society, have a long way to go before we will have reached a point at which we understand the reality of marital rape and offer victims the protection and intervention they deserve.

Sexual Conquest, Jealousy, and IPV

Aside from the obvious—marital rape—how does the sexual double standard contribute to IPV? In the interviews we conducted with both men and women, the single most common theme that emerged was men's jealousy. All or most of the men worried about or believed that their partners were sleeping ("talking") with other men. This constituted a significant threat to their masculinity, simply because an integral part of sexual prowess is the ability to keep your woman satisfied and thus not straying.[2] As a result, many men engaged regularly in hyper-controlling behavior meant to prevent their partners from having contact with other men. This, of course, is in addition to the violent outbursts and beatings that were dramatic but occurred less frequently.

Eddie recounts the night that he caught his former girlfriend with another man and probably engaging in prostitution. He admitted to beating her that night to the point that she was unrecognizable. If the description is not powerful enough, remember that Eddie is a boxer and had once beaten a man in a boxing match so badly that he killed him. Eddie's fists are, indeed, lethal weapons.

So what had happened was, come to find out she had got a hotel room at the Innkeeper on Broad Street. I would call her and she would keep going in the car. Later on that Saturday night she was coming up Fourteenth Street and I seen her, and her cousin was out there and, you know, so I told him I would pay him if he would stop her when he saw her coming, when he catch her coming up the street. So he agreed, for a fee. He took and stopped her, and when she stopped, I snuck up behind the car and jumped in, and I was like, "If you don't pull off I will break your face," you know, I told her that. So she got scared and she pulled off . . . I smacked her when I got into the car, and she said "Well, I been at the hotel with another guy." . . . When we got back to the room, you see, I knew that he used to smoke those rocks inside the cigars, so we, she took me to her room, she had cigar butts in the ashtray, and I know she didn't smoke them like that, but I know he did, the one that she had just dropped off. Then I seen her underwear by the shower and her bra, as if she had took a shower and just slipped on something to come out to drop him back off, so when I got in there and seen that I lost my mind, man, and I beat her so badly, man. I beat her so bad, until they couldn't hardly recognize her, man. Her eyes were swollen, her mouth was busted, I had chipped her teeth.

(**Eddie,** thirtysomething African American man, North Carolina)

Because masculinity is defined by such a narrow range of behaviors, with the greatest weight resting on these two aspects, breadwinning and "the bedroom," many men construct most or all of their gendered identity—as masculine men—around their success (or failure) at these two roles.

At an individual level, this may not seem so extraordinary. Men must simply get a job, work hard, make money, and satisfy their partner. However, examining this from a structural or sociological perspective, we see that success or failure in this arena is not entirely up to individual effort. As was detailed at length in Chapter 9, especially with regard to successful breadwinning, individual performance is heavily structured by external forces such as the economy, returns on human capital, and race and class discrimination (see especially Hattery and Smith 2007, 2014).

RACE, CLASS, AND GENDER: INTERPRETING DIFFERENCES ACROSS GROUPS

The precise mechanism by which failure in the breadwinner role triggers violence among men is mitigated or shaped by race and ethnicity. As noted by Kimmel (2005) and others, white men feel especially threatened when they cannot meet the role of sole provider. This is illustrated best by Darren, whose story was recounted earlier in the chapter.

In contrast, as a result of a long history of unemployment and underemployment for African American men and ready employment (as domestics) for African American women, coupled with a long history of sharing the provider role that dates back to slavery (Collins 1994; Hattery 2001; Hattery and Smith 2007, 2014), most African American men *expect* their wives and girlfriends to work outside of the home and contribute financially to the household, as noted by Eddie. For African American men, then, the frustration or "trigger" to violence arose from a situation in which their partners *refused to work* yet desired a standard of living that the men could not deliver on their own. What is interesting to note is that breadwinning is a significant trigger for both white and African American men, but the trigger is set off differently; that is, the trigger is structured and shaped by race and ethnicity, social history, and the contemporary sociopolitical climate (Smith 2008).

Similarly, sexual prowess is experienced differently for men of different racial and ethnic groups. Coming out of a stronger tradition of Protestantism and conservative Christianity, white men are less likely to assess their sexual worth by multiple sex partners but instead focus on their sexual behavior within the context of relationships that demand absolute monogamy. They are particularly threatened when they suspect that their partners are being unfaithful.

In contrast, African American men, as many scholars, including Patterson (1999), note, have the lowest marriage rates of all men in the contemporary United States (see also Hattery and Smith 2007 and Hattery and Smith 2014 for a long discussion of marriage in the African American community). Popular culture paints a picture of African American men as "players" on a sexual quest for multiple partners (Smith and Hattery 2006; Hattery and Smith 2014; Smith 2008). Yet they too are especially threatened when they believe that their wives or girlfriends are being unfaithful. Ironically, the majority of the African American men we interviewed admitted freely that they had another woman on the side but expected absolute devotion and faithfulness from their partners, whom they admitted they suspected of cheating.

This suspicion was the primary cause of a great deal of violence in their relationships. As with so many things, interviews with women confirmed this high level of jealousy that African American women were subjected to by their partners, yet the vast majority of African American women confirmed that they were not having affairs, and all reported that they were aware that their jealous partners were.

We've been discussing how beliefs about masculinity contribute to a culture that is ripe for IPV. It is also important to understand that the very nature of masculinity requires a particular, specific, compatible construction of femininity. We turn now to a discussion of beliefs about femininity.

HOW TO BE A "GOOD" WIFE: CONSTRUCTIONS OF FEMININITY AND INTERPERSONAL VIOLENCE

A Brief History of Women's Roles

Across the relatively brief history of the United States, the gender role expectations of wives have been moderately stable. This is not to say that the norm of the stay-at-home mother, so aptly illustrated in television shows such as *Leave It to Beaver* and *The Brady Bunch*, was always dominant. However, one of the authors has argued elsewhere (Hattery 2001) that despite the lack of dominance of this family form, many Americans talk with nostalgia about "the good old days" when men were the breadwinners and women were homemakers, both occupying completely separate and non-overlapping spheres of social life. Part of the lure of this nostalgia is the widespread belief that "the good old days" were really the way things "always were" until this *preferable* way of life came to an abrupt halt thanks, primarily, to the sexual revolution of the 1960s and 1970s, when women began, in greater numbers, to be educated, to enter the labor market in numbers greater than during the World War II period, and to gain some measure of control over their reproductive lives as a result of the birth control pill and legalized abortion (Luker 1985).

Despite the valiant efforts of historians such as Stephanie Coontz (1992, 1997), who uses empirical evidence to debunk many myths about family life, especially the myth of the dominance of the traditional family replete with the breadwinner father and the stay-at-home mother, this nostalgia for the 1950s has seen a powerful resurgence among politicians, the Christian Right, groups with wide appeal such as the Promise Keepers, and even TV personalities like the Duggars, whose family was featured in the HGTV show *19 Kids and Counting*. (We note that the Duggars saw their reality TV show canceled not because of a decline in interest in their lifestyle but because their oldest son, Josh, admitted to sexually abusing his siblings.) The "family values" rhetoric advanced by groups such as the Promise Keepers is appealing because it is focused on social problems, such as teen pregnancy, drug abuse, and school violence, which trouble many (if not most) Americans. The solutions proposed by groups touting "family values" rhetoric are also appealing because they focus on increasing rates of marriage, decreasing single-parent households, and promoting traditional gender roles that allow women to return to a focus on caring for the children and the home. But this is rhetoric not based in empirical realities; simply willing the divorce rate to be lower or the rate of marriage to be higher does not address the structural impediments to long-term marriage, including the economy and the strains that linger even though the Great Recession is officially over, not to mention the rate of violence in many homes. Additionally, there has never been a time when families relied more on women's wages, and thus a return to traditional gender roles, even in married-couple households, is not only unlikely but *impossible* for the majority of American families. Yet the *norm* of the stay-at-home mother survives and is preferred by many despite its lack of reality (Hattery 2001; Hays 1996).

The Cult of Domesticity

Across all of US history, the home has been women's domain. Padavic and Reskin (2002) identify the home as the "private" sphere and the workplace as the "public" sphere. Though the **public–private split** was indeed real, the assumption that economic production was relegated entirely to the public sphere is in fact false. During the agricultural era that dominated American history, many women *were also involved* in the economic production of the farm. On the typical family farms that dominated the Midwest, women were responsible for small animals (chickens), milking (on dairy farms), large vegetable gardens, and farm processes such as milk and egg production. Historical accounts (Coontz 1992, 1997; Wolf 1992) reveal that in addition to this economic work, women had sole responsibility for the home and for all of the tasks associated with it. Of course, African American women were also highly involved in agricultural work, though under slavery and the system of sharecropping that later replaced it, their involvement for centuries *brought no economic advantage to their families* (Hattery and Smith 2007, 2014).

Earlier in the chapter we outlined the structural-functionalist perspective on gender roles as proposed by Parsons and Bales (1955). Women, they argued, are the *expressive* leaders in the household, and with that position comes the work of the home, including the care of the children and, of equal importance, the care and nurturing of the husband. Thus, women were to cook a warm meal each evening. They were to design and decorate a home that was relaxing, and they were to limit the chaos in the home by teaching their young children to be quiet and calm when the man of the house arrived home each day. This ideology was later termed the *cult of domesticity*. As part of the exchange, the worker, the instrumental leader of the family using Parsons and Bales's model, earned a wage. The requirement of the husband then was to provide for the economic needs of the family by turning over at least some of his earnings to the wife so that she could purchase the necessary goods in order to run the household and rejuvenate her husband through food and a comfortable home.

The **cult of domesticity**, or the **cult of true womanhood** as it is sometimes called, is an ideology built around the idea that a woman's place is in the home. Not only did women belong in the home, but successful homemaking was critical in moving from the status of "girl" to that of "woman." Though women had always been assigned the role of keeping up the home and the family, the rise of the cult of domesticity really began in the early 1900s and reached its peak in the 1950s and 1960s. Despite a modest decline in importance, which began in the 1970s, it remains at the core of constructions of our beliefs about femininity today (Hattery 2001; Wolf 1992). This is evidenced by the empirical data that indicate that women who are married or in relationships with men continue, regardless of their employment status, to do the lion's share of the housework, and recession contributed to an increase of that gap by 4.5 hours per week (Berik and Kongar 2013). In other words, despite engaging in less paid work during the recession, men did not, on average, increase their work at home. Many women report continuing to feel the pressures associated with the work of the home, including making home-cooked meals (despite working forty hours per week), caring for their children, or arranging child care (Hattery 2001). Consider the media, for example, and television shows with titles like *Desperate Housewives* or *The Real Housewives* as well as the concomitant advertisements. The vast majority of cooking and cleaning products continue to be advertised toward women during the "soap" hours, noon to four o'clock weekdays, on HGTV, TLC, and other channels that target women, and they feature women actors who are *thrilled* with the scent of laundry detergent or the performance of a new appliance they can use to vacuum their couch cushions or window blinds.

In the early 1900s, the Industrial Revolution was in full force in the United States, and this led to the public–private split Padavic and Reskin (2002) so aptly describe. Along with the Industrial Revolution came the urbanization of the United States, and increasingly women's work "at home" no longer included working in a garden or tending to small animals. Instead, women had more time to engage in child-rearing and in caring for the home. Especially for upper-class white women, *feminism* the care of the home—decorating, cleaning, even cooking—became an art rather than a simple task. With the completion of the national rail system, for example, access to a greater variety of foods, especially fruits and vegetables, and products to decorate the home was opened up to the middle class, whereas these "luxuries" had previously been available only to the affluent (Veblen 2008). With access to more and more foods and goods—often items that were not "native" to a woman's area of residence, and thus not familiar—more and more training was required to teach young women how to make a proper home. Thus, we see the rise of finishing schools. It is also important to note that the exclusion of women from education and the professions meant that finishing schools and "professionalizing" the care of the home were the only options available for women who had intellectual or professional goals.

For a variety of reasons, the cult of domesticity, which had become an important part of the construction of femininity in the United States, reached a peak and ultimate ideological dominance by the 1950s, following two historical periods when women's involvement in the paid labor force was relatively high: the Great Depression, when women sought work to offset the lost wages of their husbands, and World War II, when women took over factory jobs left vacant by men who were sent off to war. Especially during World War II, along with earning a wage, working provided women with skills and the independence they had previously been denied (Hattery 2001; Padavic and Reskin 2002; Wolf 1992).

When men returned from the war, women were displaced from the labor market (Kossoudji and Dresser 1992). A series of laws made it legal to dismiss women from any job and replace them with veterans who had returned from war. Although some women happily left the labor force to return home, many did so reluctantly. In order to ease the pain of this dismissal as well as to meet the needs of this new woman, one who was more likely to have a college degree, who had learned a trade, or who perhaps even built cars or bombs, several forces coalesced to *professionalize* and *glamorize* the work and the life of the housewife (Wolf 1992). The work of the home was defined as *essential* to the role of being not just a good wife but also a good *woman*. Women were warned in television ads, magazine reports, and political rhetoric that their primary responsibility was to their home and the care of their family and that to fail at these responsibilities would be to doom their entire family to certain failure. Women began to be taught about the dangers of dust in their homes, for example. And women always worried that the whiteglove testers might appear on their doorstep to assess not just their skills in dusting but also their success as true women. Television and print ads for home appliances showed beautiful women vacuuming with a Hoover or doing laundry with a Maytag or cooking with a new GE oven in ways that were highly sexualized. The positive outcomes of doing housework and using these appliances were not limited to the women themselves, for these actions translated into happy husbands and successful children, or so the ads promised.

Women had demonstrated that they were intelligent and capable. They had managed every conceivable industry, from factories to health care, in the absence of men created by the demands of World War II. But the country was not ready for women to enter these professions permanently. Therefore, entire curricula were designed to educate women on the virtues of the cult of domesticity. It was believed that women were being educated and prepared for lives as housewives. We've seen a resurgence of this ideology recently. In 2005 a series of articles in the *New York Times* featured women graduates of prestigious Ivy League colleges like Harvard and Yale who "gave it all up" in order to stay at home and realize their true calling. Critics wonder about the efficiency of paying upwards of a quarter of a million dollars for an education that one will use primarily at home, and others worry that women waited too long and fought too hard for admission to these prestigious institutions—many of which did not integrate the genders until the 1970s—to "throw it all away" (Story 2005).

Many dispute this claim that women were being in some way inculcated into the cult of domesticity; rather, they argue, women were seeking a higher moral calling—they were committing themselves to the difficult and important work of mothering. As many women one of the authors interviewed as part of another study would remark, "What could be more important than caring for my children?" (Hattery 2001). Yet by the 1960s, the age of marriage was young—around twenty-one for women—as was the age of first childbirth. Fertility rates had fallen to 2.5 children per woman, and life expectancy was longer—around seventy-two years for women. The typical woman in the United States could expect to have "launched" her children by her early forties and have another twenty-five to thirty years to live. If women were staying home just for the important work of child-rearing, then we would expect to see these women enter or return to the labor force in their forties when their nests emptied and the most productive years of their careers lay ahead. However, this did not happen. Why? *Because the cult of domesticity glorified not just child-rearing but also housework.* Women were being educated to be good wives, not just good mothers, and both were considered essential qualities of good women. The socialization girls were receiving for their future roles as wives was simultaneously constructed as formal education for this "career."

While the boys in high school were taking shop class and gaining skills that would serve them in the labor market, specifically in entering the highly paid, unionized trades, women were taking home ec, learning skills that would serve them as they strove toward the ultimate goal: being a good wife, as defined by the cult of domesticity. Young women were being instructed by their teachers in the academic setting (not clubs or voluntary activities) in how to be a good wife. A young woman could read a magazine such as *Ladies' Home Journal* or watch television and be bombarded with images of women's success—as wives—being inextricably linked to their use of appliances. Relaxing in front of popular television shows of the time, which included *Leave It to Beaver* and *Peyton Place*, women (and men) were bombarded with a clear message that *essentialized housework as central to being a successful woman* as well as being a good wife. Being instructed in such a message in the landscape of the 1950s would have cemented the importance of adopting the "wife" role in the marriage. *This was not optional.*

Furthermore, it is important to realize the power of defining masculinity, as was discussed in the earlier part of this chapter, in relation to work while defining femininity in relation to the relationship. One definition leads to independence and the other to dependence. A man's ability to have a roof over his head and food in his stomach was tied to his ability to work hard and earn a living. A woman's ability to have a roof over her head and food in her stomach was tied to finding a man and keeping him and, more important, relied on his generosity toward her.

Young women today may no longer be indoctrinated into lives of second-class citizenship through such glaring messages as this, but the cult of domesticity remains dominant. As noted, especially on particular cable channels (HGTV, TLC, A&E), advertisements run from morning until late night featuring attractive women engaged in the labors of the home. One ad features Kelly Ripa, the daytime talk show host, demonstrating the thrill she receives from using her LG washer and dryer and being able to shower her children with clean and neatly folded clothing that she deposits in their drawers and closets.

Further evidence for this perpetuation of the cult of domesticity comes through examining self-help books targeted at women. A tour of Amazon.com or a stroll through Barnes and Noble reveals a plethora of books instructing women on the benefits of giving over power to their husbands or, these days, "partners." And lest you believe these ideas are simply relics from a time gone by, Laura Doyle authored several books in the late 1990s and early 2000s that offer women advice on how to become submissive to their husbands. Best-selling author Sara Horn published her version in 2013: *My So-Called Life as a Submissive Wife: A One-Year Experiment . . . and Its Liberating Results.* Doyle's book *The Surrendered Wife: A Practical Guide to Finding Intimacy, Passion, and Peace with Your Man*, published in 1999 and released in paperback in 2001, offers just this advice. A careful examination of the chapter titles is revealing: "Give Up Control to Have More Power,"

"Abandon the Myth of Equality," and "Relinquish the Chore of Managing the Finances." We offer an excerpt to illustrate our point:

> Respect means that when he takes the wrong freeway exit you don't correct him by telling him where to turn. It means that if he keeps going in the wrong direction you will go past the state line and still not correct what he's doing. In fact, no matter what your husband does, you will not try to teach, improve, or correct him. That is the essence of a surrendered wife.
>
> (2001: 35)

Perhaps more troubling than the advice that you should allow your husband to behave stupidly, as this excerpt seems to advise, is the advice to give up management of the finances. As noted in the previous chapter, one of the critical barriers to leaving that abused women face is lack of access to financial resources (Browne 1989; Gelles 1997; Hattery 2008; Koss et al. 1994).

It is precisely this power imbalance that creates a situation ripe for IPV. *The Surrendered Wife* and books like it are not simply guides to pampering your husband. If you read them carefully, they say that a woman should put her husband's needs above her own, that her problems are less important than his, and that he can behave however he chooses, even staying out all night, a right he has earned by working so hard. In fact, these guides to being a good or surrendered wife are guides to help women accept their status as second-class citizens and male domination: the man, we are reminded, is the master of the house, and the woman is not to question his decisions.

The Surrendered Wife and IPV

When one reads books like *The Surrendered Wife*, one quickly finds that the rhetoric is justified by a caveat about the "good husband." Women's concerns about giving up power are dismissed by suggesting that a good man will not take advantage of this structured power differential codified in the institution of marriage. And perhaps this is true. But there are several troubling problems with this approach.

The Surrendered Wife and the Master of the Bs

When men and women in America enter partnerships, they do so in the social landscape outlined in this chapter. Men are socialized to believe that masculinity means earning a good wage and being the master in the bedroom. As both the abusive men and their partners confirmed in our interviews, when some men experience threats to their masculine identity, they engage in IPV. They slap, kick, punch, blacken eyes, break bones, bite, berate their partners with horrible names, and sometimes even rape their partners. When women enter these partnerships believing they are second-class citizens and believing that men should have total sexual freedom, that women should serve their man's every need, and that they should put his needs above their own, then they remain vulnerable to these slaps, kicks, and blows that render them injured and sometimes dead.

Accepting even a *portion* of this inequality leaves women at risk for abuse. Structured inequality, and the acceptance of it, creates a set of social arrangements that results in four million acts of IPV *reported* per year. Perhaps the most troubling part of this pattern—which has increased in the past decade or so, as evidenced by books like Laura Doyle's and Sara Horn's—is that it is women encouraging other women to accept this form of oppression and second-class citizenship. Unfortunately, the statistics on IPV and the stories of abused women tell us that millions of women in the United States live as second-class citizens not only in the public sphere, where they experience sexual harassment (MacKinnon 1991) and wage discrimination (AAUW 2018), but also in the private sphere, where they are subjected to millions of acts of violence, emotional abuse, and rape per year. In fact, Candy's story illustrates the dilemma that many women face: they fear harassment and violence in the public sphere—sexual harassment at work, men catcalling them on the streets (Kearl 2010), men trying to pick them up in bars—and in some cases they accept oppression and abuse in the private sphere in order to avoid it in public. Candy trades violence at home, much of it quite severe, at the hand of her partner, in order to take advantage of the protection he provides from violence at work and in the streets.

Race, Class, and Gender Analysis

As we have argued elsewhere (Hattery 2001; Smith 2008), dominant ideologies, by definition, pervade the ideological landscape for everyone living in the United States, yet many individual actors, especially racial and ethnic minorities and the poor, may resist the dominant ideology or develop nonconforming ideologies (see Hattery 2001; Smith 2008; Therborn 1980).

We would argue that acceptance of and resistance to dominant constructions of femininity vary across race and ethnicity and class groups. For example, the degree to which women adopt the culture of domesticity has varied. In fact, historically, white middle-class women have enlisted the labor of African American women and Latinas they have employed as domestics (Romero 1992; see Stockett 2009 for a fictional example) as "partners" in their quest for domestic success. These women, who were working long hours for low wages, had very little time or energy left to focus on their own homes or children. Furthermore, as many scholars have noted

(Collins 1994; Hattery 2001; Romero 1992; Segura 1994), the opportunity to be a stay-at-home mother has eluded most women of color and poor whites, even during the 1950s and 1960s, when this "traditional" family form dominated in the white middle-class community.

Some might look at the gap in marriage rates, especially between African American and white women, as further evidence for a belief that African American women are more likely to resist the cult of domesticity than are their white counterparts. However, based on interviews with both African American and white women, we argue that although marriage rates differ, and there are many explanations for this (see Burton 1990; Hattery and Smith 2007, 2014; Patterson 1998), *heterosexual partnerings* do not vary. In other words, despite the fact that very few (only 10 percent) of the African American women we interviewed were legally married and almost all of the white women we interviewed were, there was no difference in the likelihood of being in a partnership or committed relationship; African American women were simply less likely to *marry* their intimate partners (Passel, Wang, and Taylor 2010). Additionally, Passel and colleagues note that there is only a small difference in the marriage rates of whites and Latinas, and that which does exist is primarily among undocumented Latinas who fear that engaging any part of the legal system, including through a civil marriage, might lead to deportation.

Before we conclude this chapter, we offer a brief discussion of some of the ways that globalization is facilitating exploitative and abusive family formations.

The Impact of Globalization on Interpersonal Violence: Human Trafficking

When most of us think about human trafficking, we think about sex trafficking. And sex trafficking is a serious international epidemic that involves sexual assault, child sexual abuse, and IPV. According to a 2016 United Nations report *Global Report on Trafficking in Persons*:

- Fifty-three percent of human trafficking involves sexual exploitation, 40 percent involves labor trafficking, and the remaining 7 percent comprises "uncategorized" trafficking and "organ trafficking."
- Nearly half (49 percent) of all victims of human trafficking are women, 21 percent are girls, 18 percent are men, and 12 percent are boys. In other words, 30 percent of all victims of human trafficking are children, and 70 percent of all victims of human trafficking are girls and women.
- The vast majority (72 percent) of those convicted of human trafficking are men.

- Though some human trafficking is local (within a country) or regional, the majority of human trafficking involves the movement of people from the "global south" (South Asia, Southeast Asia, and sub-Saharan Africa) to the wealthiest countries in the world, including the United States, Canada, western European countries, and Saudi Arabia.

(United Nations 2016)

And, though sex trafficking makes up the majority of human trafficking, we will detail in this discussion human trafficking that goes largely undetected because it doesn't appear to be trafficking and may not be defined as such, even by victims and advocates. Our specific focus here is on three types of trafficking: international adoption, international surrogacy, and marriage migration.

International Adoption

According to the US State Department, in 2017 nearly 4,714 children from ninety-nine countries were adopted by American parents. Most international adoptions are facilitated by a variety of licensed agencies that are based in the United States. International adoptions, in order to be legal, must comply with the Hague Convention, which seeks to ensure that all adoptions are in the best interest of the child and make the child's safety their top priority.

That said, there is a market for international adoptions among American would-be parents, and when there is a market, market forces, including supply and demand and competition, develop. Carney (2011) examines what he calls the "red market" for international adoptions. There are thousands of American parents willing to pay tens of thousands of dollars to adopt children from developing countries. This demand must have a supply, and as Carney documents, a system of kidnapping toddlers as well as offering poor mothers a "boarding school" for their young children, who are then trafficked into adoption, has led to the nonconsensual removal of parental rights. Another deceptive strategy involves paying parents a few hundred dollars for their children who are then "supplied" to international agencies who "sell" these children for adoption. And, in order to compete, international agencies operating in the red market offer adoptions at a slightly reduced price and for a slightly shorter wait time.

One agency in particular, Malaysian Social Services, has been accused of trafficking in children for adoption, mostly from South Asia, including India. Carney details the case of Subash Roa, whom his parents claim was stolen while he toddled around the water pump just a few dozen feet from his mother. He was sold to Malaysian Social Services by the kidnappers, one of whom posed as his mother, for the equivalent of $236 and then trafficked through Paquette Adoption Services, which has arranged 1,411 international adoptions since 1982, and placed with a family in Wisconsin. Despite Carney's efforts to talk with the adopted parents about the possibility of communicating with Subash's biological parents, which has been a strategy for making some amends in these cases, they refused. Carney's research is only the tip of the iceberg of the red market for international adoptions.

International Surrogacy

The United States is one of a small number of countries that allows for paid surrogacy; would-be parents can either identify a surrogate themselves or work with an agency to identify a surrogate. The typical surrogacy arrangement in the United States costs between $50,000 and $100,000. In 2002, India legalized surrogacy and, once again, a market emerged. Agencies sprang up in places like New Delhi that took advantage of the poverty in India and the fears of Americans that Indian surrogates would not have the means to deliver healthy babies—because of poverty, lack of a nutritional diet, lack of prenatal care, and the like—by creating a fully institutionalized surrogacy experience. Poor women in India can "rent" their wombs for $5,000 or $6,000, all the while being required to live in the clinic, where they are well fed and their activities tightly monitored. This provides a guarantee for the parents paying for her services that she is well cared for and increases the likelihood that she will deliver a healthy baby. But, Carney (2011) asks, at what price to her? According to American Adoptions (www.americanadoptions. com/adopt/the_costs_of_adopting), the cost for American parents is only $15,000 to $20,000, a fraction of the cost for an American surrogate. The clinic pockets approximately $10,000 of that, and the rest goes to the surrogate. Of course, many would argue that this is not trafficking because everyone is consenting, but critics question whether true consent can be given when Indian women are living in such abject poverty.

Marriage Migration

Immigration and international migration are nothing new. Indeed, other than the Native Americans, Alaskan Natives, and Native Pacific Islanders, the vast majority of people living in the United States—including citizens and noncitizens—arrived here via some form of international migration; they immigrated freely, they immigrated seeking asylum, or they were trafficked. The slave trade can be characterized as the first form of human trafficking.

With increasing globalization, it is estimated that in 2017 there were 258 million international migrants (United Nations 2017). And, though people migrate for many reasons, one of the drivers of international migration is family reunification. For many families, globalization has accelerated the processes for reunification and

for new immigrants to settle permanently in their adopted homelands. Family reunification policies provide one of the easiest routes to immigration for those seeking to immigrate to the United States. And, perhaps unintentionally, family reunification policies have created an easy pathway for marriage migration. Merali (2008) notes that the United States has experienced a large influx of girls and women who are marriage migrants since 2000; annually, more than half a million applications are made to sponsor a spouse to immigrate to the United States. More than half of the applications are filed by men who have married women abroad (p. 281).

In order to file a sponsorship application, the citizen, generally a man, must provide all kinds of information, including documentation of his ability to provide financially for three years.

> The husband signs a contract with the national government taking full responsibility for the sponsored bride's basic needs (including food, shelter, health, and dental care) and integration needs (training in English, social programs, etc.) for this three-year period. In the first three years after her arrival, the wife has no independent access to resources and is not eligible to receive any Social Security benefits. Unlike immigrants who come to the United States independently, she is not connected to any immigration agencies or social supports apart from her husband.
>
> (Merali 2008: 282)

Family reunification policies like the one utilized by the US immigration service may seem innocuous enough and even be considered progressive, but these policies actually exacerbate a power differential that already exists and magnify the power the man has over his wife. Not only does the woman's husband wield the power he already derives from patriarchy, but he also has power over her because he speaks English and she may not, and because she is completely dependent upon him for her survival. As we noted in our discussion of the economics of IPV in the previous chapter, women's economic dependence on their partners leaves them vulnerable to IPV. And, as the research documents, this vulnerability is extreme for girls and women who are marriage migrants. As Merali (2008) shows, international marriage migrants are subjected to all forms of IPV, including physical abuse, financial abuse, and sexual abuse, and if they attempt to seek relief from this abuse, they risk deportation. In addition, it is often the case that there is a significant age differential between the men and their migrant wives, which increases her vulnerability as well. Finally, as is typical with most forms of exploitation, marriage migration flows from underdeveloped countries like Vietnam and Thailand to postindustrial economies like the United States, Canada, and Taiwan. Most men who sponsor marriage migrants as their spouses are expatriates seeking a wife from their home community, where they have elevated status because they are American citizens.

As noted, the majority of applicants for family reunification married their spouses abroad. And, in some communities, including in much of Vietnam, only women with already low status, especially women living in extreme poverty, participate in international marriages, which further exacerbates their status in the community. As a result of her entering into an international marriage, her family is shunned from the community, it is likely that she will never be able to return to her home, and her family will not be in a position to help her should her spouse become abusive—both because they cannot afford to and because she has disgraced them.

Many men seeking international brides are seeking second or third wives. In order for the marriage to be legal and thus qualify for family reunification approval, he must divorce his current wife. Wives have very little power to resist the divorce, and in many cases it leaves them in poverty. If the wife he is divorcing was a marriage migrant herself, she may be particularly vulnerable and unable to access Social Security and other safety net programs.

Hmong Marriage Migrants

The Hmong are an ethnic group from the mountainous regions of China, Vietnam, Laos, and Thailand. The United States military recruited Hmong to assist them in fighting during the Vietnam War and then abandoned the Hmong when the US pulled out of Vietnam. And according to Evans (2002), those fighting against the United States viewed the Hmong as traitors and launched a Hmong genocide. As a result, thousands of Hmong refugees first fled to Thailand, and beginning in 1978, hundreds of thousands fled Thailand and Vietnam by boat. Denied access to Indonesia and Malaysia, after literally months floating around on boats, approximately two hundred thousand Hmong were granted political asylum in the United States; they settled primarily in Minnesota, Wisconsin, North Carolina, and central California.

Like many communities, the Hmong have benefited tremendously from the processes of globalization, which have allowed them to use the family reunification policies to reunite. This has been particularly important for the Hmong because their community is literally scattered all over the world, much like other displaced populations, such as Eastern European Jews who fled the Holocaust and Syrians who are fleeing the Middle East in the 2010s. Thus, international marriage has been a long-standing practice among the Hmong.

The Hmong community in Wisconsin has seen a significant uptick in what advocates term *abusive international marriages*. We note here that advocates like those featured in Box 10.3 do not refer to these experiences as "trafficking," and we respect that and will not either. By definition, abusive international marriages involve men living in the United States marrying Hmong women who live abroad and are not US citizens. Abusive international marriages often have the following characteristics:

- Older men marrying underage girls (under age eighteen).
- Age differences of twenty to seventy years (men who are fifty to eighty years old marrying twelve- and thirteen-year-old girls).
- Older men acquiring young wives through their sons, who make the marriage arrangement.
- Force—though the wife may be older than eighteen, her family forces her to marry out of economic need.
- Misrepresented marital status—men indicate that they are widowed or divorced and do not disclose that they are already married when they arrange for their new wife.
- Forced divorces—men force their first wives to divorce them so that they can take second or even third wives. In the process, the divorced wives often lose support, including forfeiting child support.
- Abandonment ("marry and dump")—the new bride is abandoned within the first few months of marriage, and the husband returns to the United States with the promise but not the intent of sponsoring her immigration vis-à-vis the family reunification process. A dumped wife suffers tremendous status loss and may find that she is forced into sex trafficking as her only means to make a living.

Like other marriage migrants, Hmong wives are completely dependent upon and vulnerable to their husbands. And, like many marriage migrants, Hmong wives report high levels of IPV, including physical, emotional, and sexual abuse. Additionally, because some abusive international marriages in the Hmong community involve taking second or even third wives, the negative impact is felt by the first wife and her children as well. She may experience feelings of humiliation, she may also be subjected to IPV, and often her children feel a sense of shame or abandonment.

We had the privilege to interview a Hmong woman we'll call "V," who is a survivor of an abusive marriage. Though V is not a marriage migrant herself, her story illustrates the plight of many immigrant women, including Hmong and Somali, who are caught in the web of abusive marriages and marriage migration.

V was born in Laos. When she was five, she and her family escaped Laos and settled in a refugee camp in Thailand. When she was ten, V and her family were able to move to the United States, taking advantage of the family reunification act; V's aunt lived in Milwaukee and sponsored V's family, who were subsequently resettled there. V was a bright and hard-working girl, and her aunt and other women noticed. They began to suggest to Hmong men in the community that V would make a good Hmong wife; she would work hard and be submissive. When V was twelve, a man visited her family and arranged to take her to the mall one day after school. That day V's life changed forever.

After school one day, the man arrived to take V to the mall. Though she had no reason to be suspicious, she soon realized that they were not driving toward the mall at all. When V questioned the man, he indicated that he had left his wallet at home and they were stopping at his house to retrieve it. When they got to his house, the man went inside while V waited in the car. When the man returned, he had another man with him. Neither man got into the car. V became scared and started to scream. The men pulled her kicking and screaming from the car, dragged her into the house, and held her hostage there for three days. V was raped over and over and over again until she could not walk. At the end of three days, the man took V to her parents' house and told them that he had had sex with her, and a marriage ritual was performed. Without her consent, after three days of torture, and at only twelve years of age, V was married in the eyes of the community, though not legally, to a man more than a decade older than her. She was in the sixth grade.

The rape and beatings continued almost daily, and within months V was pregnant. She delivered her first child at age thirteen, and, as a result of almost daily rape and her husband's refusal to allow her to use birth control, V had four children by the time she was eighteen.

V's husband was an extremely violent man who beat her regularly, threatened to kill her, raped her, and emotionally abused her. After she turned eighteen, rather than legally marrying her, he decided that he needed to take younger wives and began an annual trek to Laos, where he "married" countless young women using the "marry and dump" strategy outlined above; he never brought any of the wives to live in the United States. Despite the reprieve his trips provided, V grew tired of his infidelity. She appreciated the time when he was gone and she was at peace, and she realized that she needed to get out of the marriage.

Divorce is shunned in the Hmong community, and V first tried a series of mediations to address her husband's infidelities. Though the community was supportive of her demands for fidelity in her marriage, her husband continued his annual trips to Laos. After several years of enduring these trips, V sought support from the Hmong community that if he took another trip, they would support her decision to divorce. He took another trip, rationalizing it based on the fact that he had already purchased the tickets.

V's community refused to support her, so she hired a lawyer and attempted to seek some justice in the civil court system. Though she was never legally married, her lawyer was able to bring a civil lawsuit that would guarantee her a fair distribution of the marital assets.

During the trial, as V's lawyer presented evidence of the length of their relationship, the judge began to ask questions about V's age. At one point he called V and her lawyer into his chambers to confirm that she had been an underage minor when four of her six children were born. When V confirmed this, the judge immediately called the prosecutor.

Ultimately, V's (now former) husband was convicted of child sexual abuse and sentenced to prison. What follows is her statement to the court at the sentencing.

BOX 10.2	V'S VICTIM STATEMENT

V's victim statement is printed verbatim. Remember that English is not V's first language. Emphasis ours.

Thaying robbed me of my childhood; the innocent trusting of a child is lost forever due to his lies. He lied about taking me shopping and I trusted him with the innocence of a child, at the end of that day he stole my innocence and crush my trust in man. Throughout our sixteen years together he continually abused me mentally, physically, emotionally, sexually, economically, and socially. I suffered at the hands of Thaying for so long and now, still suffer from all the lies and the backlashes that he has created using the Hmong community at large to do his dirty work. I don't understand how a father, who claims to love his children, could be so cruel to his own flesh and blood by making them go through this type of public humiliation. I am extremely hurt and heartbroken for the suffering that my children have to undergo at the hands of their father. It's sad to think that I brought them into this world and I'm not able to protect them from being ostracize ridicule from the Hmong community because they are a part of me. The father that every child crave to be part of their life is the father that they fear would do harm to their mother. Words could never explain the heartache I feel when I look at my children's eyes. I only want to leave the marriage and live a separate and happy life full of love and joy with my children. I didn't want to live a life that was full of lies and deceit. I don't want my children to go through all the heartache and drama with Thaying anymore. This is the only reason I decided to file for divorce. He could not accept the fact that I want to be out of the relationship, so he aired his dirty laundry and now there are consequences for all the things that he has done to me. He was the one who cause this to come out in the open and yet he blames me for his own indiscretion.

continues

BOX 10.2   V'S VICTIM STATEMENT *continued*

Hmong communities not just locally but globally is against me, and my parents. They said that I am a traitor to Hmong people; I destroy the Hmong culture, beliefs, traditions, and reputations. My parents didn't raise a good obedient Hmong woman but a heartless woman who would demolish Hmong culture the way it was meant to be. Most of them want to kill me. The Hmong community at large are threatening and shaming my family and me for what had happen to Thaying. They have threatened to search for me and hunt me down like a squirrel in the woods. These threats are aired on Hmong radios and Hmong conference calls throughout the United States. The people who call to talk on the free conference call are from anywhere in the world. The Lor family is using Hmong black magic (tso dab and/or tso qes zeb) to harm me and my mother.

During our marriage, Thaying had made threats against me if I ever leave him. The threats that are constant are:

1. He would kill and bury me in the basement head first. This is to show the gods that I was a bad wife and does not deserve to live, and then he would cover the hole with concrete cement.
2. He would kill and bury me in the backyard then plant flowers on top of my body. That way he could just report me missing and no one will suspect that I was in the backyard so no one will find me or my body.
3. Kill me and put me in a sack, tie it with something heavy to weigh me down, and then throw me into Lake Michigan. That way my body won't float back up so no one will ever find me. These are the three common threats that he mention to me over and over throughout our marriage.

During the divorce proceedings, Thaying threatened that at the end of the divorce process, if he ended up paying child support then he would get his visa and passport ready, buy a one way airline ticket and wait until time to leave, and then he will kill me and leave the country.

Due to all Thaying's threats and the Hmong community threats, I fear that if Thaying get released from jail, I will be the first one to suffer his wrath and leave my children behind without a mother to care for them. Second in line to suffer his wrath would be my parents for testifying and supporting me. On top of my fear of being hurt from Thaying, I don't know what the Lor clan and the Hmong community will do to hurt me and my family. Thaying, his friends, and his family members have voice that if he spends ten to twenty years in jail, there would be no point for Thaying to start a

continues

BOX 10.2   **V'S VICTIM STATEMENT** *continued*

new life. His one and only goal when he gets out is to kill me then kill himself. Your Honor, the sentence that you will place on Thaying today is not just for me but for every Hmong woman out there that lacks the strength to come forward because of this type of backlashes in the Hmong community. I don't have the strength and courage to stand the backlashes either but I have to because of my safety and my children's happiness. The reason I never brought this subject up is because I respect the Hmong culture and tradition marriages. The abuse and violence is what I am fighting against in this case. *The future of the Hmong women are at stake here, looking for justice that has been deny for thousands of years because culture was frozen in time to cover up violence against women.* I am asking for the safety of my children, my parents, and me that you consider giving the maximum sentence that is allowed under the law for the crime that was committed against me.

This is not a case of tradition, culture, or practice of the old country, but simply a case of sexual assault. Please don't let this crime slide through the cracks because the perpetrator is hiding behind culture, tradition, and practices. The important thing is that we must follow the law of the land regardless of which country we live in. If culture is used by our community to explain and justify violence against women then by some force we have gone back in time to a land that we wish not to reside in. The United States developed rules, laws, and regulation to govern the people. As American Citizens we are the people. This is the land of the melting pot which has a rich culture, tradition, and practices within it borders. Every person in the United States have their own culture, tradition, and practices but are not using them as an excuse to hide violence against women. Let this case not be an exception to the rule.

Many of the first generation who were born and raised in Laos believed that what Thaying did to me was not wrong. It is his right since he is my husband. From the perspective of traditional Hmong culture, there is no such thing as rape within a marriage. They still believe that rape within a marriage is not a crime. When a girl, doesn't matter the age, becomes a wife—willingly or unwillingly—sex is a duty that the wife provides for the husband. If the husband request for sex, then the wife submit without resistance. If she resist then the violence is considered her fault for resisting. It was and still is a very difficult subject for me to speak about because cultural pressure prohibits the mention of sexual assault.

Thaying, at one point was my husband, is an evil man and will never stop what he did to me until he gets his way with whomever he is with. He will lie and twist everything around to suit his situation. To Thaying, it is his way or no way at all. I have endured

continues

BOX 10.2	**V'S VICTIM STATEMENT** *continued*

mental, physical, emotional, sexual, economic, and social abuse from him for sixteen years and he continually denies that it ever happened. *His claim is that it is his right because he was my husband and we're Hmong so that is what Hmong people do. I am asking that the court send a strong message to the Hmong community that an act of sexual assault is a crime and is not acceptable in the United States in any shape or form. Culture, tradition, and practice have no bearing on crimes that have been committed against a person be it a man or a woman.*

It would have been better if I could have said this personally today, but my safety and the safety of my children is more important to me. I feel that if I should come to court personally, I fear that my anonymity what little I have left would be compromise and jeopardize my safety. I hope that the magnitude of fear and intimidation for my safety from Thaying and the Hmong community is clear in this letter. The support that Thaying has generated in the community due to the inaccuracy that *Milwaukee Journal Sentinel* had printed which portray Thaying as the victim of cultural and tradition is overwhelming and unbelievable. The true fact that Thaying was convicted of the crime of sexual assault is not the subject but culture and tradition is.

Thank you, Your Honor, for giving me this opportunity to speak even if it is just from a letter due to safety issue surrounding this case. I ask that you search in your heart and give Thaying the sentence that is appropriate for the crime which he has committed and not to let culture and tradition weigh in on your decision but the crime itself.

Source: Court interview conducted by the authors.

V's case not only reveals the tragedies of abusive marriages, marriage migration, and child sexual abuse, but it also reminds us of the importance of intervention. We asked V if she continued to go to school while she was pregnant and after she gave birth, and she responded emphatically, "Yes!" In fact, despite having four children by her eighteenth birthday, she graduated from high school in the top 5 percent of her class and went on to earn a community college degree.

Then we asked V if any teacher had ever said anything to her or asked her anything about the context of her pregnancy, and she said "no." When we asked V if she had prenatal care, she said, "Of course." When we asked her if any of the doctors or nurses asked her anything about the context of her pregnancy, she said "no."

We asked V how it felt when the judge finally asked the question. She said she couldn't believe it. She wished someone had asked her about her circumstances earlier.

Had someone asked her, her husband's reign of terror might have been mini-mized. If someone had asked V about her pregnancies—a teacher, a nurse, a doctor—an investigation might have been launched, her abuser might have been brought to justice sooner, and V might have been free from the violence sooner.

BOX 10.3	HMONG ADVOCATES ORGANIZING IN WISCONSIN

Hmong in several Wisconsin communities have begun organizing in order to address abusive international marriage and other challenges facing their community. As a result of their advocacy, women in their community are finding the support they need to seek help and even leave abusive relationships, and Hmong men are challenging traditional beliefs of masculinity and calling for a new masculinity among Hmong men.

Source: Dabby-Chinoy 2012.

CONCLUSIONS

IPV is a cause of great injury to many women and even becomes fatal for some. It is easy to argue that "bad" men abuse their partners and that "weak" women sub-mit to it or will not leave. These explanations are appealing because they focus on individual explanations and because they suggest that as long as a woman marries a "good" man, she will be fine.

Synthesizing the arguments regarding dominant beliefs about masculinity with those regarding dominant beliefs about femininity leads to the conclusion that elements of the ideologies of masculinity and of femininity are mutually reinforcing, and together they work to maintain a system of gender oppression—an inequality regime (Acker 2006)—that leaves women vulnerable to IPV and lets men off the hook when it occurs. Thus, both systems will have to be unseated before we can expect to see a reduction in IPV. We will return to a much more in-depth discussion of this as well as a discussion of recommendations in the concluding chapter. We note here, however, that a more clear and precise understanding of these constructions of masculinity and their racial and ethnic variations will, if employed, lead to more culturally specific and effective preven-tion and intervention programs for men at risk of perpetrating IPV and women who are vulnerable to IPV, and these will be articulated in the final chapter.

When we had the opportunity to revise this book for the second edition, we felt that the book needed to be globalized in some way. Because we are scholars of family violence and not globalization, we decided to focus on and include the discussions of international adoption, international surrogacy, and marriage migration as illustrations of family violence that occurs across international borders. Children are kidnapped and sold into a system of international adoptions, women in developing countries have their bodies and their labor exploited by agencies that facilitate surrogacy, and women are forced into abusive marriages. Each of these types of violence occurs because of power and inequality; women and children with no other choice "consent" to practices that are funded by Americans, who, even if they are not wealthy by American standards, have the financial assets to purchase children, babies, and wives, often without any knowledge of the exploitive and often violent system in which they are engaged. We chose to highlight the Hmong community for two reasons: first, because they are an invisible population in the United States and we hoped to bring some attention to the challenges they are facing; and second, because one of our colleagues is Hmong and she has been conducting research on international abuse marriage migration since 2012. As she shared bits and pieces of her research with us, we knew that we needed to draw attention to the plight of so many Hmong women in the United States and abroad.

In the next chapter, we turn to a discussion of the specific role that religion—which can be considered a generator of ideology—plays in IPV and child abuse; specifically, we examine the ways in which religious leaders often fail to intervene in IPV and child abuse cases and thus contribute to its perpetuation.

RESOURCES

Her, Dorothy. 2014. *Building Our Future: Ending Abusive International Marriages.* Saint Paul Neighborhood Network. www.youtube.com/watch?v=FBiieHou8Sw. (We highly recommend this documentary, which features Hmong women talking about the abuse they have experienced and Hmong men identifying a new masculinity that leads to a reduction in violence and safe families.)

Newell, Mike. 2003. *Mona Lisa Smile.* Revolution Studios/Columbia Pictures. (This film, set in the 1950s, is an excellent example of the ways in which the cult of domesticity was taught deliberately to young women as a way to "keep them in their place.")

NOTES

1. Although it is now a part of our colloquial speech, the phrase "boys will be boys" first appeared in William Thackeray's *Vanity Fair* in 1848 (and similar forms were used earlier).

2. An article in the *New York Times* on "genital cutting" summarizes nicely the motive behind this practice, which remains widespread in Africa and the Middle East: to keep women faithful. See Dugger, Celia W. 2011. "Senegal Curbs a Bloody Rite for Girls and Women." *New York Times*, October 15.

REFERENCES

Acker, Joan. 2006. *Class Questions, Feminist Answers*. New York: Routledge.

American Association of University Women (AAUW). 2018. *The Simple Truth About the Gender Pay Gap*. www.aauw.org/research/the-simple-truth-about-the-gender-pay-gap.

Berik, Günseli, and Ebru Kongar. 2013. "Time Allocation of Married Mothers and Fathers in Hard Times: The 2007–09 US Recession." *Feminist Economics 19*(3): 208–237, DOI: 10.1080/13545701.2013.798425.

Bombardieri, Marcella. 2005. "Summer's Remarks on Women Draws Fire." *Boston Globe*, January 19. www.boston.com/news/education/higher/articles/2005/01/17/summers_remarks_on_women_draw_fire.

Bosson, Jennifer K., Joseph A. Vandello, Rochelle M. Burnaford, Jonathan R. Weaver, and S. Arzu Wasti. 2009. "Precarious Manhood and Displays of Physical Aggression." *Personality and Social Psychology Bulletin 35*(5): 623–634.

Browne, Angela. 1989. *When Battered Women Kill*. New York: Free Press.

Brownmiller, Susan. 1975. *Against Our Will: Men, Women, and Rape*. New York: Simon and Schuster.

Burton, Linda. 1990. "Teenage Childbearing as an Alternative Life-Course Strategy in Multigeneration Black Families." *Human Nature 1*(2): 123–143.

Callimachi, Rukmini. 2015. "ISIS Enshrines a Theology of Rape." *New York Times*, August 13. www.nytimes.com/2015/08/14/world/middleeast/isis-enshrines-a-theology-of-rape.html.

Carney, Scott. 2011. *The Red Market: On the Trail of the World's Organ Brokers, Bone Thieves, Blood Farmers, and Child Traffickers*. New York: William Morrow.

Centers for Disease Control (CDC). 2017. *Fact Sheet*. www.cdc.gov/violenceprevention/pdf/ipv-factsheet.pdf

Chafetz, Janet Saltzman. 1974. *Masculine/Feminine or Human? An Overview of the Sociology of Sex Roles*. Itasca, IL: F. E. Peacock.

Collins, Patricia Hill. 1994. "Shifting the Center: Race, Class, and Feminist Theorizing About Motherhood." In *Mothering: Ideology, Experience, and Agency*, edited by E. Glenn, G. Chang, and L. Forcey, 45–66. New York: Routledge.

Connell, R. W. 1990. "An Iron Man: The Body and Some Contradictions of Hegemonic Masculinity." In *Sport, Men, and the Gender Order: Critical Feminist Perspectives*, edited by M. Messner and D. Sabo, 83–95. Champaign, IL: Human Kinetics Books.

Connell, R. W., and James Messerschmidt. 2005. "Hegemonic Masculinity: Rethinking the Concept." *Gender and Society 19*(6): 829–859.

Coontz, Stephanie. 1992. *The Way We Never Were: American Families and the Nostalgia Trap*. New York: Basic Books.

Coontz, Stephanie. 1997. *The Way We Really Are: Coming to Terms with America's Changing Families*. New York: Basic Books.

Dabby-Chinoy, Chic. 2012. *Abusive International Marriages: Hmong Advocates Organizing in Wisconsin*. San Francisco, CA: Asian and Pacific Islander Institute on Domestic Violence. www.apiidv.org/files/Abusive.International.Marriages_APIIDV_4.2013.pdf.

Doyle, Laura. 2001. *The Surrendered Wife*. New York: Fireside.

Dugger, Celia W. 2011. "Senegal Curbs a Bloody Rite for Girls and Women." *New York Times*, October 15.

Epstein, Cynthia. 2007. "Great Divides: The Cultural, Cognitive, and Social Bases of the Global Subordination of Women." *American Sociological Review 72(1)*: 1–22.

Evans, Grant. 2002. *A Short History of Laos: The Land in Between*. Crows Nest, New South Wales, Australia: Allen & Unwin.

Franchina, Joseph J., Richard M. Eisler, and Todd M. Moore. 2001. "Masculine Gender Role Stress and Intimate Abuse: Effects of Masculine Gender Relevance of Dating Situations and Female Threat on Men's Attributions and Affective Responses." *Psychology of Men and Masculinity 2(10)*: 34–41.

Gelles, R. J. 1997. *Intimate Violence in Families*. Thousand Oaks, CA: Sage.

Gillooly, Patrick. 2011. "New Report Details Status of Women in Science and Engineering at MIT." *MIT News*, March 21. http://news.mit.edu/2011/women-mit-report-0321.

Hattery, Angela. 2001. *Women, Work, and Family: Balancing and Weaving*. Thousand Oaks, CA: Sage.

Hattery, Angela. 2008. *Intimate Partner Violence*. Lanham, MD: Rowman and Littlefield.

Hattery, Angela J., and Emily W. Kane. 1995. "Men's and Women's Perceptions of Non-Consensual Sexual Intercourse." *Sex Roles 33(11)*: 785–802.

Hattery, Angela J., and Earl Smith. 2007. *African American Families*. Thousand Oaks, CA: Sage.

Hattery, Angela J., and Earl Smith. 2014. *African American Families: Myths and Realities*. Lanham, MD: Rowman and Littlefield.

Hays, Sharon. 1996. *The Cultural Contradictions of Motherhood*. New Haven, CT: Yale University Press.

Hofstede, Geerte. 2001. *Culture's Consequences*. 2nd ed. Thousand Oaks, CA: Sage Publications.

Kearl, Holly. 2010. *Stop Street Harassment: Making Public Places Safe and Welcoming for Women*. New York: Praeger.

Kimmel, Michael. 2005. *Manhood in America*. New York: Oxford University Press.

Koss, M. P., L. A. Goodman, A. Browne, L. F. Fitzgerald, G. P. Keita, and N. F. Russo. 1994. *No Safe Haven: Male Violence Against Women at Home, at Work, and in the Community*. Washington, DC: American Psychological Association.

Kossoudji, Sherrie, and Laura J. Dresser. 1992. "Working Class Rosies: Women Industrial Workers During World War II." *Journal of Economic History 52(2)*: 431–446.

Kristoff, Nicholas, and Sheryl WuDunn. 2009. *Half the Sky: Turning Oppression into Opportunity for Women Worldwide*. New York: Alfred A. Knopf.

Lemert, Charles, and Ann Branaman. 1997. *The Goffman Reader*. New York: Wiley-Blackwell.

Luker, Kristin. 1985. *Abortion and the Politics of Motherhood*. Berkeley and Los Angeles, CA: University of California Press.

MacKinnon, Catharine. 1991. *Toward a Feminist Theory of the State*. Cambridge, MA: Harvard University Press.

Majors, Richard, and Janet Bilson. 1992. *Cool Pose: The Dilemmas of African American Manhood in America*. New York: Lexington Books.

Mansley, Elizabeth. 2007. "Man Up: Exploring the Relationships Between Race, Social Class, Intimate Partner Violence, and the Construction of Masculinity." PhD dissertation, Department of Sociology, University of Delaware.

Massachusetts Institute of Technology. 1999. "A Study on the Status of Women Faculty in Science at MIT.*" The MIT Faculty Newsletter XI(4)*. Boston, MA: Massachusetts Institute of Technology. http://web.mit.edu/fnl/women/women.html.

Merali, Noorfarah. 2008. "Theoretical Frameworks for Studying Female Marriage Migrants." *Psychology of Women Quarterly 32(3)*: 281–289.

Messner, Michael A. 2002. "Playing Center: The Triad of Violence in Men's Sports." In *Taking the Field: Women, Men, and Sports*, edited by M. A. Messner, 27–62. Minneapolis, MN: University of Minnesota Press.

Padavic, Irene, and Barbara Reskin. 2002. *Women and Men at Work*. Thousand Oaks, CA: Pine Forge Press.

Parsons, Talcott, and Robert Bales. 1955. *Family, Socialization, and the Interaction Process*. Glencoe, IL: Free Press.

Passel, Jeffrey, Wendy Wang, and Paul Taylor. 2010. "Marrying Out: One-in-Seven New U.S. Marriages Is Interracial or Interethnic." *Pew Research Center*, June 4. www.pewsocialtrends.org/2010/06/04/marrying-out.

Patterson, Orlando. 1998. "For Whom the Bell Curves." In *The Ordeal of Integration*, 125–146. New York: Basic Civitas.

Patterson, Orlando. 1999. *Rituals in Blood: Consequences of Slavery in Two American Centuries*. New York: Basic Civitas.

Reidy, Dennis E., Joanne P. Smith-Darden, Kai S. Cortina, Roger M. Kernsmith, and Poco D. Kernsmith. 2015. "Masculine Discrepancy Stress, Teen Dating Violence, and Sexual Violence Perpetration Among Adolescent Boys." *Journal of Adolescent Health 56(6)*: 619–624.

Romero, Mary. 1992. *Maid in the U.S.A.* New York: Routledge.

Russell, D. 1990. *Rape in Marriage*. Bloomington, IN: University of Indiana Press.

Sampson, Robert J. 1987. "Urban Black Violence: The Effect of Male Joblessness and Family Disruption." *American Journal of Sociology 93(2)*: 348–382.

Sanday, Peggy Reeves. 1981. "The Socio-Cultural Context of Rape: A Cross-Cultural Study." *Journal of Social Issues 37(4)*: 5–27.

Segura, Denise A. 1994. "Working at Motherhood: Chicana and Mexican Immigrant Mothers and Employment." In *Mothering: Ideology, Experience, and Agency*, edited by E. Glenn, G. Chang, and L. Forcey, 45–66. New York: Routledge.

Smith, Earl. 2008. "African American Men and Intimate Partner Violence." *Journal of African American Studies 12*: 156–179.

Smith, Earl, and Angela Hattery. 2006. "Hey Stud: Race, Sex, and Sports." *Sexuality and Culture 10(2)*: 3–32.

Stockett, Kathryn. 2009. *The Help*. New York: Amy Einhorn Books.

Story, Louise. 2005. "Many Women at Elite Colleges Set Career Path to Motherhood." *New York Times*, September 20. www.nytimes.com/2005/09/20/us/many-women-at-elite-colleges-set-career-path-to-motherhood.html.

Summers, Lawrence. 2005. "Remarks at National Bureau of Economic Research Conference on Diversifying the Science and Engineering Workforce." *Office of the President, Harvard University, Cambridge, MA*, January 14. www.harvard.edu/president/speeches/summers_2005/nber.php.

Therborn, Göran. 1980. *The Ideology of Power and the Power of Ideology*. London: Verso.

Tjaden, Patricia, and Nancy Thoennes. 2000. *Full Report of the Prevalence, Incidence, and Consequences of Violence Against Women: Findings from the National Violence Against Women Survey*. Washington, DC: US Department of Justice. www.ncjrs.gov/pdffiles1/nij/183781.pdf.

United Nations Department of Economic and Social Affairs. 2017. *International Migration Report 2017*. www.un.org/en/development/desa/population/migration/publications/migrationreport/docs/MigrationReport2017_Highlights.pdf.

United Nations Office on Drugs and Crime. 2016. *Global Report on Trafficking in Persons 2016*. www.unodc.org/documents/data-and-analysis/glotip/2016_Global_Report_on_Trafficking_in_Persons.pdfwww.unodc.org/documents/human-trafficking/2014/GLOTIP_2014_full_report.pdf.

Veblen, Thorstein. 2008. *Theory of the Leisure Class*. New York: Oxford University Press.

Warshaw, Robin. 1988. *I Never Called It Rape: The Ms. Report on Recognizing, Fighting, and Surviving Date and Acquaintance Rape*. New York: Harper & Row.

Wilson, William J. 2009. *More Than Just Race*. New York: W. W. Norton.

Wolf, Naomi. 1992. *The Beauty Myth: How Images of Beauty Are Used Against Women*. New York: Anchor Books.

11

RELIGION AND FAMILY VIOLENCE

What is a good enough reason for divorce? Well, according to Rick Warren's Saddleback Church, divorce is permitted only in cases of adultery or abandonment—as these are the only cases permitted in the Bible—and never in cases of abuse. As teaching pastor Tom Holladay explains, spousal abuse should be dealt with by temporary separation and church marriage counseling designed to bring about reconciliation between the couple. But to qualify for that separation, your spouse must be in the "habit of beating you regularly," not be simply someone who "grabbed you once" (Joyce 2009).

OBJECTIVES

- To provide an overview of the role that religion has played in shaping family violence—especially child abuse and intimate partner violence
- To identify the specific texts and passages that institutionalized religions rely on for shaping appropriate gender roles and parent–child roles
- To explore the ways in which institutionalized religions have responded to family violence vis-à-vis texts and passages
- To examine the responses of individual spiritual leaders to victims who seek assistance
- To provide recommendations for transforming religion from an institution that directly and indirectly supports family violence to one that participates effectively in its eradication and prevention

KEY TERMS

religiosity

theory of secularization

INTRODUCTION

There has long been tension between religious institutions and the public, as well as public institutions, including law enforcement, regarding matters of the family. While we argued in Chapter 2 that one of the barriers to intervening in family violence was the notion that it was "private," this is not so much the case for religious institutions, which have a long history and tradition of commenting on and otherwise being involved in the private matters of the family. One reason for this is the tensions that have always existed between religious institutions and the secular world. For example, one area of high tension is reproductive rights and technologies. In response to the ever-increasing ability of people to control their reproductive lives through scientific technologies that run the gamut from restricting pregnancy (birth control pills, IUDs) to increasing fertility (in vitro fertilization, egg donation), many religious institutions are organized around an ideology that prohibits the control of reproduction based on a belief that it is akin to "playing God." Religious leaders write pamphlets on these topics—the description of Rick Warren's position on divorce is illustrative—and often preach on these issues; it seems fair to assume that Rick Warren and religious leaders like him incorporate these notions into couples' counseling. In this chapter we explore these tensions and the ways in which religious doctrine and practice have shaped all aspects of family violence, including prescriptions for gender roles and parent–child relationships that set the stage for family violence. We also examine the institutional responses to the phenomenon of family violence that arise when individuals seek help from priests, ministers, rabbis, and other religious leaders. We begin with a brief overview of the history of the tension between religious institutions and the secular world.

TENSIONS BETWEEN RELIGION AND THE SECULAR WORLD

A brief overview of the relationship between religion and the secular world is an important starting point when laying the groundwork for understanding one of the ways in which religion shapes family violence and, especially, the religious response to it.

Among sociologists of religion, there is great interest in the rate at which people in a given society are affiliated with particular religions. Sociological research on religion has revealed that both the content of religious beliefs (fundamentalism as compared to more liberal ideologies) and the importance of religion in an individual's life (religiosity) shape a variety of attitudes and behaviors, ranging from beliefs about interracial marriage to voting patterns. The Pew Forum on Religious Life gathers statistics, primarily from the census but also from other national surveys, and compiles these data as well as an analysis in convenient reports. According to the data, in the United States approximately 75 percent of Americans report being affiliated with an institutionalized religion (Pew Research Center 2015). As shown in Table 11.1, just under half of all Americans (46.6 percent) identify as Protestant and 20.8 percent as Catholic. This is not surprising given that the majority of Americans trace their origins back to Protestant and Catholic countries—including Western Europe and Latin America.

The second question that sociologists of religion are interested in is the overall religiosity of people in different societies. **Religiosity** is a way of measuring both the frequency with which people attend church and the level of their belief in certain core religious principles. According to a Pew Research Center report (2015), studies on church attendance are unreliable because respondents significantly over-report, by 100 percent, their church attendance. Though 40 percent of Americans report going to church regularly, in fact only approximately 20 percent actually do. According to another Pew Research Center report (2018), the vast majority of

Table 11.1 Major Religious Traditions in the United States (2014)

	Among all adults . . . %
Christian	**70.7**
Protestant..	46.6
Evangelical churches	*25.4*
Mainline churches..	*14.7*
Historically black churches	*6.5*
Catholic..	20.8
Orthodox Christian	0.5
Mormon..	1.6
Jehovah's Witness...	0.8
Other Christian	0.4
Other Religions	**6**
Jewish...	1.9
Muslim	0.9
Buddhist...	0.7
Hindu	0.7
Other world religions...	0.3
Other faiths..	1.5
Unaffiliated	**22.9**
Atheist	3.1
Agnostic..	4.0
Nothing in particular	15.8
Don't know/refused to answer	**0.6**

Source: Pew Research Center 2015.

Americans report that they believe in God (80 percent), 33 percent classify themselves as "spiritual" but not "religious," and one in five (21 percent) indicate that they pray every day.

Thus, as the rate of Americans who report no affiliation (just over 20 percent) has been steadily rising over the past two decades, simultaneously those who are affiliated appear to be more religious—attending church more frequently and with a higher percentage expressing beliefs in core religious principles (Pew Research Center 2018). This is a perplexing question for sociologists of religion and social commentators studying the trend toward secularization, a phenomenon that has been termed the **theory of secularization**.

Peter Berger (1999), one of the leading sociologists of religion, who specializes in the question of secularization, summarizes the theory of secularization as the prediction among scholars that modernity and religion are inversely related. This inverse relationship between modernization and religion is created in large part by the rise in the acceptance and even prioritizing of science. The creationism/evolution debate is an illustration of this process. As Americans began to accept the tenets of evolution, they simultaneously began to discard their belief in creationism, which led many fundamentalist Christians to liberalize their views, and the impact on already liberal Christians was a trend toward lower levels of religiosity and, at the extreme, the rejection of religion entirely. Thus, the theory holds, as a culture or society or nation becomes increasingly modern, the people in that culture or society or nation will become less religious. This theory was developed largely by observing the changing role of religion and the relationship between religion and secularity in Europe. In short, Berger (1999) argues that in Europe the theory of secularization paints an accurate portrayal of the pathways of both religion and secular life. Europe has demonstrated a critical and severe shift toward secularization in two key ways: the declining importance of religion to individuals and the dismantling of state religions, which were common throughout all of Western Europe across the entire second millennia (roughly 500–1900). For example, Anderson (2004) notes:

> Numbers drawn from the long-term European Values Study (EVS) and other research underscore the degree to which Europe has abandoned its Christian heritage. For one thing, the pews of Europe's churches are often empty. In France, only one in twenty people now attends a religious service every week, and the demographic skews to the aged. Only 15 percent of Italians attend weekly while roughly 30 percent of Germans still go to church at least once a month. Indifference is widespread. A mere 21 percent of Europeans hold religion to be "very important." In France, arguably the most secular of Europe's nations outside of the formerly

Lutheran countries of northern Europe, the percentage is lower still, at slightly over 10 percent. As Cardinal Dionigi Tettamanzi, archbishop of Milan, lamented in the *New York Times* in October 2005, "The parishes tell me that there are children who don't know how to make the sign of the cross." Only Europe's growing Muslim population seems to exhibit any religious fervor. True, few Europeans proclaim outright atheism, and a majority still call themselves Christians. But how many are Christian in anything but a nominal sense? Not only do Europeans not go to church very often; only about 40 percent believe in heaven and only half that percentage in hell. The concept of sin is vanishing from the European mind. Just 57 percent of Spaniards, 55 percent of Germans, 40 percent of French people, and approximately 30 percent of Swedes now believe in the existence of sin.

(n.p.)

While Europe is becoming increasingly secular, the opposite appears to be happening in the United States. This is vexing for two reasons: first, the United States leads the world in terms of modernizing, and second, the majority of Americans continue to trace their ancestry to these same countries in Western Europe. This of course is predicted to change by 2050, when people of Hispanic origin will make up the majority of the US population. Thus, Berger (1999) argues that the secularization theory applies only to Europe and must be revised with regards to the rest of the world.

Berger (1999) argues further that the tension between religion and secularization has existed from the beginnings of the United States and for centuries across Europe. Most recently, this tension is evident in Middle Eastern countries, like Saudi Arabia and Iran, that are facing struggles between secular and Islamic branches of government. Indeed, in several of these countries there are two rules of law in place, the more liberal secular law and the highly conservative sharia law. Although perhaps the cases presented in the Middle East are the most obvious, secularizing forces do also exist in the United States. America's highly educated, often left-leaning elites are every bit as secular as the most disenchanted Europeans (Anderson 2004). Berger says of these elites:

Its members are relatively thin on the ground, but they control the institutions that provide the "official" definitions of reality, notably the education system, the media of mass communication, and the higher reaches of the legal system. These elites have wrought secularizing changes in law and culture over the last several decades—using the courts to drive crèche displays from public property and to end prayer or religious instruction of any kind in public schools, for example. However, they have yet to persuade the majority of Americans to embrace a secular worldview themselves.

(1999: 10)

Though this "control" may be disputable at least in some contexts—recall how often presidents across the second half of the twentieth and early decades of the twenty-first centuries invoked religious language and principles in their formal speeches as well as in their more informal remarks—it is important because it may lead to tensions in family violence prevention and intervention. Specifically, if church leaders perceive that they are "losing ground" in the public sphere, they may also interpret attempts by law enforcement and the criminal justice system to interfere in family violence—which occurs very clearly at the core of what we consider the private sphere—as further threats. As a result, they may be increasingly resistant to accepting advice or help when family violence erupts among their flock.

RELIGIOUS TEXTS AND BELIEFS THAT ARE USED TO SUPPORT FAMILY VIOLENCE

As noted by renowned sociologist of religion Peter Berger (1999) and social commentator Brian Anderson (2004), it is not only the increase in religiosity in the United States but the rise in *evangelical Christianity* in the United States and conservative sects of the other major religions—especially Islam and Judaism—in other parts of the world that are the most perplexing. This rise in conservative religions is of paramount importance to our discussion here, as it is these traditions that also resist the modernizing of gender roles—which is often a key point of tension from which intimate partner violence arises (see Chapter 10). Here we examine the specific texts from each of the major holy books and specific religious principles from each of the major institutionalized religions that are used to endorse and reinforce both *traditional family roles* as well as violence against women and children.

Judaism

According to the National Resource Center on Domestic Violence (2007), one of the major tenets of Jewish marriage is peace in the household, or *shalom bayit*. Accordingly, one of the common misperceptions is that intimate partner violence and child abuse do not occur in Jewish households. Yet there is no statistical evidence to suggest that Jewish women and children are any less likely to experience violence or that Jewish men are any less likely to perpetrate it (Tjaden and Thoennes 2000). Additionally, the National Resource Center on Domestic Violence suggests that the construction of *shalom bayit* as primarily the responsibility of wives may prevent or inhibit Jewish women from leaving violent relationships:

> *Shalom Bayit* may be a reason why many Jewish women stay in abusive relationships, in that a victim of domestic violence may be reluctant to seek help because

she may feel she failed at her role to maintain the peace in her home; she may be fearful of bringing *shanda*, or shame, on her family and the community . . . Many people falsely believe that domestic violence does not exist in Jewish homes, and this myth reinforces the silence that allows domestic violence to continue. By bringing attention to the abusive relationship, the victim has not only exposed her imperfect marriage, but she has also exposed the vulnerabilities of her community and may be ostracized or resented for doing so.

(2007: 1)

We can speculate that a similar process inhibits the disclosure of child abuse and the reluctance of families, as well as rabbis, to involve law enforcement and Child Protective Services in child abuse cases; to make child abuse public would be to expose a household that has failed to uphold *shalom bayit*.

Islam

According to the National Resource Center on Domestic Violence, there are passages in the Qur'an that have been used by husbands and spiritual advisers to justify domestic violence:

For Muslim men and women, the Qur'an is the primary source of their faith and practice. In Islam, the focus of marriage is encapsulated in the following verse of the Qur'an: ". . . they are a sort of garment for you and you are a sort of garment for them . . ." (2:188). Qur'anic verse 4:34 is often used to justify physical abuse against a wife if she does not submit to her partner's authority. It states:

"Men shall take full care of women with the bounties Allah has bestowed upon them, and what they may spend out of their possession; as Allah has eschewed each with certain qualities in relation to the other. And the righteous women are the truly devout ones, who guard the intimacy, which Allah has ordained to be guarded. As for those women whose ill-will you have reason to fear, admonish them [first]; then distance yourself in bed, and then tap them; but if they pay you heed, do not seek to harm them. Surely, Allah is indeed the Most High, the Greatest."

(2007: 2)

Spiritual leaders and abusive men may interpret this verse as requiring traditional gender roles; husbands are to be the main providers for and protectors of the family and wives are to be subservient to them. As we discussed extensively in the previous chapter, deviation from gender roles which are often perceived as threats to masculinity may be a trigger for violence. And, for a Muslim man and his spiritual advisers, this verse in the Qur'an may be seen as a religious justification for his violence. He is, after all, simply being a good husband according to religious teaching.

However, many scholars, including Laleh Bakhtiar, who is the first Muslim woman to translate the Qur'an, have interpreted this translation as charging men with the responsibility of financially and physically protecting and caring for their wives and families, not abusing them. Others have noted that the role of "protector" is synonymous with someone who has the responsibility of safeguarding the interests of another, not with someone who imposes their authority on another. If there is a disagreement between a husband and a wife, including the suspicion of infidelity, the Qur'an gives instructions on how to attempt to resolve this situation. It is the husband's responsibility to first talk to her and to then refuse to share her bed. If this fails,

> a husband may "tap" his wife in a symbolic effort to demonstrate his seriousness in the matter . . . Many scholars of the Qur'an have debated over the appropriate translation of the word "tap" as the original Arabic word carries several different meanings . . . In some texts, it is translated as "hit" or "strike"; however, many scholars believe that this is an incorrect translation of the original Arabic word, based on the Prophet's lifelong abhorrence of hitting women.
>
> (National Resource Center on Domestic Violence 2007: 1–2)

Christianity

Turning to Christianity, the dominant religion in the United States, we also see that many Bible passages have been used to justify abusive behavior, of both women and children. Again, quoting from the National Resource Center on Domestic Violence report:

> Similar interpretations have been given to Biblical texts that also focus on *gender roles within heterosexual marriages* [emphasis ours]. Traditionally, Christian teachings about the roles of husbands and wives within a marriage rely heavily on Ephesians 5:21–33 . . . Nine of the twelve verses discuss the responsibility of a husband to his wife. The remaining three verses, when taken in isolation, may be interpreted to imply that the husband has absolute authority over the family and this authority cannot be questioned, and that wives, in turn, must demonstrate absolute obedience and summarily submit to abuse from their husbands.
>
> (National Resource Center on Domestic Violence 2007: 3)

There are many passages in the Bible that have been interpreted to justify and indeed propose preference for inequalities in gender roles between husbands and wives, including the Genesis story that recounts Eve's temptation of Adam and their subsequent banishment from the Garden of Eden. Other verses include Timothy 2:9–15, 1 Corinthians 14:34–35, Colossians 3:18, 1 Peter 3:1–7, Corinthians 11:3–10, and the following from Ephesians 5:22–33, which is often cited:

> Wives, submit to your husbands as to the Lord. For the husband is the head of the wife as Christ is the head of the Church, his body, of which he is the Savior. Now as the Church submits to Christ, so also the wives should submit to their husbands in everything.

We note here that among Judaic, Islamic, and Christian scholars, there is widespread agreement that all of the texts and passages cited here are subject to interpretation and that there are keywords, such as *tap* in the Qur'an, that may be interpreted by some scholars as "strike" or "hit" and by others as something even less than a "tap." Although it is important that we recognize these distinctions in terms of the actual justification (or not) for abuse by the three most influential, institutionalized religions, we must also note that the average Christian, Jew, or Muslim is not educated in these distinctions. Furthermore, based on anecdotal evidence—our own experiences in a variety of church settings, the beliefs many of our students hold, and the experiences a dozen women seminary students shared with us as part of another project—we suggest that many of the spiritual leaders (pastors, rabbis, and imams) serving "on the ground" in literally millions of local churches, temples, and mosques are not trained in the ancient languages and semantics necessary to make these distinctions, and as a result many preach these verses in ways that reinforce traditional gender roles for their congregants. Thus, it seems clear that the likelihood is high that individuals who are in abusive relationships themselves or who, in their capacity as spiritual advisers, are counseling members of an abusive family may apply these passages "as is" and thus reinforce the notion that religious beliefs support and even dictate inequality in marital and parenting roles. Furthermore, these passages may all be extended and interpreted to suggest that one of the burdens and responsibilities of husbands is to discipline their wives and children—occasionally with physical abuse—in order to "train" them to be morally upstanding.

DIVORCE

Finally, for extremely religious women, the teachings about divorce can be an important barrier to leaving abusive relationships and homes. In all three of the major world religions we have been discussing, marriage is a lifelong, sacred commitment among husband, wife, and God or Allah. Some women may feel intense pressure, and they may be pressured by spiritual advisers, to remain in marriages despite the presence of abuse. In addition to the pressure that women may feel or self-impose, their husbands may also use religious ideologies of divorce and the sin of breaking the marriage bond to force their victims to stay in violent marriages. It is also important to realize that for many religious women, especially those who belong to marginalized religions—Jews in the South, Muslims in most of the United States—and for Christian women who live in the Bible Belt, the congregation or temple or mosque to which they belong may be their primary community of friends and support. Thus, an abused woman considering the possibility of divorce as a mechanism to end the violence[1] may realize that to separate from her husband will likely sever her relationship with her entire faith community. This is illustrated by a study of violence among Muslim American women. Participants in the study indicated a reluctance to divorce—and many women lived with violence for years before seeking a divorce—precisely because they feared losing their spiritual community or being assigned a maligned status within a community that defines marriage as central to the spiritual life of both the individual and the community (Hassouneh-Phillips 2001).

INDIVIDUAL RESPONSES TO FAMILY VIOLENCE BY SPIRITUAL ADVISERS

As stated above, there is a great deal of variability in the amount of *formal training* that individual religious "professionals"—ministers, priests, pastors, rabbis, and imams—receive. For example, though all Catholic priests must attend seminary, there is no requirement that ministers in many of the Protestant denominations attend formal seminary before they "hang out their shingle" and open up a church. This is particularly the case in denominations that are less centralized. For example, perusing the job listings posted by the Southern Baptist Convention revealed that the formal requirements for the position of "pastor" varied and were not necessarily linked to education, though ordination as a minister was required. In most Protestant churches, ordination to the pastoral office is the rite by which the church:

- recognizes and confirms that an individual has been called by God to ministry
- acknowledges that the individual has gone through a period of discernment and training related to this call (there is no credentialed training that is required, for example a seminary degree)
- authorizes that individual to take on the office of ministry.

Additionally, the degree to which spiritual leaders receive any training with regards to family violence is even more variable. Thus, though the official position of all institutionalized religions forbids violence in families, the vast majority who are ministering to their religious communities are not necessarily educated about issues of family violence, and as a result, when family violence is exposed to a spiritual leader, his response is likely to be shaped by his own personal experiences and not by the religion's official position. You may remember that although some religious organizations have recently allowed the ordination of women, the vast majority—including *all* Catholic priests and Muslim imams—are men. Additionally, some denominations, most notably Roman Catholicism, require priests to be celibate and never marry. Thus, one critique of the Catholic Church is that although priests are often called to engage in counseling for engaged couples, married couples, and parents struggling with raising children, they have absolutely no personal experience with these relationships, other than as children growing up in a family, on which to draw.

Unfortunately, the majority of spiritual advisers are not well trained to deal effectively with family violence, and in some cases the religious leader is himself the perpetrator of violence.

BOX 11.1   MARLEEN

Marleen was suffering significant abuse by her husband; he had kicked her, punched her, and even broken one of her ribs. Desperate, she went to her pastor for spiritual guidance.

Here's how one article described what happened:

Marleen's pastor was sympathetic. He prayed with Marleen—and then he sent her home. "Try to be more submissive," he advised. "After all, your husband is your spiritual head." Two weeks later, Marleen was dead—killed by an abusive husband. Her church could not believe it. Marleen's husband was a Sunday school teacher and deacon. How could he have done such a thing?

Tragically, studies reveal that spousal abuse is just as common within the evangelical churches as anywhere else.

Women who are connected to their church—regardless of denomination—face an uphill battle. They are faithful to the church and faithful to their spouses and families. Yet the modern church has not advanced in thinking about the role of women in the family.

Marleen's is a tragic illustration.

Source: Colson 2009.

Responses like that of Marleen's pastor pit intimate partner violence advocates and religious leaders against one another. Religious leaders express the fear that secular approaches to intimate partner violence will result in divorce—which violates the lifelong contract that characterizes religious marriage. Diametrically opposed are intimate partner violence advocates and educators who argue that no one should be subjected to abuse, no level of abuse should be tolerated, and advising a woman to "go home and be a better wife" is nothing more than victim blaming that exacerbates the problems of family violence (National Resource Center on Domestic Violence 2007).

INSTITUTIONAL RESPONSES IN GENERAL TO FAMILY VIOLENCE

For a variety of reasons, including the tragedy described in Box 11.1, there have been some attempts by organized religions to provide information about family violence—especially intimate partner violence—and suggest some "best practices" for dealing with family violence when it is presented to an individual spiritual adviser. For example, the United States Conference of Catholic Bishops developed a website to provide advice to parish priests who are presented with victims of intimate partner violence.

The National Resource Center on Domestic Violence makes it clear that counseling victims of intimate partner violence who are deeply faithful and embedded in a faith community is far more effective in achieving desirable outcomes if the woman's faith is respected and utilized in the counseling. Thus, collaborations between intimate partner violence advocates and spiritual leaders are critical to addressing intimate partner violence in faith communities (National Resource Center on Domestic Violence 2007).

Unfortunately, not only have the institutionalized responses of organized religions fallen short, but in many cases the organizations themselves have chosen to turn a blind eye to violence, especially when the perpetrators are members of the faith community and even leaders in the faith community (see Box 11.1 involving Marleen). Why has the primary response of religious leaders to family violence been so unsatisfying? Feminist theorists suggest that this is an expected outcome because all three of the primary world religions and religious texts came to being inside of patriarchal societies. Furthermore, though not all religious and spiritual leaders are male-identified, the vast majority who are educated are trained in organizations dominated by men, and thus the lessons of patriarchy pass even to the women seeking formal and informal religious training. And, despite recent changes in ordination practices, the vast majority of spiritual leaders, including all

Catholic priests and Muslim imams, are men. As men, they live in a cultural landscape of patriarchy and male privilege. Even if some of these beliefs and practices diminished when they entered their spiritual vocation, they grew up and lived, usually at least for some years, as adult men in a culture that affords men the privilege to treat women and children as objects for *their use*, treats violence against women and children as unimportant, and often renders the experiences of the victims invisible.

In addition, as we have argued elsewhere (Hattery and Smith 2019), institutions that are gender segregated create a culture that elevates male privilege to a status that is untouchable and reduces women (and children) to the point of having no status at all. As noted, not only are all of the major world religions male dominated, but they also, to varying degrees, can be characterized as gender segregated. Catholicism and Islam are perhaps the extreme cases—Catholic priests live in sex-segregated communities, women are not allowed to hold any positions of power, and priests are believed to be the physical embodiment of Jesus himself. In the case of Islam and conservative Jewish temples, even worship is gender segregated—other Christian denominations and liberal Jewish temples also even remain highly gender segregated, at least at the level of leadership and decision-making. When women are excluded from having a place at the table and contributing to discussions and decisions, it is no wonder that "women's issues"—including child health and safety—are absent from the debate. And when cases of abuse are leveled against spiritual leaders, the absence of women at the table certainly shapes the response, and as we shall see in the case of the Catholic Church sex scandal, which generally reinforces the privilege of men and render the allegations invisible, unsubstantiated, or unimportant.

This is exactly what motivated a group of African American women to found the Institute on Domestic Violence in the African American Community (IDVAAC). The church has always been an important social site for African Americans, and most African American women report belonging to a church and indicate that it is an important part of their lives (Lincoln and Mamiya 1990). But the church's response to intimate partner violence was minimal. Thus, the IDVAAC fills an important niche in fighting intimate partner violence in the African American community. By providing training, annual conferences, and a multitude of resources that can help spiritual leaders and congregations address the issue of intimate partner violence in their communities, the IDVAAC is an example of both empowering women and transformation. We encourage you to visit their website, www.idvaac.org/index.html. Please see the Resources section for links to other organizations pursuing similar goals.

WHAT HAPPENS WHEN THE PASTOR IS THE BATTERER?

One of the problems facing many tightly knit communities arises when men in positions of power are abusive to their wives, children, or both. There are countless stories of women abused by police officers who cannot call the police for fear they will not be believed or for fear that the "thin blue line" or culture of fraternalism among police will result in the other cops taking his side, or Native women living on Indian reservations whose abusive husbands are part of the families that govern life on the reservation (Snyder-Joy 1996).

A similar situation arises in faith communities when the pastor or any member of the church or temple leadership is the perpetrator of family violence. Obviously, when anyone in a position of power is abusive, his victims are more likely to languish in silence simply because his position is an enormous barrier to revealing the truth. Furthermore, in cases such as these, we can assume that the pastor—who is perpetrating violence—is unable to provide assistance to other victims who seek his help because of the limitations of his own experience as an abuser. This is yet another way in which religion and family violence intersect at both the individual level (the abuser and his wife or partner) and the structural level (the inability of a victim to find assistance in her house of worship). These cases highlight the importance of groups such as the IDVAAC, discussed previously.

CHILD ABUSE: THE SEX SCANDAL IN THE CATHOLIC CHURCH

Perhaps the most troubling case of the intersection of religion and family violence comes from the sex abuse scandal that has rocked the Catholic Church. Certainly, this case is devastating for each individual victim, but perhaps what is most troubling is the sheer enormity of the scandal—thousands of victims on at least three continents—and the *institutionalized* role of the church in covering up the abuse and thus allowing it to continue.

The United States Conference of Catholic Bishops commissioned researchers at the John Jay College of Criminal Justice in New York to examine the data and the cases of allegations of child sexual abuse in the United States. The John Jay report covers the years 1950 to 2002. Researchers uncovered that a total of 4,392 priests were accused of abusing 10,667 children under the age of eighteen during that period, just in the United States alone. One of the more startling findings in the John Jay report is this:

> The majority of priests (56%) were alleged to have abused one victim, nearly 27% were alleged to have abused two or three victims, nearly 14% were alleged to have

abused four to nine victims and 3.4% were alleged to have abused more than ten victims. The 149 priests (3.5%) who had more than ten allegations of abuse were allegedly responsible for abusing 2,960 victims, thus accounting for 26% of allegations. Therefore, a very small percentage of accused priests are responsible for a substantial percentage of the allegations.

(John Jay College of Criminal Justice 2004: 5–6)

During the period from 2004 to 2014, another 3,400 cases were reported, 401 cases in 2013 alone. Since 2004 some 848 priests have been defrocked and over 2,572 have been given lesser sentences because of age or illness. That said, the overwhelming majority have never set foot in a courthouse, let alone a prison.

We imagine that one might take comfort in knowing that only a small percentage of accused priests (3.5 percent) were responsible for approximately one-third of the child sexual abuse. We actually find this to be extremely troubling. Why? For two reasons: First, because it confirms the claim that these abusive priests were pedophiles. Their sexual abuse was not a single act; it was not a single mistake. These were serial rapists. Second, this confirms the cover-up. It would be impossible for any priest to sexually abuse as many victims as these 3.5 percent did without being discovered. Rather, this evidence strongly confirms our argument here that when allegations were made, supervisors engaged in inappropriate—in fact, illegal—strategies for addressing the abuse: providing inadequate counseling, encouraging confession and forgiveness, and, when the abuse continued, moving the abuser to more-remote parishes.

SEXUAL ABUSE IN ST. MICHAEL, ALASKA

Catholic missionaries came to St. Michael, Alaska, in 1899, just thirty years after the United States government purchased Alaska. Father George S. Endal arrived in St. Michael in 1936 and across a forty-plus-year career, he moved in and out of St. Michael and other remote Alaskan villages. In 1949 he met Joseph Lundowski, a non-ordained volunteer in Catholic parishes and communities across rural Alaska. Posted together in St. Michael, from 1961 to 1987, between them these two men sexually abused nearly an entire generation of children in St. Michael, nearly one hundred victims, both boys and girls. More troubling is the fact that there is evidence of communication between parish priests and the vicar dating back to as early as 1965 warning about accusations of sexual abuse by Endal, Lundowski, and the then famous Father Jim Poole, who was allegedly known for having a penchant for taking girls into his bedroom.

continues

SEXUAL ABUSE IN ST. MICHAEL, ALASKA *continued*

According to the details laid out in a lawsuit and reported in the *Los Angeles Times*, there is evidence not only for a cover-up, but also for the systematic movement of pedophile priests into the most remote and vulnerable communities: a dozen priests and three missionaries were accused of sexually abusing Eskimo children in fifteen villages and Nome, Alaska from 1961 to 1987. The flood of allegations led to accusations that the Eskimo communities were a dumping ground for abusive priests and lay workers affiliated with the Jesuit order, which supplied bishops, priests, and lay missionaries to the Fairbanks diocese. Even one victim of child sexual abuse is too many. But the case of St. Michael forces us to ask the question: what is the impact of this degree of child sexual abuse on an entire community?

Though accusations of sexual abuse of children by priests have been around for decades, the child sex abuse scandal in the Catholic Church exploded in early 2002 when hundreds of victims of Boston-area priests filed lawsuits against both the Catholic Church and Cardinal Bernard Law.

Several individual priests were tried in criminal court and given lengthy prison sentences. One of the most widely covered priest sex abuse cases ever involved Father John J. Geoghan. Like many pedophiles, Father Geoghan targeted single mothers. In the 1970s he targeted a woman in Boston who was raising not only her own children but another family member's as well. At the time, Father Geoghan seemed to be a godsend. He served as a father figure and role model for her sons, and his presence in their home many evenings a week provided a bit of a respite for her. After the revelation of the sexual molestation that Father Geoghan perpetrated against her sons, however, she was riddled with guilt (Carroll 2002).

As one *Boston Globe* article reads,

> For nearly two years, Geoghan came by to help almost nightly, always clad in his Roman collar. For the longest time, the children were terrified about the abuse, but said nothing: Geoghan fondled them in their bedrooms, sometimes as he whispered bedtime prayers. The oldest was 12, the youngest 4.
>
> (Carroll 2002)

In February 2002 Geoghan was sentenced to ten years in prison for molesting a ten-year-old boy.[2] Eventually more than one hundred and fifty victims came forward to accuse Father Geoghan of sexual abuse. These victims together filed civil lawsuits seeking monetary compensation, thus beginning the process of bankrupting several individual dioceses of the Catholic Church, including Boston, Los Angeles, and St. Paul, Minnesota. Not long after the cases in Boston, several hundred victims successfully sued the Archdiocese of Los Angeles, leading to convictions, monetary settlements, resignations, and the continued drain on the coffers of several dioceses of the Catholic Church in the United States. Not long after the allegations in Boston and Los Angeles, the crisis erupted in Europe, with thousands of victims and hundreds of perpetrators being identified in examinations of seminaries and boarding schools throughout the British Isles. Cases have emerged in other European countries as well, including Portugal, and across Latin America. Most recently, in the summer and fall of 2018, the child sex abuse scandal once again rocked the United States, when high-ranking official, Cardinal McCarrick, resigned abruptly from his post in Washington, DC. McCarrick was considered by many to be one of Pope Francis' most trusted advisers. McCarrick was not only accused of sexually molesting young men, but he was also implicated in the cover-up of hundreds of priests accused by thousands of victims in Pennsylvania.

Critical to understanding the child sex abuse scandal in the Catholic Church is understanding that the bishops in the United States, as well as the highest-ranking papal administrators in Rome, knew about child sex abuse allegations as early as the 1950s, 1960s, and 1970s. The official response to the allegations was to remind the victims that to make such an allegation publicly, if it turned out to be false, would lead to their immediate excommunication, or official separation from the church. Recall that fear of separation from the faith community is a key barrier for abused women as well. Often priests who had been accused of sexual abuse were moved from large parishes in cities and urban and suburban areas to small rural parishes. The assumption was that removing a priest to a small rural parish would limit the number of potential "whistle-blowers" and essentially render the priest's behavior "out of sight and out of mind" for his supervisors, the bishops. In fact, as has occurred over and over across dioceses in the United States, Europe, and Latin America, the removal of predatory, pedophile priests actually led to more and more victims who were simply dispersed across a wider geography. In addition to putting hundreds of new children at risk for abuse, the lack of accountability sent the message to the abuser that his behavior was not of grave concern and he was free to continue abusing.

A Tale of No Accountability

The child sex abuse scandal in the Catholic Church is deeply disturbing. But what is perhaps most troublesome is that fact that some bishops and archbishops, who not only covered up allegations of child sexual abuse but oversaw strategies for more effective cover-ups, were promoted through the ranks of the Catholic Church. Cardinal Timothy Dolan, Archbishop of New York, and recently (until 2013) president of the United States Conference of Catholic Bishops, is one of the most prominent leaders in the Catholic Church in the United States. During his term as Archbishop of Milwaukee, he orchestrated the hiding of money to protect the diocese from lawsuits and devised a plan to pay priests accused of sexual abuse to leave the priesthood (Associated Press 2013). Records released as part of bankruptcy hearings for the Archdiocese of Milwaukee, the Associated Press reported,

> provide new details on Cardinal Dolan's plan to pay some abusers to leave the priesthood and move the $57 million into a trust for "improved protection" as the Milwaukee archdiocese prepared to file for bankruptcy amid dozens of abuse claims. A Vatican office approved the request to move the money.
>
> (Associated Press 2013)

How can one make sense of Dolan's participation in the cover-up and his rise to the highest position in the Catholic Church in the United States? It is difficult to imagine such a professional climb if the Vatican were truly interested in addressing the child sex abuse scandal and eradicating child sexual abuse perpetrated by its priests. On the other hand, Dolan's promotion is quite logical if he is being rewarded for his expertise in protecting the Catholic Church and her assets. Whether it is explicit policies or loyalty to the fraternity of the Catholic Church, the bankruptcy documents suggest that Cardinal Dolan was well aware of the consequences of the child sex abuse scandal and chose to protect the church rather than hold pedophile priests accountable and protect the children of Milwaukee: "Cardinal Dolan told Cardinal Ratzinger that 'as victims organise and become more public, the potential for true scandal is very real'" (Associated Press 2013).

Some Changes Afoot in the Catholic Church

Now that these cases have begun to come to light, there are some reasons to be optimistic. On June 9, 2015, Pope Francis established a commission within the Congregation for the Doctrine of the Faith to address sexual assault issues in the priesthood and especially—for the first time—deal with bishops who have not properly handled cases of child sexual abuse in the diocese and among the priests they supervised, particularly bishops who simply moved abusive priests from parish to parish. This new development is significant in that it is the power that the bishops have, especially to move priests from one parish to another, that was never addressed as the Church fought to find ways to hide pedophilia in the ranks of priests.

On the same day that the pope announced the formation of this commission, it was also announced that the Vatican ordered former Dominican archbishop Józef Wesołowski to stand trial on child abuse (Scammell 2015). His case is particularly interesting in that while Wesołowski was assigned to the Vatican, prior to the child abuse case on which he will be tried, he was indicted for possession of child pornography. So the question becomes, how is it possible that no one in the Church leadership was aware of the behavior of a pedophile priest who was subsequently promoted to the rank of archbishop? It's not. And it is simply not plausible to insist that no one knew.

RECOMMENDATIONS FOR TRANSFORMATION

Much of this chapter has focused on the role that religion—religious beliefs, the attitudes of spiritual advisers, and the response by the administrators of institutionalized religions—plays in various types of family abuse. It should be clear that although there have been some good efforts at understanding and mitigating the role that religion plays in perpetuating family violence, there is much work to be done. The Catholic Church, which has suffered a serious and expansive scandal, has a long way to go to "clean up its own house" before Catholic clergy will be entrusted with caring for the victims in their parishes. There is little that can be done to force the type of systemic change that is necessary other than what is already taking place: protests and boycotts by Catholics, negative publicity, and expensive lawsuits.

Clergy and religious leaders need to be trained on issues of intimate partner violence and child abuse so that they can offer an appropriate response and the support that helps the victims rather than revictimizes them. This is an area in which there is much room for transformation. If religious leaders at the top levels are willing to collaborate with anti-violence advocates to develop programs that can be used to educate and train clergy who are "on the ground" and provide them with the best practices for preventing and interrupting intimate partner violence and child abuse, then the potential to save victims from the horrors of abuse is great. The work of the United Church of Christ (UCC) provides a promising example. The UCC has researched and developed a "safe book" that can be distributed to high-level leaders as well as everyday clergy. This safe book provides information on abuse as well as the best practices for its prevention and interruption. We are highly encouraged by this type of program and hope that it will be widely disseminated and utilized.

CONCLUSIONS

In this chapter we have set out to discuss three important concepts:

1. The antagonistic relationship between the secular world and the religious world, with special attention to how this impedes an appropriate response to family violence.
2. The religious texts and ideologies for the three primary world religions that are frequently cited by abusers to justify their behavior and cited by spiritual leaders when they inappropriately counsel victims to stay in violent relationships.
3. The ways in which systemic abuse by religious institutions, such as the Catholic Church, reinforces male power and privilege and allows the abuse of women and children to be perpetuated.

As we noted throughout the chapter, there is no religion that advocates violence; indeed, violence is considered to be the ultimate betrayal of trust by all of the major world religions. Although religious scholars recognize the translation problems that lead to texts that *seem* to support violence but are in fact misinterpretations of the original language, the typical priest or minister or rabbi or imam may have little access to this knowledge and information, and thus he (or she), like the members of the congregation, is likely to absorb and perpetuate the false belief that religion dictates unequal gender roles that privilege husbands and require the absolute submission of wives. The power of believing in this ideology even a little bit is that it often provides a justification for intimate partner violence and it leaves the spiritual adviser advocating for women to "go home and be more submissive" rather than leave and even divorce an abusive husband.

At the institutional level, we argued that religions are gender-segregated institutions, and this quality results in women's issues—especially child abuse and intimate partner violence—being rendered unimportant and even invisible. This problem is further exacerbated by the fact that among the ranks of religious leaders are men who are themselves involved in some of the worst abuse imaginable—including married clergy who abuse their wives and Catholic priests who perpetrate child sexual abuse. Some individual priests have molested and abused hundreds of young children. We argue, as several vocal Catholic women theologians (we note the work of Sister Elizabeth A. Johnson, Professor at Fordham University and author of *Quest for the Living God: Mapping Frontiers in the Theology of God*, 2011) have suggested, that until religions open up their leadership to women and to feminist ideals of equality, change is unlikely to occur. We applaud the victims who have had the courage to stand up and speak, for it may very well be their expensive lawsuits that eventually force transformation among institutionalized religion—especially Catholicism. We also highlighted the work of the Institute on Domestic Violence in the African American Community and the "safe book" developed by the United Church of Christ. The mere existence of these programs brings attention to the problems we have highlighted, and we are optimistic that they will lead to transformations at the local and regional level or within specific denominations that will improve the situation when victims—typically abused women—approach their spiritual advisers for help. In the next chapter, we turn to a discussion of violence in institutions. Specifically, we examine fraternities, sports, and the military and the role that institutional features play in perpetuating gender-based violence.

RESOURCES

Boston Globe archives: www.boston.com/globe/spotlight/abuse/documents/law_depositions.htm. The *Boston Globe* not only broke the Catholic Church scandal in the United States but also has archives where all of the facts of the cases, the priests involved, the cardinals who covered it up, and the trials can be examined. We highly recommend you explore this invaluable resource on your own.

United Church of Christ (UCC) Safe Book: www.ucc.org/ministers/safe/safebook.pdf.

Religion Link: www.religionlink.com. This organization describes itself as a resource for journalists writing about religion.

Christian

Peace and Safety in the Christian Home: http://godswordtowomen.org/pasch.htm. This organization is "a biblically-based international network providing spiritual insights, practical resources and positive guidance to all those who in any way address domestic violence."

The Institute on Domestic Violence in the African American Community (IDVAAC): www.idvaac.org/index.html.

United States Conference of Catholic Bishops: www.usccb.org/laity/help.shtml.

Mormon

LDS Family Services: https://providentliving.lds.org/lds-family-services. This group was established by the Church of Jesus Christ of Latter-Day Saints to help educate church leaders on issues related to domestic violence and the needs of its victims.

Jewish

Jewish Women International: www.jwi.org. This advocacy group based in Washington, DC promotes safe home environments for Jewish women and girls.

Muslim

Muslim Women's League: www.mwlusa.org. This nonprofit organization works to improve the status of women in the American Muslim community. Part of its mission is to create awareness about domestic violence within the American Muslim community. It is based in Los Angeles.

Peaceful Families Project: www.peacefulfamilies.org. An initiative of United Muslim Relief, this group produces workshops nationwide on domestic violence from a Muslim perspective. The organization is based in Great Falls, Virginia.

Multifaith

FaithTrust Institute: www.faithtrustinstitute.org. This interfaith organization based in Seattle works to prevent domestic abuse in the Islamic, Buddhist, Asian and Pacific Islander, Jewish, Latino, black, Anglo, indigenous, Catholic, and Protestant communities. It has sponsored the National Declaration by Religious and Spiritual Leaders to Address Violence Against Women.

Sakhi for South Asian Women: www.sakhi.org. This community-based organization in the New York metropolitan area is committed to ending violence against women of South Asian origin.

NOTES

1. As we note in the very first chapter of the book, the time of greatest risk for domestic violence homicide is when the relationship ends—through a breakup or divorce. One example is the murder of Yeardley Love, the University of Virginia lacrosse player who was murdered by her ex-boyfriend soon after she ended their relationship.

2. On August 23, 2003, only eighteen months into his prison sentence, Father Geoghan was murdered by another inmate.

REFERENCES

Anderson, B. C. 2004. "Secular Europe, Religious America." *The Public Interest 155*: 143–158.

Associated Press. 2013. "Top US Cardinal Timothy Dolan 'Paid Off Abusive Priests.'" *The Telegraph*, July 2. www.telegraph.co.uk/news/worldnews/northamerica/usa/10154334/Top-US-cardinal-Timothy-Dolan-paid-off-abusive-priests.html.

Berger, P. 1999. "The Desecularization of the World: A Global Overview." In *The Desecularization of the World: Resurgent Religion and World Politics*, edited by P. Berger, 1–18. Washington, DC: Ethics and Public Policy Center.

Carroll, Matt. 2002. "A Revered Guest; a Family Left in Shreds." *Boston Globe*, January 6. www.boston.com/globe/spotlight/abuse/stories/010602_dussourd_spotlight.htm.

Colson, Chuck. 2009. "Domestic Violence Within the Church: The Ugly Truth." *BreakPoint*, October 20. www.christianheadlines.com/news/domestic-violence-within-the-church-the-ugly-truth-11602500.html.

Hassouneh-Phillips, D. 2001. "Marriage Is Half Faith, the Rest Is Fear of Allah: Marriage and Spousal Abuse Among American Muslims." *Violence Against Women* 7(8): 927–946.

Hattery, A., and E. Smith. 2019. *Gender, Power, and Violence: Responding to Sexual and Intimate Partner Violence in Society Today.* Lanham, MD: Rowman and Littlefield.

John Jay College of Criminal Justice. 2004. *The Nature and Scope of Sexual Abuse of Minors by Catholic Priests and Deacons in the United States 1950–2002.* City University of New York, February. www.usccb.org/issues-and-action/child-and-youth-protection/upload/The-Nature-and-Scope-of-Sexual-Abuse-of-Minors-by-Catholic-Priests-and-Deacons-in-the-United-States-1950-2002.pdf.

Johnson, E. A. 2011. *Quest for the Living God: Mapping Frontiers in the Theology of God.* New York: Continuum Press.

Joyce, K. 2009. "Biblical Battered Wife Syndrome: Christian Women and Domestic Violence." *Religion Dispatches,* June 18. www.religiondispatches.org/archive/1007/biblical_battered_wife_syndrome%3A_christian_women_and_domestic_violence.

Lincoln, E. C., and L. H. Mamiya. 1990. *The Black Church in the African American Experience.* Durham, NC: Duke University Press.

National Resource Center on Domestic Violence. 2007. *Religion and Domestic Violence.* Harrisburg, PA: Pennsylvania Coalition Against Domestic Violence. www.vawnet.org/Assoc_Files_VAWnet/NRC_Religion.pdf.

Pew Research Center. 2015. "America's Changing Religious Landscape." www.pewforum.org/files/2015/05/RLS-08-26-full-report.pdf.

Pew Research Center. 2018. *When Americans Say They Believe in God, What Do They Mean?* April 15. www.pewforum.org/2018/04/25/when-americans-say-they-believe-in-god-what-do-they-mean.

Scammell, Rosie. 2015. "Vatican Orders Ex-Dominican Archbishop to Stand Trial on Child Abuse." *USA Today,* June 15. http://usat.ly/1ehAQc5.

Snyder-Joy, Z. K. 1996. "Self-Determination and American Indian Justice: Tribal Versus Federal Jurisdiction on Indian Lands." In *Native Americans, Crime, and Justice,* edited by Marianne O. Nielsen and Robert A. Silverman, 38–45. Boulder, CO: Westview Press.

Tjaden, P., and N. Thoennes. 2000. *Full Report of the Prevalence, Incidence, and Consequences of Violence Against Women: Findings from the National Violence Against Women Survey.* Washington, DC: US Department of Justice. www.ncjrs.gov/pdffiles1/nij/183781.pdf.

12

INSTITUTIONALIZED VIOLENCE

A woman who signs up to protect her country is more likely to be raped by a fellow soldier than killed by enemy fire.

—**Jane Harman**, California congresswoman, 2008

This chapter examines the ways in which particular features of institutions shape the violence against women, both intimate partner violence (IPV) and sexual assault, that is perpetrated by their members. We explore several institutions: the military, college campuses and fraternities, and "SportsWorld."[1] We chose to focus on these institutions because they have high rates of violence against women and they share a set of common characteristics that facilitate this violence and allow it to continue.

OBJECTIVES

- To explicate the specific institutional qualities these institutions share
- To explicate the processes inside these institutions that produce high rates of violence against women, both IPV and sexual assault
- To provide data on rape and IPV in each of these institutions
- To provide policy recommendations for reducing violence against women in these institutions

KEY TERMS

SportsWorld	rape culture
institutions	fraternalism
gender-segregated institutions	hazing

bullying	working a yes out
total institution	rape baiting
power	pulling train
riffing	college conduct system

INTRODUCTION

This chapter may seem to be a departure from all of the other chapters in this book in that our focus here is on institutions. In fact, the analysis presented in this chapter builds on the discussion in Chapter 11 that illuminated the sex abuse scandal in the Catholic Church. In our research for another book (Hattery and Smith 2019), we examine seven social institutions—the Catholic Church, the military, fraternities, **SportsWorld** (see the definition in note 1), and prisons, politics and Hollywood (the last three we do not discuss here)—and identified a set of common structures that create an environment ripe for gender-based violence. As we will demonstrate here, these institutions protect offenders in ways that allow them to continue to perpetrate violence against women—their wives, girlfriends, and peers (who we will argue are the equivalent of "family," serving alongside one another on the battlefield or studying together in the pursuit of college degrees). For the reader with a particular interest in gender-based violence and these seven institutions, we encourage you to check out our book *Gender, Power and Violence: Addressing Sexual and Intimate Partner Violence in Society Today*, published in 2019.

We begin with a discussion of institutions more generally as well as the structures that facilitate gender-based violence.

INSTITUTIONS

Sociologists define **institutions** a bit differently than most people. When most people think of institutions, they think of organizations that have some level of bureaucracy and some physical space: for example, prisons, schools, churches, banks, the Capitol building in Washington, DC. For a sociologist, all of these are institutions, but so are many other things. Sociologists do not limit institutions to only those organizations with bureaucracies and buildings; we consider an institution to be any system that has a defined set of norms that organize social life. For example, the family is an institution, education is an institution, and the entities we focus on in this chapter—fraternities, the military, SportsWorld, and college campuses—are all institutions, even though not all have a defined physical space. Each institution has a set of norms that dictate social behavior for those members of the institution. Each institution has a set or sets of rules, a hierarchical structure, and some sort of system of internal justice that regulates the behavior of members. Each institution socializes its members to develop—and later demands—a high level of loyalty; the institution is more important than the individual. In addition, each of the institutions we are analyzing in this chapter has another trait in common: they are all gender segregated.

Gender-Segregated Institutions

The term **gender-segregated institutions** generally refers to institutions that are overwhelmingly composed of one gender. It need not be the case that the institution is 100 percent one gender, but in most cases, gender-segregated institutions are 90 percent or more one gender. Though institutions can be segregated by either gender (for example, women's colleges have only women-identified students), our focus here is on institutions that are reserved for men. In the context of our discussion, the institutions we are interrogating may not be gender segregated in terms of membership, though some, like the military, are, but more so in leadership and in day-to-day interactions, like fraternities and SportsWorld. And, though there is some variation across these institutions, what is important to note here is that gender segregation produces several unique patterns that can contribute to gender-based violence.

First, gender-segregated institutions are just that, segregated, which means that there is very little, if any, routine contact between the genders. In institutions that are dominated by men, this means that they have few, if any, meaningful interactions with women as part of their daily routines. Again, the level of interaction varies, from almost no mixed-gender interactions in the military to interactions with women in which they generally have very limited roles—as cheerleaders, "little sisters," and so forth—in fraternities and SportsWorld. When men have few meaningful interactions with women, or when those interactions are framed by dominance and subordination, it makes it much easier to construct a belief system organized around "us" and "them." In the circumstances we're talking about here, the "us" is valuable or superior and the "them" is inferior. Sociologists and others refer to this process as "othering." When one group, in this case women, are designated as "other," it is easier to justify engaging in exploitation and violence against them.

Second, one feature of gender-segregated institutions is that they are overwhelmingly hypermasculine. (We remind the reader of our extensive discussion of masculinity in Chapter 10.) The term *hypermasculine* refers to an exaggerated state of masculinity, typically composed of traits like aggression, fearlessness, and violence, that is often expressed on the fields of play and of war. In other words, gender roles are rigidly prescribed—men fight or lead and women are there to serve men's needs—and traditional or hegemonic masculinity—characterized by, for instance, sexual prowess and breadwinning—is the *only acceptable gender expression for men.*

Rape Culture

Many feminists have offered definitions of the term *rape culture.* For our discussion, **rape culture** refers to a set of values and customs that minimize the impact of rape, limit the definition of rape, and relegate women to the status of sex objects whose only value is to serve men sexually. Fundamental to the concept of rape culture is the belief that "actual rape" is very uncommon and that in most cases of "rape," the victim deserved it. In rape culture, women are blamed for getting raped regardless of the circumstances. For example, a woman who is raped while running in a park is blamed for not making good safety decisions, a woman who is raped after being drugged at a fraternity party is blamed for accepting a drink, and women are blamed for being raped because they dressed "provocatively" (in fact, this has been a response to girls as young as five years old; see Costello 2014). Diana Scully (1990) notes that in her interviews with convicted rapists, they denied raping anyone and claimed that the women whom they were convicted of raping "asked for it" by walking alone at night and looking over their shoulders while they were being followed by the rapist. If this isn't evidence of the centrality of victim-blaming in rape culture, we're not sure what is!

> Legendary men's college basketball coach Bobby Knight said in 1988, "I think that if rape is inevitable, relax and enjoy it."
>
> (Moran 1988)

Rape culture is indeed everywhere, and the institutions we interrogate are no exception. In fact, as we dig deeper in our analysis of each institution, it will become clear that the hypermasculine nature of the military, fraternities, and SportsWorld exacerbates and intensifies rape culture.

Third, in institutions that women are seeking to integrate, such as the military, men often perceive these attempts as transgressions that need to be policed. Integration of any sort has never been met without a fight, and most often the fights involve violence. Think, for example, of the fire hoses, dogs, National Guard troops, and tanks that were deployed all over the South during the 1960s as the battle over integration raged, as some sought to integrate segregated spaces and demanded justice while others sought to protect segregated spaces and, in some cases, engaged in violence in order to do so. Though the battles of gender integration have not taken place on such a mass scale, the battle lines have been equally guarded. And, as predicted by feminist theorists like Cynthia Fuchs Epstein, the more women attempt to integrate male-dominated spaces, the more men will use gender-based violence—sexual assault and IPV—as a mechanism to police women's behaviors and remind them of their "place":

> The enforcement of the distinction [based on sex/gender] is achieved through cultural and ideological means that justify the differentiation. This is despite the fact that, unlike every other dichotomous category of people, females and males are necessarily bound together, sharing the same domiciles and most often the same racial and social class statuses . . . I am convinced that societies and strategic subgroups within them, such as political and work institutions, *maintain their boundaries*—their very social organization—through the use of invidious distinctions made between males and females.
>
> (Epstein 2007: 4)

Fourth, we will argue, as others have, that gender dominance in the leadership of an organization plays a significant role in both the tolerance for and the focus on preventing and intervening in cases of gender-based violence. There are a variety of reasons for this argument, ranging from the lack of experience many men have with sexual and interpersonal violence *as victims though not as perpetrators* when compared with women to the culture of brotherhood that develops in gender-segregated institutions and rises to the highest levels of leadership; this sense of brotherhood often requires the protection, at any cost, of members accused of wrongdoing. Additionally, as noted, sex-segregated institutions are typically hypermasculine and to stand up to gender-based violence may be seen as unmanly. All of these pressures, taken together, lead to cultures in gender-segregated institutions that allow gender-based violence to flourish, that ignore it or cover it up when it does happen, and that blame women for reporting it.

FRATERNALISM

By definition, fraternities are "fraternal." That said, all of the institutions that we analyze in this chapter also have many qualities that we associate with fraternities. We find Sanday's (2007) use of the term *fraternity* useful: "I use the word 'fraternity' in its broader sense to mean a group of persons associated *by or as if by ties* of brotherhood, or any group or class of persons *having common purposes and interests*" (p. 7).

Fraternalism, then, is defined as a strong sense of loyalty to and identification with one's group. Fraternal organizations, including not just fraternities but also the Catholic priesthood, sports teams, and a military unit, exemplify fraternalism. Fraternities are obviously fraternal. A complex set of initiation rituals establish not only membership into the fraternity—members refer to each other as "brothers"—but also loyalty to the organization. When a woman accuses a fraternity member of rape, she often finds that his brothers take his side and will often testify for him in a conduct hearing. We frequently hear of and read about cases in which a brother's memory of the event fades in ways that are particularly helpful to the accused and particularly harmful to the victim (see especially Sanday 2007).

The military, too, involves a process of initiation typically referred to as "boot camp." This six- to eight-week initiation is designed not only to teach new recruits about the rules and regulations of the military and the skills necessary to do their jobs but also to help them develop a fraternal bond. *Semper fidelis*, or *Semper fi*, the official motto of the Marine Corps, is Latin for "always loyal." Marines are also fond of the saying "God, Country, Corps." These mottos impart on the new recruit the belief that the institution is more important than the individual. It is this sense of "family" that is created in the military that makes it so difficult for women who are sexually assaulted by fellow soldiers who are supposed to "have their backs." And, if the assault isn't bad enough, when a soldier accuses another soldier of rape, his "battle buddies" tend to take his side and often engage in retaliation that is as damaging as the assault itself.

Within the Catholic Church, the priesthood also resembles a fraternity. Men live together, eat together—in homes with female housekeepers—socialize together, even take vacations together. And they make decisions together. Segregation also tends to produce a sort of groupthink mentality in which one perspective grows to dominate simply because it is reinforced over and over again by people with similar backgrounds and training. For example, when we examine fraternities, young men, being isolated from other perspectives, can come to hold beliefs they otherwise never would have considered, and these beliefs tend to intensify over time. It is not surprising that fraternities often get into trouble when they behave as a group in public, such as when members of the Yale chapter of Delta Kappa Epsilon shouted "no means no, yes means anal" on campus or members of the University of Oklahoma chapter of Sigma Alpha Epsilon sang racist songs while riding on a bus to a formal event.

Similarly, when priests have very limited regular contact with people who think differently from them or who live different lives—such as women or members of other religious organizations—they can develop this kind of groupthink

mentality as well. Something that would otherwise seem inappropriate or unreasonable can come to be viewed differently when everyone around you expresses a common sentiment.

Bryon Cones, in his 2010 essay, describes his experience in seminary as much like basic training in the military:

> In effect, a Roman Catholic priest is made in a way similar to a U.S. Marine. Candidates are sent away to "basic training" for an extended time, share an intense experience in a strict hierarchical system, and are encouraged to form bonds of brotherhood in that system, in fact, to draw their identity from it. Precious few non-priests are involved in the day-to-day formation of seminarians, and personal contact with parishioners, especially women, is limited and infrequent.
>
> One result of such formation is a certain loyalty to the priestly institution, such that priests identify first with their brothers rather than with those they are ordained to serve. (I still detect that tendency in myself though I was never ordained.) One product of such group loyalty has been a systemic failure among priests and bishops to report clerical child sexual abuse, some cases of which are so monstrous they should be labeled rape and torture.

Cones's description sounds eerily similar to the process of pledging and initiation in fraternities; the bonds to the other priests and the loyalty to the institution are the most important in one's life.

SportsWorld, at least the part of SportsWorld inhabited by men, is highly fraternal. Similar to fraternities and the military, there is a great deal of focus on team-bonding: there is no *I* in "team." Teammates often cover for each other when there is trouble, including "losing" cell phone footage of rapes. And, much as in fraternities, gang rape is unfortunately rather common. SportsWorld comprises a variety of varied institutions and not all teams or organizations have initiation rituals, but many do. And, often, these rituals can be best characterized as sexualized **hazing**.

HAZING

Many initiation rituals, however, go far beyond the innocuous. Anecdotally, we have been told about a "ball wash" ritual in which upper-class football players stand naked with their legs spread widely while rookies are forced to crawl, faceup, between the players legs. But it is in the world of fraternities that the most disturbing initiation rituals, many of which constitute hazing, take place.

Beyond the fact that rituals and behaviors like vomiting and posting pictures of naked women on Facebook (as fraternity brothers at Penn State did) communicate expectations of masculinity, fraternity culture is deeply rooted in the premise that men are superior to women. This deeply held value is critical to the development of rape culture in fraternities. Based on interviews with an informant, Bob described an initiation ritual that involves the pledges being treated like women, a ritual explicitly designed to reinforce women's inferior status. Sanday (2007: 168), in her investigation of a fraternity gang rape, relates a story told by Bob, who says that when the pledges arrived at the house for their initiation they were sprayed with a thick, red liquid and were forced to wear diapers. At one point, their diapers were removed and the brothers "ridiculed their genitals."

In a similar set of rituals described by Rick, a member of a different fraternity, pledges were told to wear jock straps under their clothes instead of underwear when they arrived for their initiation. The pledges were instructed to strip out of their clothes so that they were naked except for the jockstrap. Brothers pulled down the pledges' jockstraps and used basting brushes to apply Ben Gay to their scrotums. The jockstraps were then replaced and "thirty seconds later all of the pledges were writhing in pain." The brothers explained to the pledges why this ritual was necessary: "We're going to cleanse the weak, dependent, pussy out of you."

Bob and Rick both report that throughout the initiation rituals, which often go on for several hours, the brothers use derogatory language, calling the pledges "pussies," "pin-dicks," and so forth. The rituals and language used communicate quite clearly to the pledges that masculinity is valued, femininity—and by extension women—is weak and inferior, and a core element of masculinity is heterosexuality.

BOX 12.1	**HAZING DEATH AT PENN STATE**

When you think of fraternities—more so than sororities—you often think of young college women and men enjoying the freedoms that come with the privilege of being able to attend a college or university in the United States.

What you don't think about is death. Yes, college students in fraternities have a documented history of playing pranks, sexual promiscuity, as we have well documented, and scamming their professors through secret test banks buried deep in the fraternity house or today in a private google drive. They are also famous for far too much drinking!

On February 2, 2017 Timothy Piazza, 19, was pledging the Beta Theta Pi fraternity at Pennsylvania State University. Like pledges around the country he was required to consume alcohol—even though the legal age for drinking in Pennsylvania is 21—via a hazing ritual known as "the gauntlet."

This ritual cost Mr. Piazza his life.

continues

BOX 12.1	HAZING DEATH AT PENN STATE *continued*

In just 82 minutes Piazza consumed 18 drinks, leaving him with a blood alcohol level between .27 percent and .35 percent, which is more than triple the legal driving limit. Drunk, he was unsteady on his feet and subsequently fell down a set of basement stairs. Perhaps out of fear, perhaps because of their own drunken state, the fraternity brothers didn't place a call to 911 emergency for a full 12 hours after Piazza fell down the stairs. Piazza died on February 4, 2017 at Hershey Medical Center in Hershey, Pennsylvania.

All fraternity brothers involved were spared jail time for their actions.

Source: Helene Bruckner. 2018. "Students Fall Victim to Hazing Epidemic: Unity at What Cost?" *Touro L. Rev. 34*: 459 http://bit.ly/2LOzqrf.

As we have noted throughout our discussions in this book, we live in a patriarchal culture in which what women do is devalued, what women are is devalued, and what happens to women is devalued, especially when violence done to women's bodies is sexual in nature. And, by extension, we, as a culture, are extremely unwilling to take sexualized violence against men or boys, when perpetrated by other boys or men, seriously. Though this is the case in the military as well, nowhere is this more evident than in SportsWorld. As we will document, over and over and over again, the athletes who occupy the rarified air of SportsWorld, all the way from the professional ranks to high school, are given preferential treatment at all stages of the investigation, and there is tremendous public support for athletes even when they behave in the most violent and abusive ways possible, especially when their victims are women and boys.

TOTAL INSTITUTIONS

Erving Goffman, in his groundbreaking work *Asylums: Essays on the Social Situation of Mental Patients and Other Inmates* (1961), introduced the concept of a total institution. Goffman's concept of the total institution was developed based on his ethnographic research in mental institutions, or what were at the time called "insane asylums." Since he introduced this concept, sociologists have expanded it to other institutions that meet the same criteria. Of the institutions we analyze in this chapter, none meets the strict definition of a total institution; rather, we consider each to be quasi-total institutions, or institutions that have many of the same structures as total institutions. Here we provide an overview of Goffman's concept of the total institution.

A **total institution** is an institution whose primary mission is to control literally every aspect of members' daily lives; members are allowed to make very few decisions. For example, inside of total institutions members are generally required to wear a uniform; all meals are controlled in terms of what is served and when; access to entertainment is tightly restricted—for example, the institution controls whether members have access to TV or a computer or how many books they may possess at a particular time—exercise and hygiene are restricted, including how often members are allowed to shower; and members are told when to sleep and wake each day. In a true total institution members are not allowed to leave voluntarily but must be officially dismissed. Total institutions also typically have internal systems of justice, which allows those in charge to make nearly every decision with very little oversight.

Total institutions are characterized as having rigid hierarchies. As such, they are composed of a structured set of power relations. One group of people—coaches, commanders, leaders—has the power to compel nearly all of the behavior of members, can discipline them when they refuse to comply, and dictates norms for both attitudes and behaviors. Subordinates in the system report to superiors who have a great deal of power, comparatively. When it comes to gender-based violence, this hierarchy creates yet another layer of power, one that functions to create a climate wherein violence can be perpetrated, victims are afraid to report it, and there are often few, if any, consequences for the people who committed the violence. For example, in the military, many women who are raped report that the violence was perpetrated by the very supervisors or commanders to whom they report. Women report that they believed they couldn't say no to the sexual advances of a supervisor any more than they could say they were unwilling to do a particular task or engage in a particular physical activity, such as required early morning runs. Additionally, in the military, the reporting structure dictates that victims of rape report it to their supervisor. When the supervisor is the rapist, reporting is impossible. Similarly, in the context of SportsWorld, if a young man is being sexually abused by his teammate and he believes the coach knows about it and is tolerant of it, or at least looks the other way, he may worry that if he refuses, he will see his playing time reduced or, worse, he will be cut from the team.

POWER

Often ignored, like an elephant in the room, is the issue of **power** and its role in individual acts of violence, as well as the power that institutions have in dealing with gender-based violence when they occur. For many decades, feminist theorists and scholars have demonstrated that rape is not a crime of passion but rather an act of power (Brownmiller 1975; Brush 2001; Brush, Raphael, and Tolman 2003; Griffin 1979; Hattery 2008; Hattery and Kane 1995; Koss 1985; Koss et al. 1994; MacKinnon 1991; Renzetti 2001; Rich 1980, 1995). The power that men have to rape women (and other men) is rooted in their position of dominance in a patriarchal society (MacKinnon 1991). Specifically, MacKinnon argues:

> These investigations reveal that rape, incest, sexual harassment, pornography, and prostitution are not primarily abuses of physical force, violence, authority, or economics, although they are that. They are abuses of women; they are abuses of sex . . . Sexuality, then, is a form of power. Gender, as socially constructed, embodies it, not the reverse.
> (1991: 113)

As we have noted throughout the book, beginning in Chapter 3 in our discussions of theory, IPV and child sexual abuse are acts of violence that are rooted in power. For example, a key pattern in family violence is the tendency for it to be perpetrated by people with power against those without power. Stronger, older people abuse younger, weaker people. Of course, this trend reverses when parents become elderly and are vulnerable to their adult children. People with more resources—parents, adult children, husbands—are more likely to be abusive toward those without resources—children, elderly adults, wives—than the reverse. In the special case of institutionalized power, the pattern holds. Fraternity brothers, who control access to alcohol on campus, rape women who come to the party hoping to have a good time and, yes, maybe even to get drunk. Commanders rape soldiers in their units. High-profile athletes, who are often local if not national celebrities, rape women they encounter at parties, bars, local watering holes, and VIP lounges.

Each institution also experiences a dilemma: how to do the morally correct thing—reduce rape—while meeting the interests of the institution. For example, colleges and universities make it clear in all of their promotional material as well as in their mission statements that the safety and success of their students is paramount. Yet one in five women (20 percent) on a college campus are raped while they are in the institution's care. Colleges and universities experience the tension between providing for the safety of their female students and being terrified of admitting that rapes happen on their campuses, a fear driven by the concern that if parents knew that their daughters had a one-in-five chance of being raped while on campus, they would never allow them to enroll. At the end of the day, with virtually no exception that we can find, colleges and universities resolve this tension by hiding rape statistics (Karns 2015) and utilizing a process of conduct board hearings that almost never find perpetrators responsible, which results in them remaining on campus, free to rape more victims.

STATISTICS ON GENDER-BASED VIOLENCE

Approximately a quarter of women in the United States have had at least one experience with gender-based violence. That said, the statistics on various forms of gender-based violence are highly contested. Rape and IPV in particular are significantly underreported; most reliable sources indicate that only 20 percent of rapes are ever officially reported, and thus estimates of the prevalence of rape and IPV are best produced by surveys conducted by government agencies like the Centers for Disease Control and Prevention (CDC) and independent researchers. Interestingly, the data from several of the institutions we analyze in this chapter, including college campuses and the military, have nearly identical rates of under-reporting. When comparing the official statistics that government agencies require colleges and universities and the military to report with the surveys conducted with members of each institution, we find that only about 10 percent of rapes are officially reported by each of these institutions with mandatory reporting. (We note that in other research we conducted, prisons also officially report only 10 percent of all rapes.) We find this to be yet another indicator that the structures of the institutions themselves shape the experiences of gender-based violence within. That said, we utilize the most reliable sources when we provide statistics in this chapter. Drilling down into the various forms of gender-based violence reveals some very disturbing numbers. Here we provide the statistics on rape. (Refer back to Chapter 9 for the statistics on IPV, stalking, and IPV homicide.)

Rape

According to the CDC, nearly one in five women (20 percent) and one in four-teen men (7 percent) have reported that they were the victims of a completed sexual assault (Smith et al. 2018). Additionally, nearly half (43.6 percent) of all women and a quarter (24.8 percent) of all men experienced a form of forced sexual contact other than rape, including unwanted sexual contact or being forced to penetrate someone.

We turn now to an examination of gender-based violence in institutions.

THE MILITARY

The military creates an environment that is ripe for gender-based violence for a variety of reasons. In this section we will explore the special environment created by the military and offer examples of cases in which the culture of the military and the stresses of war lead to tragedy in military families. The military is a unique institution in American life for a variety of reasons, several of which create a culture ripe for gender-based violence; specifically, the military is hypermasculine, highly gender segregated, and fraternal, and it functions at least in some ways as a quasi-total institution, perhaps most importantly by having an internal system of justice completely hidden from view and review.

The military is one of the most gender-segregated institutions in American life. As the data in Table 12.1 reveal, though there is variation among the branches, in the most integrated of the branches women comprise less than 20 percent of the members and in the Marines, often considered to be the most hypermasculine of the branches, women comprise less than 6 percent of the members. For women serving on aircraft carriers or, as is the case with a woman we interviewed, in Guantanamo Bay, they may be one of a very few or in some cases the *only* woman, which further intensifies both the hypermasculine culture and the challenges to reporting. Additionally, when we examine the leadership, we see that women are virtually absent.

Data on IPV in the military are nearly impossible to get, primarily because they are not collected by the military and, when national-level data on experiences with IPV are collected, they are not organized by military status. That said, news reports and personal communication confirm that rates of IPV in the military are high. Furthermore, the military is uniquely situated because it is an institution dependent on weapons. Although this seems simplistic and straightforward, it is worth noting that the very presence of and easy access to weapons is a likely contributor to the high rates of IPV homicide that we see on US military bases. Data on risk factors for IPV homicide reveal that women living in a household where guns are present are six times more likely to be murdered, and for those whose partner has used a weapon on them, the risk for being murdered is twenty times greater than the average (Campbell et al. 2003).

Table 12.1 Women in Military Leadership (2015)

	Army	Navy	Air Force	Coast Guard	Marines
Members	15.8%	15.3%	18.5%	15.5%	5.8%
Leadership General/Admiral	1 out of 11	0 out of 11	0 out of 14	0 out of 40	0 out of 4

Source: Data from Bensahel et al. 2015.

When it comes to soldiers returning from active duty, access to weapons coupled with the fact that many are struggling with mental health issues and trying to reintegrate into family life means the transition can be tragic. For example, the military estimates that at least half of all soldiers returning from a war theater are suffering from some mental health issues, including post-traumatic stress disorder (Hoge et al. 2008). This type of stress can understandably lead to strains on intimate partner relationships and, without proper attention, may result in episodes of IPV. "I don't think there is any question about that," said Peter C. McDonald, a retired district court judge in Kentucky and a member of the Pentagon's now disbanded domestic violence task force. "The war could only make things much worse than even before, and here we had a system that was not too good to begin with" (Alvarez and Sontag 2008).

BOX 12.2	**FORT BRAGG**

The stress and strain on families in the twenty-first century has grown, and these issues are even worse for military families. Fort Bragg is one of the largest military bases in the United States, and a good number of service members being deployed to or returning from Afghanistan and Iraq pass through there. Fort Bragg families have had considerable domestic trouble, and there does not seem to be any viable solution in sight. During the height of the wars in Iraq and Afghanistan, between 2002 and 2005, Fort Bragg had 832 victims of intimate partner violence and ten intimate partner violence homicides. (We can speculate that, with far fewer troops being deployed in 2019, rates of intimate partner violence homicide today are also likely decreasing at Fort Bragg.)

An article in *Mother Jones* describes one incident at Fort Bragg that happened in 2005: "At 8:30 p.m. [Richard] Corcoran arrived at his wife's house and went after 30-year-old Michele with a gun, firing at her as she fled to a neighbor's. (She was wounded but survived.) He shot and wounded another Fort Bragg soldier who was in the house and then shot and killed himself—all while his seven-month-old daughter lay in another room."

Source: Houppert 2005.

Additionally, men coming home from serving abroad face struggles with regard to family reintegration and especially concerns about jealousy. If their wives have established or strengthened relationships while their husbands were absent, the husbands and partners may be resentful of these relationships and certainly jealous if these friendships are with men. This jealousy, especially when accompanied by mental health issues, may lead to violence. Though we will never know the exact cause of the IPV homicide epidemic at Fort Bragg, we can speculate that all of the factors here contributed to this tragedy.

When complaints are made, be they of harassment or rape by a fellow soldier or claims of IPV either on or off base, the military is unlike any other US institution in that it has its own system of justice that supplants the civilian criminal justice system. Though a military wife who is being beaten by her husband might call 911, it is far more likely that she would call the military police. And, even if she does call 911, the dispatcher is likely to defer her call to the military police, perhaps without her knowledge. Similar to the case on college campuses, military bases almost always have memoranda of understanding with the local police department so that cases on base are deferred, and thus kept internal. As a result, the vast majority of violence that military women and wives face is handled from within. It is not difficult to understand, then, that the response to the reports is not always in the best interest of the victims. As we will discuss at length in Chapter 15, the response of the civilian legal system—be it to allegations of IPV or child or elder abuse—is fraught with problems for the victims, and these problems are exaggerated in the military because of its unique nature as a gender-segregated institution and because of its desire to keep its problems out of the purview of the more critical public. As with the Catholic Church sex scandal, which we discussed in Chapter 11, when a gender-segregated institution is faced with policing its membership for violence against women or children, the outcome almost always favors the men involved and rarely addresses the needs of the victim, and the institution engages in remarkable antics designed to keep the incident from ever becoming public.

Beginning in 2011 or so, a great deal of attention began to be focused on sexual assault in the military, partly as a result of the hard work of two senators, Claire McCaskill and Kirsten Gillibrand, although other forces were at work as well. There were several relatively high-profile sexual assault cases in the news, more and more women were returning from serving in Iraq and Afghanistan and reporting that they had been raped by their fellow service members, and the documentary *The Invisible War*, on sexual assault in the military, was released in 2012. It is in this context that rape in the military garnered such high-profile national attention and it shapes our discussion here.

We compared official military data with data generated by the RAND Military Workplace Survey in order to gauge underreporting. According to the US Department of Defense (2018), in 2017, there were 6,769 rapes reported by military personnel. In contrast, the RAND survey, which was most recently conducted in 2014, reported nearly 20,000 rapes, about half of which were reported by women and half by men. It may come as a surprise that as many men as women reported being raped. This is a result of the level of gender segregation in the military, an institution that overall is not more than 10 percent women. And, though men reported as many rapes as women overall, women's risk for rape was four times higher than the risk for men: 4.3 percent of women and 1 percent of men in the military reported being raped in 2014.

Similar to IPV, sexual assault in the military is handled through an internal system of justice. In order to increase reporting, the military has designed two reporting mechanisms: restricted and unrestricted reporting. With a restricted report, no investigation will be initiated. A victim may report to the Sexual Assault Response Coordinator and indicate that the report is restricted; it may not be shared with anyone. One may wonder why anyone would bother making a restricted report, since there will be no investigation. The advantage to making a restricted report is that not only is the privacy of the victim protected, they also become eligible for mental health and other support services once a report is made. With an unrestricted report, the information will be shared and an investigation will be launched, though the military does not mandate that the investigation involve civilian law enforcement. If an internal investigation uncovers probable cause, a court-martial ensues.

Of the 5,110 unrestricted reports filed in 2017, approximately 10 percent were judged to be baseless or false, which, we note, is similar to the rate of false reporting in national-level data. Only 134, or 4 percent, resulted in a conviction on any charge at court-martial, which is only slightly higher than the rate of conviction in criminal court when rape victims report to the civilian police. Of those convicted of at least one crime in a court-martial process, most received more than one form of punishment. Only 71 percent were subjected to some kind of confinement, and even fewer, only 57 percent, were punitively discharged or dismissed. The vast majority, 81 percent, had their rank reduced, and 61 percent were fined.

No soldier deserves to be raped and no soldier should put her or himself at risk for severe illness and even death because of the fear of rape. Nothing is more tragic than lives lost, but that is to be expected in a war zone. What is not expected is for lives to be lost because of the threat of sexual violence by one's comrades, as was the case for women who died from dehydration while serving in the Middle East. They were so afraid of being raped if they left their barracks at night to go to the latrine that they stopped drinking any fluids in the late afternoon.

During the wars in Afghanistan and Iraq, women soldiers were dying of dehydration; these were certainly preventable deaths, but not all that surprising given the desert conditions. Or so it seemed.

> In 2006, Janis Karpinski, the former commander of Abu Ghraib prison, testified before the International Commission of Inquiry for Crimes Against Humanity, investigating the Bush Administration. Karpinski stated that the true cause of death for some female soldiers who served in Iraq had been covered up. She testified that the women had indeed died of dehydration, as the military had reported. However, she charged that the military failed to disclose that women were dying of dehydration because they would not drink liquids late in the day. They avoided liquids due to their fear of being assaulted when they used outdoor bathrooms in the middle of the night.
>
> (Dowler 2011: 307)

Dowler argues, and we agree, "It seems evident that a state has failed to protect its citizens when simple acts, such as urinating during convoy or going to the latrine, become markers of bravery" (Dowler 2011: 307).

Source: Dowler 2011. Reproduced by permission of Taylor & Francis Books UK.

Challenges to Reporting

There are many challenges to reporting rape in the military that are unique to the military.

- Men who are victims: men who are victims are even less likely to report than women who are victims. And it is not hard to understand why, in the hypermasculine culture of the military, a man reporting any sexual contact with another man, even nonconsensual, fears he will be labeled as gay. Also, until the repeal of "don't ask don't tell" in 2011, this assumption could lead to his dismissal. Given the high level of gender segregation in the military and the high number of men who are victims, this is a significant challenge.
- There are only a few women: a second aspect of the incredibly gender-segregated nature of the military is the fact that a victim may be one of only a few women on the ship or in her unit. Because the military (like college campuses) requires that reports of crime be shared with the community via a weekly crime report, if there are only a few women in the unit, she will be "outed"; it's not hard to understand why a victim would choose not to report when she knows that everyone she works with, reports to, and

supervises will be able to identify her. This will remain a challenge for the foreseeable future—until the military is fully integrated, or until the requirement and mechanism for reporting crimes is modified.

- One's supervisor is the rapist: in many cases, including those featured in the documentary *The Invisible War*, the rapist is one's supervisor. Given that the military is a total institution and has a hierarchical structure, making an accusation against one's supervisor is essentially professional suicide. As long as victims cannot be protected from their perpetrators, especially when he is their supervisor, this will remain a challenge to reporting.

- Retaliation: one of the most troubling aspects of military sexual assault is the retaliation the victims often face when they report. The Human Rights Watch (2015) report on retaliation found that 62 percent of victims who reported a sexual assault experienced retaliation. In other words, victims who report a sexual assault are twelve times more likely to experience retaliation than the offender is to be punished. Victims who were interviewed as part of the Human Rights Watch report noted that they experienced several different kinds of retaliation, including **bullying** and interpersonal abuse, professional repercussions, and other disciplinary actions, which might include being disciplined for underage drinking. Many victims reported that the retaliation they suffered was worse than the rape itself. Protecting victims who report is not only protecting their civil rights but also critical to increasing reporting.

- Adultery charges: unique to the military's Uniform Code of Military Justice, sexual contact, consensual or not, between people not married to each other violates the standards of adultery. In many cases that we read about and that were featured in the documentary *The Invisible War*, many women who reported a sexual assault were told that if they continued with the claim, they would be charged with adultery and face punishment, including reduction in rank or even discharge. Many women threatened with adultery charges were not married, but their assailants were! This is nothing short of bizarre, and until the policy is revised, this will remain a significant barrier to reporting.

In our conclusion we will offer some recommendations that we believe would reduce rape and IPV in the military and better address it when it does occur. We turn now to a discussion of rape on college campuses and in fraternities.

RAPE ON COLLEGE CAMPUSES

During 2014, significant national attention was focused on rape on college campuses, including several actions from the White House and statements by President

Obama, public service announcements that aired in college football stadiums, and government mandates for changes to campus policies. We argue that this attention was the result of a confluence of events, including several high-profile incidents, such as cell phone videos of sexual abuse going viral on social media and several Title IX accusations of wrongdoing at some of the nation's most elite colleges and universities, including the University of North Carolina. Several high-profile athletes were accused of rape. As we noted earlier, the military was facing serious scrutiny not only for the incredibly high rates of sexual assaults but also its mishandling of reported cases. And perhaps the president himself, Barack Obama, began to think about the fact that his own daughters were nearing the age when they would be most at risk for sexual assault. In many ways it was a perfect storm, a context in which rape on college campuses had to be addressed.

Yet rape on campus is nothing new. We've been studying rape on college campuses for more than twenty-five years, and the sad fact is that very little has changed. Of course, getting reliable statistics on a phenomenon that is so severely underreported can be challenging—estimates are that only 10 percent of rapes on college campuses are reported—but a variety of studies conducted by independent scholars and national organizations all find nearly identical prevalence rates that have been remarkably consistent over more than twenty-five years. Scholars, including Mary Koss (1985) and Robin Warshaw (1988), have conducted research on samples of thousands of college students and found that approximately one-quarter of women had been raped since coming to college. The National Health and Social Life Survey (Laumann et al. 1992) found that 22 percent of surveyed women and 2 percent of surveyed men had been *forced to do something sexual* at some time in their life. The National Women's Study found that 13 percent of surveyed women had been victims of a *completed forcible rape* at some time in their life (Tjaden and Thoennes 2000). Research conducted by the Centers for Disease Control and Prevention found that 20 percent of women, nearly one in five, reported being raped at some time in their lives (Smith et al. 2018). Taking all of these data together, we are confident that the figure that one in four or one in five women will be raped is in fact accurate, both nationally and on college campuses. This is confirmed by a report issued by the US Department of Justice in 2014, which estimated that 110,000 women are raped on college and university campuses each year (Sinozich and Langton 2014). Across the typical four years a student is enrolled in college, a half million of her women peers will be raped. Put another way, on the typical state university campus with twenty-five thousand students, research would estimate that there are hundreds of rapes per year, and over the course of four years, thousands of rape victims are walking the quad, sitting in classes, and living in residence halls on the same campus as the men who raped them.

Given the one-in-five statistic, one might conclude that 20 percent of all college men are rapists. Although it is very difficult to measure the percent of men on a college campus who are committing rape, several scholars have used survey methods to provide data to answer this question. According to one recent study (Campbell 2015), 5.6 percent of the men studied had committed an act that met the legal definition of rape. In another study, 46 percent of participants (n=173) in a study on a single college campus "reported perpetrating some form of sexual coercion" (Young et al. 2016: 803) and 10 percent reported that they used force, such as hitting or using a weapon to make their partner have sex (Young et al. 2016: 804). Some suggest that the typical college rapist, just like the typical rapist Diana Scully interviewed in prison, commits six rapes while he is in college. On a campus of twenty-five thousand students, assuming half are men, we would expect to find several thousand men who have committed an act of sexual violence. As we will see when we discuss the internal system of justice on college campuses, the fact that most colleges didn't expel a single student for sexual misconduct in the previous decade is very troubling indeed. Understanding this statistic helps us to focus on both prevention and intervention efforts. Though all men and women should receive prevention training, the majority of resources should be applied to interventions when rapes are reported; students found guilty of sexual misconduct should be expelled.

Fraternities

Fraternities play an important role on college campuses; in fact, they are often the social hub of the entire campus. Though fraternities are not true total institutions, they have features of total institutions that create a climate in which rape is common. Fraternities may not control every aspect of a member's life, but they do exercise certain forms of control that are important. At certain stages of membership, for example, behavior is tightly controlled. When men are pledging a fraternity, the fraternity demands nearly 24/7 dedication, which often results in pledges seeing a drop in their grades during the pledging semester. Desperate to seek admission, pledges will do almost anything, including, in some cases, participating in a gang rape or bearing silent witness to one. Additionally, because fraternities are the social hub on campus, the fraternity literally controls a member's reputation, especially as a marker of his masculinity. Along with initiation, these types of control over members both reinforce the fraternal nature of the fraternity—members are brothers for life—and also serve to establish loyalty to the fraternity. When a member is accused of rape, he can be sure his brothers will stand with him and defend him and the reputation of the fraternity at nearly any cost.

The masculinity that is socialized and reinforced in fraternities is one of hypermasculinity with regard to two specific attributes: alcohol consumption and sexual conquest. We draw on Sanday's 2007 book, *Fraternity Gang Rape*, extensively and we encourage you to explore it for much more detailed discussion than we can provide here. Sanday's research includes reports from students she trained as ethnographers who hung out in fraternity houses and at their parties and conducted interviews with fraternity brothers. According to Sanday, one indicator of the emphasis on excessive drinking was the praise pledges and brothers received when their excessive drinking caused them to vomit. Similarly, Sanday's student researchers reported that, well beyond verbal bragging about sexual interactions, brothers had "brag boards" where they posted notes about the women they had had sex with, going so far as to indicate those they had raped ("not gotten consent from," in their words). Today, in the age of social media, fraternities continue to use public mechanisms for sharing sexual exploits. During the summer of 2015, Penn State University banned Kappa Delta Rho from campus and the national fraternity expelled thirty-eight members from the Penn State chapter because they posted nude and semi-nude photos of women at their parties on their secret Facebook page. Investigators have indicated that some brothers could face criminal charges, but at the time of this writing there has been no prosecution. Many may wonder why fraternity brothers would engage in what appears to be really stupid behavior, posting crime evidence on Facebook. But, when we consider Sanday's frame, posting pictures on Facebook is simply the new version of the message board; a public or semi-public way to provide evidence of sexual conquest. Pictures of naked women posted on Facebook or cell phone videos of sex acts provide the evidence and also send cogent messages to pledges that this is the type of masculinity that the fraternity values.

As we have noted, fraternities control the social life on campus, not only because they host the parties but also because they supply the alcohol. On campuses with thousands of students under the legal age to drink, providing access to alcohol is a powerful tool, and as we will see, fraternities use it as part of their strategy for seducing women and, if they won't consent, raping them.

Rape Culture in Fraternities

In general, the fraternity members Sanday studied argued that when women get raped, it's because they "asked for it." From their perspective, first and foremost women ask for it by coming to the fraternity's parties. They also ask for it by accepting the alcohol the fraternity is happy to provide. They ask for it by dancing and flirting. In short, they ask for it by their very existence. Similar to other cases that are well documented in the media, including the conduct hearing in the case of Jameis Winston, the quarterback at Florida State University who was accused of rape, and a gang rape that Sanday writes about, inferred consent on the part of the victim is based on *the perpetrators'* perceptions of her sexual behavior: "She seemed amazingly eager, unrestricted in her sexual desire" (Sanday 2007: 92). Sanday and many others challenge that perception, in this case based on many accounts, including the victim's, that she was too drunk and high to consent.

Rape culture also defines women as having very few functions in society other than as sex objects: to be viewed in pornography, to dance at football and basketball games, to be ring girls in boxing matches, and to be sexually available whenever and however men demand them to be. The exceptions to this rule, of course, are mothers and other women defined as asexual, such as Catholic nuns.

As Syrett (2009) and Sanday (2007) argue, one of the defining features of fraternities is their exploitation of women as a strategy for demonstrating their heterosexual hypermasculinity. During the summer Sanday conducted her research, she interviewed several women who hung around and even lived in the fraternity house where a gang rape took place, and they identified several categories that fraternity members and other women used to describe women:

> Regulars were women who attended every party but were not girlfriends of any of the brothers. In addition to "wenches," "regulars," and "bimbos" there was a strong inner circle of women who were girlfriends of the brothers. The girlfriends came to the parties to make sure their boyfriends didn't take up with any of the other women at the party. Girlfriends didn't like the regulars and made ugly remarks about their virtue. This would seem to be fairly normal jealous behavior if it weren't for the fact that many of the girlfriends had once been regulars themselves. The various types of women never bonded with one another, as their primary interest was in the brothers, which is the way that the brothers seemed to want it to be.
>
> (Sanday 2007: 69)

In sum, rape cultures are built on the fundamental belief that women are inherently inferior to men and that their only real value is their sexual availability to men. In this context, it is not so difficult to understand how men create a rational explanation for rape: women ask for it. However, it is also true that men's sexual advances are sometimes rejected. If women's sexuality is defined as something that is generally and universally available to men at their discretion, then consent becomes an anomaly, and fraternity brothers describe a variety of strategies they employ for getting otherwise reluctant or unwilling women to have sex.

Fraternity Environment That Facilitates Rape

Rape culture can fuel particular environmental arrangements and practices that facilitate rape. In this section we provide a discussion of these arrangements and practices as well as several illustrations.

- Fraternities have space that is suitable for hosting parties; houses are generally quite large and have spaces that can be converted to dance floors.
- Fraternities are generally unsupervised, unlike residence halls, which have resident assistants and others charged with enforcing rules, including those about drinking.
- Fraternity houses are owned by their national chapters and not by the university, which means that they are required to meet the liability requirements of the chapter, not necessarily the university.
- Sororities are prohibited by their national chapters from hosting parties in which alcohol will be served. This further facilitates fraternities' control over the social or party scene of the campus.
- Fraternities control the parties and therefore control the mixing and dispensing of the alcohol. The fraternities provide all of the alcohol for women who attend the parties (brothers must supply their own beer or wine). Fraternities are known for mixing grain alcohol with sweet juice like Hawaiian punch, a concoction they refer to as "jungle juice." The punch is so sweet that it masks the taste of the grain alcohol, and it is easy to get very drunk, very quickly, especially for inexperienced drinkers.
- The house is the fraternity's turf. Scholars have noted that one aspect of fraternity houses that facilities rape is access to bedrooms. In addition, because the houses are very big and women are only allowed upstairs when accompanied by a brother, it is not uncommon for rape victims to report that they didn't know where they were, which made it more difficult for them to escape when a brother attempted to rape them.
- Fraternity houses are often off campus. In order to get women to attend a party at an off-campus fraternity house, fraternities employ their pledges to shuttle women back and forth to parties, often to and from campus. Women on the campus where we teach explained the process to us: on any given night when fraternities are having parties, they put out notifications that include the cell phone number to text for a pickup. A woman simply texts the number with her location and a pledge picks them up and delivers them to the fraternity house. When they are ready to leave, the pledges are there to shuttle them home. As a result, the women have no idea where they

are and they are dependent on pledges to get home. Women on our campus who were raped at fraternity parties talk about escaping the fraternity house and having no idea how to get home. (And clearly, no pledge is going to shuttle a woman home who is screaming that she's been raped.)

In addition to creating an environment that is conducive to rape, fraternity brothers engage in specific behaviors designed to facilitate sexual activity. Fraternity brothers argue that these strategies are just part of the sexual dance between men and women and that if they result in a sexual encounter, the encounter is consensual. Along with Sanday (2007), we disagree. We argue that these strategies are designed to manipulate consent when it cannot be obtained ethically. Sanday (2007) identifies four strategies employed by the brothers: (1) riffing, (2) working a "yes" out, (3) rape baiting, and (4) pulling train.

Riffing

According to Sanday's research, **riffing**

> means talking your way into a situation. Some brothers were better riffers than others. There is a skill involved in being good at riffing, because it involves persuading someone to do something. There are many kinds of riffs. There is the "nice guy" riff, which means offering to walk a woman home when it is late at night. By being well mannered and almost chivalrous, the "nice guy" riffer hopes to induce the woman to invite him in.
>
> (Sanday 2007: 72)

Working a Yes Out

Sanday (2007) devotes an entire chapter in her book to "working a yes out" because it is such a common strategy employed by fraternity brothers. **Working a yes out** refers to encouraging or forcing a woman to consent to sex by either talking her into it or plying her with alcohol. Verbal coercion and the use of alcohol to get women to consent are common practices on college campuses, as elsewhere. In their study of 3,187 women on thirty-two college campuses, Koss and her colleagues (1994) reported that 44 percent of women reported that they had been verbally pressured to have sex; 12 percent said that men had attempted sexual intercourse by giving them alcohol or drugs.

Rape Baiting

Rape baiting refers to strategies that a man can employ to increase the probability that he will have sex by the end of the evening, without regard to consent. In addition to the strategies already discussed, "working a yes out" and riffing, rape baiting also includes tactics for identifying potential victims. In Sanday's (2007) research, which was originally conducted in the late 1980s, she revealed a strategy that continues to be used today: marking women at parties based on the probability that a brother will be successful in "working a yes out."

> The brothers marked women who came to their parties with something called power dots . . . white being the most difficult, then yellow, then blue, red and with black being the easiest . . . I think the dots helped to mark women for other men so that they would know where to start.
>
> (Sanday 2007: 111)

In 2014, a fraternity at the University of Wisconsin, Milwaukee, was reportedly marking certain women's hands with a red X and targeting these women with date rape drugs that were mixed into their drinks. On our campus, women reported similar marking systems that are designed to target women for drugging or "working a yes out."

Pulling Train

Pulling train refers to group sex, which may be consensual or not, involving one woman and several, sometimes as many as a dozen, men. Sanday (2007) argues that men who believe that a woman can physically have sex with multiple men one after the other are delusional and are operating in the "blame the victim" mentality. And we agree that the "group sex" descriptions in her book are all acts of gang rape, nonconsensual sex forced by many men on one woman. The men, however, see pulling train differently; they conceive of this strategy as a way to facilitate sex for men who have never had it before. For a man who has not had sex and is not confident in his abilities to "work out a yes," climbing into a train allows him to take advantage of the fact that his brothers have already done the hard work of getting the woman ready for sex so he can take advantage of this situation. Fraternity brothers are not alone in buying into the flawed ideology that once a woman has consented to sex with one member of a group—such as a fraternity or sports team—she has consented to sex with all of them. For example, a jury was convinced in the trial of University of Minnesota basketball player Mitch Lee that the victim in the case could not have been raped by Lee because she had already consented to sex with his teammate a few minutes earlier.

BOX 12.3   FACILITATING A RAPE IN A FRATERNITY HOUSE

Sanday's student researchers found that fraternity brothers engaged in carefully scripted practices in order to prepare a woman for sex, consensual or not, depending on her interests. The brothers described identifying a target early in the week. They tended to choose first-year women: they were eager to enter the social scene, they were unfamiliar with the social norms, and they didn't know their way around yet. Men reported that they looked

continues

BOX 12.3	**FACILITATING A RAPE IN A FRATERNITY HOUSE** *continued*

for these women in their classes, the dining hall, or just hanging out on campus. They started to "chat them up" and "made them feel special." By midweek they had invited their target to a party at the fraternity house that weekend. When their targets arrived, they immediately got them a glass of whatever punch the brothers had concocted, typically a very sugary drink that hides the burn of the grain alcohol used to spike it. On our campus, this is often referred to as "jungle juice." Because the punch flavor hides the alcohol, it is easy to get very drunk very quickly. The brothers then reported moving on the target, putting their arms around her, dancing, kissing her, and, as long as she didn't resist or as long as she seemed "into it," steering her upstairs to a designated room.

Why a designated room? The brothers indicated that before the party started they cleared out a room of all identifiable things, posters, pictures, and so forth, which would be restored after the party. This was to ensure that if a woman reported the rape and the police brought her to the house to show them what had happened, she wouldn't be able to find the room where she was raped because, while there had been nothing memorable or personal in it at the time of the rape, the personal items were now replaced. This strategy also reduces the likelihood that she can even identify the man who raped her, because the designated room, unlike one's own room, does not contain any photographs or other visuals connected to the rapist.

The men indicated that they then maneuvered the women to the bed and started engaging in sexual activity with her, fondling her, removing clothing, kissing her, and so forth. If the woman complied, then they engaged in consensual sex. If not, the men reported that they attempted to "work a yes out," and if that failed, they used physical force and restraint in order to complete the sexual activity. As long as they had sex, consensual or not, they had met their obligation for heterosexual hypermasculinity.

When asked if the brothers considered this rape they indicated quite clearly that it was not rape, that "the women asked for it." They asked for it by coming to the party, because according to the men interviewed, it is understood that parties are for drinking and sex, and by not only consenting to come to the party but by coming enthusiastically, the women were looking for sex. We concede that there very well may be women who come to parties to get drunk and have sex, but even if that is the case, consent doesn't work that way. Consenting to attend a party is not consenting to sexual behavior. Furthermore, according to the law, each individual sexual act must be consented to, even when one has had consensual sex in the past, otherwise the act is legally considered sexual assault. There is no blanket consent. Sanday (2007) suggests, "Party women who believe that their sexual activities are all in good fun do not, perhaps, realize the extent to which they play an important role in the formation and celebration of ties of brotherhood" (p. 65).

Source: Sanday 2007.

Challenges to Reporting

Rape victims on college campuses, be they victims of fraternity brothers, athletes, or anyone else, face the usual challenges to reporting:

- They are not sure if what happened to them was rape, especially if the man who raped them used techniques like riffing or "working a yes out."
- They may feel they are partly responsible for the rape because they went to the party willingly, a belief that is clearly endemic in fraternity culture and inevitably bleeds out into the overall campus culture, adhered to by many students, including the women who attend the parties.
- They may be afraid of becoming a pariah on campus, never invited to another party.
- They may be afraid that they will face consequences for drinking if they are underage.
- They may feel ashamed and are worried that their parents will find out.

And, though there are some strategies that college campuses can develop that will decrease these challenges to reporting, such as providing medical amnesty—protection from any conduct violation for underage drinking—the primary approach that colleges and universities have employed is handling things in-house.

College Conduct Systems

There are many reasons why colleges and universities favor a sexual misconduct process (colleges and universities do not use terms such as *rape* or *sexual assault*). From our perspective, some of these reasons are good and some are highly problematic (Table 12.2).

For a variety of reasons, we recommend that all cases of rape on college campuses be reported to the local police and dealt with in the formal criminal justice system, but we understand all the reasons why victims would prefer to, and, we argue, should, have access to an internal **college conduct system**. That said, because most victims don't know that conduct processes rarely result in removing the perpetrator from campus—hundreds, perhaps thousands of campuses have never expelled a single perpetrator—they rarely end up satisfied with the process.

In the early 1980s, colleges and universities began to receive reports from their female students that they had been raped. They almost always identified the perpetrator as another student. Thus, colleges and universities, and those who work in student affairs specifically, identified a clear need to put policies into place to address rape on their campuses. Policies have varied over time—mostly due to positive revisions—and from institution to institution, but generally student conduct policies share common features.

Table 12.2 Pros and Cons of an Internal Conduct Process on College and University Campuses

Pros	Cons
Not all sexual misconduct can be easily prosecuted in court.	Colleges and universities have a vested interest in underreporting for fear (we argue, unfounded) of being ranked as unsafe.
Many victims would prefer not to have to testify in court, which might mean their parents find out.	Current best practice for conduct officers is to treat most conduct violations as "teachable moments."
Many victims want the process over as quickly as possible.	Conduct officers and conduct board members are not necessarily trained to evaluate felony sexual assault, nor do many have any training with regard to the research on sexual assault on campuses.
Many victims want a consequence for the sexual assault but may not want to see the offender go to jail.	Rarely are offenders suspended or expelled, and thus, as noted by Sanday (2007), they are free to commit more rapes.
Most cases of college rape involve alcohol and are difficult to prosecute.	
Many victims don't want their parents to know they were drinking or that they were previously sexually active.	

Sexual misconduct: The term used to describe any unwanted sexual activity, including penetration.

Hearing board: A panel of university members, generally faculty and staff, though at some universities students are also included (a practice that is considered to be extremely problematic), that hears the cases. There is tremendous variation in terms of how members are selected and how much (or little) and what kinds of training they receive.

Sanctions: Typically sanctions range from required papers on sexual assault to suspension or expulsion, both of which are extremely rare.

Complainant: The term used for the accuser.

Respondent: The term used for the accused.

Quite clearly, campus systems of justice are set up very differently from the criminal justice system. The reasons for these differences are many, but they reflect the reasons colleges and universities prefer to handle cases of rape through an internal system. For example, the differences in language reflect the fact that colleges and universities *are not* part of the criminal justice system, primarily because they cannot impose criminal justice sanctions, including incarceration, and therefore they are careful not to use language like "rape" or "sexual assault"—which have legal definitions—"defendant," and so forth. Second, the system is meant to be transformative rather than strictly punitive; those who are found "responsible" (rather than "guilty") are most often assigned opportunities to learn more about sexual assault—writing research papers, attending trainings—rather than punished by suspension or expulsion. Many defend this system as one that is less stressful for victims, results in a faster resolution, and will therefore increase reporting.

All that may be true. But, in fact, *reporting has not increased at all* since the inception of these types of policies and remains at approximately 10 percent. Only a tiny fraction, perhaps 10 percent, of those who do report go through the conduct process. In the rare case that the conduct process is utilized, it almost never results in any sort of significant punishment. Thus, the very reason given for establishing this process—that it is a more friendly process for the victim—doesn't pan out when we examine the numbers. Of equal concern is that reducing the prevalence of rape on campus is not expressly articulated as a goal, as it is with other conduct issues, such as underage drinking and drug use. For example, most conduct processes are expressly designed to reduce behavior that is detrimental to the campus community, such as underage drinking or plagiarism. In fact, as Campbell's (2015) work clearly demonstrates, failing to hold perpetrators accountable results in *a more dangerous campus community*. Frankly, it is also insulting that colleges and universities treat felony rape in the same manner as plagiarism. Not only are they entirely different kinds of misconduct, but faculty and staff are well trained to identify plagiarism, we understand the reasons it occurs—lack of understanding on the part of students, not giving oneself enough time to complete a project, ease of finding papers to copy on the Internet—and we have effective strategies for reducing it. None of this can be said about rape. The vast majority of faculty and staff, including conduct officers, are not trained to conduct the complex investigation that is necessary when a rape is reported, they are not trained to evaluate the evidence, and they are not familiar with any of the vast research literature on rape in general and rape on college campuses in particular. It is quite simply absurd that rape on college campuses is dealt with using this process.

At the intersection of rape on college campuses and sexual assault in SportsWorld is the role that the culture of SportsWorld plays in the overall rape culture on college campuses. Well beyond the violence that is perpetrated by athletes themselves, which we will discuss in the next section, research reveals an even more insidious phenomenon: rape on college campuses occurs at a higher rate on "football Saturdays," when the campus hosts a game (the home team plays at home), than on other Saturdays during the year, including when the football team is playing an away game.

BOX 12.4	**RAPE ON FOOTBALL SATURDAYS**

At colleges in the NCAA's Division I Football Bowl Subdivision, rapes have always been reported, and the allegations have often included athletes—for example, allegations at Florida State University and the University of Notre Dame, which are profiled in the film *The Hunting Ground*. Jon Krakauer's book *Missoula* (2015), which focuses on the "rape capital"—the University of Montana, in Missoula—illustrates this point as well. More recently, beginning in 2014, the Department of Education's Office of Civil Rights begun to publish a list of colleges and universities that are currently under investigation. There were fifty-five colleges and universities under Title IX investigation in 2014. As of January 3, 2019, a total of three hundred and ten colleges and universities are under active investigations and one hundred and ninety-two have had investigations completed. If you are interested in monitoring Title IX investigations, we recommend the interactive tool available at the Chronicle of Higher Education: https://projects.chronicle.com/titleix.

In one of the few academic papers on the topic of rape on football game day, the authors argue that empirical evidence shows that on Football Bowl Subdivision campuses (including the University of Notre Dame, Florida State University, and the University of Montana) when the home football team is playing a home game, rape reports by college-age women increase by 28 percent (Lindo, Siminski, and Swensen 2015). The difference between rapes reported on home game Saturdays and away game Saturdays is significant: 25 percent more rapes are reported on home games days than on away game days.

Though the data do not establish a specific causal relationship, Lindo, Siminski, and Swensen (2015) speculate that the increased party climate and excessive consumption of alcohol, much of it taking place at fraternity parties and/or fraternity-sponsored tailgate parties, is a significant contributor to the elevated rates of sexual assault on football Saturdays.

We turn now to a discussion of gender-based violence in SportsWorld, noting that this violence is perpetrated by both college athletes and professional athletes. Though IPV is certainly perpetrated by college athletes, sexual assault is by far more common and cases often rise to national attention because of the celebrity-like status of the athletes who are accused.

SEXUAL ASSAULT IN SPORTSWORLD

There is much debate about the rates of violence against women that is perpetrated by athletes. Those who argue that athletes don't perpetrate any more violence against women than nonathletes claim that we are simply more aware of these cases because of the athletes' celebrity status and the newsworthiness of their bad behaviors. Others note that it is difficult to measure rates of gender-based violence perpetrated by athletes as compared to nonathletes because crime statistics are not recorded in such a way as to identify athlete status (or any other profession, for that matter). Finally, others suggest that the relationship between high rates of gender-based violence and athlete status may in fact be a spurious one, that in fact the real relationship is one of age; that men in their teens, twenties, and early thirties are the most likely to perpetrate gender-based violence, and it just happens that this is the age range that most college and professional athletes fall into. In fact, as we will discuss in the next section, systematic and extensive systems of cover-up result in few players ever being formally arrested or charged, and thus the allegations never make it into the public record or the media where we would have access to them— so perhaps the rates are actually higher. Data from the first study that we are aware of that attempted to measure sexual violence perpetrated by athletes and compare these rates to those of nonathlete college students found that, in fact, collegiate student athletes did perpetrate more sexual violence than their nonathlete peers. In the study of one hundred and seventy-three college men, one hundred and one athletes and seventy-two nonathlete students, more than half (54.3 percent) of athletes, compared to 37.9 percent of nonathlete college men, admitted that they had engaged in sexually coercive or sexually abusive behavior (Young et al. 2016). This difference was highly statistically significant (p<.001).

In the summer of 2015, Paula Lavigne, an investigative journalist working for ESPN's program *Outside the Lines*, published the findings of her year-long examination of rape by college athletes. Clearly prompted by the case of Jameis Winston at Florida State University, in which so many things seemed mishandled, her investigation sought to determine if the case of Jameis Winston was unique or part of a larger pattern.

BOX 12.5	JAMEIS WINSTON

In 2013, the star quarterback for the Florida State University football team, Jameis Winston, was accused of rape by a Florida State student. The rape allegedly took place on December 7, 2012, at Winston's off-campus apartment after a night of partying at the Tallahassee bar Potbelly's (Bogdanich 2014). However, as many in the news media

continues

BOX 12.5	**JAMEIS WINSTON** *continued*

have reported, significant questions have been raised about the overall investigation and the timing of the investigation in particular. Though the woman who accused Jameis Winston of rape reported that the rape took place on December 7, 2012 and had a rape kit collected that confirms this, and she identified Winston as her rapist on December 10, 2012, no investigation or word of the case broke in public for nearly a year (December 2013), just prior to Winston being awarded the Heisman Trophy and leading the Florida State Seminoles to the national championship. It is difficult to argue that the delay in investigating Winston was unrelated to his role on the football field. Eventually, Winston and his lawyers agreed to an on-campus hearing that was conducted in an extremely unusual manner: Florida State University appointed a state judge to oversee the hearing, something we have never seen in a conduct process. Winston was found not responsible and proceeded to be drafted number one overall in the spring 2015 NFL draft. As of the time of writing, no criminal charges have been filed, but the accuser and Winston settled a civil lawsuit, the terms of which are undisclosed.

Source: Bogdanich 2014.

Lavigne's (2015) investigation uncovered a series of systematic practices that impacted the impartial investigation of high-profile athletes accused of a crime, and of sexual assault and IPV in particular. She argues that these practices explain the statistically significant finding that athletes are far less likely than college-age men in the same communities to be arrested and charged when they are accused. Given the finding by Young and colleagues that athletes engaged in more sexually coercive and violent behavior than their nonathlete student peers, this is indeed troubling. *In other words: student athletes perpetuate significantly more sexual coercion and violence but are significantly less likely to be arrested or charged when they are accused.*

For example, in Tallahassee, Florida, the home of Florida State University, 70 percent of athletes accused of a crime had those charges dropped or never faced charges at all, compared to 50 percent of college men at Florida State University who are not athletes. Lavigne (2015) found specifically:

- Athletic department officials involved themselves in investigations many times. Some tried to control when and where police talked with athletes, others insisted on being present during player interviews, alerted defense attorneys, conducted their own investigations before contacting police, or even, in one case, handled potential crime scene evidence. Some police officials were torn about proper procedure—unsure when to seek a coach's or athletic director's assistance when investigating crimes.

- Some athletic programs had, in effect, a team lawyer who showed up at a crime scene, jail, or police department—sometimes even before an athlete requested legal counsel. The lawyers, sometimes called by athletic department officials, were often successful in giving athletes an edge in evading prosecution, whether for minor offenses or major crimes.

- The high profiles of the athletic programs and athletes had a chilling effect on whether cases were even brought to police and how they were investigated. Numerous cases never resulted in charges because accusers and witnesses were afraid to detail wrongdoing, feared harassment from fans and the media, or were pressured to drop charges in the interest of the sports programs.

Systematic special treatment like this does not take place in a bubble; rather, it's part of a deeply embedded culture that is designed to protect athletes from any external scrutiny. At Florida State University, the athletic department hired a former football player and placed him in charge of dealing with the police when an athlete got into trouble. Based on our reading of Lavigne's (2015) report, as well as the extensive *New York Times* piece by Walt Bogdanich (2014), it is quite clear that Winston's case involved many of these types of systematic interventions. For example, in Lavigne's (2015) interview with district attorney William Meggs, he reveals the reason for the yearlong delay in interviewing Winston: the athletic department simply would not allow investigators to interview Winston. They argued that any contact with Winston had to go through them, and for an entire year they kept him from being available. Only after he won the Heisman Trophy and after Florida State won the national championship, and when there was significant outside pressure for an investigation, and when Winston had been provided an appropriate attorney who attended the conduct hearing with him, were the police allowed to interview Winston. A year after the accusation against Winston was made, Meggs made the decision not to bring any charges in the case. As noted by Lavigne's (2015) report, this type of systematic protection of athletes is not limited to Florida State University.

IPV IN SPORTSWORLD

Benjamin Morris, a statistician for the online publication *FiveThirtyEight*, conducted a sophisticated statistical analysis that involved using data reported in the

Bureau of Justice Statistics annual crime report combined with a database compiled by *USA Today* that included all arrests of NFL players beginning in 2000. Morris's (2014) analysis revealed that though NFL arrest rates for IPV were lower than the average for men of the same age group, nevertheless, 55 percent of the arrests of NFL players were for IPV and an additional 38 percent of arrests were for sexual violence. Morris goes on to note that when he compared the data by social class, one of the key predictors for perpetrating and experiencing IPV, only 20 percent of women in the upper-income bracket report an incident of IPV, the same crime that 55 percent of NFL arrests are for.

Of course, all of this is complicated by many other factors, including the fact that NFL players may have grown up with significantly less income and wealth than they have as professional athletes, which is completely different from the trajectory of the average wealthy American—who is born wealthy and stays wealthy. Thus it may be muddying the waters to look at the rates of IPV arrests among the wealthy and include professional athletes in that social class grouping without caveat. Additionally, based on research we conducted for another project (Smith 2014), we found that high-profile athletes, especially those playing football, basketball, and baseball, were less likely to be arrested than less well-known athletes playing the same sports. This is a stark reminder of the role that discretion plays when officers are called out to a case involving a high-profile athlete, whether college or professional. Thus, it is also possible to conclude from Morris's analysis that *arrest rates* for NFL players are actually lower than the *arrest rates* for nonathletes, and that *the actual incident rates are significantly higher than the arrest rates reflect.* For us, the takeaway message that Morris persuasively demonstrates is that, at least in the NFL, there is a significant problem with gender-based violence, both IPV and sexual assault.

BOX 12.6	RAY RICE

On February 15, 2014, Baltimore Ravens running back Ray Rice punched his then fiancée Janay Palmer in an elevator in a casino in Atlantic City, New Jersey. The next day, a video surfaced of Rice dragging his unconscious fiancée from the elevator, and Rice was arrested. Almost immediately, football coaches, owners, and announcers expressed their support for Rice and their disbelief that he had actually engaged in a serious act of IPV. In March 2014, Roger Goodell, commissioner of the NFL, who has the power to impose sanctions on players who violate player conduct policies, met with Ray Rice and

continues

| BOX 12.6 | RAY RICE *continued* |

determined that an appropriate sanction was a two-game suspension. Advocates working to end IPV were understandably enraged, especially given the fact that the sanction for driving under the influence of alcohol or drugs is an automatic four-game suspension. Roger Goodell and the NFL came under intense scrutiny, and Goodell modified the official NFL policy to require a six-game suspension for the first incident of IPV and up to a lifetime ban for subsequent incidents.

In September 2014, video footage surfaced of Ray Rice punching his fiancée in the face (this was in addition to the video that surfaced in February 2014). The day after the second video surfaced, the Baltimore Ravens released Rice. That same day, Roger Goodell released a statement that he had not previously seen the second video, although there is ample evidence that it was delivered to his office, and he suspended Rice indefinitely. In December 2014, Rice appealed his indefinite suspension on the grounds that he was initially sanctioned to two games under the policy in place at the time of his hearing. A court overruled the NFL and Rice was reinstated.

Source: King 2014.

The case of Ray Rice illustrates several important points, including special treatment and the problems with internal systems of justice. For example, Ray Rice received unusual treatment in the criminal justice system—he was allowed to enter a pretrial intervention program, something only 1 percent of those facing similar charges are allowed to do. Second, Roger Goodell, like coaches, athletic directors, and owners throughout SportsWorld, and no different from leaders in each of the other institutions we analyze in this chapter, did not take an incident of gender-based violence seriously. The case of Ray Rice, however, wasn't the first (or sadly the last) time that the NLF ignored instances of sexual and intimate partner violence that players engaged in.

NATE NEWTON, DALLAS COWBOYS

"The Cowboys knew about the abuse while she was still married to Nate, her book reveals, and chose to do nothing."

Of course not. This was the era when "the Cowboys" were AMERICA'S TEAM! During this time they won three Super Bowl championships in four years: Super Bowl

continues

NATE NEWTON, DALLAS COWBOYS *continued*

XXVII (1992), Superbowl XXVIII (1993), and Super Bowl XXX (1995). Newton played for the team from 1986 to 1998.

Newton was a classic abuser. He wooed his wife Dorothy—across the years of his marriage—into believing in him that he would stop drinking, that he would stop his many infidelities and that he would stop beating her. Like most violent men, he didn't do any of these things.

What makes the Newton case especially grievous is the headline of this box: that the management of the Dallas Cowboys failed to act, do anything to intervene. When she tried to meet with front office management, the appointment was canceled. Dorothy wrote a book entitled *Silent Cry: The True Story of Abuse and Betrayal of an NFL Wife.* Her book sat on the shelf, garnering hardly any attention, until the IPV cases of Ray Rice, Baltimore Ravens and Greg Hardy, Dallas Cowboys brought new attention to Dorothy Newton's expose in her tell-all book.

Source: Dorothy Newton. 2015. *Silent Cry: The True Story of Abuse and Betrayal of an NFL Wife.* Grand Rapids, MI: Zondervan Publishers.

| **BOX 12.7** | **JOVAN BELCHER** |

Just days after Thanksgiving in 2012, Kansas City Chiefs player Jovan Belcher came home in the early morning hours and shot his fiancée nine times in front of their three-month-old child. The shooting occurred after Belcher spent the night hanging out with other women and accusing his fiancée of hanging out with rapper Trey Songz (as captured in Twitter conversations). Belcher then drove to Arrowhead Stadium and, in front of his coach, Romeo Crennel, shot and killed himself.

Source: "Jovan Belcher Kills Girlfriend, Himself," 2012. *ESPN.com.*

We find it highly problematic that Belcher's homicide-suicide did not seem to move either Roger Goodell or the NFL to make any substantive comments about players involved in IPV. In fact, despite the fact, as Morris (2014) notes, that IPV was nothing new to the NFL (55 percent of the arrests of NFL players between 2000 and 2014 were for IPV), it took seeing a video, albeit of a significantly less serious case of IPV than Belcher's, involving Ray Rice, for Goodell and the NFL to pay any serious attention to the IPV being perpetrated by its players. Perhaps most perplexing in the IPV homicide-suicide of Jovan Belcher was the coverage on sports outlets like ESPN, which we monitored regularly and which focused on the tragedy of his suicide and even the death of his fiancée, but never once discussed the prevalence of athletes who engage in IPV, nor even ever label the event an act of IPV. The fact that Belcher eventually committed a homicide should have been an opportunity to discuss the fact that if IPV is not interrupted, it can end tragically in death. Some 1,500 women are murdered each year by their current or former intimate partners.

THE INTERSECTIONS OF RACE

One of the critiques of discussions like ours, as well as of the media portrayals of athletes who engage in violence against women, is that the conversation is always focused on black men. We will not simply dismiss that critique. We, like other scholars of and activists for racial equality, are deeply concerned about the images of black men that populate our media. In the spring of 2015, when the riots raged in Baltimore, there was much critique of politicians and journalists who referred to the rioters as "thugs." Even a cursory review of the images of black men on TV, in the movies, and on social media reveals quickly that black men are relegated to just a few roles: athletes, entertainers, and criminals. We were very concerned in the aftermath of the, now infamous, Ray Rice video—the security footage that showed Rice punching his then fiancée Janay Palmer unconscious (see Box 12.6)—as more and more media attention focused on athletes who perpetrated violence against women, both IPV and rape, that all of the images we saw were of black men.

So we address the issue here with transparency and logic. First and foremost, as concerned as we are about the impact that these images may have on shaping Americans', especially white Americans', attitudes toward race, we are more deeply disturbed by the possibility of not showing these images, which would ultimately erase the experiences of women who have faced tremendous violence at the hands of men. This need to expose gender-based violence supersedes our concerns about the images themselves. That said, we implore the media to engage in thoughtful analysis that helps us to understand why so many of the images we see are of black men (see Figure 12.1). We offer three explanations, based on the evidence.

- First, it's simply a numbers game. If we limit our discussion, for the moment, to college and professional football, which is reasonable given that the vast majority of the cases involve football players, black players are significantly overrepresented in both leagues. Therefore, we would expect the majority of the cases in the NFL and at least half of the cases coming from college athletes to involve black men.
- Second, when we dig deeper into the cases that are reported in the national media and compare them to those we cataloged by researching newspaper crime logs, it is no surprise that there are plenty of white athletes who are engaging in gender-based violence as well, raping women and abusing

their partners. That said, as we have documented elsewhere (Smith 2014), black players are disproportionately identified as star players, and thus their behavior garners more national attention than that of the bench-warmer. As such, when the media is selecting which stories to feature, they are more likely to select stories associated with athletes who have national name recognition—who are more likely to be stars—than those who are well known only locally. We utilized local media outlets in order to conduct our research on athletes arrested, charged, and convicted of gender-based violence, which facilitated the inclusion of many white athletes (Smith 2014).

- Third, there may be some intricacies of race that matter. For example, black athletes may be disproportionately likely to have grown up in situations in which they were exposed to violence, either in their homes or in their communities. As we demonstrated in Chapter 8, exposure to violence in childhood increases the risk that one will grow up to perpetrate violence; living in a neighborhood with high levels of gang violence also predisposes men to engage in violence as they grow up. This may be compounded by the "Cool Pose" masculinity that many black men feel constrained by, which often leads them to express and establish their masculinity through violence.

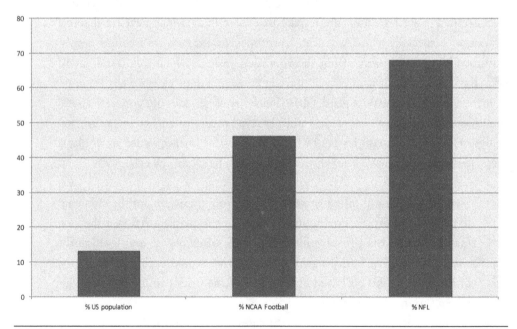

▲ **Figure 12.1**
Black Men as a Percentage of the US Population and Athletes in SportsWorld.

It should be clear from our discussion here that SportsWorld has a problem with gender-based violence. Not only do athletes, both collegiate and professional, perpetrate both sexual and IPV, but the institutions that govern their lives, colleges and professional leagues also fail to hold them accountable. These institutions seem more interested in keeping the athlete on the field or court, especially if they believe he is the key to a championship or, sadly, just another win, than in holding him accountable and offering him an appropriate intervention so that he can learn not to engage in these types of violence. Furthermore, we, like others, are concerned about the image that comes out of SportsWorld—that it is just black men who perpetrate gender-based violence. If we are honest about the reasons why more black athletes are accused of violence against women, we must interrogate the role that race plays, not only in their overrepresentation in SportsWorld but also in their overexposure to violence.

CONCLUSIONS

We opened the chapter by arguing that one of the tensions each of these institutions faces is between their moral obligation and mission to protect their members and the desire to keep the institution alive and growing. When confronted with a rape accusation, colleges and university administrators, military commanders, fraternity chapters, coaches, and athletic directors all fear that the accusation itself will lead to such a dramatic decline in the reputation of the institution that the institution will fail. Crippled by this fear, institutions respond by hiding rape allegations, which automatically results in a failure to investigate the allegation and hold the perpetrator accountable. Think, for example, about the case of Jameis Winston at Florida State University (see Box 12.5). Winston could not simply be suspended from the team during the investigation or dismissed without noting the cause, were he found sufficiently responsible. Why? Because people would have asked why. Of course, the problem of rape only grows when the perpetrators are not held accountable and dismissed. And so, on college campuses, in the military, among fraternities, and among college and professional athletic organizations, there is suddenly a crisis whose origins no one can quite figure out. We argue that, certainly, there is a short-term risk in admitting that rapes happen—at ridiculously high rates—and in dismissing perpetrators. The institutions risk hits to their reputations and the loss of people with valuable skills—commanders with combat experience; men who can dunk a basketball and might lead the team to a championship (which would bring a windfall of cash to coaches, players, owners, and even college presidents). But we argue that if these institutions can look past the short-term risk, there is guaranteed long-term gain. When a rapist is dismissed from the military, each of his victims is more likely to remain in the service, so the value of *their* experience is retained and the cost to replace them reduced. When a rapist is expelled from a college campus, the women he would have raped in the future are spared, which is obviously of benefit to them but is also of benefit to the university, which will see its rates of rape decline and its women students graduate and go on to successful careers.

Institutions will change only when it is in their best interest to do so, out of shame, to preserve their reputation, or because it becomes too costly not to. We argue that this time is now. Each of the institutions we have analyzed in this chapter has a rape epidemic and is facing significant scrutiny in the court of public opinion. Increasingly, institutions are also facing hefty lawsuits. The reader will recall that Michigan State University will pay more than $550 million in fines and settlements in the wake of the Larry Nassar sexual abuse scandal. If they are to survive, colleges and universities, the fraternity system, SportsWorld, and the military must take the short-term risk for the long-term gain. In doing so, they will be able to eliminate the moral tension, treating their members with the dignity they deserve and preserving their institution's reputation in the public eye. Finally, we urge the reader who is interested in institutional violence to check out our book *Gender, Power and Violence: Responding to Sexual and Intimate Partner Violence in Society Today* where we devote an entire chapter to each of the institutions we have discussed here, including fraternities, the military, and SportsWorld, as well as the Catholic Church, prisons, and politics and Hollywood.

In the next chapter, we turn to a discussion of unique experiences faced by members of the LGBTQ community who experience IPV.

RESOURCES

Chronicle of Higher Education Interactive Title IX investigation tool: https://projects.chronicle.com/titleix.

White House Public Service Announcements

1 Is 2 Many (intimate partner violence): www.whitehouse.gov/1is2many.
It's On Us (rape on college campuses): www.youtube.com/watch?v=LNVFPkmZTQ4.

NOTE

1. In the first edition of *Race, Sport and the American Dream* (2007), one of the authors, Smith, coined the term *SportsWorld* to refer to the complexity of the institution of sports. Sports, he argues, is much more than the games that are played on

fields or courts. SportsWorld encompasses the personnel—players, coaches, managers, owners, league commissioners—as well as properties, including stadiums and arenas, television broadcast rights that carry enormous financial incentives, and all of the ancillary functions such as travel, hotels, tickets, and of course fandom. The institution of sports is like no other, evolving from the "toy department of life" to become a major American institution embedded in our schools and colleges and in the business world as major corporate entities.

REFERENCES

Alvarez, Lizette, and Deborah Sontag. 2008. "When Strains on Military Families Turn Deadly." *New York Times*, February 15. www.nytimes.com/2008/02/15/us/15vets.html.

Bensahel, Nora, David Barno, Katherine Kidder, and Kelley Sayler. 2015. *Battlefields and Boardrooms: Women's Leadership in the Military and Private Sector.* Center for a New American Security. www.cnas.org/sites/default/files/publications-pdf/CNAS_BattlefieldsVsBoardrooms_BensahelBarnoKidderSayler.pdf.

Bogdanich, Walt. 2014. "A Star Player Accused, and a Flawed Rape Investigation." *New York Times*, April 16. www.nytimes.com/interactive/2014/04/16/sports/errors-in-inquiry-on-rape-allegations-against-fsu-jameis-winston.html.

Brownmiller, S. 1975. *Against Our Will: Men, Women, and Rape.* New York: Simon and Schuster.

Bruckner, Helene. 2018. "Students Fall Victim to Hazing Epidemic: Unity at What Cost?" *Touro L. Rev. 34*: 459. http://bit.ly/2LOzqrf.

Brush, Lisa. 2001. "Poverty, Battering, Race, and Welfare Reform: Black-White Differences in Women's Welfare-to-Work Transitions." *Journal of Poverty 5(1)*: 67–89.

Brush, Lisa, Jody Raphael, and Richard Tolman. 2003. "Effects of Work on Hitting and Hurting." *Violence Against Women 9(10)*: 1213–1230.

Campbell, Jacquelyn. 2015. "Campus Sexual Assault Perpetration: What Else We Need to Know." *Journal of the American Medical Association Pediatrics 169(12)*: 1088–1089. http://archpedi.jamanetwork.com/article.aspx?articleid=2375126.

Campbell, Jacquelyn C., Daniel Webster, Jane Koziol-McLain, Carolyn Rebecca Block, Doris Campbell, Mary Ann Curry, Faye Gary, Judith McFarlane, Carolyn Sachs, Phyllis Sharps, Yvonne Ulrich, and Susan A. Wilt. 2003. "Assessing Risk Factors for Intimate Partner Homicide." *National Institute of Justice Journal 250*. www.ncjrs.gov/pdffiles1/jr000250e.pdf.

Costello, Carol. 2014. "'Sexy' Clothes Don't Excuse Sexual Violence." *CNN.com*, October 9. www.cnn.com/2014/10/06/opinion/costello-provocative-clothes-dont-cause-rape.

Dowler, Lorraine. 2011. "The Hidden War: The 'Risk' to Female Soldiers in the US Military." In *Reconstructing Conflict: Integrating War and Post-War Geographies*, edited by Scott Kirsch and Colin Flint, 295–314. Burlington, VT: Ashgate, 2011.

Epstein, Cynthia. 2007. "Great Divides: The Cultural, Cognitive, and Social Bases of the Global Subordination of Women." *American Sociological Review 72(1)*: 1–22.

Goffman, Erving. 1961. *Asylums: Essays on the Social Situation of Mental Patients and Other Inmates*. New York: Doubleday.

Griffin, Susan. 1979. *Rape: The Politics of Consciousness*. New York: Harper & Row.

Hattery, Angela J. 2008. *Intimate Partner Violence*. Lanham, MD: Rowman & Littlefield.

Hattery, Angela J., and Emily Kane. 1995. "Men's and Women's Perceptions of Non-Consensual Sexual Intercourse." *Sex Roles 33(11)*: 785–802.

Hattery, Angela J., and Earl Smith. 2019. *Gender, Power, and Violence: Addressing Sexual and Intimate Partner Violence Today*. Lanham, MD: Rowman and Littlefield.

Hoge, C. W., D. McGurk, J. L. Thomas, A. L. Cox, C. C. Engel, and C. A. Castro. 2008. "Mild Traumatic Brain Injury in U.S. Soldiers Returning from Iraq." *New England Journal of Medicine 358*: 453–463.

Houppert, Karen. 2005. "Base Crimes." *Mother Jones*, July/August. http://mother jones.com/politics/2005/07/base-crimes.

Human Rights Watch. 2015. *Embattled: Retaliation Against Sexual Assault Survivors in the Military*. www.hrw.org/report/2015/05/18/embattled/retaliation-against-sexual-assault-survivors-us-military.

"Jovan Belcher Kills Girlfriend, Himself." 2012. *ESPN.com*, December 2. http://espn.go.com/nfl/story/_/id/8697360/kansas-city-chiefs-jovan-belcher-kills-girlfriend-commits-suicide-police-say.

Karns, M. Elizabeth. 2015. *Reporting of Sexual Assault: Institutional Comparisons, 2013*. Research Studies and Reports, Cornell University ILR Collection. http://digital commons.ilr.cornell.edu/cgi/viewcontent.cgi?article=1057&context=reports.

King, Peter. 2014. "The Ray Rice Fallout." *Sports Illustrated*. http://mmqb.si.com/2014/07/25/ray-rice-nfl-suspension-ravens.

Koss, Mary P. 1985. "The Hidden Rape Victim: Personality, Attitudinal, and Situational Characteristics." *Psychology of Women Quarterly 9(2)*: 193–212.

Koss, Mary, Lisa A. Goodman, Angela Browne, Louise F. Fitzgerald, Gwendolyn Puryear Keita, and Nancy Felipe Russo. 1994. *No Safe Haven: Male Violence Against Women at Home, at Work, and in the Community*. Washington, DC: American Psychological Association.

Krakauer, Jon. 2015. *Missoula: Rape and the Justice System in a College Town*. New York: Anchor Books.

Laumann, Edward O., John H. Gagnon, Robert T. Michael, and Stuart Michaels. 1992. *National Health and Social Life Survey*. The National Opinion Research Center at the University of Chicago (NORC). http://popcenter.uchicago.edu/data/nhsls.shtml.

Lavigne, Paula. 2015. "Lawyers, Status, Public Backlash Aid College Athletes Accused of Crimes." *ESPN.com*, June 15. http://espn.go.com/espn/otl/story/_/id/13065247/college-athletes-major-programs-benefit-confluence-factors-somes-avoid-criminal-charges.

Lindo, Jason, Peter M. Siminski, and Isaac D. Swensen. 2015. "College Party Culture and Sexual Assault." Working Paper 21828. National Bureau of Economic Research. http://nber.org/papers/w21828.

MacKinnon, Catharine. 1991. *Toward a Feminist Theory of the State.* Cambridge, MA: Harvard University Press.

Moran, Malcolm. 1988. "Knight Is Criticized Over Rape Remark." *New York Times,* April 27. www.nytimes.com/1988/04/27/sports/knight-is-criticized-over-rape-remark.html.

Morris, Benjamin. 2014. "The Rate of Domestic Violence Arrests Among NFL Players." *FiveThirtyEight,* July 31. http://fivethirtyeight.com/datalab/the-rate-of-domestic-violence-arrests-among-nfl-players.

Newton, Dorothy. 2015. *Silent City: The True Story of Abuse and Betrayal of an NFL Wife.* Grand Rapids, MI: Zondervan Publishers.

Renzetti, Claire M. 2001. "One Strike and You're Out: Implications of a Federal Crime Control Policy for Battered Women." *Violence Against Women* 7(6): 685–698.

Rich, Adrienne. 1980. "Compulsory Heterosexuality and Lesbian Existence." *Signs* 5(4): 631–660.

Rich, Adrienne. 1995. *Of Woman Born: Motherhood as Experience and Institution.* New York: W. W. Norton and Company.

Roberts, Dorothy. 1997. *Killing the Black Body.* New York: Vintage Books.

Sanday, Peggy Reeves. 2007. *Fraternity Gang Rape.* New York: New York University Press.

Scully, Diana. 1990. *Understanding Sexual Violence: A Study of Convicted Rapists.* Boston, MA: Unwin Hyman.

Sinozich, Sofi, and Lynn Langton. 2014. *Rape and Sexual Assault Victimization Among College-Age Females, 1995–2013.* Washington, DC: Bureau of Justice Statistics. NCJ 248471. www.bjs.gov/content/pub/pdf/rsavcaf9513.pdf.

Smith, Earl. 2007. *Race, Sport, and the American Dream.* Durham, NC: Carolina Academic Press.

Smith, Earl. 2014. *Race, Sport, and the American Dream.* 3rd ed. Durham, NC: Carolina Academic Press.

Smith, S. G., X. Zhang, K. C. Basile, M. T. Merrick, J. Wang, M. Kresnow, and J. Chen. 2018. *The National Intimate Partner and Sexual Violence Survey (NISVS): 2015 Data Brief—Updated Release.* Atlanta, GA: National Center for Injury Prevention and Control, Centers for Disease Control and Prevention. www.cdc.gov/violenceprevention/pdf/2015data-brief508.pdf

Syrett, Nicholas L. 2009. *The Company He Keeps: A History of White College Fraternities.* Chapel Hill, NC: University of North Carolina Press.

Tjaden, Patricia, and Nancy Thoennes. 2000. *Full Report of the Prevalence, Incidence, and Consequences of Violence Against Women Series: Research Report.* Atlanta, GA: Centers for Disease Control and Prevention. www.ncjrs.gov/pdffiles1/nij/183781.pdf.

US Department of Defense. 2018. *Annual Report on Sexual Assault in the Military.* Washington, DC: US Department of Defense. http://sapr.mil/public/docs/reports/FY17_Annual/DoD_FY17_Annual_Report_on_Sexual_Assault_in_the_Military.pdf.

Warshaw, Robin. 1988. *I Never Called It Rape: The Ms. Report on Recognizing, Fighting, and Surviving Date and Acquaintance Rape.* New York: Harper & Row.

Young, Belinda-Rose, Sarah L. Desmarais, Julie A. Baldwin, and Rasheeta Chandler. 2016. "Sexual Coercion Practices Among Undergraduate Male Recreational Athletes, Intercollegiate Athletes, and Non-Athletes." *Journal of Violence Against Women* 23(7): 795–812. https://doi-org.mutex.gmu.edu/10.1177/1077801216651339.

13

VIOLENCE IN LGBTQ FAMILIES

We began this book by making it very clear that we did not intend to write a book about family violence in which we segregated different populations by race or gender; rather, we would incorporate discussions of racial and gender variations inside of each topic. We feel strongly that this intersectional approach to the study of family violence—and most other social phenomena—is appropriate for a variety of reasons. The intersectional approach focuses on the fundamental "samenesses" rather than the "differences" among us, it allows us to see the commonalities without rendering variations invisible, and last, as we have argued elsewhere, the intersectional theory from which this perspective is derived has proven to be quite powerful in explaining the ways in which experiences with family violence, societal responses to family violence, and patterns of family violence vary by race and ethnicity, gender, sexuality, and other social statuses.

In addition to presenting data on the prevalence of violence in Lesbian, Gay, Bisexual, Transgender, and Questioning (LGBTQ) families, the focus in this chapter will be on exploring the ways in which models for predicting partner violence do and do not work for LGBTQ families. Of primary consideration will be a discussion of the intersection of gender, sexuality, race and ethnicity, and intimate partner violence (IPV). We will also explore the ways in which institutional discrimination shapes both experiences with LGBTQ IPV and responses to it.

OBJECTIVES

- To examine the prevalence of IPV in LGBTQ relationships
- To examine the prevalence of IPV among transgender and queer people
- To explore the ways in which sexuality shapes IPV and to explicate the similarities and differences across sexualities
- To explore the special case that the "closet" creates for IPV in same-gender couples

- To examine the criminal justice response to IPV in same-gender couples
- To explore the response of other agencies (for example, social services, shelters) to IPV and the challenges these present to LGBTQ victims and perpetrators
- To suggest policies and practices that would improve the ways in which agencies and institutions respond to IPV in the LGBTQ community

---

KEY TERMS

sex	cisgender
gender	queer
intersexuality	genderqueer
"true" hermaphrodite	sexuality
androgen insensitivity syndrome (AIS)	sexual orientation
gender identity	lesbian continuum
transgender	compulsory heterosexuality

INTRODUCTION

We have deliberately chosen to dedicate a chapter to violence in LGBTQ relationships because they are unique on the exact dimension that characterizes IPV: gender. As noted throughout the book, the majority of family violence is perpetrated by men against women; in short, family violence and IPV in particular are gendered phenomena. Gender is the single most powerful factor in shaping the risk for becoming a victim of violence and, even more so, perpetrating violence. In fact, gender shapes perpetration even more powerfully than it shapes victimhood; in cases of child abuse—and child sexual abuse in particular—men make up the overwhelming majority of abusers, even though children of all genders are victimized. While these patterns hold across race and ethnicity, age, type of violence, and so forth, they are significantly disrupted in LGBTQ relationships, mainly because victims and the perpetrators frequently, though not always, share the same gender identity. Violence in LGBTQ couples is *structurally different*, and thus it is important to dedicate a chapter to this phenomenon alone and explore the ways in which IPV is shaped by sexual orientation and the gender composition of the couple.

Before we begin our discussion of violence in LGBTQ couples, we must define some terms.

DEFINITIONS

Sex Versus Gender

Beginning with the second wave of feminism, a social movement that began in the late 1960s and was largely organized around women's reproductive rights and violence against women, feminists and sociologists began to think about distinctions between sex and gender. Though we have moved beyond these distinctions, as we will explore shortly, it is important to begin with them because, for nearly thirty years, this conceptual model dominated the field and strongly influenced the ways in which those of us studying IPV thought about it empirically and especially theoretically. Furthermore, at the time, this distinction was revolutionary—though not nearly as revolutionary as the current movement!

Sociologists and feminist scholars sought to distinguish between the physical body and the behaviors and practices that denote our "sex." In order to draw these distinctions, we began to talk about **sex** as representing the physical body that we are each born with and **gender** as the set of behaviors that we are socialized into and develop in order to assert our sex. Scholars argued that because of the powerful role that gender stratification plays in the United States, expressions of gender—often thought of as femininity and masculinity—were closely aligned with the two sexes: female and male. Scholars also argued that this alignment was largely socialized. In other words, boys and girls were born with different body parts, but it was their socialization—which is highly gendered and distinct—that led to the development of gender. For example, boys and girls are socialized strongly to favor certain activities—sports versus nurturing games like playing house or school—and in some cases are punished for expressing gender-incompatible preferences (Kane 2012). Thus, boys and girls will express distinct preferences that typically, though do not always, align with their gender. Feminists and sociologists, however, believed these preferences were developed out of socialization rather than being part of the biology of boys and girls. This distinction—that gender was a product of socialization and was therefore not "natural"—transformed our way of thinking about gender, for once we begin to think of preferences and personalities as *socialized*, we can begin to imagine the possibility that gender preferences and personalities could be changed or become variable. For example, if aggression is not inborn but trained, then boys could be socialized to be less aggressive. Though this is a widely accepted concept today, thirty years ago it was revolutionary.

West and Zimmerman (1987) argue that gender is in fact something that is performed and exists only when performed in relationship with another person. They suggest that when people perform traditionally gendered tasks—when women cook or when men take out the garbage—they are "doing gender." Acts of "doing gender" reinforce one's gender to oneself and others. Acts that seem to violate gender norms—gender-bending—reinforce the notion that gender is not fixed or aligned exclusively with sex. Women can embrace and exhibit masculine traits and still be women, and vice versa. Thus, feminist theorists and individuals began to explore the concept of gender-bending as a social protest, as well as evidence that sex and gender may not be as closely aligned as was previously believed. In particular, gender-bending challenged the notion that gender was a stable concept.

As the twentieth century came to a close, feminists fully embraced the notion that gender was neither stable nor rigidly aligned with sex, and they began to question the stability of biological sex. This perspective is gaining ground in scholarly and activist communities—especially among feminists—though it is not necessarily shared outside of feminist circles.

The argument that sex itself is not a stable or fixed concept has been largely advanced by the work of feminist biologist Anne Fausto-Sterling (2000). Based on her extensive reviews of both historical records and contemporary medical studies, she draws our attention to both the transgender community and the relatively common medical phenomenon known as **intersexuality**.

The concept of the instability of sex itself is a more complex argument and requires that we learn a little bit about the biology of sex. Biologists had long been aware of what they term *true hermaphroditism*, which is described by Fausto-Sterling: "A **'true' hermaphrodite** bears an ovary and a testis, or a combined gonad called an ovo-testis" (2000: 37), a condition that is quite rare. However, both female and male pseudohermaphrodites, individuals with either an ovary or a testis along with genitals from the "'opposite' sex" and other forms of what is now termed *intersexuality* (Fausto-Sterling 2000), are indeed common enough to warrant a discussion.

Based on her review of the medical literature, Fausto-Sterling (2000) argues that slightly less than 2 percent of all births involve some sort of ambiguous genitalia or reproductive organs. One example is **androgen insensitivity syndrome (AIS)**, a congenital disorder caused by errors in gene coding that block the ability of androgen receptors to absorb androgen. Androgen is a hormone in the "male" body that facilitates the maturation of secondary sex traits, including the growth of the genitals, facial and body hair, and a leaner body type. Individuals who are born with the typical male XY chromosomal makeup but who suffer from AIS will fail to develop to sexual maturity and thus will be infertile. With undescended testes, their external sex organs will appear to be female. AIS occurs in approximately one in twenty thousand births.

Gender identity refers to how individuals identify in terms of their gender. **Transgender** refers to the identity of individuals whose sex assigned at birth—which Fausto-Sterling (2000) argues is in and of itself a problematic though obviously extremely common event ("It's a boy!" or "It's a girl!")—is different from the gender they believe themselves to be. Transgender individuals may choose a variety of ways in which to achieve congruence: some choose to adopt the traditional dress and mannerisms of the gender with which they identify, some have body modification procedures (for example, breast augmentation or mastectomy), and some have gender congruence or gender affirmation surgery, including procedures to reconfigure their genitals. You may be familiar with Caitlyn Jenner's decision to transition from male to female, which is the subject of her reality TV show *I Am Cait*. The term **cisgender** refers to individuals whose sex assigned at birth is congruent with their gender identity. Finally, the terms **queer** and **genderqueer** refer to individuals who don't identify with either identity in the binary—male or female—but rather view their gender identity as more fluid. Individuals who identify as queer may prefer pronouns like *their* and *them* as opposed to *he* or *she*.

Sexuality or Sexual Orientation

Sexuality, or **sexual orientation**, is a concept that captures both an individual's tendencies in terms of sexual and romantic attraction and their sexual behavior. Sexuality is highly controversial, and there are serious debates about the degree to which sexual orientation is fixed, biologically determined, a product of socialization, or an unstable concept that exists on a continuum. Here we will not go into each of these debates, but we will summarize the scholarly literature on sexuality in order to lay the foundation for our discussion of violence in LGBTQ relationships.

For most of the twentieth century, sexuality was believed to exist in a set of fixed locations: homosexual, heterosexual, and more recently bisexual. Beginning with the work of Kinsey et al. (1948, 1953), scholars and researchers began to argue that sexuality exists on a continuum such that someone can be almost exclusively heterosexual or exclusively homosexual (the anchors of the continuum), thoroughly bisexual (the midpoint), or anywhere in between these fixed points. This notion of sexuality on a continuum reinforced the idea that sexuality is about attraction more than actual behavior. In other words, all people have a fundamental attraction (which varies along the continuum). This is distinct from their behavior, which may be based on circumstances or structural constraints other than attraction.

Scholars and activists today typically consider all nonheterosexual individuals as part of a highly complex and diverse community that includes gay men, lesbians, and people who identify as bisexual, transgender, queer, or any of a number of other identities. We adopt the acronym LGBTQ when referring to individuals in this community in order to represent the various identities while also acknowledging that, as our understanding of sexuality and gender identity becomes more complex, additional identities will likely emerge and will need to be represented. Though scholars and activists recognize the incredible diversity inside of this community, they also acknowledge that individuals in this community face some of the same prejudices and structural barriers in housing, employment, education, incarceration, and violence.

For example, D'Emilio (1983) argues that homosexuality has always existed, but the degree to which it is present as a family form is dictated by the economic system of a society. D'Emilio illustrates this point by considering the situation in colonial America. Though there is evidence of same-gender relationships then, especially among literary writers of the time who exchanged love letters even if they never engaged in sexual intimacy, there are few, if any, examples of same-gender families (same-gender couples living in a partnership together and/or raising children together). D'Emilio suggests that this is primarily a product of the ways in which an agricultural economy constrains family choices. In an agricultural economy in which the family farm is the primary economic unit, heterosexual couples who could produce a "labor force" by having several children would be the most successful. Families that could not produce children would be seriously disadvantaged and might even find it impossible to survive. In fact, adult children who never married—either by choice or by necessity—often stayed with their parents or other relatives who needed additional help on the family farm. Thus, individuals with same-gender attractions would have been constrained in pursuing relationships and families by the economic system. D'Emilio notes that both the changing social climate of the second half of the twentieth century—particularly the civil rights and women's rights movements—as well as the shifting economy and the increasing acceptability of women in the labor force opened the door for the possibility of same-gender families for the first time in the history of the United States.

Taking the Kinsey scale as a starting point, Adrienne Rich (1980) argues that sexual orientation should not necessarily be limited to *sexual* attraction but should be based on one's basic orientation toward relationships. Coining the term **lesbian continuum**, she argues that many women—including a majority of those who identify as heterosexual—establish their primary emotive relationships with other women. Rich also describes the concept of **compulsory heterosexuality**, which refers to the fact that in a patriarchal culture—where partners can provide income and a sense of protection from the outside world—it is often necessary for women to develop romantic relationships with men even when they are attracted sexually and/or emotionally to women. You will recall our lengthy discussion of compulsory partnering in Chapter 9. *Compulsory partnering* is a term we developed based on Rich's concept of compulsory heterosexuality.

The vast majority of scholars of sexuality argue that homosexuality and bisexuality have always been part of human culture (see Fausto-Sterling 2000 for a particularly detailed historical account) and exist in the animal kingdom as well. These data have been used primarily to argue that sexuality is biologically determined rather than socialized. Many scholars, including Fausto-Sterling (2000), Rich (1980), and D'Emilio (1983), would argue that despite the fact that sexuality is biologically determined—we are born the way we are—socialization and the social climate shape the degree to which any nonheterosexual identity can be expressed.

More recently, scholars of sexual orientation have also explored the notion that, though sexuality is biologically determined and then shaped by the social, political, and economic climate in which individuals live, it may also be unstable. In other words, one's sexual orientation may shift across one's lifetime. Some scholars even argue that bisexuality is not so much a fixed sexual orientation as it is a way of describing most people's sexuality; in short, most individuals may inherently have attractions—sexual, emotive, or both—to people of all genders, and the expressions of sexuality and the development of relationships are shaped by an individual's needs at a particular point in time as well as the social, political, and economic context in which they find themselves. All of that said, there are two important points to keep in mind as we discuss IPV in same-gender relationships: First, despite all of the potential variation in sexuality, our discussion here will be limited to individuals who are actually living in same-gender relationships. Second, all of the people who respond to violence—law enforcement personnel, prosecutors, judges, social workers, and so on—generally bring with them their own understanding of sexuality when they respond to violence in a same-gender relationship. Thus, all of the controversies that exist about the origins of homosexuality and stereotypes about gay men and women often influence the ways in which we respond to violence in a same-gender relationship.

STEREOTYPES OF GAY MEN AND LESBIANS

Because stereotypes of gay men and lesbians are so common and because they shape our responses to violence in same-gender relationships, it is worthwhile to discuss some of the most common stereotypes. The majority of stereotypes about gay men and lesbians are derived from a lack of understanding and a tendency to conflate sexuality and gender. The assumption is that gay men are more feminine than heterosexual men and that lesbians are more masculine than heterosexual women, and that these differences in femininity and masculinity are both biological and directly related to "being gay."

HOW DO STEREOTYPES IMPACT REACTIONS BY LAW ENFORCEMENT?

When law enforcement and other responders to IPV invoke these kinds of stereotypes about gay men and lesbians, this may adversely impact the ways they respond to same-gender IPV. For example, if an officer holds a stereotype that gay men are "drama queens," then they may underestimate the severity of an episode of IPV; the officer may conclude (wrongly) that the victim is exaggerating. Similarly, when law enforcement and other responders to IPV invoke stereotypes they hold about men and women, this may adversely impact the ways that they respond to these incidents of same-gender IPV. For example, the perception that men are the perpetrators of IPV and women are the victims may inhibit a responding officer from recognizing men who are victims or women who are perpetrators in same-gender relationships.

In addition to the problems associated with stereotypes is the issue of the gender-based conceptualization of IPV. As we have argued throughout the book, IPV is a gender-based phenomenon that developed out of, and is inextricably linked to, patriarchy and inequalities of power. That said, our reason for treating same-gender IPV in a separate chapter is that same-gender violence violates our very conceptualization of IPV—at least on the surface—and thus must be considered separately. We must address this apparent contradiction head-on. It is critical that all individuals who work with victims and perpetrators of IPV have their stereotypes surrounding gay men and lesbians and same-gender IPV debunked.

PREVALENCE

Research on the prevalence of IPV in same-gender couples reveals that the overall rates are higher in the LGBTQ community, with two exceptions: straight men report higher rates of IPV than gay men, and there are often too few bisexual men reporting violence to make solid comparisons.

Table 13.1 Lifetime Prevalence of Rape, Physical Violence, and/or Stalking by an Intimate Partner

Women		Men	
Lesbian	43.8%	**Gay**	26.0%
Bisexual	61.1%	**Bisexual**	37.3%
Heterosexual	35.0%	**Heterosexual**	29.0%

Source: Walters, Chen, and Breiding 2013.

Table 13.2 Lifetime Prevalence of Severe Intimate Partner Violence

Women		Men	
Lesbian	29.4%	**Gay**	>16.4%
Bisexual	49.3%	**Bisexual**	Too small to report
Heterosexual	23.6%	**Heterosexual**	13.9%

Severe physical intimate partner violence includes being hit with a fist or something hard, slammed against something, or beaten.
Source: Walters, Chen, and Breiding 2013.

Perhaps most interesting to note from these numbers is that women of all sexual identities report consistently higher rates of violence than men of nearly all sexual identities, with bisexual men reporting very slightly higher rates than straight women. Sexual and intimate partner violence are gendered even when we examine the rates in same-gender couples. Additionally, bisexual women report significantly higher rates of sexual and intimate partner violence than either lesbians or heterosexual women.

Although we will discuss some key differences in the ways in which same-gender IPV is experienced, there is no evidence to suggest that the types of physical or sexual violence that occur in same-gender couples are any different from that experienced by heterosexual couples: victims of same-gender IPV report being hit, kicked, punched, and having things thrown at them, and they report episodes of sexual violence. Gay men and bisexual men report sexual violence at rates between 40 and 50 percent, and 16.4 percent of gay men reported that they had experienced *severe physical violence* at the hands of their intimate partners (Walters, Chen, and Breiding 2013).

Gay men and lesbians also face significantly higher rates of violence by strangers and acquaintances. One study reveals that nearly half (42 percent) of gay men and nearly 30 percent of lesbians reported violence at the hands of family members, peers, or strangers, rates that are significantly higher than for their heterosexual counterparts. Equally disturbing is the finding that both gay men and lesbians reported rates of child sexual abuse that are significantly higher than those of their heterosexual counterparts (Tjaden, Thoennes, and Allison 1999). This is important to note because, as the 1998 murder of Matthew Shepard illustrates, homophobia that breeds the type of violence propagated against Shepard is the same homophobia that, when internalized by a gay man or a lesbian, may lead to a form of self-hatred, which, when reflected in their partner, may lead to violence.

Matthew Shepard was a twenty-one-year-old University of Wyoming college student who was beaten to death in October of 1998 because he was gay. His murder was particularly brutal in that the perpetrators lured him away from a bar, drove him to an isolated area, beat him severely, and tied him to a fence. He was discovered the next day, having survived the night, and died several days later in a Colorado hospital. The two men who murdered him, Aaron McKinney and Russell Henderson, mounted a "gay panic" defense, suggesting that they were essentially afraid of Shepard's gayness. They were sentenced to life in prison.

Source: For an overview of the murder of Matthew Shepard, visit www.matthewshepard.org/about-us.

UNIQUENESS OF IPV IN SAME-GENDER COUPLES

Though in most ways IPV in same-gender couples is no different than it is in heterosexual couples, there are some critical ways in which it is. For example, when gay men and lesbians who are experiencing violence seek assistance from law enforcement, the courts, or social service agencies, the stereotypes held by those agents often influence the ways in which they respond, and victims themselves may allow their beliefs about who is an appropriate victim (for example, not lesbian women!) to cloud their own strategies for seeking help. In terms of the criminal justice system, one study found that when all incidents of same-gender IPV were considered together, there was little difference between IPV arrests of perpetrators in heterosexual and same-gender partner incidents. However, when gay and lesbian couples were considered separately, differences in police response became more evident. Police were more likely to make arrests in lesbian IPV cases when injuries were minor. In contrast, in gay couples, more serious injury was required for an arrest to be made (Pattavina et al. 2007). Thus, a police officer's stereotypes that women are victims and men are not may lead to their readiness to arrest the perpetrator when the victim is a woman, even though the perpetrator is a woman as well, and their reluctance to make an arrest in cases in which the victim is a man, even when the perpetrator is as well.

Another challenge facing gay and lesbian victims of IPV may be their reluctance to turn over a member of their community to the police and the criminal justice system. Similar to the experiences of African American women who fear the treatment of their partners by potentially racist police, prosecutors, or corrections officers (Hattery and Smith 2018), gay men and lesbians may fear the treatment their partners will be likely to receive if they are reported and arrested. This reluctance may be exacerbated for lesbians who also identify as feminists; they may worry that they will be seen as traitors to their gender and their sexuality for reporting violence at the hand of a woman.

Finally, it is important to point out that transgender victims may face the greatest barriers to reporting. They have good reason to fear that their identity will not be respected by law enforcement and other responders, especially if they have not legally changed their identity or if they have not had gender affirmation surgery. In our research on violence in prisons we learned, for example, that when trans-identified people are arrested or sentenced to jail or prison, their assignment is based strictly on their biological sex rather than their gender identity, e.g. transgender women are placed in men's prisons and transgender men are placed in women's prisons, and they report extraordinarily high rates of violence, particularly sexual violence (Hattery and Smith 2018).

Given the unique set of challenges that LGBTQ-identified victims of IPV face, it is especially important to have services that are designed specifically to address these challenges. Rainbow Response Coalition (see Box 13.1) is an example of just this kind of organization.

BOX 13.1   RAINBOW RESPONSE COALITION

Committed to educating communities and breaking the silence around LGBTQ intimate partner violence.

What We Do

Rainbow Response is a grassroots coalition based in Washington, DC, that brings together organizations and leaders from the Lesbian, Gay, Bisexual, Transgender, and Questioning (LGBTQ) communities, along with traditional domestic violence service providers and government agencies, to increase the awareness about Intimate Partner Violence (IPV) amid the relationships of LGBTQ individuals. The Coalition works to promote education within the LGBTQ communities and beyond and identifies existing services that are provided in a manner respectful of the unique identities of LGBTQ survivors of IPV, as well as batterers.

Research and Education

Research indicates that intimate partner violence occurs at the same rate in heterosexual relationships as it does in LGBTQ relationships. In 2009, Rainbow Response released a

continues

| BOX 13.1 | RAINBOW RESPONSE COALITION *continued* |

groundbreaking report on IPV in the LGBTQ community based on surveys conducted over a year's time at various community events. This, the first report of its kind for the Washington, DC metro area, confirmed what national research has shown: 28% of respondents self-identified as survivors of IPV. Emotional abuse, physical violence, and sexual violence were the most common types of abuse experienced. Rainbow Response continues its research endeavors to help bring light to the increased and urgent need for services for LGBTQ survivors.

Rainbow Response works to engage and educate the public through outreach on college campuses and at LGBTQ community events. LGBTQ Pride Season in the District is one of our busiest times of the year. The Coalition takes an interactive approach to community education; we use a Wheel-of-Fortune style game to teach people about the specifics of same-sex violence and we host town hall discussions where individuals can share their experiences and concerns. Rainbow Response also facilitates healthy relationship workshops where individuals or couples can discuss strategies to ensure that their relationships are healthy and loving.

Advocacy

Rainbow Response has written several testimonies advocating for the increased need of an educated response to victims of LGBTQ partner violence. Recently, Rainbow Response has written to offer comments on the Office of Human Rights' proposed housing regulations to provide guidance concerning housing discrimination and protections for victims of domestic violence.

Training and Technical Assistance

One of the first lifelines for those experiencing abuse is law enforcement. Rainbow Response, along with a coalition of other LGBTQ organizations, was successful in developing training modules and facilitating specialized, in-person trainings with both the Metropolitan Police Department and DC's Court Services and Offenders Supervision Agency. Additionally, in conjunction with the Mayor's Office and several other LGBTQ organizations, Rainbow Response participates in a critical incident task force with the Metropolitan Police Department to ensure that officers are well informed and able to provide culturally competent assistance [to] the LGBTQ community.

Source: Rainbow Response Coalition website, www.rainbowresponse.org.

Other problems arise when victims of same-gender IPV seek assistance through shelters. Garcia and McManimon (2010) review the history of the shelter movement and identify two critical problems that are specific to LGBTQ-identified victims, both of which develop out of heterocentric ideologies of IPV. Because men constitute the vast majority—perhaps 85 percent—of perpetrators in both heterosexual and same-gender IPV and because the vast majority of victims of IPV are women, regardless of their sexual orientation, there are very few shelters that exist to serve men who are victims. The lack of attention to men who are victims is exacerbated by the fact that the gendered wage gap (AAUW 2018) results in a commonly held belief that men have the financial resources to leave threatening circumstances of any kind and that they are thus less in need of shelter services than women. In fact, because of a substantial and well-documented "gay wage penalty" (Carpenter 2007), gay men leaving abusive relationships may not have the resources necessary to leave successfully. Second, again based on a heterocentric construction of IPV, it is often believed that women who are perpetrators in lesbian relationships will seek access to shelters by posing as victims and thus harass, threaten, and stalk their victims (Sullivan 1997). There is not necessarily substantial evidence to confirm this fear. Again, similar to their treatment in jails and prisons, transgender victims will often be assigned to shelters (of all kinds, not just shelters that explicitly serve victims of IPV) based on their biological sex, especially if they have not changed their identity legally or had surgery. Imagine a transgender woman who is fleeing IPV being denied a bed in a shelter serving victims of IPV and being sent to a shelter providing services for homeless men. The National Coalition of Anti-Violence Programs (2015) reports that 71 percent of LGBTQ victims of IPV were denied access to shelter services. Clearly, one of the additional problems that gay and lesbian victims of IPV face is the treatment they receive when they seek help.

LGBTQ victims of IPV face significant challenges in the civil court system as well. As Calton, Cattaneo, and Gebhard (2015) note, the intervention that LGTBQ victims of IPV report seeking most often are orders of protection. And yet, at least half of all victims report being denied an order of protection. The primary barrier to successfully obtaining an order of protection are the state-specific statutes. In some states, including Montana and South Carolina, the order of protection statutes specifically prohibit LGBTQ victims from applying. In many states there is no specific exclusion of LGBTQ victims, but as is the case with all orders of protection, judges have a wide latitude and significant discretion in whether to grant the order or not. Judges who believe stereotypes about LGBTQ individuals and relationships or who may have misconceptions about IPV in the LGBTQ community may not believe the complainant and refuse to grant the order of protection (Calton, Cattaneo, and

Gebhard 2015). As we will discuss in the final chapter, this is one more reason why the inclusion of LGBTQ sexual and intimate partner violence in the 2013 reauthorization of the Violence Against Women Act (VAWA) was so critical.

Perhaps one of the most critical differences between violence in heterosexual relationships and same-gender IPV is the "closet." If one or both members of a same-gender couple are not "out," then the threat of "outing" can be particularly powerful. For example, a perpetrator of violence may threaten to out their partner if they try to leave or call the police. This alone can constitute a serious level of psychological abuse and can be exacerbated if the perpetrator is already out and thus feels no threat to their identity. Additionally, the knowledge that a victim will have to out themself if they go to the police for help or file for an order of protection may pose a significant barrier to help-seeking behavior. As noted previously, the power of the closet may be experienced most profoundly by transgender people, whose identity is even more deeply misunderstood and who face, as we have noted, significant mistreatment when they access systems designed to help victims, specifically shelter, law enforcement, and the court system.

APPARENT CONTRADICTIONS: SAME-GENDER VIOLENCE IS STILL ROOTED IN CONCEPTUALIZATIONS OF GENDER

Despite the fact that, on the surface, same-gender IPV seems to violate the most fundamental feminist premise that IPV is rooted in patriarchy and inequality in gender relations (Hattery 2008), in fact, IPV in same-gender relationships is built on the same premises as all forms of IPV: power, inequality, and the ability to dominate. This is not to suggest that the more "masculine" member of the couple will automatically be the perpetrator while the more "feminine" will always be the victim. But rather, as is the case with child abuse, elder abuse, and partner abuse, the perpetrator of violence will likely be the person with more power. This power might be physical but is more likely to be financial, emotional, or even "out" status. For example, as noted above, if one member of the couple is out and the other is not, the power inherent in the ability to out another can be translated into all kinds of abuse in the relationship, including physical, emotional, financial, and sexual.

Now we turn to an examination of violence in the transgender community.

VIOLENCE IN THE TRANSGENDER COMMUNITY

Although heterosexism is alive and well in the United States, more and more legislation and public opinion polls indicate that Americans increasingly endorse the human and civil rights of gay men and lesbians. In fact, in the summer of 2015 the United States Supreme Court ruled in favor of marriage equality, making it the law of the land. However, simultaneously and despite the public's fascination with Caitlyn Jenner, transgender men and women face significantly higher rates of discrimination, are more likely to commit suicide, and are more likely to be the victims of violence than their gay and lesbian counterparts.

Though many transgender men and women report healthy intimate relationships, there is anecdotal evidence to suggest that they can be particularly vulnerable to IPV. One study finds that half (50 percent) of transgender individuals studied reported violence—physical and sexual—in their intimate partner relationships (Risser et al. 2005). One factor that may increase the probability of IPV, especially *sexual abuse*, for intersex and transgender individuals is that they represent challenges to our binary understanding of sex and/or gender. For example, many transgender individuals report that the anticipation of a first sexual encounter with a new partner is anxiety-filled because even if they have disclosed their "status," they can never be quite sure of the reaction of a new partner.

Transgender people face significant threats of violence in sexual encounters with acquaintances and strangers as well. In some cases, people seek out transgender individuals for sex because they are perceived as sexually exotic. In other cases, even if they are forewarned, new partners may be perplexed by the appearance of the transgender person, whose very body defies our binary construction of male and female, and may respond to this emotion by engaging in violence. In fact, every year there are news accounts of trans people being severely beaten, raped, and even murdered in sex encounters with partners who either didn't know of their identity or were threatened by their bodies. Many of the perpetrators report feeling tricked, especially in cases in which they are attempting a transaction with a prostitute whom they did not realize was a transgender individual. We would argue that in many cases, the potential sex partner did actually know of the trans person's identity but felt threatened by the challenge to gender and sexual binaries that the trans body represents and responded with violence, often both physical and sexual. The rape of a transgender person is a powerful illustration of how rape is rooted in power. The rapist responds to a threat to their understanding of gender and sexuality and bodies by engaging in sex, albeit forceful and nonconsensual. Second, because intersex and transgender individuals challenge our fundamental understanding of sex and gender, in particular, intersex and trans victims are often reluctant to call the police or report the violence for fear that they will be revictimized by the very agents who are charged with their protection.

CONCLUSIONS

In this chapter, we have explored the experiences of violence faced by individuals who identify in the LGBTQ community. Overall, we argued that the experiences of these individuals are no different from those faced by heterosexuals; the violence includes physical assault, emotional abuse, sexual abuse, and financial abuse. On the other hand, sexuality and gender shape the likelihood of experiencing violence and the interactions both victims and perpetrators have when they attempt to report the violence or escape it. Specifically, stereotypes and prejudices significantly inhibit the equitable treatment of both victims and perpetrators. Thus, it is critical that agents of the institutions that deal with and interact with victims and perpetrators of violence be educated about the special circumstances faced by members of the LGBTQ community in order to ensure appropriate responses that meet the needs of the victims and perpetrators.

More specifically, we offer several recommendations. First and foremost, we argue for raising the visibility of all identities in the LGBTQ community as well as of the higher rates of violence that members of this community face. It's easier to ignore people who are rendered invisible. In our own community of Fairfax, Virginia, there is a great deal of focus on services for victims of IPV in the LGBTQ community, but we know that this is not the case universally. Second, the marriage equality decision by the Supreme Court is a step in the right direction; however, members of the LGBTQ community are not legally protected from discrimination in other areas, such as housing and employment. Nothing we as a community do to address IPV in the LGBTQ community will be significant until the law protects members of this community from discrimination and violence in other areas of life. Third, laws that prohibit discrimination would open the door to addressing many of the barriers to help-seeking that we identify, including the inability to secure an order of protection, the inability to find a safe and appropriate shelter, and the guarantee that a law enforcement officer will respond appropriately to an act of violence when it is reported.

That said, we recommend that the struggle be both at the macro level—changing anti-discrimination laws—and at the local and regional levels. With the proper training and the implementation of best practices, most of the barriers to reporting and receiving services could be removed. Shelters can be reconfigured to adequately address the needs of LGBTQ victims. Judges and law enforcement agents can be educated about the unique nature of IPV in the LGBTQ community—for example, the fear of being outed—to help ensure that cases are handled properly. We hope that our discussion adds to that of so many others in calling for identifying strategies for reducing IPV and sexual violence in the LGBTQ community, as well as for intervening appropriately when it occurs.

RESOURCES

Anderson, Jane. 2003. *Normal.* Avenue Street Productions/HBO Films. (*Normal* explores the experiences of a family in which the husband, in his forties, reveals a transgender identity and decides to transition.)

Cram, Bestor, and Candace Schermerhorn. 1997. *You Don't Know Dick: Courageous Hearts of Transsexual Men*. Northern Light Productions. (*You Don't Know Dick* is a documentary based on candid interviews with transgender men.)

Kaufman, Moisés. 2002. *The Laramie Project*. Good Machine. (This docudrama recounts the death of Matthew Shepard and explores its impact on the Laramie community.)

Peirce, Kimberly. 1999. *Boys Don't Cry*. Fox Searchlight. (*Boys Don't Cry* is a fictionalized account of the real-life murder of Brandon Teena, a transgender man who was killed after his identity was revealed.)

Pierson, Frank. 2003. *Soldier's Girl*. Bachrach/Gottlieb Productions. (*Soldier's Girl* is a fictionalized account of the real-life murder of Army serviceman Barry Winchell, who was murdered by a member of his unit after it was discovered that he was in love with a transgender woman.)

REFERENCES

American Association of University Women (AAUW). 2018. *The Simple Truth About the Gender Pay Gap*. www.aauw.org/research/the-simple-truth-about-the-gender-pay-gap.

Calton, J. M., L. B. Cattaneo, and K. T. Gebhard. 2015. "Barriers to Help Seeking for Lesbian, Gay, Bisexual, Transgender, and Queer Survivors of Intimate Partner Violence." *Trauma, Violence, and Abuse*. doi: 10.1177/1524838015585318.

Carpenter, C. S. 2007. "Revisiting the Income Penalty for Behaviorally Gay Men: Evidence from NHANES III." *Labour Economics* 14(1): 25–34.

D'Emilio, J. 1983. "Capitalism and Gay Identity." In *Powers of Desire: The Politics of Sexuality*, edited by A. Snitow, C. Stansell, and S. Thompson. New York: New Feminist Library Series.

Fausto-Sterling, A. 2000. *Sexing the Body: Gender Politics and the Construction of Sexuality*. 1st ed. New York: Basic Books.

Garcia, V., and P. McManimon. 2010. *Gendered Justice: Intimate Partner Violence and the Criminal Justice System*. Lanham, MD: Rowman and Littlefield.

Hattery, A. J. 2008. *Intimate Partner Violence*. Lanham, MD: Rowman and Littlefield.

Hattery, A. J., and E. Smith. 2018. *Policing Black Bodies: How Black Lives are Surveilled and How to Work for Change*. Lanham, MD: Rowman and Littlefield.

Kane, Emily. 2012. *The Gender Trap: Parents and Pitfalls of Raising Boys and Girls*. New York: New York University Press.

Kinsey, A., W. Pomeroy, C. Martin, and P. Gebhard. 1948. *Sexual Behavior in the Human Male*. Philadelphia, PA: Saunders.

Kinsey, A., W. Pomeroy, C. Martin, and P. Gebhard. 1953. *Sexual Behavior in the Human Female*. Philadelphia, PA: Saunders.

National Coalition of Anti-Violence Programs (NCAVP). 2015. *2015 Report on Intimate Partner Violence in Lesbian, Gay, Bisexual, Transgender, Queer and HIV-Affected Communities in the U.S.* http://avp.org/wp-content/uploads/2017/05/2015_NCAVP_IPVReport_MR.pdf.

Pattavina, A., D. Hirschel, E. Buzawa, D. Faggiani, and H. Bentley. 2007. "A Comparison of Police Response to Heterosexual Versus Same-Sex Intimate Partner Violence." *Violence Against Women* 13(4): 374–394.

Rich, Adrienne. 1980. "Compulsory Heterosexuality and Lesbian Existence." *Signs* 5(4): 631–660.

Risser, J., A. Shelton, S. McCurdy, J. Atkinson, P. Padgett, B. Useche, B. Thomas, and M. Williams. 2005. "Sex, Drugs, Violence, and HIV Status Among Male-to-Female Transgender Persons in Houston, Texas." In *Transgender Health and HIV Prevention: Needs Assessment Studies from Transgender Communities Across the United States*, edited by W. Bockting and A. Avery, 67–74. Binghamton, NY: Haworth Press.

Sullivan, C. M. 1997. "Societal Collusion and Culpability in Intimate Male Violence: The Impact on Community Response Toward Women with Abusive Partners." In *Violence Between Intimate Partners*, edited by A. P. Cardarelli. Boston, MA: Allyn and Bacon.

Tjaden, P., N. Thoennes, and C. Allison. 1999. "Comparing Violence Over the Life Span in Samples of Same-Sex and Opposite-Sex Cohabitants." *Violence and Victims* 14(4): 413–435.

Walters, Mikel L., Jieru Chen, and Matthew J. Breiding. 2013. *The National Intimate Partner and Sexual Violence Survey: 2010 Findings on Victimization by Sexual Orientation.* Atlanta, GA: National Center for Injury Prevention and Control, Centers for Disease Control and Prevention. www.cdc.gov/ViolencePrevention/pdf/NISVS_SOfindings.pdf.

West, C., and D. H. Zimmerman. 1987. "Doing Gender." *Gender and Society* 1(2): 125–151.

14

PREVENTION AND AVOIDANCE
The Early Warning Signs

But by the time I had found that out [that he was a crack addict], I was already madly in love with him. I mean, he was my world . . . He was my world. He was everything.

—**Stella**, thirtysomething white woman, Minnesota

I love the hell out of her. And it got to be love because we separated one time, and it just fucking hurts like hell. And like, somebody reached into my heart and just tried pulling it out. But I got over it. I moved on. I had another girl. Then all of sudden, she want to come back in my life. She's doing bad now. She can't get these kids together. You [his first love] was the only one who knew how to keep my life together.

—**Hank**, fortysomething African American man, Minnesota

This chapter will explore the ways that intimate partner violence (IPV) often comes as a surprise to victims because the red flags that point to its likelihood are so often masked by our constructions of romantic love. We will explicate the ways that common notions of romance can become pathways to abuse. For example, how does a gesture that is interpreted as romantic—like surprising a new lover by showing up at her workplace and whisking her off to lunch—turn into an abusive tactic that is a hallmark of stalking behavior? This chapter will be especially important for students who are off on their own at college, exploring their sexuality and learning how to forge romantic relationships without the usual escape hatches provided by parents and family life, as well as for those considering careers in social work, counseling, teaching, and any other profession that involves working closely with and mentoring young adults.

OBJECTIVES

- To examine the dominant notions of romantic love in the United States
- To examine the ways in which notions of romantic love may hide early warning signs for IPV
- To provide examples of typical patterns of romantic relationships as well as patterns that may lead to IPV and note the differences and similarities
- To provide some policy recommendations so that prevention can be more effective by noting the red flags embedded in notions of romantic love

KEY TERMS

early warning signs	jealousy
intrusion	erotic property
popping up	serial abuser
isolation	prone to anger
possession	unknown pasts
coverture	destiny
marital rape exemption	

INTRODUCTION

One of the comments most frequently heard by scholars and practitioners who work with battered women is that they did not see the first assault coming. Yet as discussed in depth by Angela Browne (1989), many violent relationships include early warning signs. In this chapter, we will explore the presence (or absence) of these early warning signs in the relationships that we learned about in our interviews, and we will then extend this discussion to an important issue that emerged in those interviews: the idea of destiny, of these two people being "made for each other," which led many of the people we interviewed to envision themselves together forever, despite the presence of severe physical violence, emotional abuse, and even sexual abuse.

"I DIDN'T SEE IT COMING!": THE EARLY WARNING SIGNS

In her interviews with battered women, Angela Browne (1989) notes that although the women repeatedly reported that the first assault often seemed to come out of the blue, in fact there were patterns of behavior in the relationship that were so consistent in their prediction of violence that she termed them **early warning signs**. These signs are intrusion, isolation, possession, jealousy, being prone to anger, and unknown pasts.

| BOX 14.1 | OPRAH WINFREY AND RIHANNA |

Oprah Winfrey Has a Warning for Rihanna: Chris Brown "Will Hit You Again"

Speaking directly into the camera, Winfrey said, "If a man hits you once, he will hit you again. He will hit you again."

—Helen Kennedy, *New York Daily News*,
March 8, 2009

Early in 2009 the world was awakened to learn that singer/songwriter Chris Brown had beaten his then girlfriend, pop star Rihanna. The news coverage brought to the forefront the issue of IPV, and one of the most important messages it conveyed was that it could happen to anyone of any race and social status. Though some may disagree with Oprah's decision to weigh in on their relationship, her comments elevated the conversation to the national level.

Source: Kennedy 2009.

As part of our work with the Fairfax County Domestic Violence Prevention, Policy and Coordinating Committee (DVPPCC), we receive the county's annual fatality report. The report, created by outside observers, looks for patterns in cases of IPV homicide. Though some cases of IPV fall through the cracks and prior to the homicide there had been no contact with police, social workers, shelters, or even hotlines, in the vast majority of cases, there were warning signs that were either ignored or never analyzed for the patterns they reveal. Here we consider one high-profile case that you should be familiar with, that of O. J. Simpson and his ex-wife, Nicole Brown Simpson.

First, we note that O. J. Simpson was acquitted for the 1994 murders of his ex-wife, Nicole Brown Simpson, and Ron Goldman. But he was found responsible in a wrongful death civil lawsuit, and he was ordered to pay a significant settlement to their families. What is important here is that, as in the cases of many battered women who are murdered each year, a review of the Simpsons' relationship demonstrates that there were early warning signs present, including previous incidents of IPV that either were not officially reported but that Nicole detailed in her diary or shared with her sister Denise, or were reported but failed to elicit a satisfactory response from the criminal justice system. We know, for example, that Nicole Brown Simpson called 911 to report at least one incident of IPV, and the police file contained photographs of her black eye. These kinds of failures lead to hundreds of homicides each year.

Here we will briefly summarize each warning sign, and then we will provide cases from our interviews that illustrate each early warning sign.

Intrusion: "Checking In" and "Popping Up"

Browne (1989) identifies **intrusion** as the batterer's monitoring the comings and goings of his partner.[1] Many abused women report that they feel as if their partners "check up on them" all the time. For example, many women report that they are required to call and check in when they are not in the physical presence of their partners. Women report being berated and often beaten when they are late or take longer than expected on an errand or a commute home from work. These outbursts of verbal venom or physical abuse (or both) can be set off by being less than five minutes late in arriving home. In a highly publicized case that came to our attention in spring 2004, an abused woman who had finally escaped after ten years of constant abuse reported that she was required to stay inside the house all day long. Her husband would call randomly at all times of the day, and if she did not answer the phone on the first ring, he would come home and beat her severely. This type of control significantly restricted her movement inside the house and rendered impossible any chance that she could step out of the house, even for a breath of fresh air. (This woman's story of abuse that made her a prisoner in her own home was aired on ABC's news program *20/20* on August 13, 2004.)

Another example of intrusion comes from Josie, whose story we discussed at length in Chapter 9. Josie's boyfriend installed wiretapping and recording technology in their home so that he could monitor her telephone conversations. In addition, he opened her mail, and on several occasions when she was out shopping with a girlfriend, she caught him spying on her and trailing her.

Popping up is another form of intrusion. As we detailed extensively in Chapter 9, many women and men reported this sort of behavior. Josie recounted how her partner would come by the nurses' station looking for her, and when he found she was at lunch with her colleagues, he later beat her.

Even without a physical assault, this type of control is a form of abuse. Intrusion reflects a lack of trust on the part of the abuser and engenders tremendous anxiety in the victim. It is also closely linked to jealousy; it is motivated primarily by the abuser's worry that when he cannot see his partner, she is probably with some other man.

If you have never been beaten or the victim of emotional abuse and controlling behavior, then you may wonder: What woman would put up with this level of intrusion and control? How does this type of behavior become part of a long-term relationship? As is the case with all of the other early warning signs, what is truly insidious about intrusion is that in a new relationship, early on, it appears to be simply an expression of love, and it is interpreted by the woman as flirtatious or romantic. For example, a new partner may call their new love during the workday just to say hello or leave messages when one or the other is out with friends or traveling. Most women would consider it romantic if their new boyfriend popped up at noon for a surprise lunch or at the end of the day to whisk her off to a romantic dinner. In many new relationships, these behaviors would be considered romantic, and they would not raise any red flags. Many women would feel swept off their feet.

Although many of us may have similar experiences and would feel or have felt equally wooed by them, such behaviors can amount to early warning signs in violent relationships. This sort of popping up and calling just to say hello usually declines precipitously in healthy relationships. As the couple moves into a more advanced relationship and trust is in place, there is less need for reassurance—often the real source of the constant phone calls and messages—and thus romantic behavior or gestures, including surprise visits, become less common and may be reserved for special occasions such as a birthday or anniversary.

Yet in abusive relationships, these forms of intrusion increase dramatically. Calling just to say hello becomes calling to check up. Popping up as a romantic surprise turns into a way to be sure that the woman is where she said she is and to control her movement, and it serves to satisfy the batterer that she is not with other men. And, as noted in Chapter 9, this sort of intrusion can lead to reprimands from supervisors or even being fired from one's job. Because these abusive patterns of intrusion begin as something that seems romantic, they are often overlooked by women until the level of intrusion is severe and the relationship has already become abusive.

BOX 14.2	IPV IN THE DIGITAL AGE

Cyberstalking and the use of technology to intimidate and abuse someone—physically, sexually, verbally, or emotionally—can of course target anyone. That said, for victims of IPV, cyberstalking is an unfortunate unintended consequence of the development of new technologies, including cell phones, GPS devices, and spying tools. For example, the National Center for the Victims of Crime, an agency that measures and tracks stalking rates, reports that not only are electronic devices used to stalk, but entire websites are devoted to providing programs that make the stalking undetectable to the victims. There is also software that an abuser can install on a victim's phone or computer that

continues

BOX 14.2	**IPV IN THE DIGITAL AGE** *continued*

captures every keystroke and sends the information to the abuser. This allows the abuser to see who the victim is talking to (via text or email) and whether she is seeking help or even googling websites that offer tools for victims. Another website allows the abuser to run his cell phone through a program that changes the number display on calls to the victim's phone. Even when the victim has blocked calls from the abuser's phone, with the scrambling device he can disguise his number to appear on her cell phone as an incoming call from "Mom" or one of her close friends (Hoopes 2014). Thinking it is her mom or a friend, she will likely answer and he can then continue to terrorize her. These are just a few examples from the world of sophisticated technologies that are being used to perpetuate violence against women. In December 2015, in recognition of the evolving nature of what constitutes "abuse" in a digital world, England and Wales passed the Serious Crime Act 2015, which expands the definition of *domestic abuse* to cover cases involving psychological and emotional torment via social media or online stalking. This is but one example of how criminal justice systems globally are contending with advances in technology.

Source: Online source of UK legislation, www.legislation.gov.uk/ukpga/2015/9//76/enacted.

Isolation: Married in Thirty Days at His House

In Browne's study of abused women (1989), she found that over time, many abusers **isolate** their partners from family and friends, and this had several negative outcomes for the women. For example, many abusers prohibited their wives and girlfriends from working and required them to stay at home, usually literally in the house, all day long. This resulted in complete economic dependence on the abuser, it eliminated any chance for the women to amass the financial resources necessary to leave, and, perhaps most important, it severely impacted the social networks of the women (see Chapter 9 for a lengthy discussion of this point). In many cases, battered women were cut off from all family and friends. This served to keep the battering a secret, and it significantly decreased opportunities for the women to escape, as they had no friends or family who knew where they were or who could pick them up and help them to leave the relationship.

As we noted in the discussion of intrusion, one might wonder, what person would put up with being isolated from friends and family? Yet like the patterns of intrusion, isolation begins slowly, it is similar to common notions of romance, and for many abused women who are leaving abusive family environments, like Debbie and Candy, who were profiled in Chapter 8, this isolation from family may seem desirable at first.

Most women will remark that when a girlfriend starts dating a new man, she disappears. It is not uncommon in new relationships for the couple to isolate themselves almost 100 percent from others. Going out with friends is quickly replaced by private, intimate, one-on-one dates. In our culture, this seems normal, just part of the "getting to know you" period in new relationships.

In healthy relationships, as the couple gets to know each other better, a pattern emerges of mixing intimate one-on-one dates and group dates or outings with friends and family. Most couples arrive at a mix that works for their relationship. In abusive relationships, however, what begins as a preference for one-on-one, intimate dates becomes an exclusivity of the relationship such that the couple rarely, if ever, socializes with others—friends or family—and the woman is typically prohibited from any socializing on her own with friends or family. In contrast, the man often continues to have "guys' nights out" with his friends and perhaps his family.

In extreme cases, as discussed in Chapter 9 as well as in Browne's book (1989), women report that they are prohibited from working and are required—through various mechanisms, such as making random phone calls that must be answered on the first ring, nailing windows shut, locking doors from the outside, covering the windows with tinfoil—to stay inside the house and see no one while their partner is away from home: at work, running errands, even socializing or on outings with other women.

Furthermore, in the case of many abused women, this isolation began early and was supplemented by forced commitments. Rose, an African American woman we interviewed in North Carolina, grew up in a terribly dysfunctional family. Her father was never in her life and her mother abandoned her and turned over custody of her to her own mother (Rose's grandmother) when she was just a young girl. When we asked her about her relationship with her mother, she indicated that she had not seen or talked to her in years and was not sure she would even recognize her.

Rose indicated that her grandmother was a good maternal figure, caring for her and nurturing her. But it is obvious that the scar of abandonment remains in Rose some forty-five years after her mother left (Rose was in her early fifties when we met her). When she turned eighteen, she moved away to attend college. She met her husband on a blind date, and things progressed quickly, based on his wishes, not Rose's:

He was just nice. I guess I should have realized he was too possessive or something then. We hardly knew each other. He always thought I should be in my dorm. He was in the army and he came home on weekends, and I would be gone. He would act like that's okay if I wasn't there and stuff like that. Once we got married, that changed. Then I had to be in a room or in the house all the time.

(**Rose,** fiftysomething African American woman, North Carolina)

Within a month or so of their first date, Rose was married. She skipped over this part so quickly that at one point in the interview, we asked her to return to this major event in her life. She spoke candidly, saying that her husband never asked her to marry him. In order to keep her away from other men, whom he clearly identified as potential suitors, he began telling people that they were married.

We never even talked about getting married, really. I just know he was telling people that we were getting married. But he never asked me. I was only seeing just him. His cousins and friends and people were saying that they heard we were getting married. We never had a wedding or anything. The next thing I know . . . I don't even think of it as a real marriage. I don't even know what I was thinking. It was only his mother, his grandmother, and uncle. They were the witnesses. We were at their house. She preached and signed the papers, and that was it. We were married. [AH: Would you have wanted your grandmother to be there?] Oh, my gosh. They probably wouldn't want to come. They wouldn't have let it happen. I wish I would have told somebody. I don't have any family here.

(**Rose,** fiftysomething African American woman, North Carolina)

This wedding seemed quite unusual to us. The more and more Rose talked about it, the more it became clear that Rose's husband used marriage as a way to both isolate Rose and possess her.

We do not interpret Rose's experience as unique; we heard other similar stories in interviews with other women. As we noted in Chapter 9, in some cases, abused women on the run moved in with men they hardly knew in order to avoid being homeless. They understood this as an *economic* decision or exchange. And although these stories have more to do with economic dependency than intentional isolation, the result is often isolation that is as severe as the type of isolation Rose's husband intended to, and ultimately did, create.

We return to a discussion of Andi, whose story we detailed in Chapter 8. Andi moved from Chicago to Minnesota within twenty-four hours of meeting a man outside of the homeless shelter. She and this man shared a bedroom and soon became sexually involved. In a short time, the relationship became emotionally, verbally, and physically abusive. Andi found herself isolated, by her choice and her actions, from any family or friends who could have come to her aid. She was literally five hundred miles from family or friends who could have helped her.

Why do women choose to enter into committed relationships, in some cases even marriages, so quickly? The answer lies, we believe, in two places: living on the economic margins and fleeing abuse or neglect in their families. In the case of Debbie, whose story we also profiled in Chapter 8, she married her husband to escape the abuse she experienced at the hands of her father. In the case of Andi, she moved across state lines with a man she did not know because she was living on the economic margins. Fleeing a toxic environment, facing homelessness in a huge urban area, and faced with what she perceived as very limited choices, she made a dangerous choice.

Possession: "You Belong to Me"

Another early warning sign is a behavior Browne terms **possession**. For Browne (1989), *possession* describes the sense of ownership that many abusers exhibit toward their partners.

Since the founding of this country, the crux of gender relations has been men's ownership of women. This is codified in both legal and religious codes. Violence toward women dates back centuries. "Throughout Euro-American history, wife beating enjoyed legal status as an accepted institution in western society" (Weitzman 2001: 41).[2] When John Adams was attending the Continental Congress in 1776, his wife, Abigail, wrote him a letter that would become famous, addressed to her "Dearest Friend": "In the new code of laws, I desire you would remember the ladies and be more favorable than your ancestors. Do not put such unlimited power into the hands of husbands" (quoted in Crompton and Kessner 2004). But John Adams and other well-meaning men were no more able to free women than they were the people they enslaved. When the founders of our country signed the Declaration of Independence, their own wives were still, in every legal sense, *their* property. Upon marriage, a woman forfeited the few rights she had—the legal term for this is **coverture**, as in the man's rights "cover" his wife's—and her husband owned her just as he owned his horse. Another example that illustrates the point: if a woman was raped, it was considered a property crime, not a personal crime. A typical punishment involved the rapist being indentured to the woman's husband, if she was married, or forced to marry her if she was single. The rationale behind this "punishment" was that a woman's virginity was essential to her marriageability;

without her virginity intact, her father had no hope of marrying her off and would be saddled with providing and caring for her for the rest of his life. Thus, a marriage, even to a rapist, solved the marriageability problem that the father of a rape victim faced. Of course, today, many citizens of postindustrial societies would find this practice abhorrent, though we note here that this does continue to happen in many rural and industrializing societies in Africa and the Middle East (Kristoff and WuDunn 2009).

Yet even today, men's ownership of women is still ritualized in a traditional American wedding: the father of the bride walks the bride down the aisle and "gives her away." This ritual symbolizes the transfer of the woman from the ownership of her father to the ownership of her husband. Based on the belief that men own their partners, if a woman engages in any interaction with another man (it need not be sexual), her husband or partner may interpret it as a threat. Just as we are justified in shooting a prowler who attempts to enter our homes, some men feel justified in reacting violently if they think another man is about to "steal" his woman. It is interesting to note here that most often his rage is executed against his partner (the possession), not the other man (the intruder). This is much like someone setting their house on fire when a prowler approaches rather than shooting the prowler to prevent his entry into the home. Perhaps when seen this way, we can better appreciate the preposterous—but common—notion that men hold that beating their partners is an acceptable and reasonable response to the fear that she will leave him for another man.

Browne's discussion of possession refers to something more, though. It also refers to the belief that when you own something, you can use it at your own discretion. This applies, according to Browne (1989), particularly to sexuality. The abused women in Browne's study recalled many experiences in which they felt that their partners tried to "possess" them sexually.[3] As noted by scholars such as Browne (1989) and Lawless (2001), this is a polite way of saying that abused women reported being raped by their partners. You will recall Debbie's story of marital rape and sexual abuse, which we reported in Chapter 8.

The issue of marital (or partner) rape is contentious. One of the outcomes of the belief that men owned their wives that was clearly reflected in the US legal system was the **marital rape exemption** (definition on p. 288). Essentially, this exemption made it legal for men to rape their wives; husbands were legally exempt from claims of rape made against them by their wives. These exemptions were part of the legal code well up into the 1990s, when the last remaining states finally dropped them (Garcia and McManimon 2010). Though the marital rape exemptions are now gone from the legal code in all fifty states, their sentiment often persists. In reality, rape is a very difficult crime to prosecute, especially when the victim and the offender know each other. It is nearly impossible if the victim has had consensual sex with the man she is accusing (see especially Hattery and Kane 1995). Furthermore, decades of informal observation of high-profile rape trials reveal that rape charges are generally difficult to prove if a victim has been sexually active (she is not a virgin) and especially if she has sex with another man in the same time frame as the alleged rape, either with her husband or with someone else. For example, recall the highly publicized rape trial of Kobe Bryant. The defense argued that the victim could not have possibly been raped because another man's semen—belonging to her boyfriend at the time—was collected as evidence along with Bryant's; she was cast as a "whore" because she had sex with another man within twenty-four hours of (though, we note, prior to) the alleged rape. The same defense was part of the Duke lacrosse rape case. As our research and that of others documents, if a woman has consented to sex with the perpetrator at any time or anyone else recently, a rape conviction is incredibly difficult to obtain. It is clear that it will take much more time before women in our society will be able to successfully charge their intimate partners with rape (Garcia and McManimon 2010).

In addition to directly articulating rape within their partnerships, many more women reported that they had sex when they did not want to or participated in sexual acts that they did not want to in order to please their husbands and avoid further violence.

Many abused women recount instances of feeling as if they are possessions, that their partners treat them as such. An example from the made-for-TV movie *The Burning Bed*, based on the real-life story of Francine Hughes, illustrates this point. The abused woman in the film, Fran, portrayed by Farrah Fawcett, is on the stand at her trial for murdering her abusive husband, Mickey. She is asked to describe the night of the murder. She recounts a night filled with violence, when she is beaten severely and then raped. As she is describing the rape she notes, "It was like he wanted to possess me." Browne (1989) also notes that rape in abusive relationships can be experienced as attempts to possess a woman by possessing her body. Interestingly, Browne also notes that women who are raped, possessed, in their relationships, are *more likely to leave or kill their partners than women who are not raped*. The stories we heard from abused women confirm this. Many women reported that when rape became a regular part of their experiences with their intimate partners, it was like the proverbial straw that broke the camel's back: they knew they had to leave.

Other Forms of Possession: Molding Her

Browne (1989) focuses primarily on sexual possession in abusive relationships. However, we interviewed many women (and men) who talked of other kinds of possession and controlling behavior. In the context of these relationships, men described shaping their partners *to be the way that they wanted them to be*. For their part, the women acquiesced, at least temporarily, until they realized that the acquiescence was dangerous for them. Though we heard this story repeatedly, perhaps the most dramatic example came from Will and Stella, whom we interviewed in Minnesota:

When I met her, I had to mold her into the ways, into the things that I like. Okay, like with the cooking and stuff. Now she can, boy, she can put some dishes together now. I had to show her, look, this is where I like to eat, this is how I like, you know, how I like my pants folded. She used to doing laundry and would pop them out like this, instead of putting the seams together. She'd just pop them and then fold 'em like that. I'd grab them, I'm like, wait a minute. You got to fold my pants like this.

(Will, fiftysomething African American man, Minnesota)

JEALOUSY AND SEXUAL INFIDELITY

Jealousy, a signal of an actual or perceived violation of the sexual or erotic property exchange, was a similarly common and a particularly threatening aspect in the relationships we studied. This finding reinforces Browne's work (1989). Virtually every man we interviewed suspected his partner of infidelity, yet less than 20 percent of the women we interviewed admitted to having an affair. In fact, though it was the men who expressed extreme jealousy, they were often the ones who were actually engaged in infidelity, and most often the woman was aware of the flings with "girlfriends" or with prostitutes.

How can we understand this double standard?[4] This is precisely the kind of question that an intersectional approach helps to explain. If we consider Kimmel's (2005) work on masculinity, Browne's (1989) work on jealousy and the need to control one's partner sexually, and Engels's (1884) and Collins's (1992) discussion of erotic property, a clearer picture of the role of infidelity in IPV emerges. First, let us consider Kimmel (2005). A primary component of a masculine identity is sexual prowess, and one way in which to establish this is to be a "player"—to have sexual relationships with many women at the same time. Thus, we can interpret the behavior of men who are engaging in sexual infidelity as simply seeking to establish their identities as "real men." Though their partners may not like this behavior, many women seemed to be somewhat tolerant of it, and the reality of men's infidelity is absolutely taken for granted by many of the men we interviewed. One man we interviewed, Akim, who had had multiple affairs during his marriage, reflected that he had learned his attitude toward women from his older friends on the street:

And they always influenced—you know—I used to watch them. They got girls, girls, girls, girls. So I, I basically picked that up . . . and actually, what they were teaching me and showing me, and the, uh, examples that I was getting from them, it was not right, but it was real, you know what I mean? Yeah.

(**Akim,** fiftysomething African American man, North Carolina)

The majority of the women we interviewed knew their partners were involved with other women. In the case of Betty, Akim's wife, she knew that he was involved in a long-term relationship with another woman.

Though men do not expect their partners to be jealous of their interactions with other women, Browne (1989) notes that jealousy is extremely common and severe among men who perpetrate IPV, and that it begins early in the relationship. Abusers are extremely jealous of *any interaction* between their partner and any other man. Abusers are jealous when their partners flirt, but they are also jealous when it is other men doing the flirting. As Josie's case illustrates (see Chapter 9), abusers are even jealous of any platonic or working relationship their partners have with other men. This extreme jealousy, even when it is unfounded, is often a trigger for violence.

MALE PERSPECTIVE ON CHEATING

Many abusers define their "outside" relationships differently than they define the relationships they suspect their wives or girlfriends of having. Typical of abusers, Hank was jealous of his girlfriend and used this unsubstantiated jealousy as a justification for emotional and physical abuse. Hank's girlfriend was in jail when we interviewed him, and when we asked Hank if he was being faithful to his girlfriend while she was serving a seven-month sentence for parole violation, he smiled and said he had some action going on the side. Here is how he put it: "I gotta get my thing thing on, you know."

When we pressed him, forcing him to deal with this apparent inconsistency, that he was admitting to cheating yet at the same time he would not tolerate any suggestion of the same by his girlfriend, he clarified things for us:

Oh, while she in prison. Nah, nah, she know about it, you see. It ain't cheating when she know about it. Hey, go ahead and do what you got to do baby, just as long as you . . . send me some money and you don't leave me.

(**Hank,** fortysomething African American man, Minnesota)

WOMEN'S EXPERIENCES WITH JEALOUSY

Most of the women we interviewed reported that they were accused by their partners of having "outside" relationships. The frequency of these accusations varied from infrequent to daily. Many women reported that their partners rifled through their pocketbooks or cell phone directories. More than one woman told of her partner engaging in extreme behavior in order to be sure she was being faithful to him. Women we interviewed reported that their partners conducted inspections of their bedsheets and smelled their panties in order to satisfy themselves that their women were being faithful as well as to send the message that if they detected any evidence of the presence of another sexual partner, they would respond violently.

Employing the concept of **erotic property** (Collins 1992; Engels 1884) helps us to unlock the power of jealousy. While establishing one's sexual prowess is critical to establishing a masculine identity, this is not the case for women. In fact, women exchange access to their sexuality for the financial support and protection of the men they partner with and marry. Further, this exchange is exclusive. Thus, a woman who is unfaithful is committing perhaps the greatest violation of the sexual contract. Under this contract, men have a right to control the sexual lives of their partners *because the women have become their erotic or sexual property*. Furthermore, when a woman commits an act of infidelity, this is perceived as an act of stealing on the part of the other man involved, aided and abetted by the woman. When women are viewed as property, they can be owned by only one man at a time. Thus, infidelity is akin to other property violations. Just as we uphold the right to defend our property, violence—at least against one's partner—is endorsed as a "reasonable" reaction to a woman's infidelity.

Infidelity is threatening on another level as well, as it suggests that a man is unable to keep his partner satisfied. This double threat to masculinity makes infidelity a potent act and one that can, and perhaps should, at least in the view of many men, be avenged by violence. The fact that in our culture we "understand" when men go into a violent rage and either beat their partners or assault the "other" men—we as a culture term these acts "crimes of passion"—further indicates the potency of this violation: a violation of the sexual contract is a direct threat to masculine identity.

Like the other early warning signs identified by Browne (1989), jealousy is common in the early stages of intimate relationships. Before a couple makes a commitment to each other, each individual often has anxiety about the level of commitment and exclusivity of the relationship. Jealousy often signals the insecurities typical of early relationships. Over time, however, in healthy relationships, as commitments are solidified and the level of trust increases, jealousy decreases. In contrast, in violent relationships, jealousy becomes more intense and more frequent as time goes on. And, as noted both here and in Chapter 10, jealousy often becomes the trigger for violent outbursts.

PRONE TO ANGER: OTHER ASSAULTS AND PRIOR RECORDS

Many scholars who study IPV report that batterers are often **serial abusers**, moving from one relationship to another and abusing each of their partners along the way.[5] As a result, abused women often report that at some point they learned about their husband's or boyfriend's previous wives and girlfriends and the violence they experienced. Browne (1989) noted that the women she interviewed reported that they did not have any knowledge of the violence that plagued their partner's past, though in many cases the men did have previous experiences, and in some cases even criminal records, for interpersonal violence, such as fighting and assault, an early warning sign she refers to as **prone to anger**.

Many of the men we interviewed had a history of violence, and nearly all— 90 percent—of the African American men we interviewed had served time in prison, mostly for violent offenses or drugs. Certainly, this time in jail and prison added to these men's experiences with violence, even if their sentences were for drugs or property crimes like breaking and entering. You may recall that Eddie is a professional boxer who killed someone with a punch in the ring just months before we interviewed him.

Cindy's story illustrates this particularly well. Cindy's abusive partner—whose violence she had escaped by entering the shelter—was the younger brother of her first love, her true love. Her first relationship, which began during her teen years, was with a man somewhat older than she, named Sam. They were involved for a few years and early on had a child together. Sam was abusive toward Cindy; he beat her several times, including hitting her with a closed fist in the face when she was a teenager and pregnant with their child.

Sam went to prison for dealing drugs, but Cindy kept in touch with him while he was locked up.[6] One day Sam called Cindy and told her that his mother had died. He asked Cindy to pick up his younger brother, Leon, and take him to the funeral. Cindy agreed. She picked up Leon and took him to the funeral, and they were "hanging out" by the end of the day. She and Leon began what would be a long-term, on-and-off, violent relationship. Soon after she and Leon moved in together, Cindy went to visit Sam in jail. She told him that she was dating one of his brothers. He asked if she was seeing this one and that one, and she repeatedly responded "no" to each inquiry. Finally, Sam said, "You're not seeing Leon, are you? He's got a lot of problems, including being violent!" She admitted that she was, in fact, involved with Leon.

In her interview, ten years after this discussion with her ex-boyfriend, Leon's brother Sam, and six children later, she admits that she should have listened to Sam's warning. She chose to ignore it and lived a decade with this terribly abusive man.

Furthermore, knowledge of his previous violent relationships could and should have been an early warning sign for Cindy. She recalled that when she left Leon the first time and entered a shelter in another town, the social worker asked her who the man was who had beaten her so badly and cut her face with a knife. When she said it was Leon, the woman showed her a long scar on her own cheek and said that many years earlier he had done the same to her, and she was indeed one of his past partners.

I can't explain I let him do it, you know what I'm sayin', 'cause I thought he was in love with me but society ain't got shit to do wit it, you know what I'm sayin', I can't even blame it on, 'cause his mama used to beat his daddy, [daddy] used to beat his mama. He ain't no mama's boy, he mean, he too mean to be a mama's boy. I ain't the first woman that he hit. I might not be the first one that he raped, you know what I'm sayin'. . . . He ain't go rape me no more, you best believe that shit, 'cause I was in the counselor's and like, I wrote my kids' name down, this lady—very educated, pretty woman, got a big ol' scar right there—she was doing financial at one of the shelters I was at before, financial care, and she looked at me, she seen my kids' name [touches the scar on her cheek], she said Leon Allen did this.

(**Cindy,** thirtysomething African American woman, North Carolina)

UNKNOWN PASTS: "I MOVED IN WITH HIM THE NEXT DAY/ MARRIED IN THIRTY DAYS"

Finally, Browne (1989) notes that among the abused women she interviewed, this lack of information regarding their partners' previous experiences with violence extended to other aspects of their lives, the warning sign she refers to as **unknown pasts**. The truth was that most abused women knew almost nothing about the past experiences of the men they partnered with.

Browne argues that this is typical of violent relationships and is difficult to detect because it is masked as romance. Abused women reported (Browne 1989; Lawless 2001) that early on in their relationships with their abusers, the men were focused on learning about them, they paid them a great deal of attention, they wanted to hear about their lives and pasts and hopes and dreams, and that at the same time they revealed very little about themselves. Many of the women interviewed by both Browne and Lawless noted that while growing up, no one had paid them this kind of attention. They were not used to being the center of attention, to being listened to. Therefore, when these men made them the center of attention and listened attentively, they did not notice that the men said very little about their own past experiences.

This sort of imbalance in information sharing has many important outcomes for the individuals involved. One outcome is that the women experience an unrealistic sense of emotional intimacy with their partners. They have shared a great deal about themselves and feel close to their partners, without recognizing the imbalance in emotional sharing. Thus, they make what appear to outsiders to be very unwise decisions that, in fact, feel very natural to them. The level of intimacy created in this new relationship may be greater than she has experienced in *any* relationship before, and thus she inaccurately assesses how much she can trust this new partner.

"WE WERE MADE FOR EACH OTHER"

We conclude the discussion in this chapter by focusing on one of the key factors that inhibits abused women from leaving their abusive partners: the notion that they belong together. Most people who have never been in an abusive relationship wonder why women who are abused by their partners would stay. Most women will remark that if they were struck even one time, they would leave.

We have not focused on why abused women stay; rather, we have attempted to tell their stories and analyze them using a more complex framework than the simple "why doesn't she just leave?" perspective that is so common.[7] Yet throughout these chapters, we have tackled issues regarding staying and leaving and mostly come to the conclusion that abused women stay for many reasons—because in the balance they will lose more if they leave or because their experiences of child abuse leave them literally impaired in their ability to respond to the violence they experience as adults. But most often, when asked why they didn't leave, abused women responded that they stay because they love him. They do not like what he does or the way he behaves, but they love him.

Acknowledging the fact that most women stay with abusive partners and understanding the reasons they do is important for advocates and agencies that work with individuals and families experiencing IPV. As we have noted in several previous chapters, women will not be able to successfully leave abusive relationships unless and until they have the resources and support to do so. As we will address in the final chapter, women need access to living-wage jobs, affordable housing, and affordable child care.

Most importantly, they need access to safety: during the first eighteen months after an abused woman leaves, she is at the highest risk for IPV homicide.

Seldom have we read accounts of the reasons *abusers* stay. Perhaps the question seems less relevant in light of the fact that most abusive men work so hard to control their partners and literally "possess them." Interestingly, no one ever seems to consider the possibility that it might be healthier for the abuser—as well as his victim—to exit the relationship. However, when one talks at length with many abusive men outside of a treatment environment, as we have done, one learns that many abusers not only rationalize their violence as a reasonable response to the behavior of their wives and girlfriends but also further rationalize the violence as a way of expressing love and concern for their partners. This is similar to the way in which some parents who physically abuse their children rationalize the abuse by indicating that "it was for their own good" or that they needed to "be taught a lesson."

Hank, whom we mentioned earlier in the discussion of infidelity, described to us a common situation: he would return home from a long day at work—he worked as a security guard—and the house would be a mess, and there would be no dinner ready. His girlfriend would begin nagging him about something, and he would explode. He would call her a "motherfucking lazy bitch." She would attempt to run out of the house and he would grab her and beat her to keep her from leaving.

Right, I got a fifth-degree assault with her . . . I get mad at her. And then I cuss at her. I call her out a name . . . But I, she provokes me, for me to put my hands on her. Now say, for instance, I want to walk out that door. She'll run in front of that door and tell me I ain't going nowhere. Get the hell out of the house, get away from her for a little bit 'cause I'm steamed, I'm mad. She done pissed me off. I'm mad. I want to walk out that door. She stand in front of the door and won't let me out. I try to move her. Pulling her, get away from the door. She holding the door, no, no. So I have to put hands on her to try to move her. She won't move, so I don't just hit her or anything, I try to get her out of the way. I try to . . . look, let me out. And she, that's a provocation to me. She throw things at me. She just pick up shit and she'll just throw it at me.

(**Hank,** fortysomething African American man, Minnesota)

After listening to Hank for more than an hour, we kept thinking, why would you stay with someone who annoys you so much? So we asked Hank, "Why do you stay with her?" He responded immediately:

I love the hell out of her. And it got to be love because we separated one time, and it just fucking hurts like hell. And like, somebody reached into my heart and just tried pulling it out. But I got over it. I moved on. I had another girl. Then all of sudden, she want to come back in my life. She's doing bad now. She can't get these kids together. You [his first love] was the only one who knew how to keep my life together.

(**Hank**, fortysomething African American man, Minnesota)

Many women also stay because the men they are with are good to their children. In many ways, what this means is that women are putting the needs of their children above their own needs.

No. I pay everything. I pay . . . and I even said that out loud in front of him. I said, I said it to one of my friends. I said, why should he leave? He doesn't contribute anything to the house. I said I pay the rent. I pay the rent. I pay the utilities. He drives my car. I put the gas in. I pay everything for the kids. I do the cooking and cleaning. Why should he leave? He's got it made. You know. And it's sad that I can realize that and I know I'm being used, but I just can't take that final step, and I think it's because the kids. They love him so much, but it's even gotten to the point where they'll say, Dad's not here again. He's out with his friends. Or, why can't Dad do something with us? You know.

(**Stella**, thirtysomething white woman, Minnesota)

And yet, when women do stay, if their children are harmed by the abuser, they often find themselves being blamed by law enforcement officials and social workers. This is especially true for African American women (Roberts 1997).

Equally powerful and intimately connected is the fact that in many cases, the man she is with, the man who beats her, saved her from violence in a previous relationship. But the most powerful cause of staying together, especially on the part of the abuser, seems to be the sense that "they were destined to be together."

We would argue that this sense of **destiny** is derived from the notion of possession. These men seek to literally possess their wives and girlfriends, to own them, to control them, to treat them as they wish, and they are completely unable to imagine that these women would ever leave them. Furthermore, many studies of women who are *killed* by their abusive partners note that the riskiest time for being murdered is at the time of separation (Browne 1989). Thus, the notion of possession woven together with the concept of "destiny" is an extraordinarily dangerous combination for abused women.

The notion of destiny is not limited, however, to abusers. Many, if not most, of the abused women we and others (Browne 1989) have interviewed speak in similar terms. Over and over we talked with women in the shelter, or in their apartments out on their own, and we always concluded the interview by asking them what would happen next. While some women reported that they were with new men because they needed a place to stay and others indicated that they were already or would soon be looking for a new man, *the majority admitted that they would probably end up back with the same men they had struggled to escape.*

CONCLUSIONS

IPV often seems to sneak up on its victims. Many abused women report that they did not see it coming. Browne's (1989) groundbreaking work on women who killed their abusive partners illustrates that while the women might not have seen it coming, there are distinct patterns in potentially violent relationships that essentially can be understood as early warning signs. The problem is that the romantic landscape of the United States, which is heavily influenced by the media—especially romance novels and movies—serves to mask the early warning signs. A great deal of attention focused on the woman, private dates, talking about her all the time, wanting to be with her all the time, and jealousy are all within the typical script of romantic behavior in new relationships. In most healthy relationships, as the relationship becomes more committed and trust is built, these patterns decline and are replaced by other patterns. Couples spend more time apart and integrate, as a couple, into their personal social networks. In violent relationships, these patterns escalate rather than diminish, and typically this escalation coincides with the onset of violence; thus, women feel caught off-guard.

We certainly do not advocate for removing romance from courtship. However, given the importance of these early warning signs in violent relationships, women ought to be aware of these patterns and learn to take a more critical look at the behavior of new boyfriends.

We close this chapter with a discussion of obsession. Being obsessed with another person to the point of wanting to possess them is typical of both men who are abusive and the women they abuse. This obsession inhibits leaving on the part of abused women and sometimes leads to murder on the part of the men. In order to reduce IPV, men must be taught that women are not their possessions to do with what they wish.

But more important—albeit more difficult to achieve—is to address the system of patriarchy that allows men to literally possess or own their partners. Any system of ownership, including slavery, capitalism, and patriarchy, that allows one class of human beings to possess another class of human beings is critical to the establishment and reinforcing of inequality regimes (Acker 2006) that will inevitably lead to and depend upon violence as a means of keeping the inequality regime intact. In this context, all forms of violence against women—including sexual harassment, rape, and IPV—must be understood as rooted not only in patriarchy but also, more significantly, in that aspect of patriarchy that defines women as the possessions of their partners. Violence is a tool that men in a patriarchal society utilize to remind women of their status as possessions, much like violence against enslaved bodies and, later, the lynching of freed African Americans was a tool whites used to remind African Americans of their status in a country ruled by a system of racial domination. When understood this way, one recommendation for reducing IPV is clearly the dismantling of all systems of domination, including patriarchy.

In Chapter 16 we will summarize the tenets and data presented in this book, and we will make policy recommendations for intervention, reduction, and prevention of IPV and the factors that contribute to its development and persistence. That said, here we suggest some practical prevention strategies that could be implemented before the system of patriarchy is fully dismantled; the wait for that to happen is a long one, and there is no reason not to develop and implement prevention strategies immediately.

The majority of public schools continue to require health education classes beginning in elementary school and continuing through the first year or two of high school. In addition to discussing health and nutrition, these courses often involve age-appropriate discussions of controversial topics, including drug use and sex education. Our primary recommendation is that age-appropriate modules or units on healthy relationships be developed and included in the health curriculum beginning in elementary school and continuing through the first years of high school. These units could be shaped around the early warning signs that Browne developed and we have expanded. As children grow older, clips from popular films, television shows, and music videos could be shown, analyzed, and discussed in order to highlight and illustrate notions of romance. Additionally, these discussions could conclude with students and teachers talking about how to interact in ways that will produce healthy rather than violent relationships. This has been tried in many communities, including by the staff at the battered women's shelter in Lumberton, North Carolina, and it has been quite successful. We should also note, however, that the parents in the local Lumberton, North Carolina, high school have been incredibly resistant to this programming—many have refused to allow their interested teenagers to participate—and therefore we acknowledge that a great deal of persuasion and education would have to be done with parents, not to mention school boards and state departments of education, before this type of programming could be implemented widely.

RESOURCES

The National Center for the Victims of Crime: www.victimsofcrime.org.

Apted, Michael. 2002. *Enough*. (This film follows the main character, Slim, played by Jennifer Lopez, through the first meeting, courtship, and marriage to her abusive husband. Many of the early warnings signs are present.)

Greenwald, Robert. 1984. *The Burning Bed*. Tisch/Avnet Productions and NBC. (*The Burning Bed* is based on the true story of Francine Hughes, who killed her abusive partner after repeatedly seeking interventions from both the criminal justice system and the social welfare system. It is also an excellent example of the early warning signs.)

Ruben, Joseph. 1991. *Sleeping with the Enemy*. 20th Century Fox. (*Sleeping with the Enemy* details the plight of an upper-class battered woman and the obsessive nature of her abusive husband.)

NOTES

1. Interestingly, both we and Lisa Brush explored this concept independently without being aware of each other's work (Merton refers to this as *serendipity*). The fact that we each came upon this concept without knowledge of each other's work suggests even more strongly the importance of this reality in the lives of battered women.

2. For an excellent review of the history of legalized violence against women, see Garcia and McManimon 2010.

3. There are other examples of men "possessing" their partners. In many cases, women reported that they had to hand over their paychecks to men, they were treated as servants who had to do all of the household labor (cooking, cleaning, laundry, childcare), and they were treated like objects who existed merely for the enjoyment of their partners.

4. There is even evidence of the double standard in the language that we use to describe men who have multiple partners and women who do. Men are called "players," for example, whereas there are virtually no positive terms for women who have multiple partners. In contrast, there are virtually no negative terms for men who "sleep around," but the negative terms for women abound.

5. Incidentally, it is also true that many abused women move from one abusive relationship to another, never able to break the cycle.

6. Sam is still in prison serving another sentence for drugs.

7. A simple search on Amazon.com will produce, in a matter of seconds, a list of literally hundreds of books that offer women advice about how to leave abusive relationships. *Defending Our Lives: Getting Away from Domestic Violence and Staying Safe*, by Susan Murphy-Milano, is but one example.

REFERENCES

Acker, J. 2006. *Class Questions, Feminist Answers*. New York: Routledge.

Browne, A. 1989. *When Battered Women Kill*. New York: Free Press.

Collins, R. 1992. *Sociological Insight: An Introduction to Non-Obvious Sociology*. London: Oxford University Press.

Crompton, V., and E. Kessner. 2004. *Saving Beauty from the Beast: How to Protect Your Daughter from an Unhealthy Relationship*. New York: Little, Brown and Company.

Engels, F. [1884] 1972. *The Origin of the Family, Private Property, and the State*. Introduction by Eleanor Leacock. New York: International Publishers.

Garcia, V., and P. McManimon. 2010. *Gendered Justice: Intimate Partner Violence and the Criminal Justice System*. Lanham, MD: Rowman and Littlefield.

Hattery, A. J., and E. W. Kane. 1995. "Men's and Women's Perceptions of Non-Consensual Sexual Intercourse." *Sex Roles 33(11)*: 785–802.

Hoopes, Heidi. 2014. "Apps to Easily Encrypt Your Text Messaging and Mobile Calls." *Gizmag*, September 27. www.gizmag.com/secure-text-messaging-phone-clients-comparison-ios-and-android/34000.

Kennedy, Helen. 2009. "Oprah Winfrey Has a Warning for Rihanna: Chris Brown 'Will Hit You Again.'" *New York Daily News*, March 8. www.nydailynews.com/entertainment/gossip/oprah-winfrey-warning-rihanna-chris-brown-hit-article-1.367300.

Kimmel, M. 2005. *Manhood in America*. New York: Oxford University Press.

Kristoff, N., and S. WuDunn. 2009. *Half the Sky: Turning Oppression into Opportunity for Women Worldwide*. New York: Alfred A. Knopf.

Lawless, E. J. 2001. *Women Escaping Violence: Empowerment Through Narrative*. Columbia, MO: University of Missouri Press.

Roberts, Dorothy E. 1997. *Killing the Black Body*. New York: Random House.

Weitzman, S. 2001. *Not to People Like Us: Hidden Abuse in Upscale Marriages*. New York: Basic Books.

15

THE RESPONSE TO FAMILY VIOLENCE

The Criminal Justice System and the Social Welfare System

OBJECTIVES

- To describe the various institutional responses to family violence
- To detail the role that health-care providers—emergency room staff, pediatricians, family physicians—play in responding to family violence
- To detail the role that shelters and other social service agencies play in responding to family violence
- To detail the role that intervention programs play in responding to family violence
- To examine the ways in which the criminal justice system responds to family violence
- To examine the ways in which the criminal justice system may increase the probability of intimate partner violence (IPV)
- To provide policy recommendations to improve our institutional response to family violence

KEY TERMS

health care	criminal justice system
domestic violence shelters	mandatory arrest laws
intervention programs	protective order
feminist models	guardian ad litem (GAL)
family systems models	domestic violence courts
psychological approaches	restorative justice

INTRODUCTION

This chapter will be devoted to an examination of institutional responses to individuals and families who are experiencing family violence. We will examine responses to both the victims and the perpetrators. As we have detailed throughout the book, one of the major issues with regard to family violence is the lack of reporting and the overall lack of attention that is paid to episodes of family violence. Most research indicates that only a fraction of family violence comes to the attention of anyone outside of the family. Furthermore, when family violence does come to the attention of outsiders, most often these outsiders are treating the *symptoms* of family violence—setting broken bones in the emergency room, giving food stamps to a woman fleeing her abusive partner, providing a change of clothes for a child who comes to school disheveled—rather than the causes. Even less often is the criminal justice system involved in a way that holds the perpetrators of violence accountable. Thus, though we will of course examine the response of the criminal justice system, this chapter will focus on the response of the health-care system, shelters, and intervention programs as well. With regard to the criminal justice system specifically, we will focus on two points of intersection between the criminal justice system and family violence: responses of the criminal justice system to family violence and the role that incarceration plays in increasing the probability for IPV. We will conclude the chapter by providing policy recommendations for dealing more effectively with all forms of family violence, and specifically the ways that service providers who regularly interface with victims—emergency room staff, school teachers, social workers—can provide better referrals to victims so that the patterns of violence themselves, not just the symptoms of the violence or abuse, are addressed.

INSTITUTIONAL RESPONSES TO FAMILY VIOLENCE

As we have seen throughout this book, when family violence occurs there are, or can be, a variety of institutional responses. The specific mission of the individual institution largely shapes institutional responses. It is important to recognize that different institutions play very different roles in addressing family violence, both because they have different missions and because their missions overlap in different ways when it comes to family violence. So, for example, medicine has as its express mission the treatment of family violence-related injury, but it may also play a significant role in detecting family violence, as we shall see below.

The Institution of Health Care

The primary mission of **health care**, as an institution, is the prevention and treatment of disease and injury. With regard to family violence, the role that health-care providers play in terms of prevention and treatment varies tremendously with the *type* of violence; for example, the prevention of child abuse and neglect is more central to the mission of health care *as an institution* than the prevention of other forms of family violence. Thus, parents with newborns are not only encouraged to bring their babies in for the age-appropriate checkups and vaccinations but often they are also offered information on age-appropriate parenting, they are asked by their pediatrician if they are having any trouble, and they may be enrolled in voluntary programs run by the local hospital or by social services agencies, such as Exchange/SCAN and Welcome Baby, that provide monthly newsletters with information and support as they navigate the challenges of parenting newborns and infants. One national program, Exchange/SCAN, the last four letters of which stand for Stop Child Abuse Now—which is present in many counties nationwide—offers a wide range of programs designed specifically to prevent child abuse and neglect. Exchange/SCAN programming is built on the assumption that a high proportion of child abuse and neglect is the result of parents and caregivers lacking accurate information regarding child development, lacking resources to meet the needs of their children, and feeling overwhelmed by the challenges of caring for young children. For example, in an attempt to prevent shaken baby syndrome, Exchange/SCAN disseminates a video to new parents on infant crying. The video, which tells the story of a baby who was shaken to death, focuses on the period that most infants go through that is characterized by higher-than-average rates of crying. The intent is to provide parents with information about these periods of crying—which typically occur between two and four months old—so that if their child's crying increases during this time, they will be less likely to be overwhelmed and will understand this is simply a normal developmental stage that will pass. Locally, Exchange/SCAN targets all mothers of newborns—they are contacted first while still patients in the local birthing center—and enrolls them in newsletter mailings, offers parenting classes and support groups, and arranges for home visits for at-risk families.

In some communities where rates of child abuse and neglect are of concern to local residents, nonprofit agencies have developed programs designed to prevent child abuse and neglect. Similar to Exchange/SCAN, the focus is typically on providing education to parents so that they will understand their child's developmental processes and parent in ways that reduce abuse and neglect and increase maximum development. The Arizona Children's Association (AzCA) is an example of just such a local agency. We feature one of Arizona Children's Association's most innovative tools: Brain Boxes.

Many of the programs like Exchange/SCAN and the Arizona Children's Association depend upon partnerships with local hospitals and clinics that provide maternity and pediatric care. Though most of the programs are developed by nonprofits, the medical community, especially pediatricians, has a vested interest in these otherwise unlikely partnerships based on both the concern that child abuse can lead to long-term and expensive health problems and the acknowledgment that parenting newborns and infants is difficult and that parents, especially new parents, need advice and help in navigating this role. In contrast, there is very little, if any, attention paid to preventing either IPV or elder abuse. Certainly, there are likely to be some programs targeting the prevention of elder abuse that might be disseminated when the adult child of an elderly parent attends checkups and appointments with the aging parent and in particular if the physician is involved in moving the elderly person into an institutional setting (for example, a long-term or Alzheimer's care facility). However, in all likelihood, the prevention information provided would focus on the types of elder abuse perpetrated by care providers and strangers rather than that perpetrated by family members themselves. When this attention on prevention does exist, it is distributed on an individual basis, as a response to concerns raised in an appointment, for example, rather than being disseminated systematically. Yet as we discussed in Chapter 6, caregiving for elderly parents and young children can be equally stressful, and the same types of abuse are likely to occur: physical abuse, emotional abuse, and in particular, neglect. This is no surprise given that the elderly often have needs that are similar to those of infants: they are unable to perform many self-care tasks, including toileting, bathing, and feeding. Thus, the risk for neglect is particularly high and similar to that faced by infants.

BOX 15.1	NEW DIRECTIONS INSTITUTE PARTNERS WITH ARIZONA CHILDREN'S ASSOCIATION

Arizona Children's Association Program: *Home Visitation with Brain Boxes*

The Bright Start program is a home visitation/family support service targeted toward at-risk families with children, birth to age five, that uses learning toys and books from a unique, patented product called Brain Boxes.

The Brain Box is a set of twelve aged and staged boxes with hands-on learning activities that promote healthy brain development. The Brain Boxes are used as tools to reinforce the basics of what anyone working with a young child, whether a parent, caregiver, teacher, or therapist, needs to know to help a child's brain develop in the healthiest way possible.

An AzCA master's-level clinician trains families in the early brain curriculum and provides in-home support and follow-up for families for a three- to twelve-month period, depending on the needs of individual families. In-home support focuses on helping families to implement the skills they have learned into their everyday routines.

continues

BOX 15.1	NEW DIRECTIONS INSTITUTE PARTNERS WITH ARIZONA CHILDREN'S ASSOCIATION *continued*

In addition to providing this interaction opportunity, in-home staff may provide additional support services that include anger management, conflict resolution, communication and negotiation skills, stress management, parenting skills, and problem-solving skills. Staff also provide information regarding infant and child development, home management, nutrition, job readiness training, housing search and location, and behavior management. In-home clinicians work with each family in the development of linkages with community resources to meet the family's needs, which may include a wide array of health services, child-care resources, respite, and domestic violence or substance abuse services. Clinicians in the program receive a minimum of one hour per week of individual supervision, as well as group supervision two to four hours per month.

Prevention programs like Bright Start represent an opportunity for AzCA to impact Arizona's youngest and most vulnerable citizens in a meaningful way. Putting a focus on the healthy development of infants and young children, as well as supporting the caregivers they rely on, positions AzCA as a leader in prevention efforts across the state of Arizona.

Source: Arizona Children's Association, www.arizonaschildren.org; New Directions Institute, www.newdirectionsinstitute.org/programs.htm.

This raises the question as to why there is very little systematic attention paid to caregiving for the elderly in contrast to that which is provided for the parents of newborns. Though we are unaware of any research focusing on this question, we can speculate that there are a variety of explanations:

- As a rule, the elderly are less likely to be viewed as being as overly needy as infants.
- In the elderly, decline may occur slowly, whereas infants are born highly needy.
- The elderly themselves may deny aspects of their decline and resist both care and advice for avoiding abuse and neglect.
- Caregiving may begin in small ways and increase over time for the elderly, whereas the reverse is true for newborns and infants, and thus the appropriate timing for information may be less clear.
- Those who provide care for the elderly may not be consistent: care might rotate among adult children or paid staff, and thus the physician may not see the same caregiver across visits.

- Though both the young and the old are devalued in our society, in this setting the elderly are likely even more devalued than newborns and infants.
- Because the variation in needs of the elderly is high relative to the needs of infants, which are more or less consistent across all healthy babies, it may be difficult or unproductive to create standard types of guides for elder care, especially if information that is not relevant in an individual situation leads to the discarding of the entire packet of information.

Finally, we note that there are *no* health-care programs that focus on preventing IPV. Though there is ample evidence that dating violence and stalking are experienced by teens—according to the Centers for Disease Control and Prevention (Centers for Disease Control 2017), 10 percent of boys and girls in high school reported experiencing *physical* dating violence—there is no systematic attempt to disseminate prevention information to *girls or boys* this age. We acknowledge that this is a very difficult topic to raise with a teenager, and certainly health-care providers may be reluctant to scare young people, yet we strongly assert that this is a critical opportunity lost. Perhaps it is not appropriate for a health-care provider to raise these issues with every patient, but we suggest two strategies for providing appropriate prevention information to teenagers and young adults: First, put literature on dating violence in exam rooms. Curious teens as well as those who may already be experiencing violence may pick up this kind of literature. And second, when teenagers and young adults seek a health-care provider in order to learn about or obtain contraceptives (for instance, to obtain a prescription for the birth control pill, have an IUD inserted, or receive Depo-Provera shots), or to seek help in terminating a pregnancy, the health-care provider can use this opening in order to provide information, even just a pamphlet, about dating violence.

Though some of our recommendations might initiate difficult conversations, they offer an opportunity to prevent (and detect) teen dating violence. Even just making information available has the potential to prevent or interrupt violence among young people and could ultimately change their lives forever. Additionally, some states have taken a "public service announcement" approach to reaching potential victims.

We also note that simply making information available in examination rooms has the potential to reach *adult* victims as well and to educate parents about the risks that their children face for dating violence. Proactive parents who pick up this information may have the courage they need to initiate conversations with their own children, and again, this may serve to prevent (and interrupt) dating violence in their own families (Figure 15.1).

Whereas health-care providers have fallen far short in terms of the prevention of family violence—with the powerful exception of efforts to prevent child abuse—they often play a significant role in detecting family violence when it occurs, specifically in the detection of both child abuse and elder abuse during the context of regular appointments. When children and older adults are seen regularly by the same health-care providers, symptoms of physical abuse and neglect may be detected; it is clearly more difficult to observe indicators of emotional, financial, or sexual abuse unless a particular complaint is made. Because neglect is often characterized by a slow decline, the key to detection is regular health-care visits, with the downside being that it may take several months, or even longer, to detect neglect. That said, health-care providers may be the best positioned of any institution to detect neglect in care and nutrition.

BOX 15.2	VIOLENCE PREVENTION

He always knows...

...where I am.

...who I'm with.

...what I'm doing.

◀ **Figure 15.1**
Poster from an
Anti-Stalking
Campaign in
New York City
in 2015.

Cell Phones... Computers... Cameras... Global Positioning Systems (GPS)
Today's technology gives stalkers even more tools to monitor, intimidate, and track victims. If you or someone you know is a victim of stalking, there is help. Please contact us.

Office for Victims of Crime
OVC
"Putting Victims First"

THE NATIONAL CENTER FOR
Victims of Crime
www.ncvc.org · 1-800-FYI-CALL

SPONSORED BY: U.S. DEPARTMENT OF JUSTICE ♦ OFFICE OF JUSTICE PROGRAMS ♦ OFFICE FOR VICTIMS OF CRIME

Source: Office for Victims of Crime.

For example, many women are annoyed by the requirement of being weighed every time they go to an appointment at the clinic, but this is one of the main ways that nutritional neglect can be detected among both children and the elderly.

Health-care providers may also be the best positioned to detect all types of physical abuse—to the elderly, children, and intimate partners—when the abuse is characterized by non-life-threatening but repeated violence. For example, health-care providers may detect things like burns, lashing, and their scars. The ways in which health-care providers treat this information are not only subjective but also vary by the qualities of the victim. As noted in Chapter 6, health-care providers are mandatory reporters of child abuse. Thus, if there are significant patterns of abuse or neglect, health-care providers may be the avenue to reporting the abuse to social workers. We underscore here the process of mandatory reporting. Mandatory reporting often involves first making a report to Child Protective Services, which may or may not result in criminal action being taken. In many, if not most, cases, CPS will identify social service and family court solutions—for example, a child may be removed from an abusive household and put into foster care without neglect charges being filed—rather than involving the criminal justice system. There are many advantages to keeping cases of neglect and mild abuse out of the criminal justice system, including shielding children from having to testify in court and avoiding incarcerating parents who may be (with proper education and mentoring) able to appropriately parent and whose incarceration and consequent removal from the family, along with their loss of wages and financial support, would be *more* detrimental to the child.

In contrast, the elderly and adults are not protected populations. Thus, when a health-care provider sees indications of abuse or neglect, they are under no obligation to report their concerns. Thus, the role that routine health-care providers play in detecting elder abuse and IPV is spotty and very much dependent on an individual provider's willingness to raise the issue with their patients. In fact, a recent study revealed that interventions in emergency rooms fall short more often than not:

> Among abused women who were identified in the emergency departments, a social worker was provided 45 percent of the time. In only 33 percent of cases did the providers determine whether the victim had a safe place to go, and only 25 percent of the victims were referred to domestic violence services.
>
> (Rhodes et al. 2011)

One of the challenges to creating mandatory reporting laws for women and the elderly is balancing patient privacy—the right of adults to control the access to their medical information—with the need to protect victims. It is a thorny issue; for example, we would never want to see mandatory reporting laws used by unsympathetic health-care providers to report a pregnancy (or an abortion) that a woman wants to keep confidential from her partner. Thus, it is a slippery slope to recommend broader-reaching mandatory reporting laws, but we do encourage the discussion of ways in which health-care providers can serve as a conduit for intervention. One compromise might be to require health-care providers to document suspected abuse and neglect in the patient's file—for example, documenting injuries, scars, visual signs of neglect—so that if and when the patient is ready to report the abuse to the authorities, they have a medical record that documents the severity, frequency, and history of the abuse.

It is also very important to note the ways in which both prevention and detection by health-care providers are significantly shaped by social class, race, and gender. All of these factors shape the likelihood of both prevention and detection, primarily by shaping the likelihood that an individual will receive routine health care and the likelihood that they will see the same provider each time, both of which are at the core of the successful prevention and detection of abuse and neglect. Obviously, the poor and those without health insurance are far less likely to receive routine health care. And, when they do seek medical care, they are significantly more likely to seek it from urgent care clinics and emergency rooms, thus decreasing the likelihood that they will see the same health-care provider more than once. Yet, as noted above, the detection of neglect and certain types of physical abuse—burns, lashes, scars—requires that the individual be seen repeatedly, over time, by the same health-care provider in order to rule out the injuries being the result of accidents, which is a common explanation abused women provide. Whereas "falling down the stairs" might be accepted the first time it is presented as the explanation for bruises or broken bones, if this excuse is presented multiple times to the same health-care provider, they are likely to be suspicious that either abuse is going on or the patient has some other condition that leads to frequent falls, such as Lou Gehrig's disease or the early stages of multiple sclerosis. Thus, although social class may not shape the likelihood of being a victim of neglect or abuse, it does shape the likelihood that it will be detected by health-care providers.

Like many phenomena in our culture, race and social class are highly correlated. Even after the passage of the landmark Affordable Care Act (Obamacare), which brought health-care options to millions of Americans, nonwhites, especially African Americans, Hispanics, and Native Americans, are less likely to have adequate health insurance or access to high-quality health care (see especially Hattery and Smith 2014). Individuals who are uninsured or underinsured continue to seek care in emergency rooms and urgent care clinics, and this care is sought only when the individuals have a significant or severe illness or injury. Even for those who have health insurance, if they are part of an underserved population or live in areas that are considered underserved, when they have regular visits with a health-care provider, the odds that they will see the same person consistently are low. As a result, nonwhite minorities, like the poor, are less likely to have access to either the prevention or the early detection that is potentially provided by health-care providers. Thus, neglect and abuse may become more severe before they are detected, and as a result they may be elevated to the criminal justice system rather than being handled through social service agencies and other noncriminal intervention strategies. As noted previously, finding social service and family court solutions to child neglect and mild cases of abuse is almost always preferable to incarceration, especially when seeking a solution in the criminal justice system would further escalate an already overly high rate of incarceration, as is the case with African American men. As with most other things in American life, the poor and nonwhite minorities have less access to the kinds of prevention and intervention strategies that may save lives, and when intervention does occur, it is more likely to be criminal rather than civil or social, which often creates more difficulty for the entire family.

Last, we note that although girls and women are more likely to be victims of all forms of family violence, the fact that men are far less likely to have regular visits to a health-care provider means that abuse and neglect among elderly men may be less likely to be detected until it has become severe. Thus, as with most aspects of life in the United States, our social location determines the role that the institution of health care can play in the prevention, detection, and intervention strategies that are presented to us.

Shelters

There are many important tools for interrupting IPV. Since at least the beginning of the 2000s, most communities have adopted a comprehensive approach to violence prevention and intervention. In many communities, this comprehensive approach involves a set of public and private (nonprofit) agencies that are woven together to address issues such as safety for victims, batterer intervention programs, support services in legal cases, and so on. We will highlight some agencies that we believe illustrate best practices in terms of the prevention of and intervention in IPV. The landscape has not always looked this way. In the very early years services were not coordinated, they were entirely voluntary, and they focused on what was considered at the time the most pressing need: safety for women and their children. Thus, the story begins with a discussion of shelters.

Domestic violence shelters (or what were once termed battered women's shelters) trace their history to the feminist consciousness-raising sessions of the early 1970s. As women, primarily in small, intimate support groups, began to disclose their own experiences with violence or those of their close family and friends, it became clear that there was a need for temporary shelter for women who lacked the assets to leave abusive relationships (MacKinnon 1991). As we discussed at length in Chapter 8, one of the biggest barriers to leaving that is faced by victims of IPV is the lack of resources that would facilitate an escape: namely, the money to rent a hotel room, finance travel out of town, and so forth. Thus, early on in the "shelter movement" (Garcia and Mcmanimon 2010; MacKinnon 1991), women began to open up their own homes to provide temporary shelter for women and their children who were attempting to escape abusive partners.

By the mid-1970s, with the vision of some very strong women as well as their financial backing and support, shelters began to pop up around the country, first in urban areas like New York and Chicago and much later in suburban and rural areas, where, unfortunately, they are still relatively rare. In fact, most people are surprised to learn that although there are 1,200 shelters nationwide for battered women, there are 3,600 shelters for abandoned animals. This reflects both a lack of financial support for abused women and victims of violence in general and a lack of understanding of the need that abused women and their children face. Most Americans grossly underestimate the level of IPV in their own communities and thus are not compelled to support the building and maintenance of shelters locally. This is particularly problematic in suburban areas, where myths about middle-class people—both the myth that they don't experience violence and the myth that they have the resources to escape violence—exacerbate this tendency to underestimate the need for shelters. The problem of underestimating the need for shelters or other temporary housing is even more underestimated in tight-knit rural communities, where everyone knows each other and violence tends to be more hidden, taking place behind closed doors out of the fear of being discovered and shunned (Hattery 2008).

Shelters fill a critical niche in the network of resources that many abused women and their children need in order to leave their abusive households successfully. In addition to providing a temporary place to live, shelters often provide opportunities for counseling for the women, as well as their children; help in navigating other social services, such as the complex system of social welfare; and help in navigating the family court system and the protection it can provide, including obtaining orders of protection and even filing separation and divorce papers. There is no doubt that many abused women would not have been able to successfully leave abusive relationships and establish independent lives for themselves and their children without a shelter.

That said, shelters are not able to meet all of the needs that abused women and their children face. In Chapter 13 we noted that victims of LGBTQ IPV often are unable to utilize any of the resources that shelters offer. For example, there are only a handful of shelters for boys and men who are victims, including gay men. Lesbian victims may find that they are not secure and safe in shelters because shelter staff are not always able to distinguish victims from lesbian perpetrators who may present themselves as victims. And, as we noted, there are currently no significant safe options for transgender victims. Additionally, one problem that all mothers face is the fact that shelters often restrict the presence of young men over the age of twelve, as they may be perceived as threatening to the other victims who reside in the shelter. As a result, mothers with teenage sons may find that they either are prohibited from using shelters or may have to make alternative arrangements for their young sons, who themselves may be victims of violence at the hands of their fathers or stepfathers. Last, there are often significant time limits that shelters impose on residents; typically, these range from thirty to ninety days, depending on both the shelter's mission and available resources. These restrictions are often based primarily on the fact that the shelter resources are stretched; each and every week they have to turn desperate women away. Thus, they limit shelter stays in order to accommodate as many women and children for *temporary* housing as they can. Some shelters employ a holistic approach that involves more than just temporary housing and includes counseling, employment training or educational support, and programming for children. In these shelters, the length of the stay is often dictated by the counseling and training goals more than the need to continuously turn over beds. Either way, shelters are a temporary stop in the journey to leaving abusive relationships. They fill a critical niche, but they are rarely a magic pill. Many abused women find that they turn to shelters more than once as they put their lives together and leave their abusive partners successfully.

We know that one of the most difficult transitions for women escaping IPV is the move into a permanent home. And the barriers to leaving are many, ranging from finding a new place to live to leaving their home safely, to raising the funds to put down a deposit and pay the first month's rent, to possibly transitioning children from one school to another. One barrier we don't often consider is the difficulty of actually moving. Meathead Movers seeks to address this barrier.

BOX 15.3	MEATHEAD MOVERS

One of the obstacles for women leaving abusive relationships is the literal move. Partnering with local domestic violence agencies, shelters, and law enforcement in Central California, Meathead Movers eliminates that barrier by moving victims of IPV free of charge.

Source: Meathead Movers, www.meatheadmovers.com.

Comprehensive Approaches

Many communities are employing comprehensive approaches to addressing intimate partner (and sexual) violence. We highlight a government program in our own community of Fairfax County, Virginia, that utilizes a comprehensive approach to violence prevention and intervention. We quote from their website:

> The Office for Women & Domestic and Sexual Violence Services offers compassionate and comprehensive state-accredited programs for women, men, teens and children who have been affected by domestic and sexual violence, stalking, and human trafficking. Our services include:
>
> - Counseling services (individual and group) for survivors of domestic and sexual violence.
> - Telephone hotline/helpline available 24 hours a day, 7 days a week to provide information and support.
> - Shelter and support services for individuals and families leaving violent situations.
> - Intervention services for abusers, including those referred by the courts for physical, emotional or verbal abuse and those who voluntarily seek services.
> - Community education about healthy relationships, effective communication skills, and how to recognize abusive behaviors.
> - Support Groups for Women, Men and Children
> - Women's Sexual Assault Survivors Group
> - Men's Support Group for adult survivors of childhood sexual abuse.
> - Women's Domestic Abuse Survivor Group. This support group is for adult women who are currently experiencing or have previously experienced domestic abuse.
> - Respect UR D8: Recognize and learn more about teen dating violence and abuse through classes at select high schools.
> - Supports the Fairfax County Commission for Women and works to promote the full equality of women and girls in Fairfax County.
>
> ("Office for Women & Domestic and Sexual
> Violence Services" 2016)

What is not apparent from their website, but what we know from our experience working with the OFWDSVS, is that many of the services they "provide" are actually not provided by their staff. Rather, they offer a coordinated response that connects victims to other agencies that provide the services they need. For example, a victim who comes in seeking support to leave an abusive relationship may be escorted to one of the local shelters that services victims of IPV. Similarly, an abusive spouse who is court-ordered to an intervention program will be referred to

OFWDSVS, which will connect him (or her) to one of several batterer intervention programs that meets his (or her) needs.

Both the OFWDSVS and the Fairfax County Domestic Violence Prevention, Policy and Coordinating Committee (DVPPCC) recognize the need to educate legislators and governing officials (in Fairfax, this is the board of supervisors) in order to ensure that laws that favor violence prevention and intervention are passed and that agencies that provide services are adequately funded. Fairfax County is not

---

BOX 15.4	A COMPREHENSIVE APPROACH

Fairfax County's comprehensive approach to violence prevention and intervention includes a community board, the Domestic Violence Prevention, Policy, and Coordinating Council (DVPPCC). This includes representatives from all of the agencies that serve victims of IPV, including the director of the OFWDSVS, the county attorney, a judge from the domestic violence court, shelter directors, the directors of batterer intervention programs, defense attorneys, members of the local bar association, the chief of police, the fire chief, members of Legal Aid, leaders in the faith community, members of the Fairfax County Commission on Women, and scholars, including one of the authors. The mission of the DVPPCC is

> to unite senior-level public officials and community leaders; to advise the Board of Supervisors on a range of domestic violence policy, legislative, and program issues; and to guide the development of a coordinated and collaborative community response to domestic violence in Fairfax County.
>
> ("Apply to be on Fairfax County's Domestic Violence Prevention, Policy, and Coordinating Council" 2016)

The comprehensive approach of the DVPPCC is unusual and highly impressive. First and foremost, it makes the prevention of violence in Fairfax a community problem, not one that is relegated to the work of a few agencies. Second, it is based on an understanding that IPV is a far more complicated problem than just a man with anger management issues. Successful prevention and intervention strategies rely on an understanding that a comprehensive approach is needed, including economic development (employment); support in churches, mosques, and temples; affordable housing for families; and support for children in local schools. In many ways the DVPPCC reinforces the argument we make through the entire book: IPV, child abuse, and elder abuse are community problems that require changes in the economy, the health-care system, the education system, housing, safety net programs, and our system of incarceration.

immune to IPV, but we are optimistic that the innovative approach employed here will ultimately result in reductions in all forms of family violence.

Intervention Programs

Intervention programs are primarily focused on providing educational programming for individuals who have perpetrated IPV. In some cases the perpetrators may be court-ordered to attend an intervention program. Both civil and criminal courts may compel attendance, often in lieu of jail time—in criminal cases—or, in civil cases, in exchange for allowing the abusers to remain in the home. In some cases offenders may continue to live with their partners and in other cases they may not, but in either case the assumption is that the two individuals will continue to have contact with each other. For example, you may remember from Chapter 12 the IPV case involving Baltimore Ravens running back Ray Rice, who in summer 2014 was caught on security camera punching his then fiancée Janay Palmer in a hotel elevator in Atlantic City. Rice was offered, and accepted, placement in a pretrial intervention program that allowed him to avoid jail time.

Sometimes, though not always, these programs are administered by the same agencies that also provide services for victims. In our home community of Fairfax County, Virginia, the county government, vis-à-vis OFWDSVS, offers the ADAPT offender/batterer intervention program to residents of Fairfax County. In Winston-Salem, North Carolina, Family Services provides a domestic violence hotline, dispatches victim advocates when a woman is raped, conducts "safety checks" on families with known violence, administers the local domestic violence shelter, and administers the local batterer intervention program. Family Services also provides the majority of the staff for the Safe on Seven program, which we will discuss later in this chapter. Family Services is essentially "one-stop shopping" for IPV.

You may recall that many communities approach child abuse and neglect through the utilization of social services programs, specifically Child Protective Services, and family court—determining and arranging child custody—far more often than engaging the criminal justice system and prosecuting and detaining the abuser. The same is true for IPV. Batterer intervention programs—which comprise a variety of tools, including mandatory education classes, attendance at substance abuse programs, anger management, and even victim restitution, which we will discuss at length shortly—are the most common approaches to dealing with the offenders in cases of IPV. In fact, not only are they the go-to model for social workers who are charged with assisting abused women and their children, but they are also the go-to model in criminal cases in which the abuser is prosecuted. Mandatory attendance is the single most common *criminal* sentence for IPV cases. In a study of

Winston-Salem, North Carolina, Harvey (2002) looked at the previous five years of *criminal* cases of domestic violence and found that of those that resulted in a conviction, 75 percent were sentenced to attend the batterer intervention program at Family Services. Thus, it is important that we examine carefully the social service program that serves as the primary criminal justice response to IPV.

Batterer intervention programs vary, in part depending on whether they are administered by counselors in private practice or, as the Family Services program is, as sort of a hybrid social service and probation or parole program. There are at least three approaches to batterer intervention: feminist models (for example, Emerge), family systems-based programs, and counseling or psychologically based models that feature various aspects of counseling and behavior modification programs (Healey, Smith, and O'Sullivan 1998).

Feminist Models

- Developed out of the feminist consciousness-raising movement that produced the shelter movement.
- Focus on power and control as the cause of IPV.
- Focus on equality as the goal of treatment and reeducation.

Family Systems Models

- Are based on the assumption that IPV is a result of a dysfunctional family.
- Contend that violence escalates as the result of the behavior of both people.
- Argue that violence is the result of an interaction; it is not the problem of one person alone.
- Focus on identifying problems in the interactions and teaching couples how to solve problems.

Psychological Approaches

- Focus on individual problems, such as a history of abuse or drug and alcohol addiction.
- Utilize psychotherapy (both group and individual).
- Utilize cognitive behavior therapy (identifying triggers and learning alternative responses to violence).

Though all of these types of programs exist around the country, in his expansive examination of batterer intervention programs nationwide, Gondolf (2015) notes that the "most prominent, or at least best-known, batterer program in the country" is "Duluth model," a psychological-counseling model that is deeply rooted in a feminist understanding of IPV as an expression of power (Gondolf 2015: 1).

THE DULUTH CURRICULUM: ISSUES OF POWER AND CONTROL AS PRIMARY TARGETS

Many batterer intervention programs adhere to, or borrow from, a psychoeducational and skills-building curriculum that is a component of the Duluth model. Developed in the early 1980s by the Domestic Abuse Intervention Project (DAIP) of Duluth, Minnesota, the model emphasizes the importance of a coordinated community response to IPV and places battering within a broader context of the range of controlling behaviors illustrated in the "Power and Control Wheel." The wheel depicts how physical violence is connected to male power and control through a number of control tactics: minimizing, denying, blaming, and using intimidation, emotional abuse, isolation, children, male privilege, economic abuse, and threats. According to the Duluth model, the batterer maintains control over his partner through constant acts of coercion, intimidation, and isolation punctuated by periodic acts of violence.

The curriculum is taught in classes that emphasize the development of critical thinking skills around eight themes: nonviolence, non-threatening behavior, respect, support and trust, honesty and accountability, sexual respect, partnership, and negotiation and fairness. Depending on the total length of the program, two or three sessions are devoted to each theme. The first session of each theme begins with a video vignette that demonstrates the controlling behavior from that portion of the wheel. Discussion revolves around the actions that the batterer in the story used to control his partner, the advantages he was trying to get out of the situation, the beliefs he expressed that supported his position, the feelings he was hiding through his behavior, and the means he used to minimize, deny, or blame the victim for his actions. At the close of each session, the men are given homework: to identify these same elements in an incident when they exhibited similar controlling behaviors. During subsequent sessions devoted to the theme, each group member describes his own use of the controlling behavior, why he used it, and what its effects were. Alternative behaviors that can build a healthier, egalitarian relationship are then explored.

Putting the Duluth curriculum into practice requires considerable skill on the part of group leaders. One group observed for this report strayed dramatically from the evening's agenda, as members succeeded in sidetracking the discussion away from their behavior into complaints about the curriculum and about their partners. Even when the agenda is adhered to, the classroom-style format can allow some members to sit back and not participate in discussions or even reflect on their behavior. Group leaders have to be vigilant against both the active and the passive ways batterers avoid taking responsibility for their abuse, both inside and outside of the group setting. Furthermore, directors of several programs have noted that the tenor of the group intervention varies substantially depending on the style of the group leaders and how they view their role (e.g., as educators who teach new skills or as therapists who confront the men's inappropriate behavior).

Source: Healey, Smith, and O'Sullivan 1998.

Shortcomings of Batterer Intervention Programs

Ed Gondolf, one of the premier leaders in the field of batter intervention, studied the best programs and the leading figures in the field to learn more about what they think works and where there are areas for improvement. In his book, *Gender-Based Perspectives on Batterer Programs: Programs Leaders on History, Approach, Research and Development*, published in 2015, he argues first and foremost that batterer intervention programs that are the most successful, by any measure, are those built on feminist principles that locate the underlying causes of IPV in constructions of gender, and that are not only deeply embedded in the community but also engaged in strong partnerships with shelters and rape crisis centers. Programs that only focus on anger management or substance abuse, without addressing gender and power, will not be effective in transforming abusive men's behavior. That being said, Gondolf (2012, 2015) also argues that to maximize success, intervention programs must be comprehensive; they must "engage with men in a fuller way," including drug and alcohol treatment, parenting classes, and "promote an emotional awareness in men" (Gondolf 2015: 165).

Gondolf also takes on squarely the critique that we, and many others, have made that calls into question the success of batterer intervention programs. He argues, based on his extensive research with thought leaders and practitioners in the field, that evaluators are using the wrong measures to assess success. Rather than focusing exclusively on recidivism, Gondolf (2015: xxii) argues

> for more nuanced and complex outcomes that recognize the process of change, rather than "snapshots" of recidivism. Qualitative studies of women's well-being, as well as women's safety and agency (i.e. the ability to exert power and enact decisions) would help broaden the outcomes beyond narrowly focused indicators.

Additionally, he suggests that evaluations focus at the micro level of the intervention, which tools and programs seem to be the most useful, and at the macro level, assess the degree to which individual programs are "getting at the cultural roots of what is a social problem" (Gondolf 2015: xxiii) (Figures 15.2 and 15.3).

In contrast, a study conducted by Gondolf (1999) reported that length was not correlated with recidivism, noting that participants in a three-month program fared as well as those in a nine-month program after twelve months.

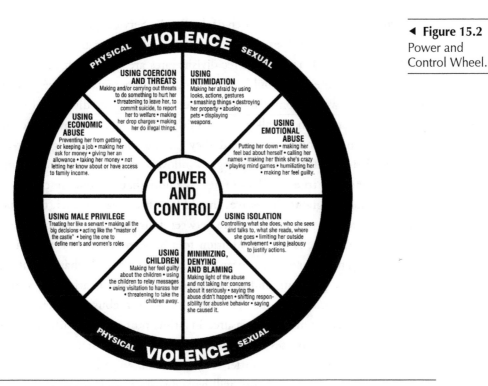

◄ **Figure 15.2**
Power and
Control Wheel.

Source: www.theduluthmodel.org/pdf/PowerandControl.pdf.

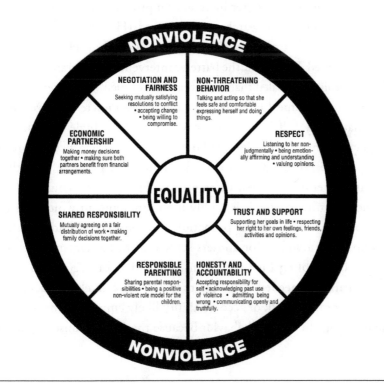

◄ **Figure 15.3**
Equality Wheel.

Source: www.theduluthmodel.org/pdf/Equality.pdf.

In general, our evaluation research of the Family Services program (conducted in 2005 and 2010) as well as the overall conclusions drawn by Healey, Smith, and O'Sullivan (1998) reveal that recidivism rates are quite high but, as is the case with other crimes, we would recommend researchers use a three-year window rather than twelve months to measure recidivism. As the director of Emerge noted, abusers can learn to talk the talk fairly easily—and our own interviews with abusive men confirm this—and they are capable of making short-term changes in their behavior. Thus, a longer window to measure recidivism is more accurate in detecting true recidivism rates. We note that this does not mean that the intervention programs themselves should last three years; rather, the data all seem to indicate that programs that are between four and nine months are effective. What we do note is that in addition to a honeymoon period that may be experienced by an abuser who has been convicted on an assault charge, sentenced to an intervention program, and desires to reestablish his relationship with his partner, just like recidivism rates in other areas—drug abuse, property crimes, and so on—recidivism must be measured in a time frame that is sufficiently long to allow the everyday stresses of life and, in the case of abusive men especially, their relationships to emerge in order to determine if an individual will go back to their previous ways of coping or will have developed new and better ways of handling stress.

The second problem that batterer intervention programs face is attendance. For example, the evaluation research we conducted (Hattery, Williams, and Smith 2005) as well as that conducted by our colleague Lynn Harvey (2002), both of which evaluated Time Out, the batterer intervention program in Forsyth County, North Carolina, revealed that more than half of men (55 percent) court-ordered to attend the Time Out program failed to complete the twenty-six sessions, and that nearly half (45 percent) never attended a single session! How does this happen? In many counties like Forsyth County, the offices of probation and parole have no jurisdiction over the Time Out program, and there is little coordinated effort between these offices. Thus, unlike court-ordered drug or alcohol treatment, which is highly monitored and in which missing a session can be a reason to revoke probation and send the offender back to jail, there is no accountability for abusers sentenced to batterer intervention programs. This is troubling for two reasons. First, the abusive person is not receiving the treatment needed and thus they are more likely to recidivate, and, second, the complete lack of accountability likely empowers the offender to continue to engage in abusive behavior because there is no consequence for doing so!

Interestingly, in their review of batterer intervention programs, Healey and colleagues (1998) identified programs that linked probation and parole with intervention services. They report, not surprisingly, that when abusers' attendance at court-ordered intervention programs is monitored, not only do they attend, but their recidivism rates go down.

> An evaluation of the probation reform showed a drop in the annual recidivism rate from 29 percent in 2005 before the reform to 24 percent in 2008, after the reform . . .. There also was a reduction in the number of men whose probation were revoked after they committed a felony from 1,052 in 2005 to 846 in 2009 (a 20 percent decrease), according to official records. The drop in "technical revocations" was nearly 50 percent.
>
> (Gondolf 2012: 189)

We suggest that this is likely for the same reasons that unsupervised intervention programs do not work: men who attend the program *are receiving treatment*, and there is a consequence associated with their abusive behavior—they are required to attend weekly sessions. Additionally, their recidivism is more likely to be detected by the probation or parole supervisor. Thus, we highly recommend that court-ordered batterer intervention programs be linked with probation services, as this combination seems to have the best chance of reducing recidivism.

THE CRIMINAL JUSTICE RESPONSE

The **criminal justice system** encompasses everything from law enforcement to corrections. For a variety of reasons, including the history of family violence, which we reviewed extensively in Chapter 2, and the overarching belief that family violence is a "family problem," for the most part, the only parts of the criminal justice system that deal with family violence are law enforcement and the courts. Unless the abuse results in significant injury or death, there is very seldom any sentencing of offenders other than to probation and possibly an intervention program like those we reviewed above or an alcohol or drug treatment program. Thus, our focus in this section will be on law enforcement and the courts.

As noted earlier in this chapter, as well as in our discussions of both elder and child abuse, neither child abuse nor elder abuse typically involves a 911 call and the arrival of a law enforcement agent on the scene. More likely, both child abuse and elder abuse cases make their way into the system either because of a report by someone concerned—a caregiver, parent, teacher, health-care provider—or because the injuries sustained require the victim to be brought to the emergency room. Furthermore, in these situations, often the cases are referred to social services first, particularly when it is a case of child abuse, in which instance the matter is referred to Child Protective Services.

Thus, although occasionally law enforcement may respond to a call about elder abuse or child abuse, the typical family violence call they respond to is one of IPV. As any police officer or deputy will tell you, domestic violence calls are the worst; they are dangerous, they are time-consuming, and they rarely result in an arrest. Thus, law enforcement agents are often reluctant to respond, if they respond at all. Countless abused women we have interviewed or seen interviewed for documentaries detail the fact that once their battering became chronic and they were known at the police department, even a 911 call rarely elicited a response.

When law enforcement officers do arrive on the scene of a domestic violence call, they typically have several difficult decisions to make: Who was the initiator? Should someone be arrested? And what other options might there be to defuse the situation? Of course, this is all on top of the fact that they have to assess their own safety, as it is not uncommon for domestic violence incidents that result in a 911 call to involve weapons. In fact, each year police officers are killed responding to domestic violence calls. According to a report by the Department of Justice Community Oriented Policing Services (Cops), which analyzed all two hundred and ten law enforcement deaths between 2010 and 2014, approximately 40 percent of all officers slain each year were killed when responding to an IPV call, and 90 percent of those officers were killed with a firearm (Lartey 2016). In fact, at the time of this writing, this hit very close to home for the authors. A police officer in Prince William County, Virginia, a community just a few miles from our home in Fairfax, was killed responding to an IPV call. It was her first day on the job. She was twenty-seven years old.

Often the first decision that a responding officer must make is to determine, if possible, who initiated the violence and thus who is the perpetrator. Though the data on IPV all confirm that, especially in cases of severe violence, the vast majority of incidents involve a man who is the perpetrator, it is not uncommon for both parties to be actively engaged in "fighting." Typically, the officer will deduce that the individual with the more severe injuries—perhaps the person who called 911—is the victim, but it is not always clear, and in some cases, as Garcia and McManimon (2010) note, officers will arrest both parties when they are unable to determine who initiated the violence.

Clearly, the primary decision facing a responding officer is whether to make an arrest. In their extensive review of police departments, Townsend and her colleagues (2006) note first that although all police departments have written protocols for responding to IPV, behaviors that they consider to constitute IPV vary:

All of the departments (99%) consider actual physical (non-sexual) assault as an act of domestic violence and 90% consider actual sexual assault domestic violence. Fewer departments consider violations of court protective orders (78%) or threatened physical (non-sexual) assault (78%) domestic violence; even fewer consider threatened sexual assault (65%), stalking (62%), verbal assault (50%), criminal trespass (46%), and property crime (43%) as domestic violence.

(Townsend et al. 2006: 25)

More troubling, their research reveals that even when there are protocols in place, the rate of following these protocols varies, as does the level of accountability for failing to do so. They suggest that failing to supervise officers' responses to IPV and hold them accountable for failing to follow procedures is a lost opportunity in terms of training officers in the most effective strategies for responding to these difficult calls.

One of the biggest changes in the policies and practices of law enforcement began in the mid-1980s and early 1990s with the Duluth model. Historically, the law enforcement response to an incident of IPV was to defuse the situation by walking the man around the block and offering to take the victim to a friend's or family member's home or perhaps even the emergency room—in short, to create distance between the individuals and give them both time to "cool off." Even when the victim demanded that the perpetrator be arrested, law enforcement agents were frequently reluctant to do so and often refused based on the grounds that they did not have probable cause: they did not "see him do anything." Countless interviews we have conducted, read about, or seen in documentaries illustrate this reality. Wearied by what they considered a lack of response, as well as a lack of accountability, feminist activists agitated for **mandatory arrest laws**. The theory behind mandatory arrest—which generally involves booking the perpetrator and holding him (or, rarely, her) for twenty-four to seventy-two hours or until they can be arraigned—is simply that in addition to creating space and a cooling-down period (though most men who are arrested rather than walked around the block become, understandably, more agitated, not less!), an arrest can provide a wake-up call that IPV will be taken seriously and has criminal consequences.

Beginning with the Duluth model, the mandatory arrest movement slowly spread across the country so that by the end of the twentieth century, virtually every state had mandatory arrest laws. Interestingly, the most recent movement is for the revocation of these laws as activists and practitioners seek noncriminal solutions to IPV. Mandatory arrest laws are quite effective in creating space between the two people involved. And in some cases, particularly when the arrest involves middle- or upper-middle-class white men who generally have not had any previous interaction with the criminal justice system, it does serve as an effective wake-up call, as it did for some of the men we interviewed. However, mandatory arrest has not been as successful as its advocates had hoped.

Both the research on mandatory arrest as well as anecdotal evidence provided by shelter staff and other practitioners who work with abused women reveal that there are some problems with mandatory arrest that have led to its suspension in some jurisdictions. One problem, identified by research relating mandatory arrest laws and intimate partner homicide, concludes that mandatory arrest laws suppress reporting incidents of IPV based on a fear of the arrest on the part of the victim, and as a result IPV that is significant enough to warrant an arrest instead goes unreported and undetected and ultimately escalates into homicide (Iyengar 2007). Other problems with mandatory arrest laws include the following:

- Because charges of domestic violence rarely end up in a conviction, the arrest, in addition to aggravating the abuser, may leave him empowered to engage in more violence and more severe violence because he learns there is no serious consequence for his behavior.

- For a variety of reasons, the women themselves often plead that the perpetrator not be arrested, or when he is, they advocate for his release and provide the bail money. They may do this out of genuine fear that he will be even more abusive when he returns home, or because they feel guilty, or because they fear other consequences of his arrest, such as lost wages if he misses work while he is on mandatory lockup, or, if he is a habitual offender, they may worry that this will violate his parole or probation and send him back to prison. For whatever reason, this behavior discourages police officers from making an arrest and from even responding to domestic violence calls at all.

- Similarly, women may refuse to testify as witnesses in the rare instances when the cases go to trial. A victim's refusals may be for all the reasons stated above, as well as the fact that once some time has passed between the initial incident and the trial, she may have forgiven him, she may have reconciled with him, he may have stopped being abusive, and so forth, and thus the couple may have lost the immediate need for a criminal justice intervention. This is similarly discouraging for police officers as well as detectives and prosecutors who have invested in bringing these cases to trial, and it often negatively impacts their willingness to invest in other cases of IPV, which in part contributes to the low rate of prosecution.

- As noted in Chapter 13, mandatory arrest laws are often problematic when officers respond to an incident of same-gender IPV because the officers—seeing the world of crime through their cultural lens—assume that violence between two people of the same gender is not at all like violence between a man who is the perpetrator and a woman who is the victim. As a result, they may be less or more likely to make an arrest based on their stereotypes about gay men and lesbians as victims or perpetrators.

- Similarly, mandatory arrest laws can be problematic in cases in which abused women are fighting back or engaging in self-defense. It is not uncommon for women in these cases to be arrested for domestic assault, when in fact they are simply responding to the violence being perpetrated against them.

In short, mandatory arrest laws have seen a cycle: they began slowly as a reaction to a lack of response on the part of law enforcement to IPV, they grew to be nearly universal, and now some jurisdictions are repealing them based on evidence that they may not always produce the best outcome. Additionally, as the movement toward handling minor cases of IPV focuses on social service interventions rather than a criminal justice response, we will likely continue to see a reduction in mandatory arrest with regards to IPV.

Orders of Protection

One of the most common responses to IPV is the **protective order**. Orders of protection vary by jurisdiction, and they can be either temporary or permanent. If an individual feels that she or he is in immediate danger and the judge agrees, an emergency order of protection will be granted immediately and without a hearing. If the complainant is not in immediate danger and/or the emergency order of protection expires, both parties will participate in the order of protection hearing, and if the judge believes there is sufficient evidence that the respondent poses a threat to the complainant, a permanent order of protection will be issued with a specific expiration date.

Orders of protection generally ban the parties from having any physical contact with each other as well as restricting the degree of proximity between the two parties; often they cannot come within fifty feet of each other. Orders of protection can also be tailored to specific circumstances, as is often the case when stalking or non-physical harassment is involved. For example, the parties may be banned from phone or e-mail contact, including text messaging.

Unfortunately, both the research and the anecdotal evidence reveal that for as common as they are, orders of protection are not very effective in preventing further violence (Garcia and McManimon 2010). For example, many abused women we have encountered reported that their partners knew exactly the distance at which the order of protection would be enforced and would position themselves just on the other side of the line—still able to harass but not violating the precise distance required in the order of protection. One woman we interviewed told of how her partner, who was also the father of her children, insisted that he would give her the child support check he owed her only if she would meet him in person. Desperate for the money, she did so. Upon her arrival at their agreed-upon meeting place, he called the police and *had her arrested* for violating the order of protection she took out on him! Another victim, a student in one of the classes taught by one of the authors, reported that her ex-husband, against whom she had an order of protection, would drive up and down her block waving a shotgun out the window, threatening to kill her. When she called the police she was told that they could not do anything because he was not violating the order of protection—he maintained the required physical distance mandated in the order of protection—and that she should call back if he shot the gun because then they could do something.

These examples illustrate the simple fact that orders of protection are only as valuable a tool as the willingness of the local law enforcement agents to enforce them. There are other problems associated with orders of protection as well. For example, they require that the victim appear in court and reveal very private information about themself. This must be done at least twice. During the hearing for a permanent order of protection, the victim must repeat this kind of intimate information while facing the person who is abusing them. This can be a very intimidating process that is frequently a barrier to getting an order of protection. Additionally, orders of protection are not enforceable in certain circumstances. For example, on a college campus, an order of protection between two students is not enforceable in the classroom. Let's consider the following scenario: if a student, we'll call her Mary, has an order of protection against her ex-boyfriend, we'll call him Tom, who is also a student at the same university, the university cannot enforce the order of protection in the classroom. Thus, Tom can obtain Mary's schedule and register for all the same classes and sit in the same classroom—no matter how small—with her. Not only have we been made aware of these cases in our own classrooms by the university's dean of students, but they confirm that every year they are faced with multiple cases of student IPV about which they must inform the faculty who are teaching these students—the victim *and* the offender—in their classes.

Finally, we note that because orders of protection are civil documents rather than criminal orders, research shows that they are not a powerful tool in the war to protect women from violence. For example, Tjaden and Thoennes (2000) report that more than 50 percent of orders of protection are violated. Additionally,

> there is growing evidence that abusers are becoming increasingly aware that they can avoid the service of orders of protection. The orders are civil documents and do not allow officers to enter the premises or force the person to accept these documents absent a subsequent court order. As a result, orders of protection may go unserved for long period of time.
>
> (Garcia and McManimon 2010: 132)

One of the challenges that deputies face in Fairfax County, Virginia is that orders of protection must be served in person and every attempt must be made to be sure the person being served understands the order. In the cases of an emergency order of protection, the deputy may be required to remove the perpetrator from the residence. Fairfax County is one of the most diverse counties in the United States. According to a report by the sheriff to the DVPPCC (2015), orders of protection are served to people speaking one hundred and fifty-three different languages. Because of the diversity of Fairfax, there are officers who speak the most common languages, including English, Spanish, and Korean, and most documents are translated into these languages, but the resources are not available to provide a person who speaks one of the one hundred and fifty-three other languages or documents in those languages. The Fairfax County sheriff's office pays an exorbitant fee to a translating service that provides, over the phone, a translation of the document to the perpetrator being served. And, in addition to the expense, there is anecdotal evidence to conclude that in many cases the perpetrator does not understand the requirements of the order of protection. As the United States becomes increasingly diverse, this will likely be a challenge faced by more and more jurisdictions.

That said, orders of protection, though they are controversial in terms of their effectiveness, remain a common tool for interrupting IPV and hopefully preventing it in the future. In Forsyth County, North Carolina, the social service agency charged with addressing IPV, Family Services, has established a unique program called "Safe on Seven" that allows them to provide trained staff at an office on the seventh floor of the courthouse where victims file the paperwork to take out orders of protection. What makes this program unique is that staff are trained in dealing with both the victims and the perpetrators of IPV. Staff are there to assist the victim in filing the paperwork as well as to make the process less intimidating; to create a safe environment for the victim, protecting her from the harassment of the offender, who may also be present; and to offer her referrals into other programs that she may need, including a shelter, support groups, and social services where she can apply for welfare.

BOX 15.5	SAFE ON SEVEN

Safe on Seven: Forsyth County Domestic Violence Center (SOS) is a multiagency service center for victims of domestic violence. The center is located on the seventh floor of the Forsyth County Hall of Justice at 200 N. Main Street in Winston-Salem, North Carolina.

The center provides a "one-stop shop" by bringing together key service providers, such as law enforcement, victim advocates, legal advocates, and social services.

Previously, victims had to seek out services at multiple locations throughout the community. The center helps minimize the difficulties victims face as they navigate the legal system. The overriding focus of the center is victim safety and offender accountability.

Clients of the center are able to obtain legal advice, advocacy, referrals, and protective orders as well as information concerning their court cases. The on-site partners include the District Attorney's Office, Family Services, Clerk of Court, the Forsyth County Sheriff's Office, the Legal Aid of North Carolina, the Department of Social Services, the Winston-Salem Police Department, and the Winston-Salem State University Center for Community Safety.

Source: "Safe on Seven."

As noted, research on orders of protection indicates that even when they are filed, they are violated more than 50 percent of the time, and a good number of them are never even served (Tjaden and Thoennes 2000). Thus, the order of protection can create a false sense of safety on the part of the victim and may actually result in increased violence or even homicide.

BOX 15.6	INNOVATIVE PARTNERSHIPS AMONG LOCAL LAW ENFORCEMENT, CHILD ADVOCACY GROUPS, AND INTIMATE PARTNER VIOLENCE AGENCIES

Tucson, Arizona is seeing an unlikely partnership in the battle to address IPV. Emerge! Center for Domestic Abuse, a local agency whose mission is to provide "the opportunity to create, sustain, and celebrate a life free from abuse" ("Working Together Helps Victims of Domestic Abuse" 2015) and the largest local provider of resources—including shelters, educational programming, education, outreach, and advocacy—has partnered with the Pima County sheriff's department, the Southern Arizona Child

continues

BOX 15.6	INNOVATIVE PARTNERSHIPS AMONG LOCAL LAW ENFORCEMENT, CHILD ADVOCACY GROUPS, AND INTIMATE PARTNER VIOLENCE AGENCIES *continued*

Advocacy Center, and the Pima County Attorney's Office. Prior to this partnership, perpetrators of IPV who were arrested were released from jail with simply a promise that they would honor the terms of the order of protection against them. And, as we have detailed in this chapter, orders of protection are not terribly effective at providing the victim safety.

Emerge! and the Southern Arizona Child Advocacy Center provide training for the Pima County sheriff's department and Pima County Attorney's Office on patterns in IPV, child abuse, and best practices as they relate to orders of protection. As a result of this partnership, beginning in January 2015, deputies in Pima County began under-cover compliance checks to ensure that perpetrators had not returned to and were not living in the victim's residence. Those that are caught violating the order are arrested. Though it's a bit too early to tell how significant the impact of these compliance checks will be, there is optimism in the community that they will prove an important strategy in reducing IPV.

Source: "Working Together Helps Victims of Domestic Abuse" 2015.

Lethality Assessment Program (LAP)

Developed in 1985 by one of the leading scholars on IPV, Jacquelyn Campbell, LAP is a tool that is designed to be administered by law enforcement agents who are responding to an IPV call and assess the likelihood that the victim is at risk for extreme danger or even homicide. When an officer administers LAP and determines that the likelihood is high for lethal or near lethal violence, they will do several things. First, the officer informs the victim that the assessment indicates that she is at significant risk for extreme danger and even homicide. Second, the officer immediately gets a victim advocate on the phone with the victim so that she will be provided with all of the resources that can reduce her risk for increased violence, including offering to get her to a shelter and schedul-ing a follow-up meeting for later that day (or the next day, if the incident occurs at night). Though LAP has been around for nearly thirty years, only recently have law enforcement departments adopted this intervention strategy. In fact, in our home community of Fairfax County, Virginia, LAP was only adopted in spring 2015.

BOX 15.7 | **DOMESTIC VIOLENCE LETHALITY SCREEN FOR FIRST RESPONDERS**

DOMESTIC VIOLENCE LETHALITY
SCREEN FOR FIRST RESPONDERS

Officer: Date: Case #:

Victim: Offender:

☐ *Check here if victim did not answer any of the questions.*

▶ *A "Yes" response to any of Questions #1-3 automatically triggers the protocol referral.*

1.	Has he/she ever used a weapon against you or threatened you with a weapon?	☐Yes	☐No	☐Not Answered
2.	Has he/she threatened to kill you or your children?	☐Yes	☐No	☐Not Answered
3.	Do you think he/she might try to kill you?	☐Yes	☐No	☐Not Answered

▶ *Negative responses to Questions #1-3, but positive responses to at least four of Questions #4-11, trigger the protocol referral.*

4.	Does he/she have a gun or can he/she get one easily?	☐Yes	☐No	☐Not Answered
5.	Has he/she ever tried to choke you?	☐Yes	☐No	☐Not Answered
6.	Is he/she violently or constantly jealous or does he/she control most of your daily activities?	☐Yes	☐No	☐Not Answered
7.	Have you left him/her or separated after living together or being married?	☐Yes	☐No	☐Not Answered
8.	Is he/she unemployed?	☐Yes	☐No	☐Not Answered
9.	Has he/she ever tried to kill himself/herself?	☐Yes	☐No	☐Not Answered
10.	Do you have a child that he/she knows is not his/hers?	☐Yes	☐No	☐Not Answered
11.	Does he/she follow or spy on you or leave threatening messages?	☐Yes	☐No	☐Not Answered

▶ *An officer may trigger the protocol referral, if not already triggered above, as a result of the victim's response to the below question, or whenever the officer believes the victim is in a potentially lethal situation.*

Is there anything else that worries you about your safety? (*If "yes"*) What worries you?

Check one: ☐Victim screened in according to the protocol
              ☐Victim screened in based on the belief of officer
              ☐Victim did not screen in

If victim screened in: After advising her/him of a high danger assessment, did the victim speak with the hotline counselor: ☐Yes ☐No

Note: *The questions above and the criteria for determining the level of risk a person faces is based on the best available research on factors associated with lethal violence by a current or former intimate partner. However, each situation may present unique factors that influence risk for lethal violence that are not captured by this screen. Although most victims who screen "positive" or "high danger" would not be expected to be killed, these victims face much higher risk than that of other victims of intimate partner violence.*

Source: Maryland Network Against Domestic Violence

Campbell and her colleagues (2003) studied the efficacy of LAP in predicting the likelihood of a future homicide and found that the presence of any of several factors significantly increases the likelihood of the victim eventually being murdered (Figure 15.4).

As their research reveals, certain factors dramatically increase the likelihood that a woman will be murdered by her partner or ex-partner. A victim whose partner has used or threatened her with a weapon is 20.2 times more likely to be murdered

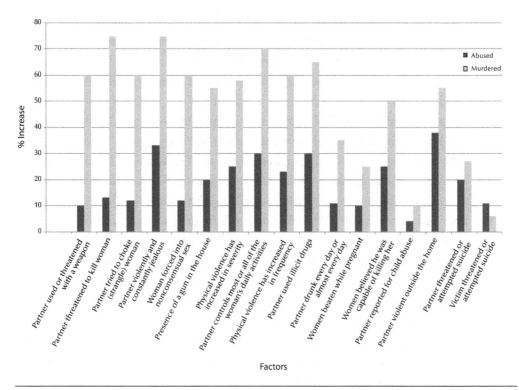

▲ **Figure 15.4**
Factors That Increase Risk for IPV Homicide.

Source: Data from Campbell et al. 2003.

than a victim who has not been threatened with a weapon or had a weapon used on her. Other factors that increase a victim's risk for homicide include: her partner threatened to kill her (14.9 times more likely to be murdered), her partner choked or strangled her (9.9 times more likely to be murdered), and her partner was violently jealous (9.2 times more likely to be murdered). Following close behind are the presence of marital rape (6.1 times more likely to be murdered) and the abuser having a gun in the house (6.1 times more likely to be murdered). Given the predictability of IPV homicide, the implementation of LAP by law enforcement is an excellent strategy, based on solid research, for identifying the victims most at risk for homicide and connecting them directly to the services that they need.

Child Protective Services as a Response to Child Abuse

As noted in Chapter 6, social service agencies, and Child Protective Services in particular, often become involved in cases of child abuse or neglect. In contrast to IPV cases, in which women can and often do seek asylum in shelters, children under the age of eighteen are not capable or legally (apart from in exceptional cases) able to live on their own. As a result, in cases in which the violence or neglect has reached a certain level of severity, children are removed from their parent(s) and transferred temporarily to foster homes. We note that the decision to remove children from their homes and place them in even temporary—let alone permanent—custody of a nonrelative is a complex decision that often involves many different agencies and considerable time. For example, in a typical child abuse or neglect case, once the initial report has been made, usually to the Department of Child Protective Services, in the Division of Health and Human Services, an investigation is launched. This investigation will generally involve a site visit by a CPS staff member and interviews by CPS staff with the child, the parent(s), teachers, the child's physician if available, and other adults who have the opportunity to observe the child. Additionally, the court will generally appoint a **guardian ad litem (GAL)**, a trained volunteer (training requirements vary by state) who will interview the child and observe them in the home in order to make a recommendation to the judge regarding the ideal placement for the child. You may recall our extensive discussion of GALs in Chapter 6. If the court determines that the child would be better suited to live elsewhere temporarily—in foster care—or permanently with other care providers, then the judge will order that the child be removed from the home, and if the placement is permanent, they will terminate the parental rights of the biological parent(s) and transfer custody to the legal guardian or adoptive parent. Thus, social services fill the gap in child abuse and neglect cases that shelters fill in cases of IPV.

As noted in Chapter 6, there are many problems associated with Child Protective Services and foster care—for example, the rate of juvenile detention is approximately seven times greater for children in foster care than for those living in a permanent home (Moarsh 2006; Pipher 1994). It is very difficult to determine when abuse or neglect is severe enough to warrant removing a child, even temporarily, from his or her parent(s). Moreover, there is a great deal of controversy surrounding this determination. These decisions are never made lightly. In some cases, when the CPS staff agree that the family has potential, they may choose to involve the family, as a whole unit, in counseling. The CPS staff at the Olmsted County Department of Social Services in Minnesota practices this approach. Operating under the assumption that most families have the potential to be healthy and safe if they are given the tools—education, resources—to do so, they take the entire family as their "client" and work with them to develop family safety plans; parents are required to attend parenting classes, children receive therapy, and social workers make regular home visits to ensure that the children are safe. Of course, the problem with this approach is when the decision to leave a family intact results in the further neglect, abuse, or even death of the child victim.

When it comes to sibling abuse, as we discussed in Chapter 7, CPS is seldom a viable option for many reasons. First and foremost, sibling abuse is rarely disclosed and even less often reported. There are, for example, no mandatory reporting laws for sibling abuse. Teachers, school counselors and pediatricians, even family therapists may have very little familiarity with sibling abuse and are very unlikely to screen for it. If it is determined that a child is in grave danger from sibling abuse, it is challenging to determine which child should be removed from the home, as both the victim and the perpetrator need the support living in the family provides. Finally, if CPS does intervene, parents will likely be required to attend family therapy, and they may be reluctant to or not be able to afford it.

We are not in a position to evaluate the various approaches to dealing with child abuse and neglect—ranging from removing children permanently from their parents' custody to working to keep families together—but we do note that underneath the controversy are advocates who care deeply about children and are seeking innovative ways in which to meet the needs of the children and keep families together, provided doing so will result in a safe environment.

In contrast to both IPV and child abuse and neglect, there are really no systems in place for providing temporary housing—shelter or foster care—for victims of elder abuse. Because a certain proportion of victims of elder abuse are already institutionalized and institutions are reluctant to identify their own faults when elder abuse or neglect is discovered, it is typically addressed by the adult children who discover it. In most cases, the elderly parent is removed from the institution (or, in cases of home care, the home health-care provider is fired), and in some cases, either civil lawsuits are filed or criminal complaints are taken out. Both of these approaches force the matter into the court system. It is more difficult to determine what happens when relatives are engaging in elder abuse and neglect. Unless it is reported to the police, we suspect that it is handled within the family. As you will recall from our discussion in Chapter 5, when elder abuse or neglect is perpetrated by family members, stress is often the primary cause. Stuck in the sandwich generation, the typical caregiver is overburdened, and this leads to what we might consider situational abuse or neglect. Thus, if the abuse or neglect is discovered by family members, they take matters into their own hands and either remove the abusive care provider or begin to provide the support that relieves the abuser from the stress of the situation, and the abuse or neglect dissipates.

Prosecution

All forms of family violence have the potential to intersect with the criminal justice system through prosecution. As noted, with regard to both child abuse and elder abuse, cases are very rarely prosecuted unless (1) they involve a perpetrator who is a nonfamily member—for example, in cases of child abduction or child sexual abuse or paid caregivers for the elderly; (2) the violence is heinous; (3) the violence is sexual; (4) the neglect is life-threatening; and/or (5) the abuse or neglect takes place over a long period of time and there is a solid body of evidence for prosecution. Of course, the number one barrier to prosecuting perpetrators of either child or elder abuse is reporting. If the abuse is handled within the family or within a social service agency such as Child Protective Services, it may not be prosecuted, especially if solutions that protect the victim and stop the abuse can be identified and implemented.

Thus, our primary focus with regard to prosecution is IPV. The first factor that shapes the probability for prosecution is whether the law enforcement agent makes an arrest. In states with mandatory arrest laws this is a moot point, generally speaking, but as noted above, with a great deal of subjectivity and discretion given to law enforcement officers even in states with mandatory arrest laws, a major barrier to prosecution is the failure to make an arrest.

Prosecutors have similar discretion; the decision to prosecute rests *exclusively* with them. Research on prosecution rates varies across time and place, but the overarching conclusion we can draw is that cases of IPV are rarely prosecuted, with prosecution rates ranging from 2 percent to 21 percent (Garcia and McManimon 2010: 118). Barriers to prosecution include:

- A lack of physical evidence. As reluctant as law enforcement agents are to respond to an IPV call, they are also reluctant to return to the scene and collect evidence.
- A lack of medical evidence. As with rape cases, emergency room staff and physicians are primarily concerned with treating the injuries as quickly as possible. Thus, unless a victim advocate accompanies a woman through her emergency room experience, it is unlikely that forensic photographs and other medical evidence will be collected (see especially Martin 2005).
- Reluctance of victims to testify. As noted previously, it is very common for victims in IPV cases to be unwilling to testify for a variety of reasons, including fear of the perpetrator, fear or guilt regarding his (or her) incarceration, a genuine desire for reconciliation and change, and the simple passage of time, which can numb and lessen the reaction to the violence by the time of the trial. This is such a serious dilemma that some jurisdictions have experimented with evidence-based rather than witness-based prosecution. This approach allows district attorneys to prosecute cases based on the physical and medical evidence without the testimony of the victim. As one can imagine, this approach

is highly controversial, primarily because, although it may be successful in gaining a conviction, it may be undertaken while disregarding the desires of the victim, usually a woman, and may add to her feelings of victimization. If she is unable to control the prosecution of the case, she may feel that the state has not worked in her best interest, even if the prosecutor believes they have. Additionally, if the sentence is not long, there is a danger of exposing her to more violence; that is, even if she refuses to testify, her partner may be furious after being prosecuted and beat her more severely when he is released.

Domestic Violence Courts

In response to all of the shortcomings and problems associated with the prosecution of cases of IPV, some jurisdictions have experimented with **domestic violence courts**. Building on specialized drug courts as their model, domestic violence courts—which can be housed in either criminal court or family court (a civil court that handles such things as divorce, child custody, child support, and so on)—focus on therapy, intervention, treatment, and restoration. Advocates who practice in domestic violence courts—attorneys as well as judges—understand that the relationships and circumstances of IPV are complex and that, in many cases, the desires of the victim are twofold: getting the violence and abuse to stop and, if possible, reconciling with the perpetrator. Thus, the approach in domestic violence courts is getting both the victim and the perpetrator the help they need, be it drug and alcohol treatment, entrance into a successful batterer intervention program, therapy and income support for the victim while the perpetrator is completing treatment, or ultimately a safe reconciliation, if that is desired.

Domestic violence courts are also based on the principle of **restorative justice**. Just because they eschew jail or prison as punishment does not mean they ignore the pain and damage done by the perpetrator. Thus, they often employ a model of restorative justice that provides an opportunity to "right the wrong" and create accountability on the part of the perpetrator. One common strategy is to require the perpetrator to listen to the victim describe the violence and abuse and its impact from their perspective. This is often very painful for the perpetrator and very cathartic for the victim. Additionally, some research on IPV indicates that it is a result of an inability of the abuser to "take the role of the other," or, in other words, to walk in the shoes of the victim. In short, the abuser has not developed an ability to empathize. If empathy can be built through a process of restorative justice, some research suggests that the possibility of successfully treating the abuser and ending the abuse permanently is significantly higher (Goodrum, Umberson, and Anderson 2001).

CONCLUSIONS

In this chapter, our goal has been to review and explore the range of responses to family violence by various institutions in our culture. We examined the role of health-care providers, the role of social service agencies (including CPS), the role of law enforcement, and the role of the courts—both criminal and family. Overall, we noted that the institution *least likely* to have any significant response to family violence, and this is especially the case with child abuse and elder abuse, is the criminal justice system. For the most part, child abuse is primarily dealt with through health-care providers and social services, particularly Child Protective Services. Often child abuse is detected during hospital and clinic visits, and many health-care providers have systematic programs focused on preventing child abuse. When child abuse does occur, it is typically handled through an investigation by Child Protective Services staff, who determine if the child can remain in the home or if they must be removed and placed in foster care until the family situation is resolved. Additionally, Child Protective Services may partner with civil court judges to recommend or require that neglectful and abusive parents attend parenting classes—run by social services agencies such as Exchange/SCAN—as part of the process of regaining custody of their children.

Elder care is rarely addressed by *any* institution. It is not a priority or even a focus for any of the institutions we have researched and discussed in this chapter. Unless the abuse is perpetrated by a nonfamily member, it rarely reaches the point of institutional intervention. Even in cases where the abuse is perpetrated by a nonfamily member, such as a home health-care provider who may be physically, emotionally, sexually, or financially abusing an elderly person, often the adult children will simply fire that person rather than bring the case to the authorities. Sadly, there has been very little to say about the institutional response to elder abuse.

Similarly, sibling abuse, for all its pervasiveness, is even less likely to be addressed institutionally, through CPS, the school system, the health-care system, in spiritual communities, or even in therapeutic settings. This is an area for real development.

Thus, most of this chapter has been devoted to understanding the role that various institutions play in dealing with IPV. As with other forms of family violence, we noted that the majority of the response is by social service agencies, namely shelters that house abused women and intervention programs that attempt to treat abusers. Unlike the case with child abuse, there is very little involvement by health-care providers, which is a major missed opportunity for both prevention and intervention.

Furthermore, although we praise the social service providers who work diligently and in many cases devote their lives to the prevention of and intervention in IPV, we note that at every turn there are serious shortcomings that result in gaps in service and populations that remain unserved or underserved, and unfortunately for both victims and offenders, the probability of success—defined as leaving an abusive relationship, reducing recidivism, or reconciling into healthy relationships—is limited. In the final chapter, we explore possibilities for the future.

RESOURCES

For a detailed report on officers killed in the line of duty and while responding to domestic violence calls, see the FBI's Uniform Crime Reports: www.fbi.gov/about-us/cjis/ucr/ucr.

Curry, Lynne. 2015. *The DeShaney Case: Child Abuse, Family Rights, and the Dilemma of State Intervention.* Lawrence, KS: University Press of Kansas. (This book details the landmark child abuse cases that have shaped family law in the United States.)

Greenwald, Robert. 1984. *The Burning Bed.* Tisch/Avnet Productions and NBC. (*The Burning Bed* is based on the true story of Francine Hughes, who killed her abusive partner after repeatedly seeking interventions from both the criminal justice system and the social welfare system. It is also an excellent example of the early warning signs as they relate to IPV homicide.)

Klaus, Olivia. 2009. *Sin by Silence.* Quiet Little Place Productions. (Filmed behind prison walls, this documentary reveals the lives of extraordinary women who advocate for a future free of domestic violence.)

Lazarus, M., and R. Wunderlich. 1994. *Defending Our Lives.* Cambridge Documentary Films. (This documentary focuses on four of the Framingham Eight, a group of battered women who were sentenced to life in prison for killing their abusive partners. It is an excellent example of the miscarriages of justice that are common in the cases of battered women.)

REFERENCES

"Apply to be on Fairfax County's Domestic Violence Prevention, Policy, and Coordinating Council." 2016. Fairfax County, Virginia. www.fairfaxcounty.gov/domesticviolence/apply-dvppcc.htm.

Campbell, Jacquelyn C., Daniel Webster, Jane Koziol-McLain, Carolyn Rebecca Block, Doris Campbell, Mary Ann Curry, Faye Gary, Judith McFarlane, Carolyn Sachs, Phyllis Sharps, Yvonne Ulrich, and Susan A. Wilt. 2003. "Assessing Risk Factors for Intimate Partner Homicide." *National Institute of Justice Journal* 250. www.ncjrs.gov/pdffiles1/jr000250e.pdf.

Centers for Disease Control (CDC). 2017. *Youth Risk Behavior Survey: Data Summary and Trends Report, 2007–2017.* www.cdc.gov/healthyyouth/data/yrbs/pdf/trendsreport.pdf.

Domestic Violence Prevention, Policy, and Coordinating Council (DVPPCC). 2015. Annual Report. www.fairfaxdvcommunity.org/files/documents/DVPPCC-FY2015-Data-Compilation-011816.pdf.

Garcia, V., and P. McManimon. 2010. *Gendered Justice: Intimate Partner Violence and the Criminal Justice System*. Lanham, MD: Rowman and Littlefield.

Gondolf, Edward W. 1999. "A Comparison of Four Batterer Intervention Systems: Do Court Referral, Program Length, and Services Matter?" *Journal of Interpersonal Violence 14(1)*: 41–61.

Gondolf, Edward W. 2012. *The Future of Batterer Programs: Reassessing Evidence-Based Practice*. Boston, MA: Northeastern University Press.

Gondolf, Edward W. 2015. *Gender-Based Perspectives on Batterer Programs: Program Leaders on History, Approach, Research and Development*. Lanham, MD: Lexington Books.

Goodrum, S., D. Umberson, and K. L. Anderson. 2001. "The Batterer's View of the Self and Others in Domestic Violence." *Sociological Inquiry 71(2)*: 221–240.

Harvey, L. K. 2002. *Domestic Violence in Winston-Salem/Forsyth County: A Study of Domestic Court Cases in 2001*. Winston-Salem, NC: Center for Community Safety, Winston-Salem State University. Report prepared for Forsyth County and Family Services and available from the authors (Angela Hattery, hatterya@gmail.com).

Hattery, A. J. 2008. *Intimate Partner Violence*. Lanham, MD: Rowman and Littlefield.

Hattery, A., and E. Smith. 2014. *African American Families: Myths and Realities*. Lanham, MD: Rowman and Littlefield.

Hattery, A., M. Williams, and E. Smith. 2005. *The Efficacy of the Time Out Intervention Program in Forsyth County*. Winston-Salem, NC: Wake Forest University. Report prepared for Forsyth County and Family Services and available from the authors (Angela Hattery, hatterya@gmail.com).

Healey, K., C. Smith, and C. O'Sullivan. 1998. *Batterer Intervention: Program Approaches and Criminal Justice Strategies*. Washington, DC: National Institute of Justice. www.ncjrs.gov/pdffiles/168638.pdf.

Iyengar, R. 2007. "Does the Certainty of Arrest Reduce Domestic Violence?" *Evidence from Mandatory and Recommended Arrest Laws*. NBER Working Paper 13186. Washington, DC: National Bureau of Economic Research. www.nber.org/papers/w13186.

Lartey, Jamilles. 2016. "Police Officers Most Likely to Die Responding to Domestic disputes." *The Guardian*. www.theguardian.com/us-news/2016/jul/31/police-officer-fatalies-department-of-justice-report.

MacKinnon, Catharine. 1991. *Toward a Feminist Theory of the State*. Cambridge, MA: Harvard University Press.

Martin, P. Y. 2005. *Rape Work: Victims, Gender, and Emotions in Organization and Community Context*. New York: Routledge.

Moarsh, M. 2006. *Understanding Gender, Crime, and Justice*. Thousand Oaks, CA: Sage.

"Office for Women & Domestic and Sexual Violence Services." 2016. Fairfax County, Virginia. www.fairfaxcounty.gov/ofw.

Pipher, M. B. 1994. *Reviving Ophelia: Saving the Selves of Adolescent Girls*. New York: Putnam Press.

Rhodes, K. V., C. L. Kothari, C. Cerulli, J. Wiley, and S. Marcus. 2011. "Intimate Partner Violence Identification and Response: Time for a Change in Strategy." *Journal of General Internal Medicine 26(8)*: 894–899.

"Safe on Seven." *Family Services (Forsyth County, NC)*. http://familyservicesforsyth.org/find-help/safe-relationships/domestic-violence/safe-on-seven.

Tjaden, P., and N. Thoennes. 2000. *Full Report of the Prevalence, Incidence, and Consequences of Violence Against Women: Findings from the National Violence Against Women Survey*. Washington, DC: US Department of Justice. www.ncjrs.gov/pdffiles1/nij/183781.pdf.

Townsend, M., D. Hunt, S. Kuck, and C. Baxter. 2006. *Law Enforcement Response to Domestic Violence Calls for Service*. Document No. 215915. Washington, DC: US Department of Justice. www.ncjrs.gov/pdffiles1/nij/grants/215915.pdf.

"Working Together Helps Victims of Domestic Abuse." 2015. *Arizona Daily Star*, January 13. http://tucson.com/news/opinion/editorial/working-together-helps-victims-of-domestic-abuse/article_700c38e2-3ed1-5667-84e3-27c453ef9ce0.html.

16

WHERE DO WE GO FROM HERE?

> In total these acts of violence are like a ritualized acting out of our social relations of power: the dominant and the weaker, the powerful and the powerless, the passive . . . the masculine and the feminine.
>
> —**Michael Kaufman**, "The Construction of Masculinity and the Triad of Men's Violence"

The final chapter of the book will first provide a summary of what we have covered so far and then proceed into a carefully laid-out prescription—based on the data presented in each chapter—for the prevention of all forms of family violence. Our proposals will include suggestions for modifying the criminal justice approach as well as suggestions for the development of more successful prevention and, when necessary, intervention programs. Unlike many texts on this topic, we will also provide suggestions for the ways in which reductions in inequalities—of race and ethnicity, social class, sexuality, and particularly gender—will likely lead to reductions in the levels of all forms of family violence. We will conclude by providing suggestions for future research.

OBJECTIVES

- To provide a brief summary of the history of various forms of family violence, the theories used to explain family violence, and the most common responses to it
- To lay out a series of prescriptions for an improved response to family violence—highlighting what works and what does not—as well as suggestions for both prevention and intervention
- To offer a perspective on the ways in which reductions in social inequalities of gender, race and ethnicity, sexuality, age, and so on would inevitably produce reductions in family violence

KEY TERMS

corporal punishment

family theories

environmental and contextual expla-
    nations

feminist theories and power theories

Conflict Tactics Scale

intergenerational transmission of vio-
    lence theory

restorative justice models

Family and Medical Leave Act

INTRODUCTION

We began this book by arguing that families—in the United States and around the world—are complicated and, when taken together, form a complex institution that is both thriving and evolving in response to changing requirements, expectations, and shifts in other institutions and social structures, including the economy and the legal system. To take one example, in June 2015, the United States Supreme Court ruled in a landmark 5–4 decision that denying gay and lesbian citizens the right to marry violates the US Constitution; as a result, marriage equality is now the law of the land. This signaled yet another change in the state of the institution of the family in response to changing societal norms.

This book does not address the issue of the changing composition of the institution of families but rather focuses on the dark side of family life: violence. Regardless of the social changes that contribute to different forms of family violence, family violence is never okay. It is never a "healthy" or "reasonable" adaptation, and it is never a solution.

SOCIAL CHANGES

There have been a variety of social changes that have shaped family violence. As we discussed at length in Chapter 2, though there are differences in forms of family violence that are prevalent throughout US history, one commonality is the labeling of family violence as a phenomenon. Prior to the mid-twentieth century, there was a high tolerance for responding to "undesirable" behavior with **corporal punishment**, and men—fathers and husbands—who were charged with the moral development of their children and wives were allowed to engage in physical violence in order to facilitate this development. As such, unless children or wives were murdered or severely injured, their physical abuse was not only *not defined* as problematic or abusive, it was fully legal and tacitly sanctioned by society. Social workers began to raise concerns about child abuse and neglect during the Great Depression, when many single mothers struggled even to provide food and shelter for their children. It was not until the second-wave feminist movement of the 1960s and 1970s that any attention was placed on spousal abuse, and this attention generated more focus on other forms of power-related abuse, including child abuse and elder abuse. Thus, family violence has largely been an area of concern and study for only fifty years or so.

The understanding of elder abuse has also largely been shaped by the societal changes that impacted the ways in which we, as a culture, defined abuse and the degree to which we considered it a concern. As noted in Chapter 2, elder abuse was impacted by an additional societal change; specifically, the changes in life expectancy across the twentieth century. At the turn of the twentieth century, the average life expectancy, though it varied by race and gender, was in the mid-forties. Few people lived long enough to become "elderly," and thus the incidence of elder abuse was relatively minor. Across the twentieth century, life expectancy soared to the mid-seventies (again, with variations by race and gender) and, as a result people lived long enough not only to become "elderly" but also to develop a series of chronic and debilitating diseases—such as diabetes, cancer, and especially Alzheimer's disease—which resulted in their need for living assistance and even institutionalization. This, in turn, contributed significantly to the increased risk the elderly face for experiencing all forms of abuse.

In the past twenty years or so, largely as a result of the work of feminist activists and scholars, definitions of abuse have also been expanded. By focusing attention on the power that exists in abusive relationships, feminist scholars illuminated the importance of expanding definitions of abuse to include emotional abuse, psychological abuse, sexual abuse, and even financial abuse and neglect. Today, it is widely accepted by scholars, activists, and practitioners that some abusive relationships may never involve physical violence, yet the impact of other forms of abuse may be just as severe, or even more severe. Additionally, it is not uncommon for abusive relationships to incorporate multiple forms of abuse. This recognition shapes our response to abusive relationships as well as our approaches to prevention.

THEORIES AND METHODS

In Chapters 3 and 4 we explored both the theories and the methods that are used by scientists who study family violence to understand, explain, and predict various forms of family violence. In sum, there are three key theoretical approaches utilized by scholars of family violence: family theories, environmental and contextual theories, and feminist and power theories.

1. **Family theories** focus on the family as a unit that is composed of a set of complex relationships. Families experience conflict, and when they do, lacking other skills, individuals may turn to violence as a mechanism for resolving the conflict or solving problems. Furthermore, for some members of families, their roles dictate that they are charged with socializing and providing care for

other members. In this capacity, some members of a family may employ violence or other abusive behaviors intentionally, believing that these strategies—for instance, the corporal punishment of children—are necessary, or the abuse may result from the intense pressures to accomplish caregiving. Last, family violence theorists acknowledge that abuse tends to follow patterns of power: those with more power abuse those with less power because "they can" and because "it works." In other words, parents may physically punish children or husbands may beat wives in response to a behavior they do not like, and it generally has the desired effect—the behavior ceases. Practitioners who subscribe to the family violence paradigm focus on interventions that involve the entire family; for example, family therapy may be used to address intimate partner violence (IPV) or parenting classes may be used as a tool to reduce child abuse and neglect.

2. **Environmental and contextual explanations** do not constitute a separate theoretical paradigm but rather are subsumed into other theoretical frameworks, including family theory, criminology theories, and even some aspects of feminist theory. Environmental and contextual explanations focus on the role that environmental stressors and context play in producing family violence. For example, research on child abuse reveals that parents of children with special needs, parents with an above-average number of children, and single parents are at greater risk for engaging in child abuse and neglect. Similarly, elder-care providers who are part of the sandwich generation—caring for both aging parents and children simultaneously—are at greater risk for engaging in elder abuse and neglect. Recognizing the role that environmental stressors and context play in producing family violence results in intervention and prevention strategies that focus primarily on the factors that put families at risk for abuse.

3. **Feminist theories and power theories** of violence focus on the role that power and privilege play in producing family violence. Feminist scholars argue that abuse almost always follows the same pattern—it is perpetrated by individuals who occupy positions of higher status, and the victims are always members of oppressed groups. For example, the vast majority of IPV involves men, who often hold positions of economic as well as physical power, abusing women; child abuse involves parents—who have every type of power—abusing children; and similarly, elder abuse is predicated on the status hierarchy of age. Last, feminist theory shapes prevention and intervention by focusing on disrupting systems of power at the structural level and encouraging the acknowledgment of power and privilege at the individual level in ways that lead to greater awareness and lessen the likelihood of using that privilege in destructive ways.

In the case of family violence, data are collected in a variety of ways, including surveys, interviews, observations, and the reporting that is required of various agencies at the local, state, and federal levels. For example, the Bureau of Justice Statistics requires that all local law enforcement jurisdictions relate all crimes that are reported, investigated, and closed annually. National studies, such as the National Crime Victimization Survey, involve calling randomly selected individuals and surveying them about their experiences as victims of crimes. Both of these methods are used to create prevalence estimates for various types of crime in the United States. Additionally, scholars may conduct interviews, surveys, or observations among smaller populations in order to learn more about a particular aspect of crime. For example, we have interviewed nearly fifty men who either were court-ordered to attend a batterer intervention program or were required to work with Child Protective Services—because they had physically abused their partners in front of their children—in order to learn more about the triggers men identify that lead them to engage in violence. These types of studies are especially useful for exploring family violence in special populations that may be less visible or even invisible in national studies, including marginalized populations, such as same-gender couples and immigrants. Last, we note that scholars of the family violence paradigm have designed survey tools, specifically the **Conflict Tactics Scale**, in order to explore the utility of family theory in explaining family violence. You will recall that the CTS has been administered dozens of times to dozens of different samples—both national samples and local samples. The primary contribution of the CTS is that it was developed based on the assumption that violence can be, and often is, perpetrated by both members of the couple, and thus it was the first tool capable of revealing the otherwise hidden phenomenon of situational couple violence.

DATA ON FAMILY VIOLENCE

Despite rigorous methods for identifying and measuring family violence, estimating the prevalence of various forms of family violence is difficult and likely to be subject to flaws that result in, primarily, underestimates. Family violence is largely underestimated because a certain amount of it goes unreported and undetected. Because developing statistical estimates of family violence relies on some sort of reporting, national statistics are likely to underestimate the actual number of victims and incidents because most incidents are never officially reported. Additionally, as noted above, though we now have social and legal definitions of abuse, the reporting of abuse requires that the victim or perpetrator define the behavior as such, or it must be witnessed by an outsider who labels it as abuse. However, because most family violence occurs inside the home, this is not common. In some cases, ideological beliefs prevent accurate identification and intervention in abuse cases. For example, there remain large pockets of parents who believe that corporal punishment does not constitute abuse, despite social norms and even laws that label it as such. In many cases, a victim's own shame may prevent them from labeling their experiences as abuse and subsequently reporting them.

That said, unfortunately, family abuse is very common. Estimates by the CDC as well as reviews of medical records suggest that as many as 10 percent or 4.5 million Americans over the age of sixty experience some form of abuse each year. The statistics on child abuse are even more startling. As many as 6.6 million children are the victims of child abuse each year, and, tragically, 1,800 children per year die as a result of abuse or neglect. The most common form of family abuse is IPV; estimates are that at least one in four women will be in an abusive relationship in her lifetime, and as many as 50 percent of all women—including many who will never live in an abusive relationship—will experience *one abusive incident*. Why is IPV so much more prevalent than either elder or child abuse? We suspect that there are two key reasons: ideological and structural. Ideologically, as we have discussed at length in this book, the long history of tolerating gender-based violence coupled with a resurgence of cultural and religious supports for rigid, and inherently unequal, gender roles result in strongly held beliefs that tolerate, if not promote, the abuse of women by their intimate partners. Structurally, one of the key differences between IPV and both child and elder abuse is the probability that a woman will have many different partners across her lifetime, whereas children will likely have only one set of parents and parents only one set of children and children only one set of siblings. Thus, in abusive households, the risk to children or elders or siblings is extremely high, but it is simultaneously extremely low in households that are free from abuse. In contrast, a woman may have eight to ten intimate relationships in her lifetime, including serious dating relationships, cohabiting relationships, and marriages, and with each subsequent partner, her risk for being abused "resets." This increased exposure to different potential abusers, which is more or less unique to women and occurs only rarely in the cases of children and elders, results in significantly higher rates of IPV than either elder or child abuse. That said, despite the fact that we know that abused women have a very difficult time leaving abusive relationships, children and elder victims have almost no chance of leaving unless the abuse or neglect is detected. As a result, for those children or elders living with abuse, the likelihood that it will be severe and long-lasting is high. IPV may constitute a single incident, after which a woman leaves the abusive relationship, or it may last her entire lifetime.

The most important recommendation we have for addressing the problems associated with underreporting and investigating gender-based violence and child sexual abuse is that the officers, investigators, hearing boards, attorneys, priests, and judges need to receive appropriate and ongoing training regarding best practices in these cases, including, for example, trauma-informed interviewing. In internal hearings, such as those that take place on college campuses, in which finding an accused person responsible would not result in removing that person's rights vis-à-vis incarceration, institutions must replace the "beyond a reasonable doubt" standard with the "preponderance of the evidence," as we argue in our other work (Hattery and Smith 2019). And, because all of the people who respond in any way to gender-based violence or child sexual abuse live in a society mired in rape culture, a culture that devalues women's experience, blames them for being raped and abused, and believes men's accounts nearly unequivocally and without proper investigation, we must address the culture.

NEGATIVE CONSEQUENCES ASSOCIATED WITH IPV

We devoted the second half of this book to an extensive and multi-chapter discussion of IPV, and in these discussions we documented the negative outcomes associated with IPV. These range from physical injury, emotional pain, and billions of dollars in health-care costs to untold losses in economic productivity, the costs of services for abused women and their children, and finally the costs associated with the criminal justice system: responding to domestic calls, detaining abusers, and adjudicating the cases.

But the biggest negative consequences associated with IPV are not the economic costs borne by a variety of institutions but rather the costs to families in the contemporary United States. Most individuals who end up in violent relationships never intended for their relationships to go this way. As we noted in Chapter 8, many of the women we interviewed, and in fact *all* of the African American women we interviewed, experienced sexual abuse or had premature, "consensual" sexual relationships—we refer to this as *premature sex engagement*—that left them impaired in their abilities to deal with romantic partners (Hattery 2009). Many of the women and men we interviewed witnessed violence in the families in which they grew up. Many of the men, and this was especially true for African Americans, witnessed severe violence, even gun murders of parents in their homes. Many men vowed that they would never treat their romantic partners and their children this way. Yet they did.

But I still look at it like this. I think as far, you know, young men, we come up and we gonna see our mothers and our fathers together. You know, we come up and we . . . get that thing going on, you know, like my moms was married to my real dad, I did see him slam her head on the car, I was in the car, I did see that one, so you know, I think, I think these young men, when we see that, when we children and as we grow up we like, I'd never do that when I get married. I get married I never do that, I ain't gonna say this, I ain't gonna do that to my wife. But when we grow up, you know what I'm sayin', not knowin', you know what I'm sayin', in our mind, that's what we really been taught to do, that how we been taught to deal with things, you know. Moms say something, she smack in the mouth or somethin' like that, that kinda stick with guys, you know. Well guys say I ain't gonna do this, I ain't gonna do that, but when they get in the situation that do exactly that, you know.

(**Manny**, twentysomething African American man, North Carolina)

The primary negative outcome of IPV is that it ruins individual lives and it ruins families. Boys who grow up *witnessing* violence in their homes have triple the risk for becoming physically violent with their own romantic partners than boys who do not (Ehrensaft and Cohen 2003). Boys who grow up in families in which their fathers (or father figures) beat their mothers learn an important lesson: that women have no value and that women's self-interests are not linked with their own. This is similar to the findings of Scully's (1990) interviews with convicted rapists who reported that "rape" was when *they* decided they forced a woman to have sex, not when the woman herself made the same claim.

Living with IPV is stressful at its minimum and lethal at its most severe. For women, living with IPV can mean having to learn how to apply makeup to cover cuts and bruises, learning to scream into a pillow so that the children will not hear, choosing homelessness, or living in a shelter in a new city or state or region of the country in order to survive. For men who are abusive, the outcomes of violence include living with someone who is afraid of you, often being separated from your children, and, in some cases, being arrested and charged with a crime and experiencing some sort of punishment, ranging from attending an intervention program *that you have to pay for*, to incarceration.

So often scholars of IPV, and we as a culture, focus on the toll that IPV takes on its victims. But men who perpetrate this kind of violence lose as well. They lose the chance to have a loving, intimate relationship with another person. They often lose the chance to raise their children or have any sort of relationship with them. They lose the chance to fulfill that part of the American dream that includes making and raising a family. And they must live with the pain that they have hurt someone they claim to love and the guilt that they have created a toxic environment for their children. By exposing their children to violence, they are contributing to the intergenerational nature of this poisonous phenomenon. Men, too, are hurt by the violence they perpetrate. Therefore, it is in their self-interest to reduce the prevalence of this social ill.

THE INTERGENERATIONAL TRANSMISSION OF VIOLENCE

Though most men who grow up in violent households do not become violent, nevertheless, those who do are at a significantly greater risk for becoming violent.

> **Intergenerational transmission of violence theory** is the belief that the predilection to be violent and abusive, especially the likelihood of perpetrating IPV, is inherited from one generation to another.

Will argues just that point. Although Will's adherence to this belief may, in part, be a mechanism to excuse his behavior, it is also clear that he understands something about the intergenerational transmission of violence in his own family history.

It's heredity, but I think some people take it a different way by heredity, you know, how they pick it up. One way, I think the main way, that I see it as, from seeing it. From you seeing it. It's not in your blood. It's actually from seeing it.

(Will, fiftysomething African American man, Minnesota)

We argue that we need to further explore the mechanism for intergenerational transmission of IPV. Unlike many aspects of socialization and social learning, we do not believe it is as simple as boys learning by watching their fathers. Rather, we learned a great deal about a possible mechanism for intergenerational transmission when we asked the men we interviewed what advice they would give their sons. Their responses fell primarily into two categories: do not get hooked up with a bad woman, and do not get played.

Analyzing the advice these men gave or planned to give their sons, we would argue that what gets passed on in the intergenerational transmission are beliefs about men and women: beliefs about gender. Men intend to teach their sons how to be masculine. They may not teach them explicitly that they should hit their romantic partners, but they teach them how to be the "man of the house," how to be in control, how to require certain behavior from their romantic partners. Furthermore, they teach their sons lessons about women. For example, they teach their sons about appropriate roles for women, about behaviors that are common in women, and about the ways in which women will try to manipulate and control them. In essence, they need not explicitly teach their sons to hit women because IPV, especially verbal abuse, will be a logical outgrowth of their general lessons about the way women are, what it means to be a man, and the roles of men and women in a relationship. If boys learn that they are the ones in charge, that women are out to manipulate them, and that *real men* keep their women in line, then it is quite likely that these boys will grow up to be perpetrators of IPV, even if they are bound and determined not to become abusive like their fathers.

As far as my son goes, I'm gonna teach him to stand up for himself, not to let anybody run over him. Just to really be cautious about who he deals with, um, to really, really get to know the person, not just having sex with them and stuff like that, to really get to know someone before you get involved with them, 'cause there's so many diseases, it's, uh, you have some . . . out there and so he just really needs to be aware of what that person likes and dislikes and see if it matches up with some of the stuff he likes and dislikes before he gets involved with her and makes a mistake.

(**Ward,** thirtysomething African American man, North Carolina)

PROPOSALS FOR CHANGE

In this section, we begin with specific recommendations that could be implemented by various institutions, and we conclude with musings about the relationship between reducing inequalities and reducing the occurrence of various forms of family abuse.

BOX 16.1	THE SOCIAL-ECOLOGICAL MODEL FOR VIOLENCE PREVENTION

The social-ecological model was developed by scholars and practitioners in the field of public health, and it has been quite successful in reducing public health problems such as smoking, drug abuse, and underage drinking. At its root, a social-ecological model

continues

BOX 16.1	THE SOCIAL-ECOLOGICAL MODEL FOR VIOLENCE PREVENTION *continued*

is based on the premise that the primary goal is preventing the targeted behavior from ever starting. The social-ecological model was developed based on research that demonstrated that any meaningful change in behaviors will only occur when campaigns target four interlocking elements: individuals, relationships, communities, and societal factors. Additionally, the model is most effective when change is targeted across all four levels simultaneously.

The Centers for Disease Control and Prevention (CDC) has developed a social-ecological model for addressing IPV (Figure 16.1).

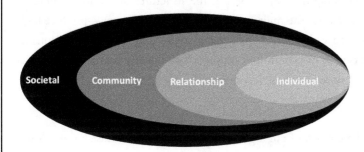

◄ **Figure 16.1**
The Socio-Ecological Model.

Individual

The first level identifies individual factors that increase the risk that an individual will perpetuate or be victimized by IPV. As we discussed at length in Chapter 9, there are a variety of factors that increase one's risk, including age, education, social class, race, and, most important, exposure to violence in childhood. Prevention strategies at the individual level are focused on providing education targeted at violence prevention and, most important, providing appropriate interventions to child victims and witnesses.

Relationship

At the relationship level, the focus moves from the individual to the relationships that increase or decrease the risk for perpetrating or becoming a victim of violence. Strategies at this level include programs that promote healthy relationships, provide training in negotiating conflict in relationships, for example, among siblings, and, as we noted in Chapters 5 and 6, helping individuals develop social support to reduce the likelihood of perpetrating or experiencing child abuse and elder abuse.

continues

BOX 16.1	THE SOCIAL-ECOLOGICAL MODEL FOR VIOLENCE PREVENTION *continued*

Community

Individuals live not only in relationships but also in communities. The focus at this level is to improve community conditions that are associated with IPV (as well as elder and child abuse, including sibling abuse). For example, we know that access to health care, jobs, and safe housing are all protective factors from experiencing or perpetrating violence. Consistent with the literature on neighborhoods, violence often spills from the sidewalks into the household, and thus a central issue for attention at this level is reducing other types of crime and violence in all neighborhoods. Indeed, we dedicated an entire chapter to exploring the ways in which the structures of specific communities—fraternities, SportsWorld, the military, and the Catholic Church—produce high rates of both gender-based violence and child sexual abuse. Our recommendations in that chapter would be central to a community approach to violence prevention and thus we encourage the reader to review those recommendations.

Societal

The societal level is where much of our argument in this book has focused: the culture, norms, and structures in society that create sites ripe for or prone to IPV. As we discussed at length in Chapter 9, structural changes in laws and the economy, such as wage equality; reduced unemployment, especially for women; and lower rates of incarceration, especially for African American men, will all result in reductions in IPV. Shifts in culture, as we discussed at length in Chapter 10, including hegemonic masculinity and the cult of domesticity, will lead to lower risks for perpetrating or becoming a victim of IPV.

Source: Centers for Disease Control and Prevention 2015.

Criminal Justice System

As we discussed at length in Chapter 15, the criminal justice system intervenes in family violence in a variety of ways; the success of those interventions is variable, however. As we argued in Chapter 15, there are seldom law enforcement or legal interventions in child abuse or elder abuse cases, and almost never in cases of sibling abuse, for a variety of reasons, most notably because the victims in these cases differ in one significant way: they are unable or extremely unlikely to report the abuse or call the police. In the next section, we will discuss other potential "sites" for intervention that may be more successful. With regard to the occasions when someone reports the abuse or calls 911, which is most likely to happen in cases of IPV, there are a number of issues that need to be addressed:

- Ideological constructs constrain responders' ability to identify abuse. As noted in both our discussion of history and our discussion of responses, part of what limits appropriate law enforcement and criminal justice responses to family violence are the long-held and intractable beliefs about punishment. As noted earlier, beliefs about child discipline and appropriate gender roles often prohibit responders from identifying abuse and intervening appropriately.
- In many cases, perpetrators have established a high level of control through using terroristic strategies; when confronted, a victim may be too afraid to admit that abuse is occurring or may refuse to press charges or testify.
- In some cases, especially cases of IPV in which victims are fighting back, responders report that they have trouble determining which person initiated the violence, and thus which person is the perpetrator and which person is the victim. Research indicates that this problem is cited frequently in cases of same-gender couple violence.
- Law enforcement personnel do not like dealing with family violence, and as noted in Chapter 15, one of the major impediments to preventing and interrupting IPV is the unwillingness of law enforcement agents to serve and enforce orders of protection.
- For many of the above reasons, prosecutors are often reluctant to pursue abuse cases, and judges are often reluctant to impose sentences that include incarceration or, for that matter, any level of accountability.
- Because some components of IPV are civil rather than criminal matters, judges rarely, if ever, impose sanctions on perpetrators that hold them accountable. In cases that land in criminal court, abusers may be sentenced, for example, to an intervention program that is not required to report the attendance of the person sentenced to the court or a probation officer.

Considering each of these shortcomings of the criminal justice system, we propose the following recommendations:

Educate, educate, educate!

All professionals who have the slightest possibility of interacting with victims of any form of family violence must be educated about the nuances of the offender–victim relationship so that they can identify abuse more accurately and respond appropriately to it. Beginning with some basic principles, such as that it is never okay to hit another person or to deny them access to the basics in terms of food, housing, and sanitation, law enforcement and criminal justice staff must be educated about the realities of family violence and myths must be debunked. As our colleague Patricia Yancey Martin (2005) demonstrated, when this type of education is provided by rape crisis centers, the interventions that take place are perceived as being more fair and appropriate by both the victim and the offender.

Incarcerate when necessary

Incarceration can serve several functions, including punishment, deterrence, and ensuring public safety. Although it has not been shown to be much of a deterrent in pre-criminal populations, it may serve as a deterrent for future violence among perpetrators of certain forms of family violence. And while incarceration is not likely to be effective for reducing recidivism among sexual abuse perpetrators, especially child sex abusers, it may be for those who engage in physical violence and financial abuse. Last, incarceration can be a way to ensure the future safety of the victims, be they children, a spouse, or an elderly parent.

Pursue alternatives to incarceration

Despite the potential that incarceration has to meet several important needs when we as a society respond to family violence, it may not always be the ideal response. Specifically, in cases in which the abuse is not severe or long-term, it may be possible to treat individuals who have engaged in abuse so that they can become stewards of healthy relationships in their own lives and continue as contributing members of society. Additionally, depending upon the severity and types of abuse, there may be both a desire for reconciliation and advantages associated with it if, and only if, the perpetrator can be successfully treated and rehabilitated and if, and only if, the victim desires to reconcile. Many victims of IPV hope to reconcile with their abusive partners, and many children could benefit from ongoing relationships with their parents, provided they can be educated and supported in non-abusive parenting techniques. Additionally, in cases of both IPV and child abuse, incarcerating the perpetrator prevents them from working and thus providing income for the family, which is generally never in the best interest of the victims.

We suggest that in some cases, perhaps most that involve an early intervention, alternatives to incarceration would be most effective in responding to family violence. Let us be clear; we believe accountability must be required. Connecting intervention programs with probation and parole services, as is the practice with substance-abuse treatment programs, would provide that accountability, ensure the completion of the re-education programs, and allow the abuser to remain employed and contributing financially to the family. We can imagine a similar model for parents who engage in child abuse. Given the high cost and other negative consequences associated with foster care, even a small probability for success of this type of model makes it worth trying.

As noted in Chapter 15, another attempt to achieve better outcomes while ensuring accountability is being explored through domestic violence courts that utilize restorative justice models. **Restorative justice models** are built on the assumption that families will try to stay together or reunite if they have the freedom to do so, and thus the resocialization of perpetrators will ultimately be in the best interest of all parties, even if the family members choose to separate. You may recall that this model can, and often does, provide not only accountability but also higher rates of re-education and a higher probability for reunification and a cessation of violence. We suggest that more jurisdictions explore domestic violence courts based in restorative justice models as alternatives to incarceration.

In the chapter on institutionalized violence (Chapter 12), we noted that one of the barriers to adequately addressing gender-based violence and child sexual abuse inside of institutions is their reliance on internal systems of justice. We argue that these systems must be radically reformed if we are to see any reduction in gender-based violence and child sex abuse in the military, on college campuses, or in the Catholic Church. Specifically:

Hold perpetrators accountable

As shown in the research of Diana Scully (1990), who interviewed convicted rapists, and studies of rapists on college campuses (Campbell 2015) as well as testimony and other evidence in the civil and criminal cases brought against the Catholic Church and Larry Nassar and Michigan State University, the majority of rapes and instances of child sexual abuse are perpetrated by serial abusers. The average rapist is purported to have raped six or seven victims. Simply put, the most efficient way to reduce the rates of rape and child sexual abuse in any of the four institutions we have analyzed in this book is quite simple: hold the perpetrators accountable, including removing them from the institution if necessary. In fact, one of the upsides to the fact that each institution has an internal system of justice is that all of this can be done without even engaging any law enforcement systems. Colleges and universities can suspend and/or expel those who are found responsible for sexual misconduct. (As a reminder, colleges and universities do not use the terms *rape* or *guilty* because their processes are not criminal proceedings.) The military can dishonorably discharge members found guilty in a court-martial proceeding, but they can also discharge a soldier for disciplinary reasons even if a court-martial is never initiated. The Catholic Church can defrock priests found responsible for child sexual abuse. When athletes commit violence against women, if they are college students, they can be suspended or expelled, just as any other college student can be. And if they are professional athletes, they can be suspended or fired from their jobs.

Revise the investigation and adjudication processes

There seems to be a tremendous amount of reluctance in each of these institutions to hold perpetrators accountable. More than 110,000 women are raped each and every year on college and university campuses, and yet the average campus doesn't expel a single student a year. In fact, in the fall of 2014, when *Rolling Stone* examined rape cases at the University of Virginia, in an article whose main source has since been discredited, they found that the University of Virginia had *never* expelled a student for rape, though they expelled several each year for plagiarism (Erdely 2014). Let us be clear, though a small part of the *Rolling Stone* article was discredited, the data on expulsions have not been. Furthermore, though some of the details in the *Rolling Stone* article were discredited, many sections were actually *corroborated.* To read about the case that broke open the scandal of fraternity rape at the University of Virginia we recommend *Crash into Me: A Survivor's Search for Justice*, by Liz Seccuro. Much of "Jackie's" story in *Rolling Stone* was actually lifted from Seccuro's memoir, which occurred in the fraternity that "Jackie" said was the venue of her assault.

As we noted in our discussion of the United States military, nearly twenty thousand men and women service members report being raped every year, and yet less than 7 percent of perpetrators found responsible receive any punishment at all, with only a fraction of those 7 percent dismissed or confined. The majority are assigned fines, have their rank reduced, and/or have their duties reassigned. As we noted in our discussion of the Catholic Church, of all of the hundreds of priests who have faced claims of child sexual abuse, only a tiny fraction have been defrocked. Many of the most egregious offenders were allowed to retire to posh communities, never facing any consequences for their behavior.

Hence, to interrupt rape across the four institutions we study, we could effectively bring to a screeching halt campus rape (including fraternity rape), military rape, rape that takes place in SportsWorld, and child sexual abuse in the Catholic Church simply by removing the perpetrators from the institution.

Let us be clear. We are not arguing that the accused's due process rights be in any way weakened. As scholars who have also written about exoneration, cases in which citizens who are innocent have spent decades of their lives in prison for crimes they did not commit, we are highly concerned about "getting it right." In fact, as we have argued elsewhere (Smith and Hattery 2011; Hattery and Smith 2018), in addition to the problems associated with incarcerating someone for crimes they did not commit, when we incarcerate the wrong person, the real perpetrator is free to continue committing crimes, and in the case of rape and child sexual abuse, this is exactly what happens. So we care deeply about getting it right, for the accused, for the victim, and for all future victims. That said, we believe that we can protect the rights of the accused to be innocent until proven guilty while simultaneously believing victims and conducting appropriately rigorous investigations of the facts in order to make a determination, in a court of law, of guilt or innocence, or, in internal systems of justice, to render the accused responsible or not. And we are confident, based on the thousands of other cases that do not involve gender-based violence or child sexual abuse that we get right every single year, that if investigators didn't rely on their own rape myths to evaluate a victim's story and if the same rigorous standards of investigation were applied in rape cases as they are to muggings and burglaries and drug deals and plagiarism, we would see justice for victims, and the rates of gender-based violence and child sexual abuse would consequently decline.

BOX 16.2	ADDING SEXUAL MISCONDUCT NOTES TO COLLEGE AND UNIVERSITY TRANSCRIPTS

The White House initiatives and directives focusing on rape on college campuses that began in 2014 and extended into 2015 served as a wake-up call for many college and university presidents and high-ranking administrators, who suddenly became aware of something those of us working in the field had known for decades: that rape on college campuses was an epidemic. Because all public colleges and universities are governed by their respective state legislatures, this panic on the part of college administrators was transferred to state lawmakers, who wanted to pass legislation designed to address rape on college campuses. And, though we applaud the desire on the part of our elected officials to focus resources on addressing the issue, in many cases they did so quickly and without much understanding of the research and best practices.

We would argue that this is the case in our current home state, Virginia. Along with legislators in Michigan, Virginia legislators passed a law that would require a notation on college and university transcripts when a student is found in violation of the university's sexual misconduct policy. Presumably this kind of violation would result in expulsion, and this is certainly the logic expressed by lawmakers and college presidents, that this notation would make it harder for colleges or universities to accept a transfer student who had violated the sexual misconduct policy, and if they did accept the transfer student, they would know that they had been found responsible in a hearing process. On the other hand, would accepting a transfer student with a known sexual misconduct violation create liability for colleges and universities? What happens if, for example, a transfer student with a known violation commits more violence that violates

continues

BOX 16.2	ADDING SEXUAL MISCONDUCT NOTES TO COLLEGE AND UNIVERSITY TRANSCRIPTS *continued*

the sexual misconduct policy—would victims be able to sue the university for accepting the perpetrator and not keeping its promise to ensure their safety? Some critiques of this new law note that academic transcripts are not rap sheets, that academic transcripts do not contain any mention of any other violations of a college or university's code of conduct, such as underage-drinking violations (except for plagiarism, which is academic misconduct). And, in our conversations, college and university registrars are uncertain as to what changes will have to be made in the transcript software they use in order to insert this kind of notation. Most colleges and universities use some version of the same software, so if all colleges and universities adopt the transcript policy, the software company would likely write code to facilitate the notation, but for the few colleges and universities who are attempting to do this on their own, this may actually present a rather significant challenge. Others argue that people deserve second chances and that this policy will effectively be a "death sentence" for a young man simply trying to get a college education.

We have several concerns. First and foremost, in the current climate, such a small number of men are found responsible of violating sexual misconduct policies and expelled that regardless of one's perspective—pro or con—this will affect a tiny number of students, perhaps no more than a few hundred per year. Second, we worry that colleges and universities already seem incredibly reluctant to find perpetrators responsible and that this "death penalty" requirement will make it even less likely that they will dispense a finding that would effectively end a young man's attempt to get a college education. Third, we do believe in second chances and in an individual's ability to change—we have to, for to believe anything less is to be left with absolute pessimism. Given that, we believe that any student found responsible of sexual misconduct should be offered an opportunity for treatment and training programs and, upon successful completion, be allowed to return to a college or university campus, perhaps as a transfer student, or perhaps to their original institution, but only after all of the victims have graduated. We want to be clear—we are not talking about some cupcake program, like the one it seems that Josh Duggar of *19 Kids and Counting* participated in, but a real program that has proven success and would verify that the participant was in fact able to return to a setting like a college or university campus and no longer be a risk. We note that we do not have this same optimism for child sex offenders, for all of the research indicates that there are very few, if any, successes in treating child sex offenders.

To read more about the transcript laws, see New 2015.

PREVENTION AND INTERVENTION

We must begin thinking of prevention of and early intervention in family abuse just as we do with regard to many health issues, including regular visits to the dentist, cancer screening such as mammography, and health screenings for conditions such as high blood pressure and diabetes. These prevention and early intervention strategies save numerous lives and save our health-care system and government billions of dollars per year. Thus, we strongly advocate a significantly greater investment in both prevention and early intervention programs, for which there are many models that could be adopted at a relatively low cost and a high payoff.

Given the prevalence of the early warning signs in actual cases of IPV (see Chapter 14), and given the relative ease in teaching about both the early warning signs and strategies for developing healthy relationships rather than potentially predatory ones, we feel strongly that well-developed and extensively integrated prevention programs could be pivotal in reducing IPV, especially dating violence among young people. Prevention programs could be built into many already existing institutions and curricula. For example, Family Services in Forsyth County, North Carolina has developed a teen program geared toward addressing all aspects of healthy relationships, including when and how to make decisions about sexual activity, reproductive health, and of course dating violence. Though attendance for this program is currently only voluntary, the staff hope to get permission from the school board to provide the healthy-relationships curriculum to the local high school health educators. In the 2017 session, the Virginia legislature passed a law that requires age-appropriate, evidence-based curricula designed to prevent dating violence, sexual harassment, and sexual violence to be provided in all public schools. Though we have significant concerns about the abstinence focus, we are optimistic about the inclusion of sexual and intimate partner violence in teen dating relationships.

Virginia Legislation Requiring Training in Healthy Relationships.
§ 22.1–207.1. Family life education.

    A.   As used in this section, "abstinence education" means an educational or motivational component that has as its exclusive purpose teaching the social, psychological, and health gains to be realized by teenagers' abstaining from sexual activity before marriage.

    B.   The Board of Education shall develop Standards of Learning and curriculum guidelines for a comprehensive, sequential family life education curriculum in

continues

---

continued

grades kindergarten through 12. Such curriculum guidelines shall include instruction as appropriate for the age of the student in family living and community relationships; the benefits, challenges, responsibilities, and value of marriage for men, women, children, and communities; the value of family relationships; abstinence education; the value of postponing sexual activity; the benefits of adoption as a positive choice in the event of an unwanted pregnancy; human sexuality; human reproduction; *dating violence, the characteristics of abusive relationships, steps to take to deter sexual assault, and the availability of counseling and legal resources, and, in the event of such sexual assault*, the importance of immediate medical attention and advice, as well as the requirements of the law; the etiology, prevention, and effects of sexually transmitted diseases; and mental health education and awareness.

C.   All such instruction shall be designed to promote parental involvement, foster positive self-concepts, and provide mechanisms for coping with peer pressure and the stresses of modern living according to the students' developmental stages and abilities. The Board shall also establish requirements for appropriate training for teachers of family life education, which shall include training in instructional elements to support the various curriculum components.

1987, c. 371; 1999, c. 422; 2002, c. 554; 2004, c. 1030; 2007, c. 32; 2008, c. 417; 2009, cc. 437, 583; 2017, c. 692 [emphasis ours].

Evidence-based "healthy-relationships" units that focus on preventing dating violence while promoting healthy relationships based on partnership, rather than on traditional gender roles that promote male dominance and female submission, could be routinely added to the health classes that all students in public high schools take in the ninth and tenth grades. These units would fit comfortably alongside already existing units on sex education, nutrition and fitness, and drug and alcohol education. We believe these types of programs hold tremendous promise for reducing the most common types of IPV—those based on the cultural norms derived from traditional gender roles. Last, we note that these programs could be developed in ways that are not "sexuality specific" such that they would prevent IPV in both heterosexual and same-gender and transgender relationships.

Both child abuse prevention programs and elder abuse prevention programs could be targeted toward those individuals who are preparing for and in the early stages of either parenting or caregiving for an elder. Identifying new parents is far easier than identifying elder-care providers, primarily because parenting begins at a certain moment that typically is initiated in a hospital, whereas taking care of an elder may begin slowly and intermittently, without a specific starting point. That said, we believe that models for preventing child abuse could be modified to address elder abuse.

BOX 16.3	COMPREHENSIVE SEX EDUCATION PROGRAMS

We are intrigued by comprehensive sex education programs that begin in kindergarten and teach young children about respect and consent, which have been successful in reducing teen dating violence and sexual assault where they have been adopted. We encourage you to examine the Spring Fever program in the Netherlands (De Melker 2015); we believe it has incredible potential if adopted in the United States.

Source: De Melker 2015.

We recommend that a variety of parenting programs and child prevention programs be implemented routinely, beginning with the initial prenatal examination and extending through childhood and the teenage years. One approach that we have seen is the monthly newsletter that many hospitals send to new parents. Each monthly installment describes the typical development that parents can expect at each month as well as the challenges that parents might face. For example, because colic often begins in the third month, the third installment often carries a discussion of colic, how to recognize it, and tips for dealing with it. As the child ages, these newsletters could be reduced to twice per year and include discussions of appropriate discipline, and for parents of preteens and teenagers, the newsletter would likely include suggestions for setting boundaries and materials that would guide discussions about sexuality, drugs and alcohol, driving safety, and so forth. Once a child enters school, these newsletters could be disseminated by the school district but include health information generated by the local pediatrics department. This type of newsletter would likely have some impact on reducing child and sibling abuse as well as improving health outcomes for children.

A similar model could be developed and designed to prevent elder abuse. The primary challenges would be identifying who needs the information and disseminating it at the right time. Because providing elder care, as noted, may begin slowly and intermittently, it may not be possible to identify appropriate recipients of the newsletters until families engage an institution, such as their health-care provider, home health-care system, or residential programs. That said, in all cases in which an adult child accompanies their parent to a health-care appointment, screening for caregiving could begin. Both the adult child and the senior could be offered information regarding the early stages of caregiving, including discussions of expectations and challenges. Regular newsletters (or other forms of contact, such as blogs) could follow, with each installment addressing different issues, such as hiring care providers, handling finances, and the kinds of physical and mental decline that can be expected. These programs would be built on the assumption that in cases of both child abuse and elder abuse, lack of information, lack of understanding about what to expect, and feelings of being overwhelmed are causes of the majority of both child and elder abuse. Thus, in a best-case scenario, this approach would reduce a majority of cases of both child and elder abuse.

Education programs such as these, however, primarily address neglect; unfortunately, much child and elder abuse takes the form of physical abuse and sexual abuse. We believe that there is very little that programming can do to prevent these types of abuse. Thus, we turn to intervention. Clearly, intervention is important in all cases, not just those involving severe abuse, neglect, or sexual abuse. As we noted in Chapters 5 and 6, there are a variety of forces that reduce the likelihood of intervention. With regard to child and elder abuse, one of the key barriers is the small probability that the victim will report the abuse or call 911. Thus, the thrust of interventions will have to be located in institutions, including the health-care system, schools, and senior day programs, where the abuse can be recognized and detected without the victim having to report it directly. Though abuse is more often identified and reported in emergency room visits, we strongly recommend that routine screening for child abuse and elder abuse be developed and implemented among family physicians and internists who see patients for their routine and non-emergency care.

As we argued with regard to law enforcement and people who work in the criminal justice system, we begin by noting that physicians and other health-care staff need to be educated about child abuse and elder abuse. They must be trained to recognize less-severe violence, abuse in its early stages, and symptoms of nonphysical abuse, namely emotional or psychological abuse and sexual abuse. Additionally, we must develop reporting mechanisms and protocols that are "easy," not time-consuming, and otherwise not prohibitive; for example, health-care providers should never worry that reporting possible abuse would in any way damage their reputations or leave them open for lawsuits. Simultaneously, we should consider developing sanctions for failing to report abuse that could reasonably be identified by a group of one's peers; these could be developed similarly to the way in which medical malpractice standards are established. These strategies would move us significantly forward in terms of intervening in both child and elder abuse. One example of this is provided by the Texas Department of State Health Services. We also remind you of the case of V, detailed in Chapter 10, who was kidnapped, repeatedly raped, and pregnant at age twelve. Had a middle-school teacher or a nurse asked about the context of V's pregnancies, the child sexual abuse and IPV she endured for decades might have been interrupted sooner.

Similarly, education programs that are required for all teachers and senior day programming staff should focus on recognizing the early signs of all forms of abuse. Because teachers and day programming staff are likely to have the most regular contact with potential victims of any nonfamily member, educating these staff has the potential to be *even more powerful* than many other intervention strategies that could be proposed. As with health-care providers, we must develop mechanisms that are "easy" and not time-consuming and ensure the professional and personal safety of the reporter. For example, the Texas Department of State Health Services allows reports of child abuse to be made online. Their department website is careful to point out that they are mandated to investigate any report that reasonably suggests abuse might have taken place ("Child Abuse Reporting Requirements for DSHS Contractors Providers" 2015). As noted in Box 16.4, the department also makes clear that failure to knowingly report the presence of abuse is an actionable offense. Furthermore, the department website makes clear that a report need only indicate the child about whom one is suspicious. Any other information—such as the name of the suspected abuser or addresses for the child or abuser—is helpful but not required. These types of mechanisms—such as online reporting and requiring only the name of the child— tend to streamline the process and, if implemented widely, would likely increase dramatically the number of cases that would be investigated in the early stages, before greater harm has been done to the victims and more severe consequences face the perpetrator. Early intervention improves the likelihood of rehabilitation and reconciliation, both of which are often desirable for both victims and offenders.

BOX 16.4	TEXAS SEXUAL ABUSE OF A CHILD STANDARD

The Family Code requires that you not knowingly fail to report any case where a child may be adversely affected by abuse. In particular, there have been some misunderstanding of the criminal laws relating to offenses against children. Sexual abuse, including sexual assault and indecency with a child, can occur even when there is no force, duress, or coercion; in other words when the minor and his or her partner are both willing sexual partners. Your own attorney can explain these criminal laws to you *so that you can then report when required by law.* [emphasis ours]

Source: "Child Abuse Reporting Requirements for DSHS Contractors Providers" 2015.

We turn now to a larger and more esoteric discussion of the types of broader social changes that would likely result in decreases in all forms of family violence.

THE BIG PICTURE: REDUCTIONS IN INEQUALITY

Our analysis and framework for understanding family violence are based on the express assumption that all forms of family violence are outgrowths of inequalities, both inequalities of status, such as gender, race, age, or sexuality, and inequalities within individual relationships. Based on these assumptions, we would expect family violence to follow general patterns: IPV will generally involve men perpetrating abuse against their partners, child abuse will involve parents and stepparents abusing children as well as older siblings abusing younger siblings, and elder abuse will involve adult children abusing their vulnerable parents. The explanation for these patterns is that individuals hold social power imbued to them via systems of domination—patriarchy, age, and so forth—and this power can be abused by engaging in violence against the person with less access to social power. At the individual level, we see the interaction of these systems of domination vis-à-vis individual access to power; for instance, IPV often takes the form it does because men typically earn more money than their partners, and this leaves women dependent upon their partners to meet their basic needs and thus vulnerable to IPV. Similarly, children and older adults are vulnerable to abuse because they are dependent economically and in so many other ways on the people who care for them. Of course, part of what becomes interesting is when abuse follows the societal patterns but defies the actual individual situation. For example, as we discussed extensively in Chapter 9, when men are unemployed and find themselves economically dependent on their partners, this creates a climate ripe for IPV. Thus, the inability to remain dominant at the individual level—as the breadwinner—often leads men to turn to the social power imbued to them by patriarchy in order to reestablish their dominance in their relationship, and this reassertion of dominance is often accomplished through the use of violence.

PRESCRIPTIONS FOR PREVENTING AND INTERRUPTING FAMILY VIOLENCE: DISRUPTING INEQUALITIES

As we have argued, much abuse is an outgrowth of social inequalities and inequalities in individual families. Thus, here we offer societal-level approaches to reducing inequality and thus reducing all forms of family violence. Though there are differences that characterize the various forms of family violence—for example, the elderly are the most vulnerable to economic or financial abuse, whereas young girls are the most vulnerable to sexual abuse—we believe that our overall argument can and should be extended to all forms of family violence. In short, as long as some people are relegated to the status of second-class citizens while others occupy positions of power and privilege, all forms of family violence will be present at rates that impact tens of millions of Americans and adversely affect our social world.

Economic Reform

One of the constant themes throughout our discussions has been the issue of economics, finances, and money. As we noted in Chapter 10, dominant ideologies of masculinity prescribe that men take on the role of breadwinner. Moreover, many, if not most, women expect that their partners will contribute significantly to the economy of the household (Bianchi, Robinson, and Milkie 2007). When men are unable to meet the economic needs of the family, they often report being nagged by their partners, and they often feel that their masculinity is threatened. In fact, scholars and family therapists alike agree that one of the most common sources of couple arguments is money: how much the family needs, who is going to earn it, how much needs to be saved, and how it is going to be spent.

We argue that most people (men and women) should be contributing economically to their households unless they are incapable of doing so—perhaps they are disabled—or unless they are stay-at-home parents, which, for men, remains relatively rare in the United States. According to the 2010 census, the percentage of men who are stay-at-home dads continues to hover below the 10 percent mark. Additionally, many men need to take more economic responsibility for their families than they do, a problem we encountered in our interviews. However, we argue that in order to make serious headway on the problem of IPV as it is associated with economics, we need to move beyond individual responsibility and demand serious economic reform. The truth of the matter is that even in the best-case scenario, where a hardworking man is working full-time, year-round, he will have to make at least fifteen dollars an hour in order to keep his family above the federally established poverty line. Yet, as most poverty experts note, living above the poverty line does not mean that you are "making ends meet" (see Edin and Lein 1997). We suspect that over time we would see a decline in IPV if we returned to an economy that offered a living wage to all employees, not just those with special skills and advanced education (Ehrenreich 2001). As we noted in Chapter 9, the Great Recession of 2007–2009 led to an uptick in IPV, especially for white women. Though we have not seen any research specifically on the impact of the collapse of the banking system and the gutting of many retirement accounts as a result of huge drops in the stock market and financial crimes, such as those perpetrated by scam artists like Bernie Madoff and those behind the Enron scandal, we can speculate that these downturns in the economy made the elderly more vulnerable and they inevitably became more dependent upon their children to assist them in meeting their daily needs. In some cases, this may result in an elderly person finding themself no longer able to pay for home health care or institutionalized care and having to move in with one of their children. As we discussed extensively in Chapter 5, this creates an environment ripe for the stresses that lead to elder abuse. Unfortunately, we may not know the full impact of the economic crisis and Ponzi schemes for decades, until the entire group impacted attempts to retire.

Economic reform that provides a living wage to men is not the only key to disrupting IPV. As discussed at length in Chapter 8, women are vulnerable to IPV because of the economic oppression they suffer. As long as women continue to earn only a portion of men's wages—currently, women earn eight cents on a man's dollar, a ratio that has remained relatively stable for the past twenty years—they will be dependent on men in order to provide economic stability for their families. The outcome of the gender wage gap is, according to Rich (1980), compulsory heterosexuality or, as we argued in Chapter 9, compulsory partnership. Abused women stay in abusive relationships because they cannot leave *and* feed their children. Abused women who do leave often jump quickly into relationships with men they barely know out of sheer economic need. They need someone to help pay the rent and stock the refrigerator. And the men with whom they jump into relationships often become abusive. Thus, economic reform that provides a living wage to all workers and reform that will address the gender wage gap are critical in that these reforms will result in women being less economically vulnerable to their partners, and thus rates of IPV will decline.

Gender Equality and Dismantling Patriarchy

In Chapter 10 we argued that IPV is a "logical" by-product of patriarchy. Inside a system of male domination, in which men are defined as superior and women inferior, in which men have social, political, and economic power and women have little to none (Zweigenhaft and Domhoff 1998), the prevailing model of gender relations is one of domination, power, and control. Acker (2006) describes this as a *gender inequality regime*. In a system designed around oppression and inequality, it is not surprising that the dominant group uses a variety of means to control the subordinate group—in fact, one would *expect* them to do so. Clearly, not all men are abusive, but as Andrea Dworkin (1987) argued, all heterosexual relationships contain the elements necessary for IPV. What is remarkable, frankly, is when some men *choose not to* exercise the power and control they have that is bestowed on them by patriarchy; it is in fact *truly remarkable that the majority of men do not engage in violence against their partners, even if they grew up witnessing it in their own families.*

Patriarchy is, at its most fundamental level, a system of privilege. Part of the privilege is, as noted, the power to choose when and how to exercise power. Another and equally important aspect of the privilege is the ability to render women and women's "interests" invisible. Scully's study of convicted rapists provides insight into this aspect of privilege:

> Since patriarchal societies produce men whose frame of reference excludes women's perspectives, men are able to ignore sexual violence, especially since their culture provides them with such a convenient array of justifications . . . *Indeed, it appears that . . . a man rapes because his value system provides no compelling reason for him not to do so.*
>
> (1990: 116)

We could easily replace "sexual violence" with "IPV," and it would accurately reflect what men who abuse reported to us. The structural rendering of the "victim" or "oppressed" as invisible allows the oppressor to feel justified in their behavior.[1] Men perpetrate sexual and IPV because they can get away with it and because they do not see the interests of their partners as inextricably tied up with their own.

In examining the relationships of men and women living with violence, several patterns emerged. As we discussed at length in Chapter 10, many men identify a similar trigger to their violence—their inability to meet the demands as a breadwinner. One of the traps of any system of domination, and patriarchy is no exception, is that it defines very rigid roles for both men and women. Women are relegated to the status of second-class citizen, with little power and few choices. Men are also relegated to a narrow set of available roles, the primary role being that of economic provider. Furthermore, this rigid role assignment is strictly enforced. How do we know? Despite the fact that men, as well as women, are eligible for the provisions of the **Family and Medical Leave Act**, allowing them time off from work when they have a new baby—or adopt or have a sick family member who needs to be cared for—less than 10 percent of men take advantage of it, and some report they are not given "permission" by employers to take advantage of this provision to which they are legally entitled (Hattery 2001). The ranks of the stay-at-home father, though growing, are relatively small, at about 8 percent (nationally). And when men do stay at home, they incur a great deal of negative feedback for this decision (Hattery 2001). Though we would never suggest that limiting men's choices to take family leave or stay at home to parent is the same as women's economic dependency on, and thus vulnerability, to men, we do note that limited roles and constrained choices are the hallmark of patriarchy and contribute in important ways to the culture of IPV.

Another distinct pattern that emerges in these couples is that men's attempts to control their partners and their use of violence are often triggered when their partners engage in behaviors that are perceived *by them* as uppity. In short, women are verbally berated, beaten, and abused when they are *acting as if they are free.*[2]

Women are abused and beaten when they take too long on an errand or return home later than expected. They are abused and beaten when they have lunch with a coworker their partner does not like—which he may define as any man besides himself. They are abused and beaten when they decide they are not going to clean up after their partners and especially if this involves cleaning up or preparing food for their partners' friends as they watch sports events, like football or boxing. They are abused and beaten when they decide to change the dinner menu or the time the meal is served. And, mostly, women are abused and beaten when they talk to or express any interest in a man other than their partner, even though the expression may simply be of friendship or collegiality. When women exercise agency, engage in their own decision-making, or attempt to wield power, they are verbally berated, beaten, and sexually assaulted. In other words, IPV is a form not only of rule enforcement (or discipline) but also of role enforcement; women need to know their place. This pattern of violence can only be explained as part of a larger system that is designed to keep women in their "rightful" place, as second-class citizens, on this earth to serve the needs of their partners. The greatest risk factor for becoming a victim of IPV is simply being a woman.

THE FINAL WORD: RELATIONSHIPS AS PARTNERSHIPS

Understanding family violence requires that we see systems of domination and the ways that they are interconnected. Family violence is a logical outcome of patriarchy, but it is reinforced by other systems of domination, such as class exploitation and racial domination. Fighting the epidemic of family violence means dismantling patriarchy so as to empower women, but it also means that roles for men must be expanded as well. When men are boxed into evaluating themselves within a narrow framework of masculinity, they will almost always fail. Thus, revising our constructions of masculinity (as well as femininity) will offer men more opportunities for success as well as a richer life experience. What does this mean? Practically, it can mean things like associating masculinity with being a good dad. Being a supportive partner can be defined as being a "real man." It means transforming heterosexual relationships into partnerships. Referring back to our discussion in Chapter 10, this would mean defining both men and women in relation to their intimate relationship and in relation to the labor market.

As long as we continue to define men primarily by their relationship to the labor market ("I am a plumber" or "I am a banker") and women primarily by their relationship to men ("Tom's wife"), we will be unable to transform heterosexual relationships into true partnerships.[3]

Destroying the notion that men must be breadwinners and women must be restricted to the role of "support" (taking care of the home and the children, being supportive of her man) and replacing it with a notion that men and women in heterosexual (or same-gender) relationships are in partnerships would have many positive outcomes. The notion of partnership suggests equality and interdependence. If one is interdependent with one's partner, then it would be against one's self-interest to sabotage or harm that partner. If men and women identified their self-interests as interconnected, then the result would be healthier, happier, more fulfilling relationships for all of us. And violence would become a rare event.

Dismantling patriarchy, however, means more than simply creating new constructions of masculinity and femininity and new norms around gender relations in relationships—both heterosexual and same-gender. For true equality to arise and for a serious reduction in IPV, women must be given access to real social, political, and economic power. Women must be paid a fair wage, they must have the opportunity for political leadership, and they must have access to social leadership as well. The same holds true with regards to sexuality. All members of the LGBTQ community, who also build relationships that are often constrained by traditional stereotypes about gender and masculinity and femininity, need to have real access to social, political, and economic power. Only when they have access to these sources of power and can live as citizens of the "first world" will they be able to build meaningful relationships free of the negative trappings of heteronormativity and thus free of violence. For this to be effective, however, disrupting systems of gender domination will also *require* the simultaneous dismantling of racial domination and heterosexual domination and reformation of the economy.

In order to live healthy, productive lives in relationships with each other, both men *and* women need to be freed from the severe economic exploitation that currently exists in the political economy of the United States. The rich continue to get rich by stealing the labor of the poor. Every time a worker is paid less than they are worth, the net gain goes to the business owner. Only when all people are paid a fair and living wage for their work, only when they are all offered opportunities for economic advancement based on fair principles, not the exploitation of others, will they be able to live in healthy relationships with each other, relationships that are free of violence. This is particularly important for lesbians, who because of the gender wage gap typically have lower overall household earnings than their straight counterparts. Indeed, as D'Emilio (1983) notes, economic freedom is essential not only to healthy same-gender partnerships but also to their very existence!

Finally, as we noted above, minority men must not be treated as second-class citizens in economic, political, or social life—and especially in the criminal justice system—if they are to develop a healthy masculine self-identity. Similarly, we cannot justify the abuse of minority women by invoking a system that devalues them and their bodies. True equality for men and women is tied to equality for *all* men and *all* women, regardless of race or ethnicity (Davis 1983). Moreover, *gender equality* is interwoven intimately with equality for children and the elderly, especially because it is women who are most often the caregivers for their children and their aging parents. Thus, the struggle for gender equality has the potential to transform all human relationships and reduce all forms of family violence.

NOTES

1. This argument can also be applied to other systems of domination, such as racial superiority and economic exploitation.

2. See Auerbach 2004, an op-ed in the *Washington Post*, for a good explanation of the interlocking web of violence, HIV/AIDS, and IPV.

3. We should note here that the same concern can be expressed about same-gender couples, though, as discussed in Chapter 12, there are obviously no gender differences present. We hope that, now that marriage equality is finally the "law of the land" in the United States, same-gender couples will not succumb to the same tendencies heterosexual couples have of living in anything but true partnerships. That said, we know, based on research about internalized homophobia, that at least some LGBTQ couples will attempt to mimic or copy heterosexual marriages, and this could be devastating to them individually and to the institution of gay marriage more broadly.

REFERENCES

Acker, J. 2006. *Class Questions, Feminist Answers*. New York: Routledge.

Auerbach, Judith. 2004. "The Overlooked Victims of AIDS." *Washington Post*, October 14. www.washingtonpost.com/wp-dyn/articles/A31115-2004Oct13.html.

Bianchi, S., J. P. Robinson, and M. A. Milkie. 2007. *Changing Rhythms of American Family Life*. New York: Russell Sage Foundation.

Campbell, Jacquelyn. 2015. "Campus Sexual Assault Perpetration: What Else We Need to Know." *Journal of the American Medical Association Pediatrics 169(12)*: 1088–1089. http://archpedi.jamanetwork.com/article.aspx?articleid=2375126.

Centers for Disease Control and Prevention. 2015. "The Social-Ecological Model: A Framework for Prevention." www.cdc.gov/violenceprevention/overview/social-ecologicalmodel.html.

"Child Abuse Reporting Requirements for DSHS Contractors Providers." 2015. *Texas Department of State Health Services*. www.dshs.state.tx.us/childabusereporting/default.shtm.

Davis, A. Y. 1983. *Women, Race, and Class*. New York: Vintage Books.

De Melker, Saskia. 2015. "The Case for Starting Sex Education in Kindergarten." *PBS NewsHour*, May 27. www.pbs.org/newshour/updates/spring-fever.

D'Emilio, J. 1983. "Capitalism and Gay Identity." In *Powers of Desire: The Politics of Sexuality*, edited by A. Snitow, C. Stansell, and S. Thompson, 100–113. New York: New Feminist Library Series.

Dworkin, Andrea. 1987. *Intercourse*. New York: Free Press.

Edin, K., and L. Lein. 1997. *Making Ends Meet: How Single Mothers Survive Welfare and Low-Wage Work*. New York: Russell Sage Foundation.

Ehrenreich, B. 2001. *Nickel and Dimed: On (Not) Getting by in America*. New York: Henry Holt and Company.

Ehrensaft, M., and P. Cohen. 2003. "Intergenerational Transmission of Partner Violence: A 20-Year Prospective Study." *Journal of Consulting and Clinical Psychology* 71(4): 741–753.

Erdely, Sabrina Rubin. 2014. "A Rape on Campus: A Brutal Assault and a Struggle for Justice at UVA." *Rolling Stone*, November 19.

Hattery, A. 2001. *Women, Work, and Family: Balancing and Weaving*. Thousand Oaks, CA: Sage.

Hattery, A. 2009. "Sexual Abuse in Childhood and Adolescence and Intimate Partner Violence in Adulthood Among African American and White Women." *Race, Gender, and Class* 15(2): 79–97.

Hattery, A. J. and E. Smith. 2018. *Policing Black Bodies: How Black Lives Are Surveilled and How to Work for Change*. Lanham, MD: Rowman and Littlefield

Hattery, A. J., and E. Smith. 2019. *Gender, Power, and Violence: Responding to Sexual and Intimate Partner Violence in Society Today*. Lanham, MD: Rowman and Littlefield.

Kaufman, M. 1987. "The Construction of Masculinity and the Triad of Men's Violence." In *Beyond Patriarchy: Essays by Men on Pleasure, Power and Change*, edited by M. Kaufman, 1–29. New York: Oxford University Press.

Martin, P. Y. 2005. *Rape Work: Victims, Gender, and Emotions in Organization and Community Context*. New York: Routledge.

New, Jake. 2015. "Requiring a Red Flag." *Inside Higher Ed*, July 10. www.inside-highered.com/news/2015/07/10/states-requiring-colleges-note-sexual-assault-responsibility-student-transcripts.

Rich, A. 1980. "Compulsory Heterosexuality and Lesbian Existence." *Signs* 5(4): 631–660.

Scully, D. 1990. *Understanding Sexual Violence: A Study of Convicted Rapists*. Boston, MA: Unwin Hyman.

Smith, Earl, and Angela J. Hattery. 2011. "Race, Wrongful Conviction & Exoneration." *Journal of African American Studies* 15(1): 74–94.

Zweigenhaft, R. L., and G. W. Domhoff. 1998. *Diversity in the Power Elite: Have Women and Minorities Reached the Top?* New Haven, CT: Yale University Press.

INDEX

Printed in the USA
CPSIA information can be obtained
at www.ICGtesting.com
LVHW072127060124
768331LV00011B/506